RESPONDING TO TERRORISM IN SOUTH ASIA

The Regional Centre for Strategic Studies (RCSS) is an independent, non-profit and non-governmental organization for collaborative research, networking and interaction on strategic and international issues pertaining to South Asia. Set up in 1992, the RCSS is based in Colombo, Sri Lanka.

The RCSS is a South Asian forum for studies, training and multi-track dialogue and deliberation on issues of regional interest. All activities of RCSS are designed with a South Asia focus and are usually participated by experts from all South Asian countries. The Centre is envisaged as a forum for advancing the cause of cooperation, security, conflict resolution, confidence building, peace and development in the countries of the South Asian region.

The RCSS serves its South Asian and international constituency by: (a) networking programmes that promote interaction, communication and exchange between institutions and individuals within and outside the region engaged in South Asian strategic studies; (b) organizing regional workshops and seminars and sponsoring and coordinating collaborative research, and (c) disseminating output of the research through publications which include books, monographs and a quarterly newsletter. The RCSS facilitates scholars and other professionals of South Asia to address, mutually and collectively, problems and, issues of topical interest for all countries of the region.

Queries may be addressed to:

Regional Centre for Strategic Studies
2 Elibank Road
Colombo 5
SRI LANKA
Tel: (94-11) 2599734, 599735
Fax: 2599993; e-mail: edrcss@sri.lanka.net
RCSS website: http://www.rcss.org

RESPONDING TO TERRORISM IN SOUTH ASIA

Edited by

S.D. MUNI

REGIONAL CENTRE FOR STRATEGIC STUDIES
COLOMBO

MANOHAR
2006

First published 2006

ISBN 81-7304-671-9

Published by

Ajay Kumar Jain for
Manohar Publishers & Distributors
4753/23 Ansari Road, Daryaganj
New Delhi 110 002

Typeset at

Digigrafics
New Delhi 110 049

Printed at

Lordson Publishers Pvt. Ltd.
Delhi 110 007

Distributed in South Asia by

FOUNDATION BOOKS

4381/4, Ansari Road
Daryaganj, New Delhi 110 002
and its branches at Mumbai, Hyderabad,
Bangalore, Chennai, Kolkata

Contents

RCSS is grateful to the Ford Foundation
for its generous support for the project on
Understanding and Combating Terrorism in South Asia
under Regional Collaborative Research Initiatives
on Non-Traditional Security in South Asia.

Preface

This study is a part of the larger project on Non-Traditional Security in South Asia, undertaken by the Regional Centre of Strategic Studies (RCSS), Colombo. The editor and contributors of this study are thankful to the RCSS and its Executive Director, Professor Sridhar Khatri for giving us the opportunity to be associated with the project.

In this study we are not addressing the question of terrorism in South Asia as such. Our focus is on the strategies evolved by the South Asian states in responding to the challenge of terrorism. However, while looking at the strategies, it is inevitable that the essential characteristics of terrorism are also understood and explained as the nature of terrorism faced in each of the South Asian countries has its own specific aspects. The study is divided into two sections. In the first section, the way in which each of the South Asian states have responded to terrorism, has been studied carefully. In the second section, some of the comparative aspects of the regional perspective, such as the role of civil societies, consequences of the strategies pursued, role of the third parties, and political economy of terrorism and responding strategies have been taken up for discussion and analysis. There is also a data paper on South Asian terrorism included at the end of this study.

Every collaborative study has to absorb the pangs of logistic, professional, and personal constrains. Such constraints cause delay in the completion of the study and at times also impinge on its quality. This study is not free from that. And yet, all the contributors deserve to be complimented for going through the discipline required and enduring the indulgence of editorial and organizational imperatives. I am also thankful to K. Yhome and R. Ramasubramanian, the conscientious researchers pursuing their M.Phil./Ph.D. studies at the School of International Studies, Jawaharlal Nehru University, New Delhi, for rendering crucial help in putting the hard and soft copies of the manuscript in line.

New Delhi
3 May 2005

S.D. Muni

1. Introduction

S.D. Muni

South Asia has had a long and diverse experience of dealing with terrorism. This experience dates back to the late 1940s and 1950s. Terrorism then was understood differently from today, since the terrorist attacks in the US on 11 September 2001. The forms and patterns of terrorism experienced in South Asia since those early years have been varied ranging from religious extremism to those resulting from ethnic, regional, systemic and politico-ideological rebellions and conflicts. In many of these conflicts terror has been employed as one of the important instruments of revolt, and terror has also been employed in strategies to curb and counter these revolts by the state. Terror emerging out of these revolts in a given South Asian country has also been endorsed, employed and even encouraged by a neighbouring state to advance its specific strategic and foreign policy objectives. This has given rise to the phenomenon of 'cross-border' terrorism.

The South Asian countries have been facing up to the challenge of terrorism through various strategies. There are, no doubt, success stories in this endeavour of fighting terrorism, but the challenge remains as serious and daunting as ever. It seems that the nature of this challenge has also been undergoing rapid transformations as a result of the evolving domestic, regional, and international contexts. However, the persistence of the challenge of terrorism also underlines the fact that the strategies pursued to cope with the challenge have not been adequate, appropriate, or effective. As terrorism has come to occupy a critical place in the global as well as South Asia's regional politics, and as much of peace, stability, and progress in a given country as well as the region as a whole depends upon curbing terrorism, it is necessary to explore the possibilities of how best to deal with it. A sense of urgency and seriousness is added here because there exists a mutually reinforcing relationship between terrorism in South Asia and terrorism at the global level in the post-9/11 context.

The Objective

To put it in a nutshell, the objective of our study is threefold, namely: (i) to identify and examine the respective strategies followed by the South Asian states in dealing with their respective challenges of terrorism, (ii) to make a critical assessment of these strategies for their failures, successes, or effectiveness over the years; and (iii) suggest possible alternatives and improvements so that these strategies become effective and viable in meeting the present and future challenges on a lasting basis. It may also be in order to examine the consequences, both positive and negative, of these strategies and the manners and styles of their pursuance on other relevant segments of public policies and social lives in the South Asian countries. While the role of the state is central in dealing with the challenge of terrorism, an attempt is also made here to look at the significant role being played by the civil society and non-governmental organizations and agencies in responding to terrorism in the region. The areas of tension as well as coexistence and coordination between the state and the non-state actors need to be identified and explored for in-depth understanding and policy implications.

Understanding Terrorism

For any assessment of the strategies to deal with terrorism, a basic and balanced understanding of 'terrorism' itself is very essential. However, the current focus on terrorism is a post-9/11 phenomenon where it has acquired a steamrolling thrust. All hitherto prevalent conceptual parameters have been submerged and flattened under this thrust. In the discourse on terrorism the notions of proxy-wars, asymmetrical and unequal conflicts, people's wars and revolutionary conflicts have lost their significance. Charles Krauthammer was right when he drew attention to the asymmetrical aspect of the conflict inherent in the 9/11 events. He said:

The asymmetry is almost comical. The whole world against one man. If in the end, the United States, backed by every great power, cannot succeed in defeating some cave dwellers in the most backward country on earth, then the entire structure of world stability which rests ultimately on the pacifying deterrent effect of American power, will be fatally threatened.[1]

The 'cave dwellers' have not been *finally and fully* defeated as yet. And to add to this asymmetrical aspect, the case of Saddam and his Iraq has also been added.

The definitional riddle of terrorism has so far not allowed the UN to come up with a universally accepted formulation. The US definition of terrorism that provides justification for the current policy approach is also not adequately persuasive. Andrei Philke's formulation on defining terrorism as it appeared in the journal,[2] *Terrorism and Political Violence* (1996), is generally followed in the US State Department's Reports on 'Global Terrorism'. It has also been approvingly cited in a Brookings study by Paul R. Pillar (*Terrorism and US Foreign Policy*, 2001). It says; terrorism is 'pre-meditated, politically motivated violence perpetrated against non-combatants by sub-national groups or clandestine agents usually intended to influence an audience'. In this definition, all the key components like 'pre-meditated, politically motivated . . . non-combatants . . . sub-national groups or clandestine agents', etc., are prone to subjective interpretations. For instance, an army officer after duty hours, an intelligence officer, an administrative officer, a senior government functionary or decision-maker may all be non-combatants from the perspective of establishment but are they so from the perspective of rebels and opponents of the establishment? In this definition the bias is clearly against the non-state actors; the state is assumed to be not a perpetrator of terrorism, which the civil society in any country would find hard to endorse. It will also be factually misleading as there are innumerable authentically recorded instances of state terrorism in South Asia and many other countries and regions.

There are other difficulties in accepting the US-endorsed formulation on terrorism. In the US policy, terrorism is a reflection of a deep sense of vulnerability arising out of the 9/11 experience. In this respect, it is tilted in against the jehadi or Islamic terrorism and seems to be overlapping with Huntington's

Clash of Civilizations[3] theory, notwithstanding various US official statements discounting the anti-Islamic thrust in its approach. Recall what Huntington said in his civilizational conflict treatise: 'Underlying problem with the West is not Islamic fundamentalism, not the ideological exchange within a particular religion, but it is Islam—a different civilization whose people are convinced of the superiority of their culture and obsessed with the inferiority of their power'. So there is a power dimension as well in the US understanding of conflict with Islam. Perhaps, the use of the terms like 'crusade' and 'axis of evil', in President Bush's early responses to 9/11 was not all that inadvertent. Charles Krauthammer rightly builds upon this thesis when he explains the US post-9/11 policy:

> On September 11, American foreign policy acquired seriousness. It also acquired a new organizing principle: We have an enemy, radical Islam; it is a global opponent of worldwide reach, armed with an idea, and with the tactics, weapons and ruthlessness necessary to take on the world's hegemony, and its defeat is our supreme national objective, as overriding a necessity as were the defeat of Fascism and Soviet Communism.[4]

Accordingly, the US post-9/11 policy also underlines a careful attempt to use terrorism as a cover for global strategic restructuring. The objective seems to be to reinforce the threatened hegemony. There are several statements by the former National Security Adviser and present Secretary of State, Condoleezza Rice, the Secretary of Defence, Donald Rumsfeld, and the former State Department Policy Planning Director Richard Hass in support of this assumption. Therefore, one has to be careful in following the US formulations on terrorism for understanding the South Asian situation. In the South Asian situation, jehadi extremism is only one source of terrorism. There are other cases of terrorism where jehadi extremism is not relevant at all, like the Naxalites and insurgencies in India's north-east, the Maoists in Nepal, the LTTE in Sri Lanka, etc. The US perspective is not oblivious of these distinctions and that is why it subtly makes a distinction between 'global' and 'regional/local' terrorism. In South Asia, terrorism at both these levels is relevant and challenging.

In any attempt towards understanding terrorism, two aspects

are critical, namely, the legitimacy and the targets of the violence. The question of the legitimacy of violence will cover unjust and excessive use of force by the state and it will also distinguish terrorism from other forms of violence such as in revolutionary struggles, people's wars, national liberations, ethnic uprisings, etc. It is in this distinction that the question of 'one person's terrorist' as another person's 'freedom fighter' assumes significance. This distinction will also, to some extent, address the question of the targets of violence. In any revolutionary struggle, guerrilla warfare or national liberation struggle, violence to weaken the enemy and target even lowly officials of the state, including the suspected 'informers' of the state who may otherwise appear to be innocent civilians, is justified. The prevalent notion of terrorism would not do that.

With regard to the target of violence, another definition of terrorism says: 'terrorism is the *intentional* use of, or threat to use violence against civilians or against civilian targets, in order to attain political aims'. In this case, any '*collateral damage* to the civilians used as human shields or to cover military activity or installation', by any of the combatants, then this will not be treated as terrorism. (*Defining Terrorism: Is One Man's Terrorist Another Man's Freedom Fighter?* by Boaz Ganor, Director, Institute of Counter Terrorism, September 1998.)

The question of the legitimacy of violence used in terrorism leads us to the question of 'root-causes' of terrorism. In the South Asian context, Sri Lanka's President Chandrika Kumaratunga made very bold and unusual comments in her address to the SAARC Summit held in Kathmandu in January 2002, soon after 9/11. She said:

> Someone once said, 'hope betrayed transforms itself into bombs'. I would add that, perceived injustice, if it is allowed to continue unresolved, would transform itself first into despair and then into violence. In today's context, the demand for the rectification of injustice is with acts of violence, which by itself raises the issues of justice in terrorist violence. . . .
>
> At this point it would be useful to remind ourselves that . . . the terrorists did not cause the partition of India and create the tragedy of Kashmir as a buffer zone. To come closer home, neither did the LTTE nor the armed Tamil militants create the circumstances for the marginalisation of the minority communities of Sri Lanka.

> Violence—social, political or physical—perpetrated by the state or the agents of the state against other states or its own people is the womb of terrorism, humiliation is its cradle and continued vengeance by the state becomes the mother's milk and nourishment for terrorism.[5]

Very few heads of state would have courage to go to this length in holding the state responsible for terrorism.

ROOT CAUSES

Taking a cue from this statement and recognizing the prevailing realities of terrorism in South Asia, the roots of conflicts that generate and perpetuate terrorism in the region may be seen at three levels: internal, regional, and global. At the internal level, the state must bear responsibility for its contribution to this menace. Two notable drifts that account for the lapses on the part of the state are, one, the rise of the sectarian state, and, two, the failure of governance on the part of the state. In 1947–8, when the South Asian states were generally brought into being (with the exception of Nepal), the character of the polity aspired to was secular, respecting the diverse and multi-ethnic, multi-religious texture of the societies of the South Asian states. Even Pakistan was no exception to this, if one recalls its founder Jinnah's vision. Slowly and gradually, however, all the South Asian states have drifted in various degrees and forms of proclaiming themselves as sectarian states based on religious or ethnic identities. India has not yet fallen in the this category but sectarian forces are well entrenched in the political processes.

The sectarian drift has naturally disturbed harmony and balance in the multi-ethnic societies of South Asia. Minorities and marginalized groups have become insecure—being pushed into a state of desperation where violence appears to be a viable and perhaps the only option for grievance redressal.

The second critical drift in South Asia has been the failure of the state in delivering good governance, i.e. balanced development, removal of poverty, and an atmosphere of social and individual security. This is a complex area where the state has not been able to cope with the triple explosion of 'information, aspirations and identity'. It is also possible to argue that, in some respects, the fast-changing global situation, with constrained aid flows and the squeeze of globalization, has added to the woes of the state. However, the state has paid very inadequate attention to the needs of the deprived sections of the society. One of the factors behind the rise of madrasa culture and jehadi extremism in Pakistan and militancy in India's Jammu & Kashmir is the lack of economic opportunities. The rural uprisings in India, including the Naxalite movement, have also resulted from years of exploitation and deprivation of the rural poor and landless.[6]

It is desirable in this respect to steer clear of the steamrolling approach to terrorism where every act of violence, particularly the one directed against the state by the defiant and rebellious groups, is treated as terrorism.

We may not be accused of overstretching the point of governance if we say that political dynamics and the manner of carrying out the struggle of power for capturing the government is also a part of governance. In this respect, none of the South Asian conflict situations may be free from the phenomenon of intertwining political vested interests with conflicts. In Pakistan, jehadi forces are well plugged in the Pakistani power structure, particularly through the army. In India, the north-east insurgencies and the Naxalite movement enjoy political patronage in one form or the other.[7] In Nepal, the monarchy had patronized the Maoists until July 2001, and even political parties had carried out their mutual rivalry through the Maoists in some cases. In Sri Lanka, the Tamil question is a major issue in intra-Sinhala political rivalries, and so on.

South Asian countries have had a somewhat broader, but not a basically different approach. While it is not our concern in this study to delineate the conceptual parameters of terrorism, it may be desirable to take a differentiated view of the phenomenon of terrorism. Care needs to be taken to separate the 'terrorism' component of a given religious, ethnic or ideological conflict from its traditional thrust. It may also be necessary that the senseless and indiscriminate use of violence even by the state is assessed for its terrorist characteristics and consequences. Accordingly, without going into further details, we must apply a threefold criteria: (a) the legitimacy of violence; (b) the instruments, extent, and forms of violence; and (c) the targets of violence to ensure if a particular mode of violence should be treated as a terrorist act or not. For instance, any violence without a legitimate cause, which is excessive and indiscriminate, and targeted against innocent and helpless people should surely be categorized as terrorist violence.

Response Strategies

It is said that language has its own ideology and words carry certain biases. In dealing with terrorism, terms like 'combating' or 'countering' necessarily carry, explicitly or otherwise, a negative, militaristic bias. These terms have very little scope for redressing legitimate grievances or accommodating justified demands of the groups in conflict. These terms are in conformity with most of the state-dominated strategies to deal with terrorism since the priority in these strategies is of fighting and eliminating rather than 'preventing' terrorism. For any lasting resolution of terrorism-generating conflicts, much more than a simply militaristic approach is required. We are therefore advisedly avoiding the use of the terms 'combating' or 'countering' here, and instead suggest that terms like 'dealing with', 'coping with' or 'responding to' be used. The last, i.e. 'responding to', may be even more desirable as it is value neutral and can cover a wider spectrum of options and alternatives including political and socio-economic approaches. This term also seems to be more compatible with the role of the state as well as non-state actors in South Asia in dealing with terrorism.

The strategies pursued by the South Asian states in responding to the varied challenges of terrorism may fall into four broad categories. The first strategy is based on *the use of force*. This strategy is invariably pursued by almost all the South Asian states. The thrust of this strategy is to use superior counter-force to suppress terrorism and insurgency. The agencies employed in the use of force range from ordinary police to paramilitary and specialized forces as well as the regular armed forces of the country. Many of these security formations have been inducted into fighting insurgencies and terrorism without proper training, equipment, and guidance. As a result, the use of force is either inadequate, or excessive, or inappropriate; and in all these conditions, it helps insurgency and terrorist forces to gain legitimacy, social support, and greater buoyancy. While the inadequate and improper use of force erodes the credibility of the state, excessive force invokes revulsion among the innocent victims and turns them against the state. Particularly instances of fake encounters, custodial deaths, arrests without trials, rape, torture, arson, looting, extractions by the police and security forces alienate people from the state and cripple its moral authority to deal with the rebellion. Such examples are found in each of the South Asian countries.

This strategy also raises the question of proper coordination and understanding between different instruments and agencies of force, i.e. between police, paramilitary and military forces, between intelligence and security agencies, between security agencies and political as well as administrative decision-making processes. In recent years, the pressure has also increased upon security agencies to carry out their operations under the constraints of human rights and social sensitivity. Some security forces in South Asian countries are adjusting to these requirements while others are indifferent towards them. The security forces are also assigned responsibilities in the resettlement and rehabilitation of victims of terrorism and conflicts. In India, the security forces have also launched special programmes (like *sadbhavana*) in the areas of health, education, and resettlement, to win the support of the people in the areas of their operations. Other countries might have also done something similar. This positive aspect of the 'use of force' strategy will also be factored into the overall discussion. South Asian countries have active National Human Rights Commissions to keep a watch on states' behaviour. The state is also giving its security forces training in human rights to help them conduct their operations in a civilized manner.

The second strategy relates to the *law and order* approach where terrorism is dealt with as a crime and sought to be curbed through legal and police methods. Almost all the South Asian states have enacted special laws and raised specialized forces in pursuance of this strategy. For such measures, the security forces exert pressure under the pretext that the existing laws and security provisions are not adequate to deal with the challenge of terrorism. In India, the enactment of the Prevention of Terrorism

Act (POTA) and the Terrorists and Disruptive Activities Act (TADA) have been debated politically as well as from the human rights perspective. In Sri Lanka, laws were also enacted to control the flow of essential commodities to the Tamil-dominated areas in the name of denying such commodities to the Tamil militants. In the process, ordinary Tamils living in the conflict zones suffered unprecedented hardships. In Nepal also the supply of food grains has been curtailed in the Maoist-dominated areas. King Gyanendra now is also changing the administrative and political structure of the kingdom under the pretext of dealing with the insurgency. The enactment and implementation of such laws get involved with the political dynamics and raise further controversies because such measures are also abused by the ruling parties to punish and harass their political adversaries. And the impact of these laws in curbing terrorism has been far from being satisfactory.

Then there is the *political and constitutional* approach to address the root causes of insurgencies and terrorism. Under this approach, steps to initiate talks and peace processes in search of negotiated settlements have been taken, and in some cases, accommodation through constitutional changes have also been offered and achieved. Holding elections and referenda to initiate or endorse a certain political decision also falls into this category. In India, to resolve the insurgency in the Punjab, the Rajiv Gandhi government even went to the extent of enabling the provincial opposition party, Akali Dal, to come to power through an election. In Assam, Rajiv Gandhi also let the Assam Gana Parishad, the principal agitators for the Assamese cause, come to power. Even before Rajiv Gandhi, there were attempts to accommodate the aspirations of the hill tribes through special constitutional provisions like the 6th Schedule of the Constitution, and political arrangements for power-sharing. The political and constitutional approaches have also enabled the state to win the hearts and minds of insurgency-affected people. Political campaigns have also been launched to isolate the terrorists and insurgents and erode the social support for their cause. In complex insurgencies and ethnic conflicts, political and constitutional approaches are a must for finding a lasting resolution of the core issues, but then the success of such approaches also depends critically on the requisite political consensus among the affected groups and their political representatives. One of the reasons that frustrated all the constitutional proposals made so far for solution of the Tamil problem in Sri Lanka has been the lack of consensus among the mainstream Sinhala parties. India's multilayered federal Constitution on the other hand has given it resilience, in this respect to produce positive results with regard to the challenges in Tamil Nadu, Punjab and the north-eastern states. In Nepal, the rewriting of the Constitution through a constituent assembly is the main demand of the Maoists and some of the political parties. In effect, they are seeking the King's exit from active politics and governance and his control of the armed forces.

Closely linked to the political and constitutional approach is the strategy of responding to terrorism through *socio-economic development* and *cultural accommodation*. Moves and actions related to human rights protection, winning hearts and minds, creating economic opportunities for the affected people, generous allocation and effective disbursement of resources for resettlement and rehabilitation, recognition of language preferences and cultural specificities, etc., constitute the various components of this strategy. It is, however, unfortunate that developmental deficiencies of the conflict-affected peoples and areas have not been seriously addressed. This is a long-term strategy and deals more with the preventive aspects of terrorism and conflicts. The political regimes and leadership have not shown patience for such long-term strategies that may not yield visible results during their span in power. The developmental approach has also been frustrated by the lack of massive financial resources required to fight the curse of under- and mal-development. Even when resources are made available, only a tiny fraction of them reach the targeted social groups and regions due to corruption and inefficiency. There are several studies showing the high levels of corruption in South Asian societies and the deleterious effects of such corruption on the countries' developmental agenda.

None of the foregoing strategies have been, or should be, pursued in isolation. An important question in assessing the identified strategies is to see as to what extent the balanced and effective coordination and integration among them has been obtained by the South Asian states in responding to the challenges of terrorism. To some extent, India has pursued these strategies simultaneously if not in a properly integrated manner, with success in a few cases like the Tamil separatist movement (during the 1960s), the Punjab insurgency, and the insurgencies in the north-east (Mizoram and Tripura), where the use of force was followed up with political and constitutional accommodation. Negotiations have also been established with the Nagas, the Kashmiris, and other insurgent groups. Sri Lanka also succeeded in resolving the JVP challenge of 1971 through a combined use of military methods and political measures. The second round of the JVP uprising was also handled similarly during 1986–90. Bangladesh defused the alienation of the Chakmas of the Chittagong Hill Tracts. But there are many more cases of failure where the responses of India and other South Asian countries to insurgencies and terrorism have been imbalanced and lopsided, resulting in complicating the challenge rather than resolving it. There is increasing evidence that more than one of the approaches mentioned earlier have been attempted in South Asian countries but it has not been possible to strike a requisite balance and harmony in their pursuance. High priority has often been accorded to the use of force and law-and-order approaches.

The External Dimension

It may not be adequate to look at these strategies within each of the South Asian countries. There are regional and global dimensions to the problem of terrorism in South Asia, and accordingly, the assessment of these strategies also needs to be made at the *regional* as well as the *global* levels. At the regional and global levels, bilateral and multilateral cooperation have become essential components of strategies to respond to terrorism. Bilaterally, we must keep in mind that in South Asia there are several instances of one country exploiting the insurgencies and internal conflicts of a neighbouring country for its strategic and foreign policy goals. Almost every South Asian country has been accused of such exploitation at one stage or another. Further, due to contiguous ethnic identities and unnatural, porous borders, insurgencies and terrorism easily spill over from one country to another. Bilateral cooperation may help in dealing with such spillovers and such help may also go a long way in helping the victim country deal with conflict and terrorism in a more effective manner.

There are several aspects of such cooperation: sharing of intelligence, military support, joint operations, border management, question of sanctuaries, shelters, refugees, flow of arms, training camps, state sponsorship and cross-border character of terrorism, financial resources, role of the diaspora, etc. Bilateral cooperation in these areas exists in South Asia in one form or another, but there is lot more that needs to and can be done. The extent to which this cooperation can go was demonstrated by India and Sri Lanka in the conclusion of the July 1987 agreement between the two countries under which the Indian Peace Keeping Forces (IPKF) fought Tamil insurgency in Sri Lanka. This attempt was vitiated by Sri Lanka's internal politics which humiliated India and forced it to withdraw the IPKF in 1990 before it had completed its task. Sri Lanka is now again seeking Indian support to meet any possible contingency where another Eelam war breaks out. For this, India and Sri Lanka have even finalized a draft on bilateral Defence Cooperation Agreement. Another example of bilateral cooperation to combat terrorism in South Asia was witnessed between India and Bhutan, when in December 2003, the latter undertook its own military operations to flush out Indian insurgent groups from its territory where they had established sanctuaries and operational bases. Imagine a situation where Bangladesh also comes forward to cooperate with India like Bhutan in this regard. Pakistan has been conducting joint and coordinated operations with the US to flush out Taliban and Al Qaida operatives from along the Pakistan-Afghanistan border, particularly in the South Waziristan area. If a similar gesture of cooperation is extended by Pakistan to India, the problem of insurgency and terrorism in Kashmir will become far more manageable for the latter.

Multilaterally, at the regional level, SAARC assumed a role for itself in the 'suppression of terrorism' as early as in 1987 when a regional Convention on the subject was adopted. But this Convention has, by and large, remained a dead letter. For many years the member countries did not ratify the Convention by making relevant domestic laws as desired. Thanks to the events of 9/11 and the launching of the 'war on global terrorism' by the US, international pressures have been on the rise since 2002 for South Asia to seriously take up the challenge of combating terrorism. The impact of such pressures was evident when at the Kathmandu SAARC Summit in January 2002, the decision to revamp the SAARC Convention on Suppression of Terrorism to make it more effective was taken. The real problem has been the absence of the necessary political will on the part of those states that look upon conflict and terrorism in a neighbouring country as a political and strategic opportunity rather than a matter of security concern. It would be useful to examine the potentialities and constraints of SAARC in playing an effective role in meeting the challenge of terrorism in the region.

The international community has always been actively interested in playing a decisive role in resolving conflicts in South Asia. The international community's dabbling in Kashmir issue stands as an obvious example of this since the late 1940s. The US, and subsequently many others, have time and again offered to play a third-party mediatory role in regional-conflict resolution. An explicit example of playing such a mediatory role in terrorism-related conflicts can be seen in Sri Lanka, where since 2000, Norway, backed by the US, EU, and Japan, is playing the role of a third-party facilitator to resolve the ethnic conflict. This role has come under severe criticism and even faced the prospects of termination, but survives. The critical aspect of the 'third party' role is the interests and stakes of the prospective third party in the resolution of conflict by playing honest broker. The demand for such third-party mediatory roles are on the rise in South Asia. Pakistan has always been keen to get a 'third party' involved in Kashmir. Nepal's Maoists, for the past couple of years, have also started asking for the involvement UN or any 'independent international agency' or actor in facilitating their talks with the King's government.

It may be useful to objectively evaluate the question of the third-party role in peace processes in terrorism-related conflicts. There are different forms of such third-party roles, from quiet persuasion to facilitation, mediation, financial incentives, peace-keeping and peace making, etc. In the post-9/11 period, terrorism has become a key global issue. There is a visible spurt in inclination and initiative on the part of the 'international community' to help South Asia in fighting terrorism, as this is considered a part of the 'global war against terrorism'. The US and UK are actively involved in the responses of the states to terrorism in Nepal, Sri Lanka, Bangladesh, India, and Pakistan through substantial military and economic support. The US is also exercising its influence on Pakistan against the latter's involvement in 'cross-border' terrorism in India's Kashmir insurgency. In some cases, the influence of these extra-regional powers in domestic approaches to terrorism is visible and even decisive. This global dimension deserves careful analysis and critical evaluation because extra-regional powers have their respective strategic objectives in South Asia, and their influences on the regional approaches to responding to terrorism are becoming stronger every day.

An important evolving form of the international community's role in terrorism-related conflicts is to act collectively in promoting peace processes and conflict resolution. In relation to South Asia, there are two concrete examples where the donors have come together to offer a collective package of financial support in the task of reconstruction and rehabilitation if the parties to the conflict make sincere efforts to resolve their conflicts. This has been done in Sri Lanka and also initiated in Nepal. In Sri Lanka, the donor community came together in outlining the parameters of the peace process and conflict resolution in the form of the Oslo Agreement. Subsequently, as a result of two donor conferences in Washington and Tokyo in 2002, an assistance package of US $4.5 billion has been proposed to both the Sri Lankan government and the LTTE if they work together towards peace and conflict resolution under international monitoring by the donor group. It is instructive that such a role for the donor group has so far been rejected by the LTTE as it does not want to be driven to peace by compromising on its political agenda. Thus while donor incentives are welcome, donor conditions are not acceptable. The donor initiative has also not made much progress in Nepal where, besides other things, the King flouted the advice of the donors and major powers by taking power into his own hands at the cost of the democratic system.

Additional Variables

While evaluating and analyzing the matrix of four strategies operating at three levels, two other variables may be factored in; namely, the *character of the state* that is responding to terrorism as also the changing character and dynamics of the insurgent and other groups in conflict that resort to terrorism in pursuance of their political goals. The state has dominant features which characterize its core behaviour depending upon its social base, coercive capabilities, and ideological orientation. It can be autocratic, democratic, sectarian, secular, welfare, national security state, autonomous, dependent, revolutionary, regressive, fascist, imperialist, and so on. This character of the state may define its response to terrorism. A national security or a militaristic state, for instance, may not be inclined to pursue the course of political and constitutional accommodation to address the root causes of terrorism. A sectarian state often precipitates ethnic conflict and terrorism. It may very likely resist plural and multicultural solutions to the minorities and sectarian adversaries involved in the raging conflicts.

Strategies for responding to terrorism will also have to be evolved in relation to the nature of the challenge posed. Accordingly, a dynamic analysis of the *changing character of the groups resorting to terrorism* is also essential. Such groups seldom remain the same as when they started their operations, in terms of their leadership, their organizational structure, their ideological posture, their demands and military capabilities, their external linkages, and so on. If our research attempt can identify and/or establish any causal or coincidental relationship between these changing aspects and the changes in the strategies pursued to deal with terrorism, a basic contribution to the existing knowledge on the subject would be made.

Outcomes

The evaluation of the responses to terrorism in South Asia will obviously be made on the basis of an assessment of the successes or failures of the strategies pursued. There are also many intermediary stages between the stark judgement on success or failure in a given case. The management, moderation, diversion, diffusion, etc., of the terrorism-generating conflict, or even the beginning and prolonging of a peace process, may constitute such stages. It would, however, be useful to project these intermediary stages into possible final outcomes in the interest of policy prescriptions. Innovative alternatives may be suggested to explore the possibilities of making the strategies pursued more effective.

Terrorism and the process of carving out responses to it *also generate political, socio-cultural and developmental consequences* in a country braving terrorism. For instance, in Nepal and Pakistan, autocratic institutions like monarchy and the military respectively have become stronger in the course of fighting terrorism. In these countries political parties have also become divided on the question of terrorism, the state's response to it, and the involvement of external players in fighting it. Diverse political considerations thus shape the strategies and the way they are executed. Leaders and political parties have strengthened or eroded themselves in other countries. Institutions have been discredited or regained their legitimacy in the course of pursuing a certain strategy or not pursuing others. There are also developmental and economic consequences of terrorism-generating conflicts and strategies pursued for resolving or coping with these conflicts. The Maoists in Nepal, for instance, are blamed for the damage to developmental projects and economic infrastructure, pushing the already poor country further into the state of misery and deprivation. At the same time, the latest International Crisis Group Report (ICG) on Nepal concludes that politics, including the centrality of the King, in the kingdom is an obstacle to the peace process. Socially, these conflicts, and the responses to them, uproot people, generate the exodus of refugees, both within and outside the country, and adversely affect women, children, and the helpless sections of society. These conflicts also create inter-state tensions, new alliances and bonds of cooperation, and redefine the strategic parameters of the region and its member countries. South Asia must be critically examined in the perspective of these consequences.

ROLE OF THE CIVIL SOCIETY

Civil society has an important role to play in responding to terrorism. This role is being and can be played in coordination with, or independently of, the role of the state. Even when the civil society plays an independent role, it can reinforce the role of the state or act as a watchdog for the lapses, failures, and excesses of the state. Media and information agencies occupy a very critical place in this respect, and their role in responding to terrorism deserves to be carefully examined. Then there are non-governmental organizations (NGO), both national and international, involved in the protection of human rights, in reconstruction and rehabilitation, in facilitating and reinforcing peace processes. Their negative as well as positive contributions in dealing with the conflicts must be assessed. There is no uniformity in the role played by the media and the NGOs. Different social and political conditions under which all these non-state actors operate shape their roles and the respective outcomes. A comparative study of this aspect in South Asia deserves attention.

FRAMEWORK OF THIS STUDY

With the perspective outlined above, this study focuses on the strategies adopted by the individual South Asian countries in responding to their specific challenges of terrorism. In view of the diversity of the challenges faced, two separate chapters on India have been included, which deal with the Punjab and Kashmir insurgencies on the one hand and that of the north-east on the other. Since the Punjab conflict has almost been resolved, the contrast in India's strategies in the Punjab and elsewhere may be illustrative. Maldives has not been included in this study as there is no serious problem of terrorism raging there. In addition to the case studies, some comparative perspectives have also been included. They deal with the political and social consequences of the strategies followed to cope with terrorism-generating conflicts, the role of third parties and of the civil society in resolving such conflicts, and also the political economy of terrorism and state responses to the menace. As mentioned earlier, there is also a data paper on the regional situation to add to the comparative perspective.

NOTES

1. Charles Krauthammer, 'Patterns of Global Terrorism', State Department, Bureau of Public Affairs.
2. Paul R. Pillar, 'Terrorism and US Foreign Policy', Washington: Brookings Institute Press, 2001.
3. Samuel P. Huntington, *Clash of Civilization and the Remaking of World Order*, A Touch Stone Book, New York: Simon and Schuster, 1996.
4. Krauthammer, 'The New World Order After 11 September', <http://www.reveatations.org.2a/New World Order.htm>.
5. Text circulated by Sri Lankan High Commission, India. Also SAARC Documents of the 11th Summit.
6. There are a number of studies on this theme. For recent comments on this see, Prakash Singh, 'The Ploughshare that Became a Pistol', *Indian Express*, 22 April 2005.
7. Maloy Krishna Dhar, *Open Secrets: India's Intelligence Unveiled*, New Delhi: Manas Publications, 2005; Ved Marwah, *Uncivil Wars: Pathology of Terrorism in India*, New Delhi: HarperCollins, 1997.

2. Responding to Terrorism in Punjab, and Jammu & Kashmir

Ajai Sahni

India has had a continuous experience with fighting insurgencies since the mid-1950s. It was, however, the Sikh fundamentalist terrorist movement in Punjab through the 1980s and early 1990s, and the Pakistan backed Islamist separatist terrorism in Jammu & Kashmir (J&K), which assumed threatening proportions in 1989 and still continues, that constitute two of the most significant challenges to unity and integrity that the country has confronted in its history since Independence.

While a relatively greater body of general literature is available on the J&K conflict, neither movement has been adequately documented or analysed, particularly in terms of the extraordinary diversity of continuous strategic and tactical innovations on both sides—state and anti-state—of these conflicts, as well as the political initiatives and actions they provoked.

It is useful to explicitly state at the outset, however, that no combination of these innovations and initiatives amounts to a consistent 'Indian strategy of response' or a coherent 'counter-terrorism policy'. Indeed, despite decades of wrestling with the problem, as George Tanham notes, 'India has not developed a coherent internal strategy for domestic law and order and separatist and insurgency problems, or a counter to Pakistan's policy of assisting these separatist movements.'[1] Tanham notes further that India has, at best, developed counter-insurgency tactics, not an overall strategy. It has, indeed, in this context, been possible to speak of a 'fruitless cycle' that has been 'repeated in an endless succession of "peace initiatives" at the highest level—regularly interrupted by escalating violence, military mobilization, coercive diplomacy and belligerent political rhetorics'[2] in a pattern that displays 'the consistency of a pendulum, swinging with insistent regularity from one extreme to the other'.[3]

This incoherence in the response has been the single most significant factor in the persistence of these movements over extended periods of time, as the gains of each tactical or policy innovation or initiative are often cancelled out before they can be consolidated by contradictory moves. The centrality of coherent governmental responses to the trajectory of an insurrection has been insufficiently understood in this context, as the discourse vacillates between the extremes dictated by inchoate and misconceived theories of 'root causes' on the one hand, and the immediate imperatives of containment and retention of the rudiments of state control, on the other. W.C. Sonderland has noted, rightly that, 'as soon as the challenge is in the open the success of the operations depends not primarily on the development of insurgent strength, but more importantly on the degree of vigour, determination and skill with which the incumbent regime acts to defend itself, both politically and militarily'.[4] Barring brief periods characterized by the requisite clarity and focus, the necessary 'vigour, determination and skill' have, by and large, been lacking in the state's responses to terrorist and insurgent movements in India. The resolution in Punjab was, in fact, the product of one such relatively brief episode of political resolve and strategic and tactical lucidity against a background of extended vacillation, drift, and active political mischief.

It is not the intention here to trace the various causes that contributed to the rise of terrorism in Punjab and J&K, but it is useful to note certain peculiarities that generally characterize terrorist movements in this context, and that are of significance from a policy perspective:

1. There is a wide gap between 'root causes', triggering factors, and the sustaining dynamic that emerges once a movement has acquired certain 'maturity'.[5] Root and triggering factors decline in significance as useful inputs for a strategy of resolution, and it is the unique sustaining dynamic that becomes critical once the state is confronted with a full-blown insurgency or terrorist movement. Simply put, even if subsequent policy correctives eliminate the presumed 'root' and 'triggering' causes, movements may still persist if the

sustaining dynamic is not addressed. Conversely, if the sustaining dynamic is neutralized, movements end even if the root and triggering causes remain entirely neglected. There is, consequently, something evidently problematic with explanations and policies which seek their justifications in 'unfulfilled collective aspirations' or within the conventional dogmas of class, economic, or political analyses. As one commentator notes in the context of the defeat of terrorism in Punjab: 'Little change was noticed in the objective conditions, and none of the adduced reasons or causes of the rise (of terrorism) appear to have been removed. . . . Once the movement collapsed, one was left wondering how could it disappear so suddenly and without leaving a trace of cultural sympathy for the "fighters".'[6]

2. Perspectives on causation and the character of terrorism have often polarized policy prescriptions between two mutually exclusive approaches: the 'military',[7] which emphasizes use of force to 'restore normalcy'; and the 'developmental', which seeks to address the 'root causes' and thus secure a victory over 'hearts and minds'. Neither approach, however, necessarily excludes the other, nor is adequate in itself. Both are founded on a partial perspective, which, in some measure, reflects an inaccurate assessment of the dynamic that is set in motion by widespread terrorism. An efficient state response requires a coordinated and comprehensive effort that addresses all aspects of this dynamic, and 'piecemeal and local solutions have no impact'.[8]
3. Another aspect of this polarization of perspectives is the presumed dichotomy of 'democratic' and 'military' solutions. This ignores the reality that the use of force is integral to all forms of governance, including the democratic, and the use of such coercive force against terrorism is 'not just a necessary expedient, but a fundamental obligation and duty of constitutional government. . ."[9]

To fail to exercise this legitimate coercive authority is . . . not an act of non-violence or of abnegation; it is not a measure of our humanity or civilization. It is, rather, an intellectual failure and an abdication of responsibility that randomises violence.

alienating it from the institutional constraints of the state. . . . In doing this, it (the state) makes innocents the victims of criminal violence, instead of making criminals the targets of its own legitimate and circumspect punitive force.[10]

In examining the counter-terrorism responses in Punjab and J&K, it is necessary to point out at the outset that, while certain commonalities may emerge, it is not useful to approach the subject with the intention of seeking out such shared or 'universal' principles. Generalization, in this context, tends to trivialize the issue, and any such formulation would be open to criticism. There are enormous strategic and tactical differences between the two theatres. Indeed it is seldom adequately emphasized that such differences are also a fact within each theatre itself. The counter-terrorism campaign in Punjab in 1989, for instance, was entirely and radically different from the campaign in 1991; similarly, the rural campaigns in the Mand region, and the confrontation in urban Ludhiana would have few points of comparison. There is, moreover, no generalized model or modus operandi that can be extracted from the Punjab or the J&K experience. The campaigns in these states are not reducible to any simple set of 'formulae', and successes—including the comprehensive success in Punjab—and arise out of a *pattern* of continuous invention, adaptation, and good generalship.

Contours of Counter-Terrorism in Punjab[11]

The counter-terrorism campaign in Punjab made several radical departures from inherited wisdom, and one of the most significant of these was the fact that it was the Punjab police which spearheaded the state's response to terrorism in the most effective phases of the fight-back. Conventional theory has generally held that once terrorist or insurgent campaigns have passed beyond a certain level of violence (this threshold varies according to the objective circumstances of particular insurrections, as well as the positions and perspectives of the state leadership), the army is the natural instrumentality of response, with the 'civil' police relegated to a supportive or secondary role. This has been the position even of those who are generally opposed to the use of the military in civil or internal disorders.[12] This has also been the standard pattern of response in most campaigns in India, as it has been in most other areas of major civil strife across the world.

This propensity has been compounded in India because of an implicit assumption that the local police force, with its personal, cultural, and political affiliations, and sympathies with the local population in an area of widespread disorder, would generally be substantially subverted. This was certainly the perception in the earlier stages of terrorism in the Punjab, with central forces often deeply suspicious of the local police. In its later stages, under K.P.S. Gill's command, however, the Punjab campaign eventually demonstrated not only that the civil police was an effective counter-terrorist force even in the most extreme circumstances, but also that the presumption of bad faith was unfounded.

There were, however, grave failings in the Punjab Police in the period before 1984. K.P.S. Gill has noted that the atmosphere of terror and collapse in the state at this time was far in excess of anything that the situation itself warranted.[13] Between 1981 and 1983, the terrorists had killed 101 civilians. Of these, 75 were killed in 1983 alone,[14] which in the prevailing state of hysteria, inspired one commentator to term it as 'The Year of the Armageddon'.[15] All terrorism is, of course, unacceptable, but this assessment was more than excessive, especially in view of the course terrorism was to take in the years to come, and indeed, also in view of the levels of criminal violence that were regarded as 'normal' in the state.[16] Yet the first years of terrorism induced a state of near complete paralysis in the police,[17] partly as a result of the unfamiliarity of the nature, randomness and brutality of terrorist violence, and substantially because of the contradictory signals emanating from the political classes in the state and at the centre. As Gill describes it:

> the shock of terrorist tactics—unfamiliar in the extreme—produced a paralysis that was compounded enormously by the conduct of politicians at the very highest level. To expect a sagacious, balanced and adequate response from district police officials against extremism that is clearly, directly, sometimes openly, encouraged by leaders at the highest level of governance, is to ask for the impossible. In any event, in the absence of a clear mandate and a firm leadership, the police, directionless and demoralised, quite simply, refused to engage.[18]

Consequently, the first phase of terrorism thrived under the protective umbrella of political patronage and cynicism, culminating in the occupation and fortification of the Golden Temple by Jarnail Singh Bhindranwale and his terrorist cadres. At this stage, Prime Minister Indira Gandhi abruptly swung to the other extreme of crude overreaction and ordered the army to clear the Golden Temple on 3 June 1984. The hastily executed Operation Blue Star virtually destroyed the Akal Takht and damaged many other buildings within the complex. Apart from the loss of life,[19] the operation inflicted incalculable psychological damage on the larger Sikh community; damage that was compounded further by the army's Operation Woodrose, intended to 'mop up' Bhindranwale's surviving associates from villages and gurdwaras across the country. Suspicious of the police and acting on poor intelligence, the troops—drawn overwhelmingly from outside the state—inclined towards sweeping and indiscriminate arrests, which eventually drove a large number of youths across the border into a welcoming Pakistan. As Operation Woodrose came to an end, Indira Gandhi's assassination and the brutal massacre of Sikhs that followed 'gave a new lease of life to a movement which could easily have been contained in 1984 itself'.[20]

The period 1984–8 saw some effort at organization within the police. In the initial period of terrorism, there had been an abject failure even to document terrorist crimes by the police, to register First Information Reports (FIR) and to draw up lists and profiles of terrorists and their organizations. These tasks were initiated after 1984, at the same time when limited cordon-and-search operations by the police and paramilitary forces commenced. The police also took over charge of the Golden Temple, which had been controlled by the army since Blue Star.

This was nevertheless a period of enormous strategic failure, as the centre resorted once again to the politics of manipulation and an inchoate search for a 'political solution'. Along with the Akali Dal, the centre reopened negotiations with the extremist All India Sikh Students Federation (AISSF), which had spearheaded Bhindranwale's terrorist forces in the pre-1984 era. The Barnala government appointed the Bains Committee, which released almost all terrorists then under detention, and there was little pretence even of a minimum sanction for law enforcement. Indeed, the then governor of the state is said to have conceded that the government was paralysed, and that the terrorists ruled by fiat and killings.[21] In March 1986, Julio Rebeiro, who was credited with the counter-terrorist rhetoric of 'bullet for bullet',[22] was brought in as the Director General of Police. The situation he confronted was grim:

> Judges appointed specially to try terrorist offences were, for much of their time, on leave or engaged in influencing their superiors to shift them out of such risky jobs. The politicians, responsible for causing the problem in the first place, refrained from even visiting villages and terrorist-affected areas out of fear. The result was that the field was left open to the terrorists and to those who wielded the gun on behalf of the State, that is, the police. It was commonly said in Punjab that the police were in charge of the rural areas of the state during the daytime. At night, the terrorists took over since the police were themselves reluctant to face the terrorists' bullets in the dark.[23]

Ribeiro remained under continuous political and terrorist pressure throughout his tenure. In April 1986, as the presence and activities of the terrorists in the Golden Temple became impossible to ignore after their 'Declaration of Khalistan', units of the National Security Guard (NSG) were flown in to flush out the terrorists in what is sometimes called Operation Black Thunder I. Political collusion was evident, when information regarding the operation was leaked out, with the result that 'no one of note was caught'.[24]

Despite the escalating rhetoric, there was little by way of a focused counter-terrorist strategy or action. The confusion was reflected in Rebeiro's statement that the police could not be expected to wipe out terrorism, but were only in a position to 'control it'.[25] This uncertainty on the role of the police and the character and magnitude of terrorism undermined operations. Thus, for instance, when the AK-47 entered the terrorist arsenal in May 1987, the dominant thinking continued to emphasize the conventional police doctrine of 'minimum use of force' against the unconstrained violence of the terrorists, and there was strong resistance to upgrading the 'civil' police's weaponry to include arms that were considered 'military'—SLRs and LMGs—and at least some of this resistance came from the police leadership itself.[26]

It was only after the dismissal of the Barnala government in May 1987 that the police began to commit itself for the first time in a conflict that, by this time, had escalated to the level of warfare. Nevertheless, in the prevailing atmosphere of political license, this only fed the violence further, and the second fortification of the Golden Temple—as well as a rising stream of atrocities within its precincts—commenced. Operation Black Thunder II, a simple siege operation, broke the will of the terrorists working out of the Temple and finally demonstrated that the Golden Temple could not be reclaimed by the terrorists as a safe haven and operational base for the remaining duration of the movement for Khalistan.

Yet the security forces in Punjab were still far from generating an efficient counter-terrorism response. There were severe inadequacies of infrastructure, weaponry, communications, organization and, critically, motivation, which had to be overcome well before the terrorists could be effectively engaged and defeated. The most significant obstacles that were overcome in the 1988–93 phase have been enumerated to include the following:[27]

1. Police stations had not been adequately manned and equipped to react to terrorist violence on their own. After Black Thunder, the capacities of sensitive *thanas* (police stations) were upgraded with the objective of making each police station capable of reacting immediately and independently to any act of terrorist violence in its jurisdiction.
2. The ratio of operational to static and non-productive force had been extremely unfavourable. In mid-1988, between 40 and 50 per cent of the 35,000-strong Punjab Police Force was, on any single day, tied down to static and entirely unproductive duties. The bulk of this number was immobilized at innumerable *nakas* (barricades) and, at best, helped create the illusion of security among the general public. In the months following Black Thunder, a large proportion of these personnel was rapidly reallocated to create an operational force that comprehended as much as 85 per cent of the total personnel available.[28]

3. The police had been infiltrated by elements sympathetic to the terrorist cause, and had been weakened by deep communal divisions within and between various police and paramilitary units. Paramilitary forces, drawn primarily from outside the state, displayed a strong anti-Sikh bias.[29] The compromised elements within the force were systematically segregated from anti-terrorist work and sensitive duties, and were given tasks that kept them away from the counter-terrorism campaign. The structural conflict between various wings of the security forces was also addressed. The various forces had been acting in isolation from, and often in competition with, each other. There was no sharing of information, and deep-rooted mutual suspicion that arose out of their traditional ways of exclusionary, often competitive, functioning. To counter this trend, joint interrogation teams were created, along with a system to share available intelligence between all forces. Over a period of time, the Punjab Police and the CRPF attained an extraordinary level of cohesion and coordination.
4. There had been a complete lack of systematic intelligence gathering and analysis. It was only after Black Thunder that intelligence operations began to achieve acceptable levels. Documentation and analysis were carried out at the ground level in each police jurisdiction. Police stations were identified and categorized on the basis of the intensity of terrorist activities, and a village-wise analysis was carried out. Gradually, unique patterns emerged from the surface uniformity of terrorist operations across the state. A continuous system of dissemination of all received intelligence to all the concerned forces was also established.
5. A coherent strategy of response to terrorist activity was lacking. On the basis of the enormous intelligence exercise initiated after Operation Black Thunder II, it became possible to carry out operations which were area, gang, and terrorist specific. The initiative progressively passed out of the hands of the terrorists and into those of the security forces. The terrorists did retain the capacity to organize unpredictable and entirely random strikes against soft targets. What they lost, however, was the impunity of

operations that they had commanded in the past. After each major terrorist strike the responsible group was targeted not only in the Punjab, but also in their safe houses all over the country. Even where such operations did not result in immediate arrest, they paralysed individual terrorists and prominent groups, reducing their capacity to act.

6. Police leadership had failed, and in the earlier phases, the police had been 'led from behind', with senior officers minimizing their own exposure to risk. As the same attitude percolated down to the field level, even the most routine police and security functions began to be totally neglected.[30] A radical policy of postings and promotion was introduced, through which sensitive areas and critical anti-terrorist operations were headed by officers (often very young officers) who were willing to confront danger and take strong personal initiatives, and who volunteered for these high-risk assignments. Those whose motivation, loyalty or bravery was suspect simply 'opted out' for softer postings, often on deputation outside strife-torn Punjab. The selected men led from the front, and were themselves led by the example of the senior-most police leadership after 1988.

The post-Black Thunder period witnessed three distinctive phases in counter-terrorist operations corresponding with the various political regimes and the radical shifts in their policies and orientation to the terrorists.

Opportunities Wasted

After Black Thunder, the then Prime Minister Rajiv Gandhi abandoned his earlier ambivalence and gave the forces a clear mandate to defeat terrorism. A swift redeployment and re-orientation of forces produced immediate results. In March 1989, a massive composite Special Operation—bringing together the forces of the Punjab Police, the CRPF and the Border Security Force (BSF)—was launched in the entire Mand area (a patch of marshland lying primarily in the Amritsar and Ferozepur districts, but flowing over into Kapurthala and Jalandhar as well), Ajnala, Jandiala, Tarn Taran and Batala (along the river Beas). The cordon-and-search combing operations in the terrorist heartland yielded a steady stream of arrests and seizures of arms, ammunition and explosives. The impact was compounded by highly focused intelligence-based operations, as well as the effective use of 'spotters'—captured terrorists who helped identify former associates. By May 1989, the anti-terrorist drive had completely blunted the capabilities of the leading terrorist groups.

At this time, a Village Defence Scheme (VDS) and a system of appointing Special Police Officers (SPO) was formulated, and volunteers among the young men and women in vulnerable villages were provided with arms and training to resist terrorist action at the local level. Plans for the defence of each village were devised, and SPOs, often army or police veterans, were placed in charge of each village operation, supported by small contingents of regular policemen where necessary. Over 10,000 men were mobilized under the VDS and SPO schemes before the end of 1990.[31]

The impact of these measures was palpable. The year 1989 registered a dramatic fall in civilian casualties, at 1,168, down from 1,949 in 1988. Both terrorist and security forces casualties, however, rose significantly, proof of the higher intensity of counter-terrorist engagement (Terrorists: 1988—373; 1989—703; SFs: 1988—110; 1989—201).[32] By the fourth quarter of 1989, the terrorists had been pushed into a corner and almost 65 per cent of all terrorist crime, 64 per cent of civilian casualties, and more than half of all killings in the state were contained within the jurisdiction of just 13 of the 217 police stations in the state.[33] At this stage, K.P.S. Gill, who conceptualized and led the counter-terrorist campaign, asserts that terrorism could have been wiped out in the state 'within another six months of sustained campaigning'.[34]

The pressure forced some changes in terrorist tactics and weaponry, as the armed gangs that had roamed the countryside were systematically engaged and neutralized. The militants progressively inclined to more surreptitious operations and increasingly resorted to the use of timed and remote controlled explosive devises, rather than the AK-47. By April 1989, handling explosives had become an integral part of training in the camps across the border, and some of the first significant seizures of plastic explosives and sophisticated IEDS and timing devises were made in May 1989.[35] Nevertheless, the impact of a continuous depletion in their ranks and critical casualties in the terrorist leadership inflicted a constant toll.

These trends were, however, reversed when the counter-terrorist impulse was diluted towards the end of the Rajiv Gandhi regime, when his discredited government, struggling against charges of corruption, announced a general election, and sought to exploit public insecurities over terrorism in Punjab 'by allowing the sore to fester a little longer'.[36]

THE V.P. SINGH AND CHANDRASHEKHAR GOVERNMENTS

Both the V.P. Singh and Chandrashekhar governments sought to bring back the era of the 'political solution' through policies intended to 'win hearts and minds'. The V.P. Singh regime demonstrated its weakness on terrorism in its first weeks, when it capitulated after Rubaiya Sayeed, the daughter of the then Union Home Minister, was kidnapped (on 11 December 1989) by militants in what was, at that time, an incipient terrorist movement in J&K. Worse, beyond a few symbolic initiatives, such as the Prime Minister's visit to the Golden Temple the day after his swearing-in, there was no coherent policy perspective on terrorism, and procrastination and drift became central to the state's responses. As the government dithered ineffectively, the hardened terrorist leaders of Punjab adopted increasingly intransigent positions, and violence escalated once again. At the same time, the terrorists' front organizations, including their newly elected Members of Parliament, mounted a relentless campaign of protests and agitations which tied down an increasing proportion of the available force in the state. Political and legal action by such fronts, many masquerading as human rights organizations, was closely coordinated with the terrorist leadership and with escalating terrorist activities. Thus, after an encounter with terrorists in February 1990, the BSF recovered a 13-point directive addressed to the newly elected Member of Parliament, Simranjit Singh Mann, from the Pakistan-based terrorist leader, Wassan Singh Zaffarwal, defining elements of this coordinated strategy.[37] The police were brought under direct attack, with police personnel who were on leave and family members of policemen being specifically targeted in a campaign aimed at demoralizing the forces. Five hundred and six policemen were killed in 1990 alone, a majority of them while they were at home on leave. Worse, 'the mounting tide of violence and open political subversion was compounded by irrational and arbitrary force withdrawals'.[38] The situation worsened further after the V.P. Singh regime collapsed and the new Prime Minister, Chandrashekhar, entered into negotiations with the terrorists—whose first demand was the removal of the then Director General of Police K.P.S. Gill; a demand that was immediately conceded. Gill was transferred out of Punjab in December 1990, and took over as Director General, Central Reserve Police Force (CRPF).

Chandrashekhar's final political gambit in Punjab was to push the state into elections in June 1991, immediately after the general elections scheduled for the rest of the country, and in the middle of a rapidly deteriorating law-and-order situation and escalating terrorist violence within the state. A large number of candidates with terrorist links joined the election process and commenced campaigning, moving openly across the state with large contingents of armed 'bodyguards'.[39] Simultaneously, groups that had proclaimed a boycott of the elections, prominently those under the Panthic Committee (Sohan Singh), unleashed a campaign of political assassinations that eventually claimed the lives of 27 candidates, as well as a number of acts of random terrorism including, prominently, the massacre of 74 train passengers on 15 June 1991. Despite the rising violence, a completely irrational force reduction occurred through this period, with the army being withdrawn and the paramilitary force presence cut back. Finally, Chandrashekhar's misconceived election gambit was aborted, though only after the new Prime Minister, Narasimha Rao, had been sworn in.

Operation Rakshak I, an army operation to flush out terrorists from the border districts, was also undertaken under the short-lived Chandrashekhar regime. While it was successful in clearing the border districts, it failed to have any significant impact on the scale of terrorism in the state and was, in fact, substantially responsible for a wider dispersal of terrorist activities as the major groups were gradually 'squeezed out' of the border districts into the Malwa and Doaba regions, with a concentration in the Ludhiana and Sangrur districts.

It is useful to examine the impact of the V.P. Singh and Chandrashekhar regimes—both committed to 'winning hearts and minds'—on the graph of fatalities in the state. Killings in all categories rose dramatically: almost as many civilians were killed in the two years under these regimes as the sum of civilian fatalities in the preceding 12 years of terrorism (1978–89: 5,070; 1990–1: 5,058 civilian fatalities). Paradoxically, the political 'soft approach' did not help save terrorist lives either, and counter-terrorism operations inflicted unprecedented casualties in their ranks as well. In 1989, under a relatively stable political dispensation, 703 terrorists were killed. In 1990, 1,320 terrorists were killed, and in 1991, terrorist fatalities rose to 2,177, as two successive regimes sought to win their 'hearts and minds'. Despite this, the terrorist ranks swelled continuously, and the 'terrorist heartland' extended itself from 13 police stations at the end of 1989, to the whole state by the end of the Chandrashekhar regime.

THE ENDGAME

The final phase of the war against terrorism commenced after the Rao government had been sworn in at the centre and Beant Singh had subsequently been elected chief minister after the state assembly elections of February 1992.

The sheer intensity of the violence in Punjab, built up continuously over the preceding two years, could hardly end with a simple change of regime, and it was some time before a coherent strategy of response was defined by the new government. It was only in November 1991 that K.P.S. Gill was returned to the state with a mandate to create the conditions for an orderly and free election to the Legislative Assembly by February 1992. Significantly, the mandate was backed with an adequate provision of forces—both the army and the paramilitary—and these were deployed in a unique pattern under what Gill describes as 'cooperative command'.

Unlike previous operations, the army and the police (both state and paramilitary) acted in complete concert, with a clearly defined institutional structure of cooperation and consultation. An officer of the rank of Inspector General (IG) from the Punjab Police was attached to each corps of the army deployed in Punjab. A Superintendent of Police (SP) was assigned to each brigade. Police contingents were attached to every army battalion, so that comprehensive and coordinated actions could be taken independently, by each unit, in all emerging circumstances. There was total sharing of all intelligence, to the extent that police control rooms had representatives of the army present, so that relevant intelligence was passed on immediately to every relevant unit. This interaction was carried right up to the highest level. The system of 'cooperative command' that was established at this stage was not compromised in even a single instance by force loyalties or personality clashes throughout the final phase of counter-terrorist operations in Punjab.[40]

There was also significant innovation with regard to the deployment of the army in this phase, under what came to be known as Operation Rakshak II: the classical pattern of saturation of 'sensitive' locations was rejected, and the army was distributed across the state in formations split down to the section level to ensure the widest possible presence. Combined with the extraordinary arrangements for the protection of all candidates, and strong preventive measures by police and paramilitary forces, the result was that not a single candidate was killed during the entire election process and, despite a boycott of the elections by all major terrorist formations—backed by threats of violent reprisals—the elections passed off relatively peacefully, though the voter turnout was low.[41]

The election of February 1992 significantly transformed the ground situation. A new government with a measure of democratic legitimacy was installed; the terrorists had failed to disrupt the electoral process; and since they had called for a boycott of the elections, no terrorists, front organizations, or candidates from the major Akali factions had contested—and these radical elements were consequently eliminated from the political scene, as was their power to exploit the instruments and institutions of democracy to further the extremist agenda. The agitational programmes of the preceding two years collapsed abruptly.

After the elections, the counter-terrorism campaign intensified with major tactical innovations. The army remained in the State, but returned to barracks, and was only called out to play a supportive role in specific operations, particularly to provide rapid-response teams to back up police action, and to provide the outer cordon in search operations.

The police leadership was reorganized to counter the growing influence of the terrorists in urban centres. Senior officers were pulled out of routine tasks in the Police Headquarters at Chandigarh, and each was assigned 4 to 5 of the 140-odd urban centres in the state. Each centre was divided into sectors along a grid, and vehicles and manpower were allocated for patrolling and pursuit duties along strategic points. With this single device, the threat to urban industrial concentrations was contained.

In April 1992, the terrorists shifted their attention to the targeted killings of security personnel. By August this strategy was to be extended to the most intensive campaign against the police and their families. The campaign peaked in August 1992 when 100 out of the total of 167 persons killed in the state were drawn from the police or from the families of policemen.

The response came in the form of three strategies. The first of these was based on the immediate identification of the perpetrators of the latest outrage, and the application of the fullest force to secure their arrest or elimination.

The second strategy focused on the most important terrorists. A police study of terrorist strikes had shown that, despite the increasing scope and range of terrorist activities in the state, and in spite of their improved striking capacity and mobility, militancy in a majority of the cases was highly localized. Even the most important terrorist leaders were found to operate within a radius of no more than 15 to 20 km from their respective villages. With this knowledge, backed by efficient intelligence gathering, it became possible to immobilize and eventually arrest or eliminate these elements. Instead of wasting resources on every petty criminal and opportunist who had joined the terrorist ranks, the available manpower and infrastructure was focused disproportionately on the leaders, the planners, and the ideologues of the movement. Among the 139 hardcore terrorists who fell to this strategy in 1992 were a dozen self-styled 'Chiefs' and some 20 'Deputy Chiefs' of various terrorist groups.[42]

The third element of the strategic response came in the wake of the August killings of policemen and their families, in the shape of Operation Night Dominance. Once again, an analysis of the pattern of terrorists' activities indicated that an overwhelming majority of the killings in the villages took place in the late evening or very early morning. All senior officers were directed to take personal charge of operations at night. From this point on, these officers would be leading night-ops three or four days in every week—*and* performing their normal duties during the day. It was Night Dominance that eventually broke the terrorists' spirit, destroying the even limited impunity with which they could act in the dark of night. Night Dominance included a number of strategies of deception, such as focal point patrolling and the clustering of personnel and vehicles in a single locality to create an illusion of force saturation far in excess of the actual availability of manpower and resources.[43]

It is useful to note that under the preceding 'soft' governments of 1990–1, 5,058 civilians, 1,003 policemen and 3,497 terrorists had been killed, and the state appeared to be teetering on the verge of disintegration. Through 1992 and 1993, 1,566 civilians, 277 policemen, and 2,911 terrorists were killed, and by mid-1993 peace had been completely restored in the state. Political parties—including the now revived 'traditional' factions of the Akali Dal—had participated in municipal and panchayat elections which had secured unprecedented voter turnouts, and a constitutional government was squarely in charge.

If there is a single lesson to be drawn from the Punjab experience, it is in the fact that each time a 'political solution' was sought through a dilution of counter-terrorism operations, through negotiations with terrorists and their front organizations, and through policies of appeasement of terrorist elements, terrorism escalated. Political solutions cannot, in fact, be implemented in situations where the terrorist has the upper hand, as extremists are essentially committed to a maximalist position, and will seek to impose their own will through terror as long as this is possible. Moreover, as long as the terrorists retain significant power, they define the character of politics itself, and inevitably distort the character of the proposed 'political solution'.

Diplomacy and international pressure played no significant role in the response to, or resolution of, terrorism in Punjab, primarily because there was a widespread ethos of the 'tolerance of terror' in the leading western countries, and because India failed consistently in projecting a coherent and convincing picture of the state's perspectives to the international community.[44] Indeed, recruitment, mobilization of finances and of political support by the extremist elements among the Sikh diaspora in leading western countries—prominently, USA, Canada, UK, and Germany—continued unhindered throughout the course of the movement, and remained vibrant even after it had been comprehensively defeated in the Punjab.

CONTOURS OF COUNTER-TERRORISM IN J&K: THE QUEST FOR *AZADI*

The incidents of December 1989,[45] which signalled that terrorism in J&K had entered into an explosive phase, were met with a pattern of shock and administrative collapse that was both reminiscent of the initial stages of terror in Punjab and astonishing in view of the enormous experience of counter-terrorism that had already been gained over nearly a decade of Khalistani violence in that state, not to mention the decades of experience with insurgencies in India's north-east. Clearly, the mechanisms of institutional learning within the government and in the various forces deployed for counter-terrorism duties were severely inadequate, if not non-existent, and each new theatre of terrorism finds the state virtually setting about to reinvent the wheel.

The failure in Kashmir is the more incomprehensible since terrorism was not an abrupt manifestation but the intensification of an ongoing and well-known process. The December 1989 incidents did not mark the 'beginning' of terrorism in J&K; low-grade terrorism and Pakistan-backed subversive activities had been a reality in the state right since the tribal invasion launched by Pakistan in 1947, and 1989 had already witnessed several incidents of terrorist attack—including the 31 July bomb blast outside the Srinagar Telegraph Office and the assassination of a National Conference (NC) worker in August—which should have set alarm bells ringing.

To believe that of the government, its intelligence agencies, the army guarding the Line of Control (LoC) in J&K and the paramilitary forces similarly employed, none had a clue of what was brewing across the LoC since at least 1986, if not earlier, would be to stretch one's credulity to unimaginable limits. Hundreds of youths were sent across mountain passes to be armed and trained in PoK, and that Indian picquets and patrols on the LoC remained ignorant of such passage speaks poorly of those responsible for guarding the frontiers. Immense quantities of sophisticated arms and ammunition were brought into the Valley without knowledge or interception. There can be no doubt that initially the trouble in Kashmir was allowed to gain momentum through sheer neglect.[46]

Unlike Punjab, the advent of high-intensity terrorism in J&K was abrupt. The terrorists were very well equipped, with adequate weapons supplies and training from Pakistan, and 1990 itself saw the security forces seizing 1,240 AK series rifles, 108 rocket-launchers, 74 rocket-boosters, 65 rocket propelled grenades (RPG) and 77 universal machine guns (UMG).[47] A total of 1,177 persons were killed in terrorism-related violence that year alone (862 civilians; 132 SF personnel; and 183 terrorists).[48]

The situation in J&K was worsened considerably by the fact that an unstable coalition was assuming only tentative power at the centre, and appeared to lack both the vision and the will to confront the realities of terror. Panic and a knee-jerk deployment of paramilitary forces, and later the army, comprehended the sum of the initial response, and the issue was at first treated as a 'law and order problem' and a 'political issue', with no manifestation of a counter-insurgency doctrine or perspective on the specificities of the situation in Kashmir. The state police, as was the case in the initial phase in Punjab, was also systematically and deeply subverted, and the paramilitary forces that had been rushed to the Valley came down heavily but ineffectually on the people. Within a few months, the state administration had broken down completely.[49]

As a result the initiative passed progressively into the hands of the terrorists, who took advantage of the overwhelmingly defensive and reactive orientation that dominated counter-terrorism policy and responses. The then Chief Minister Farooq

Abdullah resigned in disgust when the centre appointed Jagmohan as Governor of the state, after its capitulation in the Rubaiya Saeed case, and violence and intimidation in the Valley mounted exponentially.[50] The infirmities of the state were compounded by overreaction and purposeless brutality—such as the massacre of unarmed protesters at the Gawakadal Bridge[51]—which alienated virtually the entire Valley population; and political manipulation made everything worse. M.J. Akbar, in his book, says:

Politics, not policy, was the sole motivation of the eleven months of V.P. Singh's prime ministership, and blood stained more than one corner of India, as each of his 'moves' evoked an opposite if not always equal reaction. Kashmir, tragically, was emptied of its Hindus by this awful violence.[52]

Terrorism at this stage was primarily an urban phenomenon, though a campaign of intimidation against the minority Kashmiri Pandits had been extended into the rural areas of the Valley as well. However absent any clear strategy or intent to contain the terror within its original urban confines, it soon leaked out into the rural and *mufussil* areas, transforming places like Sopore and Kupwara into hotbeds of militancy, and thereafter overflowed into the Valley, into Doda, Poonch, Rajouri, and the hilly tracts of the Udhampur district fuelled by exaggerated stories of security forces' excesses and by a failure to control the movement of volunteers and trained cadres across the LoC.

By March 1993, 'the then Prime Minister felt very much concerned as to whether Kashmir was slipping out of our hands and whether the situation could be retrieved'.[53] The then Governor-General K.V. Krishna Rao noted later that,

all organs of the government, including the administration, police, doctors, engineers, teachers, and even the judiciary were subverted and terrorized, and people lost their confidence in them. A large gap developed between the administration and the people, and the people felt that it was the writ of the militants that was running in the state . . . Instead of dealing firmly with the militants, officialdom gave the impression of appeasing them, to avoid trouble . . . the police felt outmatched. Its leadership was weak and some of the officers were involved with the militants. . . . People were chary of taking their complaints to the police, for fear of information being passed on to militants. . . . In sum, the police commanded neither the respect of the militants nor that of the public.[54]

At this stage, significantly, the terrorist movement had passed out of the hands of the Jammu and Kashmir Liberation Front (JKLF), its primary initiators who sought 'independence', and into those of the more Islamist fundamentalist Hizb-ul-Mujahiddeen (HM), which had been introduced into the Valley by the Inter Services Intelligence (ISI) in September 1989, as a counter to the JKLF, and which sought Kashmir's merger with Pakistan. Over the succeeding years, Pakistan deepened this strategy, eventually and entirely marginalizing the JKLF—whose dominant faction led by Yasin Malik eventually abandoned 'armed struggle' and 'came overground' in May 1994—with die hard pro-Pak organizations such as the HM, Harkat-ul-Ansar (HuA) and, later, the Lashkar-e-Toiba (LeT) among others taking over. 'Another potent and vicious element came in the form of foreign mercenaries, commonly called Afghanis. In fact, the leadership of the militants passed on from the local commanders to the outside mercenaries.'[55] At this stage, 'The *mujahideen's* halo of heroism was gradually giving way to a painful realization among the public that because of the phenomenal expansion of the armed struggle from 1990–1993, the ranks of freedom fighters contained politically shallow people, opportunists, and even criminals.'[56]

The flip side of this 'criminalisation' was the emergence of 'renegade' groups or *ikhwanis*, surrendered militants disillusioned with Pakistan's games and the increasing role and excesses of the *mehmaan* mujahidin ('guest', i.e. foreign militants), who changed sides and began to 'assist' the security forces in their counter-terrorist operations. The first of these renegade groups came into existence in 1994 under the leadership of Kuka Parrey, who headed the Awami League and went on to become a Member of the Legislative Assembly (MLA).[57] Under their terms of surrender, the *ikhwanis* were permitted to retain their weapons for 'self defence'; they participate regularly in combat and road opening operations with the army and, during its period of activity, the Special Operations Group (SoG) of the state police; receive a regular pay; and gather intelligence. However, the *ikhwanis* have been widely discredited because of their involvement in extortion and other criminal activity, as well as widespread allegations of arbitrary action, motivated 'intelligence' feeds to the security forces and other abuses, including excesses against civilians.

Despite the visible decay within the movement for *azadi*, at a strategic level the period between January 1990 and the end of 1993 was appropriately described by Lt. Gen. Vijay Madan as 'one of the wasted efforts' on the part of the state:

> The Higher HQs at Delhi or Udhampur had no clue on how to handle matters and the higher HQs at Srinagar spent its time carrying out small unit operations rather than ensuring that a proper atmosphere was created in order to give the psychological space for manoeuvre to the cutting edge i.e. the fighting units to enable them to carry out their operations more aggressively and in a proactive manner.[58]

An Uncertain Coherence

It was under these circumstances of general and growing disarray—violence claimed 2,567 lives in 1993 in a total of 4,457 incidents—that the first coherent efforts at a coordinated response emerged. In May 1993, what its architect the then Governor-General K.V. Krishna Rao described as a 'Unified Concept' to 'effectively plan and coordinate operations' was set up at the state and field levels.[59] Variously referred to as a Unified Headquarters (UHQ) or at times, incorrectly, as a Unified Command, the UHQ comprises the Army, the Border Security Force (BSF), the Central Reserve Police Force (CRPF) and the State Police, with the Chief Minister as its chairman and the General Officers Commanding (GOC), 15 and 16 Corps, as advisers to the chairman. The role of the two corps were,

> At the field level, the two corps headquarters, in addition to their normal operational role of defence against external aggression, were to be responsible for anti-militancy operations in the State, with the exception of Srinagar city. Under the corps, the divisions were to be responsible for anti-militancy operations in their territorial jurisdiction, and all paramilitary forces meant for anti-militancy operations were to be under the operational control of the divisional commanders.[60]

A counter-insurgency grid was also established after the induction of additional manpower, and a fresh force, the Rashtriya Rifles, was raised to meet the increased demand for troops. Efforts were also made for better management of the LoC and the co-ordination of intelligence. The Intelligence Bureau, which had withdrawn most of its field units in 1990 after a number of attacks targeting its officials, restored its operations across the state.

It would be another three years before circumstances conducive to fresh elections in the state could be established, but the restoration of political processes was an explicit objective of the 1993 initiatives, as was a wide range of administrative measures intended to redress popular grievances and restore developmental processes. The latter had little impact on the ground given the degraded condition of local administration and extension services, but the return and reactivation of political parties and leaders began the slow build-up to the elections of 1996.

The year 1993 also saw the creation of the All Parties Hurriyat Conference (APHC)—a loose coalition of 23 'political parties' with close ties to the terrorist underground and Pakistan—which listed, among its prominent objectives, the projection of the 'Kashmir problem' in the international community. The APHC initiated a campaign of political harassment and obstruction in support of the terrorists, calling for *bandhs* (shutdowns), protests and demonstrations against 'human rights violations' by the security forces and other 'political' issues. The APHC emerged as one of the major sources of the transfer of funds from external sources to the terrorist groups, and many of its leaders have also been accused of misappropriating a large proportion of such funds.

Towards the end of 1993, the security forces registered two major successes which inflicted significant psychological damage on the militants. The first of these was the negotiated resolution of the siege of the Hazratbal Shrine, which had been occupied by terrorists in November 1993. The second was a sustained counter-terrorism campaign, Operation Sahayak, which was launched in October 1993 cleared Sopore town and its surrounding areas of an overwhelming terrorist presence. Gradually, some semblance of order was restored in the state's urban centres as a result of a higher and structured deployment of the forces in a 'three-tier security grid', which sought to create layers of security along the LoC, a second line to interdict infiltration-exfiltration activities in the interior, and a third 'ring' around major urban centres and critical establishments and installations. However, overall violence remained high, and escalated marginally over the succeeding years, to peak in 1996 with a total of 2,903 fatalities. Given the terrain, the sheer sprawl of the state, the presence of widely dispersed, small and isolated settlements, and the continuous stream of trained militants across the border, no pattern or attainable saturation of deployment could contain terrorist attacks, and as the militancy came under pressure in the Valley, it focused increasingly on soft targets in the sparsely populated Doda, Poonch, and Rajouri districts of the Jammu region.

The security situation in J&K kept the state out of the general elections of 1991, but efforts for the revival of the electoral process had been ongoing since mid-1993. As the general elections of 1996 approached, it was decided that J&K would be included, and also that assembly elections—the last of which had been held in 1987—would be held in the state as well, as a measure of progressive political normalization. The gigantic electoral exercise in May, followed by the Assembly elections in August, saw a significant saturation of forces across the state, and while the year registered a marginally higher trend in fatalities, the elections could be considered to have been immensely successful from a strategic perspective. Despite a boycott by the terrorist groups and the Hurriyat, the elections saw an impressive overall turnout—though polling was low in the more volatile constituencies of the Valley.[61] There were some allegations of coercive voting, with many voters complaining that security force personnel and *ikhwanis* had bullied and pressured them to go to the polling booths. Nevertheless, the elections installed a NC government led by Farooq Abdullah and restored, in some measure, an imperfect political process in the state. The elections—combined with operational successes and increasing public cooperation with the SFs—did herald a reversal of the escalating trends in the violence, and there were steady though gradual gains over the succeeding years, till the explosive developments of the Kargil 'war' and the surge in terrorist violence that followed. This was a period of visible exhaustion for the terrorist forces as well as their front organizations and popular support base, and by early 1999, despite high—though declining—levels of violence, there was a widespread belief that a permanent reversal in trends had been secured, and that the movement would wither away.

Among the factors that contributed to this outcome was the continuous reinforcement of the 'grid' under the Unified Headquarters system, which facilitated the 'recovery' of very large areas that had been virtually abandoned in the early years of panic. This was made possible through the creation of a tiered system which used the fullest available manpower for area domination and interdiction of terrorist movement and consolidation. The state police, demoralized, suspect, and marginalized in the initial stages, was also gradually mobilized in the counter-terrorism efforts, working intensively with the population while the paramilitary and military forces engaged with the more dispersed terrorist force in the harsh and mountainous terrain of the interior. Significantly, the 'grid' also relied on a substantial network of 'irregulars', including Special Police Officers (SPO), Village Defence Committees (VDC), and Dhok Defence Committees (DDC) for the protection of high pasture areas (*dhoks*), who helped hold the ground. These were backed up by reinforcements from the paramilitary forces and the army, and helped to provide a wider security net for the general population, systematically wearing out the strength of the terrorist groups.

Various 'peace initiatives' also took place during this period but with little impact on the ground. In February 1996, four 'commanders' from different terrorist outfits, grouped under the banner 'Forum for the Permanent Resolution of Jammu-Kashmir', announced their willingness to initiate unconditional talks with the union government.[62] The government responded by declaring a 24-hour 'ceasefire' on the occasion of Id, and the then union home minister held talks with the Forum on 15 February 1996.[63] Negotiations stalled when the forum rejected the government's decision to hold elections in the state and were not resumed thereafter. Negotiations with Pakistan were subsequently initiated at Islamabad, and an agreement on the setting up of a 'mechanism' to tackle the Kashmir issue was concluded in June 1996. However, escalating violence in the Valley and differences over the modalities of the proposed talks blocked the process in September 1997.

THE PENDULUM AS POLICY

A major event which impacted directly on the course of the conflict in J&K at this time was the Pokhran II and retaliatory Chagai nuclear tests of May 1998. The Bharatiya Janata Party (BJP)-led National Democratic Alliance (NDA) government had brought a new belligerence to the Indo-Pak discourse, and Pokhran II was essentially a physical manifestation of this, even as it was a grave miscalculation. The initial, if implicit, calculation that 'overt nuclearization of the subcontinent might produce some benign side effects',[64] was swiftly discredited after the initial and deceptive flurry of the 'Lahore Process'. Praveen Swami notes that:

> in the wake of Pokhran, there was no cogent understanding of the new strategic opportunities for Pakistan. After the initiation of the Lahore Process, the political establishment in New Delhi and an often-submissive military leadership concurred that Pakistan's sustained aggression in J&K would now be slowly subverted. US pressure, business interests, and above all the *a priori* assumption that nuclearisation would ensure conventional peace were among the many asinine reasons offered for the ridiculous assumption that Pakistan would choose to ignore the best opportunity it had in two decades to force an international initiative on the future of J&K.[65]

Swami asserts that 'the blast of hot air that emanated from Pokhran II, nuclear and polemical, blew firmly north towards Kargil'.[66] It blew equally towards the internationalization of the Kashmir issue—a direction that India had assiduously avoided for half a century. Robert Wirsing points out that, 'practically every privately sponsored task force on the South Asian region assembled under the auspices of major think tanks in the United States in the decade of the 1990s took an unequivocal stand against direct US involvement in the Kashmir dispute'. But the cumulative force of developments since Kargil led him to conclude that 'the prospects for significant progress on the Kashmir front to emerge from strictly *bilateral* dialogue between

India and Pakistan are bleak to non-existent'. External—especially American—intervention is increasingly considered necessary, if not inevitable, a circumstance that significantly favours Pakistan to the extent that it has set its demands so high and used every tool of manipulation and blackmail available to it—including nuclear blackmail—that anything that would seem a minimal compromise on its part would necessarily involve extraordinary concessions by India. Despite the humiliation that was inflicted on Pakistan, its forced withdrawal under clear US pressure and the substantially greater loss of life inflicted on its forces by the Indian military response—the truth is, General Musharraf continues to regard, in some sense correctly, the Kargil misadventure as a gain for Pakistan, to the extent that it brought Kashmir closer to the centre of the international focus of concern.[67]

It was after the Kargil misadventure that Pakistan-sponsored terrorism in J&K reached its most devastating scale. Apart from a quantum escalation, there was the introduction of a new tactical element, the *fidayeen* squad and high-risk or suicidal attacks, often on high security targets, which commenced with the attack on the BSF camp at Bandipora on 13 July 1999. This was just two days after the Pakistani intruders began their withdrawal from Indian territory in keeping with the US-Pakistan joint statement of 4 July in which Pakistan agreed to 'persuade' the intruders to abandon the Kargil heights. In 1999 there were another seven major *fidayeen* attacks, and 2000 saw still another seven.[68] The year 2000 also witnessed the first suicide bomber in the history of the Kashmir insurgency, when a Jaish-e-Mohammad (JeM) cadre blew up his explosive-laden car outside the Badami Bagh Army Headquarters in Srinagar on 19 April. The number of fatalities inflicted by *fidayeen* attacks was not particularly significant, but their psychological impact was overwhelming, forcing the security apparatus to tie down large numbers of troops on perimeter protection, and boosting the flagging morale of the community of jehadis, encouraging them to intensify conventional terrorist attacks. The 1999 Christmas Eve hijacking of IC 814, and the government's capitulation at Kandahar on New Year's Eve, further underscored the image of weakness and disarray in the Indian responses, fuelling an even greater frenzy of activity among the terrorists. The result was two of the worst years in terms of fatalities in J&K—2000 with 3,288 dead and 2001 with 4,507 killed.[69]

Despite increasing and risky diplomatic manoeuvres to exert some international, and particularly American, pressure on Pakistan, and despite President Bill Clinton's direct intervention in the Kargil conflict, India failed to significantly impress the international community with its case on Kashmir, and the spiral of violence continued unabated. It was the events of 11 September 2001, in the USA, that suddenly and radically transformed the international operating environment for terrorism and terrorism-sponsoring states. There was a brief season of euphoria in India as the dominant section of the leadership convinced itself that America would now fight its unending war against terrorism, and that the enterprise of international terrorism itself was imminently doomed. Increasingly, at this stage, the Indian response began to rely overwhelmingly on a shrill 'coercive' diplomatic campaign, at once to demonize Pakistan and to woo American support.

This last phase of counter-terrorism responses, which commenced with 9/11 and which still continues, reflects, on India's part, no new thinking, and a continued reactive paradigm that seeks to exploit—largely without success—the opportunities created by the action of other players, including the terrorists operating in J&K and other parts of India, the sponsoring regime in Pakistan, and the 'international community', particularly the 'global hyperpower', America. On the other hand, Pakistan has negotiated an increasingly hostile international environment with extraordinary success, executing wild, often inconceivable, adjustments that have nevertheless allowed its central objectives in Kashmir to remain unaltered. It has exacted a price in international concessions for its earlier support to terrorism, for its opportunistic withdrawal of support to the Taliban–Al Qaida combine, and for each coerced and marginal reduction in the scale of terrorism in J&K. India has, once again, vacillated between overreaction and timidity, alternately, and ineffectually, ...pting to coerce Pakistan, and suing for an unrealistic ...ed settlement. The massive military mobilization of ...n Parakram, which followed the attack on India's

Parliament on 13 November 2001, and which eventually secured nothing beyond an image of India and the South Asian region as an unstable nuclear tinderbox, was one of the most significant links in the chain of ineffectual and immensely wasteful 'coercive strategies' that have been adopted impulsively by India. At various times through the period of 'full deployment', India had argued that troop withdrawal would occur only after Pakistan ended the infiltration of terrorists into J&K and dismantled the infrastructure of terrorism on its soil. There is no evidence that either of these conditions had even partially been met when the orders for troop withdrawal went out. India simply exhausted another major policy option without significant gains, and the initiative was again abandoned to Pakistan's manoeuvrings. It is a measure of the colossal failure and wastefulness of this experiment that more Indian soldiers lost their lives in this directionless misadventure than in the Kargil war. Five hundred and twenty-seven Indian soldiers were killed in the fierce fighting to reclaim the Kargil heights; as many as 798 died unsung in Operation Parakram.[70] And even as the troops were being pulled back from the international border after, as the Cabinet Committee on Security (CCS) chose to express it, 'the armed forces had, with great distinction, achieved the objectives assigned to them',[71] a new government in J&K was already back to the appeasement of terrorists and their front organizations under the clichéd slogan of 'winning hearts and minds'.

The extremes are punctuated by responses succinctly characterized as 'more of the same',[72] which is the cyclical recourse to the operational initiatives mediated by the fractious Unified Headquarters. Periods of 'non-initiation of combat operations' and of withdrawal of forces for a variety of reasons—elections, Operation Parakram, transient crises elsewhere—have left much of the difficult terrain in J&K, particularly the sparsely populated areas of the Jammu region, periodically and in some cases chronically starved of adequate security cover. Each such dilution of operations or local withdrawal of forces is matched by terrorist moves to dominate such areas, intimidate local populations, and destroy military posts and governmental infrastructure, making subsequent reoccupation by the forces an expensive proposition. The absence of a permanent and effective security cover also undermines the confidence of local populations in the ability of the Indian state to provide effective and permanent protection, often making them sullen and uncooperative though not necessarily or ideologically hostile. The fitfulness of such an approach, moreover, impacts on the capacity of the security forces, particularly the police, the paramilitaries, and irregular forces such as the SPOs and VDCs, which operate more directly under the control of the state government and enjoy a lesser degree of legislative protection than the army, to act consistently or with determination against individuals who could abruptly be part of a 'political process', or even, in many cases, respected members of the legislative assembly or of powerful and 'legitimate' political formations.

The Unified Headquarters experiment has been substantially unsuccessful for the most part, in securing its primary purpose of effective coordination between the multiplicity of forces operating in J&K. The system has failed to overcome the often watertight compartmentalization of the army, the state police, the paramilitary forces and the intelligence agencies, which are often found to be working at cross purposes. These deficiencies were already visible by 1999 and, as one assessment of the working of the Unified Command in J&K noted, the several disparate security agencies were operating within the overall counter-insurgency (CI) grid under differing 'rules of engagement' and 'legislated authority' without the legislated means to induce coherence in implementing the CI management plan.[73] Moreover, the paramilitary forces were most hesitant to work under the operational command of the army because the ethos, training, motivation, discipline, style of functioning, and chain of command of the two forces were poles apart and impossible to bridge.[74] The problem was further compounded when the paramilitary forces were required to work with the Rashtriya Rifles, which was practically the same as the regular army, and, subsequently both indulged in one-upmanship and worked at cross purposes rather than with one another.[75]

The character and crisis of SF management in the multi-force counter-terrorism operation in J&K have received some governmental attention. In 2001, the Group of Ministers recommended that internal security and counter-insurgency responsibilities be entrusted to the central paramilitary forces and Rashtriya Rifles, and that the army should be de-inducted from these duties. The counter-insurgency role was to be gradually taken over by the CRPF, the BSF reverted to border management and the army to defence against traditional external military aggression, though it would remain available as the ultimate instrument of the state's force as a deterrent and to deal with grave contingencies.[76] There is increasing inclination to make a distinction between conflict situations where the army should have a predominant role and those where other forces can and should predominate. The prohibitive costs of employing a professional army for counter-terrorism duties for prolonged periods are also being realized. With counter-insurgency operations conducted within an indefinite time frame, the mental commitment of troops to fight cannot remain at a peak level indefinitely.[77] Even at the strategic level, the impact on the army has been debilitating, with a pressured force failing to make adequate and accurate assessments of existing and emerging threats. The aggression by what was clearly the Pakistan army in the Kargil sector in 1999 was, for instance, believed to be mujahidin terrorism and the proclaimed official projection was that it would be dealt with within a few days at the most.[78] The occupation of the Kargil heights was, in the first instance, the consequence of a strategic miscalculation which led to the vacation of these critical positions during the winter months. More significantly, professional armies are, by definition, ill-suited to deal with societal violence. It is unfair to expect a highly trained conventional military force to fight an amorphous enemy whose soldiers come as suicide bombers.[79]

None of this, however, is intended to deny the innumerable and continuous operational successes that these forces, individually and often in combination—despite the infirmities of command and control and the external limitations imposed on them—have secured over the years. Today, there are no 'liberated areas', no regions of terrorist domination, and a progressively shrinking popular base for the extremist creed. The terrorists have been confronted in their erstwhile 'heartlands' and have been beaten, again and again. 'Hearts and minds' operations by the SFs, as well as by a significantly revitalized—and, crucially, reasonably well protected—civil administration, have addressed at least the more severe elements of public resentment, and popular participation in recent elections has been comparable to other parts of the country.

Regrettably, the advantages secured at great human cost and sacrifice have been repeatedly and systematically frittered away at the altar of the reigning fiction of the 'political solution'. The SFs cannot end a terror supported from across the border in the absence of a clear mandate, a national consensus on the nature of terrorism and counter-terrorism, a political theory of closure rooted in realism, and adequate operational resources. These, unfortunately, remain stubbornly elusive within a political context obsessively focused on short-term contingencies and emergency crisis management.

Not all politics, however, has been detrimental. The restoration of electoral processes has been a critical component in the gradual progression towards relative order in the state, irrespective of the structural defects of the electoral outcome. Each election has helped restore a mechanism, however flawed, of public articulation and grievance redressal, and has created additional spaces for political moderation, which had shrunk to insignificance under the rampage of terrorist activities and extremist ideologies. The assembly elections of October 2002, for instance, installed a minority government led by Mufti Mohammad Sayeed's Peoples' Democratic Party (PDP), which had just 16 seats (all of them in the south Kashmir region)—less than its coalition partner, the Congress-I with 19, and Farooq Abdullah's ousted People's Conference (PC) with 29 seats—in an 87-seat Assembly.[80] Despite a campaign of intensified terror and intimidation and the highest level of electoral violence in the state's history, the 2002 elections had seen an average turnout of 42 per cent, and were regarded as a major moral victory over terrorism. Despite the PDP's reported proclivity for running with the hare and hunting with the hounds there was a psychological sea change in the state with the terrorist base shrinking even further. It is not possible to quantify the impact of these and earlier elections on the trends in the state, but it is clear that the restoration of the democratic process has had a demonstrably positive impact on the political and security situation in the state.

The Peace Melodrama

It is interesting that successive army chiefs have also routinely and repeatedly endorsed the reigning political dogma that the use of force or, as more commonly expressed, the 'military solution', cannot 'resolve' the problem of terrorism, and that the eventual resolution can only come in the form of a still unconceived 'political solution'.[81] There is a widespread belief that there is some simple formula or equation at the end of the Holy Grail of negotiations, which can manifest a perfect, painless, 'win-win' solution that will 'meet the aspirations' of all conflicting parties—India, Pakistan and 'the Kashmiri people'—and at the same time leave the general equations of power, demography, communal relations, and politics in the subcontinent otherwise undisturbed. This idea, unsupported by logic or history, has been a dominant impulse in the thinking of some of the most influential streams of power that have impacted on the course of events and policy in J&K. The result is, as Praveen Swami expresses it:

> Counter-terrorist operations are seen as a desultory, vaguely masturbatory activity for the boys to keep themselves occupied, while the men get down to the *real* business of finding a 'political solution' to the J&K imbroglio.[82]

This is why, while the bloody and endless business of terrorism and counter-terrorism is pushed into the background, repetitious, directionless, and historically unproductive 'peace processes' have 'hogged headlines', projecting larger than life images of participants who have little to offer beyond platitudes and opportunistic posturing.

The history of India–Pakistan negotiations over Kashmir is long and complex, and it is not the intention here to engage in a review. The extended and high profile final phase of this history commenced with the September 1998 meeting between Prime Ministers Atal Behari Vajpayee and Nawaz Sharief in New York, and an agreement to resume the 'peace process', which culminated in the 'Bus Diplomacy' of February 1999, and the 'Lahore Declaration'. Thereafter, the process has seen repeated suspensions and resumptions, including successive 'ceasefires' and cessations of 'offensive operations' by the security forces; the sterile Agra Summit; the appointment of 'interlocutors' to take 'negotiations' forward with various players in Kashmir; the vaulting declarations of the SAARC Summit at Islamabad in January 2004; and into the ongoing phase of talks under the new dispensation at New Delhi, and the altered order in Islamabad. What has persisted, through all this, is the Panglossian confidence that the process in itself and if strictly adhered to, guarantees a positive conclusion. There have, of course, been a few dissenting voices, but such dissent is an unpopular position, difficult to sustain in the current atmosphere of delusionary optimism.

To oppose or criticize a 'peace process' is to manifestly declare yourself on the side of bloodshed, of violence and of war and, consequently, is disturbingly politically incorrect. This purely semantic construction has resulted in a significant suspension of critical faculties, and has had a severe dampening and distorting influence on the discourse on the issue.[83]

Despite the transformation of the 'peace process' into an unassailable creed in both the regional and the international discourse the fact is that good intentions and a sentiment in favour of peace are not an adequate foundation for its realization. The error in the present process is that it is not reality based and represents, in the main, what has in a different context been described as the 'political realism of appeasement'[84]—a position that has historically proven disastrous for those who have adopted it and one that has a history of failure in Kashmir as well.

It is apparent in the current peace process that there is no theory of closure, certainly on the Indian side, but also in the perspectives of the 'international community' which seeks to intervene with, at best, an exceedingly imperfect and entirely deceptive projected denouement that concludes in some sort of dissection of territories, but fails entirely to address the fundamental nature of the conflict. Commenting on Vajpayee's earlier 'initiatives', Praveen Swami notes:

[the] peace initiative has costs that transcend Jammu and Kashmir—implications for the future of India as a secular state which have largely been censored out of public debate. The price of peace now sought to be brought about could, paradoxically, prove higher than the admittedly horrific loss of life that takes place each day in the troubled State.[85]

The neglect or denial of these realities is the reason why the 'search for solutions' has remained episodic and unrealistic: great hopes have been invested in electoral processes with no elaboration on how, precisely, these are expected to stem the tide of violence, or bring an end to what India has long claimed to be a movement almost entirely sustained by Pakistan; implicit faith is repeatedly expressed in the prospects of 'talks' and a 'political solution' to be 'negotiated' with discredited coalitions of lapsed terrorists and with terrorist front organizations, even as their linkages with, and almost complete dependence on, Pakistani support are exposed and derided. The 'Mizoram model' of resolution, through the corruption and outright purchase of the militant or dissident leadership, appears to be the most favoured 'solution' among Indian politicians and the state's covert agencies, ignoring the realities of the ground, the fact of a global radical pan-Islamist terrorist movement and Pakistan's persistent, ideologically driven geo-strategic ambitions.

Early indicators—while still uncertain in their detail—of the Manmohan Singh government's proposed policy do not suggest any radical shift in positions which apparently continue to ignore these broader considerations in the apparent quest for a solution to what Pakistan insists is, and India appears to reflexively accept as, the 'core issue' of Kashmir. But Kashmir is not, and has never been, the 'core issue' between India and Pakistan. The 'core issue' of this confrontation is, in fact, as Gill points out:

> the fundamentalist ideology, and the 'two nation theory' that excludes the very possibility of people of different faiths, cultures or ways of life coexisting within a single political order. The core issue, consequently, goes to the very heart and basis of India's existence, as it does of Pakistan's. The conflict . . . is an irreducible conflict between democratic liberalism and a polity based on an exclusionary religious absolutism. Those who think it can be resolved through negotiated territorial concessions with the aggressor deceive themselves no less than the Chamberlains and the Daladiers who sought to bribe Hitler into peace with similar concessions.[86]

Any negotiations within this context have historically and inevitably been exploited by the aggressors—terrorist groups, their sponsors, and their proxies—to advance their tactical objectives. The decline in violence in the post-9/11 phase has sometimes been attributed to the 'success' of the peace process, but a close study of trends indicates a secular decline in fatalities in the J&K theatre which is essentially a consequence of the changed international context, the progressive 'denial of deniability', the intense international media focus on Pakistan's support to terrorism and on the activities of Islamist terrorists, and the internal pressures that have mounted within Pakistan over this period. There is no visible correlation with the alternating periods of 'negotiations' or heightened hostilities between India and Pakistan which have characterized the last three years.[87]

This is not intended to suggest that the peace initiative and the 'political solution' are red herrings and therefore best ignored. Rather, it is the present nature of these processes and proposals, and the lack of realism in their conceptualization, that constitutes the problem. Peace initiatives and solutions must be articulated and pursued, but, equally, they must be based on 'rational choices and distinctions, not sentimentality'.[88] Praveen Swami note that:

> A real peace process in Jammu and Kashmir cannot be manufactured: it needs to emerge from real political activity, not closed-door intrigue and diplomatic manoeuvre. It will need mass mobilisation, and the creation of genuinely democratic fora in which issues, not deals, are discussed. And it will need to foreground the diverse cultural, economic and democratic aspirations of the peoples of the state, not meaningless clichés. Such a process, sadly, appears nowhere near even its beginning.[89]

CONCLUSIONS

Terrorists and their state and non-state supporters have been extraordinarily inventive in their continuous adaptation to new opportunities and challenges, and despite the extraordinary international consensus that emerged in the aftermath of the 9/11 attacks in the US, they have substantially reworked their organizational structures and operational strategies to retain significant, and in some contexts, expanded, capacities to strike. By contrast, state agencies have been 'characteristically obtuse in their responses'.[90]

Nevertheless, the course of events in Punjab and J&K have

seen continuous processes of strategic and tactical innovations on both sides of the conflict, and while it is not possible to draw out the full spectrum of political, strategic, and tactical lessons of this experience, it is useful to note at least some of the most significant of these:

1. Sectarian and collusive politics have been the most significant element in the causation and persistence of terrorist and insurgent movements.
2. In the absence of a clear sanction from the political leadership, counter-terrorism initiatives have little possibilities of success.
3. The most difficult phases of counter-terrorist campaigns are periods where terrorist violence combines with 'overground' political movements and mass mobilization. Nevertheless, overground movements have usually been, and should be, handled within the 'minimum use of force' doctrine. The use of excessive force against political mass mobilisation proved counter-productive in both Punjab and Kashmir.
4. Systems of efficient and cooperative command are essential for the success of any multi-force counter-terrorism campaign. Such systems must include the clear identification of role and function, as well as continuously responsive mechanisms for sharing of information and coordination of action between the forces. Deficiencies in systems of command and control persist in J&K.
5. Within a multi-force campaign, the role and responsibilities of the civil police are pivotal and cannot be substituted by military or paramilitary interventions.
6. Negotiations with terrorist groups are counterproductive, and while 'political solutions' can be pursued with non-violent political actors, including proxy players for the extremist groups, these must never include efforts to appease or conciliate the terrorists themselves.
7. Visible and static saturation by forces is not an efficient counter-terrorism strategy. Mobility, communications, and swiftness of reaction are critical for impact.
8. In situations of high volume and intensity of terrorist actions, enforcement agencies must selectively focus on targets that have a high 'demonstration value', such as the perpetrators

of particularly barbaric incidents or the top terrorist leadership, rather than dissipating resources on the pursuit of every offender.

9. The role of psychological operations and a well-constructed information and media strategy are critical in counter-terrorism operations. Repression of the media and information controls do not work.
10. Each counter-terrorism intervention must project and anticipate its impact on patterns of terrorism, and must include containment strategies for unwanted consequences, such as a geographical shift or spread, the introduction of new terrorist technologies, or the intervention of external (state or non-state) actors.
11. A consistent and clearly stated counter-terrorism strategy and perspective with at least a medium-term perspective is the bedrock of all counter-terrorism operations and policies.
12. Where terrorism is sponsored by hostile states, its trajectory is linked directly to the internal and external capacities of such states. Such capacities consequently must be the direct targets of counter-terrorism strategies and instruments. Diplomatic initiatives, information campaigns, non-military competitive strategies, and sub-conventional options need to be explored in order to systematically erode and undermine the capacities of such states to sustain their support to terrorism under the blanket of 'credible deniability'.
13. Where terrorism is exploited by legitimate political actors or by states as an instrument of policy, it is seldom contained within intended parameters, and evolves a logic and dynamic entirely of its own, ordinarily decimating the very forces that sponsor its initial ascent.

Notes

1. George K. Tanham, 'Indian Strategy in Flux', in Kanti Bajpai and Amitabh Mattoo (eds.), *Securing India: Strategic Thought and Practice*, New Delhi: Mansarover Publications, 1996, p. 123.
2. Ajai Sahni, 'Another Swing of the Pendulum', *South Asia Intelligence Review*, vol. 2, no. 16, 3 November 2003, http://www.satp.org/satporgtp/sair/Archives/2_16.htm#ASSESSMENT2.
3. Ibid.

4. W.C. Sonderland, 'An analysis of the Guerilla Insurgency and Coup d' Etat as Techniques of Indirect Aggression', *International Studies Quarterly*, December 1970, p. 345.
5. The idea of 'root causes' is itself suspect, and deeply influenced by rigid and unexamined theoretical or ideological paradigms and positions. These paradigms and positions have been analysed in some detail within the context of Left Wing extremism in Ajai Sahni, ' "Naxalism": The Retreat of Civil Governance', *Faultlines: Writings in Conflict & Resolution*, vol. 5, New Delhi: ICM-Bulwark Books, May 2000, esp. pp. 79-89. 'Root Causes' and elements of the 'sustaining dynamic' have also been examined within the context of insurgencies in India's north-east in Ajai Sahni, 'The Terrorist Economy in India's Northeast', *Faultlines: Writings on Conflict & Resolution*, New Delhi: ICM-Bulwark Books, vol. 8, April 2001, pp. 127–48.
6. Harish K. Puri, Paramjit Singh Judge and Jagrup Singh Sekhon, *Terrorism in Punjab: Understanding Grassroots Reality*, New Delhi: Har Anand Publications, 1999, p. 51. Praveen Swami similarly notes: 'The veteran Punjab communist leader Satyapal Dang recently suggested to me that the ways in which we have come to comprehend such conflicts is grossly inadequate. For a decade, he pointed out, what was called the Punjab problem was understood to consist of several other problems—the sharing of river waters, the status of Chandigarh, the federal demands of the Anandpur Sahib resolutions, the scars of Operation Blue Star, and so on. Yet, when peace did come about, Dang pointed out, none of these problems had in fact been resolved.' Praveen Swami, 'Clueless in Kashmir', *Seminar India*, vol. 497, January 2001, http://www.india-seminar.com/2001/497/497% 20 praveen% 20swami.htm.
7. The expression 'military', here, is used loosely to refer to the use of armed force by the state against terrorists/insurgents, whether this involves formations of the army, the paramilitary forces or the armed police.
8. K.P.S. Gill, 'Policing the Free Indian State', *The Pioneer*, Delhi, 23 August 1997.
9. Ibid., 'Endgame in Punjab: 1988–1993', *Faultlines: Writings on Conflict & Resolution*, vol. 1, New Delhi: ICM-Bulwark Books, May 1999, p. 2.
10. Ibid., p. 69.
11. This section relies substantially on a paper co-authored by K.P.S. Gill and Ajai Sahni, 'India: The Defeat of Religious Extremist Terror in Punjab', for the United Nations University, forthcoming publication; and on Gill, 'Endgame in Punjab'.
12. Even those who strongly advocate the exclusive use of the civil police to confront all internal security challenges and see a 'fundamental

conflict' between internal security duties and 'the professional instincts, traditions and ethos of the military' concede that a resort to the army is a legitimate 'last line of defence' even within 'the strict limits imposed in a constitutionalist liberal democratic system'. Cf., Paul Wilkinson, 'The Role of the Military in Combating Terrorism in a Democratic Society', in *Terrorism & Political Violence*, vol. 9, no. 3, January–June 1995, p. 89.

13. Gill, 'Endgame in Punjab', p. 7.
14. 1981: 13; 1982: 13. In the last phase of escalating violence preceding Operation Blue Star, 298 persons were killed between 1 January 1984, and 3 June 1984.
15. Chand Joshi, *Bhindranwale: Myth and Reality*, Delhi: Vikas Publishing House, 1984, pp. 126–150.
16. Even in the years preceding the advent of terrorism in Punjab, the number of murders in the state were seldom below 500 in any year, and tended to maintain a secular upward trend (1981: 555; 1982: 575; 1983: 591). In the three years after terrorism was brought under control in Punjab there were a total of 2,081 murders unrelated to terrorism (1994: 687; 1995: 686; 1996: 708). These numbers are not regarded as being extraordinary, and have attracted no exceptional comment in the media; nor was there any sense of a 'breakdown' in the state.
17. For an extraordinarily dramatic example, see Gill, *Punjab: The Knights of Falsehood*, New Delhi, 1997, p. 95.
18. Gill, 'Endgame in Punjab', p. 6
19. More than a hundred army officers and men died in Operation Blue Star, and over 550 civilians were killed in the crossfire.
20. Gill, 'Endgame in Punjab', p. 10.
21. V.N. Narayanan, *Tryst with Terror: Punjab's Turbulent Decade*, Delhi: Ajanta, 1996, p. 27; cited in Puri et al., *Terrorism in Punjab*, p. 51.
22. Rebeiro insists that the phrase was wrongly attributed to him. Cf. Julio Rebeiro, *Bullet for Bullet: My Life as a Police Officer*, New Delhi: Penguin Books, 1998, pp. 276–7.
23. Rebeiro, *Bullet for Bullet*, p. 274.
24. Rebeiro in Raminder Singh, 'Khalistan Declaration: Last Straw', *India Today*, 31 May 1986, p. 29. Rebeiro later maintained that this outcome was expected, but that the Operation was undertaken anyway because 'a message had to be delivered to the separatists'. Cf. Julio Rebeiro, *Bullet for Bullet*, pp. 284–5. Black Thunder I, however, did little to enhance the prestige of the state.
25. Rebeiro in Pradeep Mathur, 'The Retreat of Rebeiro', *Probe India*, February 1987, pp. 6–9.
26. Gill, 'Endgame in Punjab', pp. 13–14.
27. Ibid., pp. 18–27.
28. Mobile-cum-*naka* contingents—mobile units which could set up

barricades when required to block off escape routes after a terrorist incident—were constituted. Another innovation was the concept of 'focal point patrolling' under which all available vehicles in a district were brought to a single location, creating an impression of massive force and a level of saturation and mobility which did not, in fact, exist.

29. Indeed, in June 1986, Punjab Police personnel had clashed openly with the CRPF at Amritsar, and at one point, it appeared that there would be an exchange of fire.
30. The low casualty figures among personnel security force of and terrorists in the pre-1988 phase tended to reflect, at least in part, a tacit arrangement between a majority among the police and the militants that they would not cross paths.
31. Gill, 'Endgame in Punjab', pp. 32 and 45.
32. All data from *South Asia Terrorism Portal*, http://www.satp.org/satporgtp/countries/india/states/punjab/data_sheets annual_casualties.htm.
33. Gill, 'Endgame in Punjab', p. 37.
34. Ibid.
35. The flood of weapons in the state also assumed new and disturbing proportions. Till this point, weapons acquisition had to be 'financed' by the terrorists themselves through extortion and narcotics smuggling. Suddenly, in July, messages were sent out that weapons 'which had accumulated in Pakistan for which no payment is to be made' could be acquired by the simple expedient of sending 'large numbers' of terrorists across the border, Ibid., p. 34.
36. Ibid., p. 38
37. Gill, 'Endgame in Punjab', p. 40.
38. Ibid., p. 46.
39. Two hundred and eleven candidates had established terrorist links, and 34 were at that time in jail. Another 41 candidates had 'history sheets' (police records) which included offences s such as assassination, hijacking and murder. Forty-eight candidates were relatives of prominent listed terrorists. Cf. Gill, 'Endgame in Punjab', p. 49.
40. 'Endgame in Punjab', p. 59.
41. Voter turnout was 23.82 per cent. Cf. Election Commission of India, http://eci.gov.in/high_Stats/se92/StatisticalReport%20Punjab%201992.pdf, accessed 4 April 2004.
42. These included Rashpal Singh Chandran, the Chief of the BTFK (12 June); Gurjant Singh Budhsinghwala, Chief of the KLF (July 29); and Sukhdev Singh Babbar, Mukh Sewadar of the BKI (10 August). One of the last major successes for the security forces was to come in January 1993, with the death of Gurbachan Singh Manochahal, Chief of the Panthic Committee (M) and the BTFK (M) in an encounter with

security forces at village Rataul in Tarn Taran. His death was generally thought to mark the end of the real challenge of terrorism in Punjab.

43. Gill, 'Endgame in Punjab', p. 21.
44. See, for instance, Noemi Gal-Or (ed.), *Tolerating Terrorism in the West: An International Survey*, London and New York: Routledge, 1991.
45. Rubaiya Saeed, the daughter of the newly appointed Home Minister in the V.P. Singh government was kidnapped on 8 December 1989, and was released in exchange for five jailed JKLF leaders on 13 December. Mass victory celebrations in Srinagar brought the entire city to a standstill, as a stunned administration stood impotently by.
46. Lt. Gen. Vijay Madan, cited in 'Kashmir—What Went Wrong', http://www.kashmirsentinel.com/nov2002/18.html.
47. Data, South Asia Terrorism Portal, http://www.satp.org/satporgtp/countries/india/states/jandk/data_sheets/recovery_of_weapons_jan1990_to_15_Nov_2000.htm
48. Source: South Asia Terrorism Portal, www.satp.org/satporgtp/countries/india/states/jandk/data_sheets/annual_casualties.htm
49. V.K. Sood and Pravin Sawhney, *Operation Parakram: The War Unfinished*, New Delhi: Sage, 2003, p. 46.
50. Jagmohan had conspired to topple Farooq Abdullah's government at Indira Gandhi's behest in 1983, and his appointment had a very negative symbolism in the context of rising difficulties in J&K in 1989.
51. Thirty-five protestors were killed in the firing by the CRPF troops on the Gawakadal Bridge on 20 January 1990, the day after Jagmohan took charge as Governor and Farooq Abdullah resigned. Other major and counterproductive incidents in the initial months included another police firing on 1 March 1990, which left 40 protestors dead; and the 21 May firing on Mirwaiz Maulvi Mohammad Farooq's funeral procession, in which an estimated 50 mourners were killed.
52. M.J. Akbar, *Kashmir: Behind the Vale*, New Delhi: Roli Books, 2002, p. 220.
53. Gen. K.V. Krishna Rao, PVSM, *The Genesis of the Insurgency in Jammu and Kashmir, and in the North East, and Future Prospects*, USI National Security Lectures, New Delhi: United Service Institution of India, 1997, p. 20.
54. K.V. Krishna Rao, *In the Service of the Nation*, Delhi: Viking Publishers, 2001, pp. 439–40.
55. S.S. Bloeria, *Pakistan's Insurgency vs. India's Security*, New Delhi: Manas Publications, 2000, p. 341.
56. Sumantra Bose, *Kashmir: Roots of Conflict, Paths to Peace*, New Delhi: Vistaar Publications, 2003, p. 127.
57. Parrey was killed at Hajan on 13 September 2003. The expression comes from *Ikhwan ul Muslimeen* (Muslim Brotherhood), the name of the group that Parrey led before his surrender; over time, however,

ikhwani emerged as a generic term within the Kashmir context covering all surrendered militants who cooperated with or worked for the security forces. Other prominent *ikhwanis* include Liaqat Ali Khan; Usman Majid (currently an MLA); and Javed Shah (a Member of the Legislative Council—MLC—from the National Conference) who was killed on 28 August 2003. See Praveen Swami, 'India's Forgotten Army', *The Hindu*, 14 September 2003.

58. http://www.kashmirsentinel.com/nov2002/18.html.
59. Krishna Rao, *The Genesis of the Insurgency in Jammu and Kashmir*, p. 21.
60. Ibid., *In the Service of the Nation*, p. 448.
61. The turnout in the Parliamentary elections of May 1996 stood at 49.02 per cent for the entire state; the assembly elections in August saw an even higher turnout at 54.04 per cent. Source: Election Commission of India, www.eci.gov.in/infoeci/key_stat/keystat_fs.htm
62. Including the Hizb-ul-Mujahiddeen, the Muslim Jaanbaaz Force, Muslim Mujahideen and Al Baraq. See http://www.satp.org/India/J&K/Timeline_J&K.htm
63. 'Panel To Study Kashmir Militants' Demands', *Hindu*, Madras, 16 March 1996; see also, 'Setback In Talks With Militants', *Hindu*, 24 March 1996.
64. Bose, *Kashmir: Roots of Conflict*, p. 140.
65. Praveen Swami, 'The Kargil War: Preliminary Explorations', *Faultlines: Writings on Conflict & Resolution*, vol. 2, New Delhi, ICM-Bulwark Books, pp. 33–4.
66. Ibid., p. 29.
67. Refusing, for instance, to rule out the possibility of 'future Kargils', Musharraf said in an interview to the Indian news channel, NDTV, 'Let me tell you that before Kargil, Kashmir was a dead issue. To avoid Kargils, we need to resolve disputes and much depends on how we proceed on the peace track.' See, for instance, 'Musharraf refuses to rule out another Kargil', Rediff.com, 13 June 2003, http://www.rediff.com/news/2003/jun/13pak.htm?zcc=ri.
68. For a listing of major *fidayeen* attacks, see *South Asia Terrorism Portal*, http://www.satp.org/satporgtp/countries/india/states/jandk/data_sheets/major_terrorist_attachs_sfe_kargil.htm. One source places the total number of *fidayeen* attacks between mid-1999 and end 2002, at 55. Cf. Sumantra Bose, *Kashmir: Roots of Conflict*, p. 141.
69. South Asia Terrorism Portal, http://www.satp.org/satporgtp/countries/india/states/jandk/data_sheets/annual_casualties.htm. Official sources subsequently revised the numbers for year 2001. The Ministry of Home Affairs Annual Report put the numbers at 4,177; intelligence sources now offer a revised final tally at 3,796. The changing numbers reflect a process of rationalization as a number of incidents initially categorized as 'terrorist killings' were found on investigation to be otherwise.

70. 'Op Parakram Claimed 798 Soldiers', *Times News Network*, 31 July 2003, http://timesofindia.indiatimes.com/cms.dll/html/uncomp/articleshow?msid=104948
71. Sandeep Dikshit, 'Government orders withdrawal of troops from IB', *The Hindu*, New Delhi, 17 October 2002. There is a great deal of ambiguity about exactly what these 'objectives' were, and no quantifiable evidence has ever been advanced on the specifics of what was achieved.
72. Swami, 'J&K after 9/11: More of the Same', *Faultlines: Writings on Conflict & Resolution*, vol. 11, ICM-Bulwark Books, April 2002, pp. 35–62.
73. Bhashyam Kasturi, 'Unified Command for Counter-Insurgency Operations', www.stratmag.com/issue2Sep-1/page05.htm#a02.
74. Sood and Sawhney, *Operation Parakram*, p. 53.
75. Ibid.
76. Ibid.
77. Maroof Raza, 'Pakistan Sponsored Insurgency in Kashmir: A Case Study', *Aakrosh*, Delhi, vol. 2, no. 4, July 1999.
78. 'Force multipliers', *Indian Express*, 11 August 2003.
79. Ibid.
80. *The Jammu and Kashmir Government Gazette*, vol. 115, Srinagar, Sun., the 13th Oct. 2002/21st Asv., 1924, [No. 28], Part 1-B, Government of Jammu & Kashmir Civil Secretariat Law Department Notification, Srinagar, 13 October 2002.
81. For instance, on 16 September 2000, on a visit to Jammu & Kashmir, the then Army Chief Gen. V.P. Malik said that political measures were more important than military means to bring peace to Kashmir. http://newsarchives.indiainfo.com/2000/09/17/malik.html. Similarly, on 5 October 2000 the then Army Chief Gen. S. Padmanabhan, on a three-day visit to J&K, said that insurgency needed to be resolved politically but troops were duty-bound to fight the proxy war thrust by an external force using the people of the Valley. See 'New Army Chief Favours Political Solution to Kashmir', *Daily Excelsior*, Jammu, 6 October 2000.
82. Swami, 'J&K after 9/11', pp. 49–50.
83. K.P.S. Gill and Ajai Sahni, 'The J&K "Peace Process": Chasing the Chimera', *Faultlines: Writings on Conflict & Resolution*, ICM–Bulwark Books, April 2001, pp. 2–3.
84. Eric Hobsbawm, *The Age of Extremes*, New York: Vintage Books, 1996, p. 146. See also, Gill and Sahni, 'The J&K 'Peace Process': pp. 1–40, esp. pp. 3–8.
85. Swami, 'Clueless in Kashmir', *Seminar* no. 497, January 2001, New Delhi.
86. Gill and Sahni, 'The J&K "Peace Process"', p. 22.
87. See, for instance, Ajai Sahni, 'The "Peace" Carnival', *South Asia*

Intelligence Review, vol. 2, no. 4, 11 August 2003, South Asia Terrorism Portal, www.satp.org. See also, Swami, 'J&K: Withering Roses—The Peace Process Melts Down', *South Asia Intelligence Review*, vol. 2, no. 9, 15 September 2003, South Asia Terrorism Portal, www.satp.org.

88. Swami, 'Kashmir through the Looking Glass', *Seminar India*, vol. 533, January 2004, http://www.india-seminar.com/2004/533/533%20Praveen%20Swami.htm.
89. Swami, 'Clueless in Kashmir', *Seminar India*, no. 85.
90. Gill, 'Foreword', *Faultlines: Writings on Conflict & Resolution*, vol. 8, ICM-Bulwark Books, April 2001, p. 1.

3. Insurgencies in North-east: [illegible] Dimensions of [illegible] Containment

[illegible]

North-ea[illegible] internationa[illegible] the north[illegible] The region[illegible] Manipur[illegible] eight sta[illegible] Tripura[illegible]

The region[illegible] India's ind[illegible] most endura[illegible] and is [illegible] move as [illegible] [illegible] operating[illegible] and Megha[illegible] insurgenc[illegible] than a quar[illegible] 15 years [illegible] and terroris[illegible] uprisings[illegible] Nagaland[illegible] in Tripura[illegible] groups, ex[illegible] countries[illegible]

The Naga[illegible] north-east[illegible] insurgenc[illegible]

3. Insurgencies in North-East India: Dimensions of Discord and Containment

Vijendra Singh Jafa

North-eastern India is a largely mountainous region, and has international borders with Bhutan in the west, Tibet (China) in the north, Myanmar in the east, and Bangladesh in the south. The region consists of seven states: Assam, Arunachal Pradesh, Manipur, Meghalaya, Mizoram, Nagaland and Tripura. An eighth state, Sikkim, has recently been added through an amendment in the North Eastern Council Act.[1]

The region has been beleaguered, almost from the dawn of India's independence, by successive secessionist insurgencies, the most enduring being the Naga insurgency which started in 1947 and is still unresolved. In some years of intensive warfare, as many as three divisions of the Indian army and a similar strength of paramilitary forces have carried out counter-insurgency operations in Nagaland, Mizoram, Manipur, Tripura, Assam, and Meghalaya. Only one (Mizo) out of the seven major insurgencies in the north-east has been resolved. It is estimated that a quarter million human lives have been lost during the past 55 years as a result of these insurgencies and countless acts of terrorism that have taken place as a corollary to militant uprisings. There are, at present, two armed militant groups in Nagaland, 39 groups in Manipur, 37 groups in Assam, 30 groups in Tripura, and four groups in Meghalaya. The outreach of these groups extends to the neighbouring states and surrounding countries.

The Naga insurgency is the mother of all insurgencies in the north-east. It has inspired, instigated and assisted all other insurgencies in one way or the other. Arguably no other insurgency would have taken root in the region if the Naga insurgency had been effectively prevented or resolved by the government during the 1950s. One would have to go back in history to comprehend what caused the first two—Naga and the Mizo—insurgencies.

INDIRECT RULE: 'EXCLUSION' AND RECONSTRUCTION OF ETHNIC IDENTITY

The British 'Indirect Rule' in the hill areas of the north-east 'fostered the tribe over nation and tribal over national leadership'.[2] The British promoted a separate religious, social and national identity in the indirectly ruled areas, which ran counter to the growth of pan-Indian nationalism in the directly ruled areas of the country.[3] The north-eastern hill tribes were effectively excluded from the administration and socio-cultural growth of India.[4] The explicit, though self-contradictory, British reasons for segregating the hill tribes were: (1) to protect the plains from raids and plunder from the hill tribes (1873–1900); (2) to protect the hill tribes from exploitation by the plainsmen (1900–28); and (3) to foster an enlightened public policy aimed at the cultural survival of the hill tribes (1928–47). The last two were euphemisms for carrying out political, anthropological and ecclesiastical experimentation on a scale thereto unknown in the annals of colonial rule. The 'exclusion' was initially done through the creation of an Inner Line under the East Bengal Frontier Regulations of 1873. For about 90 years, the Inner Line kept the Indian culture and religion on the other side of the fence and created a controlled environment which gave the Christian missionaries an unhindered opportunity to proselytize,[5] and the administrators to provide an enormous thrust to conversion.[6] The orders issued under the Government of India Acts of 1915 and 1919 declared these areas 'backward tracts' requiring special administrative measures, and excluded them politically and judicially from the purview of the provincial legislatures and the High Court. The Government of India Act of 1935 created a totally new political status for these areas by excluding them fully from the federal and provincial legislatures and the High Court. In effect, the north-eastern hills progressively became, before India's Independence, a separate country ruled by the Viceroy through the Governor.[7]

Indians were excluded from the administration of this area.[8] The 'exclusion' also kept the hill tribes away from participation in the new democratic processes which developed in India from 1919 onwards,[9] and deprived them of an opportunity to learn political skills which could help them adapt quickly to the volatile political environment of India in which they found themselves when the British left.[10] It postponed change, making more radical and more disruptive the impact of innovations when they came.

Policy Formulation Sans Gandhi and Nehru

The liberal-philosophical approach of Jawaharlal Nehru or the humanitarian stance of Mahatma Gandhi towards the hill tribes found only superficial expression in the Constitution of India.[11] Gandhi kept himself out of the constitutional process and Nehru was too preoccupied (during 1946–9) with the partition and reintegration of India, widespread communal violence, war with Pakistan over Kashmir, and myriads of other administrative crises confronting the new nation-state to be able to give his personal attention to the Sixth Schedule of the Constitution. Left in the hands of legal pundits whose theoretical insights into constitution-making could not often compensate for their lack of experience in public affairs, and who were rummaging through the constitutional and legal analogies of the world to find a panacea for India's ethnic problems, what emerged was a patchwork policy quite unsuited to the Indian situation. The condescension with which the hill tribes were viewed, much as the American Whites had viewed the American Indians, was iniquitous and should have been unacceptable in the kind of society Mahatma Gandhi and Nehru had envisioned for India.[12] Obviously too much was left in the hands of B.R. Ambedkar whose perspective of both the American Indians and the hill tribes of the north-east was based on uninformed and outdated scholarship. The analogy given by Ambedkar was far-fetched, illogical, and even ludicrous, and has proved, in the long run, injurious to the integrity and security of India. To have compared the situation of the north-east Indian hills tribes in 1947–9 with the 'Red Indians' in the United States (US) was a tragically flawed interpretation of history. North-eastern hill tribals and their lands had been left untouched by the plainsmen of India through the centuries as opposed to the 'greatest land grab in history' and the 'most wanton bloodshed for fulfilling men's greed for land' in American history, of the Whites marching to the west by eliminating, subjugating or enclosing the American Indians in reservations. Ambedkar, while citing the analogy under examination, was ignorant of the 'complex and heart-rending' adjustments to reservation life that the American Indians had had to make, that a wild and free people were domesticated and confined by a modern war carried to their homes by professional US soldiers out to grab land for foreign immigrants, having enormous advantages in firepower and sustained by a modern economy, and that the American Indians were, at the time of Ambedkar's statement to the Constituent Assembly, and continue to be, disproportionately poor and rank at the bottom of virtually every social indicator, with worse health, higher death rates, and the highest rates of unemployment than other Americans as a whole.[13]

The word 'tribe' itself was a western concept, used loosely to mean people who are linked by the ties of language, kinship, and culture that existed prior to, and were separate from, the citizenship of modern states. They were assumed to be throw-backs and pictured as having somehow managed to inhabit the modern world without themselves being modern. They lived, according to the imperial western tradition, dangerously on the edge of state control. The British Acts of 1919 and 1935 had virtually made the north-eastern hills into a 'separate country', and, because of an erroneous understanding of the people inhabiting the north-eastern hills dictated by western concepts, this political disjunction was extended by the Sixth Schedule of the Indian Constitution in a frivolous, amateur, and illiterate manner in which the ethnicity, lands, and traditional laws of the hill people were sought to be preserved. The Sixth Schedule created a mess, an invitation to a privileged powerless existence in splendid isolation and seclusion, which has not been cleared in five decades of firefighting in the north-east.

The Assam Factor and an Unresponsive Bureaucracy

The retention of the hill tribes in Assam made the future conflict a foregone conclusion.[14] The Nehruvian integration-through-Assam model was a blunder as it 'considered Assam to be the last outpost of the Indian civilization in the east . . . entrusted with the responsibility to complete the unfinished task of integrating the tribal entities in the north-east. . . . The addition of tribal entities to Assam made her an ethnic cauldron. . . . The inter-ethnic competition for power and state privileges in such a segmented society not only gave birth to a complicated cleavage structure, but also formed the social base for a perpetual source of conflicts.'[15] A strong recommendation was made to the Governor of Assam in 1948 that the hill areas would be unhappy with Assam and would like to be centrally administered on the pattern of the North East Frontier Agency (NEFA) but this went unheeded.[16]

It was ultimately the imposition of Assamese as the official language of the state that led to the break-up of Assam and prepared the ground for insurgencies in Mizoram and Meghalaya. The States Reorganisation Commission (1953) had already set into motion hectic political activity in the hill tribal area aimed at severing their formal ties with Assam.[17] The delay, however, in Assam's political break-up stirred emotion, leading first to a more vociferous demand for a separate hill state (which gathered momentum after the creation of the state of Nagaland in 1963) for all non-Naga areas of the north-east, and later to secessionism.

There was gross insouciance, isolation, and a lack of 'empathy and sensitivity'[18] prevalent amongst the political leaders of Assam; and ineptitude, irresponsibility and arrogance symbolized the officers manning the administration in the hill areas from 1947 onwards. A posting to hill areas was often synonymous with punishment. In fact, threats by politicians to have incompetent, recalcitrant or unobliging officers posted to hill districts were not infrequent. The compliment that a particular officer was suitable for hills was tantamount to a stigmatization that he was incompetent, undisciplined, fond of the lighter things of life, and debauched by *la dolce vita*, or generally unmanageable. No wonder Nehru was of the opinion that officers who were sent to Assam's hill districts were not suited for that purpose.[19]

The Political Horsetrade

The conduct of the Indian National Congress (INC) after Nehru, and of its leaders, both at the centre and in Assam, was very largely responsible for eventually driving the peoples of the hills and the plains of the north-east towards secessionist insurgencies. Three examples should suffice for the purpose of this chapter:

1. In Mizo Hills, the insurgency was a direct consequence of rivalry between the Congress party and the Mizo Union Party (MUP). The Mizo Union was in the forefront of the anti-feudal movement during British rule and defeated the Congress party in the first elections for the formation of the District Council in 1952.[20] The ruling Congress party of Assam, however, sabotaged the District Council System (devised by the Constitution) in an effort to settle narrow political scores with the MUP. This led to the decay of the only political institution that had replaced the traditional institution of the tribal chief. The Congress-led Government of Assam first applied the brakes on financial grants. The position of the MUP weakened considerably after the 1957 elections because of their inability to secure funds for development from the Assam government. Things came to a critical pass with the *mautampui* or famine of 1959–60.[21] The District Council requested the Assam government to provide Rs. 15 lakh for famine relief on 29 October 1958. The government initially dismissed the threat of *mautam* as an invention of the tribal mind. When the famine did come, the allocation of funds and food supplies, and the efforts required for physical delivery, were inordinately slow and inadequate. The government canalized the relief through its own agencies, bypassing the District Council. Later, relief was provided through an agency known as the Mizo Famine Front, led by Pu Laldenga. As there were no roads in the south and airdrops of food was irregular due to bad weather,

the relief was largely concentrated to areas in the north, and there were a large number of deaths in the south which was inhabited by the Pawi-Lakers and Chakmas. The irony was that both the public and the government blamed the District Council for these deaths. But the controversy in which the Congress-led government of Assam was embroiled assumed a special significance when the politics of famine led to an armed insurrection in Mizo Hills seven years later.

Laldenga, who headed the Mizo Cultural Society, met Bimla Prasad Chaliha, Chief Minister of Assam, on 29 January 1960 in Shillong with members of his society to seek Chaliha's intervention in the gravely deteriorating famine situation. Chaliha was impressed by the young man, particularly when he denounced the activities of the Mizo Union and District Council, by now a pet aversion of Chaliha. The Mizo Cultural Society became the Mizo National Famine Front, and with the help of the Assam government, which used the Front to distribute relief and food supplies, it soon acquired a very significant public image. Laldenga took full credit for the belated food supplies which started arriving from June 1960. By a combination of hard work, outstanding organizational abilities, gift of oratory, gimmickry and innovation, he was able to garner tremendous popularity for himself and enlist a large number of educated young men and women in the Front. On 22 October 1961, he formed the Mizo National Front (MNF) as a political party, which was secretly financed by the state Congress party set-up. In the 1963 by-elections to the state legislature, MNF candidates defeated Saprawnga and Bawichhuka, the two stalwarts of the Mizo Union. Later, the MNF romped home with 145 candidates against 228 of the Mizo Union in the Village Council elections. This established Laldenga as a significant political force. But he had other plans. He went to East Pakistan illegally to discuss the training of Mizo soldiers and the procurement of arms with the Pakistani army. He was arrested by the Assam police while returning to India, and released on the intervention of Chief Minister Chaliha. Thus, Chaliha, the great Congressman who had participated in India's independence movement, seriously jeopardized national security in his desire to spite a rival political party, the Mizo Union.

On 30 October 1965, Laldenga addressed a memorandum to Prime Minister Lal Bahadur Shashtri demanding independence for Mizoram and expressed his willingness to fight for it. The Government of Independent Mizoram, with Laldenga as its president, was formed in December 1965. After Shashtri's sudden death, Gulzarilal Nanda was the caretaker Prime Minister for three weeks until Indira Gandhi took over as the Prime Minister on 16 January 1966. It is doubtful if senior civil servants and army commanders briefed her adequately about the developments in Mizo Hills. It appears the whole chain of information had either broken down or been subverted. For whatever reasons, both the government of Assam and the central government's own Intelligence Bureau had kept the Government of India incompletely informed about these developments. The Government of India responded to Laldenga's memorandum addressed to Shashtri by sending a Planning Commission Study Team in January 1966 to work out a strategy for the speedy development of Mizo Hills. Assam Governor Vishnu Sahai went to Mizo Hills on a four-day visit in the first week of February 1966. The Pataskar Commission visited Aizawl on 7 February 1966 to study the feasibility of separating north-eastern hills from Assam. Laldenga and his MNF cadre met all the visitors and demanded freedom from India without any reservations. However, the Joint Intelligence Committee of the Government of India did not mention the likelihood of any immediate trouble in Mizo Hills in its report of 16 February 1966, and only mentioned the possibility of the demand for independence being stepped-up a year later, in 1967. Only 12 days later, the MNF declared the independence of Mizoram on 1 March 1966, overran and took control of the entire territory until the Indian army began counter-insurgency operations which lasted 20 years.

In February 1966, the total armed force at the disposal of

the district administration was the 1st Battalion of Assam Rifles garrisoned largely at Aizawl, Lunglei, and Champhai, and 11 platoons of the 6th Battalion of the Border Security Force manning seven posts along the 180-km Mizo Hills border with East Pakistan. In February 1966, when a newly raised battalion of the Assam Rifles was in the process of being inducted in Mizo Hills, Laldenga requested Chaliha and the Prime Minister telegraphically to stop this. The telegraphic negotiations delayed the arrival of this battalion by over a month, which proved fatal.

The instructors and senior officers of the Mizo National Army (MNA) were drawn from Mizo ex-servicemen. The most useful among these were 70 Mizo Junior Commissioned Officers (JCOs) and *jawans* who had been dismissed or discharged from the army and sent home to a potentially insurgent region when the 2nd Battalion of the Assam Regiment was disbanded following a mutiny in Kashmir in 1961–2.[22] Twelve of these men (Thangzuala, Lalngura, Biakvela, Vanthanga, Lalpianga, Khualchhawna, Lalzama, Kawlvela, Khawnghingha, Vanhlira, Lalthansanga, and Padara) commanding some of the most effective units of the MNA launched some of the deadliest attacks on the Indian army and police, and reached the top hierarchy of the insurgent outfit.[23]

The history of the years 1959–66, particularly of the incidents pertaining to the Chaliha-assisted growth of Laldenga, the MNF and the MNA, is so fuzzy that both the roles played by both the central and the state agencies in these episodes and the motivations behind the policy aberrations are hard to discern. People close to Chaliha have claimed that the central intelligence agencies, and more particularly K.N. Prasad, a deputy director of the Intelligence Bureau, had misguided the Chief Minister, and this officer was responsible for Laldenga's release after the illegal visit to East Pakistan in 1964 as well as his subsequent immunity from arrest in the following months. Prasad told the present author while on a visit to Lunglei in 1968 that Laldenga had deceived him as a friend. In his statement in the Assam Legislative Assembly on 5 March 1966, Chaliha also expressed similar sentiments: 'the Mizo National Front leaders are all betrayers', he said.

2. Why the central government acquiesced to the profligacy and recklessness of the government in Assam (1955–66) that destroyed the peace and stability of Mizoram and forced the Mizos into insurgency is one of the unexplained enigmas of modern Indian history. But what is more bewildering is the manner in which both the United Liberation Front of Asom (ULFA) and the Bodo insurgencies (as well as the insurgencies in Manipur and Tripura) were engendered by the Congress party's state and central leadership, either directly or through indiscreet, imprudent, and injudicious policies.

Inevitably, some of history is necessary to understand the background. In 1905, Bengal was partitioned and Assam became a part of East Bengal. This decision was reversed in 1912 when Assam was made a Province as a result of mass protests in the Brahmputra Valley. But seven years of existence in East Bengal brought about considerable changes in the demography of Assam as land-hungry Muslims of East Bengal started migrating to Assam in massive waves, and this did not stop with the separation of Assam from East Bengal in 1912. According to the 1921 census, there were 3.5 million Bengali-speaking and 1.7 million Assamese-speaking persons in Assam. The impact of the unchecked migration was so overwhelming that a British Census Commissioner was prompted to observe in the 1931 Census Report that 'the immigrant army has almost completed the conquest of Assam'.[24] During the late 1930s and 1940s, the migration assumed political overtones when the Sir Sadulla-led government in Assam encouraged Muslim immigration from East Bengal and the Assamese Hindus construed it as a preparation for the partition of India,[25] and this provided a rationale to the Assamese fears of inundation by an alien culture. The secessionist tendencies among the Assamese Hindus date back to this period. When Nehru visited Assam in 1937 as president of the Indian National Congress, the *Asamiya Samrakshini Sabha* memorandum to him stated:

'as a means of saving the Assamese race from extinction, a considerable section of the Assamese intelligentsia has even expressed their mind in favour of the secession of Assam from India'.[26] On 1 January 1948, the Asom Jatiya Mahasabha Conference resolved that Assam should come out of the Indian union and become an independent state like Burma.[27] When it was suggested to Ambedkar in the Constituent Assembly on 6 September 1949 that District Councils in the hill tribal areas would encourage separatism, he said: 'I do not know if that prophesy could be confined only to the tribal areas. I fear that Assam itself might go.'[28] The illegal immigration from East Pakistan into Assam continued unabated after India became free. During the 1930s and 1940s the government of Assam encouraged the growth of Muslim population to prepare for the reckoning that might come at the time of independence and partition of India. During the 1950s and 1960s, the tacit encouragement to illegal immigration of Muslims from East Pakistan was a conspiracy hatched by the Congress leaders of Assam to create a vote bank for the party.[29] Muslims from East Pakistan continued to come in hordes during the first two decades of free India and voted for the Congress party in successive state and parliamentary elections. Even today, the Congress is in power in Assam because of the Muslim vote bank, and Muslims continue to pour into Assam and the rest of India from Bangladesh in the absence of a serious Indian strategy to check illegal immigration or to identify and deport illegal immigrants. In order to help this Muslim vote bank grow, a special legislation (IMDT Act) was passed in the early 1990s by the Congress governments at the centre and in Assam which prescribed complicated, wasteful, and unnecessary procedures for detecting and deporting illegal immigrants, and this undermined the Foreigners Act to such an extent that detection, trial, and deportation of illegal immigrants in Assam became, and continues to be, impossible.

It is against this background that the All Assam Students Union (AASU) and its allies started an agitation in 1979, to have illegal migrant voters' names deleted from electoral rolls and have the illegal immigrants deported from Assam. The failure of the agitation to achieve its objectives and the disenchantment of its leaders with the Government of India led to the split among its cadres, one becoming the Assam Gana Parishad (AGP) to establish its political ascendancy in Assam on the crest of the wave of popularity that it secured from the agitation, and the other becoming the United Liberation Front of Asom to fight for the secession of Assam from India. The immediate reason for the establishment of ULFA was the perceived illegal appropriation of power by the Congress in the 1983 elections. The first Hiteshwar Saikia government of 1983 was considered illegitimate by the Assamese because those elections were based on the 1979 electoral rolls which contained names of thousands of illegal Muslim immigrants from Bangladesh whose elimination from the electoral rolls and deportation was the battle cry of the AASU movement of 1979–83. The elections were boycotted by the Assamese and conducted in a garrison environment with less than 15 per cent voter, mostly non-Assamese, turnout. ULFA became a major insurgent force during the tenure of this government from 1983 to 1986.

However, in a move of great statesmanship which heralded the policy of accommodation in Indian politics, Prime Minister Rajiv Gandhi shared the Assamese perceptions and agreed to the demand that the Congress government resign and make room for fresh elections. The Assam Accord (as well as the Mizo Accord) was signed in 1985, and the AGP in Assam swept to power in 1986 (as did a non-Congress outfit in Mizoram). ULFA and AGP were, however, birds of the same feather, and ULFA continued to grow in its size and power under AGP rule.[30] The AGP government was dismissed, President's Rule was imposed[31] and ULFA was banned on 27 November 1990, followed by large-scale army operations against the ULFA from the very next day.

Then 1991 election followed. The Congress party bribed ULFA with huge amounts of money and promises to withdraw army operations and start negotiations with ULFA's high command if it enabled the Congress to win. The

ULFA issued its diktat and the Congress, led by Hiteshwar Saikia, returned to power thanks to ULFA, in one of the most peaceful elections in Assam in recent times. Saikia kept his promise and undid what the army and paramilitary forces had achieved under President's Rule. Army operations were almost brought to a halt, and 400 ULFA cadres were released from prison. Some top hard core ULFA members released from prison (Arabinda Rajkhowa, Anup Chetia, and Pradip Gogoi) were dispatched to Bangladesh to persuade their friends, particularly Paresh Baruah, to return for negotiations. These messengers never returned and issued a statement from Bangladesh for the renewal of armed struggle. Those who remained in Assam formed themselves into another armed outfit known as SULFA (surrendered ULFA), who became, with financial and administrative assistance from Saikia's government, the mafia of Assam, a bunch of criminals who looted, kidnapped for ransom, collected illegal taxes, and killed without compunction. The Congress had thus goofed again. In its desire to come back to power if forfeited national security.

3. It may be in order to mention in passing that the birth of the Bodo insurgency in Assam is also attributed to the Congress party. Within a year of AGP rule, beginning in 1986, ethnic violence erupted in the Bodo areas of Assam when the AGP government led by Prafulla Kumar Mahanta failed to meet the All Bodo Students' Union's (ABSU) demand for autonomy for Bodo-inhabited area. Assam's Congressmen were seething with discontent from the time they were made to resign as a follow up to the Assam Accord of 1985. Why Rajiv Gandhi, the architect of the Assam Accord, agreed to dismantle what he had created without giving it a fair chance is not known, except that he was persuaded by his party men who were hungry for power to agree to some unethical initiatives. A militant outfit comprising the Bodos was armed and trained by the Special Services Bureau (SSB) and the BSF as a counterblast to the AGP-ULFA combine and to discredit the Mahanta government for failing to accommodate Bodo demands. Mahanta told a press conference that the Research & Analysis Wing (RAW) was extending arms and explosives

training to the Bodos. Sanjoy Hazarika says that, 'The game was an old one: destabilize a non-Congress government by using a local grievance and using large funds that did not need to be accounted for. The hatchet man chosen for the job, Mahanta and AGP politicians say, was Santosh Mohan Deb, the then Minister of State for Home.'[32]

Geopolitical Factors

Proximity to China, Pakistan (East Pakistan up to 1971), Bangladesh and Bhutan, and the easy availability of arms, training and sanctuaries in these countries has been a major factor responsible for the growth and sustenance of insurgencies in north-east India. Almost all countries in the neighbourhood of north-east India have encouraged north-eastern insurgent groups to establish camps and sanctuaries across the border from India.

Between 1962 and 1966, five groups of a total of about 2,400 Nagas went to East Pakistan to receive training and brought back some arms. The Nagas sent a number of gangs for training and armament to China between 1966 and 1979. The first group of 200 Nagas led by Brigadier Thinuoselie went to China in November 1966. The next group of 350 Nagas under the command of Mowu Angami went in 1968 for training in guerrilla warfare and brought back considerable quantities of arms and ammunition. The Indian army captured Mowu Angami and most of his gang when they returned from China in March 1969. The third group was also badly mauled by the army before it could re-enter Burma. Large segments of the fourth (October 1974) and fifth (January 1975) China-bound groups were also destroyed or dispersed by the army. The sixth and the seventh Naga groups went to China under General Muivah and Ashikho in 1979. They settled down in Burma on their return, from where they launched many attacks inside Indian territory. The Indian army destroyed and dispersed three China-bound Naga gangs in 1968–69.

Laldenga first visited Pakistan in 1963 to discuss arms and training with the Pakistani army. This resulted in the procurement of arms and later the establishment of MNA camps in Chittagong Hill Tracts (CHT), Ruma, Rengtlang, Rangamati, Chengiachari,

Dumdumia, and Khagrasore inside East Pakistan. In November 1964, 40 MNF members went to East Pakistan and returned with arms and ammunition. Another 2,000 MNF men went to East Pakistan in 1965 for training and arms procurement. By December 1965, 800 young men had been recruited in the Mizo National Army and were undergoing training in East Pakistan. At the time of the MNF uprising in March 1966, the MNA headquarters was in Aizawl. On 3 March it moved to South Hlimen, about 30 miles south of Aizawl. On 18 March it was shifted to Reiek, east of Aizawl. By the end of the month Laldenga and the entire MNF and MNA high command had crossed the border and established their headquarters in CHT, East Pakistan. Landenga went to China for five months from November 1970 to February 1971 along with his Foreign Minister Lalhmingthanga. The MNF sent two groups to China, first in 1972 which returned with Chinese gifts of radio transmitters/receivers, arms, ammunition, gold chains, jungle warfare uniforms and boots, inflatable boats for crossing rivers, books of Mao-Tse-Tung,[33] and US currency. On its way back, two of the men were killed in an ambush by the Burmese army, and 27 of them surrendered to the Indian army in Imphal on 30 June 1975. On 23 April 1975, another group of 20 Mizos led by MNA Colonel Biakvela arrived in the Kachin area on their way to China. But after hearing about Laldenga's visit to New Delhi, they returned and surrendered to the Indian army. After the liberation of Bangladesh, Laldenga escaped to Burma. He arrived in Karachi in 1972 and stayed there until 1973. It is ironical that the ULFA and National Democratic Front of Bodoland (NDFB), hunted in the plains of Assam by the Indian army, should seek protection and sanctuary in Bangladesh, a country whose people they had earlier sought to kill or deport from Assam.

Since the early 1990s, much of the ULFA and NDFB terrorist activities in Assam has emanated from their camps in Bhutan. Bhutan, unlike Bangladesh, always acknowledged the presence of these camps but did nothing until December 2003 to throw them out, when it realized that the presence of Indian militants on its 265-km border with Assam was seriously undermining its governance of the region. King Jigme Singye Wangchuk decided in late 2003 to assert Bhutan's sovereignty over a large territory occupied by militants from India before it was too late. With the Indian army's strategic support, the Bhutan army smashed all of the 30 ULFA, NDFB, Kamtapur Liberation Organisation (a militant group of West Bengal) camps in southern Bhutan within a matter of days, killing over 100 militants and driving out the rest. Many surrendered but a large number of insurgents evidently escaped into Bangladesh, their largest haven. Bhutan very proudly announced in the South Asian Association for Regional Cooperation (SAARC) meeting in Islamabad in January 2004 that the mountain kingdom had emerged as a model of regional cooperation against terrorism. (Details of Bhutan's cooperation have been discussed in a separate chapter in this study—Editor.)

India does not have the same diplomatic leverage with Bangladesh as it has with Bhutan. The present Khalida Zia government in Bangladesh has also been accused of nurturing Pakistan's Inter Services Intelligence (ISI) operatives active in north-east India, and its help and assistance to insurgencies in the region has been described by many as a state policy dictated from Pakistan. Shy of using its military leverage, India has seen, for the past 50 years, all the major and minor insurgencies in the north-east being run from insurgent training and transit camps located in Bangladesh. In the recent past, India has identified 99 training camps of north-east rebel groups located inside Bangladesh, and the detailed list has been handed over to Dhaka for action.[34] According to a report published in *The Sentinel*, Guwahati, of 23 December 2003, there are at present 194 camps of 15 militant groups of north-east India in Bangladesh.[35]

While Bhutan watched helplessly as the militants' camps were established on its territory about 12 years ago, the establishment of these camps in Bangladesh was the outcome of a different logic and history that goes back to the assassination of Mujibur Rahman in 1973 and the emergence of an Islamic anti-Indian leadership in Bangladesh. The Islamic anti-India hold on Bangladesh is so strong that during her two terms of prime ministership, Mujib's pro-India daughter Sheikh Hasina could not demolish Indian insurgents' camps which were working under the protection of the Bangladesh army and paramilitary forces.

Collusive Politics of the Northeast: Insurgency/Terrorism as an Economic Activity

Whatever the triggering causes of the various insurgent and terrorist movements in the north-east, the proximate casual dynamic of their persistence has acquired a momentum of its own. Within the structures of this dynamic is the underground economy of terrorism/insurgency, as well as the deeply collusive nature of political and insurgent movements in these states. Most insurgencies have become resistant to resolution, substantially because a complex of vested interests in the 'overground' economy and political sphere secure significant benefits from their persistence. The 'complex collusive arrangements between various political groupings, administrators and officials, on the one hand, and different militant factions, on the other, are more the norm that the exception'.[36]

Insurgencies and terrorism in all states of the north-east are being sustained by the enormous amounts of money generated by their activities. In the initial stages of these movements, finances to fund activities were secured through raids, robberies, and kidnapping for ransom. In the second stage, where an area of influence or domination had been established, the money was much easier to come by, as ULFA discovered to its surprise in 1990: 'It was amazing, we asked for a little and they were prepared to go well beyond what we wanted,' said one ULFA leader, adding, 'that was when we realised how soft the state was, how weak the businessmen were, how much black money they had, that they could pay up and still have enough for themselves.'[37] The third stage was marked by the collusion between politicians, bureaucrats, terrorists, and businessmen who hijacked the entire Public Distribution System (PDS), the funds allocated by the central government for rural development, and the entire system of contracts awarded by the governments in the north-east.[38] A large proportion of developmental resources flow directly or indirectly to the militants themselves through a regime of collusion, extortion and intimidation. These revenues are compounded by the massive network of extortion and 'taxation' and huge incomes from lucrative illicit enterprises including drug and arms trade. Virtually every vehicle on all roads in the north-east pays a 'toll tax' at several points marking the transition from one insurgent group's area of influence to the next. In Nagaland, the National Socialist Council of Nagaland—Isak-Muivah (NSCN-IM) imposes a 'house tax' on every dwelling unit and 'professional tax' on every government employee. The compliance is total and voluntary. There is a total absence of resistance, and no faith in the ability of the government to protect private citizens and enterprises from this predatory regime. 'The businessman who paid out whopping sums as protection money was not prepared to complain out of fear. The government officer who was threatened with exposure and ridicule and forced to pass on large amounts of illicit black money, sourced to years of corruption and bribery, was silent. The tea plantation executives were afraid to call in the government, because it was seen as an extension of ULFA—and lose their managers to bullets. They paid quietly out of their large profit chests.'[39]

A complex collusive arrangement between the legitimate power elites and terrorist/insurgent groupings exists in every state affected by insurgency in the north-east. This arrangement, on the one hand, facilitates a continuous transfer of resources into the underground economy and, on the other, sustains those who hold political power. This is veritably 'a series of extra-constitutional symbiotic relationships that result in the sharing of political power, activities and jurisdictions between the legitimate agencies of the state, on the one hand, and underground affiliates of the political leadership, on the other.'[40]

In Assam, the ministers' official residences in the capital township of Dispur have traditionally provided refuge and sanctuary to ULFA insurgents or their overground supporters when pursued hotly by the army or the police. Ministers' cars have been frequently used as getaway vehicles. In Tripura the National Liberation Front of Tripura (NLFT) has close links with the Congress party, while the All Tripura Tiger Force (ATTF) has aligned itself with the ruling Left Front. The militancy in the state is substantially supported and sustained by the political patronage received by these groups. In Manipur, the outfits with which the ministers have links include the NSCN-Khaplang (NSCN-K), the People's Liberation Army (PLA), the United National Liberation Front (UNLF), Kanglei Yawol Kunna Lup

(KYKL) and Zomi Revolutionary Army (ZRA). In Manipur too, ministers regularly provide financial support and use of their official cars and bungalows to the terrorists. There is a total subversion of civilian administration in the state. Two responsible persons—a former Governor of Manipur and a secretary to the Government of India who toured Manipur recently—have told the present author that the writ of the Government of India in that state runs up to the compound walls of Raj Bhawan (Governor's Residence).[41] Recently, an outgoing Bhartiya Janata Party (BJP) Member of Parliament (MP), Thounaojam Chaoba Singh, pleaded for mercy from KYKL after the militant group had asked the MP to resign from the BJP by 15 February 2004, or face death. In his appeal, the MP said, 'I have no alternative but to beg for forgiveness. . . . If any of my actions or deeds had hurt the feelings or sentiments of any communities or peoples including Nagas, Meiteis, Kukis and Muslims, I may be forgiven.'[42] Such incidents are symptomatic of the absence of the Indian state in Manipur.

Response to Insurgency and Terrorism: Strategies for Resolution

Most modern theories of revolution have drawn heavily upon Karl Marx who thought that the causes of revolution lie fundamentally in the material conditions of life.[43] Towards the end of the colonial era, however, sedition and armed movements seeking independence from the colonizers started being projected as essentially a law-and-order problem, making it obligatory for the state to apply all necessary force to suppress its manifestations and to 'restore normalcy'. The response to insurgency and terrorism during the last hundred years has, consequently, been divided into two broad categories—the military,[44] and the developmental. The latter refers to the 'root causes' referred to by those who subscribe to the 'developmental approach' to change the material conditions of life.[45]

The record of success of military operations in eradicating terrorist movements in India, or for that matter anywhere else, has been poor. Major terrorist movements in India have normally enjoyed some foreign support and refuge in safe havens outside the country. Remnants of militant organizations are also able to find shelter in the more inaccessible terrain within the country, or to return, temporarily, to normal life among the civilian population at times when the state's coercive thrust has the upper hand. Military operations, consequently, can almost never entirely eliminate terrorist forces. Armed counter-terrorist operations, even when they are conducted with extraordinary sensitivity and respect for human rights, frequently create conditions for the further alienation of local populations, or at least for the projection of the army operating in terrorism affected areas as an oppressive occupying force. This results in the persistence and deepening of the prevailing disaffection.

Military operations have been one of the major strategies for handling insurgencies in the north-east. Sustained 'clear and hold' operations as opposed to 'search and clear' or sweep operations, were undertaken for decades in Naga Hills, Mizo Hills, and Assam, as the latter operations, howsoever aggressive, do not achieve the dual purpose of killing insurgents and destroying their infrastructure. In the Indian army's experience, massive deployment of infantry and air power, which is essential for 'search and clear' operations, is generally wasteful and often unaffordable. Aerial bombings and strafing was used in the early stages of Naga and Mizo insurgencies, but this strategy was given up for several reasons: first, because the terrain was unsuitable for the 'sweep operations' required immediately after the air strikes; secondly, adequate infantry for such operations was not available; and, thirdly, a liberal, democratic India could not continue to bomb its own civilian areas without raising eyebrows around the world.

Resettlement or grouping of villages was done in Naga Hills on a minor scale and without any legal sanction, but in Mizo Hills it was a major operation carried out on the basis of legal orders from the government, whereby almost 90 per cent of the rural population was shifted. The grouping was undertaken to (a) isolate the hostiles from villages to deny them intelligence, food, money and new recruits; (b) to have full freedom of operation against the guerrillas in the depopulated and unenclosed countryside; (c) to free more troops for operations; and (d) to build up the confidence of the villagers in the ability of the security forces to protect them so that they become willing members of the military intelligence set-up. Strategically, resettlement protected the population, united the people in positive action on the side of the government, instilled in them the will to morally and physically resist the demands of the hostiles so that some responsibility for the defence of the new settlements could devolve on the inhabitants, and provided a framework for social and economic improvement.

From the military point of view, the gains of the resettlement operations were immense. But many believe that insurgency in Mizoram was unnecessarily protracted because of the extreme emotional and physical distress caused by the resettlement of almost the entire Mizo population. There is some truth in this assertion, as there appears to be no other reason for the internal war to have dragged on for 15 years after Bangladesh's independence and the closure of MNF camps in the new country in 1971–2. The effects of grouping were perceived by the Mizos to be more in the nature of punitive 'pacification' rather than a simple counter-insurgency campaign measure. Whether the priority in a counter-insurgency campaign should be to defeat the guerrillas or to win over the 'hearts and minds' of the masses is open to debate. Works on the subject are replete with arguments in support of both. Nonetheless, as rival doctrines agree that the masses are the ultimate target, it is difficult to see how this can ever be achieved by starting the proceedings with an elemental shock to the masses. Civilian population is always the arbiter of the success or failure of both the security forces and the insurgents. The old British army doctrine that 'if you have them by the balls their hearts and minds will follow' was a very good, and perhaps often successful, colonial device, but it does not hold good in democratic countries trying to resolve their internal problems of sub-nationalism. A measure of hardship is inevitable when a whole ethnic population is identified with an insurgency. But softening of harsh conditions, and not their aggravation, is what counter-insurgency is all about. 'Examination suggests that this particular technique is unsuited to all but a very few environments and certainly not to those Third World societies in which the land, and the extensive use of it, is central to the people's way of life. Thus resettlement cannot be regarded as a cure but a symptom—a sign that government control over the people has so evaporated that the destruction of society is contemplated to protect it. This is no more a policy than are scorched earth tactics. Perhaps future counter-revolutionary exponents would be wise to regard Malaya and the New Villages as aberrations rather than examples.'[46] No wonder that undermining of this established pattern of tribal life contributed to an escalation and prolongation of the war.

In counter-insurgency, professional soldiers trained for conventional combat often follow a vicious logic of escalation, which derives from acute frustration over an elusive war which seriously undermines not only their effectiveness but the very validity of their training and organization. Hence the compulsion to accept any strategy which gives their activity a semblance of direction or purpose, anything but helplessness. When G.S. Randhawa, a retired Brigadier of the Indian army, was appointed Inspector General of Police of Mizoram after the assassination of G.S. Arya, a police officer, he adopted the strategy of impersonating the enemy to hunt the MNA in the countryside. The idea is as old as warfare itself, but in recent times Brigadier (later General Sir Frank) Kitson of the British army used his 'pseudo-gangs' of surrendered Mau Mau warriors to hunt down their erstwhile colleagues in the Kenyan jungles during 1953–55.[47] This was obviously a sinister kind of warfare which could only be indulged in as a form of colonial repression against ethnically or racially different people of nations other than one's own. Like Kitson, Randhawa sought out disgruntled members of the MNA and the fathers, brothers, sons and other close relatives of people killed by the MNA and enthused and motivated them to carry out ruthless acts of vendetta. Only one Indian newspaper wrote about this experimentation by the army.[48] Fortunately this was stopped after six months. (In 1999–2000, the Assam police also indulged in a perverted version of similar tactics with disastrous results when they brutally killed, under the command of an exasperated and misguided political leadership, several close relatives of major ULFA leaders living peacefully in the Assam countryside.)

Civil–military relations and their respective roles in a counter-insurgency operation have been the subject of considerable debate and disagreement in most democracies.[49] There is, however, no doubt that a unified command is necessary for fighting an insurgency or terrorism within a specified territory. In an area of active hostility, the army is inevitably seen by a beleaguered civil population as an enemy occupational force, and the task of increasing the material comforts of the population and rectifying their grievances remains the exclusive business of a civil administration. Moreover, army excesses (and even atrocities and wilful crimes), which are often inevitable in any intensified internal war, need a civilian watchdog. The problem of coordinating civil and military measures was a very complicated, and often a very unpleasant, business during the days of the Naga and Mizo insurgencies.[50] This was made more difficult when the warrant of precedence of civil and army officers meant for formal state functions was sought to be imposed by a highly rank-conscious Indian army in day-to-day business transactions both at the district and State levels. Pressure groups like the civil service and the press have been vocal against an administration headed by a serving military man even if the political leadership was inclined to accept it as an emergency measure.[51] But it took India almost 40 years to accept, and enforce, that the army could operate under the overall supervision of the civil authority except in operational matters where the army's independence has been recognized.

But this can work in states like Assam[52] and Jammu & Kashmir where there has been a semblance of legitimate political leadership and civil administration. In states like Nagaland and Manipur, where almost the entire political leadership has traditionally been hand in glove with the insurgents, the possibility of an effective civil authority overseeing the counter-insurgency operations is impossible.

As demonstrated by K.P. S. Gill's resounding success in Punjab (1988–95), a specially trained and motivated local police force under the outstanding leadership of a policeman is better suited for counter-insurgency operations than the regular army. One wonders why the Punjab experience in fighting an insurgency was not replicated elsewhere in the country. Gill effectively took counter-insurgency out of the realm of the army by his performance in what can be aptly described as the only totally successful counter-insurgency and counter-terrorism operation in modern history. Moreover, Gill's is the only example in free India's history when an officer has been effective in handling a secessionist insurgency by his own caste and community[53]—a task and responsibility the finest of Indian Administrative Service (IAS) and Indian Police Service (IPS) officers have either shied away from or have failed to carry out successfully.[54]

In the north-east, the police morale and training have taken the greatest beating under the mounting pressure of insurgency and terrorism. The political leadership, often hand in glove with the extremists, has never made the goals and objectives of the police force clear, and this has prompted police officers to remain passive onlookers most of the time. The state's armed police battalions are usually badly trained and carry arms which date back to the early twentieth century, though they have recently been equipped with automatic weapons and some units have been armed with AK-47s to match the insurgent firepower. Training and discipline of the Assam Police has suffered a serious setback from the time of the Assam agitation against illegal immigrants (1979–86) and the subsequent growth of ULFA and Bodo insurgencies, when the policemen were pitched against their own kith and kin with not a single Assamese police senior officer able or willing to rise to the occasion as Gill did in Punjab. Another problem has been the lack of availability of men in the police force to track down and fight the insurgents. On the pretext of providing security or batmen duties, almost 20 per cent of armed police manpower in the north-east is engaged in the households of senior officers, their duties including working in the poultry, piggery, and dairy farms or other businesses of these officers and their wives and other family members. These men, trained to fight, are engaged as cooks, cleaners, gardeners, and drivers, and many of them accompany the officers when they are posted to Delhi or elsewhere on deputation, though officially they are shown as posted in their battalions. It is reported that similar misuse of manpower trained to fight pervades the army and paramilitary forces as well.

The 'development model' predicates that massive developmental investment will eliminate the sources of popular discontent. But Ajai Sahni says: 'This assertion is, by and large, an article of faith, and in the profusion of literature reflecting this perspective, there is little evidence of a case study that would suggest that this strategy has actually been successfully implemented in any part of the world.'[55] The volume of the underground economy of insurgency and terrorism in the north-east, and the ability of this complex system to subvert all governmental interventions for economic development, has not been factored in in any resolution model by the government. The little surpluses that are left from the small incomes that accrue to the target population through development activities are duly appropriated by the militants through extortion and 'taxation'. The limited success of the developmental effort is also offset by the flight of private capital in an environment of political uncertainty and widespread extortion.

Other well-tried non-military strategies have also been experimented with: amnesties and offers of rewards, bribery and corruption, devolution of power, empowerment and the creation of new states, electoral politics, negotiations across the table, and secret negotiations in India and abroad, among others. But, except for some temporary respite from violence, nothing seems to have worked in so far as as resolution of these conflicts is concerned. Out of the seven major insurgencies only one—the Mizo insurgency (1966–86)—has been effectively resolved. But it was not resolved entirely by some deliberate act of volition on the part of the Government of India. Some other events, not connected with the Mizo insurgency, changed the geopolitical environment of the subcontinent and led to its ultimate resolution.

Although the military operations from 1966 to 1970 had considerably weakened the MNA and the grouping of villages to deny shelter, food and recruitment to insurgents has had a highly demoralizing effect on the militants and their overground supporters, it was the Bangladesh War of 1971 and the closure of MNF camps in East Pakistan that delivered the *coup de grace* to the Mizo insurgency.[56] The civil society as represented by the Church in the Mizo Hills had a significant role in ultimately getting the MNF to the negotiating table,[57] but it had very little to do with the way the MNF broke up after the fall of Dhaka. After the fall of Dhaka and the closure of MNF camps in Bangladesh, Laldenga was still fighting, albeit a losing battle, and negotiating for the next 15 years.[58]

The fact is that the entire population of Mizoram assumed the role of a 'civil society' between 1976 and 1985, if the term 'civil society' denotes forms of associations which are spontaneous, bring to completion the powerful but inarticulate forces of social union, explore various 'truth alternatives',[59] arrive at a consensus about what the truth is, and influence, through their perception of truth and reason, decision-makers on both sides of a social or political divide in resolving conflicts. If finding truth is a question of organizing civil society in a manner which will cancel out 'the fallible results', there is no civil society in Assam, Nagaland, Manipur, and Tripura.[60] Only in Meghalaya has the civil society been able to exercise some restraint on the Hynniewtrep National Liberation Council (HNLC) and Achik National Volunteer Council (ANVC) insurgencies. According to one social scientist who has explored the manner in which the 'civil society' has disintegrated in Assam violence 'has actually *excised truth* from the civil society agenda.'[61]

From 1947 India had no law to deal with terrorism until the promulgation of the Terrorist and Disruptive Activities (Prevention) Ordinance in 1985, and after the expiry of the Terrorist and Disruptive Activities (Prevention) Act (TADA) in 1995 and until the enactment of Prevention of Terrorism Act (POTA) in March 2002. Prior to 1947, the British colonial rulers adopted a model which combined criminal justice and war to deal with the terrorism in Bengal and other terrorism in India. But the history of TADA and POTA has been characterized more by its misuse rather than its legitimate use for the security of the nation. For example, the 'abysmal record of convictions': out of more than 76,000 persons arrested under TADA up to June 1994, cases against 25 per cent were dropped by the police, and out of the 35 per cent cases that were actually brought to trial, 95 per cent ended in acquittals. A mere one per cent of the persons arrested under TADA were eventually convicted. In Jammu & Kashmir, not a single case of the 20,000 registered resulted in a conviction. It is incomprehensible how the law could be stretched to the point where social activist and protestor, Medha Patkar, could be arrested under TADA. TADA was similarly applied to labour unionists and various other categories of anti-government and anti-establishment protestors, even where such protests were entirely non-violent. The sheer scale of the abuse to which TADA lent itself can be estimated by the fact that by May 1993, Gujarat, a state which until then was unaffected by terrorism, had over 17,000 persons detained under TADA, which is 32.08 per cent of the total of 52,998 detainees in the country at that time. Jammu & Kashmir, where militancy and terrorism were at a peak at the same time, had just 1,826 detainees.

Similarly, there have been some blatant misuses of the Prevention of Terrorism Ordnance (POTO) and POTA during the last two years of their existence. These include the arrest and detention under Section 21 of Vaiko, a Member of Parliament; Gopal, an editor, and eight others in the state of Tamil Nadu; the arrest of 702 persons, a large number of whom were teenagers, in the state of Jharkhand; of 240 persons in the state of Gujarat, 239 of whom were Muslims; and of Raja Bhaiyya, an alleged criminal politician in the state of Uttar Pradesh, to name a few. Not one of the arrested persons in these cases could be called a 'terrorist' as defined in POTA, and these infringements were a clear case of misuse of the anti-terrorism law for political vendetta. Among the most bizarre intended uses of POTA has been thc murder of Dalit girls in Maharashtra,[62] and a recommendation by the National Commission for Cattle to invoke POTA against gangs who smuggle cows across the country for beef.

A very valid conclusion is that the Indian executive machinery, which is incapable of effectively using powers given by its ordinary laws, resulting in near lawlessness through the length and breadth of the country, does not deserve special and extraordinary laws to handle terrorism. There are also those who argue that criminal law was only, and always, a deterrent to crime, and not a guarantee against it, and that human society would have been far happier if laws alone could eliminate the possibility of criminal conduct. The present Congress-led United Progressive Alliance (UPA) government had committed itself to the repeal of POTA and has repealed it in 2004, soon after coming to power.

The handling of the development of various secessionist insurgencies in the north-east, the manner in which they have been sought to be resolved, and the efforts by the government and its agencies to negotiate settlements has been a squalid, slovenly and dismal affair. In the process, a few retired civil servants and police officers have promoted themselves into a class of professional negotiators or peace-brokers who criss-cross the planet to negotiate with surrealistic insurgent leaders in surrealistic environments at great public expense and without achieving any breakthrough. It is a story of major failures and minor successes. Out of seven major insurgencies and over a 100 small and major armed militant groups in the north-east, only one insurgency has been resolved and only four militant groups have gone out of existence. The blame must inevitably go to the Government of India, to its political leadership and its top civil and military executive, for their total helplessness as the Naga insurgency took seven long years to develop, for their inability to change the trends when the Nagas went on the warpath and destabilization had set in, for their penchant for piece-meal solutions for trends pointing to proliferating conflicts in the north-east, for allowing the resentments of the people of other states in the north-east to fester for lack of adequate central attention aimed at redressing genuine grievances, and lastly, for their unwillingness to learn from past mistakes. As if under a divine curse, most Indians have accepted the historic fatality of the tragedy that north-east India has gone through with an equanimity that is incomprehensible.

This insouciance in the top echelons of the government is best illustrated by Bernard D. Nossiter, the *Washington Post* correspondent in Delhi who interviewed B.K. Nehru, Governor of Assam and Nagaland (1967–73), a retired member of the Indian Civil Service, and a cousin of Jawaharlal Nehru and uncle of Indira Gandhi, in 1968:

> 'The attempt to suppress the Mizo revolt and the turn to force in Nagaland (1963–73) are not simply a matter of cold political calculation. They reflect a deep strain of contempt for the Christianized tribes. This was made clear in a remarkably frank talk I had with B.K. Nehru. . . . He talked of the tribal people much as a colonial governor of an earlier day might have spoken of Indian nationalists. . . . Governor Nehru was incensed that Mrs. [Indira] Gandhi had met personally with the hostile Nagas, even though the discussions had led to no concessions'.

'You can't talk to every damned rebel who comes along with a couple of thousand guns,' he told me in his precise Oxbridge accent. 'Is this the Government of India or Bongo-Wongo? We've got a mess on our hands and will have for some time. You can't run a government along Gandhian lines. I agree with Mao. Power comes out of the end of a gun. The Nagas,' he went on, 'are petulant and spoiled children. There are times when you have to face things, kill people and be killed. . . .'

But wouldn't the new policies continue the war indefinitely? I asked. 'It is probably a good thing to prolong the fighting', Nehru replied. 'Let those people get tired of it.'[63]

NOTES

1. At the time of India's independence in 1947, the region had one state (Assam), and three Centrally Administered Areas (Manipur, Tripura, and the North East Frontier Agency or NEFA). Assam was reorganized subsequently to form the present truncated state of Assam, and three new states of Nagaland (1963), Mizoram, and Meghalaya (1972). Manipur, Tripura, and Arunachal Pradesh (old NEFA) also became states in 1972.
2. See Prosser Gifford, 'Indirect Rule: Touchstone or Tombstone for Colonial Policy', in Prosser Gifford and W.R. Louis, *Britain and Germany in Africa*, New Haven: Yale University Press, 1967, p. 391.
3. Even today Indians are called 'vais'—foreigners—by the Mizos, Kukis and other allied tribes in Mizoram and Manipur. The English were never foreigners. They were called 'saap', a derivative of 'saheb'—the ruler—and continue to be referred to by that appellation.
4. The seventeen major Naga tribes, whose languages were largely unintelligible to each other, had already invented Nagamese, a crude version of Assamese, to communicate with each other and the neighbouring Assamese before the British arrived on the scene.
5. From a Christian population of 45 in Lushai Hills District (Mizoram) and 32 in Naga Hills District (Nagaland) in 1901, almost 50 per cent of the population of these districts was Christian when the British left in 1947.
6. Most colonial officers in the hill tribal districts brazenly encouraged and facilitated missionary work. David Scott, who conquered the Brahmputra valley and the surrounding hills, wrote to W.B. Bayley, Secretary to the Governor-General of India, as early as in 1825 that 'nothing permanently good would be obtained if the British did not interfere on behalf of the tribes and prevented them from becoming Hindus.' Sir James Johnston, in *My Experiences in Manipur and Naga*

Hills (first published in 1896; reprinted as *Manipur and Naga Hills*, Delhi: Manas Publications, 1987, p. 283), wrote with characteristic immodesty that the north-east was 'the only instance in history of a body of foreigners who govern an Empire, not for their own benefit, but for the benefit of the races committed by Providence to their charge'. 'Perhaps I can justly claim a share in the spread of Christianity', wrote Colonel Shakespear, Superintendent and Deputy Comissioner of Lushai Hills, in a letter dated 20 April 1939, to Mendus, a Welsh missionary.

7. In 1942, Sir Herbert Reid, Governor of Assam, proposed the creation of a North-Eastern Frontier Province for the 'animists and Christians' of the region to be administered directly by Whitehall. It is apparent, from the way this scheme for the creation of this Crown Colony for north-east India and north-west Burma on the pattern of Hong Kong was pursued by all British officers in the north-east, that the British were aiming, through the 'exclusion' policy, at a future political status for the hill tribes which would be separate from the Indian political identity.
8. Twenty-eight Indians joined the Assam cadre of the Indian Civil Service and the Imperial Police after World War I, but none of them were posted as district officers in Naga Hills, Mizo Hills or any other Frontier Tract or in any capacity or Department of the Secretariat in Shillong from where they could either monitor or influence administration in the hill districts.
9. Rev. Michael Scott wrote about the Naga insurgency: 'We cannot evade our share of responsibility in Britain for all that has led to the present tragedy. . . . It was Britain's imperial policy which kept Nagaland isolated from India and from contact with the people and political movements of India so that there was very little exchange of ideas or mutual understanding of the people and their society when India became independent'. *New Statesman*, London, 3 September 1960.
10. This reluctance to expose the tribes to modern political institutions and to introduce modern ideas of government through an 'archaic system of hereditory rulers' was considered by the British administrators analogous to wondering 'how the city planner of a Tudor town would have designed his petrol station'. Cited in J. Gus Liebenow, *Colonial Rule and Political Development in Tanganyika*, Evanston: Northwestern University Press, 1971, p. 124.
11. Phizo and Sakhrie met Mahatma Gandhi in Delhi in July 1947. The Mahatma assured them that the 'Nagas have every right to be independent. . . . Personally, I believe you all belong to me, to India. But if you say you won't no one can force you.' In reply to a question if the Government of India would use force against the Nagas to join India, Gandhi said, 'No, not if I am alive. I will go to Naga Hills and say that you will shoot me before you shoot a single Naga.' This version

of the encounter was made available by Gandhi's Secretary Pyarelal to Nirmal Nibedon. The latter has reproduced the account in his book *Nagaland, The Night of the Guerrillas*, New Delhi: Lancers Publishers, 1978, pp. 31-35. It also appeared in *The Spectator*, London, 14 September 1962 in an article entitled 'The Naga Revolt' by George Paterson.

12. Ambedkar told the Constituent Assembly 'the position of the tribals of Assam, whatever may be the reason for it, is somewhat analogous to the positions of the Red Indians in the United States as against the white emigrants there. Now, what did the United States do with regard to the Red Indians? So far as I am aware, what they did was to create what are called Reservations or Boundaries within which the Red Indians lived. They are a republic by themselves. No doubt, by the laws of the United States they are citizens of the United States. But that is only a nominal allegiance to the Constitution of the United States. Factually they are a separate, independent people. It was felt by the United States that their laws and modes of living, their habits and manners of life were so distinct that it would be dangerous to bring them at one shot, so to say, within the range of the laws made by the white people for white people and for the purpose of the white civilization.' Draft Constitution, Sixth Schedule, Constitution Assembly Debates, p. 1025.
13. See John Ehle, *Trail of Tears: Rise and Fall of the Cherokee Nation*, New York, 1987; James Wilson, *The Original American: U.S. Indians*, Minority Rights Group Report 31, 1976. Also Roxanne Dunbar Ortiz, *Indians of the Americas* (London: Zed Press, 1984), W. David Baird, *Indian-White Relations: A Persistent Paradox*, ed. Jane F. Smith and Robert M. Kvasnicka, Washington D.C.: Howard University Press, 1976, p. 216.
14. 'Every logical consideration pointed to the desirability of the hills and plains continuing as a single political, economic and administrative unit. But, at root, the hillman suspected the plainsman, while the latter, for all their outward protestations of affection and historical affinities, had little respect for the hillman's culture and way of life. . . . Suspicion and arrogance abetted by administrative ineptitude, have been . . . the main ingredients that made for the separation of the hills and plains areas of Assam.' Nari Rustomji, *Imperilled Frontiers*, Delhi: Oxford University Press, 1983, p. 29.
15. Gurudas Das, 'Cementing the Faultlines in Assam', *Faultlines*, vol. 11, Institute for Conflict Management, New Delhi, p. 92.
16. Report of Nari Rustomji, Tribal Advisor to the Governor of Assam, 7 December 1948, Assam Records.
17. As early as 1954, Captain Williamson Sangma, MLA from Garo Hills, spoke to the Assam Assembly on the inevitability of a hill state and

cited the imposition of the Assamese language and domination by the Assamese in all spheres of life as a grave provocation. He stated that while the Assamese constituted only 50 per cent of the population of the state, they controlled 75 per cent seats in the legislature, 90 per cent of the cabinet posts, and 70 per cent jobs in the public service.

18. Rustomji, *Imperilled Frontiers*, p. 3.
19. *The National Herald*, Lucknow, 30 March 1963.
20. The Mizo Union again won the 1957 District Council though with a reduced majority of 11 out of a total 22 seats with Congress winning only one seat.
21. Mizos have dreaded the flowering of two bamboo varieties (*Melocanna bambusa soidef* and *Bambusa tuilda*, which flower every 50 years). When this happens, rats are attracted from hundreds of miles to feed on its seeds. After the seeds are eaten up, the rats attack the crop, which causes famine. There are Mizos who have seen 20 acres of paddy crop nibbled away a by rat attack in a single night.
22. The Assam Regiment is part of the Indian Army, while the Assam Rifles is a paramilitary force under the Ministry of Home Affairs.
23. When the British were faced with a similar situation in the 1930s after the dismissal of hundreds of Baluch and Pathan troops following mutiny in two battalions, they recruited these men in a specially created armed police instead of letting them loose to become criminals or rebels. This force was called the Crown Reserve Police, which later became the Central Reserve Police Force (CRPF). Lt. General S.L. Menezes, who was the Brigade Commander in Kashmir when the Assam Regiment Battalion was disbanded following the mutiny in 1961, told the present author that the British handling of the situation in the 1930s was communicated to the Defence Ministry by the army.
24. Report of C.S. Mullan, Census Commissioner of Assam, 1931.
25. Lord Wavell wrote in his Journal during his tour of Assam in 1943: 'The chief political problem is the desire of the Moslem Ministers to increase this immigration into the uncultivated Government lands under the slogan "Grow more food"; but what they are really after is "grow more Moslems".' *Wavell: The Viceroy's Journal*, London: OUP, 1973, p. 41.
26. All India Congress Committee File No. 4 (i) 1937, 13 November 1937, Rangia, Assam.
27. *The Assam Tribune*, Guwahati, 3 January 1948.
28. Draft Constitution, Constituent Assembly Debates, p. 1027.
29. It is well known in Assam that, during the 1950s and 1960s, there was a tacit understanding between the Muslim Congress leaders of Assam led by Fakruddin Ali Ahmed and Moinul Haque Chowdhury and the Hindu Congress leaders like Bishnu Ram Mendhi and Bimla Prasad Chaliha which predicated that Hindus would run the bureaucratic

machinery of Assam and the Muslims would cultivate the land. The implication was that Muslims to cultivate the land would have to be found, and they would continue to be loyal to the Congress party as long as the government kept its eyes closed to illegal immigration.

30. 'The AGP government is reported to have remained a passive onlooker in the face of the growing ULFA terrorism. They had political compulsions and saw ULFA as their second line of defence', wrote Gurmukh Singh, in 'The Militants' Progress', *The Sunday Times of India*, New Delhi, 28 September 1997.
31. 'The whole state machinery is with the ULFA', said the Indian Minister of State for Home, Sanjoy Hazarika, *Strangers of the Mist: Tales of War and Peace in India's North-East*, New Delhi: Penguin India, 1994, p. 190.
32. Hazarika, *Strangers of the Mist*, pp. 156–57. See also H.K. Borpujari, *Northeast India: Problems, Policies and Prospects,* New Delhi: Spectrum Publications, 1998, p. 96.
33. The pages of these books were used by the Christian Mizos as toilet paper while traversing dense leech-ridden jungles where water or leaves could not be used safely for the purpose.
34. The list includes 25 camps of the National Liberation Front of Tripura (NLFT), 20 of the All Tripura Tiger Force (ATTF), 18 of the National Socialist Council of Nagalim (NSCN-IM), 17 of the United Liberation Front of Assam (ULFA), 10 of the People's Liberation Army (PLA), 2 of the National Democratic Front of Bodoland (NDFB), 2 of the Muslim United Liberation Tigers of Assam (MULTA), 3 of the Achik National Volunteer Council (ANVC) of Meghalaya, 1 of the Chakma National Liberation Front , and 1 camp of the Dima Halim Daogah (DHD). These camps are in Naikhongchari, Alikadam, and Ruma in Bandarban district; Kaukhali, Nanirchar, Baghaichari, and Dighinala in Rangamati district; Kamalganj and Srimangal in Moulvibazar district, and Chunarughat in Habibganj district. Some camps exist in Dighinala, Panchari, Matiranga and Khagrachari in Khagrachari district, and Madhabpur in Habibganj district.
35. The break-up is: United Liberation Front of Assam (ULFA)—27, National Democratic Front of Bodoland (NDFB)—18; National Socialist Council of Nagalim (NSCN-IM)—18; People's Liberation Army (PLA)—12; 2 factions (BM and NB) of the Natioanl Liberation Front of Tripura (NLFT)—53; All Tripura Tiger Force (ATTF)—36; Muslim United Liberation Tigers of Assam (MULTA)—7; Achik National Volunteer Council (ANVC-Meghalaya)—9; Hinnewtrep National Liberation Council (HNLC-Meghalaya)—5; and 9 camps of other smaller militant groups. The report has given the exact location of each camp inside Bangladesh.
36. Ajai Sahni and J. George, 'Security & Development In India's Northeast: An Alternative Perspective', *Faultlines*, vol. 4, February 2000, p. 54.

37. Hazarika, *Strangers of the Mist*, p. 187.
38. During 1994–8, it was well known that the subsidised essential commodities that were made available through the PDS were diverted to the open market in all the states of the northeast, generating illegal revenues of an estimated Rs. 1,000 million per month, a large proportion of which accrued to the ULFA, SULFA, HNLC, NSCN, and other terrorist groups. The processes of this operation are exemplified by the diversion of the region's approximately 80,000 tonnes of rice and wheat under the PDS. The difference between open market prices and the PDS price in 1998 was Rs. 4.00 per kg. Most of this rice was sold in the open market, and the 'premium' shared between the political executives, civil servants, businessmen, and insurgent/terrorist groups. Whole wheat was distributed to consumers at an official rate of Rs. 5.00 to 5.50. Assam's monthly allotment of wheat till early 1998 was 30,000 tonnes, most of which was simply allocated to flour mills, many of which were directly owned by ULFA and SULFA surrogates or businessmen aligned with them in profit sharing. The flour was then sold in the black market at a hundred per cent premium, generating illegal incomes estimated at about Rs. 100 million per month. Similarly, the PDS price of salt was Re. 1 per kg; a bulk of the monthly allocation of 15,000 tonnes of salt was sold in villages at prices exceeding Rs. 3 per kg, generating illegal incomes estimated at Rs. 300 million. Villagers in Assam also paid up to four times the 'control price' for each litre of PDS kerosene oil. Similarly, 'Rural development' was another lucrative sector, and as much as 70 per cent of the funds available to Assam under this head were systematically siphoned off under a well organized network of ULFA and SULFA cadres, contractors, civil servants and members of the political executive. Of the total of Rs. 11.65 billion made available under this head during the period 1992–3 to February 1998, less than Rs. 4 billion went into legitimate schemes. There was little evidence of projects executed on the ground that supports the claim even of this fraction of expenditure. See Sahni and George, 'Security & Development In India's Northeast: An Alternative Perspective', *Faultlines*, vol. 4, February 2000, p. 54.
39. Hazarika, *Strangers of the Mist*, p. 191.
40. See Sahni, 'The Terrorist Economy in India's Northeast: Preliminary Explorations', *Faultlines*, vol. 8, p. 141. These relations are often formalized through firm—albeit secret—agreements between these power-sharing cabals. Such an 'arrangement' was arrived at between the Arunachal Pradesh Chief Minister Mukut Mithi and the National Socialist Council of Nagaland—Khaplang (NSCN-K). This Naga militant organization dominates the Changlang and Tirap districts in that state. In order to dislodge the 19-year-old Gegong Apang government, sources disclosed that Mukut Mithi and his supporters

entered into an agreement with the NSCN (K), according to which the latter guaranteed that no candidate would contest any election against Mithi's Arunachal Congress for six years in the Changlang and Tirap districts; in return the Members of the Legislative Assembly and ministers thus elected unopposed would cooperate with the NSCN (K) and follow their directions during this period.

41. Both in Nagaland and Manipur, senior state officials and political executives are paying extortion money to the terrorists, and openly negotiate the levels at which the extortion amounts from various departments are to be 'fixed'. Terrorist groups have made inroads into the functioning of government departments, including interference in government contracts, development projects, supply and bill clearances. Terrorists of the NSCN (IM), NSCN (K), PLA and the UNLF have unhindered access to government files and offices. Commercial contracts are allotted to nominees or members of various terrorist groups, who siphon off the money to finance terrorist activities. Terrorist outfits also offload rice, sugar, wheat, and other essential commodities from the PDS and distribute them among the locals at lower prices in order to gain 'legitimacy' and increase their 'base' in the state. The centre is also contemplating suspension of all funds to Non-Governmental Organizations (NGO) based in Manipur, as various NGOs are allegedly siphoning off large sums of money to the terrorists. See *South Asia Terrorism Portal*, Manipur: Assessment 2001, http://www.satp.org/India/Manipur/Assessment_Manipur.htm.
42. http://in.rediff.com/news/2004/feb/28mani.htm
43. See Theda Skocpole, *States and Social Revolutions*, Cambridge: Cambridge University Press, 1979.
44. 'Military' is, in this context, used loosely in the sense of the use of armed force by the state against militants, whether this involves formations from the army, the paramilitary forces or the armed police.
45. Huntington holds modernization responsible for breeding the processes of instability and violence in society. Samuel P. Huntington, *Political Order in Changing Societies*, New Haven: Yale University Press, 1968, p. 41. According to Gurr, relative deprivation, or men's perception of the dicrepency between their aspiration and achievement, is the basic condition of violent behaviour. He has analysed about 1,000 'strife events' in 114 polities between 1961 and 1965 and has concluded that the variables which often trigger revolution are: illegitimacy of the regime, the difficulty of communications within the country, the existence of foreign support for potential dissidents, the presence of an illegal but active Communist Party, economic discrimination, political discrimination, religious cleavage, dependence on private foreign capital, potential separatism, and so on. See Ted Robert Gurr, *Why Men Rebel*, New Jersey: Princeton University Press, 1970.

46. Major R. Marston, 'Resettlement as a Counter-revolutionary Technique', *Journal of the Royal United Services Institute*, vol. 124, no. 4, 1979, pp. 46–9.
47. Frank Kitson, *Gangs and Countergangs*, London: Barrie and Rockliff, 1960, p. 192. After Kenya, this method was employed by the British army and mercenaries against the Popular Front for the Liberation of Oman in 1957–9. A similar force called the Selous Scouts was employed by the Smith regime in Rhodesia against the national liberation movement. This role is now fulfilled by the SAS (Special Air Service) in Northern Ireland as the British army found it impossible to recruit Irish Catholics who will not find anything 'fundamentally dishonorable' in killing their own kith and kin for material benefits. See Also Frank Kitson, *Bunch of Five*, London: Faber and Faber, 1977, p. 147.
48. 'If one accepts all that is said about the special force, it would appear to be bunch of assassins—local Mizos, including former MNF—who terrorise the people, with MNF personnel as the prime targets, and contrive situations to help incriminate the MNF', *The Statesman*, Calcutta, 15 July 1977.
49. British (Kenya, Malaya, Cyprus, Oman) favour a committee at every level comprising a senior military commander, a senior policeman and intelligence officers under the chairmanship of the head of the local administration. France (Indochina) and USA (Vietnam, Iraq) have preferred a single commander system, who is a military officer.
50. The serious differences that had cropped up between the army and the civil administration in the Mizo Hills were public knowledge towards the end of the 1960s. Bernard D. Nossiter, the Washington Post correspondent in New Delhi, wrote in his book, *Soft State*, New York: Harper & Row, 1970, pp. 52–5: 'In this harsh arena, Indian civilian and military authorities have fallen out among themselves. Civilians accuse the military of inflaming the Mizos by burning their villages in retaliation for raids. The military, in turn, blame the civilians for the lack of a development program. . . . I found a colonel friend who was sorely troubled over what was happening. On the one hand, he was irritated with civilian authorities who balked at letting the army burn villages harboring rebels. But then he half-acknowledged that this served little practical purpose, apart from satisfying soldiers' demand for vengeance.'
51. In 1968, a government decision to post a serving army general as the Commissioner of Division so that he could be the overall and unified commander of all agencies dealing with the Mizo insurgency had to be reviewed and set aside within a week under pressure from the Indian Administrative Service.
52. As Chief Secretary of Assam (1997–8), the author headed the Unified Command which had the GOC IV Corp (Lt. Gen. Nirmal Chandra

Vij, later Chief of the Indian Army Staff), DGP of Assam, and local heads of central and state Intelligence agencies, the BSF and the CRPF as members. This worked very well. Earlier, during the author's tenure in Mizo Hills (1968–71), army-civil relationships were marked by considerable acrimony.

53. The largest number of Sikhs killed in Punjab by the security forces under Gill's command were from the Jat Sikh community to which Gill himself belongs.
54. It is entirely to the credit of Rajiv Gandhi that he chose, perhaps for the first time in the history of Indian administration, the right man at the right time for the right job when he appointed Gill as the Director General of Police (DGP) in Punjab in 1988. But an unthinking Prime Minister Chandrashekhar removed him at the end of 1989 soon after Rajiv Gandhi's assassination, which gave new and serious impetus to insurgency and terrorism in Punjab. One of the first things Narisimha Rao did after becoming prime minister was to post Gill back as the DGP of Punjab on a five-year tenure (1990–5) which brought peace to the state.
55. Sahni, 'The Terrorist Economy in India's Northeast', p. 129.
56. Laldenga visited China for five months from November 1970 to February 1971. On his return he removed or sidelined important moderates who were in touch with the Mizo Church leaders and looking at negotiated settlement with the Government of India as an option. Although the Chinese assured him of help, training, and arms (this offer was made use of in 1972–5), he was not quite sure of his next move and dispatched two emissaries to India in February 1971 to explore the possibility of a negotiated settlement. In this sudden move, Laldenga obviously had not reckoned with the considerable anxiety about the future of the MNF sanctuaries in East Pakistan. The Bengali demand for secession from Pakistan had turned into a mass movement with armed overtones by the begining of 1971. Many million refugees soon poured into India as the Pakistani army was deployed to crush the Bengalis, and the Government of India, pressed by mounting security problems on the eastern borders, offered general amnesty to the MNF with attractive monetary rewards and offers of rehabilitation in August 1971. It did not elicit an immediate response, but by the time the Indo-Pakistan war ended in December 1971 with the creation of Bangladesh, Lalhmingthanga, MNF Foreign Secretary, Lalkhawliana, Finance Minister Thangkima, the education secretary and 14 other high-ranking MNF personnel came over to India and surrendered. After the liberation of Bangladesh, Laldenga escaped to Burma and then to Karachi in Pakistan where he stayed from 1972 to 1973.
57. The Mizo Church leaders had taken a stand against violence from the very beginning and had told Laldenga that the Church was against

any attempt to seek help from China. In April 1967, they wrote to Saingahka, the MNF home minister (who was captured by the SF soon after): 'You have taken up this course in the firm belief that by doing so you will create better conditions for our children and the future generations to come. We admire the courage of your conviction. However, we would like to remind you that India herself has never been one nation. The Telegus are as different from the Punjabis as the Bengalis are from the Mizos, yet we together are determined to build one mighty nation. In this process, each of us has a right as well as a responsibility, and the welfare of our children in future depends on how we discharge and exercise our respective rights and responsibilities. We would also like to point out that any self-respecting government should have naturally adopted the same attitude as the Government of India has adopted towards you. It might also be realised that the Government of India, in trying to keep up this self-respect and integrity, have incurred a great loss and a number of her sons too have sacrificed their lives. We firmly believe that the government would go a step further to meet the desires of the Mizo people.' The Church leaders wrote to B.C. Cariappa, the Commissioner of Cachar and Mizo Hills, in March 1969, and attached the following remarks of Lalkhawliana, the MNF finance minister, which they had recently received: 'Knowing full well the stand of the Indian Government from the Church leaders, I am prepared to work and do my utmost to help create conditions that would lead to peaceful solution of the present situation provided, of course, the Government of India is prepared to respond to my appeal.' Although Laldenga arrived in Delhi in January 1976 and negotiated and signed a peace agreement with the Government of India in July 1976, this agreement was never implemented because his demand that he would head the provisional government of Mizoram before fresh elections were held was unacceptable to the government. After the talks with the new Janata government in Delhi also failed in May 1977, Laldenga was asked to leave India. Disillusioned by Laldenga's achievements in the negotiations, General Sawmvela, the MNA chief, surrendered with 62 senior MNA and MNF functionaries in June 1977, and declared the continuance of armed insurgency 'immoral' after the July 1976 accord. But Laldenga stayed on in the hope of a breakthrough in negotiations. The MNF split in 1978, when Biakchhunga ousted Laldenga as its president, and surrendered with his followers with arms, led to Laldenga's arrest in July 1979. He was released for negotiations after Indira Gandhi returned to power in 1980. Renewed violence erupted in Mizoram in 1982 on a command from Laldenga after the government rejected his demands. The government responded to Laldenga's blackmail by asking him to leave the country in April 1982 (he went to London), banning the MNF and MNA again, sending an unprecedentedly large force (26 battalions) to combat the renewed MNF armed militancy, and by saturating every road, town, group centre and village with troops, renewal of restrictions on movement, and dusk-to-dawn curfew. This constituted a great psychological pressure on the people who had become used to a normal tenor of life with the many ceasefires and suspensions of army operations during negotiations in the preceding five years. Everybody clamoured for a peaceful settlement and the Church made daily appeals for peace and harmony. The next two years saw the development of secret links between the Congress party and the MNF, many of the latter joining the Congress after coming overground. The Congress fought the 1984 elections in Mizoram on the platform of peace and won with an overwhelming majority. The Mizoram Congress appealed to Indira Gandhi for resumption of peace negotiations with Laldenga. He came from London on 29 October 1984, a day before Indira Gandhi's assassination. Talks were resumed a few months later, and the final Memorandum of Settlement was signed on 30 June 1985. This brought the Mizo insurgency to an end after 20 years of bloodshed.

59. See Samir Kumar Das, 'Assam: Insurgency and Disintegration of Civil Society', *Faultlines*, vol. 13, p. 114.
60. Jurgen Habermas, quoted in Samir Kumar Das, op. cit.
61. Ibid.
62. *Indian Express*, New Delhi, 17 July 2003.
63. Nossiter, *Soft State*, pp. 154–5.

4 Res...
The Pa...

Sumit...

INTRODUC...

Although ...
repeatedly ...
izations ...
his govern...
gazette. These ...
groups in ...
the Lashka...
December ...
simply ...
Musharraf ...
groups are ...
on until the ...
perators ...
separating ...

The Pakistan ...
effectively ...
close to 600 ...
operational ...
response ...
down on ...
which have ...
some measure ...
the Line of ...
Kashmir. W...
likely, inc...
decisively ...
jehad. The ...
not dissimil...

4. Responding to Terrorism: The Pakistani Response

Samina Ahmed

INTRODUCTION

Although Pakistan's military ruler General Pervez Musharraf has repeatedly pledged his intention to eliminate terrorist organizations and to eradicate extremism from the Pakistani policy, his government's response to terrorism remains far from adequate. The government did ban a number of radical Islamic groups in January 2002, including the Jaish-e-Mohammad and the Lashkar-e-Toiba, held responsible by New Delhi for the December 2001 attack on the Indian parliament, but many simply re-emerged under changed names.[1] Banned again by the Musharraf government in November 2003, a number of these groups are operating freely once again, and will continue to do so until the government takes decisive action against the perpetrators of terrorism and the institutions responsible for disseminating extremism and exclusion.

The Pakistan government has moved swiftly and relatively effectively against Al Qaida personnel, apprehending or killing close to 600, disrupting, as a result, the terrorist organization's operational capabilities within its territory. Yet the government's response is still inadequate since it has failed, thus far, to clamp down on local terrorist and extremist organizations, many of which have links with Al Qaida. The government has also taken some measures to control the infiltration of militants across the Line of Control dividing Pakistani and Indian-administered Kashmir. While such cross-border activity has reduced, it could likely increase again unless the government clamps down decisively on the extremist networks that sustain the Kashmir jehad. The situation along Pakistan's border with Afghanistan is not dissimilar. Using Pakistani territory as their base of operations and as a sanctuary, the Afghan Taliban, with the support of their Pakistani allies and ethnic kin, as well as other Afghan militants such as members of Gulbudddin Hekmatyar's Hizb-i-Islami, continue to target, with little discrimination, the US-led coalition, Afghan government personnel, and representatives of international humanitarian and development agencies.

The government's response to home-grown terrorists, including sectarian and other armed militants, has been as inadequate. Since 2002, extremists from radical Sunni Deobandi organizations, some with long-standing links to Al Qaida and their Taliban allies, have attacked western installations and personnel on several occasions. Sunni extremists, many from organizations banned by the government, are also conducting a violent jehad against their Shia sectarian rivals, resulting in tit-for-tat attacks by Shia militants. Ethnic conflict is becoming equally violent as ethno-regional rivals settle domestic scores through deadly means. Indeed, some international observers depict Pakistan as the epicentre of regional terrorism because of the state's inadequate response to the threats posed by extra-regional terrorist networks, religious extremism, and sectarian and ethnic conflict. And the military-led government's stated resolve to eliminate terrorism is increasingly questioned within Pakistan and even by some of its closest allies.

The contradictions in its policy responses have severely hampered Pakistan's ability to contain and eliminate the threats of terrorism posed to its stability, to regional security, and to the interests of its western allies. Left unresolved, these contradictions could further weaken a fragile state even as they undermine its present standing as a reliable ally in the western-led and conducted international war against terrorism. To adopt more effective military, political, and socio-economic policies, however, the military-led government will have to drastically reverse course, both in the domestic context and within its neighbourhood.

The Context

Contemporary Challenges

The dichotomy between the government's anti-terrorism rhetoric and its actions is rooted in the country's internal and external dynamics. In the internal context, domestic legitimacy continues to elude the military's reconstructed political order. To ensure regime survival and consolidation, the Musharraf government has fallen back on a long-standing alliance between the military and the religious right to counter its civilian opponents, the country's mainstream moderate political parties.[2] While the military's alliance with the mullahs might, at least temporarily, ensure regime survival, it is unlikely to result in regime consolidation. Since the military–mullah alliance has empowered the religious political right, it is emboldening in turn their militant radical Islamic allies. Ethnic conflict too has escalated because of the military's political engineering, which has excluded political actors considered undesirable by the regime and reward others for services rendered.

Despite the rapid rise of terrorist violence, the military-led government has yet to take decisive action.[3] And this hesitancy is linked to the country's external dynamics. The government's present stress on eliminating Al Qaida is based on its need for external support, mainly from the United States, to sustain and to consolidate a military dominated political order. Despite its pledges, however, Pakistan's military leadership has yet to abandon the belief that the Kashmir jehad has undermined India's hold over its part of Kashmir.[4] This use of religious extremists in Pakistan's proxy war in Indian-controlled Kashmir has its history in another decades-old conflict, which is yet to be resolved, the civil war in Afghanistan. Since the mid-1970s, the military has relied on anti-Kabul Islamic radicals to promote its perceived interests in Afghanistan.[5] This policy culminated in Pakistan's support for the Taliban during the 1990s.

Pressured by the United States after 11 September 2001, the Musharraf government appeared to have severed its links to the Taliban. It even joined hands with the US-led coalition in its war against Al Qaida and the Taliban, actively assisting in the Taliban's ouster from Afghanistan. Yet links between Pakistani and Afghan religious extremists, forged during the years of the civil war, remain intact and are unlikely to be severed so long as Pakistan fails to take effective action against the Taliban and their Pakistani supporters on its soil. However, so long as the Pakistani military remains dependent on the mullahs for regime survival, pro-Taliban Pakistani Pashtuns will continue to provide support and succour to their Afghan ethnic kin.[6]

DOMESTIC AND EXTERNAL DETERMINANTS

Terrorism has become one of the focal points of policy in the United States and elsewhere since the 11 September terrorist attacks and the subsequent US-led global war against terrorism. Yet the international community should have shown more concern about the causes and manifestation of political, ethnic, and religious terrorism in countries such as Pakistan much before 11 September. The absence of international pressure, Pakistani policy makers failed to address these real security threats to their citizens and to regional and global security. On their part, influential international actors, including the United States, were little concerned because Pakistani religious violence and political and ethnic extremism was not perceived as a direct threat to their own national security.

Yet Pakistani ethnic, political, and religious terrorism and extremism has a long history and must be understood within the context of the state's domestic politics. Since Pakistan's independence, popular support for religious extremism has been limited to a very small segment of its largely moderate population; yet religious extremists have, over the past two decades or more, become a threat to Pakistani security and regional and global stability because of state patronage, for the most part by military rulers.[7] This patronage has been bestowed with two objectives in mind; to combat the military's civilian contenders, and to undermine the standing of Pakistan's regional adversaries and competitors, India on Pakistan's eastern and Afghanistan on its western borders. As a result of this patronage, the mullahs have gained political clout. Their growing domestic strength has also, over time, translated into a degree of autonomy from their military patrons, encouraging them to adopt domestic and regional agendas that do not necessarily dovetail with those of the military.[8]

Despite the evident threat posed by religious and sectarian extremism, the military is reluctant to part ways with its Islamic extremist allies who have, in the perceptions of Pakistan's authoritative decision-makers, played a valuable role in the past in the domestic and external context, and who continue to play a useful role in advancing the military's regional agendas and in helping the military retain its control over the state.

The military's continued political dominance and thus its preferential access to the state's resources, in turn, remains at the heart of ethnic extremism and conflict in Pakistan. Using the external threat to justify an ever-increasing defence burden, the military has neglected human development in the state.[9] The disproportionate expenditure on defence at the cost of human development has widened the gap between the rich and the poor on the one hand, contributing to widespread poverty. And on the other, the state's skewed priorities have created an environment within which terrorism flourishes.

The state's failure, for instance, to provide education has directly contributed to the growth of madrasas (Islamic seminaries) which, at best, preach an exclusive religion, while the most orthodox and extremist madrasas indoctrinate and train militant jehadis. Lacking educational opportunities, hundreds of thousands of Pakistanis are forced to send their children to these nurseries of extremism, where they are exposed to the extremist philosophy of jehad. The military and the mullahs alike have relied on the jehadis produced in these militant madrasas, the former as recruits for its external and the latter as foot soldiers of both its domestic and regional jehads.[10] Because the jehadis serve the military's external purposes, little has been done to assert state control over the functioning, curriculum, or sources of funding of madrasas. As a result, the culture of the jehad continues to flourish, creating armies of zealots intent on eliminating their sectarian rivals and the perceived enemies of Islam in the region.

Because the politically dominant military is also ethnically skewed, the centralized authoritarian rule and the absence of representative institutions also contributed to inter-ethnic tensions and conflict in the multi-ethnic, multi-regional society of Pakistan.[11] Since the military is mainly Punjabi in composition, especially within the higher echelons of the officer corps, excluded ethnic communities are alienated by the state's neglect of human development even as the centre exploits their resources to finance the Punjabi-dominated military's needs. During periods of direct military rule, ethnic communities have been deliberately excluded from the ranks of the military, particularly the Baluch and the Sindhis, and, in pre-1971 Pakistan, the Bengalis. More often than not, lacking democratic avenues to voice their grievances and to articulate their demands, they have attempted to resist political repression and state exploitation by both peaceful and violent means.[12]

To counter ethnic and/or political dissent, the military has opted for divide-and-rule strategies, aligning itself to ethnic partners of its choice and then using them against its ethnic opponents. The military's propensity to use coercion to counter ethnic opposition and dissent has exacerbated ethnic–state tensions and conflict. Because the military's ethnic allies have also been allowed to resort to all available means, including force, against their ethnic rivals, the end result is an increase in armed ethnic violence and ethnic terrorism.

If the military's domestic policies have contributed in large part to religious extremism and ethnic conflict, its external preferences have strained Pakistan's relations with its neighbours, even as they have contributed to domestic extremism and terrorism. Although the military's interventionist polices in Afghanistan, for instance, are motivated by the perceived need to offset threats from a hostile neighbour, they have destabilized not just Afghanistan but also Pakistan itself. Because the military's chosen Afghan allies have been Islamic extremists, their links with their Pakistani counterparts have contributed to religious terrorism in Pakistan. And because the civil war in Afghanistan has resulted in a flourishing cross-border trade in arms and drugs, it has contributed to political terrorism and the criminalization of the Pakistani polity. Because of the continued conflict in Afghanistan and the lack of governmental authority, the cross-border trade in drugs and arms continues to finance terrorist and extremist networks in Pakistan.[13]

In the context of Pakistan's relations with India, too, the military's reliance on Islamic extremists to conduct a proxy war with its main regional adversary has empowered home-grown religious terrorists. And many of these jehadis, who are the product of the mainstream political Islamic militants and their networks of mosques and madrasas, have their links to extra-regional terrorist networks, including Al Qaida, united by their anti-Western jehad.[14]

Although the international community is far more aware than it was in the pre-11 September period, of the threats of Pakistan-based extremism and terrorism, the contradictions in the policies of influential actors, particularly the United States, are only serving to undermine the global war against terrorism. Although the US and other influential actors are pressuring Pakistan to end its support for jehadis operating in Indian-administered Kashmir, the effectiveness of this international pressure is undermined by external, particularly US, support for the Pakistani military because of the latter's perceived utility in the US-led war against terrorism in Afghanistan. Pakistan's external allies, particularly the United States, still seem to overlook the casual relationship between military intervention, crises of governance, and the escalation of religious, political, and ethnic terrorism and extremism in Pakistan. Moreover, even as the US and its western allies focus their attention on the elimination of regional terrorism in Pakistan and its neighbourhood, they have yet to understand that their support for Pakistan's military-dictated political status quo will undermine their attempts to curb and eliminate terrorist-related activities within and from Pakistani territory.

THE BACKGROUND

SETTING THE STAGE

From the time of Pakistan's independence from colonial rule to its disintegration in 1971, democratic governance had eluded the state. Created overnight by a colonial master anxious to shed its troublesome Indian empire, Pakistan's colonial heritage was to mar its political development. Because its Muslim League leadership knew little about the people they now governed, lacking a popular base, reluctant to give up their newly acquired political power, they chose to put off the creation of constitutional, representative institutions of governance, opting instead to rely reliance on an inherited civil and military apparatus to retain control.[15] Contemptuous of their weak political overseers, suspicious of civilian dissent, and schooled during colonial rule in the use of coercion to offset the demands for participation and representation, the servants of the state soon became its masters.

Indirect rule by civil and military bureaucrats was substituted for direct control by the military following the 1958 coup, exacerbating internal tensions along overlapping ethnic and regional lines. Under the decade-old military dictatorship of General Ayub Khan, the majority Bengali population understandably rejected centralized, authoritarian state structures, which deprived them of the opportunity of translating that numerical majority into power and influence through democratic institutions. The Punjabi-dominated military's political dominance and its usurpation of the state's resources irked other smaller minorities such as the Sindhis, the Baluch, and even the Pashtun in the West wing, as much as they did the Bengalis in the East wing. Since successive military governments relied on coercion and co-optation to offset domestic dissent, they only succeeded in widening the gap between the rulers and the ruled. The military's refusal to transfer power to popular hands after the first general elections in 1970, and its resultant use of force to quell Bengali dissent fuelled an all-out civil war for secession in the East wing.[16]

The military's alliance with the mullahs also made its first appearance during the Yahya regime when Jamaat-i-Islami vigilante groups were used against Bengali civilians. Atrocities committed by Islamic extremist groups such as al-Shams and al-Badar were to be replicated in a truncated Pakistan, justified not as in the East Pakistani case on the grounds of nationalism, but in the name of Islam.

Having suffered a humiliating defeat at Indian hands, the military transferred power to civilian hands. In truncated Pakistan, religious radicals were soon sidelined and ethnic tensions temporarily subsided as political leaders joined hands to help reconstruct new constitutional and democratic frameworks of governance. By the 1973 constitution, the first in the country's history to be created and adopted by political consensus, Pakistan was given a federal, parliamentary framework. Although considerable power, political, administrative, and fiscal, was vested in the centre, the constitution also included provisions for the devolution of power to the provinces.

Since there were democratic avenues of bargaining and competition, ethnic tensions initially subsided, only to be revived in a more violent shape when Prime Minister Zulfikar Ali Bhutto chose to overlook democratic norms and neglect democratic institutions. During the Bhutto period, too, the partnership between the military and the mullahs was consolidated. The military's antipathy to Prime Minister Bhutto and his Pakistan People's Party (PPP) government was based partly on the elected government's attempts to assert civilian control over the military, which included the dismissal of a number of military chiefs and the imposition of constitutional curbs on the military's political role. The military also distrusted Bhutto's Sindhi ethnic background and resented his party's revolutionary rhetoric.[17] However, it was Bhutto's propensity to ignore democratic norms, including the dismissal of the opposition National Awami Party-led government in Baluchistan and the subsequent ban on the party, which led to Baluch resistance against central control, giving the military an opportunity to regain lost political ground.

Since Bhutto opted to use the military against Baluch dissidents, an empowered and resentful military high command soon ousted him, using the mullahs as their chosen instruments to destabilize an elected government. Claiming that the 1977 elections had been rigged, the military-backed mullah alliance, the Pakistan National Movement, launched a protest movement demanding Bhutto's dismissal. In July 1977, Army Chief General Zia-ul-Haq deposed Prime Minister Bhutto and imposed direct military rule.

STATE-SPONSORED EXTREMISM

The Internal Jehad

Under Zia-ul-Haq, the military openly acknowledged the religious right as its chosen civilian partner. The military–mullah alliance was based on mutual need. Facing domestic opposition, Zia attempted to justify his military rule on the grounds of religion. Zia's Islamization agenda, which included the creation of a parallel system of Islamic legislation and judiciary, benefited the religious political extremists who had failed thus far to make any political in roads against their moderate secular allies.[18] Because the Zia regime preferred the Sunni Deobandi parties to their moderate sectarian rivals, Deobandi extremists and their anti-Shia philosophy flourished. The regime, for instance, devised legal instruments based on the Sunni Hanafi code and created institutional mechanisms, such as Shariat courts, to enforce this Islamic legislation. The dominance of the Sunni legal code marginalized and excluded minority religious and sectarian groups such as the Shias, Christians, Hindus, and Ahmedis.[19] When Sunni extremists also acquired access to fiscal resources and weapons as a result of the Afghan jehad, the result was the sectarian violence that plagues the Pakistani state till today.

Zia's policy of promoting extremist Sunni Islam, which included attempts to impose the Sunni code of Islam on all Islamic sects including the Shias had resulted in widespread Shia resistance, the first organized opposition to the military regime.[20] Since the Shias were now perceived as a potential threat, the regime was even more forthright in its support for its extremist Sunni partners. For instance, for the very first time in Pakistan's history, the state extended fiscal patronage to madrasas with the Sunni Deobandi madrasas becoming the main beneficiaries of the state's largesse. As Deobadi madrasas flourished, the ranks of Sunni militants grew. And the jehadis produced by these madrasas were to be given another external agenda: to help their Afghan religious kin capture power in Afghanistan.

The External Jehad—The Afghanistan Lineage

The Zia government's decision to align itself with the Afghan religious right was motivated by Pakistan's strained relations with its western neighbour. The backdrop of this strained relationship is a disputed border, the Durand Line, an 1893 agreement between the British Indian Empire and the Afghan monarchy. Rejecting the legitimacy of the agreement, successive Afghan governments, including the present set-up in Kabul, have refused to formally accept the inclusion of the Pashtun-majority borderlands bordering on Afghanistan into Pakistan on the grounds that the Pakistani Pashtuns should have been given a choice to join either the Afghan motherland or Pakistan. Since its relations with Pakistan have been strained ever since Pakistan's independence, Kabul has also aligned itself with Pakistan's main regional adversary, India, and before 1989 with the Soviet Union, to gain protection against its larger, militarily powerful Pakistani neighbour.

On their part, Pakistani governments, military and civil alike, have actively intervened in Kabul's internal affairs for decades, partly motivated by the perception that, as the successor state of the British Indian Empire, Afghanistan falls rightfully under Pakistan's sphere of influence. Pakistani interventionist policies are also perceived as insurance against Afghan attempts to undermine the loyalty of Pakistani Pashtuns. Pakistani attempts to influence Afghanistan's internal dynamics have centred on support for anti-Kabul dissidents of an Islamic hue, since nationalist Afghan dissidents could conceivably back Pakistani Pashtun nationalists, unlike Islamic radicals whose aim is, at least ostensibly, to unite the Islamic umma (nation).

Afghan Islamic extremist groups opposed to the Afghan monarchy, and later to Sardar Daud's regime, were given sanctuary by Pakistan during the 1970s. But it was not until the Afghan civil war of the 1980s that Pakistan could fully exploit Afghan domestic dissent. Backing Islamic militants, the mujahidin (holy warriors), with the support of the United States and other anti-Soviet states, including Saudi Arabia and China, the Pakistani military helped to destabilize the pro-Soviet government in Kabul. The military regime used jehadi madrasas, which were provided financial support by the Saudis and other Middle Eastern states as they fought their own sectarian proxy war against revolutionary Iran, to recruit and train the Afghan mujahidin.[21] The military regime also benefited domestically. US diplomatic backing and financial support helped to sustain the Zia regime against its domestic opponents.[22] Yet the policies of the military regime were to transform Pakistan into the regional base of religious, political and ethnic extremism and terrorism, with Pakistani citizens becoming the primary victims of the state-sponsored Afghan jehad.

As a result of Pakistan's involvement in the Afghan civil war, the drugs traffic that was used to finance the mujahidin soon became and has remained an integral part of the Pakistani black economy. This lucrative cross-border trade in drugs has financed terrorists of every hue even as it has penetrated the institutions of the Pakistani state. At the same time, sophisticated arms, provided by external backers to the Afghan dissidents, re-entered and have continued to flow back into Pakistan. As a result, internal conflict, religious, ethnic or political, in Pakistan has become increasingly violent.

The Zia regime's divide-and-rule policies have also contributed, in no small part, to the widening of ethno-regional and religious fissures within Pakistan. In the ethnic context, for example, the military regime had helped to create a new ethno-regional movement of Muhajirs (Urdu-speaking migrants from India and their descendants), represented by their party, the Muhajir Quami Movement (MQM), to neutralize its Sindhi opposition.[23] Because the MQM had emerged out of the Jamaat-i-Islami, which was then a Muhajir-dominated party, its leaders and cadres had imbibed from their parent religious party a belief in the utility of violence for political ends. Since Pakistan's warring ethnic communities, such as the Muhajirs, gained access to Afghan arms and some of its more extreme political factions were financed by Afghan drug money, ethnic reprisals became increasingly bloody. And Pakistan's external jehadis were also to turn their attention inwards as the Soviets departed from Afghanistan.

CONTINUITY OVER CHANGE

While the United States and many other extra-regional supporters of the Afghan jehad departed from the Afghan scene after the Soviet withdrawal in the late 1980s, the civil war in Afghanistan continued unabated, as did the intervention of external actors including the Pakistanis, the Iranians, and the Indians, each hoping that their chosen Afghan clients would capture the state. On their part, the Saudis and other Middle Eastern state and sub-state actors were equally keen to export their brand of Wahabi Islam to South-West Asia, partly to undermine Iran's regional standing and partly to gain domestic support and/or assuage domestic unrest by claiming to be the guardians and advocates of Sunni orthodoxy.

Zia's sudden demise in a mid-air explosion in 1988 and the military's subsequent decision to transfer power to civilian hands meant more continuity than change in Pakistan's internal dynamics and in its foreign policy. In fact, the military retained control over areas of particular sensitivity in foreign policy, including the policy towards India and Afghanistan. The military also continued to intervene in domestic politics. After the first two elected PPP and PML-N governments of Benazir Bhutto and Nawaz Sharif were dismissed by the military before they completed their respective terms of office, both political leaders decided, in their respective second terms of office, to accept the military's external preferences without question. In the context of the Afghan policy, this continuity translated into continued Pakistani backing for Sunni Afghan Pashtun extremists, culminating in Pakistan's role in supporting and sustaining the Pashtun Islamic militia, the Taliban.[24] Emerging out of Pakistani Deobandi madrasas in the North-West Frontier Province (NWFP) and Baluchistan, the Taliban captured Kabul and were close to eliminating the remnants of their ethnic and political foes when their progress was rapidly reversed as the result of US-led military action.

Jehad Extends to India

The military's support for the Afghan Islamic extremists also extended to their Pakistani counterparts because of another regional jehad; this time against Indian control over its part of Kashmir. Until the late 1980s, the military had refrained from backing the Kashmiri resistance, having learnt its lesson from failed military interventions such as Operation Gibralter in 1965. The outbreak of an anti-Indian insurgency in 1989, however, provided new and more rewarding opportunities of intervention. As in the case of Afghanistan, in Indian Kashmir, too, the military opted to back the more religiously orthodox of the Kashmiri dissidents and also infiltrated non-Kashmiri Islamic extremists across the Line of Control.[25] As the Taliban extended their control over Afghanistan, the military also redirected Pakistani jehadis towards a new cause, the liberation of Muslim Kashmir from Hindu India's control.

Because many of these jehadis were recruited from Pakistani Deobandi madrasas, these religious seminaries flourished as a result of state patronage and external, mainly Middle Eastern, financial and political support. Yet the military's decision to support the anti-Indian jehad in Kashmir had major repercussions for Pakistan itself as the Pakistani jehadis also looked inwards, engaging in a violent domestic jehad against their Shia foes in Pakistan. Sectarian violence became the norm as the Shias, with Iranian backing, fought back. But even when civilian governments, such as Nawaz Sharif's second government, attempted to bring Sunni terrorists to book, they faced both external and domestic obstacles. In the domestic context, attempts by elected governments to curb Sunni terrorism were undermined by Taliban support for their Pakistani Sunni allies, and their refusal to hand over even indicted Pakistani criminals guilty of sectarian murder. In the domestic context, efforts by elected governments to bring sectarian terrorists to justice were thwarted by the military's protection of its anti-Indian jehadi cadre.

Ethnic divisions and political polarization also became more fractious because of the military's constant interference and its divide-and-rule policies. When ethnic violence in Karachi reached threatening heights, the military, for instance, created a rival wing of the MQM—MQM (Haqiqi). The result was carnage as terrorists from both MQM wings targeted each other.[26] Shia–Sunni strife also became more vicious as Sunni terrorists aligned to the Taliban attacked Shia professionals and their places of worship at will, and then took sanctuary in Taliban-controlled Afghanistan, where they also benefited from the links they had established with Osama bin Laden and his Al Qaida network.

Because of the insurgency in Indian-administered Kashmir, where the mujahidin's cross-border attacks took an increasingly high toll, Pakistan's relations with India became strained and acrimonious. In 1999, when Prime Ministers Atal Behari Vajpayee and Nawaz Sharif attempted to normalize relations and to resolve the long-standing dispute on Kashmir, the path of rapprochement was supported by Pakistani public and political opinion, the sole exceptions being the military's mullah allies who rioted in the streets of Lahore, the Punjab capital and venue of the 1999 summit.

In any event, the budding rapprochement between India and Pakistan was sabotaged by the Pakistani military. Army Chief General Pervez Musharraf's decision to supplement the proxy war in Kashmir with a military operation across the Line of Control in the Kargil district of Indian-administered Kashmir almost escalated into an all-out war. The Kargil misadventure also proved the beginning of the end of civilian rule in Pakistan. When initial gains rapidly changed to reverses, taking a high casualty toll, and with Indian threats of an all-out war, the Pakistani military decided to cut its losses. US intervention, motivated by concerns of an India–Pakistan war escalating to the nuclear level, was to bear fruit resulting in a Pakistani agreement on an unconditional withdrawal. Facing domestic criticism, Prime Minister Nawaz Sharif placed on the military the sole ownership of the misadventure. In October 1999, the military struck back, ousting the elected government and imposing military rule.[27]

RESPONDING TO TERRORISM

CHANGING COURSE?

For Pakistan's fourth military ruler opportunity struck when 11 September changed his standing with the international community. From an international pariah, General Pervez Musharraf was transformed into one of the closest and most desirable of allies for the United States and much of the western industrialized world when he decided to join the US-led war on international terrorism, abandoning Pakistan's Taliban allies for close co-operation in the battle against the Taliban and their Al Qaida allies and patrons in Afghanistan.

Pakistan's response to international terrorism continues to receive plaudits globally. Sanctions such as those imposed by the United States after the military coup have been removed, as has international pressure on General Musharraf to resume the democratic transition. On the contrary, the United States and others are pouring billions of dollars in grants and loans into Pakistan, helping the military establishment entrench its hold over the state.[28] Yet the military's policy choices and directions underscore a basic contradiction in its response to terrorism. While the government through the use of its security agencies has made impressive gains in disrupting foreign terrorist networks, apprehending hundreds of foreign Al Qaida personnel and supporters, most of whom have been handed over to the United States, it has made little effort to use its security apparatus to equally good effect with regard to the home-grown terrorist groups.

While the security agencies have taken action against some domestic terrorists, using military force and the judicial system, the state's response is sporadic at best. Domestic legislation to curb the inflow of terrorist finances remains far from adequate. The military-led government has yet to take any action to assert its control over the jehadi madrasas. While General Musharraf has time and again stressed the need to eradicate terrorism by addressing its root causes including poverty and political alienation, his government's economic performance in the past four years has increased the percentage of citizens who live under the poverty line. The military's political distortions have also increased domestic alienation, and have contributed to an incremental rise in sectarian and politically inspired ethnic terrorism.

Terrorist Networks and Terrorism Financing

Pakistan's military-led government's inadequate response to terrorism is evident in the half-hearted manner in which it has dealt with home-grown jehadi and sectarian groups. Terrorist and extremist organizations banned in January 2002 re-emerged under changed names. Banned again by the government in November 2003, most operate as freely as they did in the past, once again under changed names.[29] Moreover, no action has been taken under the Anti-Terrorism Act of 1973 against the leader of any prominent Sunni jehadi or sectarian group.[30] This inadequate response can be attributed to ambiguity in the military's policies towards the external jehad in Indian-administered Kashmir and Afghanistan. In the Afghan context, too, well-informed international actors, including, ironically, the US former Ambassador to Afghanistan, Zalmay Khalidzad, believed that the Pakistan military is at best turning a blind eye to the activities of the Taliban on its soil, and was therefore complicit in the Taliban's cross-border attacks on the US-led coalition and the Kabul government. Until the military also takes a strategic rather than a tactical decision to abandon the jehad against India, it will not move decisively against the militant organizations that are most active in the proxy war or against the madrasas that produce jehadis for Kashmir.

Leaders of sectarian and extremist organizations such as Maulana Azhar Masood of Jaish-e-Mohammad and Hafiz Muhammad Saeed of Lashkar-e-Toiba (renamed the JD), which were banned after the attack on the Indian parliament in November 2001 and included by the United States in its list of terrorist organizations because of their involvement in terrorist acts in Indian-administered Kashmir, were only temporarily detained under the Maintenance of Public Order (MPO),[31] and not under the more stringent Anti-Terrorism Act. In 2003, Saeed was not only free but was also openly calling for an anti-western jehad at a public rally in the Pakistani capital, Islamabad, where it is near impossible to assemble without the knowledge of the law-enforcing agencies.

To meet its obligations under Resolution 1373, which makes it mandatory for states to take action against all acts of terrorism within and from a country's territory, Pakistan should have charged the organizations or individuals responsible for perpetrating acts of terrorism across the Line of Control dividing Indian and Pakistani Kashmir, under its Anti-Terrorism legislation.[32] Had it done so, the leaders and many of the members of the Lashkar, the Jaish and the Pakistan-based Hizbul Mujahidin would have been charged accordingly since they have, on several occasions, taken responsibility for militant acts in Indian-administered Kashmir. President Musharraf and his military-run government, however, continue to justify the insurgency in Kashmir on the grounds of a justifiable and internationally legitimate struggle for self-determination.[33]

The Musharraf government has also failed to adequately monitor and regulate terrorist funding. With no oversight over the funding of the madrasas, for instance, the military has no way of ensuring that monies do not flow from the religious extremists running jehadi madrasas to the Taliban, and conceivably to their Al Qaida patrons. Institutionalized legal constraints on terrorist funding are weak. Pakistan has yet to even meet its obligations under Security Council Resolution 1373 to effectively curb all flows of terrorist funds through official and unofficial banking channels by signing the International Convention for the Suppression of the Financing of Terrorism.[34]

Pakistan has yet to enact effective anti-money laundering legislation. As a result, monies to terrorist and extremist organizations continue to flow through unofficial channels known locally as *hundi* or *hawala*. As long as these channels continue to function so will the flow of funds to domestic terrorists, many of whom are responsible for attacks against western targets in Pakistan and/or are involved in regional jehads. Existing legislation such as the Banking Companies Ordinance 1962, which gives the State Bank authority to oversee the functioning of banking companies to check dubious transactions, are also clearly inadequate since they do not specifically address the issue of terrorist financing.[35]

Mullah–Military Alliance and the Madrasa

The government's reluctance to clamp down on extremists operating in Indian-administered Kashmir also explains, at least in part, its policies towards madrasa reform since many of the Deobandi and Salafi/Wahabi madrasas induct, indoctrinate, and train the foot soldiers of the Kashmir jehad. In fact, Pakistan's support of the Kashmir jehad has encouraged the rapid growth of the most dangerous madrasas such as those run by the Lashkar-e-Toiba. The managers of these madrasas are virulently anti-western and their graduates are the most likely to join local terrorists networks with links to Al Qaida.

The wide gap in the military-led government's anti-terrorist rhetoric and reformist policies and its actions is also motivated by domestic exigencies. In the domestic context, the military's emphasis on regime survival and regime consolidation has guided its response to issues such as madrasa reform.

Perceiving the mainstream political parties, particularly the Pakistan People's Party and the Pakistan Muslim League (Nawaz) (PML-N) and their allies in the Alliance for the Restoration of Democracy (ARD), as the main threat to his military-dominated political order, General Musharraf has revitalized a long-standing alliance between his military and the mullahs, represented by the six-party Muttahida Majlis-i-Amal (MMA).[36] This military–mullah alliance has paid political dividends to both parties. With state patronage, the mullahs managed to gain an unprecedented numbers of parliamentary seats in the October 2002 national elections, enabling them to form the NWFP provincial government, and, with the military's support, to join the ruling PML-Q-led coalition government in Baluchistan. The mullahs repaid the military by endorsing the military's political order through their support in parliament for the 17th constitutional amendment which extended Musharraf's self-assumed presidency until 2007 and transferred powers from the head of government, the prime minister and the parliament to the president, the indirectly elected head of state.[37]

However, legitimacy continues to elude the military and its political and constitutional engineering. As a result, the military remains dependent on the mullahs for support within and outside parliament. To retain that support, the military has taken great care to refrain from intruding on the mullahs' turf, which includes the jehadi madrasas run by the Islamic right-wing parties, some of which have close ties to the most militant of sectarian organizations.

In October 2002, Musharraf had publicly vowed to combat terrorism through newly devised plans and strategies, and the government's pledges included madrasa reform to ensure that these Islamic religious seminaries would no longer propagate the jehad, provide military training to young *talibs* (students) and would not preach religious, sectarian, and political hatred and intolerance. But Musharraf's plans for madrasa reform, which included the registration of madrasas, state regulation of their curriculum, and monitoring of their funding, is yet to be given legal cover and implemented on the ground. The government's sole achievement is the establishment of three model madrasas, with a standardized curriculum based on an expanded and modernized version of the madrasa course, the *Dars-e-Nizami*, to include other subjects such as the sciences and mathematics. But while these model madrasas have some 300 students, more than 1.5 million *talibs* continue to attend thousands of unregulated madrasas, including many with a jehadi and extremist bent.[38]

The Pakistan government had enacted a draft law for the registration and financial regulation of madrasas, the Deeni Madaris (Voluntary Registration and Regulation) Ordinance, subsequently approved by Musharraf's cabinet in June 2002.[39] Despite its inadequacies, including its requirement for voluntary, as opposed to mandatory, registration, the law did include mechanisms for oversight overseeing funding, including foreign grants and donations, as well as mechanisms to monitor the admission of foreign students by relevant government ministries. However, when faced with the concerted pressure of the madrasa managers who run the madrasa boards, Musharraf backtracked, choosing to pass the buck on madrasa reform to a parliament in which the mullahs have gained inordinate political influence with the military's support. Moreover, the civil bureaucracy has been given the task of convincing the five different non-governmental madrasa boards to first accept madrasa reform, before a law is introduced in the parliament even though the mullahs themselves control these boards.

Since the madrasa managers are unwilling to make concessions, and the government lacks the political will and/or the interest to reform the madrasa sector, the mullahs continue to teach as they see fit, induct *talibs* as they see fit, and accept and use funds without any governmental oversight.

Clearly Musharraf has failed to demonstrate the resolve to check the abuse of mosques and madrasas by religious extremists. During the 2002 polls, the MMA had used mosques and madrasas to conduct its anti-American and pro-Taliban election campaign. The mullahs continue to abuse these religious platforms to propagate their extremist Islamic agenda. In July 2004, the military-led government reached an agreement with the MMA to curb terrorism and sectarianism by preventing the use of the mosques and madrasas to preach sectarian hatred and support for terrorist causes.[40] Verbal agreements of this sort, however, are unlikely to reform the mosque and the madrasa until there is legislation to back them; and even more importantly, until the mullahs and the military translate their rhetoric into reality.

Responding to Ethnic and Sectarian Extremism

In Musharraf's Pakistan, as in the past, sectarian and ethnic politics has transformed into conflict because of governmental policies and preferences, since the desire to retain and consolidate power takes precedence over the need to address ethnic and sectarian grievances. As a result, those sectarian and ethnic actors, who have been provided an opportunity to expand their political clout and power-base through state patronage, have also attained considerable autonomy in the exercise and abuse of that power. Alienated and excluded religious sects and ethnic groups, on the other hand, are being forced to counter their rivals through all available means, including the use of force, since the institutions of the state are perceived as partisan in nature.

(a) *Sectarian Violence*: The Musharraf government is averse to ending past policies of extending state patronage to Sunni religious trusts and madrasas which continue to receive *zakat* funds; or reforming the legal and judicial structures, such as Shariah courts which empower the religious right at the cost of the more liberal, secular segments of Pakistani public opinion.[41] Since the Musharraf government has yet to place meaningful curbs on the jehadi madrasas, they continue to promote sectarianism and use violent means to conduct their internal jehad. Moreover, to neutralize the political opposition, Musharraf has extended state patronage to Sunni politico-religious parties, such as the Jamaat-i-Islami, which has, for instance, been handed the control of local government institutions in the most volatile of cities, Karachi. Although the government has taken action against sectarian extremists belonging to the most militant of politico-religious parties such as the Sipah-i-Sahaba—arrests are often made—but such cases are rarely pursued in court. Hence the perpetrators of religious and sectarian conflict go free. Such governmental inaction and hesitancy has only succeeded in strengthening the bargaining position of religious extremists.

Continued easy access to arms and the proceeds of the cross-border drugs trade with Afghanistan have also empowered sectarian extremists, whose attacks have become far more lethal than the past. Once confined to a few centres in Pakistan such as Karachi and Multan, sectarian terrorism has now spread to outlying areas such as Baluchistan where, for instance, an attack on a Shia mosque in the provincial capital Quetta on 5 July 2003 left 54 dead and dozens wounded.[42] Instead of responding to the threat with all the tools available to the state, coercive, judicial, and political, the Musharraf government has attempted to sidestep the issue, pinning the blame for the Quetta attack, for instance, on external attempts to destabilize the Pakistani state. Ironically, the pro-Taliban Sunni extremist organization, Lashkar-e-Jhangvi, an ally of the Taliban, has accepted responsibility for the attacks on the Shia Hazaras in Quetta, who are strongly anti-Taliban.[43]

The government's failure to use its law enforcing agencies effectively to penetrate Sunni extremist networks and to identify and then try individuals or organizations responsible for sectarian terrorism has resulted in tit-for-tat attacks by Shia militants. In May 2004, for instance, after suicide attack killed 18 people at the Shia Hyderi Mosque in Karachi, in what was most likely a retaliatory attack, Mufti Nizamuddin Shamezai, the pro-Taliban head of the Deobandi Jamia Binoria madrasa and a member of the central committee of the Jamiat Ulema-e-Islam (Fazlur Rehman), the MMA's largest component party, was gunned down in the city. A day after Shamezai's assassination, the bombing of a Shia mosque in Karachi resulted in at least 16 persons killed and another 38 injured, many seriously. If this cycle of violence has exposed the government's failure to follow through on its pledges to eradicate domestic terrorism, its manipulation of the political process, including its divide-and-rule strategies, could also result in the kind of ethnic conflict that brought cities such as Karachi to a standstill under another military ruler, General Zia-ul-Haq.

(b) *Ethnic Conflict*: For the Musharraf government, much like its predecessors, the imperatives of regime legitimacy have resulted in the institutionalized enforcement of centralized structures of governance. Existing constitutional and legal frameworks have been completely transformed. As a result of the 17th amendment to the 1973 Constitution, supreme authority is vested in the military itself, represented by the Army Chief General Musharraf. The constitution's federal framework, including all provisions for regional autonomy, is therefore only present in form. New structures of local government have been created to provide the military with a new, locally based clientele, and to undermine provincial autonomy. All policy flows from the centre; fundamental rights are undermined by arbitrary checks on the powers of the judiciary; there are severe constraints on the functioning of opposition political parties; and the military has, through its political and constitutional manipulations, stifled all avenues of political representation.[44]

The military-led government also exercises centralized control over the economy, with the centre utilizing a disproportionate share of revenues generated by the provinces as well as externally derived resources, mainly to finance the activities of the Punjabi-dominated military state apparatus. As defence expenditure continues to rise, not only is socio-economic development and redistribution hampered, but the Punjabi-dominated military's position is further strengthened. The resultant uneven economic development has perpetuated socio-economic disparities between the dominant and peripheral ethnic communities.[45] The absence of provincial autonomy and the consolidation of centralized authoritarian policies of governance and the centre's exploitation of their resources has increased perceptions of exploitation and alienation amongst excluded ethnic communities, particularly the Sindhis and the Baluch.

To contain ethnic dissent, the military has adopted strategies based on co-optation and coercion. In Sindh, for instance, the military has prevented the largest party in parliament and its main political opposition, the PPP from forming the government, opting instead for a PML-Q-led ruling coalition of convenience, which includes the MQM. Attempts are underway to further weaken the PPP by either inducing or coercing its provincial legislative representatives into switching their loyalties. In Baluchistan, too, where Baluch resentment against central control and exploitation of the province's resources poses a real threat to the military's institutional interests, to contain and control the Baluch opposition, represented in a number of small ethno-regional parties, the military has forged an alliance with the religious right, the MMA, which has been given some of the most attractive portfolios in the PML-Q-led coalition government.[46]

The dangers of this political manipulation are evident. Since the MQM represents the Muhajirs and the PPP represents the province's Sindhi speakers, Sindhi-Muhajir tensions are again on the rise. The military's political engineering in Karachi is also fuelling armed violence between the Muhajirs represented by the MQM and the predominantly Pashtun MMA.

The MQM, which dominates the Sindh provincial government and hence the administrative and law-enforcing agencies in the province through Governor Ishratul Ibad, and the MMA, which runs the local government structures created by Musharraf, are in bitter rivalry for the control of the richest city in Pakistan. Each side is accusing the other of resorting to terrorism in an attempt to destabilize the state. The MMA, for instance, has blamed the MQM for the attack on the Karachi corps commander; for the assassination of madrasa leader and Jamiat Ulema-e-Islam (JUI) member Mufti Shamezai; and the killing of 11 MMA activists in the May 2004 provincial by-elections in Karachi. Beside calling for Governor Ibad's arrest and removal, the MMA has accused the MQM of recruiting and using terrorists against its political opponents in Karachi.[47] The MQM in turn has accused the MMA of complicity in the attack on the corps commander, calling upon the central government to take action against madrasas, describing them as factories that produce religious terrorists.[48] MQM leaders have also called upon the MMA parties to differentiate between jehad and terrorism.

Since the Muhajir-dominated MQM continues to control the provincial government through Governor Ibad, with Musharraf's backing, and while the MMA's predominantly Pashtun Jamaat-i-Islami continues to run Karachi's local government, this infighting between Musharraf's allies could deteriorate into the Muhajir–Pashtun-like violence that had destabilized Sindh's urban centres in the past as both sides are well armed.

In Baluchistan, too, the Baluch, resentment of the shift in the delicate ethnic balance in favour of the Pashtuns following the influx of hundreds of thousands of Afghan refugees, ethnic tensions could assume a dangerous form. Using its presence in the Baluchistan government, the MMA is mainly interested in advancing the interests of its fellow Pashtuns. Baluch resentment against the centre's exploitation of the province's natural resources is also assuming dangerous proportions, taking the shape of armed attacks against military or paramilitary personnel and oil and gas installations.[49] The centre's manipulation of the political process and the continued absence of representative institutions and forums for ethnic bargaining and negotiation will inevitably fuel this resentment even further. Should the military be tempted to use coercion to suppress this dissent, Baluchistan could revert to the province-wide violent insurgency between dissidents and the state security apparatus of the 1970s.

LOOKING AHEAD

It serves Pakistan ill that its military rulers have yet to understand the importance of responding to terrorism and extremism in substance as well as in form. Without stringent state controls over the functioning, funding, and curriculum of the madrasas, for instance, the jehadis these madrasas produce will continue to threaten the Pakistani state and citizens as much as they will continue to undermine regional and global stability. It is therefore imperative that the government enacts legislation that will provide for official oversight over the madrasa sector. At the same time, it is equally important to ensure that there is sufficient funding and resources for public education, giving Pakistani citizens an alternative to the madrasa for their children.

Pakistan must also urgently enact legislation to prevent the flow of funds to terrorists and other extremists. It is in its interest to do so. The longer the government delays using all means at its disposal to prevent terrorists and extremists from acquiring fiscal assistance, the more likely it is that these home-grown networks of terrorists will continue to flourish, threatening to target Western interests in Pakistan thus undermining the state's standing in the eyes of its global partners. It is imperative that Pakistan uses all possible means, military, intelligence, legal, and judicial to bring ethno-political and sectarian terrorists to book. It is not just enough to capture non-Pakistani terrorists. Home-grown ethnic extremism and sectarian terrorism has, in more ways than one, become an even greater threat to the Pakistani state and its citizens.

But to do so the Pakistan government will have to make a strategic shift in its policy towards the Kashmir jehad. The longer it fails to do so, the greater the threat of international sanction and the risk of war with India. In any case, Pakistan-based jehadis in Indian-administered Kashmir are as much at war with Pakistani citizens since their jehad is also internal. And it is this internal jehad that has become the greatest threat to Pakistani stability and security. The Pakistan military must also acknowledge the need to restrain domestic actors from supporting their Afghan Taliban kin. If the international forces continue to be on the receiving end of Pakistan-based Taliban violence, they could well decide to take action against the source of this threat. Even if that eventuality does not come to pass, the cross-border trade in arms and narcotics will continue to finance and fund Pakistan's own extremists and terrorists if the links between Pakistani political actors and Afghan dissidents remain intact.

Above all, the Pakistan military should understand that it is in its own interests to return to the barracks and to restore the democratic transition. In the absence of genuinely pluralistic, representative institutions, ethnic alienation will only continue to grow among the smaller, excluded ethnic groups. A functioning federal system which provides for tangible regional autonomy through the devolution and the decentralization of authority will restore the faith of Pakistan's citizens in their state. Moreover, by refraining from manipulating the constitutional and political structures of the state, by restoring representative and heterogeneous institutions of governance, and by allowing political freedoms to function, Pakistan's decision-makers would be well on the way to effectively tackling the many challenges they presently face.

NOTES

1. The banned groups included the Jaish-e-Mohammad, Sipah-e-Sahaba Pakistan, Lashkar-e-Jhangvi, Lashkar-e-Toiba, Tehreek-e-Nifaze Shariat-e-Mohammadi, Tehreek-e-Jafaria, Sipah-e-Mohammad and the Harkat-ul-Mujahidin.

2. See, 'Pakistan: The Mullahs and the Military', *Asia Report*, no. 49, International Crisis Group, Brussels, 20 March 2003.
3. By official estimates, 330 persons have been killed in 82 incidents of terrorism in Pakistan since 2003. '330 killed in 82 incidents of terrorism: National Assembly told', *Dawn*, 18 June 2004.
4. 'Unfulfilled Promises: Pakistan's Failure to tackle Extremism', *Asia Report*, no. 73, International Crisis Group, Brussels, 16 January 2004, p. 13. (This was written before General Musharraf's visit to India in April 2005, where there were notable signs of shift in his position on jehadi terrorism in Kashmir. – Editor.)
5. Frederic Grare, *Pakistan and the Afghanistan Conflict, 1979-1985*, Oxford: Oxford University Press, 2003, p. 89.
6. The Jamait Ulema Islam (Fazlur Rehman) which runs the provincial government in coalition with the pro-Musharraf Pakistan Muslim League (Quaid-i-Azam) in Baluchistan and the Muttahada Majlis-i-Amal government in the NWFP is a staunch supporter of the Taliban. Both provinces border Afghanistan.
7. '*Pakistan: The Mullahs and the Military*'.
8. Assassination attempts on President Musharraf could conceivably have been the work of religious extremists, once aligned with and patronized by the military.
9. Hasan Askari Rizvi, 'The Military', in Anita M.Weiss and S. Zulfiqar Gilani, *Power and Civil Society in Pakistan*, Oxford: Oxford University Press, 2001, p. 210.
10. See 'Pakistan: Madrasa, Extremism and the Military', *Asia Report*, no. 36, International Crisis Group, Brussels, 29 July 2002.
11. Omar Noman, *Pakistan: A Political and Economic History since 1947*. London: Paul Kegan, 2nd edn., 1990, p. 21.
12. Samina Ahmed, 'The Military and Ethnic Politics', in Charles H. Kennedy and Rasul Bux Rais (eds.), *Pakistan 1995–1996*, Boulder, Colorado: Westview Press, 1995, pp. 106–7.
13. Hamid Khan, *Constitutional and Political History of Pakistan*, Oxford: Oxford University Press, 2001, p. 683.
14. K. Alan Kronstadt, 'International Terrorism in South Asia', Congressional Research Service Report, Washington DC, 3 November 2003, p. 2.
15. Noman, *Pakistan: A Political and Economic History*, p. 9.
16. Samina Ahmed, 'Centralization, Authoritarianism and the Mismanagment of Ethnic Relations in Pakistan', in Michael E. Brown and Sumit Ganguly (eds.), *Government Policies and Ethnic Relations in Asia and the Pacific*, Cambridge, Mass: MIT Press, 1997, pp. 99–100.
17. Ahmed, *Military and Ethnic Politics*, pp. 110–11.
18. Khan, *Constitutional and Political Histroy*, pp. 627–8.

19. Since the 1950s, Deobandi extremists had conducted an internal jehad against unacceptable Sunni sects, targeting in particular the Ahmedis. As a result of Deobandi pressure, Prime Minister Zulfikar Ali Bhutto's government was to declare the Ahmedis a non-Muslim sect, in an attempt to appease the mullahs in the mid-1970s.
20. Mumtaz Ahmad, 'Revivalism, Islamization, Sectarian and Violence in Pakistan', in Craig Baxter and Charles Kennedy (eds.), *Pakistan 1997*, Boulder, Colorado, 1998, pp. 101–2.
21. Pakistan: 'Madrasa, Extremism and the Military', p. 11.
22. Hasan Askari Rizvi, *The Military and Politics in Pakistan 1947–1997*, Lahore: Sang-e-Meel, 2000, p. 270.
23. Ahmed, 'Centralization, Authoritarianism and the Mismanagment of Ethnic Relations', p. 108.
24. Larry Goodson, 'Foreign policy gone awry: The Kalashnikovization and Talibanization of Pakistan', in Craig Baxter and Charles H. Kennedy, *Pakistan 2000*, Boulder, Colorado: Westview Press, 2001, p. 151.
25. Robert G. Wirsing, 'Kashmir Conflict: The New Phase', in Charles H. Kennedy (ed.), *Pakistan 1992*, Boulder, Colorado, Westview Press, 1993, p. 149.
26. Ahmed, *Military and Ethnic Politics*, pp. 121–2.
27. 'Pakistan: Transition to Democracy?', *Asia Report*, no. 40, 3 October 2002, p. 11.
28. The Bush administration has announced a five-year $3 billion aid package for Pakistan, half of which would be allocated for defence.
29. In an admission that the groups have re-emerged, Interior Minister Faisal Saleh Hayat disclosed his government's intention to take action against banned organizations operating under changed names. Syed Irfan Raza, 'Banned outfits with new names to face action', *Dawn*, 11 June 2004.
30. The Anti-Terrorism Act of 1997, as amended in 2001, covers acts of terrorism outside the country by any Pakistani citizen or organization.
31. Under the MPO, any person can be detained for a period of one month without being produced in court.
32. Security Council Resolution 1373 requires member states to 'prevent those who finance, plan, facilitate or commit terrorist acts from using their territories for those purposes against other countries and their citizens'.
33. According to Musharraf, the Kashmir jehad 'is not government sponsored. It has its own dynamics. Jehadi groups are not terrorist groups. There are splinter groups which are maligning the jehad and jehadi organizations.' 'Kashmir Only Dispute Between India and Pakistan', *The News*, 5 February 2003.
34. 'Unfulfilled Promises', p. 14.

35. Ibid.
36. The component parties of the Muttahida Majlis-i-Amal (United Council of Action) are the Jamiat Ulema-e-Islam (JUI-Fazlur Rehman, JUI-F), Jamiat Ulema-e-Islam (JUI-Samiul Haq), the Jamaat-i-Islami, the Jamiat Ulema-e-Pakistan (JUP), the Jamiat Ahle Hadhe, and the Islami Tehrik Pakistan.
37. 'Unfulfilled Promises', p. 16.
38. Given the lack of data, it is near impossible to determine their exact number which is estimated between 10,000 and 20,000.
39. 'Madrasas, Extremism and the Military', pp. 25–6.
40. Shakil Shaikh and Naveed Ahmad, 'Govt, MMA agree on Registration in Wana', *The News,* 7 July 2004.
41. 'Madrasas, Extremism and the Military'.
42. 'Unfulfilled Promises', p. 10.
43. Ibid.
44. See *State of Human Rights in Pakistan in 2003*, Lahore: Human Rights Commission of Pakistan, 2004, pp. 15–42 and 213–21.
45. Sofia Mumtaz, 'Nationalism, Ethnicity and the Mohajir Political Movement in Sindh', in Sophia Mumtaz et al., *Pakistan: The Contours of State and Society*, 'Oxford: Oxford University Press, 2002', p. 125.
46. 'Unfulfilled Promises'.
47. 'MMA protests against terrorism', *Dawn*, 12 June 2004; 'MMA wants Sindh governor sacked', *Dawn*, 2 June 2004.
48. 'MQM warns of attack's serious repercussions', *Dawn*, 12 June 2004.
49. 'Gas supply affected after rocket attack', *Dawn,* 3 May 2004; '18 Rockets Fired at Frontier Corps Checkpoint', *Dawn*, 4 May 2004; '6 Rockets Fired Near Gwadar Airport', *Dawn*, 21 May 2004.

5. The Challenges of Terrorism: Bangladesh Responses

Abul Kalam

INTRODUCTION

Territorially speaking, and considered from the point of the size of economy, Bangladesh is a relatively small state, but civilizationally perhaps it has a sense of belonging to the larger entity of South Asia and to the regional body of South Asian Association for Regional Cooperation (SAARC) that it mooted. It is currently the South Asian and SAARC identity which has placed Bangladesh on a different plane, and that again both regionally and globally has Bangladesh in the business of responding to terrorism. As more and more Bangladeshis in recent years have been seeking jobs abroad and/or migrating, legally or illegally—and as in consequence a newer and formidable Bangladeshi Diaspora seems in the making—Bangladesh can hardly de-link itself from its neighbourhood and the wider milieu of nations. The Bengalis of Bangladesh thus have been developing what Howard Stein calls a sense of 'psychogeography' a mental map of a belonging, even though spatially they may be situated in other countries of the world.[1]

At this particular juncture of post-Cold War history when globalization has redefined not only the understanding of the national frontiers and the nation-state but also the global landscape and international relationships, it seems difficult to conceptualize the definition of a nation-state like Bangladesh in terms of 'living space' of 1,44,000 sq. km (55,126 sq. miles) of its territorial boundary. This state has also see to the nation's image and security of its people, keeping in mind the well-being of the increasing number of Bangladeshis living abroad. The devastating terrorist attacks of 9/11 in the US had a chain reaction effect on relationships.

Bangladesh may take pride in its regional and civilizational bounds, its increasing exogenous links and in the relative ethnic cohesion and socio-cultural homogeneity of its dense population, but the country has in recent years developed an acute image problem internationally. Traditionally it had a popular image of being a 'moderate Muslim nation', but that image has in recent years been changing. Even before 9/11 the former US President Bill Clinton, appreciative of the country's moderate image, did include Bangladesh in his South Asian itinerary, but had to cutback his schedules in Dhaka due to looming terrorist threats. Currently some describe Bangladesh as a 'base of Taliban'[2] from which the terrorist groups with a 'deadly cargo' were likely to launch attacks using radiological substances,[3] while others describe it as a 'cocoon of terror'.[4] The CSIS (Canadian Security Intelligence Service) also warned that Bangladesh might emerge as a terrorist haven. Concern was also expressed over attacks by Islamic terrorists in collusion with Osama bin Laden's Al-Qaida and the GOB's alleged unwillingness to crack down on terrorism.[5] Bangladesh often takes the position that there is no scope for terrorists to operate in Bangladesh;[6] instead the GOB focuses attention on the nation's democratic and secular values.

Apart from its present image of being a terrorist hub, Bangladesh in the meantime also featured for three consecutive years in the Corruption Perception Index (CPI) of Transparency International as 'the most corrupt country of the world'.[7] The country also draws flak from the international community for the intensely fractious nature of its national politics. There is an almost breathless political confrontation between the ruling Bangladesh National Party (BNP), which is currently leading a four-party coalition government, after the national elections held in October 2001, and the mainstream political opposition, the Awami League (AL), which led the country into independence in 1971. The latter returned to power for a term in June 1996 after an embittered political struggle and held the reins of power until the October 2001 elections. Between the two contentious political parties there has been a long history of bitter mutual antipathy, blame-game, political bluff and trickery of all sorts that vitiated the country's socio-political environment. Both seemed bent upon self-justification and/or mutual exclusion through vilification of the opponent by whatever means available, including terrorist tactics.

Internationally and regionally as well, an environment of fear, domination. and subordination prevails, coupled with multi-pronged threat perceptions of terrorism. The questions that need to be addressed in this context include, what were the terrorist threats perceived internationally and regionally in recent years, and how were they responded to by the actors concerned and what were the ramifications of all this for a country like Bangladesh? How does terrorism manifest itself in Bangladesh and what have been the experiences of the country in dealing with them? How did the government and other segments of the society respond to the menace of terrorism? And finally, what measures can be visualized to effectively surmount the challenges of terrorism nationally in Bangladesh, as well as across societies in order that the world can conceivably be a better place to live in?

Keeping the foregoing pertinent questions in perspective, this chapter argues that terrorism in Bangladesh, while not a new phenomenon, has a chain-reaction relationship with the changing international and regional situations as well as with the deteriorating nature of national politics and policies. It is viewed that the country's responses to terrorism have been problematical, even though there are positive elements in them. While responding to terrorism Bangladesh needs to pursue concurrent and multi-pronged efforts building on positive changes, if the menace of terrorism is to be overcome and societies across boundaries are to move toward a more peaceful world.

In order to advance such an argument the chapter begins by appraising the notional aspects of terrorism, as is presently viewed, and takes into account the conceptual parameters or the options currently offered to cope with them in the shifting environment of relationships across societies. It then analyses international and regional responses to terrorism before and after 9/11 and in that backdrop, considers the ramifications for Bangladesh and the consequent Bangladesh responses to them. Next, the multifaceted nature of terrorist legacies and manifestations confronting Bangladesh in the problematic circumstances of its evolving socio-economic policies and the resulting challenges are taken up for a perspective of its policy responses to terrorism. Then the shifting nature of its responses to terrorism in the new era are assessed with an analysis of the means applied and evaluating their effectiveness as well as identifying positive elements in them. The conclusions sum up the findings and offer ideas for both scholarly reflection and rethinking at various layers of policymaking.

It is natural to expect that a country like Bangladesh will respond coherently in a world that has been evolving in a borderless fashion. A predominantly Muslim country, Bangladesh can barely be expected to remain unaffected by the ongoing perceived global struggle, or to use Samuel Huntington's political allegory, 'clash of cultures' between 'Islam and the rest'. Power wrangling and a climate of fear generated by ethnic brawls in the region may have been equally unhelpful. However, given the current predicament of the increased scale of terrorism in Bangladesh, the country seems to be in a tight spot and needs to reappraise its strategic policies if it is to regain its 'moderate' image and sustain itself as a viable nation-state in the volatile circumstances of regional conflicts and an unpredictable environment of international relations.

Analytical Frame and Perspectives

Terrorism is not a new phenomenon in international relations, but it has played on fears of insecurity in recent years nationally, regionally as well as globally. It has undergone a significant metamorphosis in the understanding and consciousness.[8] It seems that for analysing and evaluating the responses in a country like Bangladesh one has to appraise and understand terrorism at four different, though inter-related levels: the conceptual plane and objective, the actor's level, the expanding nature of weaponry used and the changing context of technology, and finally, the widening ranges of terrorism at the spatial level.

At the conceptual plane, terrorism may appear as of nebulous elasticity, but it does contemplate an employment of diverse strategies with an increasing spiral act or threat of violence. The objectives include exacting revenge, intimidating or influencing an audience, with premeditated and, purposeful violence employed in a struggle for political power and, implementing its ideology, demeaning and/or defeating the perceived opponent. The actors may be elusive individuals, an organized bunch of criminals, gangs of hooligans, sub-national groups/political elements, or even states/governments. The system of weaponry may vary from situation to situation but includes generating funds and/or acquiring resources by whatever means available, hijacking and hostage-taking, imperilling travel means and air lines/sea-links, using bio-chemicals, acid-throwing, use of gas and poisoning of drinking water, as well as dramatizing and publicizing by varied psychological means of intimidation and physical violence. The contextual level is enhanced and upgraded by newer instruments and weapons available, including chemical and biological weapons, and weapons of mass destruction (WMD), being sold to unscrupulous agents, to cyber terrorism and so on.[9]

Spatially, as the actors indulging in terrorism may be of varied origins, analysis has to be inclusive of the intra-national and/or national concerns, then cross-border, and, finally, global/international dimensions. Spatially also, for a long time, terrorism has been experienced in almost every society as a low intensity conflict. What seems new today is that it has innovated a newer magnitude of killing devices, and assumed diabolical ways to kill and injure people and destabilize governments by inflicting colossal damage. Up until now, there was an element of ambivalence regarding terrorism. It was often perceived as someone else's problem, whether the fight was taken up against oppressive governments, misgovernance or alien rule. Since 9/11, however, there has been a shared, an almost universal need for responding to terrorism with effective means. There has also been a growing collective resolve worldwide to respond to terrorism, even though there has not been any universal consensus on the strategies required to counter it with responses that contain, transform, and/or eliminate the terrorist upsurge.

The causality of terrorism in terms of roots and manifestations at the regional and international levels, it appears, calls for an all-encompassing conceptual framework for an in-depth appraisal and understanding, but responses to terrorism at those levels are often manifest in 'combat' and/or 'fighting' the symptomatic behaviour, rather than curing or healing the underlying disease so that the symptoms do not recur. The conventional approach that still seems to linger is one of strategic-military deterrence; it was advanced by the strategic-deterrent theorists who are inclined towards the reasoning that a threat must be confronted by a credible counter-threat, that force must be met by counter-force. Hence they tend to see 'counter-terror' or 'anti-terror' with the use of 'force' to 'combat' the *evil* as the answer.

As against such arguments, the peace theorists of various shades generally emphasize upon social diagnosis of conflict and an appraisal of the underlying phenomenon of conflict. The emphasis may perhaps be on a compassionate appraisal of the feelings of those who have resorted to acts of violence or terror and consider how best their feelings can be accommodated, their needs be met, and consequently the situations of conflict, violence or of terror be assuaged or alleviated towards peaceful change. The idea is to get outside the 'terror/counter terror' paradigm bedevilling relations within, between and among nations, to *transcend* or 'to move relationships beyond' to a new plane of interactions, by breaking the current terror-insecurity nexus.

In the contemporary contexts of terrorism in Bangladesh, and also in the global society, it seems imperative to consider the causality of relationships, how and why organized crime, violence, and insecurity relate to each other. Indeed, at the national level one may surmize a critical nexus involving terrorism, crime/violence and insecurity, with both police and politicians playing intervening roles in reproducing a terrorist upsurge in Bangladesh, as is expressed in the coupling of triangles in Fig. 5.1.

It is premised that effective responses to terrorism in a country like Bangladesh, in terms of approaches and instruments, quite often fail to take into account the prevailing nexus, being oblivious of the deep-seated causes or roots of terrorism. In the foregoing conceptual frame, one cannot but place in perspective the need for alternative strategies towards change and suggest a readjustment of thinking. The chapter makes a plea for utilizing

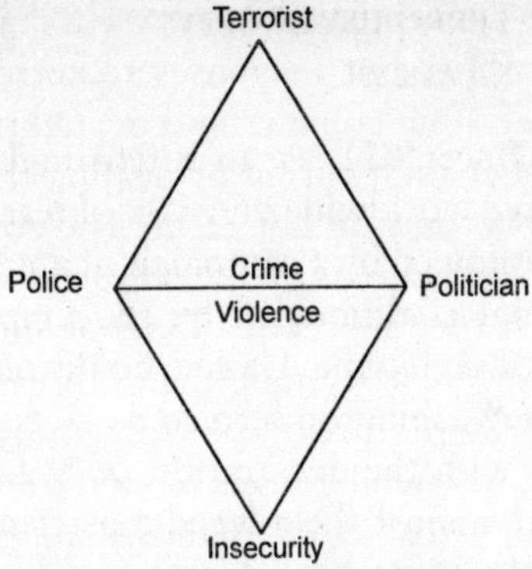

FIG. 5.1: A COUPLING OF TRIANGULAR NEXUS: TERRORISM, CRIME/VIOLENCE AND INSECURITY

innovative options and ways available towards conflict transformation, without ignoring the terrorists' methods.

Keeping the foregoing conceptual frame in perspective, it may now be useful to address the recurring phenomenon of terrorism and its linkage components at the international and regional levels, and then to focus on an analysis of the situation emerging in Bangladesh.

Multilevel Terrorist Threats: Challenges Facing Bangladesh

By the 9/11 attacks international terrorism staged its biggest show in front of the world TV cameras, as hijacked planes felled the twin towers of the World Trade Center and attacked the Pentagon, the pillars of American commerce and defence. The world was then suddenly awakened to the reality of terrorism and faced the challenge to pull together for an even stronger assault.[10] Indeed, since then international terrorism and competing anti-terror strategies have been in sequential dancing acts in dramatic or melodramatic fashion. It became apparent that terrorism was no longer a myth, that the responses to it had to be 'global and all-encompassing', with multilevel components such as political, economic, cultural and psychological.[11]

International Terrorism and its Fall-out in Bangladesh

Internationally, since 9/11 as an intensified scale of violence involved an elusive worldwide network of terrorist functionaries at work, it was followed by a campaign of anti- or counter-terror by a multinational coalition led by the unipolar global actor. The sharp response by the US-led coalition to international terror was, what Washington termed as 'acts of war', began on 7 October 2004 with the declaration of 'war on terror'.[12] The war was directed against the alleged mastermind, the Al Qaida terror network of Osama bin Laden based in Afghanistan, then run by the Taliban regime. Following the liquidation of the five-year old pro-Laden Taliban government in Kabul in the course of the US-led multinational military operations—initially code-named 'Operation Infinite Justice' and renamed later 'Operation Enduring Freedom'—Washington perceived WMD, as the greatest threat to its security.

The U.S. then broadened its anti-terror strategy on 29 January 2002 to include some selected countries—Iraq, North Korea, and Iran—named as the 'axis of evils', and outlined a doctrine of 'regime change'. The objective has been to 'prevent regimes that sponsor terror from threatening America, or (its) friends and allies' with nuclear, chemical and biological weapons.[13] America's post 'Ground Zero' anti-terror campaign sent a clear signal to the perpetrators who flattened the twin-towers that they would not escape a wounded Pentagon's vengeance. And the new century's planet circling shockwaves of multi-billion dollar 'war on terror' sent a simple signal: one global alliance or another.[14] A new doctrine was also made operational on 17 September 2002, dubbed as the doctrine of 'pre-emptive strike' in the twin tasks of 'containment and deterrence' based on the assertion that the US must be able to exercise its right of self-defence by its own pre-emptive actions to prevent the terrorists from further hurting the country. All this marked the dawning of the Anglo-American alliance's efforts to bring together 'freedom-loving peoples' against the perceived 'axis of evil'[15] The coalition's subsequent invasion of Iraq, even without UN sanction, and the ongoing anti-terror and pacification campaign manifested a deep commitment to 'combat terrorism' by whatever means available or resources required.

For Bangladesh it was a difficult moment of reckoning, as during the 9/11 attacks an interim caretaker administration (ICA) was overseeing the country's run up to the national elections. The ICA was prompt to condemn the terrorist attacks on the US, in which some Bangladeshi citizens had also perished. It joined the 'International Coalition Against Terrorism', denounced all acts that run counter to human values and divine religions, including Islam, and agreed to allow the US and the anti-terror multilateral coalition; the use of its air space, offering refuelling facilities for possible military action against the Taliban regime in Afghanistan.[16]

Meanwhile, the newly elected Government of Bangladesh (GOB) brought together a coalition which included staunchly Islamic elements, such as the Jamat-e-Islami, who opposed the country's very creation and are known for their strong sympathies for the Taliban. The government also included some other elements with 'fundamentalist' views such as the Islami Oikkya Jote (Islamic United Front). However, the GOB's policy response to the pattern of developments in Afghanistan was a reaffirmation of the position taken by the caretaker administration, as a 'staunch' western ally, conforming with the desire of the international coalition.[17] On three counts there might have been a sense of compulsion: (i) Protecting its major trading interests with the US, the UK, and Europe, (ii) a donor-dependent country, Bangladesh is likely to be isolated from the unipolar international system; and (iii) the substantial Bangladeshi diaspora in both the US, and the UK, must have had an influence in the GOB's policy stance, as the diaspora contributes significantly to the country's economy.

Therefore, cognizant of sensitivities of the country's location in Asia's Muslim neighbourhood, Bangladesh was supportive of the anti-terror strategies of the US-led multinational coalition. It backed officially all actions taken under the auspices of the UN in conformity with the UN charter and international implementation of the UN Security Council (UNSC). Dhaka sees itself bound by the 9 December 2002 Resolution 1368, adopted unanimously condemning the 9/11 attacks and paving the way for subsequent military action. It is committed to UNSC Resolution 1373—the 'most powerful response' in the war on terrorism—obligating all UN member states to take far-reaching domestic legislative and executive actions designed to prevent future terrorist activities. It also sees her bound by relevant international Conventions and Protocols relating to international terrorism, and support the international security regime.

When the military action by the US-led coalition against the Ba'thist regime of Saddam Hussein in Iraq was underway, Bangladesh was among the first countries to place restrictions on the movement of Iraqi diplomats in Dhaka, even though after its liberation in 1971 Iraq was one of the first countries in the Arab and Muslim world to extend diplomatic recognition to Bangladesh. As a major peacekeeping nation Bangladesh frequently re-stated its eagerness to participate in international efforts towards the reconstruction of Iraq should there be a consensus based on UN sanctions. However, anti-US sentiments ran high in the country across the political spectrum, but speculations were ripe that Al-Qaida outfits had spread to Bangladesh, as indeed to other South Asian countries, which fuelled allegations of 'cross-border terrorism' among various South Asian countries.[18] The leadership of the country's mainstream opposition, the AL, played a major role in fuelling this allegation, even though the terrorist upsurge in the country had started during its own rule (discussed below). In the aftermath of anti-Taliban operation in Afghanistan, when the US had tightened the belt of its homeland security as a host-recipient of international travellers, Bangladesh was also included among 25 other 'Terror Risk' countries, 24 of which have Muslim majority.

TERRORISM IN SOUTH ASIA AND BANGLADESH'S POSITION

In South Asia Bangladesh forms part of the chain-link of 'cross-border terrorism', a bedevilling notion which generally tends to give vent to a low-cost option of a 'proxy war strategy'. Such a strategy apparently meant to sanctify self-fulfilling interpretations to the contentious state of their relationships, even though it serves no more than a 'double-edged sword', enabling the sponsor state to point fingers at the abuses of a target state, but the former remains equally open to the same kind of terrorist attack.[19]

The post-colonial environment of conflict and hostilities that ensued between and among the newly created entities in the region in the aftermath of 1947 partition furthered a terrorist environment in the region. The deteriorating relations between India and Pakistan, the region's major power protagonists, has ramifications for other countries of the region, including Bangladesh.

When India sees itself as the target of terrorist violence in its north-east, Bangladesh is often perceived among the countries providing sanctuary to Pakistan's Inter-Services Intelligence (ISI) operatives, who are allegedly engaged in organizing terrorist actions against India since the 1960s[20] (see Table 5.2). Bangladesh–Pakistan intelligence establishments are believed to act in tandem in assisting the insurgents of India's north-east. India even views the Pakistani High Commission in Dhaka as the 'nerve center' of ISI activities in promoting terrorism and insurgency in India.[21]

Both India and Bangladesh are also cntangled into 'push-in' of alleged illegal refugees from Bangladesh and 'push-back' of alleged Indian (Bengali) Muslims into Bangladesh. India perceives its own security concerns as being aggravated by a combination of an upsurge of jehadi terrorism and an influx of over 20 million illegal Bangladeshi Muslims into its adjoining Indian territories in the north-east, which is set to change the demographic composition of these areas and is likely to create another situation of insecurity in the north-east.

In India a perception prevails that Khaleda Zia during her previous tenure as Premier encouraged and allowed a large number of volunteers to fight in Afghanistan against the former USSR and subsequently in Jammu & Kashmir, and that the current government led by her party looks upon the fundamentalist and jehadi elements as its objective allies, and hence wants to use these elements to keep India destabilized externally and to weaken the pro-Indian Awami League and its allies internally. India also sees a link between the terrorist groups in its north-east and the alleged Bangladeshi Islamism outfits, that the GOB has given a free hand to its military-intelligence establishment to collude with the ISI. It is also believed that there are as many, if not more, terrorist training camps in Bangladesh territory as there are in Pakistan and that more Indian fugitives wanted for their involvement in acts of terrorism in Indian territory have been given shelter in Bangladesh than in Pakistan.[22] Bangladesh strongly denies all these allegations, but it seems that almost every element of the deterioration of India-Pakistan relations has had its spillover effect on Indo-Bangladesh relations.

There is also an element of domestic political mix in India's perception vis-à-vis Bangladesh, as it is felt in New Delhi that India's 'secular parties and organisations' and large sections of the 'so-called liberal media have mis-projected' any action against illegal migration from Bangladesh as anti-Muslim. India alleges that Bangladesh only pays lip-service to the so-called war against international terrorism, that like Pakistan, Bangladesh is insincere in implementing the UNSC Resolution 1373 against terrorism, unwilling to act against either the anti-India elements from the north-east or the jehadi terrorists who pose a threat not only to their own country and India, but also to the entire region and the world (see Table 5.3). Hence it is felt that, unless the international community pressurizes the Bangladesh government to start acting against the jehadi and other terrorist elements operating from Bangladesh territory, the region and the world might witness 'another nasty surprise'. It is lamented that the international community has not paid as much attention as it should have to the signs of Bangladesh emerging as a new hub of pro-bin Laden jehadi terrorism.[23]

Bangladesh, in its turn, also sees itself as a target of regional 'cross-border terrorism', with transnational tie-ups along various factional identities. There are sub-national actors of various shades who grew amid growing socio-economic antagonism, and/ or ethnic resentment. The Purba Bangla Sharbahara Party (Party of the East Bengal Wretched) and Purba Bangla Communist Party (led by Siraj Shikdar) were believed to maintain cross-border links and were among those who were perceived as trying to destabilize the country from its inception.[24] The government then declared them outlaws and dealt them with iron hand, using brutal means, including political assassination and murder. The 'Bangabhumi movement' based in West Bengal, has also brought together cross-border operatives who enjoy the sympathies of India's right-wing coalition, and seeks to carve out a separate 'homeland' for the Hindu refugees migrating to India from East Bengal since 1947 partition. After the assassination of Sheikh Mujibur Rahman and overthrow of the one-party BAKSAL (Bangladesh Krishak-Sramik Awami League) regime in 1975, India has often been blamed for harbouring in its territory anti-Bangladesh insurgent groups. Such groups included Kaderia Bahinee (forces of Kader), led by a Liberation War veteran and staunch Mujib adherent, Abdul Kader Siddiqui, and the Chakma rebels of the Chittagong Hill Tracts (CHT). The identified terrorists, called 'listed criminals' in Bangladesh, sometimes fleeing from law or from state's hot pursuit, extremist religious fanatics, and such other cross-border insurgents, forced or illegal migrants, economic and/or political refugees who serve as breeding grounds for cross-border terrorism on either side, create bitterness in bilateral relations. Listed criminals of Bangladesh are often reported to have found safe refuge in India, while India quite often gets embroiled into what it believes 'hot pursuits' of criminal gangs or extremists well inside Bangladesh territory. Finally, a perception prevails in Dhaka that India aligns itself with the mainstream opposition AL in tarnishing the regime's image so as to isolate the GOB internationally, but the alleged Indian intrusion into Bangladesh maintained its pattern and was even worse during the five-year rule of the Awami League (see Tables 5.6 and 5.7). Thus Indo-Bangladesh 'cross-border terrorism' has become submerged with mutual threat perceptions and the dividing nature of regime politics of both polities.

Bangladesh's neighbour in the east, Myanmar, twice expelled over two and half lacs of its Arakan citizens, the so-called 'Rohingyas', into the country's south-eastern territory, once in the late 1970s and then again in the 1990s. On both occasions these resentful and uprooted Rohingyas served as the breeding ground for terrorists against the Myanmar janta and, in consequence, led to cross-state counter-insurgency operations by the Myanmar authorities. Rohingya refugees organized themselves into insurgent groups, such as the Arakan Rohingya National Organisation (ARNO) and the Rohingya Solidarity Organisation, who procure arms for their own ends and often supply arms to other extremist groups and criminals in Bangladesh including those in Dhaka.[25] All these serve as agents of cross-border terrorism, vitiating neighbourly relations between Bangladesh and its eastern neighbour, and also serve as sources of escalating terrorism within the country and across the borders as well.

Last but not least, are those operatives who maintain 'narcotic-criminal' links, involved in drug-trade, trafficking of women and children as well as in illegal arms trafficking within and beyond the region. Bangladesh is known both as a transit and a recruiting point in this narco-arms-criminal link. Chittagong district, especially its port area, remained a major route for the drug trade and arms smuggling.[26]

Apart from the perceptual divide over cross-border terrorism, there are other lingering issues vitiating Indo–Bangladesh bilateral relations. Discussions with India remain largely stalled to balance trade (extremely favourable to India), prevent illegal cross-border trade, delimit a small section of river boundary, demarcate and fence the porous 4,095 km land boundary, exchange 162 miniscule enclaves, allocate divided villages, etc. In Bangladeshi perception when the world is becoming borderless in the new era, India's attempts to fence off high-traffic sections of the porous boundary appears un reasonable even offensive. Dispute with India also lingers on over New Moore/South Talpatty Island in the Bay of Bengal that prevents maritime boundary delimitation.[27] Attempts have been made to address divisive issues at various levels, but due to fundamental differences between the two countries over the issues of illegal migration, terrorism and other cross-border issues there has not been much common ground. As a result, there has been recurrence of violent incidents along their common borders, which create serious tensions in their bilateral relations.

Terrorism in Bangladesh: Old Legacies and New Threats

Despite its relative homogeneity and ethnic cohesion, Bangladesh also experienced terrorism in the CHT, a strategically placed territory to its south-east located between India and Myanmar.

The 'terror'/insurgency and anti-terror or counter-insurgency campaign in the CHT involving tribal rebels and the GOB needs to be placed in its historical as well as current contexts. The CHT population, inclusive of 13 tribes, have been victims of misperceived policies of all kinds that placed their destinies into a quagmire. After 1947 partition, the CHT tribal leadership chose to take a position against the Radcliffe award of being included in Pakistan. Later, the ill-conceived 'developmental' policies pursued by the Pakistani regime displaced over 100,000 people of tribal origin, who were affected by the Karnaphuli hydropower dam project meant to generate electricity for the entire region. The dam was built with Canadian aid without proper environmental assessment, compensation or rehabilitation of those who were affected, causing serious discontent among the tribal people. Later the anger of the tribal people was fuelled by the various political factors. One of them was the political stance taken by the local Chakma tribal chief, Raja Tridiv Roy who in 1971 chose to side with the Pakistani janta against the Bangladesh Liberation War. He also served the military regime as a minister and encouraged tribal hostility towards the Liberation War and the post-liberation Government of Bangladesh.

However, a tentative Indo–Bangladesh understanding in the aftermath of the liberation, to liquidate any kind of insurgency directed against both, did not permit the tribal insurgents to go very far but eventually the failure of the newly established government of the country to accommodate the cultural sensitivities of the tribal people fuelled their anger. Following an internal upheaval in Bangladesh in the mid-1970s there was a change of guard in Dhaka, in particular the toppling of the pro-Indian AL regime in Bangladesh which led to a change in the Indian perception of neighbourhood security. India was alleged to have armed and provided sanctuary to the tribal insurgents across the border which had its lingering effects on the CHT tribal insurgency. The GOB's response to maintain security since 1976 has been counter-insurgency strategies such as the deployment of armed forces against the CHT tribal insurgents, combining tactics of counter-guerrilla operations, pacification and relocation of Bengali population in some of the insurgent prone areas of the CHT. A negotiation-cum-peace approach was also in-place so as to address the issue of autonomy for the CHT tribal region. An outcome was the Local Government Council Act of 1989, by which 22 government departments were transferred to them.[28] The implementation of the Act entailed administrative rearrangements in CHT as a division, its conversion into three districts, elections to the district councils and other local authorities so as to provide a greater say to the tribal people in managing their own affairs. Peace negotiations also continued to decide how best to ensure autonomy for the CHT to the satisfaction of the tribal population, address the status of the Bengali population who were relocated earlier, and settle the lingering 'land question' to meet the needs of both tribal and non-tribal people, etc. But for a long time peace seemed an elusive 'on-again and off-again' process.

After the AL came to power in Bangladesh in 1996 India played an intervening role—albeit unofficially—between the AL government and the CHT insurgents. India's intention was perhaps to strengthen the hands of a perceived friendly regime in Bangladesh which would support effective cooperation with India against the anti-Indian insurgents in the Northeast, while playing down its official involvement in the CHT insurgency. A peace accord was eventually signed in 1997 between the Parbatya Chattagram Jano Sanghati Samity (PCJSS) and the GOB, leading to the creation of the autonomous CHT Regional Council, with the insurgent leader Shantu Larma as its Chairman. Despite the return from India of most of the CHT tribal people and the creation of an autonomous CHT Regional Council, peace in the CHT still seems tenuous, with continuing tribal infighting and a power struggle between the diehards opposed to the peace accord, and the GOB itself is blamed by the PCJSS for its lack of initiative in solving the outstanding CHT issues.

The outstanding problems, as the PCJSS Chairman feels, include the failure to make the Council effective, to start the functioning of Land Commission, to withdraw army camps in the CHT, to assign the three hill district councils due responsibilities, and to rehabilitate the repatriated as well as internally displaced *Jumma* (hill people) refugees. There are other differences too. While the previous government failed to make strident efforts to implement the accord given the strong opposition to it in the country, the current government, consistent with its election promise, seems to have taken the stance that it might review the 1997 Peace Treaty to determine if its clauses were in conformity with the Constitution. It seems also not willing to withdraw the army camps unless there is a change in the security situation nor to expel the settlers as that would be against its own promises as well as against the constitutional rights of the citizens to settle anywhere in the country. The PCJSS, however, sees the continued presence of army camps in CHT against the terms of the treaty. It also sees the unwillingness to withdraw the settlers as an attempt to 'Islamize' Chittagong Hill Tracts.

Internecine clashes continue between the pro-accord PCJSS and its opponent United People's Democratic Front (UPDF). Tribal leaders have alleged that a legislator of the ruling party, Abdul Wadood Bhuiyan, Chairman of the Chittagong Hill Tracts Development Board (CHTDB), is instigating violence against the indigenous people. Therefore, the PCJSS Chairman Shantu Larma threatened to cancel the certificates of permanent residence of the settlers in the CHT area.[29] Against this backdrop of an ever-looming threat of new insurgency in CHT, stance of the anti-peace accord diehards, continued presence of some of the tribal insurgent leaders in India and given its own constitutional stance, the BNP-led government appears reluctant to iron out the differences with PCJSS leadership over the implementation of the 1997 peace accord. Apart from the unsettled nature of the CHT peace accord, terrorism in Bangladesh also manifests itself in the country's political culture and power wrangling, as mentioned earlier. The prevailing political culture in Bangladesh is such that individuals and/or political parties are not used to concede defeat nor accepting election outcomes. Political parties and groups almost routinely use the terrorists to intimidate voters so as to influence the outcome of elections, thus challenging the very legitimacy of the entire political processes.

In the context of the political evolution in much of the developing world, Bangladesh may not be an exception in all this, but what seems unique is the acute nature and intensity of political confrontation, giving the country a quarrelsome image. In a polity like Bangladesh, where politics features as an all-pervasive public function, where family and dynastic considerations dictate politics there seem to be no ground rules guiding power contention for either pursuit or resolution of conflict resolution. In the chess-game for control of authority in Bangladesh, there is little scope for mutuality of concessions or recognition of mutual needs to accommodate the greater interest of the nation.[30]

Following from above is criminalization of politics in Bangladesh. When politics is so polarized, an outcome is bound to be criminalization and 'mastaanization' of the society, germinating an overall sense of sheer insecurity and lawlessness, even though the politicians themselves also often become victims of such terror. But the most frequent victims are often the soft and the weak, or those requiring care—female gender, the minorities, children, elderly, businessmen, community and social leaders. The social hoodlums turn themselves into very many varieties, such as cross-border operatives, with external links or patronage promoting some 'hidden agenda'; but 'cross-border' terrorists do also include organized gangs of criminals involved in arms trafficking, drug rings or those involved in human trafficking. Many of them also form smugglers' rings, becoming illegal trade operatives who often tie up with armed gangsters operating between Bangladesh and its neighbours. The Indo–Bangladesh smuggling trade may be cited as a case in point. While the official level of trade flow between India and Bangladesh stands at approximately US $1 billion, the unofficial or informal/smuggling trade is known to be more than official trade flow between the two neighbours. This smuggling trade itself features as a major facilitator of cross-border terrorism, as the arms smuggling serves as key to cross-border operations, including illegal arms sales, drug and human trafficking. Many of those involved in all these underworld vices include powerful political functionaries.[31]

The issue of funding terrorism is relatively less critical in a poor but terror-prone country like Bangladesh. Whatever questions have been raised on funding have never been properly addressed or answered convincingly. The GOB has a tradition of not making public the reports of the official probe committees. In the absence of official findings of the relevant government agencies and committee reports concerning all the related aspects the issue has become a matter of sheer speculation involving the underworld of terrorist outfits, drug lords and all other kinds of illegal operatives, including the Al-Qaida chain moving through the Persian Gulf to India's north-east and Myanmar. However, the underground route of parallel banking channel, known as the *Hundi* or *Hawala* route, offering illegal transaction, or money laundering as it officially called, are often cited as a major source of terrorism in Bangladesh. The *Hawala-Hundi* operatives not only deprive the country from a large chunk of the foreign exchange earnings but they also maintain their links with the illegal arms-drug trading, human-trafficking and smuggling rings to the great detriment of the nation's ultimate interest.

Mounting Surge of Terrorism in Bangladesh and Varying Responses

It is generally believed that, like most other nations, Bangladesh has an expressed commitment and a resolve to overcome the challenges of terrorism. At the official level it has consistently condemned acts of terrorism in all its form and manifestations. However, it seems always easier to articulate an official position than demonstrate that in policy action. In the two sections below an effort is made, first of all, to measure the state of terrorism in Bangladesh and the responses at both GOB and non-official levels, and, then, to assess what those approaches could attain so far, coupled with an indication of the positive aspects of the approaches.

STATE OF TERRORISM AND THE RESPONSES

Terrorism in the country in the post-Cold War era has been on the rise since the mid-1990s when the government and the opposition political parties, led by the AL, became drawn into an intense power wrangling. Between 1994–6, for instance, the political culture of *hartal* (strikes and closures) nearly wrecked social stability and peace, causing restlessness and havoc on the nation's economy. Both sides in the political divide used the terrorist elements to intimidate the opponent and the society became almost a hostage to the political game-play. The pattern of political confrontation and power wrangling continues unabated.

Terrorism, more recently, has been on the rise in the capital city, Dhaka (see Table 5.5), the port city of Chittagong, and to most other urban areas. A spate of major bombing explosions in Dhaka, Bogra, Mymensing and other areas caused alarm in social circles and public life (Table 5.1). In the south-western districts of the country (which include the districts of greater Khulna region) the governments over the years found it extremely difficult to root out or control the terrorist outfits. The violent crime rate—which not only includes rapes and murders of children, young and old men and women, but also politically motivated assassinations, bombings, acid attacks against women, and the pillaging of houses, sometimes even entire village—has never been higher (see Table 5.4). In September 2002, a UN report expressed 'mounting concern over the breakdown of law and order in the country'. International donors threatened to hold foreign aid if the situation is not improved. Soon after the UN report was released, the World Bank representative to the country declared there was a 'high level of human insecurity in the country and an 'anti-poor' criminal justice system,' and warned that the deterioration of law and order now poses the greatest threat to the country's continued development. Thus Bangladesh has been on the verge of losing its earlier image as a 'moderate' nation. In the regional as well as in the international media increasingly it has been getting a bad name for itself as a lawless and violent country.[32]

In the backdrop of such ominous developments caused by terrorism and lawlessness, the GOB tried a few alternative approaches to contain and control the increasing spate of terrorist violence. These include (1) coercive approaches, (2) peace approaches in the CHT; (3) general amnesty approaches; (4) negotiating approaches; (5) approaches towards the Jehadi-Islamic groups; and (6) cross-border bilateral approaches. Let us look at them carefully.

1. COERCIVE APPROACHES OF THE GOB

(a) An ongoing law and order approach, with the day-to-day action by the police and other security agencies, as the part of the overall maintenance of peace and enforcement of law.

(b) Operation Clean-Heart was officially launched by the Home Ministry in Aid of Civil Power, even though the operation was actually controlled from the PMO (Prime Minister's Office). Launched on 17 October 2002, it included the following steps:

(i) a directive on 5 November asking all licensed arms holders to deposit their weapons by 15 November;
(ii) banned trading in firearms of all types until further orders and furthermore;
(iii) the deadline was once advanced by a week till 21 November;
(iv) declared illegal all the legal arms, which were not deposited by the deadline;
(v) security forces—consisting of 24,023 Army personnel, 339 Naval troops, and a large number of the paramilitary Bangladesh Rifles (BDR)—began raiding 'crime zones' in all parts of the country, including the capital Dhaka, and sought to curb extreme 'law and order situation', i.e. of murder, rape, extortion, kidnapping and hijacking all over the country;
(vi) security forces arrested 11,280 people, including 2,482 listed criminals/terrorists, and seized 2,028 weapons and 29,754 rounds of ammunition;
(vii) Passed the Joint Forces Indemnity Act 2003 (2 February 2003), indemnify all actions, including deaths and torture, during the Army-led anti-crime drive across the country.

(c) Operation codenamed 'Spider Web'—a 26-day operation—was launched on 19 July 2003, with 14,000 personnel from the police, BDR, the Ansar—militia auxiliary force, and the coast guard. The idea was to check the decline in law and order in the south-western districts of Bangladesh (covering Jhenidah, Kushtia, Chuadanga, Meherpur, Jessore, Khulna, Satkhira, Bagerhat and adjacent districts) after all regular defensive measures and combing operations by police had failed. This operation primarily targeted the outlawed left-wing extremist parties' active in the region, but had largely failed.

(d) Ordered a Special Forces' operation, 'Operation Spider

Web II' (October 2003), deploying around 4,000 personnel of the BDR, armed police battalion, police and Ansars launched the operation on 16 October to crack down on the armed extremists in the south-western districts following some high profile political killings. Stern actions were taken against the terrorists, but most outlaws went into hiding and re-emerge immediately after the end of the drive. As the strident steps failed to stop widespread killings, clashes and violence in the outlaws' hotbed of greater Khulna region continued, the GOB ordered further combing operations by the joint forces, but had little success.

(e) 'Mass arrest' approach (on the dates of declared strikes and movements) was especially adopted in April 2004 following the threat by the AL-led opposition to topple the GOB by 30 April 2004, and over 10,000 people have been arrested towards the close of April.

GOB's Instruments in Coercive Operation

Application of the instruments of law applied by the GOB in its coercive operations includes the following:

(a) section 54 of the code of criminal procedure, arrest without warrant;
(b) non-bailable, Special Powers' Act (enacted in 1973), under which anybody can be arrested and charge sheeted;
(c) legislative measures such as anti-women and children repression acts, ecological and environmental acts passed to deter and punish the criminals;
(d) Speedy Trial Act passed and Speedy Trial Courts have been set up;
(e) special joint forces called Rapid Action Team (RAT), modified into Rapid Action Force (RAF), and, finally, rechristened as Rapid Action Battalion (RAB) have been placed into action to cope with the rising web of terrorism and violence and given additional training under the armed forces division, and also provided with special equipment;
(f) anti-money laundering measures: following the lead of the Vienna Convention under the banner of the United

Nations (1988), requiring all member states to declare money-laundering a punishable offence, the GOB passed the Money-Laundering Prevention Act-2000 in April, 2002, under which Bangladesh Bank (BB) has been entrusted with the responsibilities to track down any illegal flow of resources, police the financial dealings and suspicious transactions. A Task Force headed by a BB deputy governor, with representatives from police, revenue and banks is at work, and the BB has also established anti-money laundering department which issue guidelines to all banks/financial institutions for procurement of extra-information/papers while opening accounts for their customers and for inland remittances.[33] All this is meant to fight against financial crimes, but due to corruption and official lax enforcement proved difficult.

2. PEACE APPROACHES IN THE CHT

GOB's peace approaches to containing the CHT insurgency towards implementation of the 1997 peace accords signed by the GOB with the CHT insurgents have been in process. Politically, such an approach became contentious within the insurgent movement, with the dissenting militants of the UPDF, erstwhile adherents of the Shantu Larma, insisting on 'full autonomy', demanding their distinctive cultural identity as *Jumma* (hill) people and exclusive rights in the hills, while Larma himself threatened to launch a movement if the peace accord was not implemented in its entirety. On the other hand, the Bengali settlers, now forming almost half of the CHT population feel concerned about their rights to reside and earn a livelihood in the region. The country's major political parties also sharply differed in their approaches. While the previous AL Government (ALG), which signed the accord, had failed to implement it expeditiously, the current ruling coalition sees it as inherently discriminatory in nature because it allows the tribal people to posses exclusive rights to own property in the area and to contest elections to the local government while denying similar rights to the citizens from other parts of Bangladesh.[34] Review and face-to-face meetings were occasionally held between the GOB ministers and the PCJSS team, including its Chief, but there was no substantial progress towards either conflict resolution or implementation of the stalled peace accord. However, most recently some *positive elements* have surfaced in the CHT peace process through informal dialogue. These include:

(i) a Cabinet-level subcommittee of the GOB met the PCJSS leadership on 17 April 2004 and agreed to delegate the authority to oversee development in the CHT to the CHT Regional Council in line with the peace accord;
(ii) employment for the refugees repatriated from India is under special consideration;
(iii) TK15 crores have been allocated towards job creation for members of PCJSS;
(iv) agreed to take up the land issue in the next phase of negotiation.[35]

3. GENERAL AMNESTY APPROACHES

GOB's general amnesty approach, first declared in 1999, to outlaws of the self-styled *Sarbahara* (the self-styled left radicals) party leaders and activists operating in the south-western region on condition that they lay down arms and return to normal life. It resurfaced in the wake of the failure to improve law and order in the region despite special drives. When amnesty was declared over 2,700 operatives of underground political activists responded to a general amnesty, bringing peace to the region after decades of violence. But outlawed activities rebounded in 2003, prompting the GOB to take a set of stern actions, including joint operations, as mentioned earlier. The approach has *positive* ingredients, as it conceivably sees the failure of coercive approaches, requiring an understanding of their position through compassionate appraisal of their needs, and seeks to bring the outlaws back to normal life.

4. NEGOTIATING APPROACHES

GOB's negotiating approach is an outgrowth of the general amnesty approach, as some members of parliament of the battered south-western region felt inclined to negotiate the conditions of the outlaws returning to normal life after they lay down their arms and abandon the path extremism. The whole idea is to bring a negotiated end to violence and to restore peace. The GOB itself also, reeling under the failure of the operations, was planning to reach an understanding with the extremists, offering them schemes of rehabilitation, coupled with written guarantees that there will be no legal cases against them.[36] Like the amnesty approach, it has *positive merit*, as it contains elements of mutual recognition or understanding of their common needs, for the extremists to return to normal life and for the GOB to restore security and peace.

5. APPROACHES TOWARDS THE JEHADI-ISLAMIC GROUPS

GOB's approach towards the Jehadi-Islamism groups had shifted over time. The AL had used the *Jamat-e-Islami* as its political ally during the movement against the BNP Government in the mid-1990s, and hence was initially hesitant to alienate them by taking stern action against them. Later as the *Jamat* leaned towards the BNP in its movement against the ALG, the latter used to blame the BNP-*Jamat* alliance almost instantly for every act of terror in the country, without any proof or evidence, and often took quite repressive measures against all suspected 'terrorists'. With the change of guard, the BNP-led Government, given its composition, was naturally cautious not to alienate its political ally, and quite often the suspected Islamist terrorists were *released on bail and eventually the charges against them were dropped*. The Government has, however, *banned* one Islamist group called *Shahadat-e-al-Hikma*. It was also *protective* of the Ahmadiya sect's mosques at Nakhalpara, Dhaka, and at Sarishabari, Jamalpur, which often became targets of attack by the anti-Ahmadiya mob of Islamists. However, the *publications of the sect were proscribed*, perhaps as a measure of appeasement of the Islamists, even though the sect was not declared anti-Islamic, as demanded by the Islamists. In December 2003 the Prime Minister reportedly asked *the concerned government agencies to launch a 'massive manhunt' for the clandestine extremist groups with alleged external links*.[37] It appears that the GOB has been playing tight rope between self-justification and political expediency on the one hand, and the real need for cracking down of the extremist outfits on the other.

6. CROSS-BORDER BILATERAL APPROACHES

Cross-border bilateral approaches involved the Bangladesh-India pair, which combined both political game-play and negotiations. All this followed high-level political contention between the two countries over existence of anti-Indian terrorist camps and push-in/push-back operations of alleged illegal migrants/Bengali Indian Muslims. Alongside the legacy of blame game, protest notes and counter-notes, summoning of diplomats, public accusations, there has also been common commitments to uphold the regional undertakings. These included the SAARC Regional Convention on Suppression of Terrorism (1987), the SAARC Convention on Narcotic Drugs and Psychotropic Substances (1993) and SAARC LAW, and such other laws to which there is common regional commitments. The official levels of bilateral problem-solving mechanisms include the following:

(i) Regular Flag-level meetings between the local/zonal commanders of the BSF (Indian border security forces) and the BDR.
(ii) Official level meetings of the Deputy Commissioners and Police Superintendents of the bordering districts of the two countries.
(iii) Joint Working Group (JWG) meetings of the border security establishments of both the countries, at the level of the Director-Generals of the BSF and the BDR.

At all these levels both sides take up issues from petty border events to higher levels of terrorist incidents. Both sides often officially exchange the lists of alleged of anti-Indian camps (varying from 76 to 150) in Bangladesh and alleged 'listed criminals' from Bangladesh who are alleged to find shelter in India. While both sides almost routinely repeat mutual assurances and agree to step up vigilance along the border to check crimes, the successes are tenuous. Similar meetings between the Bangladesh and the Myanmar authorities have proved more useful towards containing cross-border terrorism between the two countries. Most recently an air of *positive change* seems visible in efforts to modify the relations between the two countries. These include:

(i) An Indo-Bangladesh accord followed after India agreed to review a list submitted by Dhaka of terrorists who had allegedly taken refuge in India.[38]

(ii) Bangladesh has also agreed to share the information with India on the biggest ever haul of arms uncovered in Chittagong on 2 April 2004.[39]

(iii) India's current High Commissioner to Dhaka, Veena Sikri, has been more *proactive* than her predecessors, but seems *careful to avoid the language of blame*, and has been *non-formal in her approach* while meeting not only the GOB leaders, but also cross-sections of people like businessmen and from the media to clear up the air of misgivings. This may serve as a replicable approach for diplomatic wings of both countries.

By carefully avoiding the blame-game and official-level of the structured approach of the past, it is believed, that both India and Bangladesh may be able to minimize their differences over the contentious issues that bedevilled their bilateral relations. However, bilateral communication at higher levels of state dignitaries with an appreciation and recognition of the mutual security needs of both the peoples may perhaps facilitate greater understanding and cooperation.

The positive elements in the above mentioned approaches of GOB, could be exploited to a fuller extent to ensure greater stability at home and better understanding with the neighbours. In addition to this, the positive contribution by a few other social segments in the country towards dealing positively with terrorism and violence may be mentioned:

1. Civil Society Role: Search for Alternative Approaches: Bangladesh has a strong stream of civil society groups consisting of the non-governmental organisations (NGO), human rights activists, progressive media and secular/enlightened intellectuals. It may be useful to highlight the roles being played by some of

them so that alternatives approaches and options may be considered.

1. Known as the country of the NGOs, Bangladesh has quite a large number of rights groups, including human rights and environmental groups, both national and international, who often raise concerns over the increasing spate of terror and violence affecting the various segments of society. Many of the NGOs have profit and/or political motives, but a sizeable number of them are also non-profit, non-partisan and publicize/act on terrorism and human rights issues objectively. These include the *Ain-o-Shalish Kendra* (Law and Conciliation Centre), Democracy Watch, *Odhikar* (Rights), Institute of Human Rights, Bangladesh Human Rights Bureau, National Association of Women Lawyers, the Society for Environment and Human Development (SEHD) and the Bangladesh Environmental Lawyers Association (BELA). Many of them monitor and write about human rights abuses, speak publicly against attacks on religious minorities through press briefings, campaigns and press releases, and take up the cases of the rape and child victims in courts, and motivate people to resolve conflicts through Alternative Dispute Resolution (ADR). Some like the BELA continue to pursue the cases of eco-terrorism in the courts and even dare to confront powerful GOB agencies and bodies.
2. Enlightened intellectuals (eminent poet Shamsur Rahman and university professor Humayun Azad even risked their lives), the United Forum of Citizens against Communalism, progressive social groups/student activists, secular intellectuals and journalists act as public opinion mobilizers, and have formed human chains on the thoroughfares and in the Press Club premises, etc.
3. While much of the print and electronic media in Bangladesh is politically partisan and/or privately owned, journalists and media reporters in general have been very articulate and active in reporting terrorist incidents, even sometimes putting in jeopardy their own safety and security (Table 5.4). However, their moral courage needs official appreciation, protection, and social support.

4. Business chambers, shopkeepers, and trade bodies more lately have assumed a more proactive role. They have arranged protest meetings, processions and shutdowns of their own against the rising spate of terrorism and violence which jeopardize their lives and businesses. They also decided to try ADR methods as a way of conflict resolution between and within their business establishments, and have been insisting that the GOB-Opposition come to talking terms and *avoid confrontational politics* like calling *hartal* or in the case of the GOB going for repressive measures.[40] Such proactive role assumption by vital segments like businesses could offer strength and intensity to peaceful change in a fractious political community like Bangladesh.

2. A joint approach towards 'social inclusion' has surfaced most recently even in the wake of a rising wave of crime and violence. An example was set by the Grameen Bank (GB), the country's leading micro-credit organization, when it joined hands with the SP, Nilphamari district, the local Union Parishad Chairman, the local school headmaster and the Imam of the mosque in the presence of hundreds of people and converted a whole village to the idea of leading a normal life. The village, Kisamat Dogachhi, was earlier known as a village of thieves, thugs, robbers and criminals for over 100 years, but all 85 of the villagers, along with their 10 sardars (leaders), who were criminals for generations, vowed to lead an honest lives in return for the GB's micro-credit to their female members for income generating activities.[41] It was indeed an unique public display of a joint leadership role. The art was no longer one of exclusion or punishment for crime committed but of *social inclusion* of those who lost the track of moral destiny but felt persuaded to return to normal life in return for the prospect of their needs being met.

An Overall Assessment of Responses

At this stage, it seems proper to make an overall assessment of what has been achieved so far towards the elimination and/or containment of terrorism in Bangladesh. The GOB itself has persevered to stem the tide of terrorism in the country by adopting numerous approaches. These include the ongoing coercive approaches—inclusive of law and order, operations by special forces, mass arrests, which were coupled with instruments of force considered appropriate. There was then the GOB's approach towards the Jehadi-Islamists, the CHT peace process, general amnesty, negotiations, and cross-border dialogue. Apart from the government's approaches there was also the role assumption by the civil society groups and a joint approach meant towards social inclusion of the identified criminals.

Despite the adoption of multifarious coercive approaches by the GOB and alternative approaches by others, terrorism in Bangladesh remains problematic, with the GOB's responses showing an increasingly upward swing in the use of force to counter the rising spiral of violence, without making any serious dent in the tide of terrorism which has kept up its upswing move from the beginning of the new century through the current year (see Table 5.4).

One of the most spectacular victims of the lawlessness has been a distinguished lawmaker of the opposition AL, Ahsanullah Master, a veteran freedom fighter murdered by assailants on 7 May 2004. Within a fortnight of that incident came yet another (21 May 2004), a bomb blast in the Holy Mazar of Hazrat Shah Jalal in Sylhet town in the country's northeast, a second such episode in the same holy location within a period of five months. The blast killed two persons on the spot, and injured, among others, the new UK High Commissioner to Bangladesh, Anwar Choudhury, the first among the ethnic minorities to be elevated to such a high profile position in the British diplomatic service, 'a son of the soil'—born in the district but came to join the Friday prayers in the Mazar mosque apparently to show his respect to the holy shrine.[42] Even though no one publicly claimed responsibility for the attack on the UK High Commissioner, it was as a 'case of targeted killing' by the Islamists, acknowledged a senior GOB leader.[43]

The terrorist-insecurity nexus in Bangladesh, as represented in Figure 5.1, thus remains unbroken, the network could not be liquidated and social stability, security and peace in the country remain as fragile as ever. The operations adopted by the GOB under coercive approaches failed to produce the intended results due to a faulty strategy, lack of intelligence, alleged police tip-offs to criminals and announcements about the drive before its launching forewarning the terrorists and their ring leaders, and prompting them to go into hiding. As a result the police failed to catch any of the major ringleaders or to recover in the course of their drives any significant amount of arms and ammunition accumulated by the terrorists. Indeed, media reports in the country frequently suggest a police, politician and criminal link. It is believed that the police forces are highly susceptible to bribes, and completely incapable of waging Bangladesh's battle against terrorism.[44] The political parties are also blamed for hiring thugs to terrorize hostile constituencies and to intimidate or kill opponents, as is alleged in the case of Ahsanullah Master.[45]

Even while launching the anti-terror drives by the special forces, the GOB itself tacitly recognized such police-politician-criminal links, with the police failing to play their part as normal law and order forces. The Special Forces' operations were overseen by the PMO, rather than by normal police department/home ministry channels. Both the people-at-large and the businesses were initially relieved and welcomed the operations. During the operation many ruling party supporters were also arrested and even ministers were not exempted from speculative search. However only a small number of legal arms were deposited, the majority of the terrorists and their illegal weapons remained outside the reach of the joint forces. Many terrorists have gone underground and while many others have fled the country. Even though the border and airports have been monitored closely, most of the listed terrorists have eluded the vigilance of the joint forces. That would not have been possible without help and support from the police hierarchy and GOB/political establishments.

Thus the joint operations by the GOB did not produce the desired results, as it lost momentum after some time, degenerating eventually into an exercise in political vendetta.[46] Yet major arms hauls by the joint forces in Bogra, CHT, and in the Chittagong port area in recent months, are reminders that such operations can make a difference, given freedom of action from the police-politician-criminal nexus.

Bangladesh thus seems holed up in a dark tunnel of terrorism and violence, and escape from its spiralling pattern would require miraculous efforts. The paradigm in Fig. 5.2 is suggested as an alternative to the current disquieting pattern, with the coupling of a changed triangular nexus: communication/ADR, peace and security. The idea is to move forward, enabling the nation to break with the past so that the community as a whole may endeavour to seek alternatives to the vicious circle of terrorist-insecurity nexus involving the police, politicians and the terrorists. Examples in this direction, though not very common, are there in some of the more recent endeavours of the GOB itself, from CHT peace process to general amnesty, and then on to negotiated efforts and cross-border exchanges—all of which offer some elements of fresh thinking. Some of the civil society groups have also set examples, as have human rights activists, self-sacrificing progressive intellectuals and journalists. Last but not the least, is the exemplary instance of social inclusion (as against social exclusion by mob reprisals, arrests and jail, etc.) set by the Grameen Bank in cooperation with the SP, the school headmaster and the Imam of the mosque, which has to be replicated a million times.

In essence, the plea, as placed (in Figure 5.2) is for a 'paradigm shift' at all levels involving all the stakeholders, police, people, politicians as well as the policy-makers—shifting away from the competing/coercive strategies of 'terror and anti-terror' to a transcendental level—'to go beyond' to a new plane of interactions. To such an end all have to relate their behaviour to mutual feelings and needs, and, accordingly, to transform them-

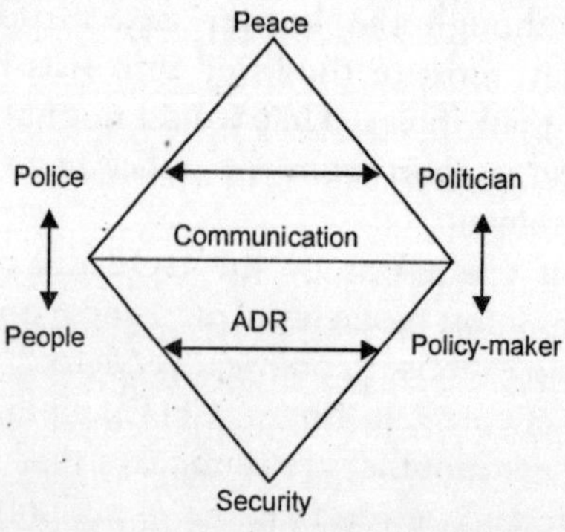

FIG. 5.2: A COUPLING OF TRIANGULAR NEXUS: COMMUNICATION/ADR, PEACE AND SECURITY

selves in the process of adjusting positions, interests, values and meeting everybody else's ultimate needs.[47] The objective, as is enshrined, is both peace and security for all. The process for a society like Bangladesh is not an easy one, as the government, with all its functionaries, the politicians and the civil society groups have to work hand-in-hand by overcoming their traditional mutual perceptions of being adversaries. Communication and reconciliation are primary prerequisites, placing priority on truth and mercy, justice and peace in the conceptual framework.[48]

For Bangladesh a number of successive events, including the brutal murder of a distinguished MP and attack on the UK High Commissioner in Dhaka, should serve to propel a sense of urgency and break the GOB's inertia. The outcome of elections in India and the most recent Singapore initiative to organize regionally against the terrorist outfits may be perceived as harbinger of additional opportunities for Bangladesh to re-establish its moderate image in the international community.

CONCLUSION

The paper addressed the multilevel challenges of terrorism facing Bangladesh in the new era and the country's responses to them. To this end, it made a conceptual appraisal of terrorism in its contents and manifestations in the shifting environment of relationships across societies and took into account international and regional responses to terrorism before and after 9/11 and their ramifications for Bangladesh as well as the consequent Bangladesh responses to them. It also identified the country's responses to the multifaceted terrorist threats facing it nationally, coupled them with an assessment of the means applied and considered their effectiveness. The analysis in the Chapter suggested a chain-link relationship of terrorism in Bangladesh with the terrorism and anti-terror strategies beyond its borders. It viewed the country's responses to terrorism as problematical, but also touched upon elements of positive changes in them.

Some thoughts will now be offered concerning the competitive strategies of terror or anti-terror played out across societies at the national, regional and international levels, emphasizing the need for cooperative understanding at those levels, and the need to change the mindset of those concerned with deciding the destinies of the peoples.

Of immediate concern is the subject of terrorism confronting Bangladesh. It hardly needs saying that, despite the use of numerous approaches and instruments, Bangladesh has failed to contain terror and the spiral of violence affecting the country and the neighbourhood. It may well be true that what a perceptive analyst calls[49] a 'psychosis' of fear and despair generated both by terror and frightful anti-terror strategies which affected all levels of relations from national to regional and international and had a spillover effect in Bangladesh.

Bangladesh in recent years has suffered serious loss of face and earned for itself a bad name and reputation as a lawless and violent nation. As already stated, it is facing a gigantic crisis in preserving public order. The violent crime rate—which includes rapes and murders, politically motivated assassinations, bombings, acid attacks against women, mob reprisals and the pillaging of entire villages—has never been higher. Traditionally regarded as 'moderate', the Bengalis, overall, are known to be peace-loving, open and broad minded, non-fundamentalist and free to share the values of different cultures, unless something directly affects them or hurts their feelings. Still the people of the country have fallen prey to terrorism and it is now a huge problem for the nation.[50] The levels of corruption, lawlessness, disorder, and the increasing spate of terrorism continue to put off investors, both domestic and international, retard the nation's overall growth and development. These are symptomatic of a vicious cycle, as they invite further poverty, more disorder and a greater terrorist upsurge. Bangladesh is thus doomed in a terrorist quagmire from which it must find a way out, sooner or later.[51]

Reform of the police and/or beefing up the power of the police or deployment of the military, may not lead the country anywhere. The GOB itself tacitly recognized the failure of the police methods and hence decided late on 28 April 2004, to form a counter-intelligence unit at the divisional level, to be headed by a Director-General in the police force for surveillance of the activities of police personnel. This may prove even more divisive, as some within the police force have already resented the creation of such a counter-intelligence unit.[52] Indeed, continued use of strong-arm tactics might prove self-defeating, even counter-productive, if democracy is to be sustained in the country.

The linking of socio-political approaches with military methods may offer the best available strategy to contain terrorism (see Fig. 5.2). Here are some tips for consideration. To begin with, there is scope for rethinking in the arena of constitution and governance. There may be a greater devolution of power from the centre to the local bodies, ensuring people's empowerment and recognition of their rights. It is pertinent to ensure transparency, accountability, and proportional representation—guaranteeing representation of both genders and minorities in decision-making. Shorter tenure for the incumbent government from five to four years or so may have a refreshing effect on the country's tense power rivalries.[53]

Secondly, country's lingering confrontational politics, providing a climate favourable for the terrorists to operate has to end. The BNP-Jamat alliance cannot deny the fact that it has failed to fulfil its election commitments to curb terrorism and check corruption, nor can it ignore the logic that it does provide an environment conducive for the Jehadi terrorists to operate. It is a failure in governance. However, to curb terrorism a spirit of communication and mutual exchange between the government and the opposition has to replace the current violence-prone culture of *hartal* and boycott, with a mutual recognition of shared needs. The government needs to complete its tenure no doubt, but it also must allow the opposition a sense of shared power and space for participation. To such an end, people expect the politicians to 'do the undoable' in national interest to communicate. The former UK High Commissioner in Dhaka, David Carter[54] implored both sides in Bangladesh politics to behave as leaders of socio-economic change, and perhaps *not* serve as constraining agents, i.e. of violence and terrorism.

There is then corruption, an unmitigated evil in Bangladesh, which needs correct diagnosis and uncompromising remedy. The social scientists often link it to anarchy and terrorism. Its phenomenal upswing has been a cause for lament, anger and social frustration, calling for increased moral and ethical vigilance. However, in order to eradicate it, the root causes of corruption be addressed not merely from a moral high ground[55] but also in the context of existing socio-economic realities. Much of corruption may be linked to the existing structure of socio-political and bureaucratic hierarchy, and a thorough overhauling or restructuring at that level seems overdue to bring sanity to the administration. An independent anti-graft body, long overdue, is yet to take shape.

There is, then, a huge mass of un- or underemployed youths, numbering 30 to 40 million, who remain the potential source of terrorism in Bangladesh. Many of them are educated but without proper jobs or opportunities to build their career. And many of the frustrated youths easily fall prey to the terrorists' trap and are often hired as *mastaans* (hoodlums) by the political thugs and gangsters for their own ends. It requires a gigantic effort to turn them away from terrorism and convert them, to the nation's advantage, into a work force. Towards such an end, the entire education-sector needs overhauling. The madrasa education, a breeding ground of fanaticism, must be integrated with an enlightened mainstream educational order, ensuring *equal* opportunities, without eroding the value of positive religious content.

There is also the image of public order. While Bangladesh is facing a calamity of sorts in maintaining public order and the rule of law, experiences suggest that the GOB alone cannot restore public order, rule of law and social sanity. A country that came into existence through a Liberation War, embracing a secular ideology, cannot afford to be painted as a nation dominated by Jehadis, thus creating a crisis in its relations with neighbours. Instead of maintaining the high moral ground of the so-called 'ostrich-syndrome',[56] it is imperative that the issue of terrorist camps and violent incidents like the bomb blasts are thoroughly probed for clarity and to place the country's image back on track and establish the GOB's own credibility. To attain such ends a coalition of GOB functionaries and social forces must also work jointly so that public order and sanity are restored. The GOB has to work with the positive elements of social change, as cited earlier. As in the UK, an Independent Security Commission may be constituted to go into the depths of some of the issues mentioned here so that trust can be rebuilt and sanity may be rehabilitated.

As to the CHT peace process, the latest informal approach

seems a step in the right direction. A compassionate understanding of the decades of neglect of the tribal population and their sufferings has to be kept in perspective, coupled with a conscientious appraisal of their feelings and needs. A 'roll-back' mindset towards the peace accord must give way towards restoring confidence and building on positive gains made so far. Persuasive efforts must continue to convince the contending parties of the merits of peaceful co-existence of different communities.

Externally, a political partnership with the regional and international communities seems equally critical so as to restore the nation's capacity to act and retract its image. The Indo–Bangla bilateral relations must be put on track, on a 'win-win' basis with no scope left for misunderstanding, given the binding nature of common security as well as vital commonalities of culture, history and geopolitical interests that bind both the peoples. All this requires considered thinking on the part of the peoples and leaderships of both countries.

On the issue of cross-border terrorism, a perceptual divide seems to hinder a common policy between India and Bangladesh, especially touching on the issue of the alleged Pakistani links. Indo–Bangladesh relations are marked by what Bangladesh Foreign Minister Morshed Khan, once described as *man-abhiman* (self-respect and ego), i.e. temporary annoyance between a pair-in-love. However, in spite of the regime changes of varying types in New Delhi a lingering feeling prevailed for a long time in India that Bangladesh, a country liberated from the brutalities of Pakistan with India's help, chose to tie up with Pakistani intelligence establishments in destabilizing India. Many Bangladeshis, on other hand, feel bewildered by the turn and twists of Indo–Bangladesh relations, because they see themselves as non-fundamentalists and wedded to a similar ideology as India. Neither the perceptual divide nor the issues of bilateral stakes seem insurmountable. Indeed, given the improvement in the regional political climate in recent months, between India and Pakistan, it seems no longer a difficult proposition to revitalize mutual confidence and to work towards common security objectives through mutual empathy and understanding.

Both Bangladesh and India may explore newer approaches

in the management of their relations. With their 'bond of blood' of 1971, both the countries may have renewal of cultural and historical identities as well as rebuild their relations on common potentials of economic and developmental synergies. Bangladesh can never gain by destabilizing India, as the latter has emerged as a natural choice of Bangladeshis looking for education or medical treatment. Similarly, Bangladesh has already emerged a strong destination for Indian products, being placed very high in India's export market. Both should forge freer trade and investment relations, not unmindful of the interest of the weaker economy. A stronger Bangladesh along India's eastern courtyard can only be in India's best interest. The new political climate ensued by the recent elections in India must be seized to harmonize and cement Indo-Bangla bonds in the greater interest of both the peoples. The friendly visit to New Delhi by the Bangladesh Foreign Minister immediately after the Indian elections in 2004 appears to have signalled the GOB's positive commitment to move in the direction.

Related to the above is the issue of political partnership with the regional and international community. This is equally critical for Bangladesh. A common approach to terrorism at the regional level is a crying need. Such an approach should enable Bangladesh to have binding relations with all the nations of South Asia, coupled with recognition of mutual interests and needs. In order to promote such an end, language of blame of the past has to give way to cooperative understanding. Time and again Bangladesh called for stronger unity and cooperation among South Asian Countries so as to build a defence shield to safeguard themselves from the negative impact of globalization and international terrorism.[57] Such official stance must be matched with concrete steps at the national level as well as bilaterally and regionally. The GOB's most recent decision to join the Singapore-initiated 8-nation Nucleus Steering Committee (NSC) to remove misperceptions of Islam in the West and to take steps to cooperate in responding to terror in the region may be in the right direction.[58]

Internationally, the attitudes to 'terror' demand some reappraisal, requiring changes in the very assumptions, structures and practices applied for dealing with it.[59] The 'war on terror', which is a 'number one' priority in American foreign policy at present, and words such as 'democracy', 'security' and 'civilization' have been used as banner in 'anti-terror war';[60] but neither democracy, security nor civilization have so far been better served.[61] The truth is that in popular perceptions in Bangladesh and across the Muslim world, in Asia and in Europe, there is scepticism, perhaps disdain about US intentions and its proclaimed principles. Yet 'defeating terrorism' or 'combating terrorism' remains a priority which drives the lone superpower not only to unilateral military action but also to seek multilateral cooperation to the end,[62] irrespective of the feelings they generate in the rest of the world about the means applied or supported. Full US backing to the brutal strategies of Israeli annexation and occupation of the Palestinian territories in violation of UN resolutions, Israeli state terrorism and its assassinations of the Palestinian leaderships, massacres and killings pursued by Ariel Sharon against all those supposedly involved in the new Palestinian *Intifida* cannot but hurt human sentiments, and generate the empathy of a largely Muslim population as in Bangladesh.

Hence it is time to reflect on the issue of the nature and exercise of power used in attaining the intended objectives of 'democracy', 'security' or 'civilization'.[63] The Al-Qaida, does not seem to be on the wane even after the destruction of its structure and hide-outs in Afghanistan. The 'al Qaidaism', if there is something like this, continues to galvanize the *umma* (global community of believers) against the perceived oppressors, and may even be growing stronger every day, under its so called patriarch and mastermind, Osama bin Laden.[64] It has to be recognized that a poor, crowded but predominantly Muslim society like Bangladesh cannot remain unaffected by such widely propagated belief system.

Moreover, if the US-led alliance is to win the 'war on terror', liberate people and check the spread of senseless violence, it has to 'recognize the obvious: that means are as important as ends'.[65] The abuses of power revealed by the world media in the wake of Iraq's 'liberation' should be an eye opener; for the US has alienated many of its own allies, with the regimes protected and/or known as American loyalists becoming even more distanced from their people. Increasingly the US, as the global leader, finds itself disengaged from many of the world's most pressing problems like illiteracy, poverty, malnutrition, killing diseases, etc. It sounds so generous of the US to offer help to train and strengthen Bangladesh police force or develop the computer database necessary to trek down cross-border terrorist movements and combat terrorism more effectively,[66] but the real needs of a society like that of Bangladesh would be to get away from the poverty trap. The US and Western help could play a critical role in this.

Returning to the issue of terrorist challenges facing Bangladesh and the country's responses to them, it is imperative that the lessons of the past are taken in earnest and the current challenges are met with meticulous care and urgency. The tales and intensity of terror are of deep consternation and despair, and the country cannot simply play them down. The pride of historical role perceptions as well as the strains of more recent occurrences must be left behind. The nation must resolve to start afresh, with positive thinking, if it is to move forward. As part of refreshing intent, an-all party national convention, a full session of the national parliament, a special summit of the SAARC nations on terrorism, etc., may be considered so that consensus may be reached on steps that would be effective in dealing with terrorism, both nationally and regionally.

TABLE 5.1: TERRORISM IN BANGLADESH: BOMB BLASTS, 2000–3

Year	Date	Place	Killed	Injured
2003	13 February	Dinajpur	0	3
	17 January	Dariajpur village, Tangail district	8	8
2002	13 October	Khulna	0	1
	11 October	Rangmati town	3	2
	28 September	Sathkhira town	3	125
	1 May	Gurdaspur up-zila (sub-district), Natore	1	25
	25 April	Dhaka	0	2
	10 April	Kushtia	0	0
	27 February	Dhandoba, Barisal district	1	1
	4 February	Chittagong Press Club	1	3
	5 January	Barisal	0	2

2001	14 October	Sirajganj	0	2
	25 September	Sylhet town	2	0
	25 September	Shullah, Sunamganj district	4	0
	24 September	Mollarhat, Bagerhat district	8	100
	3 September	Makahati Bazar, Munshiganj	0	13
	25 August	Feni town	0	7
	15 June	Narayanganj town	21	100
	3 June	Baniachar, Gopalganj district	10	25
	31 May	Duttapara in Tongi	0	5
	23 April	Dhaka	0	2
	17 April	Rajshahi district	1	0
	14 April	Dhaka	8	0
	20 January	Dhaka	6	50
2000	25 December	Dhaka	0	0
	24 December	Dhaka	2	18
	21 November	Khulna	0	4

Note: Compiled from English language media sources.

Sources: South Asia Intelligence Review, Weekly Assessments & Briefings, vol. 1, no. 22, 16 December 2002. South Asia Intelligence Review (SAIR), http://www.sair.weeklyassessmentsandbriefings#assessment2.htm/(16 December 2002).

TABLE 5.2: ALLEGED ANTI-INDIAN INSURGENT ORGANIZATIONS LOCATED IN BANGLADESH

1. The National Liberation Front of Tripura (NLFT),
2. All Tripura Tiger Force (ATTF),
3. The National Socialist Council of Nagaland-Isak Muivah (NSCN-IM),
4. The People's Liberation Army (PLA),
5. The United Liberation Front of Assam (ULFA),
6. The National Democratic Front of Bodoland (NDFB),
7. The Muslim United Liberation Tigers of Assam (MULTA),
8. The Achijk National Volunteer Council,
9. The Chakma National Liberation Front (CNLF)
10. The Dima Halam Daoga.

Note: Estimated number of alleged camps of the anti-Indian insurgents in Bangladesh varied from 15 to 156, the last number is cited by the Indian Intelligence.

Sources: B. Raman, An Update, op. cit.; Ganguly, 2002, op. cit.; Habib, 2003, op. cit. News From Bangladesh (Daily News Monitoring Service) (www.banglades-web.com). PTI (24 October 2003), 'BSF hands over list of 78 "militant camps" to BDR', *The Daily Star*.

TABLE 5.3: ALLEGED MILITANT ISLAMIC ORGANIZATIONS IN BANGLADESH

1. Shahadat-e-al-Hikma
2. Jamaat-ul-Mujahid-ul-Bangladesh
3. Jamaat-e-Yahia Trust
4. Hizbut Tawhid
5. Al Harakat-ul-Islamia
6. Al Markaj-ul-Islami
7. Jamaatul Falaiya
8. Tawhidi Janata,
9. World Islamic Front
10. Jumaat-as-Sadat
11. Shahadat-e-Nabuat
12. Harkat-ul-Jehadi-e-Islami, Bangladesh (with links to Adarsa Kutir, Al Faruk Islamic Foundation and Hataddin, Bangladeshi Islamic NGOs)
13. Al Khidmat.
14. Bangladesh Islamic Manch (Platform) (BIM).
15. The Islami Solidarity Bangladesh (ISB)
16. Servants of Suffering Humanity International, Dhaka
17. Al Harmann Islamic Institute, Dhaka
18. The Al Muzahid Party
19. Jagrata Muslim Janata Bangladesh (JMJB) (formed in April 2004 in the north-western districts).
20. International Khatme Nabuyat Movement (IKNM).

Note: The names of the above 20 Muslim militant organizations operating in Bangladesh have been reported, even though only a few of them have created news. Security agencies have reportedly identified 48 'training centres' across the country of some of the Islamic organizations. The Shahadat-e-al-Hikma (SAH) was officially proscribed by the GOB with effect from 9 February 2003.

Sources: http://www.satp.org/satporgtp/sair/index.htm (12/05/2004); *The Daily Star* (Dhaka); Bangladesh Assessment, 2003; Habib, 2003, op. cit.

TABLE 5.4: TERRORIST INCIDENTS IN BANGLADESH, 2001–3

Year	No. of incidents	Type of incidents
2001	3,283	Homicide
	1,707	Robbery
	422	Toll-collection
	1,047	Hijacking
	473	Rape
	372	Repression of women and children
2002	3,361	Homicide
	2,279	Robbery
	1,007	Hijacking
	858	Rape
	552	Repression of women and children
2003	3,832	Homicide
	3,078	Robbery
	389	Toll collection
	877	Hijacking
	867	Hostage-taking
	866	Rape
	23	Suicide after rape
	713	Repression of women and children
	115	People died in the hands of the law and order forces
	1,296	People injured in the hands of law and order forces
	65	Journalists injured
	19	Journalists arrested
	2	Journalists taken as hostage
	3	Journalists harassed
	91	Journalists threatened

Note: Different Bangladesh Human Rights organizations, which gave the above figures, however, differed on the number of people who were victims of terror and its types. The above figures represent the approximate estimate. Ain-o-shalish Kendra, which normally takes up the case of the rape victims to the courts suggests that the number of rape victims in the year 2003 went up as high as 1182. While the press is generally free in Bangladesh the journalists reporting terrorist incidents have often been targeted by terrorists, but the above data reported such incidents as a separate category only for the year 2003.

Sources: Compiled by the author from Parvez Khan, 'Aparadh Berechey, Noya Prabanata Hatyakanda Nrishangshata', http://www.Prothomalo.net.htm/ (1 January 2004); Shaikh Nazrul Islam, 'Year of Soaring Crimes', http://www.thedailystar.net web edition, vol. 4, no. 214 (1 January 2004).

TABLE 5.5: TERRORIST INCIDENTS (IDENTIFIED AS HOMICIDE/ MURDERS) IN DHAKA CITY, 2002

Area (Thana)	No. of incidents	Area (Thana)	No. of incidents
Mohammedpur	77	Shabujbagh	21
Mirpur	72	Uttara	20
Tejgaon	70	Kreaniganj	59
Sutrapur	38	Gulshan	22
Khilgaon	41	Kotwali	24
Lalbagh	28	Dhanmondhi	19
Kafrul	32	Hajaribagh	15
Shympur	35	Kamrangirchar	15
Ramna	26	Cantonment	8
Badda	29	Airport	7
Motijheel	28	GRP	11
Demra	30	Other (Medical Rept.)	22
Pallabi	26		

Other violent types as terrorist incidents

Types of murders	No. of incidents	Types of murders	No. of incidents
Mysterious Murders (as recorded in police reports)	123	Death due to doctor's maltreatment	3
Stifled to death	36	Smashed under elephant	1
Slashing by sharp weapons	45	Killed by inaccurate strike	20
Burned to death	31	Killed in attempted escape from Jail	1
Death by knifing	45	Suicide	28
Murder by beating	44	Dead body recovered without head	12
Murder by hammer or rod	6	Skeleton recovered	1
Mob beating/reprisal	7	Murdered after rape	35
Brush-fire	21	Abnormal mother killed child	1
Killed by hand bomb	4	School child butchered into 8 pieces	1
Killed by strangulation	27		
Killing by bullet	252		
Killing by crossfire	6		

Persons killed by police forces	7
Terrorist victims by social backgrounds	
Younger persons	473
Older persons	50
Women	49

Teen-aged girls	47
Children	44
Girls above eighteen	36
Teen-aged boys	36
Newly borne children	13
Prisoners	9

Source: Compiled by the author from Syed Farook Hossain, 'Shantrer Janakder dhorar aagei gootieyae gaeloo jowtha avijhan', *Saptahik Robbar* (19 January 2003), pp. 15–16.

TABLE 5.6: ALLEGED ARMED INDIAN INTRUSIONS INTO BANGLADESH TERRITORY DURING 1976–95

Years	Incidents (%)	Persons Killed (%)	Persons Injured (%)
1976–80	8	2	4
1981–5	6	9	7
1986–90	10	31	14
1991–5	24	25	25

Note: During the 30-year period until 2001, a total of 350 people were allegedly killed, and over 250 people were injured.
Source: Nasreen Huq, 'No Medals for Death in Defence of Motherland', *Holiday* (27 April 2001), p. 16.

TABLE 5.7: ALLEGED BSF ARMED INTRUSIONS INTO BANGLADESH DURING THE FIVE YEAR RULE OF THE BANGLADESH AWAMI LEAGUE

Year	Armed Intrusions	Dead	Injured
1996	130 times	13	18
1997	39 times	11	11
1998	56 times	23	19
1999	43 times	33	38
2000	42 times	39	28
2001	12 times	11	65

Source: Shah Monowar Jahan, 'BSF-aer Goolitae pantch bochoraye 147 Jon Bangladeshi nihata', *The Daily Dinkal Jahan* (20 April 2001), p. 1.

NOTES

1. Howard F. Stein, *Development Time, Cultural Space: Studies in Psychogeography*, London: University of Oklahoma Press, 1987, p. 3.
2. *Time Magazine* (15 October 2002). See also Bangladesh - Terrorism - News and Latest Information.htm (2004), http://www.einnews.com/Bangladesh/frames/frames.php3?wid=34877673
   'Amnesty International's Report'. *http://www.obokash.com/amnesty.transparency.htm*
3. 'Transnational Threats Update', *The Centre for Strategic and International Studies*, Washington, DC (June 2003).
4. *Far Eastern Economic Review* (4 April 2002).
5. http://www.apanterrorism.com/Regional Headlines.htm/ (10 December 2003).
6. *The Independent* (12 December 2003), 'No Room For Terrorism in Bangladesh', http://independent-bangladesh.com/news/dec/12/12122003mt.htm#A1.
7. http://www.obokash.com/transparency.htm/.
8. Pervez Iqbal Cheema, 'The Challenge of Terrorism after September 11: A Pakistani Perspective', in Moonis Ahmar (ed.), *The World After September 11: Challenges an Opportunities,* Karachi: Bureau of Composition, Compilation and Translation, Press, 2003, p. 58.
9. Jessica Stern, *The Ultimate Terrorists,* Cambridge: Harvard University Press, 1999, pp. 11-30; Grenville Byford, 'The Wrong War', *Foreign Affairs*, vol. 81 (July–August 2002), pp. 34–43.
10. Alan Shipman, *The Globalization Myth*, London: Icon Books Ltd., 2002, p. 13.
11. Fred Halliday, *Two Hours That Shook the World*, London: Saqi Books, 2002, p. 31.
12. Shipman, op. cit., p. 13.
13. *The Economist* (London), (2 February 2002), in Ammara Durrani, 'The U.S. War on Terrorism: A Non-U.S. Perspective', Moonis Ahmar (ed.), op. cit., p. 108.
14. Shipman, op. cit., pp. 62–3.
15. Ibid., p. 13.
16. TERRORISM-REGIONAL HEADLINES' (APAN Terrorism Regional Headlines.htm), *Justice Latifur Rahman Chief Advisor of the Caretaker Government quoted,* http://www.terrortuesday.impactsonsouthasia.response.htm/. *Terror Tuesday Impact on South Asia — Response — Bangladesh Government.htm* (South Asia Terrorism Portal: Institute for Conflict Management).
17. http://www.bangladesh.assessment.2000.htm/.coalition/international
18. Sridhar K. Khatri, 'Understanding and Combating Terrorism in South Asia', in Moonis Ahmar (ed.), op. cit., p. 152.

19. Ibid
20. B. Raman, http://www.SouthAsia—An Update/Analysis/htm/BANGLADESH&JIHADITERRORISM—*An Update.* Paper no. 887/ Group BANGLADESH & JIHADI TERRORISM/htm/(07. 01. 2004) (hereafter Raman, An Update).
21. http://www.satp.org/satporgtp/countries/India/states/tripura/terrorist_outfits/NLFT.HTM. Bangladesh Assessment, 2001–3 (hereafter Bangladesh Assessment).
22. Ibid., Sanjay K. Jha, 'Mounting tensions over Illegal Migrants and Terror Bases', http://satp,orgto/sair/Archives/1_29htm#assessments3; Raman, An Update, op. cit.
23. Raman, An Update, op. cit.
24. Ibid.
25. Bangladesh Assessment, 2003, op. cit.
26. Ibid.
27. http://www.cia.theworldfactbook.bangladesh.htm.
28. http://www.rangamatihilltracts.htm.
29. Bangladesh Assessment, 2003, op. cit.
30. Matamat (11 June 2003), 'Terrorism in Bangladesh: Causes', http://matamat.com.com/user.php?op=userinf&uname=antony_(hereafter), http://www.matamat.com.2003.htm/.
31. Binalakshmi Nepram, *South Asia's Fractured Frontier: Armed Conflict, Narcotics and Small Arms Proliferation in India's North East*, New Delhi: Mittal Publication, 2002; Neila Husain, 'Proliferation of Small Arms and Politics in South Asia: the Case of Bangladesh', *RCSS Policy Studies*, 7 (May 1999) (Regional Centre for Strategic Studies, Colombo.)
32. Ganguly, op. cit.
33. Murshid Kuli Khan, 'Anti-money laundering measures: Global scenario vis-à-vis Bangladesh perspectives', *The Daily Star* (25 October 2003), p. 6.
34. Bangladesh Assessment, 2002, op. cit.
35. http://www.thedailystar.net/ (18 April 2004).
36. Rezaul Karim, 'Govt ponders amnesty to outlaws in the southwest', *The Daily Star* (24 October 2003), p. 11.
37. Haroon Habib, 'Islamic Militancy: The Shadow Lengthens', South Asia Intelligence Review, Weekly Assessments & Briefings, vol. 2, no. 24, 29 December 2003. http://www.satp.org/satporgtp/sair/Archives/2_24htm # Assessments3 (hereafter, Habib, 2003).
38. http://www.Bangladesh.terrorism,2004.htm/.
39. http://www.thedailystar.net/ (vol. 4, no. 315, accessed on 18 April 2004)
40. http://www.thedailystar.net/ (accessed on 4 April 2004)
41. http://www.thedailystar.net/ (accessed on 22 April 2004)
42. http://www.thedailystar.net/ (accessed on 22 May 2004)

43. Finance Minister Saifur Rahman, quoted in (http://www.thedailystar.net/ accessed on 29 May 2004).
44. Ganguly, 2002, op. cit.
45. http://www.dailystar.net/_(accessed on 9 May 2004).
46. Ganguly, 2002, op. cit.
47. Wallace Warfield, 'Public-policy conflict resolution: The nexus between culture and process', in Sanole and Merwe (eds.), op. cit., pp. 195–7.
48. Lederach, op. cit., pp. 24–35.
49. Michael Howard, 'What's In a Name? How To Fight Terrorism', Foreign Affairs (January/February 2002), http://www.foreignaffairs.org.
50. (http://www.antony.matamat.2003.htm/).
51. Ganguly, op. cit.
52. News From Bangladesh (Daily News Monitoring Service), http://www.bangladesh-web.com/.
53. http:///www.antony.bangladesh.matamat.com/.
54. http://thedailystar.net/ (accessed on 26 April 2004).
55. (http:///www.antony.bangladesh.matamat.com/),
56. Habib, 2003, op. cit.
57. http://www.APAN.Terrorism.RegionalHeadlines.24-25thjune 2003.htm/.
58. The Daily Star Web Edition. http://thedailystar.net/ vol_5 no. 29.htm (accessed on 25 June 2004).
59. Francis, op. cit., p. 9.
60. Colin L. Powell (January/February 2004), 'A Strategy of Partnerships', Foreign Affairs, http://www.foreignaffairs.org/2004/1htm.
61. Michael Mandelbaum, 'The Inadequacy of American Power', Foreign Affairs (September/October 2002), www.foreignaffairs.org.
62. Powell, op. cit.
63. Francis, op. cit., p. ix; Jason Burke, 'Think Again: Al Quaeda' (May-June 2004), http://www.foreignpolicy.org/2004/1htm.
64. US to train, 29 April 2004, http:www.einnews.com/Bangladesh/frames/frames.php3?wid=34813738
    Bangladesh/Rangamati Hill Tracts.htm, http://www.foreignpolicy/2004/1htm.
65. Samuel R. Berger (May/June 2004), 'Foreign Policy for a Democratic President', *Foreign Affairs*, http://www.foreignaffairs.org/2004/3.1htm.
66. http://www.einnews.htm/ (1 May 2004); http://www.thedailystar.net/ (20 May 2004).

6. State Responses to Terrorism: The Case of Sri Lanka

Ketheshwaran (Kethesh) Loganathan

Introduction

At the outset, it must be recognized that the term 'Terrorism' cannot be taken for granted. It needs clarification. The impact of 9/11 has led to a situation where all forms of armed resistance to state repression and state-sponsored terrorism are conveniently lumped into the category 'Terrorism'. This includes the use of force to advance an ideological or political cause. 'Terrorism' is also used by states to justify their responses in the form of 'counter-terrorism' with all the features that terrorism itself contains. These responses by the state are in turn used by the non-state actors to justify their own responses. Hence, the cycle of terrorism and counter-terrorism.

The features of terrorism and counter-terrorism in Sri Lanka may be broadly listed as follows:

1. Conscious attacks on unarmed non-combatants and civilians by both the state and non-state actors as part of a politico-military strategy;
2. Extra-judicial killings (on the part of the state) and indiscriminate assassinations and killings of civilians by non-state actors as part of a politico-military strategy;
3. Torture and rape by both state and non-state actors;
4. Extortions, bribery and taxation as part of a politico-military strategy by both the state and non-state actors; and
5. Underage recruitment and deployment in combat as a conscious politico-military strategy.

Terrorism, in short, be it by the state or non-state actors, focuses on 'terrorizing' civilians into submission or compliance, even though it may be justified in relation to ideology and political cause, or just self-defence.

Terrorism uses methods that contravene all norms and standards of conduct, whether legal, moral or human and in turn justifies these acts by citing the 'extra-legal', 'immoral' and 'inhumane' conduct of the 'other'. In other words, one is the mirror image of the other and they feed on each other. The causes of terrorism, therefore, cannot be separated from the response, and the response itself may create new 'causes'.

Another hypothesis which needs to be examined and which has particular relevance to the Liberation Tigers of Tamil Eelam (LTTE) phenomenon in Sri Lanka is that that non-state actors, as in the case of the LTTE, can take on a position which is independent of the causes that led to armed revolt in the first place. And, therefore, even serious attempts by the state to address the causes may not find favour with the organizational goals and aspirations of the non-state actor. This is because the original ideological and political cause that leads to the taking up of arms gets degenerated into the use of terrorism for ensuring the organizational hegemony and political ambitions of its leaders.

For instance, it may be argued that the LTTE does not see itself as a part of the Tamil people. On the contrary, it sees the Tamil people that it claims to solely represent to be a part of itself. In other words, it perceives itself to be a state. How does the 'legitimate' Sri Lankan state respond to a 'self-perceived' state in search of legitimacy? How do the Tamil people respond in such a situation? This is the challenge that needs to be further examined.

Before we focus on the main theme of the chapter, it is imperative that the specific context of the origin and subsequent metamorphoses of terrorist organizations and their stated political goals be delineated. This is attempted in the following section.

TAMIL MILITANCY AND ITS METAMORPHOSIS TO TERRORISM

The primary causes of Tamil militancy were clearly institutionalized discrimination, Sinhala chauvinism, and state-sponsored anti-Tamil pogroms. Tamil nationalist politics was already on the political and electoral agenda in Sri Lanka from the time of independence due to discrimination in the spheres of language and employment which largely affected the professional and the middle classes.[1] The Tamil militant movement in the 1970s was characterized by extreme youth alienation stemming from discrimination in the sphere of education, most inappropriately labelled by the government as 'standardization'.[2] Ironically the discrimination against Tamil students in the sphere of education was due to the state response aimed at pacifying the alienated Sinhala youth who led the Janatha Vimukti Peramuna (JVP) insurrection of 1971.[3] The cumulative impact was that, in the process of attacking some of the causes of youth unrest and militancy within the Sinhalese community, the Tamil youth was victimized and alienated.

The discriminatory policy in the sphere of education, coupled with increasing youth unemployment at the national level, led to the Tamil youth, in particular school students, to actively engage in the Tamil nationalist struggle. Undoubtedly the increase in state violence, anti-Tamil riots and the recounting of memories of discrimination by elders at home, as well as teachers at schools, would have contributed to the politicization of Tamil school students. Key personalities in the Tamil youth movement, who later emerged as leaders of Tamil militant organizations, including Sivakumaran, Pathmanabha, Prabhakaran, Varatharajaperumal, Sritharan (Sugu), either dropped out of school or used the school as a medium of struggle.[4] The formation of the Tamil Student Federation and later the General Union of Eelam Students was a manifestation of the role being played by the Tamil youth, in particular, the school students.

The passage of the 1972 Constitution made yet another dent in ethnic relations largely due to the removal of minority safeguards in the preceding Soulbury Constitution, and the pride of place given to Sinhala-Buddhism. While it is undeniable that the 1972 Constitution had many progressive features such as the vesting of the sovereignty of the country with its people as well as the Chapter on Fundamental Rights and Freedoms and the Principles of State Policy, the balance of forces tilted decisively towards Sinhala-Buddhist majoritarianism. As noted by K.M. de Silva, 'the new balance of forces, of which the principal feature is the dominance of the Sinhalese and Buddhists in the Sri Lanka polity, was effectively consolidated. . . . Indeed the new Constitution accurately reflected the balance of forces'.[5] Or as Rohan Edrisinha and N. Selvakkumaran observed, 'the veneration of the notion of the will of the people, the rejection of most of the minority safeguards introduced by the Soulbury Constitution and the absence of other provisions for the protection of minority groups and individuals, enshrined the notion that majority decision making was the cardinal, if not the only feature of a democratic society . . . had disastrous consequences for national unity'.[6]

The leader of the Federal Party, the precursor of the Tamil United Liberation Front (TULF), S.J.V. Chelvanayagam, widely known as the father of Tamil nationalism, resigned his seat in Parliament in protest. It is pertinent here to note that a Tamil youth at a public meeting in the Jaffna esplanade, following the announcement by Chelvanayagam, placed a blood mark on his forehead, in place of the traditional saffron mark (*pottu*). The symbolic gesture of *veeram* (bravery) combined with a subtle warning against *throham* (betrayal) was, it soon became apparent, more than symbolic. Soon after the 1972 Constitution was adopted, A. Thiagaraja, a Tamil Congress Member of Parliament, who had voted for the 1972 Constitution, and V. Kumarakulasingham, a Tamil supporter of the ruling party, Sri Lanka Freedom Party (SLFP), headed by Prime Minister Sirimavo Bandaranaike, were shot at.

The electrocution of seven Tamil civilians attending the International Tamil Conference in Jaffna in 1974, attributed to firing and baton charge by the police, further hastened the introduction of militancy into the Tamil nationalist struggle. Additionally, the Tamil youths became exposed to ultra-nationalist rhetoric by Tamil mainstream political parties which had formed themselves into a joint front, namely the Tamil United Liberation Front (TULF). The TULF in its election manifesto in the run-up to the 1977 general election declared that, 'the TULF seeks the mandate of the Tamil Nation to establish an independent, sovereign, secular, socialist state of Tamil Eelam that includes all the geographical and contiguous areas that have been the traditional homeland of the Tamil-speaking people in the country'. It was clear that the TULFs increasingly strident ethno-populist rhetoric was succeeding in firing the imagination of Tamil militant youths, and the TULF had no option but to continue to humour them. Tamil militancy had arrived on the scene.

INTERNECINE KILLINGS AND TERRORISM:

The Tamil militant organizations that made their presence felt as politico-military organizations, prior to but in particular following the anti-Tamil pogrom of 1983, are the LTTE, the Eelam People's Revolutionary Liberation Front (EPRLF), the Eelam Revolutionary Organizers (EROS), Tamil Eelam Liberation Organization (TELO), and the People's Liberation Organization of Tamil Eelam (PLOTE).

It is following the anti-Tamil pogrom of 1983 that some of these organizations began targeting Sinhalese civilians. Prior to that the targets of the militant groups were primarily 'traitors'—a term used to justify the killings of Tamil politicians who were either members of national 'Sinhala' political parties, in particular the SLFP and the United National Party (UNP), and Tamil personnel of the security forces. The notable targets included Alfred Duraiappa, former mayor of Jaffna and a leading member of the SLFP who was gunned down in Jaffna on 27 July 1975 allegedly by Prabhakaran. As Narayan Swamy, an expert on the personalities as well as the *modus operandi* of the LTTE observed: 'It was Prabhkaran's first murder, and the first major assassination by Tamils.The assassination created a sensation in Sri Lanka. It also made Prabhakaran famous. His name soon acquired a halo and for the first time Jaffna youth began hearing about a secret group which called itself the Tamil New Tigers (TNT).'[7] Another sensational killing was that of a Tamil CID police officer, Bastampillai, who was lured into an ambush.

The anti-Tamil pogrom of 1983 led to a quantum leap in militant actions by the Tamil Resistance which had now acquired a politico-military character. While these organizations stepped up their attacks on 'legitimate' military targets, which included army camps and police stations, terrorist attacks against

Sinhalese civilians also began to be seen as 'legitimate' by these organizations. The precursor of what was to follow was the twin attacks on two Sinhalese settlements in the border villages adjoining the Tamil districts of Mullaitivu and Vavuniya. Altogether more than 80 Sinhalese settlers were massacred.[8] This was followed by an attack on two Sinhalese fishing villages of Nayyaru and Kokilai in the vicinity of the previous massacres. Around 60 Sinhalese civilians were killed in these attacks.

But the most heinous attack on Sinhalese civilians, which went deep into the Sinhala-Buddhist psyche, was on Anuradhapura, a Buddhist holy city, in April 1985 on 'Poya Day'—a day of religious observances by devout Buddhists. An LTTE hit squad swooped on the city and mowed down civilians and pilgrims, including children, in a gory massacre. This signalled the acceptance, particularly within the LTTE and EROS, for the need to take the struggle deep into 'enemy territory'. The subsequent bombings of civilian infrastructure and economic targets by the LTTE and EROS included the CTO, the Pettah bus stand, the Central Bank, etc., which took a heavy toll amongst civilians. The war was no longer confined to the north-east and the armed struggle was no longer confined to resistance.

As this author has argued elsewhere:

> The distinction between 'liberation struggle' and 'terrorism' had become blurred. The armed struggle was never mass-based; it reduced the people to the status of 'observers' or contributors to the coffers of the 'sole protectors'. Those among the people who were inclined towards national reconciliation and accommodation were branded as 'traitors'. In addition, the 'battle' was no longer against the State and its organs. Non-combatant civilians, particularly in the 'border areas', became legitimate targets. 'Terrorism' also came to be used to shape events—either (hopefully) to provoke a backlash, and thereby further legitimize the role of 'sole protectors', or take the war to where it hurt most and, in the process, demonstrate invincibility—and, of course, to weaken and erode the peace constituency.[9]

The killing of TELO leader Sri Sabaratnam and 200 TELO cadres by the LTTE in the streets and the fields of Jaffna in mid-1986, and the attack on EPRLF in December 1986, signalled the beginning of a bloody fratricidal conflict which was to consume the lives of hundreds of Tamil youths who lost their lives fighting one another rather than fighting the state. In fact, more Tamil youths were killed in fratricidal conflicts during 1986-87 than in combat with the security forces. This was despite the fact that only a year earlier the LTTE had joined the united front, the Eelam National Liberation Front (ENLF), comprising the EPRLF, EROS, and TELO, which had been formed in 1984. This was also despite the fact that all four organizations (i.e. LTTE, EPRLF, EROS, and TELO), including the PLOTE and TULF, together formulated a common negotiating position at the Thimpu Peace Talks of July and August 1985, and collectively called themselves the 'Tamil Delegation' while making joint written submissions at the talks. This included the formulation and submission of the 'Thimpu Principles'. In addition to the fratricidal conflicts, the subsequent killing of Tamil intellectuals and politicians (i.e Amirthalingam, Pathmanabha, Rajanai Thiranagama and Neelan Tiruchelvam) who did not subscribe to the LTTE's way of thinking and doing created a vacuum in the political landscape of Tamil politics, as well as narrowed the scope for involvement by the intelligentsia.

But it would be incorrect to say that the LTTE was the sole perpetrator. The internal killings that took place within the PLOTE during the 1980s are a case in point. Others included the assassination of TULF politicians Dharmalingam, Alalasundram, and others by TELO in mid-1985, the forced conscription of adults and children, and the killing of sympathizers of the LTTE by the EPRLF and its allies in the post Indo–Lanka Accord period of 1987–90, the hegemonic politics and thuggery of the PLOTE in Vavuniya during the early 1990s, the rampage of the EPDP as a 'para-military' during the early 1990s under the patronage of President Premadasa, and the use of violence to silence its critics even while functioning as a parliamentary party, all contributed to the rot that began to set into Tamil militancy and created distortions in their transformation into mainstream democratic parties.

Successive governments and their military-intelligence apparatuses also contributed to the rot through the creation of 'para-militaries' which were accountable to no one but their 'handlers'. The tendency to use the ex-Tamil militant organizations as instruments in the military campaign against the

LTTE, rather than empowering them as political parties by evolving a package based on substantial autonomy for the north-east, further discredited non-LTTE Tamil organizations which came to be stigmatized as 'para-militaries'. In short, all of the above contributed to the metamorphosis of the Tamil resistance from the initial idealism, selflessness, and revolutionary fervour to terrorism, fratricidal killings, and the denial of the fundamental rights to pluralism, political diversity, and life.

The Role of the State and Responses

State Terrorism as Counter-Terrorism

The response of the state to the nascent Tamil youth militancy that was emerging in the mid-1970s was typical. It adopted a two-pronged strategy: to initiate a process of finding a political settlement to the Tamil Question and to facilitate it by softening up the Tamil militancy. The killing of an SLFP Tamil politician and mayor of Jaffna, Alfred Duraiappah, as well as a Tamil policeman, Bastiampillai, by Tamil youth militants in the mid-1970s, referred to in the previous section, rocked the Colombo establishment. The SLFP-led government, headed by the late Sirimavo Bandaranaike resorted to the mass rounding-up of Tamil youths, but failed to net the actual killers. This forced many youths to go underground or into exile, only to return with a vengeance.

The run-up to the general elections in 1977 opened up a space for addressing Tamil grievances. The UNP, seizing the opportunity to swell its minority vote bank, clearly admitted to the validity of 'Tamil grievances' and the need to remedy them. Many of the UNP leaders admitted that the Tamil speaking people were facing many problems and it is the lack of solution to these problems which led them to demand a separate state. This is only before 1977. The party in the course of 1977 election promised that, if it came to power, it would address Tamil grievances in the fields of education, 'colonization',[10] use of the Tamil language and employment in the public and semi-public corporations.

On being elected with a five-sixth majority leading to the virtual decimation of the SLFP and ethnic polarization, with the

TULF becoming the main opposition party in Parliament, the UNP government headed by J.R. Jayawardene in its First Policy Statement in Parliament on 4 August 1977 declared its intentions to summon an All Party Conference to resolve the Tamil Question. However, one week later anti-Tamil riots, widely believed to be state-sponsored, broke out.[11] This was also widely believed to be Jayawardene's strategy to soften up an increasingly shrill Tamil nationalist rhetoric by the TULF which threatened to set up its own Constituent Assembly of Tamil Eelam. Interestingly, Prime Minister J.R. Jayawardene, at a special debate on the riots, following the adjournment of the National State Assembly, in referring to the rhetoric of the TULF declared, 'if you want to fight, let there be fight; if it is peace, let there be peace. . . . It is not what I am saying. The people of Sri Lanka say that'. This was said at a time when Tamil militancy was still in its infancy and by no means posed a serious security threat to the state or to the territorial integrity and sovereignty of the country.

Jayawardene repeated the same challenge and justification after the cataclysmic state-sponsored anti-Tamil pogrom of July 1983, in a broadcast to the nation. He maintained complete silence when the pogrom was on. In a futile attempt to deflect responsibility by introducing legislation in Parliament to bar political parties that espouse secession and to deprive members of such parties of their civic rights, he declared, 'We are very sorry that this step should be taken. But I cannot see, and my Government cannot see, any other way by which we can appease the national desire and request of the Sinhala people to prevent the country being divided, and to see that those who speak for division are not able to do so legally'.[12] Interestingly, in an interview given to a foreign daily just a fortnight before the anti-Tamil pogrom, Jayawardene stated, ' I have tried to be effective for some time but cannot. I am not worried about the opinion of the Jaffna people now. . . . Now we cannot think of them, nor about their lives or of their opinion of us'.[13]

The strategy of softening the people into submission was pursued simultaneously with the strategy of appeasement. In the 1978 Constitution, which replaced the Westminster model with a Gaullist-type executive presidential system, Tamil was recognized for the first time as a 'National Language', while recognizing Sinhala as the only 'official language'. Further, the Chapter on Citizenship recognized only one status of citizenship, thereby removing the earlier distinction between citizens by 'descent' and citizens by 'registration', which discriminated against Tamils of recent Indian origin or the 'Plantation Tamils'. But even here the implementation was tardy. The question of the statelessness of Plantation Tamils continued while no legislation was passed in relation to the language issue which would have given effect to the constitutional provision.

The UNP government also introduced the District Development Councils (DDC) in 1981 by way of introducing decentralization of administration. Although it was introduced countrywide, it was expected that this would address Tamil aspirations and grievances. However, as President Jayawardene himself admitted to a delegation of Buddhist clergy, which had sought a meeting with him regarding their objections to the setting-up of the DDCs, they had powers that did not go beyond that of Urban Councils and Village Councils. The DDCs were merely appendages of the central government and were not vested with executive authority. As a cabinet minister was to say in a parliamentary debate on the DDC Bill, 'this Bill has nothing to do with the Tamil problem. This Bill is a democratic evolution of power in the interest of the people of Sri Lanka. . . . it is in the interest of a unitary government decentralizing power to its own people throughout the island'.[14]

As regards the TULF, it had considerably reduced its nationalist rhetoric and was prepared to accept the DDCs, not as a solution to the Tamil Question, but as a means of ensuring some development activities for the north-east.

The fears of the Tamil politicians had been justified. A few days prior to the elections for the DDCs in Jaffna, there was another incident of state-sponsored violence in response to an action by a Tamil militant group. On 31 March 1981, the Jaffna Library was set on fire by goon squads brought to Jaffna by a cabinet minister aided and abetted by security personnel. A house belonging to a Tamil parliamentarian was also set on fire. On the day of the elections on 4 June 1982, the people came out and voted for the TULF in defiance of the state and the Tamil militants who had called for a boycott. This is a telling testimony to the failure of the two-pronged strategy of appeasement and terrorising the Tamils into submission that was followed by the government of the day during this period. The strategy did not succeed in either appeasing or suppressing Tamil aspirations and revolt.

The policy of political and physical intimidation of the Tamil parties and people by successive governments, however, failed to stop the spate of violence unleashed by the Tamil youth militancy. The state's response was to further intensify its strategy of collective punishment to terrorise the civilians into submission. In 1978, the LTTE was proscribed, and in July 1979 the Prevention of Terrorism Act (PTA) was passed in Parliament. This was the beginning of the dark days for the Tamil people. All legal and constitutional safeguards with regard to arrest, detention and protection against self-incrimination were abrogated. Suspected 'terrorists' could be detained without trial for 18 months and confessions extracted under detention were admissible in courts. It is believed that sometime in 1971, President Jayawardene directed the Army Chief to control and possibly eliminate, within a period of six months, the problem of 'terrorism' from the whole of the island country, particularly Jaffna district, but in accordance with the law of the land.

Aside from the fact that the scourge of terrorism (to the state) and the resistance or liberation struggle (to the Tamil militant movement) persist, to this day, the PTA symbolized the full force of state terrorism which became a key prop of the state's response to Tamil militancy and resistance during this period. However, it proved to be ineffective in the long-run, although in the short-term there was a lull in militant activities in Jaffna soon after the passage of the PTA. But ultimately, it is durability which ensures success or failure. In that sense the PTA was a monumental failure as a means of effective state response.

As the University Teachers for Human Rights (Jaffna) observed, 'this is an example of how misleading it could be to interpret cause and effect by only taking into account events over a small period of time. A viable operation would have involved a political solution, an amnesty and low-key intelligence gathering over a long period. To send a few battalions to Jaffna and knock people about for six months was an entirely misconceived operation—especially when the militants were no more than a few dozen in number. It was more a provocation.'[15]

The response from the Tamil militants after a lull was intensified leading to the ambush of an army convoy by the LTTE in Jaffna on 23 July 1983. What followed was carnage unprecedented in the annals of anti-Tamil riots commencing in 1958. That it was state-sponsored was without a doubt and was well documented. The casualties in terms of the lives lost, entirely Tamils, ranged from the official figure of 300 to 2,000 according to Tamil sources. The massacre of Tamil political prisoners held under the PTA highlighted the brutality of state terrorism. What was particularly galling was the announcement by President Jayawardene to bar political parties that espouse separation from entering the legislature and to deprive members of such parties of their civic rights. (Broadcast to the Nation).

Hence, the 6th Amendment to the Constitution was passed in Parliament on 4 August 1983. It basically required any person holding elected office to take an oath affirming that he/she would not directly or indirectly, in or outside Sri Lanka, support, espouse, promote, finance, encourage, or advocate the establishment of a separate state within the territory of Sri Lanka. By this act the moderate TULF ceased to be in parliament, while the Tamil politico-military organizations could not care less. What needs to be noted for the purpose of this chapter is that the state response ironically paved the way for the moderate Tamil parliamentary party to be replaced by the Tamil politico-military organizations as the vanguard of the Tamil resistance. It was yet another case of a knee-jerk response by the state which actually contributed to the gwoth of Tamil militancy from its infant stage.

The Sri Lanka state failed to realize that draconian measures like the PTA and rule by Emergency, interspersed by state-sponsored pogroms, were precisely what gave legitimacy to Tamil youth militancy as a national liberation struggle. The need to address the genesis of Tamil militancy, which mobilized around the secessionist demand for 'Tamil Eelam', was never seriously considered. The post-1983 period witnessed an escalation of the conflict interspersed by 'talking while fighting'. This period also brought in the regional and international factors, leading to the present situation where the ethnic conflict, as well as conflict resolution, has become irreversibly internationalized. We now turn our attention to these aspects.

FLAWED NEGOTIATIONS: RESPONSE TO INDIAN MEDIATION

THE ALL PARTY CONFERENCE OF 1984 AND THIMPU PEACE TALKS OF 1985 [16]

Following the anti-Tamil pogrom of July 1983, which led to the exodus of Tamil refugees to Tamil Nadu (India) and expressions of solidarity reflective of cross-border ethnic affiliations, the involvement of India was predestined. Indian Prime Minister Indira Gandhi, in a clear declaration of intent, announced in the Indian Parliament that she was establishing a 'Sri Lanka Relief Fund' and called on 'fellow citizens, including those living abroad, to contribute generously to the fund and thereby express their anguish and sympathy for the unfortunate victims of this senseless violence in a tangible and positive manner.[17]

What followed was not only the offer of a safe haven to Sri Lankan Tamil refugees, but also the facilitation of an external sanctuary to the various Tamil politico-military organizations. The key beneficiaries of India's moral and material support were the LTTE, TELO, EPRLF, EROS and PLOTE. The representatives of these politico-military organizations, along with the seasoned parliamentary party, TULF, comprised the Tamil Delegation at the Thimpu Peace Talks of 1985.

Prior to that, two emissaries were sent by Prime Minister Indira Gandhi to Colombo. The first was Foreign Minister Narasimha Rao, who delivered a stern warning to President Jayawardene to stop the carnage. This was followed by a diplomatic initative when G. Parthasarathy (GP), a retired diplomat and educationist, was sent to Colombo for discussions with President Jayawardene. His mandate was to urge Colombo to convene an All Party Conference which the TULF would attend. A proposal was also drafted by 'GP', later came to be known as 'Annexure C', which envisaged the setting up of one or more Regional Councils by amalgamating the pre-existing DDCs, with legislative powers for subjects devolved to it. The chief executive, of the executive arm, would be the Chief Minister and his Council of Ministers, backed by a regional public service. The subjects to be devolved were to be open for negotiations, including the unit of devolution.

It was an offer that Jayawardene could not refuse. And so began the process of a two-pronged strategy by India. The first was to strength the resistance capacity of the Tamil militants to demonstrate to Colombo the non-viability of a military solution. The second was a diplomatic initiative aimed at getting the two parties to the conflict to agree on a negotiated political solution. Thus began a flurry of initiatives culminating in the 'Parthasarathy Proposals' and the All Party Conference (APC) of 1984, in which the TULF grudgingly agreed to participate at the prodding of New Delhi.

While the APC meandered its way to an inconclusive end, the Tamil militant groups were, as already noted, beginning to consolidate themselves. In April 1984, three Tamil organizations had joined to form the ENLF. The following year, in April 1985, the LTTE took the decision to join the united front. The Tamil militant groups had emerged into a 'politico-military' entity with tremendous clout which clearly enjoyed the patronage of the Government of India.

Meanwhile, the assassination of Indira Gandhi on 31 August 1984 by her Sikh bodyguards led to her son, Rajiv Gandhi, assuming the mantle of the Nehru family and the helm of the Indian polity. The perception that he was 'pro-west' and not fettered by his mother's deep-rooted suspicion of the western powers gave fresh hope to Colombo. Jayawardene sent Minister of National Security Lalith Athulathmudali to New Delhi for discussions with the newly installed Indian Prime Minister. Indian Foreign Secretary Romesh Bhandari, who openly spoke about his friendly relations with the Jayawardene family, was largely instrumental in thawing the strained relations between Colombo and Delhi.

At the summit meeting between President Jayawardene and Prime Minister Rajiv Gandhi in New Delhi in June 1985, it was decided that the time was appropriate to commence the process of negotiations. On India's part, an indication was given that pressure would be exerted on the Tamil militant organizations to agree to a ceasefire and engage in direct negotiations. And pressure was in fact exerted when the Tamil militant organizations were told by a key official of the Government of India that 'Indian soil and sea' would no longer be available if they refused to engage in direct talks with the Sri Lankan government. An assurance was, however, given that India would not be a party to any process that would undermine the self-respect of the Tamil people and the militant organizations.[18]

This paved the way for the peace talks of July and August of 1985 between the Sri Lankan government and the Tamil politico-military organizations, mediated by the Government of India and held at a third venue, in Thimpu, the capital city of the Kingdom of Bhutan. The foregoing account lays out the basic politico-military and geopolitical background to the Thimpu Peace Talks of 1985. We now turn to some procedural and structural issues that led to its collapse.

The 'Thimpu Talks' lasted two rounds. During the First Round, which lasted from 8 to 13 July, the Sri Lankan government delegation put forward a draft legislation for the devolution of power. These proposals were only marginally different from the one which was placed before the All Party Conference of 1984 and which had been rejected by the TULF. It once again demonstrated that the Sri Lankan state was incapable of placing before the Tamil polity far-reaching proposals which would be seen as a viable alternative to the pitched-up demand for Tamil Eelam.

The Tamil delegation on its part declined to negotiate any proposals that had already been rejected by the TULF at the APC and placed before the government delegation a set of 'four cardinal principles' (popularly known as the 'Thimpu Principles') as a framework for the formulation of any proposals that the Government of Sri Lanka may wish to forward to the Tamil delegation. These four principles are:

(a) Recognition of the Tamils of Sri Lanka as a distinct nationality;
(b) Recognition of an identified Tamil homeland and the guarantee of its territorial integrity;
(c) Based on the above, recognition of the inalienable right of self-determination of the Tamil nation;

(d) Recognition of the right to full citizenship and other fundamental democratic rights of all Tamils, who look upon the Island as their country.

When Round Two of the talks recommenced on 12 August, the leader of the Sri Lankan government delegation, H.W. Jayewardene, in a prepared Statement rejected the 'Thimpu Principles', stating emphatically that: 'if the first three principles are to be taken at their face value and given their accepted legal meaning, they are wholly unacceptable to the Government, They must be rejected for the reason that they constitute a negation of the sovereignty and territorial integrity of Sri Lanka, they are detrimental to a united Sri Lanka and are inimical to the interests of the several communities, ethnic and religious in our country'.*

The gap between the government's set of proposals and the Thimpu Principles was not just a difference of opinion or perception, but one that was operating on two totally different ideological and conceptual planes. The government's proposals, while going beyond the decentralization and delegation of power envisaged in the pre-existing District Development Councils' system, were nowhere close to the devolution of powers available in the Indian constitution. Further, it failed to recognize the ethnic conflict in Sri Lanka as a National Question.

The Thimpu Principles, on the other hand, were a strident call for the recognition of the Tamil people as a nation with its inalienable right to self-determination. The decision to forward the Thimpu Principles was not only an assertion of Tamil nationalism, but also a strategic move to avoid placing concrete proposals which were seen as a premature abandonment of the goal for which arms had been raised—namely, a separate state of Tamil Eelam. The Thimpu Principles, therefore, could not have been anything other than an articulation of an Ideal, bereft of constitutional and legal niceties.

The Thimpu Talks were destined to collapse since neither party to the conflict was prepared to abandon its rigid position. Nor was the ground situation conducive for any serious negotiations. Interestingly and predictably, both the Sri Lankan government

*Author's personal notes. Author was personally present at the Thimpu Talks as a part of the Tamil Delegation.

and the Tamil organizations were relieved that the Thimpu Talks had collapsed. As Jayadeva Uyangoda has rightly argued, there were no favourable prerequisites for a negotiated settlement of the conflict at the time of the Thimpu Talks:

> Behind the rhetoric of negotiations and the reality of failure was indeed one important dynamic in conflict formation and conflict resolution . . . the Sri Lankan armed conflict had not reached a stage of settlement that can be worked out through negotiations at all. It was too early for the Sri Lankan government to come to a compromise with Tamil militants, because the government still believed that the guerrilla war could be defeated by military means. It was too early for the Tamil militant groups too to abandon the armed struggle in favour of a negotiated settlement, because they had just begun what they perceived as a 'liberation war'.[19]

A further complicating factor was the role of India as mediator with a multiple agenda. It was evident that New Delhi, particularly during Mrs Gandhi's leadership, was acutely averse to the involvement of western powers, as well as Pakistan and Israel, in the militarization of the Sri Lankan security forces. The attempts by President Jayawardene to canvass support from, what may be termed as, the London-Washington-Pretoria-Tel Aviv-Islamabad axis was perceived by New Delhi as an attempt to 'isolate India in the region by facilitating the strategic presence of the forces inimical to India's perceived security interests . . .'. Mrs Gandhi in her telephone conversation with President Jayawardene on 5 August also strongly disapproved of Sri Lanka seeking external military support.[20]

Further, although India's direct involvement in Sri Lanka's ethnic imbroglio did serve to enhance the resistance capacity of the Tamil politico-military organizations, New Delhi also gave a guarantee to Colombo that it would not support the demand for a separate state of 'Tamil Eelam'. While Colombo, realizing the futility of confronting India, sought to neutralize the regional power's role by co-opting it, the Tamil Resistance saw India largely as an external sanctuary necessary to advance its armed struggle for 'national liberation'. Each party to the conflict needed India on its side, while simultaneously harbouring apprehensions and suspicions regarding India's role as an 'honest broker'.

And herein lay India's failure to mediate a just and a durable solution to the Ethnic Question, despite the fact that the Thimpu Talks were doomed to fail even before they commenced. While the failure of the Thimpu Talks was due more to factors intrinsic to Sri Lanka's ethnic conflict and less to India's role as a mediator, suffice it to say India was always burdened by a multiple agenda and, in the process, lost focus. Further, India was too deeply involved as a 'party to the conflict' through its policy of strengthening the Tamil Resistance on the one hand, and applying a heavy-handed approach against it on the other. Further, the perceived role of Indian Foreign Secretary Romesh Bhandari as being sympathetic towards Colombo and Jayawardene made it impossible for him to function as an 'honest broker', in the perception of the Tamil organizations. In the process, India failed to gain the confidence of both parties to the conflict. In fact, both sides regarded India with deep suspicion. Yet, each side had to convince India of its sincerity while exposing the 'other', in a gambit to win over India, while isolating the other.

The Indo–Lanka Accord of 1987 and Problems in Internalizing the Accord

Following the collapse of the Thimpu Talks, New Delhi persisted with its attempts at a negotiated settlement while continuing to enhance the resistance capacity of the Tamil politico-military organizations. However, a warning was also sent to them through the deportation of three influential personalities within the Tamil politico-military organizations. That two of them were allowed to return is also indicative of the tendency for knee-jerk reactions and *ad hocism* employed by India under the tenure of Romesh Bhandari.

India, however, reassumed a more coherent and cogent role following the Thimpu fiasco. New Delhi decided to initiate direct talks with Colombo. This was indicated in a press release issued by the Ministry of External Affairs on 31 August 1985, declaring that, 'a comprehensive paper has been drawn up covering all issues of importance and relevance. This detailed draft could serve as the basis for negotiations towards a mutually agreed Accord by the parties concerned.' This was a clear indication from New Delhi that it was going to persist with its role as a 'mediator' whether the parties liked it or not. Thus began a process of 'proximity talks', with New Delhi speaking to Colombo as well as the Tamil organizations on the broad contours of a constitutional and a political settlement, culminating in a set of proposals referred to as the 19 December Proposals, which provided for substantial devolution of power to the bifurcated northern and eastern provinces, with institutional linkages between the two. A provision for their amalgamation was also provided subject to a referendum to ascertain whether the peoples of the two provinces wished to merge as a single unit of devolution or remain as two distinct units. In addition to devolution of power, shared rule at the centre was envisaged through the creation of the office of Vice President, presumably to involve the Tamil parties in power-sharing at the centre.

The Sri Lankan government, much to the chagrin of India, launched a major military offensive aimed at recapturing Jaffna, known as the Vadamarachchi Offensive. New Delhi was forced to intervene to frustrate President Jayawardane's resolve to seek a military solution of the Tamil issue. The intervention was made through a symbolic airdrop of essential food items for the besieged people of Jaffna. This compelled Sri Lanka to seek a political solution leading to the July Indo–Sri Lanka Agreement. This agreement provided a framework for the resolution of the Tamil problem and also committed India to come to Sri Lanka's help if Tamil militants were to take up arms. Under the provisions of this agreement the Indian Peace Keeping Force (IPKF) went to Sri Lanka to maintain peace and implement the agreement. The Accord itself addressed the issue of demilitarization as well as the establishment of regional autonomy for the north-east. As to whether the unit of devolution would be a merged north-east or not was to be determined by a referendum.

One of the peculiar features of the Indo–Lanka Accord, which perhaps led to its eventual collapse, was that it meant different things to the different actors. To President Jaywardene, it was more a case of making a virtue out of a necessity and to ensure that the IPKF disarmed the Tamil militant organizations, which his own security forces had failed to do. To the Indian Prime

Minister, the Indo–Lanka Accord was not purely a case of doing Colombo a favour. In a speech at a public meeting in Madras (presently Chennai) he said that the Accord 'secures everything that the Sri Lankan Tamils had demanded, short of breaking Sri Lanka's unity. . . . It represented major concessions by the Sri Lanka Government to the Tamil demands and Tamil sentiments.'[21] To India, the Indo–Lanka Accord also articulated its security and geopolitical concerns. The Annexure to the Accord clearly stipulated that Trincomalee or any other port, including foreign broadcasting organizations, would not be permitted to prejudice Indo–Sri Lanka relations or India's interests.

Within Sri Lanka, the left and social democratic forces, including human rights organizations and peace-oriented NGOs, welcomed the Accord. The JVP, with its anti-Indian hegemony line and ethno-populism, opposed the Accord and engaged in violence leading to the imposition of a 36-hour curfew. Ironically, Prime Minister Premadasa, a prominent member of the ruling UNP, was a bitter critic of the Accord and decided to absent himself from the signing ceremony. The attack on Rajiv Gandhi by a naval rating prior to his departure from Colombo is indicative of the strong opposition to the Accord from sections within the political as well as the military establishment.

To LTTE leader Velupillai Prabhakaran, the Indo–Lanka Accord was something that was foisted on him and in a rare public speech in Suthumail, Jaffna on 4 August 1987, just one week after the signing of the Accord by Rajiv Gandhi and Jayawardene, he implied that the responsibility now lay squarely with India. He further emphasized to the Tamil people who had gathered to listen to his speech, 'let me make it clear to you here, beyond the shadow of a doubt, that I will continue to fight for the objective of attaining Tamil Eelam. . . . The Liberation Tigers yearn for the motherland of Tamil Eelam.'[22]

To the non-LTTE Tamil militant organizations who had a meeting with Rajiv Gandhi in New Delhi on the eve of his departure for Colombo to sign the Indo–Lanka Accord, it was a case of guarded optimism. Rajiv Gandhi assured the representatives of these organizations (i.e. EPRLF, TELO, PLOTE, and ENDLF) that the Government of India would not let the Tamils of Sri Lanka down and asked them to place their trust in him. He also assured them that they would not be subject to any humiliation during the handing over of arms. An assurance was also given that all Tamil militant organizations who laid down their arms would be accommodated in interim arrangements.[23] The seasoned Tamil parliamentary party, TULF, while expressing its gratitude to the Government of India, assured its support to Rajiv Gandhi's efforts 'to find a solution to our problem, put an end to our suffering and enable us to live in safety and security with freedom, honour and dignity'.

The major flaw in the Indo–Lanka Accord was that there was no agreement signed between Colombo and the representatives of the Tamil politico-military organizations. Further, there was no consensus, even within the ruling UNP, with Prime Minister Premadasa, on his assuming office as President, eventually calling on the IPKF to withdraw, in effect abrogating the Accord. Further, the intransigence and adventurism of the LTTE in militarily taking on the IPKF, the obstructions placed by Premadasa to the implementation of the 13th Amendment to the Constitution when a flawed electoral process in the north-east led to the formation of the EPRLF-led North-East Provincial government, the arming of the LTTE, ironically by Colombo in its fight against the IPKF, and the sheer frustration of the North-East Provincial government leading to a provisional unilateral declaration of independence and going into exile, all contributed to the collapse of the Indo–Lanka Accord.

Perhaps the assassinations of Rajiv Gandhi in 1991 and President Premadasa in 1993 by the LTTE symbolized how a well-intentioned instrument which was externally mediated as a means of resolving the ethnic question in Sri Lanka can lead to a morass of problems if these intiatives do not become internalized. But the process of germinating 'home grown' solutions also had its drawbacks as the People's Alliance (PA)–LTTE Talks of 1994–5 demonstrated. We now turn our attention to the state's attempts at direct negotiations without external facilitation or mediation. In this, it is now imperative to also focus on the character of the LTTE as the primary non-state actor and its own agenda in the negotiations.

Direct Negotiations: People's Alliance and LTTE Talks of 1994

The defeat of the UNP regime in the parliamentary elections of August 1994 was predictable. The preceding 17 years under UNP rule had witnessed the widening and deepening of authoritarianism. 'Political stability' was deemed to be an essential prerequisite for the successful implementation of the 'Open Economy' package of the International Monetary Fund (IMF) and the World Bank. 'Stability' was, however, to be effected through repression and the suppressing of dissent. The Tamil Resistance, however, was another 'ball game' altogether. It simply refused to fade away. The pursuit of hegemony by the LTTE in its project to emerge as the 'sole representative' of the Tamil people and the entry into the political mainstream by non-LTTE ex-Tamil militant groups also paved the way for more internecine conflicts within the Tamil national movement. Nor was there any democracy to speak of in the Tamil areas, irrespective of whether it was under the control of the security forces or the LTTE. The non-LTTE Tamil organizations similarly failed to effect a transformation and internal democracy. Instead, they began to assume the schizophrenic character of 'legitimate' parliamentary parties and 'hated' paramilitaries.

It was in this context that the victory of the PA under the leadership of Chandrika Kumaratunga at the general elections was seen as 'fresh winds' blowing across the land. Or so it was perceived by the secular, democratic forces, including broad sections of the Tamil populace. The Tamil people felt justified in extending their support to the PA when the newly elected Prime Minister, Chandrika Kumaratunga, offered unconditional talks to the LTTE. This was followed by the relaxing of the economic embargo that had taken a heavy toll on the Tamil people, particularly those living in LTTE-controlled areas.

Despite this initial enthusiasm, it later transpired that the LTTE was guarded from the outset, as stated by Anton Balasingham in his recent book on the PA–LTTE Talks: 'From the outset, Prabhakaran, the leader of the LTTE, was sceptical of Chandrika's gesture. He felt it was a political gimmick to win the support of the Tamils and Sinhalese for the forth-coming presidential elections.'[24]

Despite these apprehensions, the LTTE went ahead and released 10 police detainees as a 'gesture of goodwill and understanding' and declared that its was prepared for ceasefire and unconditional talks. Thus began the run-up to the direct negotiations between the PA government and the LTTE in Jaffna in 1994–95.[25]

In a study on Confidence Building Measures (CBM), Isak Svensson argues that despite a 'reasonable, intuitive assumption' that CBMs during intra-state peace processes have a positive correlation with successful negotiated settlement, a quantitative survey of almost forty intra-state processes in the 1990s showed that some of the CBMs used had a 'counter-productive effect'. [26] Let us look into the Sri Lankan case.

There was no paucity of CBMs in the 1994–5 PA–LTTE talks. In fact, there was a plethora of CBMs starting with a partial lifting of the economic embargo by the PA government within two weeks of assuming power. This was promptly reciprocated by the LTTE through the release of 10 police detainees, the offer of ceasefire and call for unconditional peace talks. The government, once again, responded by making a unilateral gesture to 'restore, as far as possible, electricity, repair the major highways and part of the irrigation schemes, as further normalization of civil life'.[27] However, these measures could not be sustained in the absence of concrete measures on the ground. While the government maintained that it was doing its utmost to ease the embargo and to ensure the smooth flow of essentials, the LTTE alleged that the military was impeding such flows. The LTTE underscored the importance of the issue of the 'economic blockade' when its leader Prabhakaran, in his first press statement of 2 September 1994 officially reciprocating the government's peace initiative and the partial lifting of the embargo, stressed that: 'The new government could claim to have done justice only when the essential commodities freely available to the Sinhala people are made available to our people.' This theme was to be repeatedly stressed, but in different forms and tones, right through the period of negotiations.

And when President Kumaratunga finally expressed in her letter of 9 March 1995 to LTTE leader Prabhkaran that the demands of the LTTE, including the total lifting of the embargo and the ban on fishing in the north and the east 'could have serious military repercussions', it was cited as ample proof by the LTTE of its perception that military considerations were overweighing other considerations. The LTTE theoretician and spokesperson, Anton Balasingham, in his analysis of the 1994–5 talks, in fact, pointedly referred to this particular phraseology used by Chandrika Kumaratunga. He observed, 'Yet, it was the first time that President Kumaratunga admitted openly, without any evasions and ambiguities, that granting the LTTE's requests would trigger serious military implications and that it would amount to compromising national security.'[28] The Sri Lankan government, on its part, accused the LTTE of precisely the same thing, namely, that its demands were determined by its own military designs. The reason cited was the insistence by the LTTE that the Pooneryn army camp should be removed to facilitate the opening of the Pooneryn–Sangupiddy road and that its armed cadres should be allowed free movement in the Eastern Province.

One aspect of the CBMs which the LTTE resented was the various unilateral measures taken by the government in 'easing the hardships of the Tamil People'. This was seen by the LTTE as a covert means of isolating and alienating it from the Tamil populace. A case in point was the initiative taken by the government to unilaterally implement its reconstruction package. On 13 February 1995, the government announced the appointment of a Presidential Task Force for the rehabilitation of the north-east province. The Task Force was given a period of three months to implement its programme, which included the electrification of Jaffna, the repair of major roadways leading to Jaffna, the reconstruction of the Jaffna Public Library, and repairs to the Jaffna General Hospital. The reconstruction package was very much Jaffna-centric.

The unilateral decision was communicated to the LTTE in a letter dated 16 January by President Kumaratunga. In that letter she 'informed' the LTTE leader, V. Prabhakaran, that the government would be commencing work on the main areas of reconstruction, mentioned earlier, and requested the LTTE to 'make arrangements' to receive the technical officers and to 'facilitate their work'. The LTTE was not directly represented in the Task Force.

Although the LTTE was subsequently requested to participate in the Presidential Task Force, it was more of an afterthought, and by that time the damage had been done. The apparent CBM had become a source of suspicion. In any event, what the LTTE had proposed was its participation in the Authority for Reconstruction and Rehabilitation as the authentic representative of the Tamil people. It may also be noted that the notion of separating 'Tamil interests' from 'Tiger interests' and the 'weaning' of the Tamil populace from the Tiger 'influence' figured prominently in the broad strategy of the Kumaratunga government. The LTTE, on the other hand, was firm that it constituted the sole legitimate representative and mediator of Tamil interests. In sum, the CBMs in place, rather than building mutual confidence, introduced a strong element of suspicion as well as contestation. As Isak Svensson has argued:

> Drawn from the old Roman practice of divide and rule, the strategy to use positive measures to create or increase a split within an opponent, can be a powerful weapon. In this way confidence building measures could be used as, to paraphrase Clausewitz, the continuation of war by other means. This corresponds to the problem of differentiating between offensive and defensive strategies, as CBMs can be perceived as offensive.[29]

Another feature of the 1994–5 talks was that they were largely centred around an exchange of letters channelled through the International Committee of the Red Cross (ICRC), and the four rounds of direct talks. The tone of the letters degenerated from expressing hope and confidence to questioning the motives and intentions of the other. It may be argued that the absence of a facilitator was a major cause for the heavy reliance on the exchange of letters as a means of communicating the respective positions. In a letter of 3 February 1995 from S.P. Thamilchelvan, leader of the political wing of the LTTE and the head of its delegation, to K. Balapatabendi, secretary to the President and head of the Sri Lankan government delegation, relating to the controversy pertaining to Foreign Monitors, the LTTE observed: 'We think that it would be more appropriate that these sensitive and serious issues can be discussed and amicably resolved through direct negotiations at the next round of talks.' It is indeed ironic that the LTTE should now stress the importance of a third-party facilitator/mediator in the ongoing talks, with Norway as the facilitator. We will return to this theme in the next section.

The 1994-95, the PA–LTTE talks, perhaps, was the forum where the interconnectedness between Substance (or core issues) and Process was discussed extensively—but with no agreement reached on the relative importance of each at a given conjuncture. The PA government's position, perhaps, was most explicitly stated in a letter of 9 March 1995 by President Kumaratunga to LTTE leader Prabhakaran, when the negotiations were already beginning to go awry: 'The government has also insistently stated that negotiations to (these matters) need not delay the commencement of political talks since the two could proceed parallely'. The letter further proposed that 'talks regarding the political settlement of the ethnic problem should commence on any dates between 2nd to 10th April. . . . Our package of proposals for a political settlement would be sent to you in advance.' These talks, of course, never took place. The LTTE pulled out leading to the commencement of Eelam War III, hence reinforcing the commonly held belief that the LTTE shuns negotiations on core political issues as that would necessitate the public abandonment of its goal of a separate and a sovereign State of Tamil Eelam.

The LTTE's perspective on this issue, on the other hand, is best brought out by Balasingham in his analysis of the 1994–5 talks in his book *Duplicity in Politics*: 'there was a total misreading in the government circles that the LTTE was avoiding political negotiations. . . . It was our concern that a permanent political settlement should satisfy the political aspirations of the Tamil people and also alleviate the apprehensions of the Sinhala masses. We knew this to be a difficult task. It would require a great deal of mutual dialogue; possibly over a long period of time. It was precisely for this reason we wanted the urgent day to day problems of the people to be addressed and resolved in the initial stages of the dialogue'. Suffice it to say the LTTE took a position that was contrary to the 'parallel' process preferred by the government. The LTTE instead consistently placed its preference for a 'stage by stage' approach that basically meant arriving at a congenial atmosphere based on agreements on humanitarian and military issues before embarking on political negotiations.

The LTTE's reluctance to commence political negotiations has been seen by many political analysts, particularly from the south, as the most deficient aspect of the negotiation process in 1994–5. Lakshman Gunasekera, a columnist and political analyst known for his progressive and secular views, typifies this view in the following analysis:

> Even in the face of persistent calls by the PA Government for the peace talks agenda to include negotiations on the 'substantive issues'—that is the basic substance of a political solution—the LTTE has refused to agree to such an agenda. The LTTE refused to do so in the first round of talks in 1994–5 and even now has not made any positive indication. The only 'substance' the Tigers have said they are prepared to talk about are to do with what they call 'normalisation' of condition in the North East.[30]

The process of resolving the 'stage by stage' approach of the LTTE and the 'parallely' approach of the government never took place, other than the repeated statements of their respective positions. It is not the intention here to look into the pros and cons of the stance taken by both sides then. What is relevant now is that the current debate on gradual versus simultaneous approach to mutual confidence building and addressing the core issue of resolving the conflict in the Norwegian facilitated peace process is a continuation of the 1994–5 talks. But, before we look into the ongoing Norwegian facilitated peace process, the question is, what are the lessons that could be derived from the failure of the Thimpu Peace Talks of 1985 and the PA–UNP talks of 1994–5? As far as the 1994–5 PA–UNP talks are concerned, it is clear that there was a genuine commitment to the process by both the government and the LTTE. However, the process itself had different meanings and connotations to the parties to the conflict.

While to the PA, the process was equated with political negotiations, to the LTTE it was seen as an essential prerequisite for the creation of 'normalcy' for the Tamil people and a 'stable and a congenial atmosphere' on the ground. Political negotiations on substantive issues, aimed at addressing the causes of the conflict, were to come much later. In fact, to the LTTE, normalization and the removal of the 'day to day' problems of the people were the 'substantive' issues. To the PA government, on the other hand, securing a commitment from the LTTE that it was prepared to embark on political negotiations on alternatives to a separate state of 'Tamil Eelam' was paramount. In the process, the parties began to see each other with suspicion and began searching for 'hidden agendas'. And the hidden agenda was, in fact, determined by military and strategic interests by both sides. Ultimately, militarism won the day and the peace process, predictably, remains stalemated.

NORWEGIAN FACILITATED PEACE PROCESS: A PARADIGM SHIFT TOWARDS APPEASEMENT

Following the decision of the Government of Sri Lanka (GoSL) and the LTTE to accept the good offices of Norway as facilitator, Erik Solheim, Norway's envoy to the process, met LTTE leader Prabhakaran on 1 November 2001. Immediately following the discussion, Solheim convened a press conference in the LTTE-controlled Kilincochchi to announce that the LTTE was prepared to engage in official negotiations on arriving at a negotiated settlement to the conflict within a united Sri Lanka.

A congenial environment for direct talks was further created by the formation of the UNP-led coalition government headed by Prime Minister Ranil Wickremesinghe following the general elections of 5 December 2001. The LTTE, which denounced and successfully resisted and rolled back the 'War for Peace'* military campaign of the People's Alliance-led government and identified President Kumaratunga as its chief antagonist, felt comfortable in dealing with the UNP-led government which contested the general elections on the platform that there should be direct talks with the LTTE and indicated its support for an LTTE-controlled interim administration for the north-east.

With the renewal of the peace initiatives facilitated by Norway, following the formation of the United National Front (UNF) government, the LTTE once again asserted its right to conduct negotiations as a legitimate organization and with equality and

*The failure of 1994–5 talks led to the outbreak of Eelam War III. In this war, President Kumaratunga succeeded in snatching control of Jaffna from the LTTE. This war is described as a 'War for Peace'. –Editor.

dignity. This was to entail the lifting of the ban—a demand supported by the Tamil National Alliance (TNA), which had secured a convincing majority of the parliamentary seats for the north-east. It is abundantly evident from statements and interviews given by LTTE's chief negotiator and political adviser, Balasingham, and the head of the political wing of the LTTE, Thamilchelvan, that the LTTE would not agree to direct negotiations with the government without the ban being lifted. It also demanded that the LTTE should not be proscribed by the government if the two were to engage with each other in talks. The demand of the LTTE's de-proscription, on the other hand, was viewed with extreme suspicion by broad sections of the Sinhala polity as a ruse by the LTTE to have the international ban lifted. The JVP, in particular, was strident in its demand that the ban should only be lifted once the LTTE gave up the demand for Tamil Eelam and laid down its arms.

Prime Minister Wickremesinghe, in his Policy Statement of 22 January 2002, cited the deproscription issue as being central to future negotiations and hinted at the possibility of having the ban lifted:

> The main issue for the commencement of talks with the LTTE is the international and local ban on the LTTE. . . . I see two fundamental matters which we should consider in this regard. The first is the guarantee of the honesty of the LTTE as regards the Peace Talks. The second matter is preventing adverse effects any local arrangement would have on the international ban on LTTE. Based on these two factors, under the umbrella of a 'security net' amendments governing the regulations of the local ban should be considered whilst safeguarding international opinion (emphasis added).

This declaration of 'intent' by Prime Minister Wickremesinghe was welcomed by the LTTE immediately.[31] Wickremesinghe further added that 'the de-proscription of the LTTE will be a recognition of the legitimacy of the Tamil people's struggle. It is not a concession by the government but an acknowledgement of our position as the authentic representatives of the Tamil people.'

At this stage, it may be useful to look a bit more closely into the de-proscription issue, from a national as well as an international context. The LTTE was first banned in Sri Lanka in

1979. Following the Indo–Lanka Accord of July 1987, the LTTE and other militant organizations were granted amnesty. However, the 6th Amendment and the PTA remained on the statute books. The ban on the LTTE was once again imposed with the outbreak of hostilities on 11 October 1987, and revoked with the commencement of the Premadasa government-LTTE talks in 1989. During this period, the LTTE formed the People's Front of the Liberation Tigers of Tamil Eelam and registered it as a political party with the Election Commissioner. When the talks and the ceasefire collapsed on 11 June 1990, the ban was not reimposed. Neither did the Kumaratunga government reimpose the ban when the PA–LTTE talks of 1994–5 collapsed.

The LTTE was eventually banned in Sri Lanka on 27 January 1998 under the then prevailing Emergency Regulations, following the bomb blast at Dalada Maligawa on 25 January 1998. With the PA government allowing the Emergency to lapse in the face of having lost the majority in Parliament, the president issued orders to proscribe the LTTE anew under Section 27 of the PTA on 4 July 2001. The foregoing account clearly reveals that the imposition and the lifting of the ban on the LTTE are nothing new and have kept pace with politico–military developments within Sri Lanka.

As regards foreign restrictions or the proscription of the LTTE, the first foreign government to ban the LTTE was India. The ban was effected in June 1991 following the assassination of Rajiv Gandhi. The US Statement Department designated the LTTE a terrorist organization under the Anti-Terrorism Act of 1996 on 8 October 1997. Following the 11 September 2001 terrorist attacks in the United States, the LTTE was included in a list of organizations under an Executive Order signed by President George Bush on 23 September 2002, blocking the assets of organizations and individuals linked to terrorism. On 28 February 2001, Britain included the LTTE in a list of 21 international organizations recommended for proscription under the Terrorism Act of 2000. On 21 December 2001, Australia named the LTTE as a terrorist organization whose assets would be frozen. Australia cited this as a follow-up to the United Nations Security Council resolution 1373 of 28 September 2001, to suppress the financing of terrorism.

The international community, however, never wanted this ban on LTTE to come in the way of advancing the Sri Lankan peace process. For instance, in an exclusive interview to a special correspondent of the *Daily News* (21 January 2002), US Ambassador Ashley Wills said: 'If the Sri Lankan government decided to deproscribe the LTTE . . . that would be its sovereign decision. In the right circumstances, the US will understand why that decision was taken.' He further added, 'if the Sri Lankan government felt it necessary to lift the ban on the Tigers that would be noticed by my Government, but it will not determine our actions'.

In this context, it is necessary to recall that the day following the ban on the LTTE by Britain, the British Hgh Commission issued a statement that the ban 'should have no bearing on the peace process in Sri Lanka'. The statement further added that 'the UK strongly urges both the Government of Sri Lanka and the LTTE to begin peace talks as soon as possible'. This sentiment was repeated recently, when British High Commissioner Linda Duffield declared that the lifting of the ban on the LTTE in Sri Lanka would not bind the ban imposed by her government.[32] Likewise, the other key actor, the Government of India, although not intervening directly on the deproscription issue, has consistently taken the position that the conflict would have to be solved through negotiations with the LTTE.

The message from the 'international community', hence, was clear: go ahead and lift the ban on the LTTE, if it is an obstacle to commencing negotiations. And this is precisely what the GoSL did. The government eventually lifted the proscription on the LTTE and also took the decision that, although the PTA would remain in the statute books, the provision would not be used in any arrests or detentions during the peace process. The strategic question as to how to utilize the de-proscription of the LTTE as a leverage to secure definite commitments and guarantees from the LTTE which would satisfy the LTTE's demand for 'equality' while ensuring that the LTTE 'earns' the de-proscription was never given serious consideration. 'Appeasement' towards the LTTE, in short, was the approach adopted by the UNF government, and, is appears, advocated by key actors in the international community.

Be that as it may, on 22 February 2002, the GoSL and the LTTE signed a Ceasefire Agreement (CFA). The stated objectives of the CFA were: (i) to bring an end to armed hostilities; and (ii) to create a positive atmosphere in which further steps towards negotiations on a lasting solution can be taken. A Sri Lanka Monitoring Mission (SLMM) comprising Scandinavian countries but headed by Norway was set up to monitor the CFA. The SLMM was mandated to make a ruling on ceasefire violations, with no powers of enforcement.

The Head of State, President Kumaratunga, claimed that the UNP-led government had not consulted her on the contents of the CFA and accused the government and Norway of marginalizing her from the process. Civil society organizations and the human rights lobby also felt that inadequate attention had been given to human rights in the CFA. The opposition parties and the non-LTTE Tamil parties, which refused to recognize the LTTE as the 'sole representative' of the Tamil people, felt that the CFA was flawed since the SLMM was not given access to LTTE-controlled areas. Despite these concerns, it is indisputable that there was overwhelming support for the CFA, and immense relief amongst broad sections of the populace on both sides of the ethnic divide, that the guns had fallen silent.

Following the signing of the CFA and a period of preparatory work, official Track One negotiations commenced in September 2002. These talks came to be labelled by the parties as 'sessions in Round One'. 'Round One' was defined as approximating the stage of normalization and de-escalation. Since then there have been six sessions of negotiations in Round One of official talks between the GoSL and the LTTE, held in venues outside Sri Lanka. Norway chaired these negotiations. Appendix 6.1 gives an overview of the key decisions taken at these talks and some issues related to those decisions.

Ironically, it was precisely during the period of the CFA that the LTTE stepped up its gross human rights violations, including political killings, child conscription, extortion and abductions. This led to the US State Department repeatedly demanding that the LTTE should renounce terrorism between 'word' and 'deed'. The discrepancy in the LTTE's position on terrorism in words and deeds constrained the US from inviting the LTTE to the

Washington Conference of the Donors in April 2002. This was the precursor to the Tokyo Conference in June 2002, where Sri Lanka's Western donors and Japan put together a promised package of US $4.5 billion for the development of Sri Lanka as a whole, and the rehabilitation and reconstruction of the conflict-ravaged north and east.

A discussion on the international context would not be complete without looking into the role of Norway in the ongoing peace process. One area that needs to be re-examined is its hitherto dual role as the facilitator/mediator and monitor. As a facilitator/mediator, Norway's primary concern is to the peace process and not rocking the peace boat. As such, when it comes to its role as the head of the SLMM, it has sought to subordinate its monitoring role to its mediatory role, to the extent of turning a blind eye to gross ceasefire and human rights violations by the LTTE and sometimes the government. In the context that the SLMM has no powers of enforcement, it has to rely on 'naming and shaming' as the main instrument of deterrence. This Norway has unfortunately desisted from doing for fear of embarrassing the LTTE. It also goes contrary to its agenda of empowerment and legitimization of the LTTE as a 'partner' in the peace process. The outcome of this deficiency has been the virtual granting of a licence to the LTTE to engage in child conscription and political killings.

It is in this context that Norway should take seriously the recommendation made by a team of concerned academics and intellectuals (i.e. Tyrol Ferdinands, Kumar Rupesinghe, Paikiasothy Saravanamuttu, Jayadeva Uyangoda and Norbert Ropers) in their monograph 'The Sri Lankan Peace Process at Crossroads', that its should 'Explore together with the parties how the leadership of the Sri Lanka Monitoring Mission (SLMM) could be handed over to another country without endangering the stability of the truce in order to ensure no conflicts of interest between the roles of facilitator and of the monitor.'

Ironically, and paradoxically, it is India's multiple agenda and geopolitical interests and concerns which may ultimately bring it back on the scene with renewed vigour and changed strategy, but not necessarily as a mediator. Perhaps, it is a reality that neither Colombo nor the Tamil polity and resistance can ignore. In any event, Norwegian facilitation has clearly factored in India's role as a regional power through prompt consultations with New Delhi as the process evolves. This is bound to intensify in any future dispensation.

NOTES

1. For a useful overview of state discrimination and non-violent forms of agitations by Tamil parliamentary parties see Chapters 1 and 2 in Ketheshwaran Loganathan, *Sri Lanka: Lost Opportunities*, University of Colombo, 1996.
2. The policy of 'standardization' while attempting to balance the imbalances between the districts and ensure that more rural Sinhala youths would be assured of places in the universities, introduced a form of 'affirmative action' based on ethnicity. As a result, the number of Tamil students entering science-based courses declined from 35.3 per cent in 1970/71 to 19 per cent in 1975, with the most affected hailing from Jaffna schools.
3. The JVP revolt in 1971 was suppressed ruthlessly by the use of force by the Sri Lankan government. Subsequently, the Sinhala youths affiliated to the JVP were lectured on the virtues of conformism and non-violent political action. An estimated 75,000 people were killed during this revolt. Eventually, the JVP has emerged as a mainstream political force sharing power since the 2004 elections. This transformation has come only after another round of revolt during the late 1980s and early 1990s. A serious study of this transformation is due, but beyond the scope of this chapter due to time and space constraints –Editor.
4. Varatharajaperumal, who later became the Chief Minister of the north-east Provincial Government following the Indo–Lanka Accord of 1987, is perhaps the exception because, on his release from prison in 1976, he entered the Jaffna University and graduated, before once again being drawn into the vortex of Tamil militancy.
5. K.M. de Silva, *A History of Sri Lanka*, University of California Press, p. 530.
6. R. Edrisinha and N. Selvakkumaran, 'Constitutional Changes in Sri Lanka under since Independence', in *Sri Lanka Journal of Social Sciences*, 1990.
7. M.R. Narayan Swamy, *Tigers of Lanka: From Boys to Guerrillas*, p. 56. It may be added that the TNT was to later emerge as the Liberation Tigers of Tamil Eelam in 1977.
8. The two farms were settled by Sinhalese ex-convicts following the 1977 anti-Tamil riots.

9. Ketheshwaran Loganathan, *Sri Lanka: Lost Opportunities*, p. 189.
10. The term 'colonization' in the post-colonial Sri Lanka context refers to state-sponsored settlement schemes built around irrigation schemes, which was perceived by the Tamils as an encroachment into the 'traditional homeland' in the north-East aimed at changing the demographic composition.
11. A Commission of Inquiry headed by retired Chief Justice M.C. Sansoni, which was set up to identify persons and organizations responsible, found that the law enforcement machinery of the state, in particular the police, had failed to contain the violence and were, in many instances, guilty by association. Politicians and members of parliament belonging to the ruling party were also accused of fomenting violence.
12. 'Broadcast to the Nation' on 29 July 1983.
13. *Daily Telegraph*, 11 July 1983. Cited in, 'Sri Lanka: Racism and the Authoritarian State', *Race and Class* (1984), vol. 26, no. 1, p. 127.
14. Cabinet Minister Nisanka Wijeratne, 'Parliamentary Debates' (Hansard), 21 August 1980.
15. Rajan Hoole, 'Sri Lanka: The Arrogance of Power, University Teachers for Human Rights' (UTHR) (2001), p. 49.
16. This section is largely based on Chapter 4 of *Sri Lanka: Lost Opportunites*, by this writer, and the author's recollections as a member of the Tamil Delegation at the Thimpu Talks.
17. *Daily News*, 13 August 1983.
18. Personal recollections of the author.
19. Jayadeva Uyangoda, 'Negotiations for Conflict Resolution: Lessons from Sri Lanka's Recent Past'.
20. S.D. Muni, *Pangs of Proximity*, New Delhi: Sage, 1993, p. 52.
21. Cited in 'Indo Sri Lanka Agreement', Foreign Affairs Reports, July–August 1987 (Indian Council of World Affairs, New Delhi), p. 211.
22. English translation of speech in M.R.Narayan Swamy, 'Tigers of Lanka', p. 251.
23. The author was present at the meeting with Indian Prime Minister Rajiv Gandhi which took place on 28 July 1987.
24. Anton Balasingham, *The Politics of Duplicity: Re-Visiting the Jaffna Talks* (Surrey: *Fairmax*, 2000).
25. There is an abundance of literature available on the LTTE–PA Talks of 1994–5. For some useful discussions see Liz Phillispon, 'Breaking recurring themes in the the cycles of war and peace in Sri Lanka', CSGG Research Paper 3, London School of Economics, 1999; Jayadeva Uyangoda, 'Negotiations for Conflict Resolution', *Pravada*, 2000, vol. 6, nos. 7 and 8; Anton Balasingham, *Politics of Duplicity*. P. Rajanayagam, 'Govt-LTTE Negotiations 1994–5', in Kumar Rupesinghe (ed.), *Negotiating Peace in Sri Lanka*, 1998; and Isak Svensson, 'Confidence Building Measures in Intrastate Conflict: Lessons

from the 1994–5 Peace Process in Sri Lanka', (Department of Peace and Conflict Research, Uppsala University, 2001).
26. Ibid., Svensson, 'Confidence Building Measures'.
27. Letter of 9 September 1994 from Prime Minister Chandrika Kumaratunga to LTTE Leader V. Prabhakaran.
28. Balasingham, *The Politics of Duplicity*, p. 109.
29. Svensson, 'Confidence Building Measures', p. 26.
30. Lakshman Gunasekera, 'Is the LTTE ready to share power?', *Sunday Observer*, 20 May 2001.
31. Tamil Net Website, 23 January 2003.
32. *Daily News*, 26 January 2002.

APPENDIX 6.1

AN OVERVIEW OF TRACK ONE NEGOTIATIONS FACILITATED BY NORWAY

1ST SESSION OF TALKS AT SATTAHIP, THAILAND (16–18 SEPTEMBER 2002)

DECISIONS

To set up a Joint Task Force for humanitarian and reconstruction activities. This would involve a 'partnership between the GoSL and the LTTE' and will have the responsibility for identifying, financing, and monitoring urgent humanitarian and reconstruction activities in the north and east. The priorities were identified as (a) stepping-up humanitarian mine action, and (b) accelerating resettlement and rehabilitation of IDPs.

SOME ISSUES

(i) The concept of 'partnership between GoSL and the LTTE' was seen by sections of civil society and polity to be contrary to the principle of inclusiveness in negotiations. Others viewed it as the only pragmatic step given the prevailing situation.
(ii) The nature, composition, and legality of the proposed Task Force became a contentious issue, particularly since the LTTE was firm that any mechanism should not place them in a situation of 'subordination' to Colombo and should ensure for itself control over funds to be allocated in the north-east.

2ND SESSION OF TALKS AT ROSE GARDENS, THAILAND (31 OCTOBER–3 NOVEMBER 2002)

DECISIONS

(i) It was agreed to set up the following sub-committees comprising nominees/members of GoSL and the LTTE. The proposed Joint Task Force was given the form of a 'Sub-Committee on Immediate Humanitarian and Rehabilitation needs in the N-E' (SIHRN). The priority areas were identified as (a) resettling and rehabilitating IDPs; and (b) rehabilitating war-affected widows and children.

(ii) The formation of the Sub-Committee on De-escalation and Normalization to ensure resettlement, the return of private property and the resumption of economic activities was agreed to.

(iii) Author decision was the setting-up of a sub-committee to commence work in connection with relevant political matters. To quote: 'The parties will jointly and separately address in depth, at the current stage of the peace process, relevant subjects such as other peace processes, political solutions to ethnic conflicts, models and systems of governments, issues of post-conflict transition, coordination of international assistance, and reconciliation processes.'

Some Issues

The Sub-Committee on Immediate Humanitarian and Rehabilitation Needs (SIHRN) was not perceived as an interim instrument linked to a constitutional reform process. In fact great pains were taken to demonstrate that it was not an interim administration. This was once again seen as a pragmatic and innovative measure to accommodate LTTE concerns that the formation of an interim administration within existing constitutional provisions would be tantamount to it accepting the Sri Lankan constitution. It is a moot point as to whether it would not have been more prudent to create an interim administration giving the required 'pride of place' to the LTTE, but yet bringing it within the ambit of a constitutional reform process.

This issue has once again surfaced in the present context and in the run-up to the proposed Tokyo Donor Conference in June 2003. This will be dealt with in the concluding section of the Appendix.

3rd Session of Talks in Oslo, Norway (2–5 December 2002)

Decisions

(i) Responding to a proposal by the leadership of the LTTE, the parties agreed to explore a solution founded on the principle of internal self-determination in areas of historical habitation of the Tamil speaking peoples, based on a federal structure within a united Sri Lanka.

(ii) The parties also agreed to the setting-up of the North-East Reconstruction Fund (NERF).

(iii) The LTTE was to engage in a partnership with the UNICEF to draw up an action plan for restoring normalcy to the lives of children.

SOME ISSUES

The decision to 'explore' federal structures was generally hailed as a breakthrough. The 'Oslo Declaration' was also perceived by sections of civil society and polity as a case of the LTTE having abandoned its demand for a separate state. However, there is another body of opinion that it is premature to arrive at the above conclusion, since the LTTE committed itself to only 'explore' a solution based on a federal structure. It is also not clear whether the two parties have the same understanding of the concept of 'federalism' and whether that commitment has become 'internalized' within the two parties, or whether it is only a response to international pressure to start negotiating a political and constitutional settlement.

4TH SESSION OF TALKS AT ROSE GARDENS, THAILAND (6–9 JANUARY 2003)

DECISIONS

(i) The Sub-Committee on De-escalation and Normalization becomes defunct in view of issues relating to High Security Zones (HSZs) in Jaffna. The LTTE had, before the talks, decided to pull out of the Sub-Committee to express its dissatisfaction over the extent of the HSZs in Jaffna.

(ii) An Action Plan for an accelerated Resettlement Programme for the Jaffna District, with support from the UNHCR was agreed upon.

(iii) The parties indorsed the rapid establishment of the north-east Reconstruction Fund (NERF) and the recommendation to select the World Bank as the custodian of the Fund.

(iv) The parties agreed, 'To commence a process of discussion of human rights issues'.

(v) The formation of a Committee to 'ensure the effective inclusion of gender issues in the peace process' was agreed to.

SOME ISSUES

(i) The key issue is whether there is any precedent for an international fund managed by a multilateral agency and audited by an international auditor in a pre-settlement situation like Sri Lanka. If not, is this then a unique Sri Lankan case experimented on by the multilateral agencies and the international donor community? It is also pertinent to mention that as in the case of SIHRN, the NERF has remerged as an issue in the run-up to the proposed Tokyo donor conference in June with the LTTE expressing dissatisfaction over the ineffectiveness of SIHRN and delays in setting-up NERF. This will be elaborated in the concluding section of this note.

(ii) Another issue relates to the High Security Zones in Jaffna which are perceived by both the LTTE and broad sections of the Jaffna populace as an intrusion into their means of livelihoods (since fertile agricultural lands come under the HSZs) and freedom of movement. The security forces on the other hand have been stressing on their security considerations since demobilization of the LTTE is not on the agenda.

5TH SESSION OF TALKS IN BERLIN (7–8 FEBRUARY 2003)

DECISIONS

(i) The parties reported that the 'agreement on World Bank custodianship of NERF is close to finalization and will be signed within the next week'.

(ii) Ian Martin, former Secretary-General of Amnesty International, was involved to 'draw up a roadmap for human rights issues relating to the peace process'.

(iii) A commitment was made by the LTTE to cease recruitment of children.

SOME ISSUES

(i) The actual signing of the agreement with the World Bank, which was to have taken place 'next week' never materialized and the status of NERF remains ambivalent.

(ii) The announcement by the LTTE as regards its decision to cease recruiting children and the call along with the GoSL for a 'roadmap for human rights issues' was generally welcomed, but with some caution given the past gap between word and deed.

6TH SESSION OF TALKS IN HAKONE, JAPAN (18–24 MARCH 2003)

DECISIONS

(i) In order to prevent several incidents at sea, which included the sinking of a LTTE trawler suspected to be smuggling arms by the Sri Lankan navy, the parties agreed to 'strengthen the mandate and capacity' of the SLMM.

(ii) They also agreed to expand some preliminary issues and a framework for political matters into a 'complete plan' at the 7th Session of the talks.

(iii) Following a proposal by the GoSL to prepare for local government elections in the north and east, the LTTE offered to favourably consider the holding of such elections.

(iv) The parties asked their international human rights adviser, Ian Martin, to draft a Declaration of Human Rights and Humanitarian Principles, the planning of a programme of human rights training for LTTE cadres and government officials and the strengthening of the Human Rights Commission of Sri Lanka to enable it to develop the capacity for increasingly effective monitoring throughout the country.

SOME ISSUES

It is generally believed that the human rights roadmap plan presented by Ian Martin to the parties was not viewed favourably by the LTTE; hence the request to him to come up with another draft for the next round of talks. This development was viewed with deep suspicion and disappointment by sections of civil society, which hold the view that a human rights agreement should inform the peace process at the outset. It was also widely held that the government itself was not too enthusiastic about a human rights agreement.

SHIFT IN THE PEACE AGENDA: INTERIM ADMINISTRATION

The 7th session of talks was put off with the LTTE sending a letter to Prime Minister Ranil Wickremesinghe dated 21 April 2003 that it had 'decided to suspend its participation in the negotiations for the time being, and to not attend the Tokyo donor conference in June 2003. However, the LTTE stressed that it was still committed to a negotiated settlement and was not pulling out of the peace process. The reasons cited for their decision to suspend participation in the direct talks included: (i) Dissatisfaction at not being invited for the international donor conference in Washington on 14 April 2004, in preparation for the major donor conference scheduled to be held in Japan in June; and (ii) delays in restoring normalcy in the 'Tamil areas' and in addressing the grievances of the internally displaced.

Further, on 21 May 2003, the LTTE, in a letter addressed to the Norwegian deputy foreign minister requested him to inform Prime Minister Ranil Wickremesinghe that the LTTE wanted an 'interim administrative structure' to be set up with 'adequate powers to undertake north-eastern reconstruction and development activities'. The LTTE made the response from the government to its request a factor that would determine its decision to participate at the scheduled Tokyo Donor Conference or not.

The Tokyo Donor Conference of June 9–10 went ahead without the LTTE's presence. While the government gave a pledge to arrive at innovative mechanisms of delivery for the north-east, the international community 'took the opportunity to support the establishment by the parties of the necessary administrative structure for the effective reconstruction and development of the North and East'. The donors further stressed on the concept of 'partnership' between the GoSL and the LTTE with 'adequate safeguards[r] secure the interests of all other communities'. The Conference also emphasized the need for 'flexibility by the Government of Sri Lanka and the LTTE in accepting various forms of assistance from the donor community', and the donor community 'expressed its willingness to assist capacity building to enhance good governance so as to ensure accountable, transparent, speedy and efficient implementation of projects supported with its assistance'.

Following the Tokyo Donor Conference, the much talked about Human Rights benchmarking and the Ian Martin HR Roadmap and the impending discussions on core political issues were placed in the backburner. The agenda shifted towards the setting up of interim arrangements and administration.

7. Tackling Insurgency: The Nepal Case

Deepak Thapa

Since 13 February 1996, Nepal has been caught in a vortex of violence initiated by the Communist Party of Nepal (Maoist), CPN (Maoist), in an attempt to establish a 'new people's democracy' through a 'people's war'. Since then nearly 10,000 people have lost their lives in the fighting that has spread throughout the country, and at the time of writing, there seems no end in sight to it.

There have been two ceasefires since 1996: the first between July and November 2001, and the second between January and August 2003. But despite the promise of relief from the violence neither resulted in anything. Rather, the renewal of hostilities since both ceasefires has been more violent than the previous stages. After the end of the first ceasefire, the Nepali army, which had been watching from the sidelines, also went into battle and since then the ferocity of the fighting has increased a great deal.

This chapter is an attempt to outline how the Nepali state has responded to this internal crisis, which has taken the form of a veritable civil war. It begins with a brief political outline of the country since the founding of the modern state of Nepal, and then looks briefly at the many attempts at rebellion by non-state actors before the beginning of the 'people's war'. The last section deals with the Maoist uprising itself and the state's response to it, before concluding with some recommendations.

POLITICAL BACKGROUND

The nation-state of Nepal was founded during 1768–9, when Prithvi Narayan Shah, the ruler of Gorkha, a small principality in the central hills of Nepal, conquered the Kathmandu Valley at the end of a campaign that had lasted nearly 25 years. Until then, what is of today Nepal was made up of various tiny kingdoms and principalities.

King Prithvi Narayan Shah and some of his descendants did not stop with Kathmandu and continued with their expansionary campaign. By the early nineteenth century, the Gorkha empire spanned an area from the Teesta river in the east up to the Sutlej river in the west, and reached down from the Himalayas in the north to the Gangetic Plain in the south. Unfortunately for the Shah kings, their aggressive military successes collided with the other great power on the rise in India—the English East India Company. In the inevitable clash of arms, Gorkha (or Nepal, as the British called the kingdom after the name Kathmandu Valley was known by) was defeated after a war which lasted several years, and had to surrender a fair chunk of the territory it had conquered in the preceding years. The country's physical borders have remained more or less fixed since then.

Court intrigues had begun soon after the death of Prithvi Narayan Shah and intensified in the aftermath of the war with the British. Following a period of instability during which the country saw a succession of prime ministers, in 1846, a young courtier, Jang Bahadur Rana, emerged as the undisputed leader. He established the Rana dynasty of all-powerful prime ministers and reduced the monarchy to a purely ceremonial role. Rana rule finally ended in 1951 when King Tribhuvan, with the help of democratic forces led by the Nepali Congress Party and independent India, restored the glory of his throne and a new government consisting of both Ranas and commoners was formed.[1]

The experiment in coalition did not last long and led to a period of instability that was to plague the nation for almost a decade. The country saw a total of ten governments between February 1950 and the first parliamentary elections in 1959. In those elections held under a new constitution, the Nepali Congress won a landslide victory and B.P. Koirala became the first democratically elected prime minister of Nepal in May 1959. But his tenure was to last a bare 18 months and he was ousted in December 1960 by King Tribhuvan's son, King Mahendra, who scrapped the constitution, banned political parties, dissolved Parliament, and put many political leaders behind bars.

In 1962, Mahendra introduced the 'partyless' Panchayat system of governance, which essentially devolved a great deal of power upon the king while allowing for some semblance of democracy. Things did not change until 1990, that is, when a mass movement by political parties, including the Nepali Congress and an alliance of Communist Parties, forced the king, Mahendra's son Birendra, to disband the Panchayat regime and usher in multiparty democracy once again.

An interim government of the Nepali Congress, the communists, and the palace loyalists, led by Nepali Congress president Krishna Prasad Bhattarai, was given the task of drafting a new constitution and holding general elections to a Parliament. A committee consisting of representatives from the Nepali Congress, the communist alliance, and the palace put together a constitution and elections were held in May 1991. The Nepali Congress mustered a majority and formed the country's first elected government in more than 30 years under Girija Prasad Koirala.

The Koirala government lasted three years before internal bickering within the ruling party reached unmanageable proportions. The prime minister's response was to dissolve Parliament and call for an election in November 1994, which resulted in a hung Parliament. As the largest party in Parliament, the Communist Party of Nepal (Unified Marxist–Leninist) formed the government under Man Mohan Adhikari. But since his party did not have parliamentary majority, it was vulnerable to attempts to dislodge it. This soon became a reality in September 1995 when Adhikari was replaced by a coalition led by Sher Bahadur Deuba of the Nepali Congress with support from smaller parties, including the Rastriya Prajatantra Party (RPP), the party of those formerly associated with the Panchayat regime. It was while Deuba was prime minister that the CPN (Maoist) began its insurgency.

Adhikari's ouster was to see the beginning of coalition politics that was to plague the country for a full five years. Deuba did not last long either and neither did any of the other governments that followed. Table 7.1 shows the various governments that took office during the tenure of the second Parliament.

In May 1999, the third general elections since the 1990

TABLE 7.1: GOVERNMENTS DURING THE SECOND PARLIAMENT 1994–9[2]

Dates	Prime Minister—Party	Coalition partners
Nov. 1994–Sep. 1995	Man Mohan Adhikari—CPN (UML)[a]	
Sep. 1995–Mar. 1997	Sher Bahadur Deuba—Nepali Congress	RPP,[b] NSP[c]
Mar. 1997–Oct. 1997	Lokendra Bahadur Chand—RPP	CPN (UML), NSP
Oct. 1997–Apr. 1998	Surya Bahadur Thapa – RPP	Nepali Congress, NSP
Apr.–Aug. 1998	Girija Prasad Koirala—Nepali Congress	
Aug.–Dec. 1998	Girija Prasad Koirala—Nepali Congress	CPN (ML)[d]
Dec. 1998–May 1999	Girija Prasad Koirala—Nepali Congress	CPN (UML), NSP

Notes: [a] *Communist Party of Nepal (Unified Marxist-Leninist)*
[b] *Rashtriya Prajatantra Party*
[c] *Nepal Sadbhavana Party, a party that claims to champion the cause of the people of Tarai origin.*
[d] *Communist Party of Nepal (Marxist-Leninist), which split from CPN (UML) in March 1998. The two parties subsequently united in February 2002 as the CPN (UML).*

restoration of democracy were held. The Nepali Congress emerged victorious once again and it formed a government under Krishna Prasad Bhattarai. But his term did not last even for a year, and in March 2000 Girija Prasad Koirala ousted him to become prime minister once again.

On 1 June 2001, King Birendra and his immediate family along with various members of the royal family were killed in a bloody massacre perpetrated by the crown prince, who too lost his life. As the next in line, Birendra's brother Gyanendra ascended the throne.

In July, Girija Prasad Koirala resigned paving the way for Sher Bahadur Deuba once again to take over as prime minister. Deuba called for a ceasefire with the Maoists and three rounds of talks were held with the rebels. In November 2001, the Maoists retreated from negotiations and resumed the fighting. Deuba imposed a state of emergency, outlawed the CPN (Maoist) and its fraternal organizations and termed the insurgents 'terrorists'.

As per constitutional requirements, the emergency was ratified by a two-thirds majority, including by the main opposition CPN (UML), at the end of three months. But when the time came for a second ratification after six months, Deuba was instructed by his party not to extend the emergency; he went ahead anyway and called for a parliamentary session to push through the ratification. And when the party leaderhip pulled him up for taking such a unilateral decision, he even dissolved Parliament and called for fresh elections in six months. Deuba was expelled from the Nepali Congress, and he formed his own outfit, the Nepali Congress (Democratic).

As the elections approached, it became obvious that given the unrelenting Maoist activity in the hinterland, and particularly after two devastating attacks on government posts in early September, it would be impossible for the people to come out and vote. The political parties reached a broad understanding on this issue and authorized Deuba to apprise the king. Deuba recommended the postponement of elections by more than a year. The next day, on 4 October 2002, the king, instead, removed Deuba from office for his 'incompetence' to hold elections as promised and assumed executive authority.

Since then the king has appointed three prime ministers: in October 2002, Lokendra Bahadur Chand, in June 2003, Surya Bahadur Thapa, and in April 2004, Sher Bahadur Deuba once again. It was during Chand's prime ministership that the Maoists and the government agreed to a ceasefire and two rounds of talks were held. The talks were sabotaged when the Royal Nepal Army (RNA) killed 19 arrested Maoists even as the ceasefire was in progress, and refused to curtail their movements at district headquarters. The Maoists walked out of the talks in August 2003.

Opposition to the State: Pre-1990

The course of Nepali history until the 1990 restoration of democracy has been full of bumps. There were conspiracies and assassinations within the Palace, mostly limited to a small circle of rulers, which did not affect the country at large. But the nature of the Gorkha conquest and subsequent Rana rule meant that there were anti-state stirrings at various stages of Nepal's modern history. Much of the resistance came from new territories subjugated by the Shah rulers. According to Mahesh Chandra Regmi:

> The Rai inhabitants of the Dudhkoshi–Arun region were the first to organise a rebellion soon after the region came under Gorkhali control in 1773. During the war with China, the Murmis of Nuwakot, the Rais of Majhkirat, and the Limbus of Pallokirat again rose up in revolt. The Limbus even joined the Chinese side in large numbers to fight against the Gorkhalis. In the trans-Bheri region, the defeated states rebelled against the Gorkhali rule during the Chinese invasion. . . . Similar insurrections were reported in Accham and Doti.[3]

Gorkha retribution for rebellion was very high-handed. Execution was a preferred method of penalty. In other cases limbs were amputated or the caste status was degraded.[4] However, once the worst was over, the state took a more reconciliatory stance and various forms of amnesty were granted to the rebels.[5] That, however, did not end the opposition to Gorkha rule. As Table 7.2 illustrates, different ethnic groups did rise up against the state, but given the diffuse nature of these uprisings, they did not actually provide a credible threat to the state itself.

It was only in the twentieth century that some form of organized opposition against the state represented by the Ranas began to be seen in Nepal. The Rana regime represented an

TABLE 7.2: ETHNIC UPRISINGS IN NEPAL

Year	Incident	Area
1770	Limbu revolt and expulsion	East of Arun
1793	Murmi (Tamang) revolt	Nuwakot
1808	Khambu (Rai) revolt	Bhojpur
1858	Gurung (Sukhdev) revolt	Lamjung
1876	Magar (Lakhan) revolt	Gorkha
1877	Gurung (Supati) revolt	Gorkha
1950	Kiranti insurgency	Eastern hills

Source: Adapted from Harka Gurung, 'Rastriyeta ra janajati', Social Science Research Council Essay Collection, in press. (Adapted from www.nepalresearch.com.)

epoch that led to much impoverishment of the countryside, resulting in large-scale migrations into India. The Ranas were also afraid of outside influences entering Nepal, which could challenge their hold on the state, and kept Nepal completely isolated from the outside world. But because a continuous stream of people was migrating to India to escape penury from the hills, it led to a substantial settlement of Nepalis in India. And it was from these Nepalis in India that the first stirrings against the Ranas began in that country, mainly in the form of newspapers published there.

Within Nepal itself, it was only in 1936 that a popular organization calling for political reforms came into existence. But the Nepal Praja Parishad did not last long. In 1940 all the leaders of the Parishad were arrested and four of them were executed. That, however, was only the beginning since a more sustained form of opposition began in India with the establishment of the Nepali National Congress in Benares in 1946, and the Nepal Democratic Congress in Calcutta in 1948 and B.P. Koirala was elected president. Both had the overthrow of the Rana regime as their primary objective. The two parties united in 1950 to become the Nepali Congress and made a changeover from their earlier strategy of non-violent opposition to an armed rebellion against the Ranas. The pomp and pageantry of the Nepali army was not able to sustain a fight against the rebels and the fighting, which was joined by sections of the Communist Party of Nepal established in 1949, went on for three months. The success of the insurrection was the first instance of an anti-state movement succeeding in forcing the capitulation of the establishment.

Even as the political games continued between 1951 and the 1990 People's Movement, there were a number of incidents which challenged the state directly. While some were insignificant in scope, others had the potential to disrupt the functioning of the state. The major episodes and the government reaction are outlined here in brief.

A. *The Gorkha Dal Uprising*: The Gorkha Dal had been formed by a group of disgruntled Ranas who were against the Rana–Congress coalition, and who tried to incite the army to rise against the government. But determined response by the government nipped the incipient revolt in the bud, before it could foment any trouble that could have led to a clash of arms.[6]

B. *The Raksha Dal Mutiny*: In January 1952, the Raksha Dal, a paramilitary force created largely out of the Mukti Sena, the Nepali Congress's army against the Ranas, staged a revolt and thrust its leadership to K.I. Singh, a former Mukti Sena commander. Singh had been in custody in Kathmandu since 1951 for staging a rebellion against the 'Delhi Compromise' and had been forcefully disarmed by government troops with Indian help.[7] The government moved in and forced Singh to flee the country.[8]

C. *Bhim Dutt Pant rebellion*: In April 1953, a popular peasant leader, Bhim Dutt Pant, led a band of around 700 farmers in the area around Dhangarhi in western Nepal in an attempted revolt supposedly inspired by K.I. Singh.[9] A weak Nepali state again had to seek Indian military assistance to suppress the movement. Pant himself was killed in an encounter in August.[10]

D. *Nepali Congress Insurgency*: After the overthrow of the B.P. Koirala government, the Congress leaders who had fled to India began rebuilding the party structure in exile. Even though many of the leaders were in jail in Nepal, the Nepali Congress was able to put together an underground organization in many parts of Nepal, and, in autumn 1961, the Congress launched a campaign of sabotage and violent attacks against the government, presumably with covert support from Indian Prime Minister Jawaharlal Nehru.[11] It was an attempt by the Congress to force the king to come to an understanding with the rebels,[12] but after the Chinese launched a surprise attack on India in October 1962, India quickly told the rebels to cease their operations. The short-lived Congress insurgency was not able to achieve much despite its escalation in a number of places. A total of 77 people were killed on the rebels' side while government forces suffered 31 dead.[13]

E. *The Jhapa Uprising*: Events following the royal takeover of 1960 had seen a split in the Communist Party of Nepal (CPN) into pro-Peking and pro-Moscow factions. While the latter decided to side with the king, the former was wracked by further divisions and the Nepali communist movement saw a plethora of groups operating more or less independently of each other. It was in this situation that a Naxalite-inspired uprising took place in the eastern Nepal district of Jhapa in May 1971, in a campaign against supposed 'class enemies'. Eight people were killed by the revolutionaries.[14] But the would-be 'revolution' ended with the government moving in quickly to suppress it.

F. *Yagya Bahadur Thapa Revolt*: In yet another attempt at an armed action by the then banned Nepali Congress, Captain Yagya Bahadur Thapa led a group of revolutionaries into the eastern Nepal hills to try to join up with presumed mutineers from the army. But an information leak resulted in Thapa's band being surrounded and decimated by government troops. Around 40 of Thapa's comrades lost their lives in the army action, while he himself and Bhim Narayan Shrestha were arrested and later executed in February 1979.[15]

G. *The 1980 Student Unrest*: In April 1979, students clashed with the police over a minor incident, and it soon snowballed into a full-scale countrywide unrest which acquired political overtones. Police action reportedly led to the death of around 20 students.[16] The month-and-a-half-long disturbances ended when King Birendra announced a national referendum which gave the people the right to choose between a 'reformed' Panchayat system and a multiparty system. The former won the voting held in May 1980 through a result that is widely believed to have been rigged.[17]

H. *The Congress Satyagraha*: The Nepali Congress decided to launch a satyagraha against the Panchayat system in May 1985 with protest programmes all over the country. However, it came to an end after a series of bomb blasts in Kathmandu and elsewhere in the country in May. Seven people were killed. Although the Janabadi Morcha based in India claimed responsibility, a popular view remains that it was perpetrated by insiders in the palace itself in an attempt to discredit the Congress movement.[18]

THE 'PEOPLE'S WAR' OF THE CPN (MAOIST): FEBRUARY 1996–NOVEMBER 2001

As a prelude to the 'People's War', the CPN (Maoist) led by its elusive general secretary (now its chairman), Prachanda, made use of its political wing, the United People's Front Nepal (UPFN), to launch its 'politico-ideological preparation' in mid-1995. In September 1995, the coalition government under Sher Bahadur Deuba of the Nepali Congress came to power. As a response to the growing activism of the UPFN/CPN (Maoist) in the western Nepal districts of Rolpa and Rukum, the government launched the now-infamous 'Operation Romeo'. According to the home minister, Khum Bahadur Khadka, a 'special security programme' was begun in Rolpa in early November. Providing justification for the police operation, Khadka said that 'some criminal-minded persons carried out such activities as murdering and assaulting local residents, stopping the victims from informing the police about the incidents and the patients from going to hospital, and violently attacking security personnel, thereby creating tension and terror in the district.' He also said that police teams had been dispatched to eight village development committees (UDCs); 70 persons had been arrested prior to the security operation and 117 since; and a number of guns and *khukris* had been recovered from houses.[19]

In a newspaper interview a month later, Baburam Bhattarai, the chairman of the UPFN, provided his own version of 'Operation Romeo': '[A]round 1500 policemen including a specially trained commando force sent from Kathmandu have been deployed to let loose a reign of terror against the poor peasants of that rugged mountain district in western Nepal', he said. 'So far about one thousand people have been arrested, of whom about three hundred are kept in police custody or sent to jails under fictitious charges while the rest have been released on bail or after severe torture. The people arrested range from 12 to 70 years of age and most of them have been subjected to inhuman torture while in police custody. . . . More than ten thousand rural youths, out of a population of two hundred thousand for the whole district, have been forced to flee their homes and take shelter in remote jungles. The armed police operation is still continuing and the virtual reign of white terror seems endless at the moment.'

There is no doubt that the police were very high-handed in their dealings with the local population.[20] This only succeeded in alienating a large number of people, a fact that has been documented by various analysts.[21] That seemed to be just exactly what the CPN (Maoist) wanted. For although it had won three of four parliamentary seats in the 1991 elections, testifying to its support base in these two districts, it would have found it difficult to count on popular support for an armed uprising. It is no wonder then that, for the first few years, much of the action of the 'People's War' was limited to Rolpa and Rukum and the surrounding areas where, thanks to the government, the Maoists were able to build a support base that acted as a springboard for their growth nationwide.

On the political front, however, the first indication that the Maoists were readying for an armed movement came on 4 February 1996, when Baburam Bhattarai presented a list of 40 demands to Prime Minister Deuba, warning that if no steps were taken towards meeting their demands by 18 February they would be forced to take up arms.[22] The UPFN list included abrogating both the 1950 and the Mahakali treaties with India; introducing work permits for foreign workers in Nepal; whittling down the privileges of the royal family; drawing up a new constitution through a constituent assembly; declaring Nepal a secular nation; etc.

At that time, the UPFN/CPN (Maoist) represented only one of three major groups on the far left of Nepal's communist movement. That the government itself did not consider the implied threat to be cause for much concern becomes clear when we consider that Deuba left for India a week later. On 13 February, five days before the deadline expired, the Maoists struck in three districts, signalling the beginning of a conflict that has claimed 9,633 deaths at the time of writing this paper.[23]

From the very beginning of the conflict, there was a difference of opinion within the government as to how to tackle the Maoist issue. While Deuba made it clear that he was willing to talk to the Maoists and find a political answer, his home minister, Khum Bahadur Khadka, was for total suppression.[24] The latter even went so far as to suggest that the government would be able to tackle the Maoists in a matter of days.[25] There were also views like the one expressed by law and justice minister, Bhim Bahadur Tamang, who wondered how it would be possible to find a political solution by negotiating with a group which did not believe in the constitution to begin with.[26] To his credit, Deuba convened an all-party meeting to look at the Maoist issue on 5 March, but the meeting ended without any resolution, primarily because the ruling Nepali Congress itself was not represented at the meeting, and the participants accused the government of only doing it for form's sake.[27]

Thirteen months after the 'People's War' began, Deuba was replaced by Lokendra Bahadur Chand of the Rastriya Prajatantra Party with support from the CPN (UML). With a powerful deputy prime minister in Bamdev Gautam of the CPN (UML), it was clear who actually ran the show. With a communist-backed government in power, violence ceased for some time as an attempt was made to resolve the issue politically.[28] The government set up a task force to look into 'Maoist Activities and a Search for Solutions' under CPN (UML) Member of Parliament Prem Singh Dhami, in April 1997.

The Dhami Commission report, which was the first systematic effort by the establishment to delve into the underpinnings of the Maoist movement, was presented to the government in August 1997. The report provided a thorough analysis of the growth of the Maoists, their organization, battle strategies and future plans, and outlined recommendations to be followed by the government, which were strikingly similar to the socio-economic reforms demanded by the Maoists. It also admitted that the police actions were brutal and many innocents had been targeted, and emphasized the need to bring the CPN (Maoist) into the constitutional process and to make a formal offer for talks to the UPFN (Bhattarai).[29]

But by then the situation on the ground had changed a great deal. When local-level elections were held in May 1997, the Maoists called for a boycott. Due to the Maoist threat, polls could not be held in 87 VDCs. As a result, the district development committees could not be formed in 15 districts in western Nepal.[30] The implicit understanding between the government and the Maoists came to an end with the latter's resort to violence.

The RPP-CPN (UML) government's reaction was an attempt to pass an act entitled the Anti-Terrorist and Destructive Crime (Control and Punishment) Act in July on the active initiative of the Deputy Prime Minister and Home Minister, Bamdev Gautam, who was also deputy general secretary of the CPN (UML). The law, which was partly an attempt to address a police complaint that the Maoists they caught were being easily released by the courts, would have given the police wide-ranging powers against the Maoists.[31] What is noteworthy is that even though the government had not declared the UPFN/CPN (Maoist) to be a 'terrorist group', it was intent on pushing through a law that specified 'terrorist' activities.

The draft of the bill itself had been prepared earlier and circulated among MPs during Deuba's tenure. But it was the renewal of Maoist hostilities that prompted the Chand government to revive it. The Cabinet had approved the bill in July, but it could not be presented in Parliament due to vociferous opposition from civil society and other left parties protesting the extreme measures outlined in the proposed act, which came to be popularly known as the 'Black Law'.[32] Mary Des Chene writes: 'The point opposition of the A-T [Anti-Terrorist] Act pressed upon was that the government cannot both reject the constitution in practice and institute anti-democratic laws while rhetorically drawing on the constitution and the law as the source of its legitimacy as a democracy.'[33]

Within a couple of months the political situation changed once again at the centre as Surya Bahadur Thapa, also of the RPP, ousted his party colleague, Chand, and formed yet another minority government with the support of the Nepali Congress and the Nepal Sadbhavana Party. The new government left alone the 'Black Law', but did push through revisions to the 'Crimes against State and Punishment Act, 2046 vs',[34] as a sop to the police who were pushing for stricter laws in the fight against the Maoists.

Surya Bahadur Thapa had to make way for Girija Prasad Koirala in April 1998, as the Nepali Congress formed a minority government with support from the CPN (Marxist-Leninist), a splinter group from the CPN (UML). Koirala did try unsuccessfully to pass the Anti-Terrorist Act.[35] By then the Maoists had announced the existence of a Central Military Commission under Prachanda, on the second anniversary of the 'People's War' on 13 February 1998. Koirala was under great pressure to bring the situation under control for two reasons: conducting local elections in the areas where they could not be held earlier; and holding parliamentary elections due in a year's time. In the west, the Maoists seemed to be consolidating their grip even as they continued their attacks on the police. That was the situation when the government, in May 1998, launched the infamous Kilo Sierra Two Operation in 18 districts. This was a 'search and kill' operation which, according to the police chief of the western region, was using extreme measures. In his words: 'If they [the Maoists] don't respect the Constitution, we don't have to stick to the Constitution and take them to court.'[36]

It was during this period that the killings reached the highest point in the fighting that had begun in February 1996 and continued till the declaration of a state of emergency in November 2001. Around 500 people were killed in a campaign that was characterized by excessive brutality, and the violence has been attributed as a major cause for the swelling of Maoist ranks. In a nation-wide opinion poll conducted in early 2001, 30 per cent of the people in the mid-and far-western parts of Nepal believed that police violence was to blame for the increase in Maoist activity as opposed to a national average of 19 per cent.[37] The Maoists too have claimed as much. 'In the main areas of struggle when massacres in dozens were carried out in one village after another, the poor peasants inspired the Party continuously asserting "let the Party continue [the] People's War for which they were ready to sacrifice everything",' writes Prachanda, and goes on to say that, 'Hundreds of women victims of barbaric rape by the reactionary joined the People's War with hatred. . . .'[38] But regardless of the human cost, the violence of the police onslaught seems to have put the Maoists on the defensive, and the May 1999 parliamentary elections were conducted without much hindrance. The Maoists simply called for a boycott but did not attempt any disruptions like they had in the 1997 local elections. Analysts believe that the Maoist behaviour was the result of the Kilo Sierra Two Operation, and the rebels were not too keen on another round of repression.[39]

With the victory of the Nepali Congress with a majority mandate in the elections, the challenge before the new Prime Minister, Krishna Prasad Bhattarai, was dealing with the Maoists. In December 1999, Bhattarai formed a 'High-Level Committee to Provide Suggestions to Solve the Maoist Problem' under Sher Bahadur Deuba, who was prime minister at the time the 'People's War' began in 1996. In February 2000, the government further authorized the Deuba committee to hold talks with the CPN (Maoist), and in response, Prachanda set forth three demands,[40] and declared that if those conditions were fulfilled, the rebels would be ready for talks and even suspend military operations during the talks period.[41] But without support from his own party and the party president, Girija Prasad Koirala, there was not much Bhattarai could do. The latter's overtures towards the Maoists were seen as soft-pedalling an issue that needed firm action. In March 2000, Koirala removed Bhattarai and became prime minister once again, declaring that his first priority would be 'to restore [the] law and order situation in the country to protect the lives of the people'.[42]

Bhattarai's removal saw a resumption of Maoist attacks on the police as they strove to rid the countryside of all government presence. As part of their campaign, they were able to deal a strong blow to the government by attacking Dunai, the district headquarters of Dolpa, in late September 2000. The Dunai attack is significant for two reasons. One, it was the first time that the insurgents were able to take over a district headquarters, which provided a great psychological boost to the Maoists. The second was that after the Dunai debacle, the Nepali army, which had so far steered clear of engaging the Maoists, was mobilized for security duty in 16 district headquarters. The army's deployment, however, did not mean that it had been called out to fight the Maoists—not yet.

Not long after, the Koirala government represented by the Deputy Prime Minister, Ram Chandra Poudel, met a CPN (Maoist) central committee member in the first-ever meeting of that kind, which led to hopes that, perhaps, a breakthrough could, after, all be achieved through talks. But the optimism died after the Maoist leadership accused the government of showing bad faith by releasing a top Maoist leader only after he renounced his party at a press conference.

Meanwhile, the Deuba committee had been busy with its work even though the prime minister who set it up was long gone by then, and had been replaced by Koirala who did not look upon

Deuba with favour. The Deuba committee had sought suggestions from a variety of sources, including political parties. The response from the latter was generally quite unenthusiastic and in at least one case, the RPP, the committee was accused of not being very clear about its mandate.[43] However, in November, the Deuba committee submitted its recommendations to the government.[44] The recommendations were pretty substantive and dealt with a host of issues that it believed went to the roots of the Maoist insurgency. The suggestions foresaw an overhaul of the country's socio-economic structure, and among its conclusions was the fact that it believed that the Maoist support base had not become larger; rather it was the result of the ineffectivenss of the government machinery. The main point though was that it stressed that talks should be the way forward in dealing with the Maoists. But Koirala, who was continuing with police operations even as he tried to entice the Maoists for talks through the back door, simply ignored the Deuba report and nothing more has been heard of it since.

Events moved in another direction in February 2001 when the CPN (Maoist) declared that their Second National Conference had adopted 'Marxism-Leninism-Maoism and Prachanda Path' as the party's 'guiding thought', and indicated its desire 'to have dialogues with all concerned sections to call an all-section conference of all political parties, organisations and representatives of mass organisations in the country, election of an interim government by such a conference and guarantee of people's constitution under the leadership of the interim government so as to finding out a political solution to the country's present crisis-ridden situation'.[45]

Since one of the main stumbling blocks to any meaningful dialogue with the rebels was their insistence on an election to a constituent assembly, public pressure mounted on the government to come up with a suitable response. Accordingly, the government released the names of 294 individuals who were in police custody on charges of being sympathizers or members of the CPN (Maoist). But that did nothing to soothe the Maoists who had been demanding that the whereabouts of 73 people be made public. They said that only three out of the 73 names had showed up in that list.[46] And in April, the fighting took on a heightened ferocity as the Maoists attacked two police posts in the far west within a week of each other killing 70 policemen. They also declared that there would be no talks with the government until Koirala resigned.[47]

It did not help matters for Koirala that dissent was rising within his own party. Leading the charge was Deuba who believed he would be able to talk to the Maoists. There was also a variance of views between the prime minister and the king on mobilizing the army. As its supreme commander, the Constitution has given the king the right to deploy the army but on the advice of the National Defence Council (NDC) consisting of the prime minister, the defence minister, and the commander-in-chief.[48] The Koirala government had prepared the Integrated Internal Security and Development Plan (IISDP) for those districts most affected by the Maoist insurgency and which would be implemented with security provided by the army. But when it came to fighting the Maoists directly, the army was more than reluctant. The army chief even caused a political uproar by demanding a consensus and a firm commitment from all political parties, and a clear set of guidelines from the government, before allowing the army to move.[49] In effect, the government was left with just the police to tackle the Maoists.

The tussle between the palace and the civilian government over control over the army had begun much earlier and it was in reaction to this that the government had planned the creation of a paramilitary force which would be under its command. A task force had presented a proposal in April 2000 for setting up the Armed Police Force (APF) that would be answerable to the home ministry. Given the reluctance displayed by the army to take on the Maoists, especially in the aftermath of the Dunai debacle, in January 2001 the government had introduced an ordinance to establish the APF specially dedicated to fighting the Maoists. But it was only in October of that year that the APF came into existence. Much happened in the meantime.

On 1 June 2001, King Birendra and his entire family were killed in a gruesome massacre, and Gyanendra ascended the throne. The Maoists tried to take advantage of the ensuing chaos by trying to convince the people that Gyanendra had conspired with Indian and US intelligence agencies to kill Birendra. When that did not work, they went back to their attacks on the police.

As part of their renewed operations, in late July they attacked a police post in Rolpa and took 69 policemen hostage. The Koirala government immediately despatched the army on a rescue mission, but when the soldiers failed to confront the Maoists even after sustaining three injuries and pot-shots at their helicopters, Koirala resigned as prime minister in July. He was replaced by Sher Bahadur Deuba who said that 'his first priority is to solve the Maoist issue'. He announced a ceasefire and Prachanda responded the very next day with a similar declaration. To demonstrate its sincerity, the government began releasing those charged with association with the CPN (Maoist), while both sides prepared negotiating teams for direct talks.[50]

Between July and November 2001, three rounds of talks were held between the government and the rebels. At their second meeting, the Maoists presented their demands, among which were a constituent assembly, an interim government and a republic. Although the Maoists dropped their demand that Nepal be declared a republic, the major obstacle was the demand for a constituent assembly, which the government, backed by most of the other political parties, refused to consider. On 21 November, after three rounds of talks had been held, Prachanda indicated in a statement that the talks had been a failure. Two days later, on 23 November, the Maoists attacked the army signalling the end of the ceasefire.

Army in the Fray

Sher Bahadur Deuba called the Maoists' resumption of hostilities a betrayal, and on 26 November his government imposed a state of emergency, suspending all fundamental rights. The government also promulgated the Terrorist and Destructive Acts (Control and Punishment) Ordinance and the CPN (Maoist) was declared a 'terrorist' organisation.[51] Deuba also said that there would be no further talking until the rebels disarmed. In April 2002, the ordinance was passed by Parliament to become the Terrorist and Destructive Acts (Control and Punishment) Act (TADA), to remain effective for two years.

As mentioned earlier, when the time came for the emergency to be ractified by Parliament after three months by a two-thirds majority as per constitutional requirements, it was easily achieved and it seemed for a time that the parliamentary parties had finally found a united cause against the Maoists. In exchange for its support, the CPN (UML) did extract an undertaking from Deuba that he would agree to constitutional amendments which would address the issues raised by the Maoists. But when the government sought a second extension in May, all the political parties, including the Nepali Congress establishment represented by Koirala, were not in favour. The argument was that TADA gave enough authority to the security forces to handle the Maoists. Initially, Prime Minister Deuba seemed to agree, but within days he changed his stance and informed an all-party meeting that his government would be seeking a six-month extension in parliament. He also called for a special parliamentary session to push through the extension.

Koirala, as Nepali Congress president, suspended Deuba from party membership for refusing to call off the special parliamentary session. Deuba reacted by dissolving Parliament instead, called for fresh elections in November, and reimposed the emergency through an ordinance two days after the earlier one expired. He also led a breakaway faction from the Nepali Congress,[52] and was adamant that he would hold the elections as promised although almost everyone was sceptical about the polls given the security situation in the countryside.

But two major Maoist attacks on government troops in early September sent the political establishment scurrying to develop an alternative strategy. A series of all-party meetings was held, and on 29 September it was decided that Prime Minister Deuba would be given the authority to explore constitutional means to either defer the polls by six months or reinstate the dissolved parliament. On 3 October, Deuba met King Gyanendra to recommend deferment of the elections by more than a year. The next day, in an unexpected move, the king removed the prime minister for his 'incompetence' as he had not been able to hold the elections as scheduled, and himself assumed executive authority.

In line with other political parties, the Maoists also condemned the king's move, terming it a 'feudal retrogression' that had been carefully orchestrated since the murder of King Birendra.[53] But the statements gradually toned down with reference to King Gyanendra, and on 3 December 2002, a press release from Prachanda stated that the CPN (Maoist) had formed a 'central dialogue team' since it recognized that 'it is possible and necessary to talk to all political forces as well as the present manager of the ancient regime in order to find a peaceful, positive and forward-looking political solution to the crisis facing the country'.[54]

Unknown to the public at large, the palace-appointed government of Lokendra Bahadur Chand had begun secret negotiations with the Maoists. On 29 January 2003, just days after the assassination of the chief of the armed police force in Kathmandu, the Maoists declared a ceasefire after the government met their demands that the Interpol 'red corner' notice be called off; the term 'terrorist' which the government had tagged onto the Maoists be removed; and the bounty on the heads of top Maoist leaders be withdrawn.[55] The Maoists soon announced their negotiating team led by Baburam Bhattarai, the convener of the United Revolutionary People's Council (URPC) of Nepal, which is the 'embryonic Central People's Government Organising Committee' of the Maoists (i.e. the Maoist 'government'), while the government set up its own team under Deputy Prime Minister Badri Prasad Mandal.

Two rounds of talks were held between the two sides, and at the second meeting on 9 May, a code of conduct was agreed upon and the Maoists presented their list of demands for the government to consider. But the movement led by the parliamentary parties forced Chand to resign at the end of May and his replacement, Surya Bahadur Thapa, had to begin anew. For more than two months after his appointment, Thapa's government seemed more busy with staving off criticism than talking to the Maoists and assuring them of its good faith even though it reiterated its commitment of honouring the agreements reached with the previous government and appointed two members of the Cabinet to hold dialogue with the Maoists.

When towards the end of July it became apparent that the Maoists were tired of waiting for talks to renew, and the leaders who had come above ground slowly began to fade away from public view, a frantic government invited the rebels for another round of talks. This was held on 17 August, and the government put together its own response to the Maoists' position paper presented at the second round of talks. But by then it was just too late, and the Maoists' insistence on a constituent assembly demonstrated that the rebels were in no mood for negotiations. It just so happened that, on the day the two sides were sitting down for talks in the western Nepal town of Nepalgunj, in Doramba of Ramechhap district in eastern Nepal the army gunned down 19 people, mostly Maoist cadres, in cold blood.[56] On 27 August, a statement from Prachanda said that they were pulling out of the ceasefire, stating that 'both the "concept paper" of the old state presented at the third round of negotiation politically, and the massacres of the 19 people in Doramba by the Royal Army militarily, have declared the calling off of the negotiation process'.[57]

GROWING MILITARY BURDEN

When the army was dragged willy-nilly into the conflict, it was a force quite unprepared to take on a battle-hardened adversary. Although armed with weapons superior to the Maoists'.303 rifles snatched from the police, and traditional muzzle-loaders, thc standard issue SLRS were decades old. But with security having been given the highest priority, the army could go on a shopping spree which has had a direct effect on the country's finances. Table 7.3 by Dhruba Kumar shows the rapid escalation in the allocation to defence in the years since 2001.[58]

The expenditures indicate not only the cost of arming the military with modern weapons but also an increase in the number of personnel employed by the army and the APF. From a force that had only 50,000, in the past three and a half years it has grown by 50 per cent to reach a strength of 75,000. Similarly, the APF is now 20,000-strong. These expansions happened only in 2001–3.

Despite these developments experts believe that the Maoist conflict is not winnable. Even securing government installations and curbing Maoist activities will require the government to increase its fighting force. The army itself thinks that it will require battalion-level forces in each of the country's 75 districts instead of the company-strength troops stationed in the majority of the districts.[59]

TABLE 7.3: BUDGETARY ALLOCATION UNDER SELECTED HEADINGS (IN RS 000)

Fiscal year	Total expenditure	Regular expenditure	Defence	Home
1990/1	19,791,000	7,465,000	1,113,888	750,307
1995/6	51,647,800	22,821,500	2,193,900	1,935,200
2000/1	91,621,335	43,512,746	3,816,488 *	5,959,678 *
				+1,856,000 **
2001/2	99,792,212	49,321,941	5,829,776 *	7,528,693 *
2002/3	96,124,796	57,445,121	7,282,496	7,535,899
2003/4	102,400,000	60,555,000	7,184,221	7,053,671

Notes: * Indicates actual and revised estimates.
** Amount allocated to raise the armed police force.

Source: *Budget Speeches* Kathmandu: Ministry of Finance, documents of the years indicated.

THE EXTERNAL DIMENSION

In the escalation of the fighting against the Maoists since November 2001, the Nepali government has had to rely quite extensively on the goodwill of foreign countries. It is clear that the Nepali army would not have been able to deal with the Maoists on its own had it not been for the extensive assistance it has received from outside. Assistance has come in the form of the supply of the armaments as well as moral support for the government. While India, the US, and the UK have also provided military assistance, other influential countries like China and the European Union have endorsed the government's handling of the Maoist issue.

INDIA

It is a commonly held view by a section of the Nepali population that India is in one way or another behind the Maoist movement. Although no facts to prove this thesis have been presented, it still has a strong resonance within Nepal. On a more reflective plane, however, a case can be made, not of direct Indian complicity but of India allowing the Maoists a free hand to organize without hindrance. Nepali opposition groups have historically used India as a base in their fight against the state, going back to the early days of modern Nepal. The CPN (Maoist) is only the latest to follow in this tradition using the nearly 2,000-km-long open border between the two countries to move to and fro freely.

The Maoists are quite indignant at any suggestion that their activities would be constrained if the Indian land-mass was not accessible to them.[60] But events have clearly shown that the Maoist leadership is pretty much based in India even though they may make periodic visits to the hills of Nepal. To cite just two examples, it was in Siliguri of West Bengal that Nepal's top left leaders met Prachanda in August 2001 during the first ceasefire, while the general secretary of the CPN (UML) met Prachanda again in Lucknow in November 2003. India itself was pretty blasé about Maoist activities in India. For nearly five years since the beginning of the 'People's War', various forums were organized in India by pro-Maoist organizations and New Delhi turned a blind eye to it all. The India-based All Nepal Unity Centre is one of the front organizations of the CPN (Maoist) that the Nepali government believes is used to channel funds collected from the large number of Nepalis working in India.

The ferocity of the Maoist challenge to the Nepali state and its likely implications on India itself seems to have dawned on the Indian establishment pretty late in the day. As S.D. Muni notes: 'Law and order being treated as a state subject, the Central government in India absolved itself of any responsibility in restraining and containing the activities of the Maoists along the Indo-Nepal border. Even the June 2001 establishment of a coordination committee of the South Asian Maoists was just taken routine note of by the Indian intelligence agencies without any policy decision at the political level.'[61]

Similar observations have been made by a former Indian ambassador to Nepal: 'India, too, must accept its share of responsibility—it has been a passive spectator for far too long, despite the obvious dangers it poses to its own security', writes K.V. Rajan. He further said, 'There is no excuse for the fact that despite frequent communications from the Nepalese side, Maoist leaders for the past few years have been moving freely across the border, holding meetings with senior Nepalese politicians on Indian soil, without Indian agencies apparently knowing about it.'[62]

But despite the delay in waking up to the Maoist threat to its own security and to the bilateral relations between the two countries, and even the long-term implications on the regional geopolitical situation, India has taken serious steps to contain the Maoists. An indication of this came from India declaring the Maoists to be a terrorist organization during Indian Foreign Minister Jaswant Singh's visit to Nepal in September 2001, even though the Nepali government itself applied the appellation only after the first ceasefire ended two months later.[63]

India was the first country to declare its support of the emergency imposed on 27 November 2001. The Indian Prime Minister, Atal Behari Vajpayee, telephoned King Gyanendra and Prime Minister Deuba and offered 'whatever assistance was required' to fight the Maoists, while the Indian embassy in Kathmandu said that 'India will seal its borders and not allow its soil to be used to launch attacks on security forces in the neighbouring country'.[64] In keeping with this commitment India placed a ban on the All Nepal Unity Centre and arrested its general secretary, Bamdev Chhetri, who is also a central committee member of the CPN (Maoist), and extradited him to Nepal. So far, more than a dozen top Maoist leaders have been arrested in India, including two politbureau members, C.P. Gajurel in August 2003 and Matrika Yadav in February 2004, and the prize catch, the former general secretary of the party, Mohan Baidya (aka Kiran), in Siliguri in March 2004.

But the greatest help from India has been in the form of armaments supply. The Nepali army had been entreating unresponsive governments for the replacement of its standard issue rifle of 1960s' vintage, a plea the Deuba government had taken into consideration and agreed to. Even before the Maoist attack on the army, a Nepali army team had already been to India to procure arms at 'friendly prices'. And a day before the emergency was declared, the Nepali army chief had stopped over on his way back from abroad and appealed to his Indian counterpart to speed up delivery of armaments.[65] Supplies from India began soon after, first with the donation of two helicopters and an unknown numbers of arms. Thus far, Nepal has received two more helicopters, nearly 100 mine-protected vehicles (MPV), 25,000 Indian-made INSAS rifles, and a number of military transport vehicles, all at heavily discounted prices.[66] In total, Indian military assistance to Nepal has amounted to nearly Rs. 5 billion (US $70 million).[67]

The proactive Indian role in countering the Maoists, especially the arrests of its top leaders, has had the Maoists seething with such reactions as this from Baburam Bhattarai: 'Comrade Kiran was arrested with the active role of Indian rulers. It has bared the nexus between the neo-monarchy of the post-royal palace massacre and the reactionary rulers of India who believe in an indivisible India.'[68]

THE UNITED STATES

A major ally of the Nepali government in its fight against the Maoists has been the United States. Joining the chorus of countries offering assistance to the US in the aftermath of the September 2001 attack was Nepal. Prime Minister Deuba even offered overflights and refuelling facilities to the US as it prepared to invade Afghanistan. When the Maoists resumed hostilities in November, the US government readily agreed to provide help. It did not help the Maoists that their statements, expectedly, have always been full of anti-US rhetoric, or that they killed a locally hired US embassy staffer soon after.[69] The arrival of a new ambassador, Michael Malinowski, in December 2001 added further impetus to US assistance to Nepal.

Malinowski is a flamboyant figure who made it a point to visit military bases around the country and make statements describing the Maoists as terrorists,[70] and is among those who advocates forcing the Maoists to the negotiating table with a bloody nose. He played a major role in placing Nepal on the radar screen of the US State Department. It was an indication of his success that US Secretary of State Colin Powell dropped in during a tour of South Asia in January 2002 and declared: 'We fully acknowledge the government of Nepal's right to protect its citizens and institutions from terrorist attacks.'[71]

Powell also met Nepali army officials and listened to their request for military support. In May 2002, Deuba travelled to the US and asked President George W. Bush himself for military aid. That was not long in being promised as the US government requested Congress for US $20 million for Nepal apart from the regular aid coming in as development assistance. Of this, US $15 million was meant for helicopters and US $5 million for night-vision goggles and protective and communications gear.[72] The US $20 million aid was later reduced to US $17 million, with US $14 million earmarked for 2002 and US $3 million for 2003, as a result of the US Congress' cut-down of aid globally.[73] In April 2004, the US announced a further US $14 million in military assistance for 2004.[74] The US also provided a consignment of 5,000 US-made M-16 rifles in early 2003 in a separate procurement deal which was not related to the military assistance, while a further 20,000 of those rifles have been requested.[75]

In April 2003, Nepal and the US also signed the Anti-Terrorism Assistance Programme, further cementing the growing ties between the two militaries. In April 2003 itself the US government placed the CPN (Maoist) on its list of 'Other Terrorist Groups'.[76] This was followed by the CPN (Maoist) being designated under the US Government's Executive Order 13224 on terrorism financing in November 2003, and then its inclusion in the 'Terrorism Exclusion List', in April 2004.[77]

THE UNITED KINGDOM

Given the historical ties between Nepal and the United Kingdom (UK), mainly on account of the Nepalis serving as Gurkhas in the British Army, it was natural that the British government should take keen interest in what is happening in the country. It even appointed a Special Representative for Nepal in February 2003 in a bid to coordinate its policy with that of India and the US.

After the ceasefire ended in November 2001, like other countries, the UK too expressed its support to the government and also pledged military assistance. According to *The Guardian* newspaper, Nepal was to receive £6.7 million from the UK from its conflict prevention fund. The funds would be used to procure 'two Mi-17 support helicopters, explosive ordnance disposal equipment, logistical equipment, communications equipment and equipment in support of the military intelligence support group with the UK assisting the Royal Nepalese Army in setting up'.[78] There were also reports in the press that the UK was also planning to provide Nepal with two 'spy planes',[79] but there has been no confirmation either way of this.

Conclusion

The Nepali state has proved itself quite incapable of dealing with the Maoist insurgency from the very beginning. In retrospect, it is clear that had the various governments introduced the kind of reforms proposed by the Thapa government in August 2003, the Maoist movement could, perhaps, have been nipped in the bud. Instead, it resorted to the use of the heavy hand, which only served to fuel the insurgency, which did not have much of a popular base to begin with, let alone the military capability it now demonstrates. Even when matters had got out of hand in late 2000 and early 2001, with the prime minister and the king not seeing eye to eye on the deployment of the army, all that the government attempted was a further increase in its fighting power by raising an Armed Police Force. Ultimately, the military was handed the task of bringing the Maoists back to the peace process in a considerably weakened position. But that has also raised the profile of the army in the Nepali public arena like never before. As long as the Maoists' 'People's War' rages on, any government that comes to power will be caught in a cleft stick, of trying to balance the army's aspirations with the need to rely on the army to preserve the integrity of the state. Finding the right balance will be a sore challenge for a newly democratized polity like Nepal's.

Postscript

The writing of this paper was completed before the following major developments have taken place in Nepal:

1. The failure of the second Deuba government, appointed in April 2004, either to hold elections or to bring the Maoists to the negotiating table was used by King Gyanendra as a pretext for assuming power under his own direct leadership on 1 February 2005. He placed all the top political leaders under detention, imposed emergency and press censorship, stopped all political activity, and appointed a Cabinet of staunch royalists.

2. This has brought about some alienation between the king and the international community, with the latter asking for the restoration of the democratic process in order to effectively deal with the Maoist challenge. Military and other assistance to Nepal is being adversely affected as a result of the international community's pressures on the king, who is trying to diffuse these pressures by highlighting the priority of the terrorist challenge posed by the Maoists.

3. While a military stalemate continues between the Royal Nepal Army and the Maoists in rural areas, the king's regime continues to keep political activities in the kingdom contained. While some of the top political leaders have selectively been released, restrictions on their movements, communications and organized political actions are in place. There are also signs of the administration being reinforced under the command of royalists and old Panchayat hands.

4. There were reports in March 2005 of a serious political division among the Maoists, between the supreme leader Prachanda and the principal ideologue and erstwhile number two, Baburam Bhattarai. There are conflicting assessments of this split within the Maoists. It is believed that Bhattarai has been stripped of all his organizational positions and is being kept under strict surveillance. There are allegations that the palace has played an active role in getting Bhattarai marginalized as he is seen as an obstacle to any possible deal between the Maoists and the royal establishment.

NOTES

1. B.P. Koirala writes that the three groups never met in session and that everything was negotiated with India playing the middleman. B.P. Koirala, *Atmabrittanta*, Kathmandu: Himal Books, 2003.
2. Adapted from www.nepalresearch.com.
3. M.C. Regmi, *Imperial Gorkha*, New Delhi: Adroit, 1999, p. 11.
4. Ibid.
5. Ibid., p. 12.
6. Anirudha Gupta, *Politics in Nepal*, New Delhi: Kalinga, 1993, p. 61.
7. Ibid., p. 54.
8. Ibid., p. 70.
9. Surendra K.C., *Nepalama Communist Andolan ko Itihas* (The History

of the Communist Movement in Nepal), Kathmandu: Bidyarthi Pustak Bhandar, 1999, pp. 73–4.
10. Gupta, *Politics in Nepal*, pp. 80–1.
11. Martin Hoftun, Williom Raeper and John Whelpton, *People, Politics and Ideology: Democracy and Social Change in Nepal*, Kathmandu: Mandala Book Point, 1999.
12. Leo Rose and Margaret Fisher, *The Politics of Nepal*, Ithaca: Cornell University Press, 1970, p. 109.
13. Lok Raj Baral, *Oppositional Politics in Nepal*, New Delhi: Abhinav Publications, 1977, p. 72.
14. Krishna Hachhethu, *Party Building in Nepal: Organisation, Leadership and People*, Kathmandu: Mandala Book Point, 2002, p. 37.
15. Surya Mani Adhikari, *Nepali Congress ko Itihas* (A History of the Nepali Congress), Bhudipuran Prakashan, 2002.
16. Rishikesh Shaha, 'Politics in Nepal, 1980-1990: Referendum', *Statement and Triumph of People Power*, New Delhi: Manohar, 1992, p. 49.
17. Ibid., pp. 88–9.
18. Hoftun et al., *People Politics and Ideology*, pp. 103–4.
19. *The Kathmandu Post*, 15 November 1995.
20. See *Human Rights Yearbook 1995, 1996* for details.
21. See, for example, Shobha Gautam, Amrit Baskota and Rita Manchanda, 'Where There Are No Men: Women in the Maoist Insurgency in Nepal', in *Women War and Peace in South Asia: Beyond Victimhood to Agency*, ed. Rita Manchanda, New Delhi: Safe, 2001. Various newspaper articles by Shobha Gautam and Amrit Baskota in 1998 provide graphic details of police atrocities during that period and subsequent to that as well.
22. Nepal Rastriya Buddhijibi Sangathan, *Nepal ma Janayuddha—Bhag Ek*, (The People's War in Nepal—Part One), Kathmandu, 1997, pp. 19–22.
23. INSEC, E-bulletin, 14–20 May 2004.
24. *Janabhavana*, 14 Fagun, 2052, quoted in *Nepalma Janayuddha*.
25. *Deshantar*, 13 Fagun 2052, quoted by Gurung et al., n. 28.
26. *Lokpatra*, 20 Fagun 2052, quoted in *Nepalma Janayuddha*.
27. *Shree Sagarmatha*, 23 Fagun 2052.
28. Harka Gurung, Ananda Aditya, Surendra K.C., Chuda Bahadur Shrestha and Sudheer Sharma, *An Overview of Recent Armed Conflict in Nepal*, Kathmandu: New Era, 2001.
29. *Nekapa (Maobadi) ko Chirphar*, 2058 BS, p. 72.
30. *Manabhadhikar Barsha Pustika* (1997), p. 21.
31. Deepak Thapa, 'Day of the Maoist', *Himal South Asian*, 2001.
32. See Appendix A of Mary Des Chene, '"Black Laws" and the "Limited Rights" of the People in Post-Andolan Nepal: The Campaign against the Proposed Anti-Terrorist Act of 2054 vs', *Himalayan Research Bulletin*, 18 (2), for full text of the bill.

33. Ibid.
34. Ibid.
35. Ibid.
36. Deputy Inspector General of Police Sahabir Thapa (presently Inspector General of Police of the Armed Police Force) quoted in *The Kathmandu Post*, 8 July 1998.
37. *Political Opinion Survey Nepal 2001.*
38. *The Worker*, no. 5, 1999.
39. Harka Gurung et al., 2001, p. 45.
40. The demands were: (1) make public the whereabouts of a central committee member of the CPN-Maoist along with others who had been 'disappeared'; (2) begin the process of releasing arrested workers and sympathizers; and (3), stop 'state terrorism' and begin the process to investigate the incident of arson and killing in Rukum district (in which an entire village had been torched by the police that same month for sheltering Maoists), provide compensation, and take action against the guilty.
41. Private communication from Prachanda to Durga Subedi.
42. *The Rising Nepal*, 23 March 2000.
43. See *Janayudha ra Shanti: Bichar ra Sam̐bhavana*, SAP-Nepal, 2057, for suggestions provided by the political parties.
44. See ibid., for text of the recommendations.
45. *The Himalayan Thunder*, vol. 1, no. 1, 2001.
46. Amnesty International, 2002.
47. *Drishti*, 13 March 2001.
48. The provision of a National Defence Council was one of the compromises reached during the drafting of the 1990 constitution, thus allowing for less-than-total control of the civilian executive over the army. As a prelude to activating the Council, Koirala had appointed a defence minister, in a departure from the tradition of the prime minister looking after defence affairs.
49. *Kantipur*, 21 April 2001.
50. To his credit, Deuba attempted to weaken the Maoist constituency by announcing a few measures as a sop to marginalized groups and declared that land reforms would be introduced, despite intense opposition from within his own party.
51. The Terrorist and Destructive Acts (Control and Punishment) Ordinance was a revised version of the act pushed by the Chand government in 1997. See, www.icj.org/IMG/pdf/Report_Nepal.pdf for an English translation of the ordinance which later became an Act.
52. Despite Deuba's claim to represent the 'real' Nepali Congress, the Election Commission in September decided in favour of Koirala. Deuba had to content himself with naming his party the Nepali Congress (Democratic).

53. Press statement by Prachanda, 5 October 2002.
54. *Janaawaj*, no. 38, 5 December 2002.
55. The Interpol notice had been issued in August 2002, while the reward for the capture or killing of top Maoist leaders had been announced in April 2002. The reward ranged from Rs. 5 million for top leaders, Rs. 2.5 million for field commanders, and so on down the line.
56. The National Human Rights Commission has indicted the Nepali army for the massacre of the 19. See www.nhrc-org.np for its report on Doramba.
57. Press statement from.Prachanda, 27 August 2003.
58. Dhruba Kumar, 'Consequences of the militarisation conflict and the cost of violence in Nepal', *Contributions to Nepalese Studies*, vol. 30, no. 2, p. 181.
59. Navin Singh Khadka, 'Alms Race', *Nepali Times*, 28 May-3 June 2004.
60. See, for instance, the review by 'Laldhoj' of *Understanding the Maoist Movement of Nepal*, ed. Deepak Thapa in 'Proverbial Blind Men's Portrayal of an Elephant', *The Worker*, no. 9, www.cpnm.org.
61. S.D. Muni, *Maoist Insurgency in Nepal: The Challenge and the Response*, New Delhi: ORF-Rupa, 2003, p. 58.
62. K.V. Rajan, 'Nepal', in *External Affairs: Cross-Border Relations*, ed. J.N. Dixit, New Delhi: Konark, 2004, p. 101.
63. Sushil Sharma, 'Nepal row over US support', 26 September 2001, www.bbc.co.uk
64. 'King Gyanendra, Deuba receive call from Indian PM', *The Kathmandu Post*, 29 November 2001.
65. 'Emergency eve: Nepal Army chief came calling', *The Indian Express*, 29 November 2001.
66. Khadka, 'Alms Race'.
67. Kumar, 'Consequences of the militarisation conflict', p. 182.
68. Baburam Bhattarai, 'Raised Questions on the Arrest of Com Kiran', *The Newsletter*, First Issue, 16–30 April 2004.
69. The Maoists shot dead another local US embassy worker in November 2002.
70. In a speech in Kathmandu, Malinowski said: 'The Maoists have shown themselves to be a ruthless enemy by their tactics in the field and through terrorist attacks against both government and innocent civilian targets. . . . Working in tandem, and with the full approval and coordination of the government of Nepal—in a spirit of cooperation not interference—our governments can help Nepal defeat the Maoist threat. 'International Solidarity against Terrorism', remarks by Malinowski at a programme of the Foundation of Nepalese in America, Nepal Branch, 12 September 2003.
71. *The Rising Nepal*, 19 January 2002.
72. K. Alan Kronstadt, 'Nepal: Background and US Relations', Report for Congress.

73. Ibid.
74. www.nepalnews.com, 18 April 2004.
75. Ibid.
76. *The Kathmandu Post*, 2 May 2003.
77. According to US embassy press releases, the designation under Executive Order 13224 'blocks the CPN (M)'s assets in the US or held by US persons wherever located and bars most transactions or dealings with the organization', while the Terrorism Exclusion List puts travel restrictions on the target group.
78. David Hencke, 'Blair "sneaked aid to Nepal military"', *The Guardian*, 5 August, 2002. The helicopters were delivered in March 2003.
79. nepalnews.com, 5 May 2004.

8. Bhutan's Response to the Challenge of Terrorism

Wasbir Hussain

It's called the Druk Yul or the Land of the Thunder Dragon. But Buddhist Bhutan, nestled in the Eastern Himalayas[1] with a population of a little more than 700,000,[2] had been spared the 'thunder' of the global menace called terrorism until bands of Indian insurgents crossed over from the adjoining Indian states into the kingdom's dense and un-policed southern jungles in the early 1990s. These separatist rebels belonging to the United Liberation Front of Asom (Assam) (ULFA),[3] National Democratic Front of Bodoland (NDFB),[4] and later, the Kamatapur Liberation Organization (KLO),[5] soon converted vast wooded stretches into their home, complete with firing ranges, football and volleyball fields, etc. To push ahead with their armed struggle for independent homelands outside New Delhi's control, these rebel fighters used their Bhutan bases, located amidst more than 6,000 sq. km of tropical forests, as staging areas to launch hit-and-run strikes on Indian security forces just across the porous 440-km-long border that the kingdom shares with the Indian states of Assam and West Bengal. After most strikes, these rebels would return to their Bhutan hideouts to escape the pursuing Indian soldiers.

Bhutan's Royal government woke up to the militants' presence, and its possible consequences, only after 1994. While Thimphu was silent till mid-1994 about the setting up of well-entrenched bases by the ULFA, it actually went out to deny the presence in the kingdom of the ethnic Bodo rebels, those belonging to the NDFB, then known as the Bodo Security Force (BSF).[6] Soon thereafter, Bhutan not only admitted the presence of the foreign militants, including the NDFB, it also took up the matter with the Indian government, and began to tackle the threat in close coordination with New Delhi.

Around the time that these Indian militants entered Bhutan and set up bases there, the kingdom's southern parts were witnessing unprecedented political activity by a section of people of Nepalese origin, a movement that Thimphu sought to regard as an 'act of terrorism'. The stirring among the Lhotshampas or the Nepali-speaking people concentrated in southern Bhutan, was triggered off by the Royal government's attempt to impose the indigenous Drukpa culture on them in areas of dress and language. Agitated, a section of the ethnic Nepalese-speaking population formed the People's Forum for Human Rights (PFHR) in 1989.[7] Organized in Nepal by Tek Nath Rizal, a former member of Bhutan's Royal Advisory Council, the PFHR started distributing pamphlets in late 1989 inside the kingdom. Thimphu reacted swiftly, and many were arrested. Rizal too was arrested in Nepal and handed over to Bhutan where he was held in prison for nearly ten years.[8]

Soon thereafter, in mid-1990, some of the Lhotshampas formed the Bhutan People's Party (BPP) in India. The party organized demonstrations in southern Bhutan in September and October 1990, demanding civil rights and drastic changes in the political system. Bhutan was bent on clamping down on this uprising and described the section of people of Nepalese origin engaged in the movement as 'anti-nationals'.[9] In the wake of the Bhutanese crackdown, this section of the southern Bhutanese population began to flee the kingdom through India to the safety of Nepal. Till mid-2004, an estimated 100,000 refugees from Bhutan were still living in seven camps in eastern Nepal run by the United Nations High Commissioner for Refugees (UNHCR).

Even today, despite Thimphu's persistent denials, many believe that the ULFA rebels were 'welcome guests' in Bhutan since 1991, 'whose services were thought to be useful in dealing with the people of Nepalese origin in the country.[10] Denying such suggestions, Bhutanese officials, during extensive conversations with this author, made two major points: (1) Bhutan had not and would never embark on such misadventures at the cost of jeopardizing its age-old bond of friendship with India, and (2) Bhutan regards the 1990s' uprising by some of the Lhotshampas as an act of terrorism, and, therefore, it was illogical for anyone to suggest that Thimphu would have enlisted the support of a foreign militant group or groups to tackle a bunch of 'anti-nationals' at home.[11]

That controversy aside, the presence of the Indian militants became the kingdom's top national agenda, and both the masses as well as the Royal government began to worry about the threat to the country's security and sovereignty. Starting with its 75th session in 1997, Bhutan's National Assembly or Parliament extensively debated the issue in sessions every year,[12] and put in place contingency measures, like evacuation of civilians, etc., to be executed in the event of any military assault to expel the insurgents. Bhutan slowly began to tighten its noose around these rebels by ordering its citizens in southern Bhutan not to sell or provide rations to the militants and threatening to book anyone found to be directly or indirectly backing these rebels under the National Security Act (NSA).[13]

Unlike Bangladesh, which has always been denying New Delhi's claim that there are at least 194 Indian rebel camps in that country,[14] Bhutan while admitting the rebels' presence within its territory had been extremely cautious in its response to the problem. Thimphu was aware of the fact that its army was small and inexperienced in counter-insurgency operations. It was against any immediate military offensive to reduce the possibility of the rebels attacking soft targets, like Bhutanese civilians travelling between the landlocked southern and western parts of the kingdom through West Bengal and Assam. These concerns had made Thimphu ward off India's pressure for tough action against the militants. Instead, King Jigme Singye Wangchuk decided to try and persuade the insurgents to leave his country in a peaceful manner. Then began the official talks between the Royal government and the rebel representatives from 1998 onwards. Even after six rounds of such talks with the rebel leaders, no breakthrough was achieved. Then, on 15 December 2003, convinced that the rebels had no plans to pull out on their own, King Wangchuk unleashed his small military machine of just about 6,000 Royal Bhutan Army (RBA) soldiers and a small contingent of the Royal Body Guards (RBG) to take on the heavily armed insurgents and flush them out of the kingdom.

Thimphu claimed, a month later, that its mission was successfully accomplished. The timing of the assault, 12 years after the Indian rebels had opened shop inside the kingdom, is another story.

ULFA Sets Out for the Dragon Kingdom

By the mid-1980s, north-eastern India's largest state, Assam, was in the grip of the ULFA, a rebel group formed by six radical Assamese youths on 7 April 1979 to achieve a 'Sovereign, Socialist Assam.' Heavily armed ULFA cadres killed, kidnapped and threatened tea planters and businessmen across the Brahmaputra river valley, and generally unleashed a reign of terror. This was because the separatist outfit was busy gathering funds to purchase military hardware and was sending its cadres for advanced weapons training to Myanmar, Afghanistan, and other suitable destinations. Among those assassinated by the ULFA was Surrendra Paul, chief of the Calcutta-based Apeejay Group of Industries that has several tea plantations in Assam. Surrendra, who was shot dead during a visit near the eastern Assam district town of Tinsukia on 9 April 1990, was the brother of Indian-born British business tycoon Lord Swaraj Paul.

The influential tea industry, whose annual turnover from the tea-growing business in Assam is more than Rs. 3,000 crore today, exerted tremendous pressure on New Delhi to adopt some tough measures to rein in the ULFA. In a secret operation on 8 November 1990, a chartered aircraft landed at an abandoned airfield at Sookerating near Tinsukia, 550 km east of Guwahati, Assam's capital, and evacuated around a dozen panic-stricken executives and their families belonging to the multinational Unilever Group that had seven tea plantations in the area.[15] These executives were under threat from the ULFA. The perilous security situation of the day could be gauged by a remark of the then Indian Minister of State for Home Affairs, Subodh Kant Sahay, who said, 'The whole (state) machinery was with the ULFA.'[16] New Delhi had to act. It dismissed the state government, then headed by a regional party, the Asom Gana Parishad (AGP) with Prafulla Kumar Mahanta as chief minister. This happened on the night of 27–8 November 1990. Simultaneously, the Indian government launched the first-ever systematic counter-insurgency operations against the ULFA codenamed 'Operation Bajrang'. The Indian army smashed the ULFA's central headquarters deep inside the Lakhipathar jungles, near Tinsukia. The rebels were on the run.

By the end of 1990 and early 1991, the ULFA had set up well-entrenched bases inside southern Bhutan, mainly in the district of Samdrup Jhongkar, bordering western Assam's Nalbari district. The NDFB and the KLO followed suit. Unlike in Myanmar, where Indian insurgent groups like the ULFA had allies like the Kachin Independence Army (KIA), an anti-Yangon guerrilla group, in Bhutan they had none. The Himalayan kingdom was chosen by the ULFA, and later the NDFB and the KLO, because southern Bhutan, where it set up base, was not properly policed. Besides, the area was densely wooded and located just across from Assam. The other major factor in these Indian insurgents' decision to venture into adjoining Bhutan was the fact that the country had only a small army which was totally untrained in counter-insurgency exercises, and therefore posed very little military threat to them.[17] Above all, Bhutan, with its access to Assam, West Bengal, and Arunachal Pradesh, served as an excellent staging area for the separatists who could return to the safety of their camps in the kingdom after carrying out violent strikes in Indian territory.

The Indian intelligence community as well as analysts had put the number of ULFA camps alone inside Bhutan at 36. These included the outfit's general and council headquarters, a security-cum training camp, and a crack strike squad called the Enigma Unit. However, at the time it launched its military assault on the rebels in December 2003, Bhutan had officially stated that its troops were battling 'in excess of 3,000 extremely well armed militants' and that there were 30 Indian rebels camps: 13 belonging to the ULFA, 12 of the NDFB and 5 KLO.[18]

As the weapons recovery later revealed, the Bhutanese were right in stating that they were battling a group of 'well armed' Indian rebels. According to the Royal Bhutanese Army (RBA), more than 500 AK 47/56 assault rifles and 328 other assorted weapons including rocket launchers and mortars, along with more than 100,000 rounds of ammunition, were found or confiscated in the course of the operation inside the kingdom.[19]

An anti-aircraft gun was also found at the site of the ULFA General Headquarters (GHQ) located at Merengphu in the district of Samdrup Jongkhar. ULFA rebels interviewed by this author within ten days of the RBA–RBG offensive in Bhutan—after they fled the kingdom and surrendered to the Indian security forces—admitted that the militants possessed sophisticated weapons, including anti-aircraft guns. 'We had in our arsenal weapons like AK 81 and 56 rifles, 60 mm mortars, anti-aircraft guns, universal machine guns and a variety of rocket propelled grenades including RPG 7 and RPG 2', Utpal Bharali, 31, an ULFA sergeant who was among those who surrendered to the Assam police, said.[20] He added that an Afghanistan-trained rebel,[21] Satabda Kumar, was the chief instructor of the ULFA's artillery squad inside Bhutan. Kumar, he said, was also the commander of the group's GHQ in the kingdom. The Bhutanese government and security establishment had every reason to be worried.

Thimphu Wakes Up

'We got to know of the rebels' presence only in 1995. By that time, they had already established several camps', Bhutan's Ambassador to India, Dago Tshering, said in an interview.[22] The Envoy added, 'The development and economic activities slowed down due to the presence of these rebels who subjected innocent people to extortion, threats and coercion. Besides, the mobility of our people got restricted and border trade with the Indian states of Assam and West Bengal suffered.' Tshering said several primary and high schools located in the vicinity of the rebel bases in southern Bhutan had to be shifted or closed down and Sunday markets too stopped operating.

There were also instances of the militants attacking Bhutanese civilians and government officials, both inside Bhutan as well as while travelling through Assam. Four Royal Bhutan Police personnel were killed when rebels attacked a police station at Nganglam in southern Bhutan. Again, in 1998, a convoy of a senior RBA officials was ambushed in the town of Patshala across the border in western Assam. In five separate incidents on 20 and 21 December 2000, Indian militants killed a total of 15 Bhutanese citizens, including women and children, who were travelling through Assam, and 19 others were injured.[23] Besides, five Bhutanese vehicles were attacked, three of which were torched. A Bhutanese immigration officer Sonam Dorji was kidnapped after the rebels hijacked his Toyota Hilux and set it ablaze.[24] That the rebels' presence was impacting really adversely was borne out by the fact that these serial attacks were carried out inside Assam by the Bodo Liberation Tigers (BLT), an outfit opposed to the NDFB that was operating out of bases in Bhutan.

The Bhutanese were initially puzzled, for neither did the BLT have bases in the kingdom nor was it seeking independence from India, unlike the other Bodo[25] ethnic rebel group, the NDFB. The answer was not difficult to find. 'Initially, we could not believe it when we heard that it was the BLT who [*sic*] carried out these attacks on Bhutanese vehicles and citizens. After all, we had no quarrel with the BLT and in fact we have the common objective of having the NDFB camps removed from Bhutan as soon as possible. It was later confirmed that the BLT had indeed carried out these attacks to pressurize the Royal government to evict the NDFB militants from Bhutan since NDFB's demand for an independent Bodoland was affecting the BLT's objective for statehood [within India] for the Bodos', Bhutan's home minister told the 79th Session of the country's National Assembly which was held in June–July 2001.[26]

The militants' presence was also having its impact on Bhutan's extremely cordial bilateral ties with India. Questions were raised on whether Thimphu was in any way extending support to the rebels after a few junior foreign ministry employees were found arranging money transfers on behalf of the ULFA. At least one instance had surfaced in which the Royal government, in July 2002, admitted that the ULFA had managed to use the cover of diplomatic baggage to send money abroad. Investigations by the Bhutanese police unearthed the fact that between January and July 1996, $38,000 and Rs. 300,000 were sent abroad in two instalments through diplomatic baggage. A Bhutanese government statement on the issue said: 'While it is true that two junior employees of the Protocol Division were found to have received money and extended some assistance to the militants, this was purely on the individual level and had nothing to do with the Royal government of Bhutan.'[27]

The two employees of the Bhutanese foreign ministry's protocol division were later identified as Wangchuk Dorji and Lhaba Tshering. Investigations revealed that Dorji had received Nu 40,000 (equivalent to 40,000 INR) from a senior ULFA functionary who went around as Deepak Das, towards visa fee, air fare, etc., for his (Dorji's) travel to the United Kingdom on 22 November 1999. He was earlier said to have received Nu 68,000 from the same ULFA leader on 12 April 1996 'for business purpose to buy Chinese shoes'. The same day, Dorji was said to have received an additional Nu 118,000 for conversion to US dollars from the same rebel leader.[28] The Royal government had later terminated the services of these two foreign ministry employees, and filed a case against them at the Thimphu District Court. The Bhutanese home minister had informed the National Assembly during its 79th Session in June–July 2001 that seven persons against whom there was concrete evidence of extending assistance to the militants had been prosecuted under the National Security Act (NSA) and the courts had awarded life imprisonment to three of them.[29] It is not known whether the two employees, Dorji and Tshering, were also among those seven. The Royal government had to start getting tough as the people's representatives or the Chimis from Mongar and Trashi Yangtse districts had raised the issue in the National Assembly of some Bhutanese nationals supplying rations to the militants. The 78th National Assembly proceedings, for instance, noted: 'They (the Chimis) expressed their deep regret and disappointment that some individuals motivated by greed were involved in transporting rations to the camps of the militants for personal gains.'[30]

In mid-2000, media reports started appearing in Assam that V. Namgyal, a Bhutanese army brigadier, who was the security-in-charge and military adviser to King Wangchuk was helping the ULFA in procuring arms and ammunition from various foreign sources.[31] An English daily from Guwahati alleged in a news report in its 1 July 2000 edition that Brig. Namgyal had helped the ULFA by arranging to bring in an arms consignment from Tibet to Deothang in Bhutan on 8 April 1999.[32] Thimphu denied charges that the Royal government was helping the rebels in any way, and such news reports gradually stopped appearing in the media. The Royal government, armed with the mandate of the

National Assembly to resolve the problem of the presence of foreign militants in the kingdom, started putting in place measures to choke the rebels. The representatives of the Bhutanese people, after all, had been unanimous in stating that the rebels' presence posed a very serious threat to the security and sovereignty of the kingdom. The National Assembly speaker too is on record as having said: 'The anxiety over the situation has robbed the Bhutanese people of their sleep and made their food tasteless'.[33]

THE NOOSE TIGHTENS

It was in 1996 itself that King Wangchuk drew up a plan to restructure the Royal Bhutan Army (RBA) although the issue of the ULFA and NDFB rebels' presence in the kingdom was first discussed at the National Assembly in 1997. It was decided to deploy RBA contingents on the Assam–Bhutan border, from the southern towns of Kalikhola to Daifam, which share a porous border with Western Assam. Beginning in 1998, the RBA and the RBG underwent winter training at facilities within the country, covering courses on 'assault pioneering, low intensity conflict and jungle warfare'.[34] The chief of the RBA informed the 78th Session of the National Assembly in June–July 2000 that 4,000 officers and men of the RBA were being deployed between the towns of Kalikhola and Daifam, on the border with India, to check the rebels' activities.[35] Around the time when the rebels first made their foray into Bhutan, and for long after that, just about 500 RBA men were deployed along the entire 266 km length of the border with the state of Assam.[36]

Thimphu was soon beginning to realize that its army was grossly inadequate in numbers to deal with the security situation. By the year 2000, the strength of the RBA was increased from 8 to 14 wings. Still, its strength was too small. The RBA chief, briefing Bhutan's public representatives, had stated that in order to increase the army's strength with properly trained soldiers, it was necessary to train 800 recruits every six months.[37] To achieve this in a short time, the duration of the training at the Military Training Centre at Wangdue Phodrang was reduced from nine to six months.

Driven by the prevailing security situation, the Royal government gave up its initial reluctance and agreed to raise a people's militia by the middle of 2003. More than 200 leaders of development committees of the districts and blocks met with King Wangchuk on 14 May 2003 in Thimpu.[38] At the meeting, a senior army officer asked the rural leaders to select the most capable men between the ages of 18 and 45, to be given a three-month training course by the RBA. He said that they would be given the same remuneration and facilities as regular soldiers. At district-level meetings since 1998, the local leaders have urged the king to organize militia training so that young Bhutanese men could help 'defend the security and sovereignty' of their country. At the time Bhutan launched the military strike against the rebels in December 2003, the strength of the people's militia stood at 800.[39]

Even while repeatedly emphasizing that Bhutan would use force to evict the foreign militants from its soil only as a last resort, King Wangchuk was clearly preparing for a possible military assault from late-1999 itself. On 2 August 1999, the king issued a communication highlighting the security concerns and the measures to be implemented and followed up on a priority basis to deal with the ULFA and Bodo rebels in emergency situations. He issued a set of further instructions on 1 November 1990, pointing out various immediate measures to be taken to strengthen security in the areas affected by the presence of the militants. A board of officers was constituted, consisting of senior officers from the RBA headquarters and the concerned field commanders to examine and prepare a detailed plan of action and work out the budgetary needs. Slowly but surely, the Royal government was getting ready to take on the rebels.

The king visited the Royal Bhutan Polytechnic at Dewathang, also in the militant-infested southern region, and explained the security threat to the students and staff members. This polytechnic is the country's only institution for imparting technical education, and is therefore an important establishment. Being located next to the RBA camp, the polytechnic was exposed to security risks and a decision was taken to shift it out. By March 2000, the polytechnic was shifted to the Royal Technical Institute at Kharbandi, and the complex that was vacated was occupied by Wing XI and Wing XII of the RBA in April that year.

Apart from slowly pushing ahead with measures like recruiting and training army personnel and building houses to accommodate them in the strategic locations in the vicinity of the militants' bases, Thimphu was getting its act together to ensure that funds were available to meet any eventuality. Up to June 2000, the Royal government had spent Nu 660.70 million to meet the cost of the RBA's immediate needs, including construction works, essential administrative requirements and purchase of equipment to improve and strengthen the security in the areas affected by the rebels' presence.[40] Two helipads were also built in the area for emergency operations by the security forces. By mid-2000, the Army Welfare Fund that was set up by the king in 1976, had a reserve of Nu 642.918 million. The RBA chief informed the National Assembly in 2000 that this reserve fund was being used for emergency security needs. Again, the National Assembly (79th Session) was informed in June–July 2001 that the Council of Ministers had approved a contingency plan with a total budget of Nu 410 million to meet the challenges in the event of an armed conflict with the rebels. The plan included provision to keep open all the internal highways and motor roads, bridges and communication systems, ration and fuel reserves, medical back-up systems, etc. By the middle of 2003, King Wangchuk was talking of raising the contingency budget to meet emergency situations from one billion to two billion Ngultrum (1 Ngultrums = 1 Rupee; approximately Nu 42 to 1 US dollar).[41] Such a huge contingency fund was being kept ready because, in the king's own assessment, 10 of the nation's 20 districts were going to be directly affected in the event of a conflict with these militants.[42] The districts of Samdrup Jongkhar, Pema Gatshel, Trashigang, Mongar, Zhemgang, Samtse, Chukha, Dagana, Tsirang, and Sarpang were all at risk because the militants had camps there or travelled through them. According to the Royal government's estimates, around 304 villages with a population of more than 66,000 Bhutanese people were at risk.

On most of these preparations Bhutan was keeping its staunchest ally, India, informed. There were continuous communications between Thimphu and New Delhi on the ways and means of dealing with the militants and, on several occasions, face-to-face meetings between leaders of the two nations at the highest level. One of the key meetings that took place between the two sides was on 14 September 2003, when King Wangchuk called on Prime Minister Atal Behari Vajpayee in New Delhi.[43] During this trip which spread over five days, the Bhutanese monarch also met Deputy Prime Minister L.K. Advani, who was also India's Home Minister, and other leaders. Authoritative sources said a decision to go for a military assault by way of a pincer attack with Indian troops providing a human wall on their side of the border was taken during these meetings in New Delhi.

The ground for the crucial September 2003 meeting was prepared by Brajesh Mishra, India's then National Security Adviser, who was sent to Thimphu by Prime Minister Vajpayee on 27 March 2003. New Delhi confirmed that Mishra, during his meeting with King Wangchuk as well as other Bhutanese government leaders, did discuss the issue of the Indian rebels based in the kingdom.[44] Then, Indian Army Chief General N.C. Vij himself paid a three-day visit to Thimphu from 8 May 2003, where he called on King Wangchuk as well as other Royal government leaders.[45] But it was during General Vij's meeting with the chief operations officer of the RBA that the two army chiefs were said to have discussed the general modalities of the military assault. C.D. Sahay, Chief of the Research & Analysis Wing (RAW), India's external intelligence agency, was also said to have impressed upon Thimphu the urgent need to dismantle the Indian militant camps inside the kingdom.[46] There were clear signs that New Delhi was getting restless and Thimphu was at last ready to shed its indecision and go ahead with a military campaign to oust the foreign militants from the kingdom. But the Royal government would still not give up on holding talks with the rebels in case a military confrontation could be avoided.

The Parleys

The 78th Session of the Bhutanese National Assembly in 2000 adopted a four-point resolution in accordance with which it expected the Royal government to deal with the problem of militancy in the kingdom.[47] The resolution said:

- Every effort must continue to be made to find a peaceful solution, through a peaceful dialogue;

- All supplies and rations to the militants must continue to be stopped;
- All persons found assisting the militants must be prosecuted under the National Security Act;
- If there is no other option left, military action will be taken as a last resort.

While Thimphu had been fairly successful in implementing two of the resolutions, cutting off ration supplies and taking tough action against a few of its citizens found aiding the rebels, it was finding it hard to convince the insurgents to leave the kingdom in a peaceful manner. But the Royal government was bent on initiating a dialogue with the rebels to try and convince them to pull out of Bhutan of their own. From 1998 until October–November 2003, Bhutan tried its best to reason with the ULFA and NDFB rebels to leave the country peacefully. The process failed.

The first meeting with the ULFA was held on 20 November 1998. The Royal government was represented by the home minister himself and an official of the ministry, while the ULFA was represented by its Finance Secretary Chitraban Hazarika and a local commander. Since the two ULFA representatives were only middle-level leaders in the outfit's hierarchy, the Bhutanese side explained to them that it was 'very important for talks to be held with their top leadership who would be capable of taking decisions'. The second meeting between the ULFA and the Royal government was held on 7 May 1999. This time, ULFA Commander-in-Chief Paresh Baruah, the rebel group's most powerful leader, led the ULFA delegation while Bhutan was represented by the home minister and the chairman of the Royal Advisory Council, besides three councillors.

The Bhutanese leaders made the following points to the ULFA team:[48]

- Their (the rebels') presence infringed on Bhutan's sovereignty and security, caused the people great inconvenience and could harm Thimphu's close ties with India;
- Bhutanese territory could turn into a battlefield if Indian soldiers were to enter in pursuit of the rebels;
- It was futile to fight the might of the Indian army and that

their objective of achieving independence for Assam was unrealistic;

- They should relocate their camps and leave Bhutanese soil immediately.

The ULFA leaders' response was:

- The ULFA was bent on fighting for an independent Assam till it was achieved;
- They were forced to enter Bhutanese territory because of Indian army operations in 1992 as Bhutan was Assam's immediate neighbour and its jungles provided them the safest sanctuaries;
- The militants were aware that their presence had created a difficult situation for Bhutan and that they had discussed the issue within the organization. But they were in the preparatory stage of their struggle for independence and were not ready to leave the jungles of Bhutan;
- Their camps elsewhere were not secure and convenient and so they could not leave the kingdom.

During the meeting, Paresh Baruah told the Bhutanese side that although he was the group's senior most military commander, he did not have the authority to remove their camps from Bhutanese territory, and agreed to come to Bhutan soon for the third round of talks along with ULFA Chairman Arabinda Rajkhowa. According to Bhutanese government publications, he also stated that the ULFA would require at least one and a half-years before leaving the kingdom. For 11 months, there was no response from the ULFA, until Paresh Barua telephoned a top-ranking Bhutanese leader in April 2000. The Bhutanese leader made it clear that he and his Chairman Rajkhowa must come to Bhutan for talks before 15 June 2000. The ULFA Commander-in-Chief explained that they were unable to come to Bhutan due to security risks in view of Thimphu making public the details of the talks through presentations in the national assembly, leading to wide media coverage. He proposed to once again send the group's finance secretary and a senior adviser, an offer rejected by Thimphu. The Royal government insisted the top duo come for the talks before 15 June when Baruah telephoned a second time.

For two years no meeting took place between the ULFA and the Royal government. Finally, the third round of talks were held over three days, 11, 14 and 18 June 2001, at the central secretariat at Thimphu. Bhutan's Home Minister Thinley Gyamtsho led the Royal government delegation while the ULFA was represented by its Finance Secretary-cum-Assistant General Secretary Chitraban Hazarika and the group's Political Adviser Bishnujyoti Burhagohain. When the Bhutanese leaders handed over a list of nine ULFA camps and asked the rebel leaders of their plans, Hazarika and Burhagohain said they had the mandate from their chairman and the executive council to inform the Bhutan government that the group was willing to close down four of these camps and also reduce the strength of the remaining five camps.

The ULFA leaders, in response to being asked for specific dates by which they could shift their cadres out of the kingdom, said they would require time until December 2001 when the monsoons would be well over. According to the minutes of the third round of meeting signed by the Chairman of the Royal Advisory Council Rinzin Gyaltshen and ULFA Finance Secretary Chitraban Hazarika on 18 June 2001, the two sides agreed to meet again to find a solution to the problem of the remaining five ULFA camps in Bhutan and ensure a total pull-out of the rebels from the country.[49] For the first few months after this agreement, the Bhutanese seemed to be satisfied with the ULFA's response. 'ULFA rebels have already closed one camp located inside our country and are in the process of winding up three more bases besides reducing the number of their cadres here', Bhutan's Home Secretary Tasho Pema Wangchuk said on 27 December 2001, four days before the agreed deadline was to end.[50] The Royal Government later confirmed that while the ULFA closed down four camps by 31 December 2001, as agreed upon, these camps were soon relocated within the kingdom.[51] Therefore, when the military assault eventually began in December 2003, the RBA discovered as many as 13 ULFA camps in the country's southern region.

Thimphu was simultaneously trying to enter into negotiations with the NDFB, so as to make this rebel group also agree to withdraw its cadres from the country. It was only on 6 and

7 October 2000 that the Royal government could hold the first round of talks with the NDFB. The rebel group was represented by its vice-president, general secretary, and publicity secretary. The second round of talks was held seven months later, on 15 May 2001, in which the NDFB was represented by its President Ranjan Daimary, alias D.R. Nabla, and Publicity Secretary B. Erakdao.

The Royal government placed the same argument before the NDFB leaders, that their illegal presence was an affront to Bhutan's territorial sovereignty, and was causing hardship to the Bhutanese people. They must, therefore, remove their camps and leave the kingdom. In response, the NDFB leaders said that they had been compelled by circumstances to establish camps in Bhutan. They said that, as asked by the Royal government, they intended to leave Bhutanese territory but could not give an assurance at this stage when they would be able to do so.[52]

The Last Sitting

At the next two national assembly sessions, in 2002 and 2003, the Royal government was unable to report any breakthrough in the talks with the rebels. Exasperated, the Bhutanese representatives, during the 81st Session of the National Assembly, held from 28 June to 18 August 2003, gave a mandate to the Royal government to 'make one last attempt' at persuading the militants to leave the country. The resolution that was adopted at this session was clear that, should the talks fail, then, as a last resort, the RBA would have to be given the responsibility of removing the militants from Bhutan. Based on this mandate, Bhutan's Home Minister Jigmi Thinley, who was also the Prime Minister, invited the ULFA, NDFB, and KLO leaders to Thimphu for talks. While the ULFA and the NDFB sent middle-level leaders for the talks, the KLO did not respond at all. The Royal government had been trying to bring the KLO over for talks since 2000, but the group did not respond. In April 2003, the Royal government had sent a delegation led by the chairman of the Royal Advisory Council to meet the middle-level leaders of the KLO. At this meeting, the KLO representatives were asked to inform their top leaders to come for talks with the Royal government.[53] Home Minister Thinley, in a desperate bid to find a peaceful solution to the problem, met separately with ULFA leaders in October 2003 and the NDFB leaders in November 2003.

A Bhutanese foreign ministry statement issued from Thimphu on 15 December 2003, the day the military assault began, gave details of what the Royal government had told the rebel leaders during the last rounds of talks:

> During the talks [in October–November 2003], the militants were told, with great restraint and patience, that the Royal government cannot tolerate their presence any longer. They were reminded that their entry into Bhutan was no different from a foreign invading army, and their conduct showed no regard for our laws. It was made clear to them that they were not refugees seeking humanitarian protection, and that their refusal to leave would result in a senseless and fratricidal conflict. They were also told that the senselessness of a confrontation lay in the fact that Bhutan has nothing to do with their hopes and aspirations. Every life lost in the foreign soil of Bhutan for them would be a waste. . . . They were also advised that the moment had arrived when they should try to find a solution within the constitutional framework of the Republic of India.

The tenor of the language that Thimphu used with the rebels was much harsher than anytime before, indicating that the Royal government was getting impatient. That the countdown for the inevitable, a military assault, had indeed begun became clear when Bhutan gave a notice in the 13 December 2003 edition of *Kuensel*, the country's national newspaper, that it was left with no option but to entrust the RBA with the 'sacred duty of removing the militants from our sovereign soil in accordance with the decision of the 81st Session of the National Assembly'. Troops of the Royal Bhutan Army and the Royal Body Guards were closing in on the rebel bases. Across the border, crack Indian Army soldiers, veterans in counter-insurgency operations, were deployed in strength. The trap was laid.

The Assault

ULFA Lieutenant Domeswar Rabha, 39, had just finished his morning meal at 8.30 on 15 December 2003, when the sounds of mortar fire at a distance rattled him and eight fellow rebel fighters in the jungles of southern Bhutan. 'I was shocked, it was an attack on our main military base, the General Headquarters (GHQ). How could the Royal Bhutan Army do this to us?' Rabha, a hard-core rebel fighter trained by the Burmese insurgent group, the Kachin Independence Army (KIA) in 1988, said of his first reaction that morning during an exclusive interview with this author at a safe house in the northern Assam town of Mangaldai on 22 December.[54] A group of nine rebels, under Rabha's command, were engaged in clearing the jungles near the ULFA GHQ at Merengphu, in Samdrup Jongkhar district in southern Bhutan, when the RBA began its offensive. He was perhaps among the first batch of several militants who surrendered to the Indian security forces within a week of Thimphu's offensive. 'We have been operating out of camps inside Bhutan for many years now, and had good relations with the Bhutanese, including many of the officials who used to visit us. We are surprised, therefore, over the Bhutanese attack on us', Subhash Kalita, 40, another surrendered ULFA rebel said.[55]

These statements by surrendered ULFA insurgents make it clear that the militants were caught by surprise when the RBA and RBG soldiers began the operations at 9 a.m. on 15 December 2003 under orders from King Wangchuk. While the rebels had perhaps taken the Bhutanese for granted all along, Thimphu was preparing itself mentally, administratively, and militarily for just such a possibility—a military strike against the militants. That perhaps had been Thimphu's strategy all along, not to give the rebels any indication of the fact that its military could actually strike against them at some point of time. King Wangchuk had even visited ULFA camps on more than one occasion. The rebels claimed the king had visited the ULFA GHQ in 2002. 'We saw the King, but do not know why he had come. Our leaders told us later, he had come to enquire as to what we were doing', said ULFA rebels, Naziruddin Ali and Surya Boro who had surrendered in the wake of the Bhutanese assault.[56]

Buddhist Bhutan had last gone to war against any foreign force 138 years ago, when they fought the British. That was the Anglo–Bhutanese war of 1865 in which the British Army defeated Bhutan's then Deb Raja or temporal head, Sonam Lhendup, and came to exercise much influence on the nation's affairs.[57] Besides, that victory gave the British unhindered trans-Himalayan access for trade with Tibet.

On 14 December 2003, a day before launching the assault, King Wangchuk telephoned Indian Prime Minister Atal Behari Vajpayee and briefed him about the Royal government's plans. Announcing the launch of the military offensive in the Indian Parliament, within hours of the Bhutanese soldiers closing in on the rebel bases in the kingdom, Foreign Minister Yashwant Sinha said New Delhi was firmly behind Thimphu at this hour. Making a suo moto statement in the Lok Sabha and the Rajya Sabha (lower and upper houses respectively of the Indian Parliament), Sinha said Prime Minister Vajpayee has conveyed to King Wangchuk that the government and people of India 'stand firmly and solidly' behind the Bhutan government at this critical juncture and would provide all necessary support as requested, till the task was completed.[58] He said that the Indian Army was also taking necessary measures to intercept the movement of militants from Bhutan into India. The federal authorities, Sinha said, had advised the Assam and West Bengal governments to remain alert to deal with the situation arising out of this action, including sealing the borders and maintaining peace.[59] The Indian Army admitted that it was providing 'logistic support' like airlifting the injured RBA soldiers and other casualties in the course of the operation and that the offensive itself had been launched by the RBA and the RBG entirely on their own.

Ultimatum given, and a strategy put in place in full consultation with Prime Minister Vajpayee and the Indian Army, the Bhutanese troops made their advance to take on the rebels located in bases bordering the Indian states of Assam, West Bengal, Sikkim, and Arunachal Pradesh. If the Indian rebels thought the Bhutanese military machine was rusty, inexperienced, and battle wary, they were proved wrong. With the Indian army breathing down the rebels' neck just next door, providing a shield and waiting to trap the fleeing rebels, complete with artillery equipment and other military hardware, the rebels put up minimum resistance and the Bhutanese military tasted success soon enough. The RBA rained 81 mm mortars on the key ULFA bases, forcing many of the rebels to flee. The rebels retaliated with 51 mm mortars and grenades,[60] but it was never a full-scale fightback. Within 24 to 48 hours, RBA soldiers dislodged the ULFA rebels from their Central Headquarters (CHQ) at Phukaptong and GHQ at Merengphu, both in the district of Samdrup Jongkhar.[61] The main NDFB camp at Tikri in the same district, another NDFB camp in Nganglam sub-district, and several KLO camps in the nearby Samtse district also fell to the Bhutanese military.[62]

On 19 December, the fifth day of the operations, Indian Army Chief Gen. N.C. Vij said in New Delhi that Bhutan has handed over the first batch of seven captured rebels to the Indian Army that included 'key underground leaders'.[63] ULFA Publicity Secretary Mithinga Daimary (real name Deepak Kachari) who was one of them was eventually handed over to the Assam police and was produced at a court in Guwahati, the state capital, on 26 December 2003.[64] Top Assam police officials went on record saying the NDFB publicity chief B. Erakdao too was captured by the RBA. But Erakdao's whereabouts or whether the RBA had actually captured him in the course of the operations still remain a mystery. On 26 December the Indian army presented ULFA's 78-year-old ideologue, Bhimkanta Burhagohain, the oldest member of the group who was based in its Bhutan bases, before the media at the northern garrison town of Tezpur, 180 km from Guwahati.[65] Earlier, the media had reported that Burhagohain had been killed by the RBA while he was leading a group of non-combatants living in the camps for surrender to the Bhutanese forces, holding a white flag. A top army official said that after Burhagohain and three other senior ULFA members were handed over to them by the Bhutanese authorities on 25 December 2003, they 'expressed their willingness to surrender'.[66] Burhagohain read out a statement during his appearance before the media at the Indian Army's IV Corps Headquarters at Tezpur calling upon his comrades-in-arms to surrender. Later, when he was produced at a court in Tezpur, Burhagohain denied he had surrendered, saying he had been captured and that he would continue pursuing the ULFA cause. The Indian Army preferred to remain silent and refrained from joining issue with the veteran ULFA leader. Burhagohain and three of his comrades, 'Major' Robin Handique, Bolin Das and 'Major' Amarjit Gogoi, are currently in prison, in judicial custody.

That the ULFA and the NDFB were rather unwilling to fight the Bhutanese troops was indicated in the several responses by the top leaders of the groups. On 16 December, within 24 hours of the RBA offensive, ULFA Chairman Arabinda Rajkhowa sent a communication to King Wangchuk, appealing for a halt to the military operations, citing the traditional bond between the people of Assam and Bhutan. He said in his communication, e-mailed to journalists in Guwahati, that the Indian army was involved in the offensive and that Bhutan should not let the kingdom be used to target 'innocent people, including non-combatants like women and children'.[67] Later, in a telephone interview with this author on 26 December 2003, ULFA's elusive Commander-in-Chief Paresh Baruah made the following remark: 'At first, we thought it was the Bhutanese Army that was fighting us, so we asked our soldiers not to fight (back) and leave. Some retaliation followed later when we realized that it was the Indian Army that was actually fighting us'.[68] Whatever strategy the ULFA or the NDFB rebels may have adopted in the face of the Bhutanese assault, it was apparent that there was very little resistance from the militants. This was also borne out by the fact that the Bhutanese military suffered very little casualties: 11 RBA soldiers had died and 36 others suffered injuries.[69]

Like the ULFA, the NDFB too had gone out of its way to send a message to Thimphu not to treat it as an enemy. In a statement to *The Sentinel*, an English daily from Guwahati, on 17 December 2003, Major B. Susranggra, NDFB's military chief, said: 'The Royal Government of Bhutan and His Highness must not consider us as the enemy of Bhutan and we can never think of Bhutanese government as well as its citizens as our enemy. We shall always uphold the age-old friendly relationship between the neighbouring people of Bhutan.'[70] The ULFA also sought help from Beijing (this development will be dealt with later in this chapter), a request that was turned down outright by the Chinese authorities.

Missing Links and Timing of the Assault

If the timing of the Bhutanese military assault needs to be analysed, there is a need to focus on the missing links and unanswered questions as well. The Royal government would like to insist that there was no hidden reason for timing the crackdown at that juncture other than the mandate of the 81st Session of the National Assembly, held between 28 June and 18 August 2003, which wanted Thimphu to try and persuade the rebels 'one last time' to leave the kingdom, or expel them by using military force. 'The military crackdown was our ultimate option. The last round of talks were held in October–November, 2003 where the KLO went unrepresented as it did not respond to our invitation. Middle-level ULFA and NDFB leaders who came for the meetings said they were unable to leave the kingdom immediately,' Aum Neten Zangmo, Bhutan's foreign secretary, told this author in a telephone interview from Thimphu on 16 December 2003, Day 2 of the operations.[71] But why was the military assault carried out at that time and not earlier? The National Assembly since 2000–1 had been in favour of a policy of persuasion, and if that failed, the rebels were to evicted by force. This makes it pertinent to try and zero in on the possible trigger factor for the RBA–RBG offensive in December 2003.

The Indian and Bhutanese security establishments were stung when they learnt about the launch of the Bhutan Communist Party (Marxist-Leninist-Maoist) on 22 April 2003, the 133rd birth anniversary of Lenin.[72] The BCP circulated pamphlets in the Bhutanese refugee camps in Nepal and in areas inside Bhutan, which revealed that the new party's objective was to 'smash the monarchy' and establish a 'true and new democracy' in Bhutan.[73] Both New Delhi and Thimphu were quick to put the KLO under the scanner. Security agencies soon came to the conclusion that the KLO was active and had pockets of influence in the strategic north Bengal areas of West Bengal, and could act as a bridge between the Maoist guerrillas in Nepal and the newly emerging Maoist force in Bhutan. Formed on 28 December 1995 by some radical members of the Koch-Rajbongshi tribe, the KLO has been fighting to achieve a separate Kamatapur state by carving out territories from Assam and adjoining West Bengal where the community has a sizeable population. Indian intelligence agencies were at the same time aware of the fact that the KLO had provided sanctuary to fleeing Maoist rebels from Nepal, that the outfit had acted as a link between the Maoists and the radical left-wing activists in Bihar and that it received help from the Maoists in setting up a number of explosive units in north Bengal.

Ultimately, it could have been the emerging Maoist threat to Bhutan that may have been the key factor that made King Wangchuk shake off his long dilemma and act decisively. There had always been, of course, intense pressure from New Delhi to oust the Indian insurgents as well as the threat the rebels' presence posed to Bhutan's own sovereignty and development. Bhutan's Ambassador in India, Dago Tshering, told this writer after the military operations were over that he had 'not heard of the Bhutan Communist Party'. Tshering, however, thought there was a 'distinct possibility' of the rebels having had a nexus with 'certain people' in Bhutanese refugee camps in Nepal or the Maoist rebels themselves.[74] The missing links and unanswered questions relate to such key statistics as the number of rebels killed or captured, the actual number of militant fighters who were inside Bhutan, and their whereabouts in the wake of the Bhutanese military operations. For instance, a statement from the Bhutanese foreign office on 17 December 2003 said the RBA was battling 'in excess of 3,000 well-armed' Indian insurgents. Within three to four days, from 15 December when the offensive was launched, Bhutanese authorities started saying that rebels of the ULFA, NDFB and the KLO had been 'dislodged' from all of their 30 camps inside the kingdom, and that the Bhutanese troops were engaged in pursuing the fleeing rebels to 'flush them out' of the country.

On its part, the Indian army, which had admitted to providing 'logistic support' to the RBA,[75] had stated that its troops were deployed in strength all along the Indo–Bhutan border to prevent the entry of fleeing militants into India. Till Day 11 of the operation, that is, 25 December, the following hard statistics compiled from official statements have emerged: rebels killed inside Bhutan, 120 (as stated by the Indian army's Eastern Command chief); rebels killed by Indian army while trying to sneak back, 19 (army spokesman, IV Corps, based in Assam); surrendered, 45 (army spokesman, IV Corps); rebels captured, 36 (army sources); and the number of women and children belonging to families of rebels handed over on 24 December 2003, by Bhutan to India, 64.

This accounts for a total of 284, although many of the 64 people handed over to India cannot be regarded as rebel fighters as they were mostly non-combatants. On 2 January 2004, Indian Army Chief Gen N.C. Vij said in Guwahati that 650 militants had been killed or taken into custody in the wake of the operations inside Bhutan.[76] He did not provide any break-up of the figure. The question arises as to where have the remaining 2,300 or so rebel cadres disappeared? After all, Thimphu had said they were battling more than 3,000 fighters. Are they still inside the inhospitable jungles of Bhutan, being pursued by the Bhutanese military? If so, how have the militants been surviving? What has been their source of food?

With the Indian army stating during the time that its troops were solidly manning the border, it becomes difficult to think that the rebels had sneaked into Assam or West Bengal in large numbers in the wake of the Bhutanese offensive. It was also unlikely that most of the rebels had mingled with the locals in Bhutan as identifying outsiders in the thinly populated nation would not have been difficult. Answers to some of these questions are not forthcoming. Nevertheless, considering the geography of the region, it is possible that the rebels managed to escape into the neighbouring Indian states of Assam, Arunachal Pradesh, and Meghalaya, and some of them may have managed to move onwards to Myanmar or Bangladesh or even Nepal, days before the Bhutanese military assault had actually begun. Besides, the Bhutanese figure of its troops battling 3,000 or more rebels from 15 December onwards could itself have been either inaccurate or outdated. 'The figure on the number of rebels was just a good guess. How could anyone expect us to know exactly how many rebels were inside Bhutan?' Ambassador Tshering remarked.[77]

BHUTAN'S ACTION: ECHO IN SOUTH ASIA

The military action by Bhutan against the Indian rebels did create an immediate impact in South Asia in so far as the war against terror is concerned. The following immediate responses were noticed in the South Asian region:

- Bangladesh reacted by saying it had sealed its borders with India to prevent Indian rebels fleeing Bhutan or Myanmar from entering its territory.

- The arrest of 34 ULFA militants in and around Dhaka on 2 January 2004 and the rocket attack on the ATTF chief's apartment in downtown Dhaka are some post-Bhutan offensive developments that cannot be missed out.[78]
- The Bangladesh Home Ministry decided to crackdown on Indian militants, and keep such operations secret, obviously due to Dhaka's official stand that no Indian rebels were operating from that country.[79]
- There were strong indications of Myanmar tightening its noose on Indian rebel groups like the NSCN-K and the ULFA that have bases in the country.[80]

The Indian government seized the initiative and used the forum of the South Asian Association for Regional Cooperation (SAARC), which was holding its 12th Summit in Islamabad in the first week of January 2004, to call upon nations in the region to actively clamp down on terror. Pakistan could not have missed this strong statement by India to fight terrorism in South Asia as well as globally. Prime Minister Atal Behari Vajpayee, addressing the summit, said: 'I would like to draw attention to the courageous action taken by His Majesty the King of Bhutan and his government against insurgent groups which were trying to use Bhutanese territory to launch terrorist activities in India. It is an outstanding example of sensitivity to the security concerns of a neighbor which is at the same time in the direct long-term security interest of Bhutan itself.'[81] Earlier, on 1 January 2004, Indian Foreign Minister Yashwant Sinha had urged SAARC countries to emulate Bhutan in flushing out insurgents from their soil.[82] New Delhi's remarks and the Bhutanese Prime Minister Jigme Thinley's strong plea for the adoption and effective implementation of the protocol on terrorism during the summit were points that have not gone unnoticed. In an indirect reference to Pakistan's role, Thinley, during his address at the summit, said the recent attempt to assassinate Pakistan President Pervez Musharraf was a rude reminder of the need to root out terrorism.[83]

Post-9/11 and now, after Bhutan's military operations against the insurgents, India's neighbours, as also all those engaged in the global war against terror, have started talking a similar language, that terrorism needs to be curbed with a firm hand.

The Chinese response to a rather dramatic ULFA move must also be seen as part of this trend. ULFA Chairman Arabinda Rajkhowa put out an appeal to the Chinese leadership on 25 December 2003 to provide safe passage to the rebels from Bhutan for temporary shelter in China.[84] Rajkhowa in his fax communication to the Chinese leadership said: 'We have come under massive attack of Indo–Bhutan joint forces and our combatants have been forced to retreat up to the Sino–Bhutan border due to all out air and artillery campaigns.'[85] Beijing was quick to turn down the ULFA plea and cautioned that it had alerted its frontier forces to prevent any intrusion of Indian militants. A Chinese embassy spokesperson in New Delhi said the Chinese frontier forces were quite capable of preventing the entry of Indian rebels into their country and that they were closely monitoring the development of the situation.[86]

It is not that China or sources in China have always maintained a distance from Indian separatists. Indian insurgents had not only visited China in the past for help, but had also received assistance from sources within the country. NSCN-IM General Secretary Thuingaleng Muivah is on record as having said that the Naga rebels had earlier obtained arms from China and Pakistan.[87] Of course, Muivah's claims do not match Indian media reports in 2000 which talked of a Chinese 'agency' supplying machine guns and AK-47 rifles to rebel groups in India's north-east. A crossed cheque of half a million dollars encashed by a Chinese firm in Beijing has ostensibly revealed the source from where the top Naga militant group, the NSCN-IM, was getting arms. The news reports talked of NSCN-IM arms procurer Anthony Shimray having flown from Bangkok to Beijing in September 2000 and holding talks with the 'Chinese agency' in Kunming.[88] The report may or may not be correct, but China had always been looked upon by several north-east Indian rebel groups as their ideological source.

A Lesson Learnt

Bhutan seems to have learnt a lesson, and learnt it well. So, when the present author asked Ambassador Tshering after the operations had ended, whether the Indian insurgents could return to the kingdom that had been their home for 12 years, he replied, 'There is no guarantee, we can't, therefore, sit tight.'[89] Two possibilities are worrying Thimphu: attempts at retaliation by the rebels who could attack soft targets, either inside the kingdom or civilians passing through Indian territory, in the bordering states of Assam and West Bengal, secondly, the Royal government is unwilling to rule out the chances of the rebels returning to the densely wooded southern parts of the country.

For nearly three months since January 2004, when the RBA and the RBG ended their operations against the Indian rebels, Thimphu was engaged in working out a strategy to put in place a mechanism to tackle future threats. This led to the first Bhutan–India bilateral meeting on 'border management and security matters' in New Delhi on 9 and 10 March 2004. While Ambassador Tshering led the Bhutanese delegation, which included the country's Home Secretary, Penden Wangchuk, the Indian side was led by Additional Secretary in the Ministry of Home Affairs K.P. Singh. Four main decisions were arrived at in the meeting:[90]

- Both nations agreed to strengthen security along the international border along the Indian states of Assam and West Bengal.
- New Delhi agreed to train the Royal Bhutan Police (RBP), besides making available facilities to them for training, etc.
- The Indian Border Roads Organisation (BRO) has been entrusted with the task of upgrading and maintaining the roads leading to the kingdom from the adjoining Indian states of West Bengal and Assam.
- The two sides agreed to establish an 'institutional mechanism' between the home ministries of the two countries to evolve ways to improve coordination between district authorities on either side of the border.

The New Delhi meeting in March 2004 has been very important from Bhutan's point of view. The small size of its military and the police had been making the Royal government a bit uneasy. The strength of the RBA is just about 6,000. The strength of the RBP is even lower. Moreover, since the police in Bhutan have virtually no experience in handling security matters at a more broader and complex level, and have no training in dealing with militancy, Thimphu has been laying much stress on the training of its police force by the Indians. Intelligence gathering is another area that is worrying Bhutan. The Indian intelligence agencies are expected to provide specialized training to a small group of Bhutanese police and military officials on this aspect. 'Now, there is no way for the Bhutanese to find out what the militants on the other side of the border could be planning,' Ambassador Tshering said. This explains the haste with which Bhutan has been pursuing the Indians to train its police and tiny intelligence set-ups. The Royal Government is unlikely to be complacent any more.

Thimphu, however, is against pursuing a confrontationist approach any longer. A comment in the government controlled *Kuensel*, posted on its Internet edition (www.kuenselonline.com) on 27 December 2003, sums up the Royal government's post-operations stand:

> It might seem a little odd to ask that there should be no hard feelings at the end of it all, but it is characteristic of Bhutan and the Bhutanese people that the overriding emotions even now are regret and empathy. When we assure the people of Assam and West Bengal of our continued friendship, it includes the militants. Oddly enough there has never been any animosity during the entire operations, only a feeling of regretful necessity. At the end of it all, the Bhutanese people will not celebrate victory but will express our sentiments in prayers and butter lamps. . . .

NOTES

1. Longitude 88° 45′ and 92° 10′ east; Latitude 26° 45′ and 28° 15′ north.
2. Projected population in 2002 was 716,424, *Bhutan in Focus*, booklet published by the Royal Bhutanese Embassy, New Delhi (2003), p. 8.
3. For a comprehensive profile of ULFA, see <http://www.satp.org/satporgtp/countries/india/states/assam/terrorist_outfits/ulfa.htm>.
4. For a comprehensive profile of NDFB, see <http://www.satp.org/satporgtp/countries/india/states/assam/terrorist_outfits/ndfb.htm>.
5. For a comprehensive profile of KLO, see <http://www.satp.org/satporgtp/countries/india/states/assam/terrorist_outfits/klo.htm>.
6. On 30 July 1994, in a telephone interview from Bhutan's capital Thimphu, the country's then Home Minister Dago Tshering had said:

'There are no Bodo [pronounced Boro, but at times spelt as Bodo due to etymological connotations as the word has a Tibetan origin] militants taking shelter in any of our villages or towns. But our southern foothills have a 6,132 sq km of dense tropical forest contiguous to Assam and West Bengal. It could be possible that some Bodo insurgents cross over from time to time.'Wasbir Hussain, *The Telegraph*, Calcutta, 31 July 1994, Bhutan says no rebels hiding; Centre clears Army action against Bodos.

7. Chitra Tiwari, 'Maoist crisis spreads in Himalayas', *The Washington Times*, 24 May 2003, see <http://washingtontimes.com/world/20030524-120741-9529r.htm>.
8. Ibid.
9. Ibid.
10. Bibhu Prasad Routray, 'An Examplary Onslaught', *Bharat Rakshak Monitor*, vol. 6, no. 4, January–February 2004, New Delhi, <www.bharatrakshak.com/monitor/issue-4/routray.hmt>.
11. Bhutanese Ambassador in India, Dago Tshering, made remarks to this effect during an interview with the author in New Delhi on 18 March 2004.
12. 'Proceedings and Resolutions of the 79th Session of The National Assembly', compiled by National Assembly Secretariat, Thimphu, Bhutan, p. 5.
13. These measures were part of the three-point resolution passed by the 77th Session of the Bhutanese National assembly in 1999. See Proceedings and Resolutions of the 78th Session of The National Assembly, pp. 133–4.
14. 'Bangla denies presence of ultra camps', *The Assam Tribune*, Guwahati, 10 January 2004.
15. Sanjoy Hazarika, *Strangers of the Mist: Tales of War and Peace from India's Northeast*, New Delhi: Viking, 1994, p. 197.
16. Ibid., p. 190, cited in Wasbir Hussain, 'Multi-force operations in counter terrorism: A Viewfrom the Assam Theatre', *Faultlines, Writings on Conflict and Resolution,* New Delhi: Institute for Conflict Management, vol. 9, July 2001, p. 41.
17. Bhutanese officials have confirmed in interviews with the author that the strength of the Royal Bhutan Army is now around 6,000, meaning that when the Indian insurgents first made their foray into the kingdom, the RBA's strength was even smaller.
18. Press statements from the Royal Bhutanese Embassy, New Delhi, 15 and 17 December 2003.
19. Report in *Kuensel*, Bhutan's national newspaper, posted on its internet edition on 27 December 2003 (www.kuenselonline.com).
20. Interview with the author at an Assam police safe house in the northern district town of Mangaldoi on 22 December 2003.

21. A top surrendered ULFA rebel, Munin Nobis, interviewed by this author on 23 October 2002 at Guwahati, said top Pakistani ISI officials had arranged trips of senior ULFA leaders, including Commander-in-Chief Paresh Barua and Nobis himself, to Afghanistan via Pakistan's North West Frontier Province in December 1990 and January 1991. The ULFA leaders, apart from other engagements, had met with the frontline Mujahidin leader of the time, Gulbudin Hekmatyr. More than a dozen ULFA activists had undergone advanced artillery training at the hands of the Afghan Mujahidin trainers.
22. Interviewed by the author at the Bhutanese embassy in Chanakyapuri, New Delhi, on 18 March 2004.
23. 'Proceedings and Resolutions of the 79th Session of The National Assembly', pp. 166–9.
24. Ibid.
25. Bodo is Assam's largest plains tribal group.
26. Proceedings and Resolutions of the 79th Session of The National Assembly, p. 168
27. Media report, cited in Bibhu Prasad Routray, 'An Exemplary Onslaught', *Bharat Rakshak Monitor*, vol. 6, no. 4, January–February 2004.
28. Media report, cited in Jaideep Saikia, 'Autum in Springtime: The ULFA battles for survival', *Faultlines, Writings on Conflict and Resolution*, Institute for Conflict Management, New Delhi, vol. 7, November 2000, p. 43.
29. 'Proceedings and Resolutions of the 79th Session of The National Assembly', p. 111.
30. Ibid., p. 100.
31. 'Bhutan Govt. actively Aiding ULFA Activities', *The Sentinel*, Guwahati, 1 July 2000.
32. Ibid.
33. 'Proceedings and Resolutions of the 78th Session of The National Assembly', p. 2.
34. Bhutanese officials in interviews with the author.
35. 'Proceedings and Resolutions of the 78th Session of The National Assembly', p. 105.
36. Interviews with Bhutanese officials.
37. 'Proceedings and Resolutions of the 78th Session of The National Assembly', p. 167.
38. Kinley Dorji, 'A Militia Against Terror', *South Asia Intelligence Review* (www.satp.org), vol. 1, no. 46, 2 June 2003.
39. Interview with Bhutanese Ambassador in India, Dago Tshering, New Delhi, 18 March 2004.
40. RBA Chief General Lam Dorji's statement at the 78th Session of the National Assembly in June–July 2000.

41. Dorji, 'A Militia Against Terror'.
42. Rinzin Wangchuk, *The People Must Defend Their Country*, Kuensel internet edition (www.kuenselonline.com), Thimphu, posted on 17 May 2003.
43. *The Hindu*, 15 September 2003 < http://www.hindu.com/2003/09/15/stories/2003091509081200.htm>.
44. Media briefing by Indian government spokesman in New Delhi on 30 March 2003, <http://www.meadev.nic.in/news/20030330.htm
45. 'Indian Army Chief visits Bhutan', report in < http://www.eoithimphu.org/news31.html>.
46. 'Ulfa bases raided in Bhutan', 13 August 2003, <http://indiamonitor.com/news/readCatFullNews.jsp?ni=981&ct=International>.
47. Proceedings and Resolutions of the 78th Session of The National Assembly, p. 101.
48. Ibid., pp. 114–17.
49. 'Proceedings and Resolutions of the 79th Session of The National Assembly', pp. 104–7.
50. Telephone interview with the present author from Thimphu, 27 December 2001.
51. *Kuensel*, Thimphu, 13 December 2003.
52. 'Proceedings and Resolutions of the 79th Session of The National Assembly', pp. 102–3.
53. *Kuensel*, Thimphu, 13 December 2003.
54. Wasbir Hussain, 'We picked up our AKs and fled', *The Sentinel*, Guwahati, India, 24 December 2003.
55. Ibid.
56. Ibid.
57. Bhabani Sen Gupta, *Bhutan: Towards a Grass-root Participatory Polity*, New Delhi: Konark, 1999, pp. 25–6.
58. Press Trust of India (PTI) news report, New Delhi, 15 December 2003.
59. Ibid.
60. Statement by Lt Gen J.S. Verma, the Indian Army's Calcutta-based Eastern Command Chief, cited in Wasbir Hussain, 'Bhutan :Going For The Kill', Outlookindia.com (www.outlookindia.com), 22 December 2003.
61. Press statement from the Royal Bhutanese Embassy, New Delhi, 17 December 2003.
62. Ibid.
63. 'Seven captured militants handed over by Bhutan', Press Trust of India, New Delhi, 19 December 2003.
64. Front page photograph in *The Sentinel*, Guwahati, India, of Mithinga Daimary at a local court, 27 December 2003.
65. '"Mama" Mystery solved, calls for surrender', *The Sentinel*, Guwahati, 27 December 2003.

66. Statement to the media by Lt. Gen. Mohinder Singh, GOC IV Corps, Indian Army at Tezpur on 26 December 2003. See "Mama" Mystery solved, calls for surrender', *The Sentinel*, 27 December 2003.
67. Hussain, 'Thimphu silent on toll; ULFA, NDFB urge King for restraint', *The Sentinel*, Guwahati, 18 December 2003.
68. Hussain, 'We asked cadres to leave Bhutan', *The Sentinel*, Guwahati (www.sentinelassam.com), 27 December 2003.
69. Interview with Bhutan's Ambassador in India Dago Tshering in New Delhi, 18 March 2004.
70. Hussain, 'Thimphu silent on toll; ULFA, NDFB urge King for restraint'.
71. Ibid., *Bhutan: Going For The Kill.*
72. 'Maoists form unit in Bhutan', *The Times of India*, 18 May 2003.
73. Ibid.
74. Interview with the author in New Delhi, 18 March 2004.
75. General Officer Commanding-in-Chief of the Indian Army's Eastern Command, Lt Gen. J.S. Verma, while speaking to the media at his headquarters in Kolkata on 16 December 2003, *The Sentinel*, Guwahati, 17 December 2003.
76. 'India may choke rebels in Myanmar, 650 rebels neutralized in Bhutan: Army Chief', *The Sentinel*, Guwahati, 3 January 2004.
77. Interview with the writer, New Delhi, 18 March 2004.
78. United News of India, Dhaka, 3 January in <www.deepikaglobal.com>.
79. *The Daily Star*, Dhaka, Internet Edition, 5 January 2004.
80. Hussain, 'Anti-rebel offensive by Junta: Myanmar scene hazy, claims by NSCN-K differ', *The Sentinel*, Guwahati, 8 January 2004.
81. 'PM calls for trust, lauds courageous action of King', *The Sentinel*, Guwahati, 5 January 2004.
82. 'India tells SAARC: Emulate Bhutan to flush out insurgents', *The Assam Tribune*, Guwahati, 2 January 2004.
83. *The Sentinel*, Guwahati, 5 January 2004, 'All rebel leaders captured: Bhutan', *The Sentinel*, Guwahati, January 2004.
84. 'Arabinda SOS to China for safe passage, shelter', *The Sentinel*, Guwahati, 28 December 2003.
85. Ibid.
86. 'China turns down ULFA plea for safe passage', *The Assam Tribune*, Guwahati, 1 January 2004.
87. The Rediff Interview/NSCN (I-M) General Secretary Thuingaleng Muivah, 25 January 2001, <http//www.rediff.com/news/2001/jun/25inter.htm>.
88. 'NSCN ultras negotiate arms deal in China', *The Pioneer*, New Delhi, 31 October 2003.
89. Hussain, 'Bhutan: The Shadow of Militancy Lingers', *South Asia Intelligence Review* (satp.org), vol. 2, no. 36, 22 March 2004.
90. Ibid.

9. Responding to Terrorism: Political and Social Consequences in South Asia

Lok Raj Baral

CONCEPTUALIZING TERRORISM

The definition of terrorism provided by the United States government and others who joined the bandwagon after the attack on the US on 11 September 2001, has broadened its scope to include some of the local and regional rebellions. Violent movements being launched against the continued exploitation by a few in the name of symbols, stability, and identity or democracy may be conveniently branded as terrorist. However, attacks by the fundamentalist groups such as Al Qaida and others who carry out their missions for spreading religious and fanatical hatred can broadly be accepted as terrorist. Conflicting opinions may arise on all such definitional and operational missions as all terrorist movements are carried out with uncommon objectives and with varying strategies, methods, and tactics.

Terrorism which itself is an amorphous term and its activity is not easy to address either by the state or by other domains of civil society. In some countries, terrorism originates from religious bigotry and in some others, the issue of identity, the desire to have an honourable and secured life or the objective of a democratic system and freedom becomes the motivating factor for resorting to extreme forms of actions that are characterized by violence, killings, extortion, and crimes of various kinds. When other channels fail or are perceived to have failed by the involved actors, conveniently branded as terrorists by the opposite side, the former use coercive intimidation to further their goals. This term the originated from French Revolution and the Jacobins' *systeme, r'egime de la terreur.*[1] Stating what terrorism is not, Walter Laquer has said:

> No definition of terrorism can possibly cover all the varieties that have appeared throughout history: peasant wars and labor disputes and brigandage have been accompanied by systematic terror, and the same is true of general wars, civil wars, revolutionary wars, wars of national liberation and resistance movements against foreign occupiers.[2]

Taking South Asia, the conceptualization of terrorism does not differ basically as the anti-terrorist legal measures adopted by each country suggest. For India, terrorism means 'intentions to threaten the unity, integrity, and security of India or to strike terror in the people or any section of the people by using bombs, explosive substances, firearms or other lethal weapons'. For Pakistan, 'terrorism is to strike terror or create disturbances by using bombs, explosive firearms or inflammable substances. It also includes an act of gang rape, child molestation, or robbery coupled with rape'. For Sri Lanka, 'terrorism means causing the death of any specified person, committing any other attack upon such person, which would be punishable with death or imprisonment for seven years'. Nepal considers terrorism as 'any act or plan of using any kinds of arms, grenades, or explosives with the objective of hurting the sovereignty or the security and law and kingdom of Nepal'.[3]

The spread of fear and, threat of violence for individual and collective damages to be inflicted on the adversary to achieve the set objectives are singled out—beside other elements—to characterize terrorist acts. Such activities are carried out either openly or clandestinely by resorting to ambush laid out to inflict damage to the adversaries. Some also think that even terrorist methods (violence) can be legitimate weapons for achieving humanitarian objectives such as democracy, freedom, social and political justices, if they are beyond the reach of people. Nepal's B.P. Koirala defended his violent action launched against the absolute rule of the king in the early 1960s, stating that the Nepali regime shored by force needed to be overthrown by force alone because of the lack of other alternative peaceful channels of public dissent. The hijacking of Royal Nepal plane after it took off from Biratnagar with three million NRs and other violent activities were treated as part of the democratic struggle.[4] During the Indian Nationalist Movement too, many freedom fighters had resorted to violence with the sole objective of overthrowing the British rule in India.

This chapter tries to identify the causes of terrorism and the approaches being developed by way of redressing if not completely eliminating them. The other aspect of the chapter is the focus on the impacts or consequences produced by the emergent trends of terrorist violence in South Asia. Since the scope is too wide to embrace for a detailed analysis, attempts will be made to single out some key factors responsible for giving rise to terrorism, though many such causes, responses, and consequences are neither uniform in nature nor unilinear in dimensions. We can only broadly identify some general and some specific variables, which are as follows: structural, strategic and external. Under the structural aspects, social, political, and ideological dimensions are included. The strategic responses deal with the trends of military security in South Asia and processes of negotiations being conducted by the involved parties from time to time. The external aspects encapsulate the major trends and events concerning the bilateral, regional, and international responses to terrorism. These variables have accompanying consequences for each country. But the terrorist movements have not assumed much regional character because of the insularity of each of them. Country or specific origins and dynamics of terrorist activities might have been influenced by external situations but cannot be compared with international terrorist movements as those launched by the Al Qaida and the like.

STRUCTURE AS SOURCE OF TERRORISM

The structure of societies and polities together with continued exploitation of people by the designated members of the upper caste, class, and political elites is taken as the factor responsible for terrorism. For, these elites have not been able to transform themselves into new, progressive elites regardless of the nature of political systems. As a result, steeped in the tradition of disparity and exploitation, the South Asian region in general inherits a peculiar mixture of socio-economic and political structures in addition to producing new breeding grounds for modified parochialism such as the rise of religious and sectarian factors which also contribute to violence and terrorism.

The pre-partition division of the Indian psyche continued to overwhelm the post-partition developments, with the political parties and other disparate social and regional groups using religious, communal, regional, and other cards to establish their own respective identities. And the conventional 'democratic state' as derived from the British tradition, could not show its full capacity to cope with such trends. Moreover, the wounds of partition continued to fester with the declining appeal of political ideology espoused during the anti-British movement. Being fractious and socially conflictual, politics in India, with the passage of time, passed through turbulence in several respects, the most important being the end of the monolithic nature of the Congress party and the emergence of alternative organizations.

The emergence of the Naxalite movement in West Bengal in the late 1960s and later in Andhra Pradesh and in some other pockets of Bihar, Uttar Pradesh and Madhya Pradesh could stir Indian minds. As Frankel has pointed out, 'Democratization has fragmented political parties along state, sub-regional, caste and religious lines, creating unstable coalition governments, paralyzed from within, without the capacity to carry out unfinished reforms.'[5]

Ideological Decline and Rise of Identity Politics

Post-colonial South Asia has traversed along the road of ideological ambiguity, political uncertainties, continued social and economic disparities, religious bigotry, and regional conflicts. When political ideology is subordinated to the powerful trends of parochialism, the political elites too do not lag behind in making religion and communalism weapons for political mobilization. Moreover, such powerful trends have greatly affected politics and society.

The factors and forces responsible for India's partition and their indelible impacts on the later subcontinental developments continue to haunt many countries of the region. The political roadmap of Pakistan was soon forgotten with the passing away of leaders of national stature. The emergence of political religion as a powerful force for laying the foundations of nation-states and compromises made by sacrificing the integrative elements of nation building on secular and progressive agendas produced more fissures in both the nation and the politics of South Asia. India's pre-partition ideology which was supposed to set the course of the post-partition national landscape, soon frittered out, losing the 'normative organizational pillars' of the state—secularism, socialism, and democracy.[6]

However, many more transmutations and changes have taken place in both the ideological and the functional patterns of state and regimes. Democracy in the conventional sense, and having no capacity to transform the entrenched exploitative nature of the state and government, has no relevance despite being based on electoral politics. South Asian countries, irrespective of the character of their polities, are still not as much transformative and progressive as their aspirations demand. Nor are the new democratic elites who are catapulted into positions of power intent on making a departure from the past tradition of governance. So whatever ideologies the new elites embraced have not been translated into action in their actual spirit. As it has been pointed out, 'the growth of community conflict has coincided with "the deinstitutionalization of the Indian state where both the normative and the organizational pillars of the post-independence Nehruvian state, secularism and socialism, have weakened"'.[7]

Our probe into the structures of societies and politics in South Asia would not be apt without alluding to the issue of identity politics. When political ideologies become too weak to address the multifarious problems facing these societies and polities, a vigorous search for an agenda to mobilize people becomes significant. And such agenda has been found in ethnicity, language, culture, and regionalism, and in various other forms of sub-national identities. Many scholars may find them a discursive phenomena of today's social and political dynamics as no crafting of institutions capable of meeting these trends is possible because of the subordinate roles to be played by such institutions. Some South Asian countries in general, regardless of regime features, have failed to make a distinction between social pluralism and democracy. Since ethnicity is based more or less on bonds of different language, religion, race, tribe, caste, sect, etc., all of them contribute to forming 'social pluralism' which accepts the existence of associations. Pluralist democracy denotes 'a democratic polity characterized by social pluralism'.[8]

The tendencies of South Asian countries to be more preoccupied with the state-centric approaches to the complex problems rather than to be more conversant with social pluralism and inclusive democracy have given rise to divisive as well as conflictual trends in societies and polities.[9] Moreover, as democratic elites themselves have become more segmented by not reading into the psyche of ethnic minorities, the countries have deep-rooted ethnic conflict showing no immediate resolution to it. So democracy alone does not fill the gap if the ruling elites who come from the dominant community do not become sensitive to the other communities. The Brahmin/Chhetri dominance in the Hinduized polity of Nepal and the continued feudal control in the people's politics in Pakistan have made political regimes exclusive, thus perennially marginalizing the minorities, ethnic groups, Dalits, women, and other incapacitated sections of South Asian countries. The psychology of a homogenized ethnic nation in Sri Lanka might have been reinforced by the rise of the DMK in Tamil Nadu. Because the majority Sinhalese community of Sri Lanka suffers from a minority complex as it perceives its minority Tamils as linked to Tamils of India and of other parts of world. The minority fear psychology seems to have made the Sinhalese more concerned about their own homeland and hence the stubborn attitude of the latter.[10]

The structures of South Asian states in general are conflict-laden due to entrenched social rigidities—caste distinction and its continued impact on politics irrespective of the nature of regimes, sharpened minority psyche and its radicalization for a variety of reasons for empowerment of weaker sections. The symbiotic relationship between the Indian Hindu and Nepali Hindu orthodoxy has been identified with the recent declaration of the Hindu lobby accepting the Nepali monarch as the emperor of the world as well. These developments have dampened the prospects of secularization of politics as well as of democratization on the basis of popular sovereignty. The constitutional provision for declaring Nepal as the Hindu monarchial state, and adherence to the traditional practices and rituals by the king have made the intentions of the Nepali ruling elites suspect to the ethnic groups. Non-Hindu religious groups and ethnic communities didn't celebrate the Constitution Day on 9 November, 1990 on the grounds that it (Constitution) was discriminatory in nature and spirit. Thus, in the given context, the fear of ethnic and Dalit communities is created more by the prospect of the continuation of the historically entrenched disparity. And the use of religion for political purposes contradicts both the concept and the spirit of social and political pluralism based on popular legitimacy of power.

The other countries with a Muslim majority have been harder hit by inter-religious and inter-sectarian violence. Such trends have given rise to the trends of terrorism that work as a double-edged sword internally and externally. Patronized by the states, the North-West Frontier Province (NWFP) and Sindh show an uneasy relationship with the centre dominated by the Punjab. The three provinces have therefore become the sites of perpetual inter-ethnic and inter-sect conflicts. It has been said that 'Pakistan's ethnic conflicts are a complex product of uneven economic development, inequitable distribution of resources, lack of representative political institutions, and a coercive state appratus'.[11] Based on Islam and fed by suspicion and fear, the conception of the nation-state and the flawed policies have become the source of conflict.

The preoccupation of the less privileged provinces with the very question of identity, and the tendency of privileged elites to impose their own agenda of national identity, has stultified the process of emotional integration of all into a unified nation-state. Moreover, the treatment meted out to the Ahamadiyas as a non-Muslim minority, the Ulema's opposition to progressive social policies pursued by the state during the Bhutto regime, and the conflict between the Muhajir community in Sindh and the specific tribal problems of Baluchistan and NWFP have always been the fertile grounds for all kinds of terrorist groups.

Added to these areas of conflict, the trend of making religion as the weapon for mobilization has transcended the boundaries of states. The globalization of terrorism based on religion has therefore created unprecedented crises for nation-states. So the conventional approach to tackling the problems of countries affected by terrorist violence are not adequate as they are generally based on force as the last resort to the resolution of the crises. Not only Pakistan but all the post-colonial states are increasingly becoming vulnerable to such trends.

The foregoing narrative simply tries to impress that the country's social, economic, and political structures are in fact the breeding grounds for what we call here 'terrorism'. The built-in crises stem from a variety of sources which continue to perpetuate the divisions within societies. Other variables such as the failure of the political system to be more inclusive and judicious in the distribution as well as sharing of resources and power out people in a frenzy against the established order. In addition, lack of political direction (Nepal and Pakistan in particular) and intermittent obstructions standing in the way of democratic evolution are no less contributory to the rise of terrorism. Increasing reliance on military security has squeezed the people between the insurgents and the army and police of the state. So even if responding to terrorism is a must on the part of the state, people become fed up with the coercive approach to the problem alone, thus trying to flee their places of residence.

The general South Asian trends of migration or the refugee conditions have corroborated the fact that cities in South Asia are increasingly becoming the hubs of criminal activities, the response to which is becoming difficult for the states. Finally, the social fissures created by the incompetent states are the negative consequence. The ethnic, religious, regional, caste, class, and gender divisions are the rising phenomena of South Asian states.

Conflict Management Strategies

The systemic approach is concerned with the capacity of a political system to tackle the problem of terrorism. First of all, it is necessary to find a link between the state structures and their dynamics and the causes of the rise of terrorism. If it is due to the failure of the system and its actors, then the remedies lie in reinventing the capacity of the state. If the causes are beyond the scope of the state, then other approaches have to be found. Social disparity, failure of poverty alleviation, lack of institutionalization of political processes, corruption, rise of political religion and tensions created by it within the country and across-the international boundary have to be examined. How the aberrations that have been creeping into the political systems have created systemic crises can be traced in all the countries. In Sri Lanka, the origin of the Liberation Tigers of Tamil Eelam (LTTE) can be traced to the failure of the state to recognize the Tamil language at par with Sinhala. The motivating force of the Janatha Vimukthi Peramuna (JVP) or People's Liberation Front, a pro-Sinhala left-wing group was ethnic in that it wanted to offset the Tamil pressure for more accommodation in the political process. There was intense competition for political power, which is "the most sought after resource", and ethnic groups too scrambled for it. But 'from independence onwards, Sri Lanka has been unable to devise a stable and sustainable constitutional framework within which processes of political and economic competition can be regulated in a peaceful and democratic manner.'[12] The intense feeling of deprivation on the part of the Tamils, and the intense feeling of economic exploitation on the side of the state coupled with the strong sense of Sinhalese chauvinism goaded both of them into taking the terrorist path. The deliberate anti-Tamil policy adopted by the Sinhalese goes back to the 1920s, with the nationalist freedom movement splitting along ethnic lines. The Tamils wanted an equal share in the legislative council, which was rejected by the Sinhalese. Subsequently, since the 1950s, the language issue started dominating the political agenda, which eventually provoked the Tamils to take up arms against the state.[13]

The political approach has been partly successful in India. The Punjab crisis is a success story while the Assam agreement with the Asom Gana Parishad in 1985 turned out to be divisive with many other terrorist outfits coming to the fore.[14] Now the entire north-eastern areas are infested with insurgencies of one kind or the other. Although the Government of India has held several rounds of negotiations with the Nagas, Mizos, and Assam insurgents, lasting peace is still elusive in those areas. Some critics point out that the centre has treated 'insurgency in the north-east as a law and order issue', or in the case of Assam, it has given 'a communal colour by focussing on the Bangladeshi immigrants'.[15] Elections are held in Assam, Mizoram, Nagaland, and Tripura, but terrorist activities continue to haunt the Indian state.

The political approach seems to have become bogged down in the Kashmir conflict due to the intermingling of a variety of factors such as external support of both military and non-military nature, the role of political religion across the country, linkages with similar groups in the adjoining countries, and geo-strategic location. For sustaining any terrorist war, the role of certain foreign powers becomes essential, though this aspect has been nullified by the Indian success story on the issue of Punjab (Khalistan).[16] The distribution of ethnic groups through many neighbouring states of South Asia has the tendency of internationalizing the separatist movement, but it has been able to intensify the agendas of separatism since the break up of Pakistan. All separatist struggles that straddle the entire region have not however led to the creation of yet another state in the region. Terrorism is rampant in some Naxalite affected states—Andhra Pradesh, Bihar, Uttar Pradesh, and Madhya Pradesh—but the intensity of violence has been put somewhat within manageable limits by the Indian state.

And all political responses to addressing the Maoist problem in Nepal have failed due to some of these reasons: lack of unified approach of various political forces, including the King, political parties, and state functionaries; lack of power of the elected government to deal with the Maoist problem; a contentious political system to which the Maoists have not reconciled; the king as the key player of Nepali politics; failure of political parties to conduct in accordance with the spirit of constitution; rigidity of the constitution because of some unalterable elements; and the unchanged power structure despite the acceptance of popular sovereignty. As this aspect will be dealt with separately, it is sufficient to state that the feudal character of the state and the unbroken elite tradition of the country have a lot to do with the non-resolution of Nepal's basic problems.[17]

'Bangladesh is a more homogenous nation' because of its more than 95 per cent Bengali-speaking population. Sometimes other ethnic groups feel threatened by the increasing trends of Islamization in the country, but the worst communal clashes are not reported. Yet, 'while Bangladesh has failed to ensure the social and political space to ensure a peaceful, pluralist political system, there have been no demands or activities that threatened the integrity of country'.[18] Nevertheless, the Chittagong Hill Tracts (CHT) region became a major area of conflict for a long time. Inhabited by ten tribal groups and occupying 5,138 sq. miles (one-tenth of the whole territory of Bangladesh), the CHT people demanded autonomy but the government rejected their demand on the grounds of perceived threat to Bengali nationalism. Stretching over 24 years, the CHT area reeled under guerrilla warfare until the signing of an accord in December 1997. Signed by the Parbatiya Chattragram Jana Sanghati Samity (PCJSS), political wings of Shanti Bahini, many of the provisions of the accord remain to be implemented. Nevertheless there have been no fresh terrorist activities, but other criminal activities such as 'killing, dacoity, abduction are being committed by some tribal groups'.[19]

The Bangladesh parliamentary system, adopted after ousting the military-led government in 1990, has suffered from numerous cancerous symptoms or elements of decay. Inimical relations between the two major political parties led by the two begums—Sheikh Hasina and Khalida Zia—who happened to be the daughter and wife of Sheikh Mujibur Rahman and Zia-ur-Rahman respectively, have not set any trend of tolerance and respect for each other that in turn could help consolidate the democratic culture. On the contrary, politics has been criminalized by what Bangladeshi scholars call *Mastans*, who are considered a resource for winning elections which are merely turning into a new 'cracy', i.e. 'electocracy'. Elections do not empower the people. Neither are they the symbol and substance of participatory democracy. Sometimes the failure of law and order is so dismal that the people do not believe in the capacity and sanctity of the police and other organs of the state. When minorities, women, and other communities and regional groups cannot find any space in the political system, aggressive articulation of their interests would always be an alternative. And sometimes, the inability of Bangladeshi elites to prepare themselves for change has given grounds for conflicts.

Military and Political Response

Responses to terrorism by the South Asian states can be categorized in both general and specific terms. In a comparative perspective, however, all the states have relied heavily on military response because of their much lower capacity to deliver goods and services to the people. Broadly, we can categorize these approaches as systemic (political), military, strategic and tactical, bilateral, regional, and global.

So even in the stable democratic systems of India and Sri Lanka, the military approach to contain both internal and cross-country terrorism is increasingly becoming paramount despite the importance being attached to the political approach. Now all the countries irrespective of regime types are militaristic in orientation, though a few South Asian countries have shown that they can manage conflicts with combined military and political strategies. India's handling of the Punjab conflict is an example. The ongoing terrorist movements in India have, however, created grievous effects on Indian democracy such as 'the militarization of the Indian imagination; the government's accretion of emergency powers; the devaluation of debate and dissent; the assault on liberals and the idea of liberalism; the spread of Hindu self-hatred; and the turn to a more managerial, technical view of politics'.[20]

The response to terrorism in South Asia is primarily military-oriented and is invariably cumbersomely discursive. Over dependence on the military means that ignores all other options for non-traditional security is increasingly becoming easier for South Asian political elites who more or less find anchorage in the status quo. The security provided by the military has the characteristics of docility on the part of citizens because of its coercive nature which demands obedience to its behaviour. As has been pointed out by Jayadeva Uyangoda, 'The behaviour, a one-way commitment to political obligation, demands an unwavering loyalty to the state, its sovereignty, its territorial integrity, its stability—in short, to its security'.[21] However, the coercive state structures that are conveniently used for combating terrorism have helped develop the psyche of militarization—that the military alone can redeem the situation and hence needs to be beefed up at the cost of other elements of comprehensive security. And military response to terrorism or to other conflicts is so narrowly comprehended that even democratic elites elected by the people have become hostage to such an approach.

Militarization is generally understood by the power elites as an increase in number of army, curtailment of other activities for enabling the army and other agencies of the state by diverting huge resources at the cost of development etc. The swelling of budget for security in recent years has shown that all the South Asian countries give first priority to military security though the sources of terrorism or other violent conflicts are traced to the mal-construction of state. 'Indeed, the present is a period of reconstituting South Asia's economics, politics, social structures, cultural relations, identities, inter-state relations, political beliefs and most of the civilizational processes'.[22]

Since the politics of negotiation has suffered a set back in many cases,[23] the military options have been accompanied by the use of draconian laws and ordinances plus a number of other coercive measures. The Prevention of Terrorist Act (POTA) 2002 in India, Pakistan's Anti-Terrorism (Amendment) Ordinance, 1999, Nepal's Terrorist and Destructive Activities (Control and Punishment Ordinance), Sri Lanka's Prevention of Terrorism (Temporary Provisions) Act have been used in recent years, contrary to the vociferous criticism of opposition parties.

The Indian parliament had enacted POTA on 28 March 2002 with the objective of 'arming the state with an adequate judicial mechanism to bring terrorists to book'. Earlier, in 1985, the Indian government had enacted the Terrorist and Disruptive Activities (Prevention) Act (TADA). It has frequently been reported that POTA has been allegedly misused by the law enforcement agencies of some states, though 15 states and six union territories have not used POTA. However, 301 cases affected 1,600 persons. Some states—Manipur, Tripura and Assam—have avoided using POTA maintaining that other laws are adequate to 'tackle terrorism'.[24] Coming as it did under fierce criticism, the Union Cabinet approved an ordinance to amend POTA if the Central Review Committee of Parliament came to the conclusion that functionaries of various state governments had abused it.

It seems that such ordinances and laws have not made any difference insofar as the prevention of terrorism is concerned. On the contrary, in all those countries where these measures are adopted for curtailing insurgency or terrorism, there has been a general complaint of their abuse by the agencies of the state. Terrorist acts or otherwise, all South Asian states are oriented to a coercive administrative and military culture which normally frustrates options that could mitigate the crisis precipitated by insurgencies.

Has the military response mitigated the feeling of insecurity in South Asia? Is terrorism being tackled as a result of the pressures being exerted by the military? Answers to these questions are both yes and no. Yes in the sense that at a time when other political institutions and the civil society fail to find alternative means for providing security to the people, the military becomes the last resort. But, unfortunately, instead of making the army as the last means, the South Asian states make it the first thus wittingly or unwittingly endangering the very existence of democracy. Since terrorism has some distinct characteristics, it cannot be uniformly addressed after a certain period of time. The non-military option therefore needs to be adopted if terrorist activities carried out for certain mission are to be permanently settled.

Although all the South Asian states, except India and Sri Lanka, have given greater preference to the military option because of the mal-governance or lack of a clear roadmap of the political systems they want to embrace, all their efforts to respond to terrorism are also bizarre and reactive. India's response to the developments in the north-east and Kashmir is a mixtures of both military and non-military options, though the containment of the terrorism or separatism that has sustained since independence is possible through the military option. However, the Government of India has not completely abandoned the political option in the north-east, as elections are held, and negotiations conducted either directly or through back-channel diplomacy. Given the strategic location of the north-east and India's northern neighbour China, being an adversary, the external linkages of the insurgents became a factor for sustaining insurgencies. The supply of weapons and other logistics allegedly flowing from

China into the region continued until quite recently until both countries took steps towards mending fences.

Bhutan's proximity to the Indian north-east, particularly Assam, has been beneficial for insurgent groups wanting to either secede from India or achieve maximum autonomy. The terrorist groups, United Liberation Front of Assam (ULFA), National Democratic Front of Bodoland (NDFB), and Kamatapur Liberation Organization (KLO), are such insurgent groups that have been using Bhutanese territory to mount their insurgency. India had all along been putting pressure on Bhutan to flush out the terrorists from its territory to which Bhutan had not obliged because of its own direct contact with the insurgents. It was frequently reported that the Bhutanese government persuaded the insurgents to leave Bhutan without having to resort to force. The 81st Assembly Session of Bhutan, held from 28 June to 18 August 2003, authorized the government to hold more rounds of negotiations with the warring groups in order to make them leave the country. At long last, 'Operation All Clear' was conducted by the Bhutanese army to destroy the 30 camps spread across the southern districts of Bhutan. At the time the strength of the terrorists was estimated to be over 3,000.[25]

The Indian army which also is engaged in combating terrorism in Assam and Arunachal Pradesh, helped the Bhutanese army to evict the insurgents. The insurgents belonging to the Arunachal Dragon Force (ADF) also found refuge in Bhutan. After having been flushed out from there, they are expected to find shelter in Burma and Bangladesh thus showing that some sort of nexus has been established in other countries.*

Meanwhile, the central government's effort to end the 56-year-old insurgency in Nagaland suffered a setback in 2003 following the reiteration of the demand for a separate homeland by a separatist group. 'Our demand for a sovereign state is irreversible', said the S.S. Khaplang group of the National Socialist Council of

*These insurgents have also been seeking support and shelter in Bangladesh territory. There are reports of these Indian insurgent groups enjoying the Bangladeshi government's patronage. India's attempts to persuade Bangladesh to cooperate in dealing with these insurgents have so far failed to evoke response. –Editor.

Nagaland (NSCN-K) in a statement. Yet, New Delhi had continued negotiations with the other group as the ceasefire since 1997 was holding. It seemed that group rivalry rather than the mission was the cause for the rupture because the centre was holding talks with the Isak-Muivah faction of the NSCN. Frantic efforts were also being made to hold talks with the six banned groups in Mizoram and Agartala hoping to enhance the prospects of the National Democratic Alliance in the elections.

The military option adopted by the government has contained the insurgency but it has not helped settle the issues raised by separatist groups. The north-east's political problems therefore remain unaddressed ever since the eruption of violence in the area. However, the military option has paved the way for ceasefire and negotiations. It seems that the unfolding trends both in India and outside, of encouraging unified approaches to the resolution of conflicts will change the scene. This aspect will be dealt with in this paper, but it can be stated that the terrorist groups fighting for autonomy or a separate nation would eventually settle for more state-oriented federalism in India.

Nevertheless, all these groups are facing the heat of military pressure. At a time when the world is more or less united under the threat of national and international terrorist movements, military options can at least deter their forward movement against the organized state. The failure of all insurgencies in India to achieve their core objective—separation or autonomy as demanded by them—suggests that the other options can be put in place on the basis of military support. India's pluralist democracy is an added advantage for the accommodation of interests of various warring groups notwithstanding their own problems of rivalry and competition.

The military response is more visible in the Kashmir theatre because of the nexus developed between the various insurgent groups and Pakistan. Four major (including Kargil) and several small local wars have been waged by both the countries in addition to low-intensity conflicts of a permanent nature. The trend of increased defence expenditure and preoccupation with the threat of terrorism continues to make both India and Pakistan vulnerable. And to everyone's surprise, the South Asian region could not make any departure in the post-Cold War world. On the contrary, defence expenditures continue to show an upward trend every year. India's defence expenditure crosses more than 24 per cent of the share of central government expenditure.

Terrorism in Kashmir and its extension to other parts of India is being responded to both politically and militarily. The support to the new government of Jammu & Kashmir led by Mufti Mohammad Syeed and the centre's decision to hold talks with the Hurriyat group are some of the indications of the non-military option being pursued. Moreover, the recent rapprochement between India and Pakistan and its impact on the ongoing insurgency and terrorism is likely to be helpful in reducing terrorism. Hinting at Pakistani support to terrorist groups, the former Deputy Prime Minister and Home Minister L.K. Advani said that 'Islamabad would wake up to the fact that Pakistani society itself has had to pay a high cost because of continuing support to terrorism', and that India 'has the requisite strength and determination to foil the campaign of cross-border terrorists sponsored by the Pakistani ruling dispensation'.[26]

It seems that all the terrorism-affected countries are increasingly relying on the military for thwarting the terror menace. Pakistan is a typical case as the nature of terrorism is rooted in tribal divisions, religious and sectarian considerations, and minority rights. Instead of addressing these problems, which are germane to terrorism and other forms of political conflicts, the use of military is the obvious choice for any government. So 'defence expenditure has left three profound effects on Pakistan's society. First, the size of the army, its expansion through and linkages with the West created a praetorian state' thus making democracy a major casualty. Second, the army has emerged as an autonomous institution as if it is the guardian of the state. In the opinion of Rasul Baksh Rais, it has 'informal links alliances with some ultra-religious nationalist groups, some sections of the media and powerful social groups in recruitment areas.' Third, the military spending has taken the lion's share of national resources.[27]

Pakistan's separatist Baluch conflict, the MQM movement in Sind, tribal warfare in NWFP, are conflicts intensified by the increasing trends of sectarianism and fundamentalism. Pakistan's strategic support to the Taliban regime in Afghanistan and the terrorist factions of the Sipah-e-Sahaba until its turnaround following the Al Qaida attack on the twin towers of the World Trade Center in the US on 9/11 in 2001 had provided enough grist to the breeding of fundamentalism. And the sprouting of religious schools (madrasas) in Pakistan and other countries of the region could also be attributed to the rise of sectarian violence. During the heydays of Talibanization in Afghanistan, most arms dealers, smugglers, and drug traffickers of Pakistan used Afghanistan as a sanctuary thus threatening not only the socio-economic fabric but also creating deep and long-term effects on the country itself.

Reports about the Al Qaida and Taliban activities along the Afghan–Pakistan border and the alleged relations between the Taliban and Pakistan have been exposed in the US press and by intelligence sources, allegations which Pakistan denies stoutly. Castigating such reports as 'artificial linkages', the Pakistani foreign ministry says, 'operations in the war on terrorism on the Pakistan side of the Afghan–Pakistan border have been and will be conducted exclusively by the Pakistani forces'.[28] However, these denials have been contradicted by Afghanistan authorities who maintain that Pakistan still continues to help the Taliban as the Pakistan's establishment is stated to be 'nostalgic' about the former. Time alone will prove how far such conflicting stories about the duality of Pakistani deals—hunting and collusion with the Taliban—are true. As of now, both the US and Pakistan are on a massive hunt for Osama bin Laden and the Taliban along both sides of the Afghan–Pakistan border.

The 21-year-old Sri Lankan ethnic war is militarized on both sides because of the armed clashes and efforts made for scoring military victory by both sides. But both have also realized that the military approach would lead them to nowhere as it is basically a political problem requiring to be resolved politically. So many times both have agreed on ceasefires as well as for talks through third-party mediation. Violence has erupted intermittently, provoking the Tamils to warn the government that any delay in ending the ethnic bloodshed which has claimed 60,000 lives since 1972 could lead to a break up of the country itself. Since the majority Sinhalese did not accept the LTTE proposal for an interim arrangement which weighed heavily in its favour, the road ahead seems difficult for a negotiated political resolution to the crisis.

INSURGENCIES AND CONSEQUENCES

Both insurgencies and political instability have adverse effects on democratic stability and overall development of South Asian countries. If India has been able to maintain its territorial integrity in the midst of insurgencies and regional diversities, Sri Lanka is struggling hard to contain the effects of the LTTE. Although the LTTE has not given up its goal of Eelam, its participation in peace talks despite threats of restarting the violent war has allowed both parties to heave a sigh of temporary relief. From a developmental point of view, the country is divided into war and peace zones with the latter carrying on economic activities normally while the northern and eastern parts of the island nation suffering from violence and economic stagnation. Yet it is to the credit of Sŕi Lankan parties and leaders that the democratic structure has not been dismantled by ethnic war. In the recent parliamentary elections some Tamil parties, supposedly close to the LTTE, have also won seats.

Pakistani President General Musharraf says that Kashmir runs in Pakistan's blood, and people taking up arms against India—militants—are 'freedom fighters' for Pakistan. This spirit continues to shape Indo–Pakistan relations. In addition, Pakistan is itself embroiled in tribal, ethnic, sectarian, and regional conflicts, the consequences of which are important for democracy and development, with both short- and long-term effects. The gun culture is being accepted as a necessary element of society with both the military dominated government and various tribal and religious groups taking shelter under the gun. Armed to the teeth and permanently marred by divisiveness, the Pakistani people are deprived of freedom and democracy. Nor is the Pakistani state prepared to introduce progressive socio-political reforms for the emancipation of its downtrodden. Moreover, its India-centric foreign and defence policies, prompting the country to be militarily prepared, have also affected democratic stability.

The overall consequences of the Maoist People's War in Nepal are disastrous from both short- and long-term points of view.

Originating from the movement for the restoration of democracy in 1990, some breakaway communist groups eventually formed the Communist Party of Nepal (Maoist) in 1995. This party started the People's War on 13 February 1996 as a response to the government's crackdown on its activities in the remote western hill districts.

Concentrating basically on the far western hills and the most backward regions of the country, the Maoists' psychological as well as actual strength increased by leaps and bounds, making it a formidable force, second only to the organized army of the state, the Royal Nepal Army (RNA). First, the Maoists started attacking the police force demonstrating the strength of the Maoist insurgents, and then finally taking on the RNA following the failure of the second round of talks in November 2001. Moreover, the Maoists could drive a wedge between the elected government and the army which seemingly worked under the control of the king contrary to the spirit of the constitutional monarchy as underlined by the 1990 Constitution. The three preconditions put up by the army before the government—to declare the Maoists as terrorists, to proclaim a state of emergency before the involvement of the RNA, and to implement an integrated programme in the Maoist affected areas—followed by the speeches made by the Commander-in-Chief of the RNA indirectly apportioning blame on the political parties and leaders gave an inkling that the RNA was not at all inclined to cooperate with the government. These developments led to the resignation of Prime Minister G.P. Koirala and the appointment of Sher Bahadur Deuba who accepted the demand of the army for using it in counter-insurgency operations. The formation of a unified command structure consisting of the RNA, the Armed Police Force and the Police under the RNA, and the supply of sophisticated weapons from Belgium, India, and the US, has strengthened the fighting capacity of the state security agencies but the Maoists' capacity has also not waned, contrary to the army's claim about its actual strength. About 10,000 people have lost their lives, adding up the figures every passing day (see Table 9.4).

The CPNM entered into negotiations with the Deuba government in 2001 and with the Chand and Thapa governments in

2003, though the latter two prime ministers were appointed by King Gyanendra after he assumed executive power in October 2002. Sensing that the Deuba government had a limited mandate to negotiate with the Maoists as some of the demands put up by the latter—abolition of the monarchy and the setting up of a constituent assembly to draft a new constitution—were beyond its scope because of the rigid constitutional positions on such issues, the Maoists eventually decided to invade the army barracks in Dang, Syangja, and Solukhumbu, which resulted in the imposition of emergency and the use of the army against the Maoists. The Terrorist and Destructive Activities (Control and Punishment) Ordinance was imposed declaring the Maoists as terrorists. However, the Maoists used the ceasefire assumed earlier to strengthen their political and military positions. The leaders deputed for negotiations could meet as many varied people as possible to popularize their political agendas.

The two negotiations conducted by the Royal government in 2003 could not be successful due to lack of trust on both sides. The government punctured the last talks when the army killed 19 captured Maoists in Doramba of Ramechhap district while negotiations were on at Hapur village of Dang district. This incident of the killing of unarmed people by the security force spurred the Maoists' negotiation team leader to bluntly ask the government whether or not the agenda of a constituent assembly was to be accepted by the government or not. On 27 August issuing a statement of the end of the ceasefire, the Maoist supremo Prachanda said:

> The rationale for ceasefire, code of conduct and talks process is now over for the time being. . . . But the royal army of old regime started to violate the code of conduct from the very beginning of the announcement despite the fact that our people's salvation army was totally devoted to the ceasefire. . . . The concept paper [of the Government] could not address even the demands of parliamentary parties who believe in multiparty democracy and constitutional monarchy. . . . We rejected the proposal totally and made it clear the fourth round of talks will be held only if the establishment brings a new proposal of going for a constituent assembly. . . .[29]

The three rounds of peace talks have failed forcing both the embattled parties to resort to military means. But their social, political and economic consequences are incalculable.

Displacement of Peoples

One of the serious consequences of insurgencies is displacement of people from their countries or places of residences. In India, many streams of displaced persons mingle as, for instance, Bhutanese Nepalis, Kashmiri pundits, Tamils of Sri Lanka, Hindus of Bangladesh, to mention a few. It appears that very few people are repatriated once they have left their homes.

The Maoist insurgency in Nepal has disturbed the life of the people in general and poor villagers in particular. The poor villagers of the hills and mountains have been displaced and have found their way into India or other towns of Nepal. Those who can afford to live in cities have taken refuge there and those who are poor have gone to India for employment. Kathmandu, the Nepalese capital, is overburdened with the displaced population. Schools are invariably closed for fear that children will be forcibly recruited into the Maoist guerrilla army. Squeezed between the Maoists and state security forces, the villagers face a horrendous crisis of survival.

Meanwhile, stories of indiscriminate killings, blatant violations of human rights by the security forces and the Maoists pour into the offices of the media and human rights groups prompting the latter and foreign governments to raise their voice against such violations. Murders of family members, threat, forceful contribution, order to leave, kidnapping, destruction of property, loss of employment opportunities, indiscriminate arrests, hassling by security forces and the Maoists, dwindling economy, broken social infrastructure, insecurity of women and cases of sexual harassment are routine in the country. It has been reported that by March 2003, the total number of Internally Displaced Persons (IDP) was 7,343 in 56 districts. The NRCS information mentioned in the Nepal IDP Research Initiative finding suggested that 37,000 unregistered IDPs in addition to others who have registered. The total figure of IDPs could be between 1,00,000 and 150,000 (see Table 9.2). Yet the Ministry of Home Affairs mentioned only 2,500 IDPs and the estimated loss of property and infrastructure as about NRs 405,456,714. The districts badly affected by the Maoist violence register the following numbers of IDPs (see Table 9.5): Rolpa 54,000 (25.70 per cent), Rukum 52,000 (27.60 per cent), Salyan 21,000 (9.85 per cent), Dang 12,000 (2.60 per cent), Achham 21,000 (9.80 per cent), the total in five districts being 160,000 (12.25 per cent of total population).[30] These figures rise every day because of intensified Maoist activities in villages where the they continue to dominate.*

A report prepared by the USAID in Nepal states that the Maoists collect a 5 per cent tax on the salaries of all teachers and health workers, disrupt some school days with strikes, obligatory political meetings or Maoist students association activities. Sometimes they intrude into classrooms to intimidate teachers.[31] The fear psychosis is greater in the villages as parents fear that the Maoists, will abduct their children for recruitment. Despite the rumours circulating across the country that the Maoists recruit mostly from the hill ethnic groups and Dalits, the other

TABLE 9.1(a): TEN DISTRICTS WITNESSING NUMBER OF PERSONS KILLED DURING THE PEOPLE'S WAR (13 FEBRUARY 1996–9 DECEMBER 2003)

S. No.	Districts	By State	By Maoists	Total
1	Rukum	653	158	811
2	Rolpa	522	228	750
3	Dang	517	191	708
4	Achham	150	151	301
5	Salyan	209	70	279
6	Kailali	156	80	236
7	Surkhet	166	49	215
8	Banke	154	58	212
9	Jumla	144	65	209
10	Bardiya	174	33	207

Source: Informal, INSEC Publication.

*The United Nations has recently drawn attention to the fact that the number of IDPs in Nepal is far more than the registered figure of 8,000. It could be as high as 400,000. Some estimates mention even 1 million, a large part of which has migrated to India in search of security and livelihood. *The Hindu*, 23 April 2005; Also, *The Hindustan Times*, 23 April 2005. –Editor.

TABLE 9.1(b): NUMBER OF VICTIMS KILLED IN CONNECTION WITH 'PEOPLE'S WAR' (13 FEBRUARY 1996–9 DECEMBER 2003)

Year	By State	By Maoists
1996	59	22
1997	16	32
1998	334	75
1999	328	141
2000	179	219
2001	244	390
2002	3,297	1,351
2003	1,277	504
Total	5,734	2,734

Source: Informal, INSEC Publication.

TABLE 9.2: INSEC IDP ESTIMATES (JANUARY TO DECEMBER 2002)

Development Region	Displaced people
Eastern	398
Central	4,994
Western	4,911
Mid-Western	3,405
Far-Western	3,856
Total	17,564

Source: *Human Rights Yearbook 2003*, INSEC.

TABLE 9.3: NUMBER OF DISAPPEARED PERSONS FROM 2057 TO 2060 *MANGSIR* (APRIL 2001–NOVEMBER 2004)

Category	No of Person
Security Group	587
Rebel	111
Unknown	19 (18+1)
Total of Male	651
Total of Female	66
Total disappeared	717

Source: National Human Rights Commission, Nepal.

TABLE 9.4: CUMULATIVE KILLINGS DUE TO CONFLICT FROM FEBRUARY 1996 TO 19 JANUARY 2004

Category	Total
Police	1,107
Armed Police	174
Royal Nepal Army	370
Maoist	5,000 over
Civilians	1,140
Total	7,791

TABLE 9.5: NUMBER OF DISPLACEMENT FROM THE FIVE SELECTED DISTRICTS (JANUARY 2004)

District	Total Population (2001)	Estimated Number IDPS	Percentage of Displacement
Rolpa	210,004	54,000	25.70
Rukum	188,438	52,000	27.60
Salyan	213,500	21,000	9.85
Dang	462,380	12,000	2.60
Achham	231,285	21,000	9.80
Total in 5 districts	1,30,5607	160,000	12.25 of the total population

Source: Community Study and Welfare Center (CSWC), Kathmandu, Nepal.

castes of the hills and Tarai are not excluded. 'Most forces are commonly estimated by informed non-Maoist sources at 5,000/6,000 Red Army combatants, their most qualified, best trained and disciplined conventional military force; and 15,000 combined armed militia (in less disciplined conventional military force); and dedicated political agents and activists. The Maoists themselves claim that these groups, taken together, number about 100,000 persons'.[32]

Political Consequences

Generally, the South Asian countries have inherent problems and crises of governance which constitute the causes and consequences of insurgency or terrorism. The terrorist groups have been able to capitalize such issues as are dear to the people. So the fallout of the failure of governments in South Asia is heavy despite several plans and agendas of change made by them. Taking the Maoist agenda in Nepal, it can be said that it has tried to address the fundamentals of Nepali politics. The failure of the political parties to raise any of the substantive issues affecting the people has left the field free for the Maoists. Other agendas concerning social and economic reforms are no less important. Now it has been admitted that, given the context of Nepali historical development and the monarchy's own way of asserting power when the opportunity arose, constitutional monarchy of the British variety would not be tenable. So there would either be a monarchy or no monarchy.[33] Such a conclusion lends weight to the Maoist agenda of the republican system, however vague this agenda might be.

Unlike India, Pakistan, and Sri Lanka, insurgency in Nepal has certain negative effects on political and the developmental aspects of the country. For, the first casualty was the established parliamentary system as the king, taking advantage of the situation, took executive power into himself in October 2002. Similarly, economically, frequent strikes, *bandhs*, lockouts and violent activities have brought the country to a standstill. The latest tactics of blocking district headquarters and imposing an embargo on the movement of goods to remote areas and other coercive measures adopted to harass the government have sent prices rising, creating difficulties for the ordinary people. Now people cannot move smoothly from one place to another because of the hazards of bus travel and threats to life.

Nepal's response to the Maoist insurgency was characterized by oscillation, with the government taking contradictory positions in its treatment of the Maoists. On the one hand it went to the extent of withdrawing the terrorist tag on the eve of the peace talks and applauded the Maoist leader, Prachanda, for his bold decision, and on the other, it once again labelled them as terrorists once the Maoists retreated from the talks. It is also intriguing that the RNA which had set preconditions for its involvement in combat operations until 2001 is now fighting the insurgents without the declaration of emergency and other conditions because it is under the direct rule of the king. Now the army feels that it has a free hand on the issue despite its occasional declaration that it has been carrying out counter-insurgency operations under the direction of the government. Accusation of violations of human rights and killing of innocent people on the fictitious charge of their being Maoists are often refuted by the army in frequent press briefings.*

The post-9/11 development has changed the context with Pakistan taking a u-turn in its relations against the Taliban and other fundamentalist forces in the region and across the world. Pakistan held a steadfast attitude towards adhering to the additional protocol against the suppression of terrorism in the South Asian Association of Regional Cooperation (SAARC) Summit in January 2004. The social and political consequences of terrorism in South Asia are both perceptual and substantive. Peoples of the region perceive that terrorism has emerged as an enduring force to reckon with, which cannot be rooted out as easily as the elites of the militarized states think. Its mobilizational capacity, intensity, and commitment are unprecedented. Yet such perceptions are also nullified by the states with many of them resisting the pressure of terrorists.

It has been alleged that the institutions of madrasas in India, Pakistan, Nepal, and Bangladesh are suspect for their role in working as breeding grounds for terrorism. 'All across the globe, these once revered and venerated centres of learning are now seen as "nurseries of sedition", "factories of fundamentalists" and "hotbeds of terrorism".'[34] The sprouting of madrasas in the Tarai belt of Nepal had become an eyesore to the Indian government as these educational institutions were/are seen as the training camps of pro-Pakistani terrorists. The Pakistan government itself was/is no less worried about the misuse of madrasas and seems to be keeping them under strict scrutiny in the post-9/11 period. The flow of external money to sustain the madrasas

*The writing of this chapter was completed before King Gyanendra's takeover of power directly under his own leadership on 1 February 2005. Even the author of this paper, Professor Baral was arrested just for attending international academic conferences under the emergency regulation of 1 February 2005.–Editor.

in different countries is also producing negative consequences as these institutions with religious orientation do cater to the specific interests of the new generation of youths.

External Response to Terrorism

The 9/11 incident not only altered inter-state relations but also encouraged the trend of militarization of South Asian states. Abandoned for a long time, some of the states suddenly started receiving attention from the only super power—the US—and its allies, as well as of other regional powers like India. Taking specifically, the Nepali Maoist insurgency, could the US and India have come out openly in support of the Nepali government had there been no 9/11 terrorist attack on the US? Many agree that the terrorist agenda could reach out across the world simply because of the threat posed to the US interests. India, a proximate power, didn't brand the Maoists as a terrorist outfit prior to 9/11. Later, surprisingly, India was prompt in declaring the Maoists as terrorists even before the Nepali government did, promising 'all possible support' to the Nepali government.[35]

In April 2003, the US and the Nepali government entered into a new anti-terrorist agreement and the former has committed to provide assistance to Nepal. Observers are of the opinion that 'US involvement in Nepal has been more active, visible and unprecedented', to which India has grudgingly reacted. US assistance to Nepal is in the form of a package of equipment, supplies, and training.[36] The other major donors are the United Kingdom and India who supplied helicopters, weapons and parts for the RNA to increase the capacity of the RNA.

The continued Maoist insurgency has multiple effects in the country. The RNA's demand to further increase its force level from the existing 72,000 and the heavy costs to be involved in it are likely to have horizontal effects on the socio-economic and political domains. The RNA claims that the Maoist People's War has been considerably blunted as a result of counter-insurgency operations following the supply of sophisticated weapons including night vision helicopters to Nepal by the US, the UK, and India. During 2002–3, $17 million had been committed by the US for defence equipment, while the UK and India provided

6.5 million pounds sterling, and INR two billion for military related materials and INR one billion additional assistance, respectively.[37]

In the wake of a series of Maoist attacks on the district headquarters and military installations in March 2004, the international community including the United Nations Secretary-General Kofi Annan has made a fresh appeal for opening the dialogue between the government and the rebels. The UN appeal has received a favourable response from all sides but the government. Rejecting the UN offer, the Nepalese home minister said that the government 'didn't need any kind of foreign mediation to resolve the Maoist problem'.[38]

The externalization of terrorism has also created a difficult situation for some countries affected by terrorism. Pakistan seems to be feeling the heat of the US pressure for taking more stringent steps towards flushing out the Taliban and the Al Qaida groups from its soil. The US has claimed that its persuasion not to escalate terrorism in Kashmir has worked resulting in the new rapprochement being developed between India and Pakistan. President Pervez Musharraf's declaration that Pakistan has already decided to reduce 50,000 military personnel unilaterally is also likely to yield a positive response from the Indian side. Meanwhile, the US declaration that Pakistan is a 'major non-NATO ally' is welcomed by the latter, who is hoping that it would further qualify Pakistan for new arms purchases from Washington.

CONCLUSION

One of the greatest negative effects of terrorism in South Asia is the gun culture contributed by both the states and insurgent groups. The scourge of terrorism does not promote democracy and agendas of human security—education, health, food, and freedom from fear. The social and political consequences of terrorism are increasing alarmingly in countries whose intrinsic capacity to manage crises is low. Such disastrous consequences have been observed in Nepal following the intensification of the internal war. There has been a total disruption of social and political relations across the country.

The king's action of bringing the military into political centre stage and sidelining the elected government has made Nepal's future all the more uncertain. The situation only demonstrates the decadent state, whose survival is only anchored to a military solution. Since the trend of militarization is both a mentality and reliance on force, its spiraling effects are far more serious than the rulers tend to believe. Thus, such a trend of militarization militates against a political approach to any crisis faced by a country. Any political option is likely to risk the positions of hard-core elites of South Asia. The king of Nepal in particular would lose a great deal or even risk his throne if the forces against his active role did not rest short of the end of monarchy or a powerless monarchy as in Britain. Pakistan has tribal, regional, and sectarian groups whose missions are not only political. Hence the military will not lower its guard. Other countries irrespective of the nature of regimes do realize the need for non-military solutions to insurgency problems, but they seldom adopt them unless pushed to the brink. Yet Bangladesh concluded the peace agreement with the Chakmas in 1997. Sri Lanka too has tried to resolve the Tamil crisis politically through third-party mediation or bilaterally despite the setbacks suffered by the peace process.

However, the political consequences of insurgencies are country specific and vary both in effect and in intensity. In India and Sri Lanka, the political processes have not been affected wholly despite negative impacts created by protracted violent conflicts in some parts of those countries. India has some bright spots too because of its capacity to manage some of the worst forms of conflicts. In some other parts, it has, however, used the carrot and stick method.

From a political point of view, Nepal's Maoist war has crippled the parliamentary process owing to a common objective of the traditional forces represented by the king and the Maoists who, in the beginning, too wanted to destroy the parliamentary institution on the plea that it had failed to serve the people. When the king embarked on the course of assuming executive power in 2002, much of the ground had already been laid, the last being the inability of the government to hold general elections. Lately, however, the Maoist agenda of a constituent assembly and a multiparty system does not go against the spirit of liberal democracy, but how the Maoists would conduct this in accordance with the spirit of pluralist democracy in the future is not yet clear.

Both foreign and native observers share the view that the Maoist demand of a constituent assembly is a strategic ploy to capture power and then to penetrate into the army by contriving divisions within the parties and between the king and the parties. Yet, given the context of Nepal, such an argument seems to be untenable. Nevertheless, unless the Maoists convince other political parties, civil society, and the international community about their commitment to a liberal multiparty democracy in practice, such doubts will continue to remain as strong as ever. In April 2004, the apex leaders of the party—Prachanda and Baburam—once again appealed to the agitating parties to trust them about their commitment to republican democracy and also to forge a joint action for achieving this objective.

The rising insurgency in South Asia has put a heavy burden on the state which in turn is increasingly becoming ineffective and dependent on force to tackle the overarching socio-economic and political problems. Since the state itself is on the decline due to its inability to address the emergent crises politically, militarization or securitization in the conventional sense is the inevitable approach.

NOTES

1. As mentioned in P.R. Chari, 'Combating Terrorism: Devising Cooperative Countermeasures', in Shridhar K. Khatri and Gert W. Kueck (eds.), *Terrorism in South Asia*, Delhi: Shipra, 2003, p. 426.
2. Walter Laquer, *The Age of Terrorism*, Boston: Little, Brown and Company, 1987, p. 11, ibid., p. 428.
3. S. Sanyal, 'International Laws to Control Terrorism: A Comparative Study', *Aakrosh* (Delhi), 7:22, January 2004, pp. 62–3.
4. Narhari Acharya (ed.), Bisweswar Prasad Koirala, *Nepali Kangresska Char Dashak* (Four Decades of Nepali Congress), Kathmandu: Sambadsar, 2053 vs, p. 67 and chapter on 'Gandhibad: Chintan ra Charcha' (Gandhism: Thought and Discourse).
5. Francine R. Frankel, 'Introduction: Contextual Democracy: intersections of society, culture and politics in India' in Francine R. Frankel et al.

(eds.), *Transforming India: Social and Political Dynamics of Democracy*, New Delhi: Oxford University Press, 2000, p. 20.

6. Vinita Damodaran and Maya Unnithan-Kumar, 'Emerging Perspectives on Postcolonial India', in Vinita Damodaran and Maya Unnithan-Kumar (eds.), *Postcolonial India: History, Politics and Culture*, New Delhi: Manohar, 2000, pp. 18–19.
7. Amrita Basu and Atul Kohli, 'Community conflict and the state in India', in *Journal of Asian Studies*, 56, no. 2, May 1997, p. 321.
8. Narendra Subramanian, *Ethnicity and Populist Mobilization: Political Parties, Citizens and Democracy in South Asia*, New Delhi: Oxford University Press, 1999, p. 8.
9. Ibid., p. 2.
10. Interview with *India Today*, 15 September 1985. See details in, Lok Raj Baral, *Regional Migrations, Ethnicity and Security: The South Asian Case*, New Delhi: Sterling, 1990, Chap. 4.
11. Kavita R. Khory, 'The Ideology of the Nation-State And Nationalism', in Rashul Bakhsh Rais (ed.), *State, Society and Democratic Change in Pakistan*, Karachi: Oxford University Press, 1997, p. 131.
12. Jagath P. Senaratne , 'Reflections on the Secessionist Insurrection in Sri Lanka: Consequences for Sri Lanka, and Lessons for the International Community', in Khatri and Kueck, *Terrorism in South Asia*, p. 250.
13. Kumar Rupesinghe , 'Developing a Cooperative Framework for Dealing with Terrorism', in ibid., p. 405.
14. Walter Fernandes, 'Why is Assam Burning?', *The Hindu*, 8 December 2003.
15. *The Hindu*, 18 January 2004.
16. Lok Raj Baral, *Migrations, Ethnicity and Security: The South Asian Case*, New Delhi: Sterling, 1990.
17. Lok Raj Baral, 'Threats to Democracy', *Kathmandu Post*, 28 November 2003; 'Nepal in Crisis; Insurgency, Destruction and Development, *Himalayan Times*, 28 January 2004.
18. Matiur Rahman, 'Impact of Terrorism on Development and the Democratic Process: Bangladesh's Perspective', Khatri and Kueck, *Terrorism in South Asia*, pp. 164–5.
19. Ibid.
20. Kanti Bajpai, 'The Effects of Terrorism on Indian Democracy', in Khatri and Kueck, *Terrorism in South Asia*, p. 188.
21. Jayadeva Uyangoda, 'Security's Insecurity: South Asia's States, Socieities and Citizens in the Age of Globalization', in Rajesh M. Basrur (ed.), *Security in the New Millenium: Views from South Asia*, New Delhi: India's Research Press, 2001, p. 117.
22. Ibid., p. 127.
23. Saji Cherian, 'POTA: Misused Priorities', South Asia Intelligence Review, New Delhi, 27 October 2003.

24. *Peace & Conflict* (Delhi), vol. 7, no. 1, January 2004.
25. *IPCS Newsletter* 10/98 as cited in P.R. Chari, 'India's Defence Expenditure: Can it be Reduced?', Colombo: RCCS Occasional Paper 12, June 2000, p. 9.
26. *The Hindu* (Delhi), 5 November 2003.
27. See for details, Rasul Bakhsh Rais, 'Mixed Up Priorities: Governance and Defence Spending in Pakistan', *RCCS Policy Studies 21*, Colombo: RCSS, 2001, pp. 40–1.
28. Cited by AFP in *New Yorker Magazine*, 1 March 2004. See also *The Kathmandu Post*, 2 March 2004.
29. Nepalnews.com, 27 August 2003.
30. Community Study and Welfare Centre (CSWC), Kathmandu, 2004 as cited by Dilli Ram Dahal in an unpublished paper 'Plight of Internally Displaced Persons (IDPs) in Nepal', 1 February 2004.
31. Western Nepal Conflict Assessment Report, Mercy Corps/USAID, 2004.
32. Ibid.
33. See Lok Raj Baral, 'Rajtantraki Lok Tantra?' *Kantipur*, 9 March 2004. See also Baral's interview in the *Deshantar Weekly*, 11 April 2004.
34. Aisha Sultanat, 'Madrasas in India', Institute of Peace and Conflict Studies, Issue Brief No. 14, November 2003.
35. The Indian government's dilemma of how to deal with the Maoists and the government has been evident since the beginning of the People's War in 1996. On the one hand it has provided military assistance to the government, and on the other it adopted a soft attitude towards the Maoists along the border so much so the reports of a meeting of between Maoist leaders and leaders of Nepali parties' leaders came out in the local press. Perhaps by way of dispelling such an impression, the Indian authorities handed over two prominent Maoist leaders—Matrika Yadav and Suresh Ale Magar—in February, inviting bitter condemnation from the Maoists.
36. For other details of India and other governments' positions, see S.D. Muni, *Maoist Insurgency in Nepal: The Challenge and the Response*, New Delhi: Rupa, 2003, pp. 49–67.
37. For a detailed study of the militarization and its consequences, see Dhruba Kumar, 'Consequences of the Militarized Conflict and the Cost of Violence in Nepal', *Contributions To Nepalese Studies*, Kathmandu, vol. 30, no. 2, July 2003, pp. 167–216.
38. *Kathmandu Post*, 28 March 2004.

10. Terrorism in South Asia

Ayesha Siddiqa

INTRODUCTION

Today terrorism is recognized as one of the major menaces ailing South Asian states and societies. Unfortunately it is difficult to take a mechanical view of terrorism because it is as much about strife within societies as between states. What is it that compels ordinary people to take up arms against fellow citizens or human beings? What are the elements within the societies that opt for extreme measures? Finally, what are the societal attitudes that allow violence to spread like wildfire in a given society? These are some of the vital questions that need clarification. What makes this inquiry important is that one also needs to understand the societal motivations and attitudes that compel ordinary people to become part of a violent mechanism of holding a dialogue with an adversarial group or country. However, such an inquiry is not be possible unless one evaluates the nature of terrorism in individual states and the region in general.

This chapter aims to look at the problem of terrorism in individual states and the impact it has had on the society, finally looking at how the civil societies have considered this threat or responded to it. One of the basic hypotheses of this paper is that one would fail to get a civil society reaction in South Asia similar to what one saw in the US primarily because of the peculiar identification of the issue in individual states.

TERRORISM: THE PROBLEM

Before one embarks upon an analysis of civil society reaction to the menace of terrorism and violence, it would be fair to admit that conceptualizing terrorism in the region is not an easy task. Not only does one not come across a consensus definition, but it is also highly problematic to define all or most acts of violence as terrorism. The internal political dynamics of the states and the fact that most of the violence is caused by the state or non-state actors due to secessionist movements make it difficult for the civil society to take clear positions. It is also a fact that while not every act of violence can be termed as terrorism, South Asian societies are increasingly under the siege of violence perpetrated by non-state actors. Moreover, there is the issue of state terrorism and states' perpetration of violence or terrorism. As far as the state's involvement in terrorism is concerned two issues can be observed: first, states using force against their own citizens in pursuance of their defined political goals. This refers to conditions where the constitutional or legal framework of a state does not allow for secessionist movements or violence to support such a move. However, the question which then needs to be asked is, does the legal authority automatically confers upon a state the moral authority to use force against its people? second, the state's involvement in creating terror networks or groups. The question here is, how does one then absolve a state from its responsibility of being part of a terror network?

It is very difficult to define terrorism in South Asia using the same definition or parameter as the US. Therefore, it is also difficult to find a consensus in the civil society regarding the issue of the definition of terrorism or methods to curb the menace. It is a fact that after 9/11 the South Asian states' focus on this problem has increased. However, this does not necessarily mean that violence perpetrated by non-state actors was not happening in the region even before the US and the international community became aware of it. There is no evidence to suggest that incidents of violence have increased dramatically in the region after 9/11. From an analytical perspective the major issue is to draw a line between the state's monopoly of violence and the violence of non-state actors. This becomes increasingly difficult in conditions where the political system is ridden with poor governance and lack of justice. Thus this is an issue that needs to be dealt with thoroughly at both the academic and the policy-making levels. Unless there is this clarity, it would be difficult to visualize a concerted effort at the level of the civil society to fight violence. Given the complex nature of the issue, this chapter will refer to terrorism as violence. Before embarking upon a detailed analysis on the subject, it is vital to point out that civil society's reaction to terrorism is responsive to the nature of the problem and the linkage between the perpetrators of violence and the civil society. In cases where the issue pertains to poor governance or mismanagement by the state or state violence, it is difficult for the civil society to completely shun those who are responsible for violence just because they are non-state actors and, technically speaking, do not have a monopoly over violence. Terrorism in South Asia cannot compare with the US where the perpetrators of the 9/11 crisis were motivated by an agenda foreign to the land where the act of terror was carried out. So one would not find drastic variations in South Asian civil society's response to the problem that remains poorly defined. This is not to suggest that the common people in the region support terrorism or violence, but that they find it difficult to apply straight jacketed concepts for interpreting the issue.

TERRORISM: THE SOUTH ASIAN CANVAS

Terrorism in relation with South Asia cannot be treated with a single or even a broad brush. Needless to say, terrorism or violence by non-state actors in pursuance of particular political objectives is not a new phenomenon for this region. However, the fact is that the attention this issue has received at this juncture is linked with global developments post-9/11. The new definition of terrorism that is being pursued by the West sees terrorist activities primarily as violence pursued by networks like Al Qaida. These networks do not necessarily have a regional or national agenda even though such organizations operate in parts of the South Asian region as well. This is different from the violence that has traditionally been seen in the various regional states. This is a case in which various groups and individuals use violence with much more focused political objectives. This differentiation, according to people like I.A. Rehman of the Human Rights Commission of Pakistan, is important. According to Rehman, while the political objectives in pursuance of the rights of certain people in relation to a particular territory are more acceptable, the aims of organisations like Al Qaida are certainly not acceptable.[1] While one can debate his perspective, the fact remains that people are willing to make such a differentiation. There are others who question the fundamental logic of America's drive against terrorism arguing that it is reflective of a certain bias.[2] Such views, in fact, are reflective of the deep divide within the civil society that results in a lack of clarity as to how the subject should be treated and whether it is possible to look at the problem through a single lens.

9/11 has surely had an impact on the thinking of the states and civil societies of this region regarding terrorism. It is a mix of factors including diplomatic compulsions, external pressures and an awareness to the threat of terrorism that has drawn reactions from the governments and people. Nonetheless, the reaction continues to be mixed and varies with every state. This is because terrorism has different a shape or form in every country. In fact, the nature of terrorism and its causes vary from state to state. In broad terms, however, there are two categories that can be identified: (a) terrorism induced and conducted in partnership with global terror networks, and (b) acts of violence in pursuance of the rights of people. It is necessary to understand these categories because the attitude of the civil society varies accordingly.

Terrorism: Extension of Global Terror Networks

The two regional states that fall in this category are Pakistan and Bangladesh with the former qualifying for this slot more than the later. It is in both these countries that there is evidence of a linkage between local networks/groups and Al Qaida. This particular category is different from the other two discussed in a later section because the threat is intertwined with the growth of religious ideology in these countries. The issue, therefore, is not of a group of people struggling for their rights or for a piece of territory, as is obvious in the other two cases, but of imposing a peculiar politico-ideological system on the rest of the society. The increase in the influence of the religious right is a development which supports the connection between the local groups and Al Qaida as an external factor. However, one needs to look more carefully at both cases in order to determine the magnitude of the problem.

The impact of religious-ideology as a source of violence makes the case pretty complex. This is certainly true in Pakistan where Al Qaida as a phenomenon and a network developed during the 1980s and the 1990s. There are a number of local militant groups in both countries, especially in Pakistan, which have linkages with Al Qaida. The years of partnership in a war against the Soviet Union brought a large number of militants from Pakistan, Bangladesh and other Muslim countries together. Most of these militants used Pakistan as a base for further movement into Afghanistan. Again, the Taliban regime, which was in control of the large segment of Afghan territory, had links with religious seminaries in Pakistan. In fact, there are some who see Taliban as a creation of Pakistan's military intelligence agency, the ISI. Indubitably there was a direct linkage between the ISI, the various militant groups fighting in Kashmir, and other parts of the world, and the Taliban.

The militant network that emerged over the years and grew uninterrupted up until 11 September 2001 had some kind of support from the Pakistani military establishment. The Taliban's reason for supporting Osama bin Laden and his terrorist network which is his support in financing activities in different parts of the world was also the reason the ISI continued to cooperate with him. In any case, the groups that fought in Kashmir or other parts of the world like Bosnia, Chechnya, and the southern provinces of China and Central Asia shared a common religious ideological bias. The fact of the matter is that there were a number of groups such as Pakistan's Jaish-e-Mohammad and Lashkar-e-Toiba that had links with bin Laden.

Similarly, there were religious groups in Bangladesh that were sympathetic to bin Laden's ideology. This was the superstructure on which the terrorism network inside these two countries was established. However, underlying this top layer was another secondary layer of organizations that operated within the countries or within the region supporting movements of territorial nature, especially the struggle in Kashmir.

What is important to note is that the support for the global terror network for Al Qaida developed through the same process and in parallel to the increase of ethnic and sectarian violence and religious extremism in both countries. In fact, the overall environment in these countries allowed Al Qaida to make inroads and develop contacts with local groups. Terror, as a tool for furthering the state's political interests, was encouraged and violence ignored for the same reason. The militants were viewed as an asset and a necessary part of the military strategy that hugely depended on the militants to further the state's proxy war goals. Once conflict started in Kashmir, though not initiated by Pakistan.[3] The ISI did not take long to build more and smaller jehadi organizations, which were launched into Indian Kashmir to fight a religious war there.[4] From 1990 to 2000, the number had proliferated from one to nine (these figures only pertain to the major jehadi organizations). This resulted in the groups strengthening themselves and making inroads in the civil society because the society or groups on the margins of the society were the recruiting grounds for the militant organizations. This particularly refers to the issue of madrasas acting as recruitment centres for militant organizations. The various sectarian groups that received funding from a number of Gulf and Middle Eastern states were later deployed on other fronts depending on the tactical needs of the military planners. Meanwhile, the authorities did not bother to do any umpiring between the competing interests of these groups, and the Sunni and Shia militant groups continued with their violent battles fought on competing ideological principles similar to the conflict one saw between the Protestants and the Catholics in Ireland.[5]

The aforementioned mechanism, however, meant toying with the basic social dynamics of the society and allowing militant groups sufficient space to grow and transform the dynamics of the civil society. Of course, poverty and underdevelopment contributed towards attracting members of the civil society to join militant organizations, not to mention the role played by religious seminaries in propagating jehad and motivating people to lay down their lives for a cause that was strictly defined by the militant leadership.

This also applies to Bangladesh where an increase in violence appears to have coincided with rise in religious fundamentalism that started around 1993. The religious groups politicized faith and tried to increase their nuisance value by calling people to jehad.[6]

LOCAL BATTLES BY NON-STATE ACTORS

The second category relates to all those cases where some form of freedom struggle or violent secessionist movement has emerged primarily due to the peculiar domestic political environment. In some cases, however, there is also strong evidence of external linkages of such violent struggles. In any case, external sources do tend to play a major role in the supply of armaments, which further fuels the conflicts.

The countries that are ridden with domestic political problems leading to violent movements include India, Nepal, and Sri Lanka. In India's case, there are problems in the north-east, Kashmir, and Tamil Nadu. Violence was also witnessed in Indian Punjab during the 1980s, but since the situation seems to have been brought under control, it will not be mentioned further. What is important to note, nonetheless, is that all of these cases have occurred in bordering areas where the possibility of external help is greater or where there is an issue of division of communities between two states.

Furthermore, the problem of sub-nationalities vying for greater power and autonomy can be traced to the history of the region, especially the manner in which most of the regional states obtained their independence from the British colonial power. In some cases, it is necessary to go even further back into history basically to determine that it was the British rule that consolidated the region politically. This is particularly true of the Indian subcontinent where a consolidation did not take place despite hundreds of years of Mughal rule. Hence, the political divisions that emerged after the British left were not necessarily sensitive to the socio-political realities of the region. The administrative and political systems that were introduced after independence of these states were even more insensitive to the sub-nationalities and their politics, often resulting in poor governance and mismanagement of sub-nationalities and communities spread all over South Asia. There were also cases where the issue of sub-nationalities was created due to the peculiar politics of the colonial power. For instance, in Sri Lanka's case, the Tamils were brought into the country as labour and when the British left no measures were ever taken to address the problems of this community or redress their grievances vis-à-vis the majority. In addition, the centralized system of governance did not help in addressing the issue of multiple nationalities living in politically centralized states. Continued poor governance not only eroded people's faith in the state, but it also urged sub-nationalities to seek independence or greater autonomy. Such sub-nationalities assert their independent identities (it could be religious or ethnic) to enforce their right for independence or to gain greater rights. It is not a coincidence, however, that most of these tension spots are border areas. This, in fact, is another crucial dimension of the sub-regional relationship in the region. In some cases, like Tibet and Kashmir, the territorial disputes between neighbouring states have had serious implications for the relationship between the various sub-national groups.

In India, the north-eastern states of Manipur, Tripura, and Assam are problematic sub-regions where insurgencies and secessionist movements have resulted in violence. A similar situation prevails in Kashmir where the friction between the central government in New Delhi and the state, poor governance and corruption, underdevelopment and lack of opportunities, and influence from the neighbouring state were some of the factors that resulted in producing a hostile population. The violent movement that started in Kashmir in 1989, which New Delhi later blamed on Pakistan, in fact echoed the growing resentment of the treatment meted to them by the central government and the state authorities.

Poor governance is again the issue that created friction and violence in Nepal where the Maoists took up arms in the mid-1990s. The neglect of the common people under the multiparty system led the Maoists to protest the system of injustice.

Similarly, the Sri Lankan case denotes the friction caused by the injustice meted out to a minority at the hands of a majority. The political problem dates back to the 1950s, when the Tamil community politically protested against the Sri Lankan government's decision in 1956 to declare the language of the majority, Sinhala, as the only official language, completely ignoring the Tamil minority. Later the constitutional enactment of 1972 removed all safeguards for the minorities. It was in this sense political environment that Tamil militancy, including the LTTE, was formed in 1972. Ethnic violence has gradually escalated in

Sri Lanka, more in reaction to the majority Sinhala community's refusal to accommodate legitimate Tamil aspirations. This refusal was also reflected in the reactive, state-supported, ethnic violence on the Tamils of unprecedented magnitude in July 1983. In this two-way ethnic violence, according to one estimate, the battle thus far has claimed about 50,000 Tamil lives, made thousands homeless, and forced a large number to flee the country.[7] The organization, the LTTE, was launched primarily to achieve the political objective of liberating the Tamil minority and creating a homeland for this community through the employment of military means. Therefore, it comprises a liberation force with sufficient supplies of weapons including certain categories of major weapons system like naval gunboats. Since the 1970s, the country has experienced violence including assassinations, bombings, and suicide bombings, which has had a severe impact on the security and socio-economic development of the state and the society.

The common denominator in all these cases is that the insurgencies represent friction within the societies, which is then capitalized upon by groups and individuals that are often seen as representing the interests of the people rather than the state itself. This factor, in fact, is a hindrance in generating a consensus amongst the various stakeholders in the society to curb violence.

Victims of Violence

Such categorization does not mean that the victims of violence in each of the three cases are any different. Besides the general erosion of peace and security in the respective states, violence has affected socio-economic development in the countries or in the concerned regions. In fact, there are two models that one can observe as far as the impact of violence is concerned. The first model relates to situations where violence has affected the overall socio-economic conditions of a country and transformed the basic face of a society. The second model relates to cases where tension has affected development in certain areas and not the entire state. Here, the reference is to bigger states like India where the geographical vastness and diversity limits the impact of violence mainly to areas that suffer from violence.

Referring to the first category and specifically looking at Pakistan's case one finds that an increase in violence has had a negative impact on the society and economy of the country. The free hand that was given to militant groups during the decades of the 1980s and the 1990s created a situation where religious extremism, which represented the ideological hallmark of these organizations, divided the society resulting in an increase in sectarian violence. Reportedly, there were a total of 774 people killed and 1,172 injured in cases of sectarian violence.[8] This is the most obvious or direct cost of violence. There are other indirect costs as well such as a general growth in violence, greater influence of religious extremist organizations in universities and other centres of learning, worsening of the attitude of the larger civil society regarding women, proliferation of narcotics and small arms, and others. All these issues might not necessarily be driven by terrorism, but what is important to understand is the connection between policy-making, religious-ideological extremism, violence and the aforementioned results (see Fig. 1).

Obviously once the state condones or supports militancy and religious extremism as a policy it creates greater room for militant organizations to operate. However, this is not a stand-alone activity. The general increase in intolerance and religious extremism

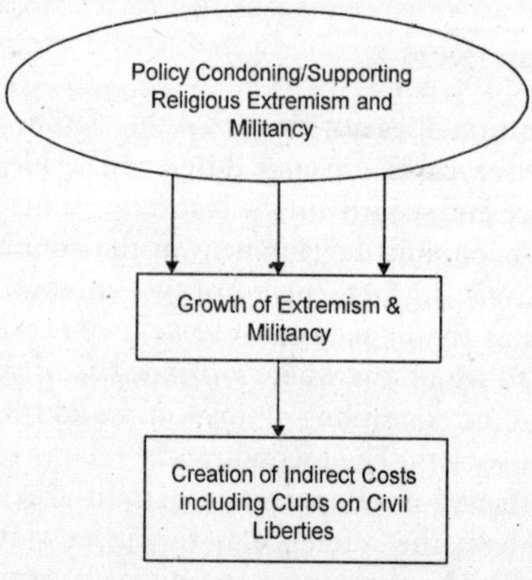

FIG. 1: THE CYCLE OF VIOLENCE.

that accompanies such developments has a huge opportunity cost in its own right. This kind of a policy perspective has negative implications for civil liberties, especially of minority groups like women and ethnic and religious minorities. The state can play a major role in altering the attitudes of the society and reducing or increasing the space for groups to coexist or to embark upon violence.

It is a fact that in both Bangladesh and Pakistan violence has increased since the rise in religious extremism. It is in such a situation that weapons or all other elements that aid violence proliferate in the society. So, one cannot take it as a simple coincidence that drugs and weapons have proliferated in both countries. The linkage between narcotics and weapons was established from the days of the early Afghan jehad of the 1980s, during which the CIA and the ISI provided cover and support for drugs and small-arms trafficking.[9] This linkage is evident in other places as well such as India's north-east.[10] It is vital to understand this linkage not only to get a sense of how terrorist groups arm themselves or finance their struggle, but also to evaluate the indirect costs. Narcotics and weapons proliferation, for instance, nourishes violence in a society and increases the problem of drug addiction which in itself threatens peace and stability.

The general increase in violence and intolerance in a society which is linked with political or ideological extremism is also detrimental for the economic growth of a country. The most obvious example is Pakistan. Although there were no figures available to show how terrorism has impacted economic progress,[11] sources that were interviewed spoke about violence affecting foreign direct investment in the country.[12] This condition also prevails in other countries like Sri Lanka where tourism, which is a major industry, was affected due to terrorism. It is but logical for investment and economic growth to retard in areas ridden with violence. The impact is more severe in smaller countries or places where violence is widespread and has many forms like ethnic, sectarian or other kinds of violence. In this situation it becomes difficult to contain the negative costs to particular territories because the threat is far more widespread.

This situation is different from the other cases/models mentioned earlier where negative implications can be limited to particular areas. This, however, is by default and not by design. It in fact happens in cases where insurgencies or movements exist in particular pockets of a country. Again, just because the affect is limited to a region it does not make a case less critical. The agony of the people of those regions or the suffering that they experience due to violence cannot be ignored. There is in fact a need for detailed studies of the economic and opportunity cost of violence in subregions. One very obvious case is that of Indian Kashmir where the population has suffered at the hands of both the state's security forces and the non-state actors. According to available data, about 148 people were killed during 2002–3. This brings the total number of people killed from 1998 to 2003 to about 17,500. In addition, there were approximately 252 buildings damaged during the same period which included government buildings, schools, religious places and houses. The report also mentions that the number of psychiatric patients in Kashmir is around 36,000 for the year 2003.[13]

This is not to say that one case is better than the other because there are similarities in both cases in terms of victims of conflict. One of the groups most affected by violence are women. Rape, for instance, is a tool used by state forces and terrorists alike, which violates the civil liberties of women. What must be noted is that in traditional societies like South Asia's, rape is not just a personal trauma, it is also a social stigma which does not bode well for the future of a victim. Hence, this is a tool that is used in embattled areas in all the regional states. In any case, females have to face other problems like greater vulnerability once their male members die in local skirmishes or through acts of violence. The condition of women in Kashmir, where they have to suffer at the hands of militants and the state's security forces, is hardly enviable.[14] There is no difference, however, between women as victims or as warriors. Women have been used in suicide bombings and other killings in Sri Lanka and other battlegrounds as well, not to mention the child-soldier phenomenon that is rampant in countries like Sri Lanka and Nepal.

REACTION OF THE CIVIL SOCIETY

Despite this picture which is definitely bleak, one finds a muted response of the civil societies of the region towards terrorism.

One of the major issues in this regard relates to the definition of terrorism. Although the significance of curbing violence in South Asia cannot be denied, the fact is that the definition of terrorism given by the US after 9/11 does not take into consideration the problematic socio-political structure of this region.

The fact is that most civil society organizations are at odds with the American definition of terrorism. And this is what often leads to their muted response to the issue. Interestingly, this kind of response applies to all the three categories mentioned in the earlier section of the chapter. A number of individuals and non-governmental organizations working in different sectors were approached regarding their views on terrorism and approaches towards fighting the menace. In all cases there was a verbal recognition of the fact that terrorism or violence was a threat and that it was detrimental for the peace and security of individual states and the region. However, there was hardly the kind of sentiment to counter the threat in the same fashion as is prevalent in American society. The lack of a comparable reaction cannot be termed as insensitivity of the South Asian civil society towards terrorism, but it denotes the peculiar perspective in each of the individual states and how the civil society has defined the issue or what remedies it has visualized in dealing with the threat. After all, violence and terrorism are real threats in the region and have cost thousands of lives and added to the existing poverty and underdevelopment of the region and its peoples. The varied perceptions will be explained in the following subsections.

REACTION OF THE NGO COMMUNITY

The NGO community is one of the most vibrant segments of the formal civil society in the region. This community, however, due to some structural issues has failed to look the matter squarely in *the eye*, which makes it necessary to understand the angle of the various segments of this community. In most cases it was not possible to find any organization working directly on the issue of terrorism. However, they tend to deal with it indirectly, which in itself poses a problem in terms of concentrating on terrorism.

First, the fact is that most of the NGOs worth any mention deal primarily with development, gender, poverty alleviation/reduction, human rights, and similar other issues. Second, terrorism per se does not necessarily fall in the ambit of their primary responsibility. Third, the NGOs that deal with development or gender issues fail to find any synergy between their current activities and focusing on terrorism. This relates to the basic structural problem of the NGOs where activities are mostly funded and are carried out to meet the requirements of the donor organizations. The projects, in most cases, allow for focused work in a particular area. This does not necessarily allow for expansion of work to other related issues. Fourth, there also appears to be an issue of the lack of intellectual capacity of the organizations to expand work to other areas. For instance, organizations working on gender might recognize that the emancipation and development of women calls for a change in the mindset of the larger community and that religious-ideological extremism, which also tends to breed militancy, plays a key role in forming attitudes towards women. However, there appears to be an inability to broaden the debate to consider issues like militancy and terrorism and the threat these pose to the freedom and rights of women.[15] This is a situation that one finds across the board in most countries or particular regions where women are suffering due to violence. The question of rape in high-tension areas like Kashmir, India's north-east or Sri Lanka is being flagged, but is not necessarily analysed in the larger framework of terrorism.

There is also the issue of voluntarily limiting the organizational agenda and limit the work to areas where results could be delivered without confronting the state or the establishment. This has certainly happened in some cases or issue areas. For example, major NGOs, especially international organizations, found it very problematic to focus on the proliferation of small arms and light weapons. Despite the urging of their head offices in other countries, there was a huge reluctance to tackle a subject which might be held as extremely contentious in the region.[16] One of the specific reservations in this case was that the concerned NGOs did not want to get into an issue area which might impede their core activities. This, in their view, could happen if the authorities did not approve of their work or if it drew a reaction from people engaged in violence. However, there are a number of smaller local NGOs as well that work on issues of small arms and light weapons proliferation and in doing so flag the problem of violence generated by the proliferation of armament in the state and society. Nonetheless, the fact remains that the majority of NGOs find it problematic to focus on terrorism. As already stated, the issue here is of delving into subjects which might pose problems for them in delivering results where they can. For instance, organizations working on education or rural development were of the view that they could possibly help a community better through improving conditions that might indirectly help in countering terrorism.

Getting positive results through engaging directly with terrorism is something that might not necessarily be beneficial to the same degree. Thus, a lot depends on the nature of the NGO itself. Service-providing NGOs in particular have limited capacity to tackle the issue as compared with NGOs involved with advocacy work. Such organizations, nonetheless, use other advocacy or analytical tools to help communities curb violence. For example, there are organizations working on conflict resolution or rights of minority groups, etc.[17] This is not to undermine the contribution of these NGOs, but to argue that their approach might produce results only after a long gestation period.

It is a fact that in countries where there are insurgencies generating violence, public opinion is divided on how to deal with the issue. This is because the civil society or the local communities are not entirely opposed to those involved in violence. The Maoists in Nepal, for instance, are seen by some as a group that could deliver the public from the poor governance of the authorities.[18] Such friction can be found in other places as well, such as Sri Lanka, Kashmir or India's north-eastern states where the civil society's perceptions appear to be equally influenced by the high-handed behaviour of the state authorities. In certain political circumstances it becomes difficult for people to draw a distinction between the coercion and violence of the state forces and the non-state actors. Although one can make a case for external intervention playing a major role in border areas, one cannot entirely ignore the negative role played by the state's poor governance as a factor that spurs violence or renders greater political influence to violent non-state actors. These are situations where, in fact, it becomes difficult for the civil society to take a decisive position against terrorism.

What must be noted that in South Asia the problem of terrorism or violence is far more complex than it is in the US or the West. Here, it is not a matter of a civilizational divide with some outside elements threatening peace and security of an individual state or the region. While there are accusations of external involvement or cross-border infiltration, there is also the issue of local populations being involved in violent movements. This not only tends to divide the sympathies of the people, but it also thwarts any official effort to muster the complete support of the local population. Finding a consensus becomes difficult despite the fact that innocent people are equally terrorized by the non-state actors and not just by the state authorities. Moreover, taking a clear position against violence becomes difficult given the diverse ethnic structure of the societies in the region. A Tamil, for instance, would find it difficult to take a position against that segment of its population engaged in militancy. What complicates matters further is when the militant is seen as pursuing an agenda which is subscribed to by other segments of the population as well. So some segments of the population might have a problem with violence, but the very fact that the violence is in pursuance of a popular political agenda often makes it difficult for the majority population to draw a clear line in support of or against the terrorists.

The nature of violent movements in the region cannot be ignored. These movements are inherently different from what the US has encountered. The idea is not to condone violence in any form or shape—and it is a fact that not all secessionist movements or acts of violence could be justified—however, it is very difficult to take positions in a situation where the lines are fuzzy and it becomes increasingly difficult to treat all acts of violence with a broad brush.[19] This is where one also begins to understand the indirect approach adopted by advocacy NGOs in dealing with violence. The fundamental understanding is that violence in a society cannot be condoned, but it is a problem that must be solved through building greater tolerance in society. Civil society organizations in the region, like NGOs or others, find it extremely problematic to define violence in South Asia purely as terrorism. This is another structural problem that does not help in generating a consensus approach. Defining secessionist movements as terrorist activities is highly problematic because of their peculiar nature. According to B.G. Verghese, 'secessionist movements are the manifestations of extreme frustration rather than ideological . . . '.[20] In societies ridden with the problem of an imbalance between the majority and the minority (this includes ethnic and sectarian) it becomes difficult to take strong positions.

The other structural limitation that one comes across in civil society finding a solution to violence is the lack of capacity. The state in any case has greater outreach and the policy mechanism to carry out a concerted effort. Surely such an effort is lacking, especially in cases where the state itself has been involved in aiding or abetting violence or the perpetrators of violence. This anomaly relates particularly to Pakistan's case where there is a strong evidence of linkage between state and non-state actors.[21]

REACTION OF THINK-TANKS

In the earlier subsection one looked at the issue of the NGO community's potential contribution to curbing violence and one of the conclusions was that this was not possible due to a number of reasons. One of the explanations was the lack of clear definition of what falls in the ambit of terrorism. This is an important issue which one would have expected the academic or the think-tank community to solve. Indeed, one does come across analytical work on the subject in most countries of the region.

Three major trends in studies of the subject became evident from the available literature. First, there are studies that are descriptive and present the case mainly in politico-strategic terms.[22] Since most of the think tanks focus on arms control, disarmament, and strategic issues, it is natural for these to review the issue mainly from a foreign relations and military perspective. Second, certain literature tends to look at the issue not in a holistic manner, but with an emphasis on pinning responsibility on state actors for perpetrating or supporting terrorism.[23] Although one cannot deny the involvement of states in the political affairs of their neighbours, and this is an element that one can find in most conflict areas in the region, one cannot entirely ignore that internal dynamics also provide impetus to violence. Thus, also comes across another set of literature that basically denies accusations or lays counter-accusations. Finally, there is the new literature that looks at the issue mainly from the prism of the post-9/11 American definition. However, there is a dearth of work that can explain the phenomenon or the problem as it pertains to South Asia.

MEDIA'S RESPONSE TO TERRORISM

The divisions in the polity and society of a given state condition the media's response to violence and terror. The fundamental constraint on the media's ability to take a firm position on the subject is due to its structural inability to present or carry out analyses. This weakness can be observed across the board in the region. Since the media's prime responsibility is to report events or crises, rarely does one find in-depth analyses of the issue. In fact, there are two basic trends that can be observed here: (a) the media debate following the official line of argumentation, and (b) conforming to a favoured position presented by a particular group. According to this approach, the print media tends to either hold external forces responsible for the acts of violence or blame it on the problematic policy-making of the authorities. Where secessionist movements are concerned, the vernacular or local language press is more likely to reinforce the popular notion. One rarely finds any original or objective arguments being presented by the media. Even when the issue relates to global terror networks, the print media takes the popularly accepted position. For instance, in the case of Pakistan the media can be found either reporting on events or presenting a position which is not dramatically opposed to the extremist groups.

The electronic media in all countries tends to present the official position as it is primarily controlled by the state or is influenced by the official position.

POLITICAL PARTIES' PERSPECTIVE

The political parties of a country represent a segment that is most representative of the civil society and also plays a key role in forming opinions. As far as violence in the society is concerned, one would generally find all political parties of regional states opposing violence in their respective states. However, this does not necessarily translate into an agreement on the definition of terrorism or policy formulation on how to control the menace of terror and violence. Like other segments of the civil society, the political parties seem to have taken up the anti-terrorism agenda after 9/11, but one has to carefully sift through the reactions to analyse the reality of the attitude of various political parties. One has to be mindful of drawing a distinction between two sets of agendas: (a) one dictated by the US or following the American call to counter terrorism, and (b) one specific to regional terror.

As far as Washington's call to counter terrorism is concerned, there are three sets of reactions that are obvious. First, while generally condemning terrorist attacks against the US, parties find it difficult to entirely support the US war against terrorism. This perspective is particularly reflected in the opinion of political parties of the smaller countries like Nepal and Bangladesh. Again, there is a difference of opinion between the ruling party or coalition and those in opposition, especially in situations where there is interaction between the concerned state and the US. This is obvious in the case of smaller countries like Bangladesh, Nepal, and Sri Lanka where the governments have aligned with Washington.[24] One also finds a general resentment against the American agenda of war against terrorism in *frontline* states like Pakistan, where religious parties are vocal in condemning Washington's attack on Afghanistan and the military action in Pakistan's tribal areas. The secular parties, in fact, are also uncomfortable about totally supporting America's actions.[25] However, the opposition is fairly muted with no evidence of any strong resistance. Despite calling for a protest against military action in the tribal areas, the coalition of opposition parties, the Alliance for Restoration of Democracy (ARD), did not manage to organize any action. Similarly, the alliance of religious parties, the MMA has also not been very active in this regard. This is despite its majority in the Frontier province.[26] This attitude can only be explained in terms of the general fear that any strong opposition might be met with coercive force from the military, or the fact that no political stakeholder is willing to take a position contrary to Washington's. The US, it must be remembered, plays a crucial role in the country's domestic politics as well.

Second, one finds support for the American war agenda in the ruling party in Pakistan, which must be seen primarily in the context of the alignment between Islamabad and Washington. It is not necessary that the political leadership of the ruling party is entirely convinced about the American agenda. Third, the reaction from India where though there is a general support for fighting terrorism, one can also sense a discomfort about totally agreeing with the US's onslaught against terrorism.[27] The reactions of the two largest states of South Asia on this issue are interesting and complex in their own regard and linked with their bilateral relations as well. On the one hand, the leadership of both countries is not completely at ease subscribing to the US military actions in Iraq. On the other hand, they find it politically expedient to be part of the war against terrorism in pursuance of their respective political objectives. In Pakistan's case, the objective appears to be the political survival of the military in Pakistan. In any case, the military is under pressure to cooperate since it was the one that had a hand in erecting the terror network.[28] Islamabad, it must be noted, has also joined the American bandwagon to seek an alignment with the US, which is traditionally sought to counter India's politico-military force in the region.

The Indian case is more complex because here the issue is of New Delhi appreciating the worth of aligning with the US in its war against terror primarily because it might help India get rid of its own problems of terror, especially that which is perpetrated by its neighbour, Pakistan. It is a fact that India has suffered at the hands of terrorism, a situation that cannot change without American involvement, particularly Washington's pressure on Islamabad to stop aiding and abetting militant networks in Kashmir.[29] Hence, one sees major political parties in India, including the BJP, supporting the general agenda of war against terror.[30] The BJP has been trying to muster support for its policy in the political circles.[31] Its failure to retain power in 2004 elections has not deterred it in this respect.

However, the BJP's inclination, as some in India's political scene believe, is also driven by the party's election agenda. This was certainly the view expressed by Ashok Kapoor, media spokesman for the Samajwadi Party in Uttar Pradesh.[32] The Congress party has been equally sceptical of the then official position condemning the government's role in mishandling the crisis in Gujarat and Kashmir.[33] It is a fact that when it comes to the issue of terrorism in the domestic context that opinion appears divided in most countries. This is due to the structural complexity of the issue. There are a few aspects that one must consider in this regard.

First, it is difficult for political stakeholders to take a solid position because of their own involvement in incidents of terror and violence. It is a fact that in all countries of the region the political leadership does take recourse to violence as a tool. Second, it is not possible for the political stakeholders to take a clear position against terrorism, particularly in states like Bangladesh and Pakistan where the religious parties are part of a coalition, or there is an indirect partnership between the religious parties and the ruling party, or where the state is involved in aiding and abetting terrorists. In Pakistan's case, for instance, most of the religious parties that form the alliance of religious parties were involved with militant groups or the global terror network. Similarly, the Awami League in Bangladesh was accused of links with religious-extremists groups and parties for political expediency.[34] Third, in cases like Pakistan's, political parties are averse to taking a position because of their lack of involvement in the policy-making process. Decisions relating to militant organizations fall in the ambit of the military rather than the political leadership.[35] Fourth, supporting the anti-terror agenda is difficult, especially in situations where the government's recipe is highly questionable. This refers to Islamabad's policy of creating anti-terror courts much before 9/11, in response to the growing incidence of violence in the country. However, these courts were seen as a tool for state coercion.[36] Moreover, they failed to fulfil the objective because the government could not provide protection to the judges of the ATCs, resulting in the killing of a few judges. Finally, the political leadership's reluctance to address the issue of poor governance which generates incidents of terror and violence is a major hindrance in solving the problem. In India's case, for example, the traditional emphasis is on blaming Pakistan for most incidents of terror. While this is true to a large extent in some cases, terrorism is a problem which requires a more holistic approach.

CONCLUSION

To sum up the debate on civil society reaction to terrorism or countering terrorism in South Asia, the primary conclusion of this chapter is that there is no consensus on this issue. Although the region has suffered from violence and terror for a long time, it is mainly after 9/11 that the issue seems to have gained attention.

In dealing with the subject one has to differentiate between the American anti-terror agenda and the problems faced by South Asia. In fact, the issue of terrorism is fundamentally quite different from the US's definition of it. Unlike Washington, which is concerned by the presence of a global terrorism network targeting American economic and security interests, the violence that one sees in South Asia is multifaceted. This is not to suggest that one should not be concerned about the global terror network like Al Qaida. On the contrary, the region has gained special emphasis and attention because networks like Al Qaida have originated from this region and have expanded across frontiers not only in South Asia, but in other parts of the world as well. Religious ideology is one of the crucial elements that form the basis of a coalition between Al Qaida and the local militant/terror groups.

However, this is a problem that is beyond the ability of civil society to solve, because some of the states have themselves been responsible for breeding and aiding such groups. So it makes sense for the US to build links with the official channels in its efforts to putt an end to the menace. But a religious ideology-driven violence is just one aspect of the problem. There are societal problems as well, including poor governance, poverty, underdevelopment, lack of justice, and inequitable distribution of resources which generate a lot of the violence one sees in the region today. A solution therefore has to be based on adopting a holistic approach to the problem.

It is also a fact that elements which formally represent the civil society such as the NGOs, think tanks or the political parties suffer from certain structural problems which hinder them from playing a dynamic role in this regard. The core constraint nonetheless is on how to define terrorism. The socio-political dynamics of individual states and the region bar any stakeholder from taking substantive initiatives to eradicate of the menace.

NOTES

1. Discussion with I.A. Rehman, Islamabad, 16 February 2004.
2. Interview with Maulana Fazlu Rehman, Islamabad, February 2004.
3. Robert G. Wirsing, *India, Pakistan and the Kashmir Dispute*, London: Macmillan, 1994, pp. 208–11.
4. Interview with Lt. General Alam Jan Mehsud, Rawalpindi, April 1994.
5. For a comparison see Martin Dillon, *God and the Gun*, New York: Routledge, 1999.
6. Ruchira Joshi, 'Terrorism in Bangladesh', in Dipankar Sengupta and Sudhir Kumar Singh, *Terrorism in South Asia*, New Delhi: Authors Press, 2004, pp. 79–80.
7. Sengupta and Singh, *Terrorism in South Asia*, pp. 57–60.
8. 'Cost of Conflict between India and Pakistan', Mumbai: Strategic Foresight Group, 2004, p. 32.
9. Alexander Cockburn and Jeffrey St. Claire, *White Out*, London: Verso, 1998, pp. 255–72.
10. Binalakshami Nepram, *South Asia's Fractured Frontier*, New Delhi: Mittal Publications, 2002, pp. 69–124.
11. One of the problems of accessing data relates to the unwillingness of the authorities to share information that would link violence with lack of economic progress. The situation becomes highly problematic where the state itself has a role in aiding and abetting terrorist organizations.
12. Discussion with Akbar Zaidi, Muscat, January 2004.
13. 'Cost of Conflict between India and Pakistan', pp. 62–3, 66.
14. A. Subramanyam Raju, 'Women and Terrorism in South Asia: Some Observations', in Adluri Subramanyam Raju, *Terrorism in South Asia*, New Delhi: India Research Press, 2004, pp. 325–36.
15. Discussion with Farzana Bari, member of an NGO in Pakistan working on democracy, Islamabad, February 2004.
16. Discussion with heads of Action Aid, Safer World, Oxfam, etc., London, December 2003.
17. Interview with the head of Shirkat Gah, Ms Khawar Mumtaz, Lahore, 29 March 2004.
18. Sengupta and Singh, *Terrorism in South Asia*.
19. Discussion with Foqia Sadiq Khan, Research Fellow, SDPI, Islamabad, November 2003.

to end the conflict is unlikely to be met. Unless conflicts in a state have an international spillover effect, the third-party role is also viewed as interference in the internal affairs in the region.

The years since the emergence of SAARC have shown how swiftly politics in South Asia oscillates between conflict and cooperation, confrontation and constructive diplomacy. The two regional agreements on the Suppression of Terrorism (signed in 1987 and 2004) are a case in point. While the 1987 convention resolved, 'to take effective measures to ensure that the perpetrators of terrorist acts do not escape prosecution and punishment', it fell short of taking specific counter-terrorism measures pertaining to the financing of terrorism. The 2004 Additional Protocol to the Regional Convention on the Suppression of Terrorism deals with this issue specifically, by making it a criminal offence to willingly or with knowledge make financial contributions to any terrorist cause. At the international level, the UN Security Council adopted Resolution 1373 in 2001, obligating all members to take specific actions to combat terrorism. This went beyond the 12 international treaties that bind only those that accede to them. Accordingly, 'all member states are required to deny all forms of support for terrorist groups; to suppress the provision of safe haven, sustenance, or support of terrorists; and to share with other governments, information about any groups practicing or planning terrorist attacks. It also bars active and passive assistance to governments.'[1] Finance and related support for terrorist activities is now under the international microscope with states undersigning to cooperate so as to deal with this issue effectively. Third parties can provide considerable support in helping to choke the finances of terrorist organizations through the institutionalization of checks on money transfers through domestic and international banks. Since most of the funds come from sources outside the state facing terrorism, this form of intervention and support would be invaluable.

The South Asian Terrorism

Although protracted conflicts have been prevalent in South Asia for more than 50 years, 'there is hardly any cause of terrorism which is uniformly applicable to all South Asian countries. Yet, some critical variables can be identified. These include, persistence of poverty and accompanying deprivations (like unemployment), low levels of literacy, limited access to health services, years of misgovernance, which have made violence the only means of bringing about a change, and the alienation of whole cultural or ethnic groups brought about by threat to life by frequent communal violence and destruction of means of livelihood.'[2] Moreover, there are those other issues that can create, and have created, terrorism-generating conflicts, spilling over national boundaries. These can be briefly summarized as: (i) territorial disputes inherited from the colonial past and the demarcation of land and maritime boundaries; (ii) sharing of water resources of common rivers; (iii) intra-state conflict involving ethno-linguistic and religious groups with cross-border affiliation; (iv) conflicting economic interests; (v) smuggling and illegal cross-border activities; and (vi) what has been termed 'illegal immigration and demographic drift' which includes migration of Bangladeshi citizens to India, and the presence in Pakistan of a large Afghan population.

Specifically, Pakistan continues to grapple with ethno-religious-political problems resulting in fissures which threaten to dismember the country. The fratricidal conflict between Shias and Sunnis is one of Pakistan's most intractable problems. There are other divisions along sectarian lines as well: Gilgit–Baltistan in the Northern Areas; Parachina and Peshawar in the NWFP; Lahore, Faislabad, Jhang, Multan, Mianwati, Sargodha, and Dera Ghazi Khan in Punjab; and Karachi in Sindh province. The ethnic clashes in Sindh were compounded by violence which the state had first created by its repression of the Balochi tribesmen and Bengali separatists.

India has borne the brunt of different forms of terrorism over the years, ranging from cross-border terrorism in Kashmir, the movement for a separate 'Khalistan' homeland in Punjab, the movement in southern India by the LTTE, insurgency in the north-east where the demands are either for secession, separate statehood or greater autonomy to the Maoist militancy from Andhra Pradesh, Chhattisgarh, parts of Madhya Pradesh, Orissa, and Bihar. In the case of the north-east, the 'root causes' of terrorism stem from a feeling of alienation, marginalization from the mainland, a desire to protect the ethnic identities as well as the protection of inter-ethnic claims to territory. The People's War Group, which straddles the states of Andhra Pradesh, Orissa and Maharashtra, is another example of left-wing extremism facing India. Its objective is to usher in a new democratic revolution by installing a people's movement through a people's war. With the passage of time both insurgencies and terrorism have operated together in India. It is pertinent to note that terrorism is the operational means or tactics used by insurgents, which makes dealing with the causes of terrorism more important than anything else.

Terrorism in Nepal commenced in 1996 with the establishment of the Nepali Communist Party (Maoist) to fight a 'People's War' against decades of misgovernance, illiteracy, social discrimination and deprivation. Facing rampant and excessive terrorist violence on the one hand, and increasing fatigue and waning tenacity on the other, there was a strong attempt to resolve the problem by the government. The negotiating process prompted by a Maoist ceasefire, commenced in 2003 by involving all protagonists to the conflict. It must be mentioned at this point that Nepal had the support of the United States government, both militarily and economically, in moving towards a peace process. India played a role by providing similar support in addition to developing better mechanisms for border management and intelligence sharing.

Bangladesh faced its own set of terrorism-generating conflict in the Chittagong Hill Tracts in the south-eastern region. An armed struggle was launched in opposition to demands for national integration with Bangladesh in 1973. This went on for a period of 24 years, until 1997, when the government reached a settlement with the insurgents in a peace negotiation. Bangladesh also confronted some terrorist organizations in its south-western region, namely, the Naxalites and the 'Sarbohara', which were offshoot political factions of ultra-left political organizations.

Sri Lanka has suffered the consequences of severe ethnic and class competition and conflict for decades. The struggle between the Sinhala and Tamil ethnicities since the mid-1950s has been one of the most violent and protracted terrorism-generating conflicts in the world. The political estrangement of the Tamils from the Sinhala-dominated Sri Lankan state is the fundamental process that gave birth to secessionist violence.

Bhutan has been viewed by India as indifferent to terrorism. The Assamese terrorist organizations (NDFB and ULFA) had sought shelter in the southern plains of Bhutan in the 1990s. India sought active military intervention to root out the terrorist camps from the Royal Bhutanese government. At the same time, the Indian government was unwilling to send its military into Bhutanese territory. This was not only to respect the latter's sovereignty, but also in the interest of maintaining cordial relations between the two countries. The insurgent groups worked this situation to their advantage and occupied substantial territory inside Bhutan as sanctuaries and safe areas. Eventually, the Bhutanese government launched a military campaign in December 2003 on these terrorist camps, culminating in the elimination and surrender of the top cadres of the terrorist outfits.

It is salient to say that in managing political dissent, all South Asian states have extensively applied the colonial mindset of coercive use of state power. There has been lesser use of persuasive or assimilative approaches to conflict management. This has set the direction for managing internal political dissent for decades, whose residual effects continue to linger. At the outset, there has been strong resistance to 'third-party intervention' in resolving terrorism-generating conflicts in the region (even internally), whether it is in the form of mediation, facilitation, consultation, or arbitration. The World Bank-arbitrated Indus Water Treaty between India and Pakistan is one of the few exceptions, although accusations of breach of treaty obligations are often heard. The other exception of course is the role of Norway as a facilitator in the peace process in Sri Lanka.

Nevertheless, there have been attempts to use back-channel negotiations, civil society involvement, NGO participation as well as the use of rehabilitated militants in resolving conflicts. NGOs could play a significant role in highlighting, for instance, the requirements of militant groups and the limits of governments to the demands of the perpetrators of acts of violence. They could project and assess the impact of the conflict on the society at large. In India, for example, there are no such models for NGO participation in conflict resolution. There are, however, individuals or groups of individuals who have done some work in conflict areas. NGOs have played a marginal role even in Sri

Lanka where the conflict between the JVP and the Sinhalese witnessed no such role-play. These attempts, miniscule as they are, have been subsumed by the larger overriding emphasis of the use of armed force by the state. It is useful to first examine the varied kinds of third-party interventions in conflict situations. This will set the stage for examining the role of third parties in resolving terrorism-generating conflicts in the region.

Types of Third-party Intervention/roles in Conflict-resolution

A heightened sense of collective responsibility exists today in responding to internal conflicts, which is based on a fear that non-combatants are at serious risk of large-scale violence. Armed organizations operating outside the purview of traditional authority structures endanger post-conflict stability. Many internal conflicts spill over into the international domain, putting an additional drain on already overburdened crisis-management resources.[3] Experiences of multilateral third-party intervention can be drawn from the Cold War context, where such interventions were intended only to deter recurring inter-state frictions. In this context, multilateral forms of third-party intervention were designed to monitor ceasefire arrangements after the negotiation of a settlement.[4]

The United Nations, which is primarily meant to build and sustain international cooperation, grapples with the new security threats by referring to its charter provisions, much of which have come under intense scrutiny because of states circumventing these very provisions. Thus, while Article 2 (7) of the UN Charter states that the UN should not intervene in matters that are essentially within the domestic jurisdiction of the state, Chapter VII allows that 'the Charter shall not prejudice the application of enforcement measures'. This implies that if a domestic conflict is construed as a threat to international peace and security, the Security Council may sanction a mandate to intervene. The articles under this Chapter leave it open to interpretation by states to defend their national interests against what they construe to be 'acts of aggression on its territory' with the use of force.

For instance, the United States has interpreted the provisions of Article 51 (Chapter VII) and built a case for 'the discriminate use of force' in dealing with asymmetric threats such as terrorism. In order to implement discriminate force, the US and other countries that seek to make a similar adaptation would need to make significant new investments in international cooperation. To support the precision-capabilities, cooperation in the military and intelligence domains is required. In addition, international cooperation will be necessary for successful coercion because others can help by leveraging adversaries or their supporters, or simply because there is strength in numbers.[5] There is broad agreement that a campaign against international terrorism, sustained over a long period, must be fought and won. In the process, states sponsoring or supporting terrorism will also face consequences, military or otherwise. And Article 51 of the UN Charter backs Washington's military response to terrorism in this regard.[6] A side issue is instructive. Being the only superpower, the United States finds it difficult to enact a role as a third party in terms of credibility. The issue of non-proliferation that has beset the world community underlines this problem.

Traditionally, the term 'third-party intervention' connotes the involvement of a set of people, or an individual, who become involved in a conflict in order to help the disputant parties to either resolve or manage the conflict. The various forms of observed third-party intervention are distinguished by the degree of power that the intervener exercises over the process and outcome of the conflict.[7] Thus, disputes may be subjected to: (i) legal rulings through adjudication or binding decisions by means of arbitration, (ii) mediation through means of threats and a range of inducements to reach a settlement, and (iii) facilitation by way of arranging meetings, promoting understanding, and guiding productive discussions. Numerous terms abound in third-party literature, but a six fold typology of pacific third-party intervention, geared mainly to the international level is instructive.[8]

1. *Conciliation*, in which a trusted third party provides an informal communicative link between the antagonists for the purposes of identifying the issues, lowering tension, and encouraging direct interaction, usually in the form of negotiation.

2. *Consultation*, in which the third party works to facilitate creative problem-solving through communication and analysis by making use of human-relation skills and social-scientific understanding of conflict dynamics.
3. *Pure Mediation*, in which the third party works to facilitate a negotiated settlement on substantive issues through the use of reasoning, persuasion, effective control of information, and the suggestion of alternatives.
4. *Power Mediation*, which encompasses pure mediation with the additional feature of use of leverage or coercion through forms of promised rewards or threats of punishments; it may also involve the use of the third party as a monitor and guarantor of the agreement.
5. *Arbitration*, wherein the third party renders a binding judgment arrived at through consideration of the individual merits of the opposing positions and then imposes a settlement which is deemed to be fair and just.
6. *Peacekeeping*, in which the third party provides military personnel in order to monitor a ceasefire or an agreement between antagonists, and may also engage in humanitarian activities.

A perceptive assessment of successful mediation strategies as a form of third-party intervention was made by William Zartman. His concept of 'hurting stalemate' seems to suggest that involvement will only be effective when a 'ripe moment' exists. This ripe moment occurs when there is a mutually hurting stalemate and where unilateral solutions are blocked.[9] This insight suggests that third parties can, in theory, induce ripe moments through the creation of hurting stalemate. With sufficient leverage, third parties can reduce the likelihood of intransigence on the part of a belligerent who resists bargaining in order to seek large anticipated gains from continued conflict, or terrorism, as the case may be. Third parties can also speed up the movement towards negotiation through imposition of deadlines and other strategies in order to decrease the perceived attractiveness of military options. Thus, the emergence of a resolving formula follows from a readjustment of the belligerent's power relations and the elimination of alternative strategies through concerted coercive efforts by third parties.[10]

Third parties can avail themselves of a range of inducements and respond to threats of punishment to obtain the desirable outcomes. However, the determination of outcomes is subject to the defining characteristics of the third party. The first consideration is the intervening party's own capabilities and connection to the conflict. Second, one must consider the status and ripeness of the conflict for resolution. Third, the character of the disputant parties and their decision-making systems influence intervention. Fourth, is the comparison of the cost of intervention to the cost of not intervening.[11] The most common form of third-party intervention is that of the military type, involving actual presence in a disputant country, military aid, hardware, alliance partnership, and, last but not the least, coercion. The Indian Peace Keeping Force (IPKF) in Sri Lanka is a prime example of such third-party military intervention in South Asia. If one were to consider the ethnic conflict in Cyprus, economic leverages of joining the EU, although acting as catalyst, have failed in terms of bringing an end to the conflict. For more than 40 years, Greek-majority and Turkish-minority Cyprus has been a bone of contention between Turkey and Greece. Lures for eventual membership to EU for Turkey have not resulted in anything concrete thus far. Factored into this of course are the complexities of the Turkish–EU accession talks that make it difficult for an immediate resolution of the ethnic confiict, economic advantages notwithstanding.

Ultimately, states are motivated by their own interests, whether offensive or defensive, to act as a third-party. While the former includes promoting international stability and protecting its foreign policy goals in conflict situations, the latter seeks to prevent rival powers from expanding their spheres of influence.[12] Another dimension can be added to this equation—offensive–defensive interests in the light of the new age of terrorism that permeates all borders and boundaries. There is considerable debate on whether impartiality is an important characteristic of third parties so that they can fulfil their role of engendering trust between the adversarial parties. Neutrality and impartiality of third parties is the general refrain. An alternative view posits: 'if the acceptance of mediation is based on a cost-benefit calculation, then the assumption that mediators must be perceived as impartial, needs to be revised. A pre-existing good relationship with one of the parties may aid effective communication and facilitate development of creative proposals. The adversary party may see such a relationship as evidence that the mediator can effectively pressurize the other party into a settlement. The mediator's success and reputation rides on their ability to deliver their ally into a settlement. And thus again, the adversary party may be reassured that the mediator is strongly motivated to reach an acceptable settlement.'[13]

Important to the whole question of possible third-party role assumption is the reliance by democracies on the power of constitutions in resolving terrorism-generating conflicts. 'This misconception is based on the belief that constitutions, by themselves can guarantee stability without the backing of security capabilities to enforce the provisions of constitutions. This tradition is in keeping with the emphasis given to security in modern stable democracies. Stable democracies are fully aware that constitutions can endure only as long as there is a security establishment to enforce the provisions in constitutions.'[14] Commenting on the conditions for domestic peace, Hans Morgenthau notes, 'peace among social groups within the nation reposes upon a dual foundation. The disinclination of the members of society to break the peace and their inability to break the peace if they should be so inclined. Individuals will be unable to break the peace if overwhelming power makes an attempt to break it a hopeless undertaking'.[15] Delving further into the debate, democratic legalists would assert that because liberal democratic regimes share an affinity with international legal processes and institutions, they tend to be more willing to depend on the rule of law for external relations.[16] Their argument depends on the notion that norms regarding limited government, respect for judicial processes and regard for constitutional constraints carry over into the realm of international politics.[17]

Clearly, therefore, a third party can assume the role of conflict resolution under varied circumstances to help resolve conflicts that generate terrorism. The role can be assumed without invitation, or by a multi-state request, or by a request from the adversary parties. What national interests of the third-party would be met by this role is also an important factor. It is possible that such third-party involvement would be projected as the need of regional or global security concerns. Yet, more often than not, the interests of the third party can themselves become part of the problem and further extend the conflict. 'Evidence from a "duration model of interstate conflict" demonstrates that diplomatic management efforts make important contributions to the resolution of interstate disputes, but it is not equally successful throughout the life cycle of a conflict. In short, the relationship between third-party mediation and a conflict's duration is non-linear with respect to the timing of diplomatic initiatives.'[18]

The introduction of international, ideologically driven and catastrophic terrorism complicates third-party roles and makes them more complex and risk-prone. Modern terrorism is capable of striking across oceans and continents. This makes the third party itself vulnerable to terrorist action. How this development would impact on third-party role-playing is an area yet to be explored. In fact, the role of the third-party is fraught with serious national security risks which makes the role not only difficult, but also imposes political costs on the leaders of state/s wishing to be third parties. They can easily become a third party to the conflict instead of being a third party to its resolution. For instance, if one of the adversarial states to the conflict is unable to manage or control the terrorist groups operating from its territories, the third party's role gets into serious difficulties. Can a third party use its economic, military, and geopolitical leverages to pressure one adversary to conform to acceptable norms of state conduct and responsibility? This would quickly erode the third party's credibility and acceptability and make its role unacceptable both politically and morally. Furthermore, in defining the success of third-party intervention, the vital point is that those who decide to intervene have an obligation to develop their own definition of success. 'Whatever standard of success is adopted, the operation itself must have an efficient, responsive decision-making system. Decision makers must be held accountable for their decisions. The operation must take measures to ensure that its forces are not taken hostage or targeted directly by the combatants. The intervening group must retain and exercise control and timing of the intervention; else they will lose the initiative.'[19]

Events of 9/11 and thereafter have forced a new dynamics over terrorist-related conflict. Third party-role assumptions have to be reinvented within such a backdrop. Some suggested role assumptions of third parties in South Asia could be: (i) ending logistics and related support; (ii) choking off finance (control mechanisms); (iii) policing and monitoring; (iv) exchange of intelligence information; (v) joint patrolling and controlling the flow of weapons; (vi) institutionalization of a mechanism for speedy trials; (vii) incorporating international law provisions into domestic law and making it legally-enforceable; (viii) development cooperation (by way of offering short or medium term political and social mobilization support owing to reconstruction initiatives);[20] (ix) denial of safe haven to terrorist organizations; and (x) resort to international 'facilitative diplomacy'.

The focus of international cooperation has evolved, from an emphasis on containing a well-known set of politically motivated groups, often with overt state sponsors, to addressing more amorphous, less hierarchical terrorist movements. Therefore, the conventional military component of counter-terrorism is likely to be limited in the future as compared to the past. The vast bulk of counter-terrorism cooperation is likely to be in the form of more comprehensive intelligence sharing among states and among police-establishments worldwide.[21] Walter Laquer argues that the only effective weapon in the hands of democracies against terrorism has been the infiltration of the terrorists' ranks and the use of informers. This cannot be obtained in current conditions without international cooperation.

An examination of the actual cases of such involvement in and outside South Asia would provide interesting facets by drawing useful parallels and lessons. What makes third-party role acceptable or credible or negative is an area that would also be worth considering.

Responding to Conflict-generating Terrorism in South Asia

It has been well stated and widely accepted that 'terrorism constitutes the use of force to achieve a political objective by targeting innocent people'.[22] However, after the events of 9/11 it has also become apparent that terrorism has changed its characteristics in terms of 'increased lethality, increased accessibility to weapons and technology, sophistication and operational competence and more importantly, force-multiplying effect of state-sponsored terrorism'.[23] The assistance that governments have deliberately or unwillingly provided to terrorist organizations has often ended up enhancing their striking power and capabilities.

Conflict-related terrorism is a mode of operation of resistance groups or movements that enjoy the support of at least some of the local population and are normally engaged in more than one type of violence. In the age of catastrophic terrorism, a lowest common denominator for conflict-generated terrorism is the deliberate, politically motivated use of, or threat to use, violence against civilians or civilian targets by a weaker side in an asymmetrical conflict.[24] Dealing with terrorism in the larger context of a 'global war on terrorism' by relying too much on the use of military force, has not proven to be particularly effective. This is true of the conflicts in Kashmir and Chechnya.[25]

In the South Asian region, 'state-sponsorship of terrorism' acquires different interpretations and forms of support to terrorist organizations, often at the cost of neighbouring states. Typically, state-sponsorship of terrorism ranges from allowing use of territory to set up camps or 'shelters', financial support (even donations and collection of funds openly in the name of a terrorist cause), rampant trafficking in weapons and related hardware, training facilities and use of its intelligence agencies, and last but not the least, earning goodwill and publicity for their cause in domestic and international forums. The old adage, 'one man's terrorist is another man's freedom fighter' holds true in this regard. 'Having themselves spawned, encouraged, aided and abetted terrorism in neighbouring countries, the border areas of South Asia have become the familiar arena of terrorism.'[26]

There, is all the same, a common thread that runs through the approaches used by the states to deal with internal political dissent. It is of a colonial mindset, bringing to bear the operational doctrine used by the British in handling political dissent and protests. The extensive use of the military, armed police, and paramilitary forces in dealing with what were essentially political movements in the post-independence South Asian states contributed in no small measure to the complexities being faced today. The use of coercive power of the state, instead of its potential and skills to evolve inclusive and assimilative strategies, has resulted in political dissent becoming armed uprisings in the decades that followed. This approach to governance set the direction for managing internal political dissent and continues to hold sway today, even as the content of armed resistance to the state has assumed the greater technological, financial and international dimensions of terrorism.

So far an excessive reliance on the use of force has not worked well in most of the conflicts in South Asia. Broadly, the instruments of dealing with internal conflicts (later translating into terrorist activities) are the use of the state police and intelligence networks, physical security agencies, paramilitary forces, the army, and in the case of India, 'two new additions were made to the counter-terrorism set up: (i) a multi-disciplinary centre for joint analysis of all the intelligence input and (ii) a counter-terrorism division in the Ministry of External Affairs to co-ordinate the diplomatic aspects of counter-terrorism.'[27]

In India, the response to terrorism has had a number of effects on the democratic functioning. It has led to the militarization of the Indian imagination, to the government's accretion of emergency powers, to the devaluation of debate and dissent, and to an assault on liberals and the idea of liberalism. It has also led to a more managerial, technical view of politics.[28] Expanding this further, terrorism would appear to involve a political cost that tends to undermine democratic values and institutions. To be able to deal with the problem, strong methods are used, which only leads to a sense of alienation in the areas affected by terrorism.[29] India has in recent decades sought to deal with conflict-generating terrorism through either non-military or military solutions. The latter option has been used to inculcate a sense of security amongst the affected people, isolating them, wearing the insurgents/terrorists down, and bringing them to the negotiating table to reach a political settlement.[30]

An understanding of the functional differentiation between counter-terrorism and anti-terrorism activities would be constructive in delineating the areas for a possible role of third parties in South Asia. Thus, 'while counter-terrorism can be seen as a security task performed by the security component of a national or international authority, the use of political, legal, economic, civil society and other peace-building instruments for the purposes of both countering and preventing terrorism can be broadly referred to as anti-terrorism'.[31] As terrorism-generating conflicts are a very specific type of violence, the tools that could be adapted to serve anti-terrorist needs effectively should be selected from the gamut of peace-building instruments.

While there is no question that terrorism-generating conflicts are ultimately best addressed by a peaceful resolution of the primary issues of the conflict itself, the extent to which this link should be politically established and recognized is less clear. The strategy of separating anti-terrorism from ongoing political negotiations, and from the peace process in general, might seem to offer the parties to the conflict a way out of the vicious circle of violence and the need to respond to it. Moreover, the approach of tying the peace process and anti-terrorism operations too closely together to the point of making one entirely conditional upon the other, can neither lead to a lasting peace settlement nor effectively address the security challenge posed by terrorism. This was dramatically demonstrated by the link between terrorism and the peace process in the context of the conflict in Chechnya in the mid-1990s. Two high-profile terrorist attacks by the Chechen rebels forced the government to sign the hasty Khasav–Yurt agreement. This was backed by neither political will nor economic resources; it also did not lead to post-conflict peace building.[32]

The problem in the South Asian region has now grown beyond internal and regional conflict with the involvement of terrorists from outside the region playing a part in conflicts. This can only be addressed through international cooperation and support in counter-terrorism measures. The socio-economic and political costs of the conflicts have proven to be too high for states to be able to singly deal with and resolve conflicts that generate terrorism. Keeping these realities in perspective, some valuable lessons can be drawn from the experience of third-party intervention in South Asia, and beyond.

Third-party Intervention in the Region

Third-party involvement in conflict-generating terrorism in South Asia is not new. India has carried out this role at the behest of the contending parties time and again. India was invited by the Sri Lankan government to help in resolving its ethnic conflict between the Sinhalese and the Tamil minorities. India is also assisting the Government of Nepal in tackling the Maoist insurgency. In 1998, the Maldivian government had requested Indian military intervention to help avert a coup, after which India withdrew its troops. On the other hand, the conflict between India and Pakistan has been referred to a third party (arbitrator), as were the Rann of Kutch and Indus Water disputes. As for the conflict in Kashmir, India took the issue to the UN but subsequently had to resile from this position owing to extraneous circumstances. As things stand, the official Indian position is opposed to any form of third-party role in Kashmir, it being a domestic issue to be resolved bilaterally.

The conflicts within the states of South Asia have shown both varied possibilities and results from the role of third parties. On the one hand exists the arbitration mode of third-party involvement in conditions where the parties to the conflict simply wish for a settlement. The India–Pakistan conflicts over the Rann of Kutch and Indus water distribution were successfully arbitrated. Yet attempts to resolve the Kashmir conflict by any form of third-party intervention (as defined in the previous sections) is not on the anvil. This is despite the fact that in 1947 Prime Minister Nehru in his address to the Constituent Assembly of India posited that 'in order to establish our bonafides we have suggested that when the people are given the chance to decide their future this should be done under the supervision of an impartial tribunal such as the United Nations Organization'.[33] A formal complaint was lodged in 1948 and a Commission was appointed to investigate facts and play a mediatory role in easing tensions. The UN Commission on India and Pakistan (UNCIP) comprising a five-member mediation team obtained India's agreement on the modalities of the appointment of a plebiscite administrator and his powers. The UN Security Council Resolution of 13 August dealt specifically with the establishment of a ceasefire, truce agreement, and determining the future status of Kashmir in accordance with the will of the people (holding a plebiscite). The acceptance of the UN Security Council resolution by the governments of India and Pakistan resulted in a ceasefire agreement coming into force in 1949—which was patrolled by the UNMOGIP till 1971—when a new ceasefire line was established. But by 1957 UN mediation attempts reached a dead end, and were abandoned. The UN lost its role as a third party in resolving the India–Pakistan conflict to the Soviet Union after the 1965 war.[34]

India does not accept the role of UNMOGIP after the 1971 war on account of the fact that the Shimla Accord reached in 1972 emphasized the bilateral approach in resolving differences between the two countries. In the interim, Pakistan continues to accept the role of UNMOGIP. So an anomalous situation exists as to its legal status and jurisdiction. Additionally, the plebiscite issue was made untenable by Pakistani military presence in Kashmir. 'After many India–Pakistan wars, feelings of suspicion and insecurity, led India and Pakistan to a search for support from outside the region. It is in this background that the role of superpowers assumed significance. From the beginning, the United Kingdom—by virtue of being the erstwhile colonial master—and the United States hoped to prevail on India through an UN-sponsored face-saving formula. This is so that the disputed state could join Pakistan, and eventually help the free world in defending against expansionist designs of Soviet communism. The British declassified documents show the attempts by Great Britain and its Western partners to influence and interfere with the mediation activities of the UN.'[35] The external powers did not get directly involved in the India–Pakistan security dyad in the regional security framework per se. Rather, their role was in the form of sponsoring or facilitating regional competition as a crucial part of Cold War imperatives.[36]

India prefers to resolve the Kashmir issue bilaterally, perceiving efforts at successful resolution in this fashion to be in keeping with its national security concerns. Pakistan, for obvious reasons, prefers to involve a third party. However, the good offices of the United States are known to function as an informal and voluntary facilitator in both emphasizing restraint in actions and bringing an end to confrontation and hostilities. To the extent that a third party was tacitly involved in dealing with the 'global war against terror' in South Asia, India has frequently sought US leverage over Pakistan in ending cross-border terrorism. The US as a third party has used economic leverages over Pakistan to curb and resolve terrorism-generating conflicts. This is extended to and even contingent upon reform and change in Pakistani domestic polity. The 2002 National Security Strategy of the US enunciates the use of economic leverages by way of developmental aid, helpful trading terms, and offering high-level technologies in exchange for cooperation in the war on terror.

In any case, the implications of 9/11 on South Asia are such that they have granted a tacit 'legitimacy' to an American role. 'The US has succeeded, as never before, in positioning itself as an influential factor on the Kashmir question between India and Pakistan. The repeated claims by the US to remain closely and permanently engaged on the Kashmir issue give it a unique advantage to be in a position to influence both the claimants to Kashmir.'[37] Ultimately, the Kashmir issue will have to be resolved through an India–Pakistan agreement, initiatives for which have been afoot since 2003. In any case, 'the war on terrorism cannot be won without American leadership, which requires working with other existing relationships. In this regard, Washington has real dilemmas regarding Pakistan. As Paul Wolfowitz observes, "Pakistan has a government that cannot deliver everything we would like . . . and we don't have the ability to simply say if you don't do, we will cut off our whole relationship." In the same vein, India's unrivalled capacity and willingness to help Afghanistan has been stultified because Washington worried that Pakistan would be upset. Actually, if Indo–Pak relations are truly on a new course, Afghanistan represents a cause on which we could both work together most productively.'[38] Significantly, therefore, US–Pakistan relations make the United States suspect as a third party.

The initial Indian involvement in Sri Lanka dates to the 1983 riots that had besieged the island nation. Prime Minister Jayawardene's mishandling of the situation led to the first open intervention by India, when Indira Gandhi sent G. Parthasarathy as a special emissary to Sri Lanka to help reach a settlement. But by early 1984, Tamil militancy had turned into a full-fledged war of liberation. Yet the Indian emissary continued his quiet diplomacy, which ultimately resulted in a set of proposals which came to be known as 'Annexure C'. This attempt also came to naught, and the assassination of Prime Minister Indira Gandhi considerably weakened the Indian position. Talks were then transferred to 'neutral' Bhutan in 1985 and the Indian third-party role drifted from the use of the good offices to a mediatory role. Two rounds of talks did not amount to any tangible gain and the process was stalled.

Then in keeping with the Indo–Sri Lanka Accord, an Indian Peace Keeping Force (IPKF) was mandated in 1987 to assist the democratic implementation of the Indo–Sri Lanka Accord so as to facilitate the holding of elections and the cessation of hostilities. But the domestic imperatives of the Premadasa government and the decisions it took obstructed the IPKF from completing its tasks effectively and it had to withdraw its forces amidst allegations of partisanship and ineffectiveness. In the Sri Lankan context, the role of a third party leads to two conclusions. The first is the failure of the use of military intervention, and the second is of reasonable success of a third party as a facilitator.

The IPKF experience in Sri Lanka was circumscribed by the Tamil demands in Sri Lanka and the Indo–Sri Lanka Accord, which proved to be unacceptable to the opposition in Sri Lanka at that time.[39] (The opposition comprised major segments of the Sinhalese Community and the LTTE.) 'Part II of the India–Sri Lanka Accord pertained to the fulfillment of the government's obligations vis-à-vis devolution of power with certain safeguards. In return, the Tamils and the LTTE were to give up arms. Once this was enforced, elections were to be held where the Tamils would vote; which they did by electing the EPRLF to power. Part III dealt with the issue of merging the northern and southern provinces.'[40] In evaluating the IPKF campaign it became apparent that President Jayawardene had found it difficult to diffuse the reservations of the opposition and within his party to the Indo–Sri Lanka Agreement. Added to this fact was that the LTTE had resiled from its earlier position of supporting such an agreement and had subsequently withdrawn support from the devolution package, all of which served to make the IPKF role unsustainable.

The Government of India's mid-term appraisal on the other hand stated, 'law and order was, by and large, restored in the northern and eastern parts of Sri Lanka. India's basic objective in sending its forces to the country was basically to preserve its democratic set-up and territorial integrity seriously threatened by various militant groups, and also to ensure that the legitimate aspirations of its Tamil minorities were not neglected in the governance of that country. These objectives were achieved in large measure.'[41] Alternatively, the failure of Indian intervention in Sri Lanka has been attributed to 'the unfortunate lack of political will and diplomatic skill on the part of the Government of Sri Lanka that drew India into the conflict. And, India's own domestic politics and electoral compulsions from Tamil Nadu forced New Delhi to get itself entangled in Sri Lankan internal affairs.'[42]

Third-party intervention in Sri Lanka, in hindsight, points to the lack of coordination between political and military strategies. As a result, military success could not be translated into political gains. It is the domestic political dynamics that led to this problem; the political leadership was struggling to retain legitimacy in Sri Lanka. The Indian political leadership, having sent peacekeeping forces to Sri Lanka, found itself unable to find a political solution. Clearly, for India, 'intervening in Sri Lanka was an important domestic political factor. It was also to counter the Sri Lankan government, which had started looking for external support to counter Tamil militancy. This had security implications for India'.[43] Involvement of third parties in terrorism-generating conflicts leads to the aforementioned conditions. The state that accepts third party's role carries a strong burden, but the third party is burdened no less.

In the second instance of third-party involvement in Sri Lanka, the Government of Norway was invited to assist the peace process (in the backdrop of a ceasefire) in Sri Lanka in 1998. Norway's interlocutors took up the role of assisting the parties in their efforts for a peaceful resolution, acting as a facilitator and not as a party to the negotiating table per se. In their capacity as a third party, the Norwegians were successful in facilitating an understanding between the parties, clarification of the respective negotiating positions, and bridging the gap between the positions of the parties.[44] Yet, the negative impact of Norway's involvement in the peace process cannot be overlooked. The peace process ended by creating divisions within both the Sri Lankan political leadership and the LTTE hierarchy.

Norway's 'back-channel success story' in the facilitation of negotiations between the PLO and Israel also has important lessons for South Asia as independent international support. In both instances, Norway has been 'successful in mobilizing development assistance, including reconstruction and reconciliation'.[45] The IPKF and the Norwegian examples also draw attention to the challenges in both approaches to third-party intervention. A decade after the IPKF pulled out of Sri Lanka, there were nostalgic references to its attainments. It was felt that had the IPKF been allowed to finish its task, the Tamil issue would have been resolved. On the other hand, Norwegian facilitation, its success notwithstanding, has divided the political leadership in the Island state. Sri Lankan President Kumaratunga objected to the concessions made to the LTTE by Prime Minister Wickramasinghe. Consequently, fresh national elections were called in the country in an effort to resolve the political impasse arising from the consequences of Norwegian involvement. The Norwegian brokered peace process created a split within the LTTE leadership as well. Karuna, the commander of the Batticola-Ampari district has revolted against Prabhakaran, the supreme leader of the LTTE. The former had allegedly sounded out the Sri Lankan government about negotiating a separate ceasefire in the eastern province.

After the withdrawal of the IPKF, India had distanced itself from playing a third party-role in Sri Lanka during 1990–2002. However, after the peace process started with Norwegian facilitation in 2003, India has re-asserted its interest in the outcome of the peace talks. As a consequence, Norway, Japan, and other countries involved in assisting the Sri Lankan peace process have close consultations with New Delhi. The Sri Lankan government has also been keeping New Delhi informed on a regular basis on the peace process. In the Sri Lankan peace process, many countries have played a third-party role of a different kind by providing international development and assistance in the form of an international safety net.

In international conflicts, particularly in Northern Ireland and

South Africa, the US has successfully played the role of a facilitator in the peace process. In the case of Northern Ireland, there was also a more direct role, with a senior military officer working out a disarming process. American economic investment, continuing and sustained lines of communication with the disputant parties had served to facilitate the process further. By offering its good offices and increasing its stakes in the socio-political and economic context of the conflict-situation, the United States put to good use the method of 'facilitative diplomacy'. One lesson that can be drawn from these experiences is that humanitarian assistance, development projects, and direct funding offer important avenues for third parties to leverage the resolution of terrorism-generating conflicts. Obversely, unilateral military interventions tend to lengthen the expected duration of a conflict. To be successful, in fact, all parties to the conflict must come to the conclusion that at least at this time, continued fighting presents too low a pay-off than expected.[46]

Interestingly, an important question has been posed regarding the moral and ethical issues in third-party intervention. 'Is there a question of ethics involved in intervening in conflict-related situations? Did India promote its power through military intervention in South Asia on moral grounds?'[47] In explaining Indian intervention in Sri Lanka, J.N. Dixit argues, 'while morality and absolute norms should govern politics, in actuality, it is not so. This is simply because human conditions remain imperfect.'[48]

Conclusion

The events of 9/11 have brought home the point that international terrorism undoubtedly involves participation by elements from outside the disputant countries. It is also controlled by elements outside the disputant states, if not facilitated by one of the disputants itself. In other words, terrorists have an agenda that extends beyond that of the sponsoring state. It has an additional characteristic of separate groups working for one purpose. Thus, local efforts should match international endeavours in resolving terrorism-generating conflicts. In the context of the South Asian region, the SAARC Additional Protocol on Terrorism signed earlier this year is a step in this direction. Towards facilitating the prevention, suppression and eradication of the financing of terrorism, the Protocol seeks to 'establish and maintain a financial intelligence unit'. Significantly, while providing for the right to seize, confiscate funds or other assets by state parties, the Protocol envisages the protection of third parties: 'The provision of Chapter 8 shall be implemented without prejudice to the rights of third parties acting in good faith.' Without a doubt, the real and dangerous third party to conflicts today are terrorist groups who have carved for themselves an autonomous space over which no one has full control. For third-party intervention to be plausible in present times, it has to be backed by commitment by the third party and the international community to deny financial, moral, and ideological help to the terrorist groups. Curbing the transfer of money to terrorist organizations is ultimately the main source for containing and perhaps even defeating conflict-generating terrorism. Towards this end, both domestic and international law have to work in tandem in enforcing and implementing financial-support flows to terrorist activities. Third-party intervention can be a potent instrument if it focuses on denial of support of any kind to terrorist organizations. Eventually, assimilation instead of alienation from the national mainstream will remain the key to ending terrorism-generating conflicts. Third-party roles in this arena are still evolving, even as they have facilitated the dialogue process amongst adversary parties.

There is no denying that terrorism is the response of the weaker side in conflicts in an asymmetric power balance. South Asia has seen many examples of it. In the post-Second World War period, most conflicts around the world have had a terrorism content, be they in Algeria, Kenya, Malaysia or Cyprus. In South Asia, international intervention has mostly been with regard to the issue of Kashmir and nuclear proliferation. The most interested third party is the United States because South Asian nuclear rivalry has posed serious challenges to its non-proliferation policy.[49] Various roles for third-party intervention have been articulated with regard to resolving the Kashmir conflict. The ability of the United States to be a third party in 'good faith' has been long hampered by the compulsions of its geopolitical interests in Pakistan, Afghanistan, and Central Asia.

Some other inter-state issues in South Asia have seemed more amenable to third-party roles in Sri Lanka, the Chittagong Hill Tracts, and north-eastern India. Nonetheless, they are best managed through a national process, combining military and political initiatives. But the lesson for the future is not a comforting one. 'States have learnt that they can use non-state actors to inflict major de-capacitating strikes on an adversary without having to be held accountable for their actions.'[50] That is where third-party role would require to be widened through international consensus and cooperation against terrorism.

NOTES

1. 'Responding to Terrorism: What Role for the United Nations?' Report of the International Peace Academy, October 2002.
2. Muchkund Dubey, 'Anatomy of Terrorism in South Asia', *The Hindu*, 1 January 2003.
3. David Carment and Dane Rowlands, 'Evolutionary Models and Third Party Intervention in Ethnic Conflict', Online Articles and Papers, The Norman Paterson School of International Affairs, Carleton University, 1998.
4. Ibid.
5. Ariel E. Levite and Elizabeth Sherwood-Randall, 'The Case for Discriminate Use of Force', *Survival*, vol. 44, no. 4, Winter 2002–3.
6. Therese Delpech, 'The Imbalance of Terror', *The Washington Quarterly*, Winter 2002.
7. Ronald J. Fisher, 'Methods of Third-Party Intervention', *Berghof Handbook for Conflict Resolution*, Berlin, April 2003.
8. Ibid.
9. William Zartman, 'Alternative Attempts at Conflict Management: Concepts and Processes', in G. Winham (ed.), *New Issues in International Crisis Management*, Boulder: Westview Press, 1989.
10. Carmant, 'Evolutionary Models'.
11. Chester Crocker, 'Lessons on Intervention', in *Managing Conflict in the Post-Cold war World: The Role of Intervention*, Report of the Aspen Institute Conference, 2–6 August 1995, Aspen, Colorado, 1996.
12. William Zartman and Saadia Touval, 'International Mediation in the Post-Cold War Era', in *Managing Global Chaos*, ed. Chester Crocker, Fen Hampson and Pamela Aall, Washington DC: USIP Press, 1996.

13. Ibid.
14. Neville Ladduwahetty, 'Security Implications of Regional Power in Sri Lanka', *LAKIMBA-Sri Lankan Issues*, 8 January 1999.
15. Hans Morgenthau, *Politics Among Nations*, New Delhi: Kalyani Publications, 1997.
16. Sara McLaughlin Mitchell, 'A Kantian System? Democracy and Third Party Conflict Resolution', paper presentation, Annual Meeting of the American Political Science Association, Georgia, 2000.
17. Beth Simmons, 'See You in "Court"? The Appeal to Quasi-Judicial Legal Processes in the Settlement of Territorial Disputes', in *A Road Map to War: Territorial Dimensions of International Conflict*, ed. Paul F. Diehl, Nashville: Vanderbilt University Press, 1999.
18. Patrick M. Regan, 'Third Party Interventions and the Duration of Intrastate Disputes', *Journal of Conflict Resolution*, February 2002.
19. Crocker, 'Lessons on Intervention'.
20. For an account of the role of the third party in conflict areas see Stephan Klingebiel, 'Impact of Development Cooperation in Conflict Situations: German Experience in Six Countries', in *Economic Dimensions of Conflict*, Development Policy Forum of the German Foundation for International Development, 30 November 2001.
21. Ian O. Lesser, 'Coalition Dynamics in the War Against Terrorism', *The International Spectator*, February 2002.
22. Walter Lacquer, *A History of Terrorism*, New Brunswick, NJ: Transaction Publishers, 2002.
23. Bruce Hoffman, 'Terrorism Trends and Prospects', in *Countering the New Terrorism*, ed. Ian O. Lesser, et al., RAND, 1999.
24. Ekaterina Stepanova, *Anti-terrorism and Peace-building During and After Conflict*, Stockholm: SIPRI, June 2003.
25. Ibid.
26. Dubey, 'Anatomy of Terrorism'.
27. B. Raman, 'India's Counter-Terrorism Strategy', www.rediff.com, 4 April 2003.
28. Kanti Bajpai, 'The Effects of Terrorism on Indian Democracy', in *Terrorism in South Asia: Impact on Development and Democratic Process*, ed. Sridhar K. Khatri and Gert W. Kueck, Delhi: Shipra, 2003.
29. Arun Jaitley, 'Terrorism and India', *Lalit Doshi Memorial Lecture*, 2 August 2002.
30. N.S. Jamwal, 'Counter-Terrorism Strategy', *Strategic Analysis*, vol. XXVII, no. 1, January–March 2003.
31. Klongebiel, 'Impact of Development Cooperation'.
32. Ibid.
33. From *Independence and After*—a collection of the more important speeches of Jawaharlal Nehru from September 1946 to May 1949, the Publications Division, August 1949.

34. C.S.R. Murthy, 'The United Nations and the India Pakistan Conflict', in *Conflict and Peacemaking in South Asia*, ed. P. Sahadevan, New Delhi: Lancers, 2001.
35. Ibid.
36. P. Sahadevan (ed.), *Conflict and Peacemaking in South Asia*, New Delhi: Lancers, 2001.
37. S.D. Muni, 'Terrorism and Interstate Relations in South Asia', in *Terrorism in South Asia: Impact on Development and Democratic Process*, ed. Khatri and Kueck, Delhi: Shipra, 2003.
38. K. Shankar Bajpai, 'Born in the USA', *The Hindustan Times*, 18 March 2004.
39. P.R. Chari, 'The IPKF Experience in Sri Lanka', *ACDIS Occasional Papers*, Chap. 2, 1995.
40. Lt. Gen. A.S. Kalkat, 'The IPKF in Sri Lanka: 10 Years On', www.rediff.com, March 2000.
41. Government of India, Ministry of External Affairs, *Annual Report*, 1988–9.
42. Rohan Gunaratna, *Indian Intervention in Sri Lanka: The Role of India's Intelligence Agencies*, Colombo: South Asian Network on Conflict Research, 1993.
43. J.N. Dixit, 'IPKF in Sri Lanka', *USI Journal*, vol. CXIX, no. 497, July–September 1989.
44. Vidar Helgesen, 'Peace and Reconciliation: Norway's Experience', The Indonesian-Norwegian Human Rights Dialogue Seminar on Transnational Justice and Human Rights, Jakarta, 29 April 2002.
45. Ibid.
46. Patrick M. Regan, 'Third Party Interventions and the Duration of Intrastate Disputes', *Journal of Conflict Resolution*, February 2002.
47. Ralph Buultjens, 'The Ethics of Excess and Indian Intervention in South Asia', *Ethics and International Affairs*, 1989.
48. Muni, *Terrorism in South Asia*.
49. Sahadevan, *Conflict and Peacemaking in South Asia*.
50. Delpech, 'The Imbalance of Terror'.

12. Political Economy of Terrorism: Sustenance Factors and Consequences

Mahendra P. Lama

Introduction

In the South Asian context, most of the recorded terrorist movements have been the offshoots of a particular malaise.[1] The causes behind terrorism have been mostly country-specific. There are several factors that could be attributed to terrorism in the region. They vary from a strident assertion of group identities as manifested in their demand for political independence, like that of the Mizos, Nagas and Khalistanis (Punjab) and Jammu and Kashmir Liberation Front in India, and Pakhtunistan in Pakistan, to change in demographic equations triggered by both intra-country induced and external migration like that of Chittagong Hill Tracts in Bangladesh, and Assam in India. They also range from the practice of internal colonialism as manifested by constant regional disparity as in Balochistan, Pakistan,[2] to the demand for political independence by the Sri Lankan Tamils in the north-east of Sri Lanka; and brutal and massive human rights violations ranging from social discrimination and disenfranchisement as in southern Bhutan to economic alienation as reflected by the poverty, forced land colonization and landlessness in Andhra Pradesh, Madhya Pradesh, Orissa and Bihar.

This also includes the ethno-cultural discrimination and alienation as in the case of the Muhajirs in Pakistan, extreme regional disparity and, more importantly, the attempt to bring about structural changes in the polity by the Maoist elements in Nepal and historical dislocations and poor post-independence adjustments as in Nagaland in India. The attributes, ranging from religious persecution and fundamentalist indoctrination to non-functioning or mal-functioning of democracy, and protracted misgovernance to environmental dislocation, do figure rather prominently in some of these theatres of terrorism in South Asia.[3]

There are consistent efforts by the extra-regional powers to create a political constituency for themselves to meet their strategic goals. For example, US policy towards Pakistan after the Soviet occupation of Afghanistan in 1979 was primarily aimed at creating forces, mostly of the fundamentalist variety (like the Mujahidins), to fight against the Soviet troops in Afghanistan. South Asian countries have also been clearly involved in encouraging, hosting and aiding terrorists from neighbouring countries. The ULFA's presence in Bhutan, overt support to the LTTE by India, insurgents in Bangladesh, free movement of the Maoists of Nepal in India, and the well-known support extended by Pakistan to terrorism activities in Jammu & Kashmir are blatant manifestation of cross-border abetment of terrorism. A relatively peaceful country like Bhutan is also now inflicted and infested by terrorism. A report mentioned that 22 Bhutanese were found guilty of aiding terrorist groups active in India's north-east and 123 more are facing trial on the same count.[4]

The increasing coordination of the terrorists, insurgents, and radical groups with their counterparts in neighbouring countries, such as that of the MCC of India with the Maoists of Nepal, the insurgents in the north-east with the LTTE, and the other militants from neighbouring countries has added a critical dimension to the entire management of militancy in South Asia.

There are equally complex and diverse factors which have sustained terrorism in the region. These factors include the retributive spirit against the heavy clampdown by the state authorities, the mobilization of a newer generation of fighters, the diaspora support to engagement of terrorist groups in commercial ventures, and the international nexus and coalitions of terrorist groups to tactics of fear and persecution.

Cost and Impact of Terrorism: Study Techniques

Although the application of economic methods in studying terrorism and its impact has been made by a range of scholars and experts from across the continents,[5] there is scattered literature on the economic costs of terrorism mostly providing very broad examples and estimates.

Though there are quite complex and intricate linkages within which a range of sets and subsets act and react to assess, absorb and thwart the economic costs of terrorism and other militancy related violence and destruction, it is possible to roughly put together the short- and long-term costs and impacts in a diagrammatic framework. A quantitative analysis of such costs is a complex task. It is difficult to quantify or isolate the impact of particular events in complex situations with a range of socio-economic matrices and logistical intricacies characterized by varying features of political economy within a particular national set-up. The strike targets themselves vary, ranging from commercial institutions to military posts and civic installations to school buildings and religious institutions. There are at the same time a number of attempts to make qualitative assessments of how terrorist violence and other militancy related activities have impacted upon national budgets, production structure, investment and trade performance, and the socio-economic growth of a particular country.[6]

Unlike the inductive framework used primarily in the political science approach to assess the costs of terrorism,[7] the economic analysis if done in a proper politico-social context can actually help in understanding and making policy applications in the following four areas:[8]

(i) Account for strategic interactions among opposing interests, e.g. the terrorists and the authorities and between both the instigating and target countries.

(ii) Ascertain how terrorists are apt to respond to policy-induced changes and to analyse how governments react to terrorists-induced changes to their policy-making environment. This comes under the rational choice model based on microeconomic principles.

(iii) Underscore how independent pursuits of well-being by the agents may be at odds with socially efficient outcomes. Thus government failures may also result from well-intentioned policies. This comes under the ambit of the theory of market failures.

(iv) Evaluate theoretical predictions and policy recommendations.

However, there are of late some rather specific studies, particularly in the context of the devastating 11 September 2001 attack on the World Trade Centre in New York that have tried to look into the costs in terms of both direct and indirect fallout.[9] One such serious effort was made by the Joint Economic Committee of the US Congress which argues that: (i) terrorism imposes a negative supply-side shock on the economy which raises costs and inefficiencies, and (ii) expenditures on security divert labour and capital resources towards the productions of necessary but lower productive activities.[10] Gary Becker and Kevin Murphy estimated that the immediate loss of both human and non-human capital caused by this attack ranged from $25 to $60 billion or about 0.2 per cent of the economy's physical assets and 0.6 per cent of the total productive assets.[11]

In the case of South Asia, there have not been any serious and systematic attempts to study the economic impact of terrorism and insurgency despite the fact that this region has remained one of the most important theatres of terrorism, insurgency and other militant activities. There are internal reports prepared by governmental agencies, most of which remain outside the public access, deliberations and reviews. A number of institutions of late have been trying to put together the economic costs.[12] Though these attempts do not have any rigorous applications of economic method and techniques either, they have largely brought forward data and information which could go a long way in providing inputs to any serious economic analysis.

Conflicts and Terrorism: Some Economic Attributes

The issue of deprivation in the form of centre-periphery debate very often appears in the fulcrum of most of these conflicts. Equally critical has been the skewed distribution of the available natural resources both within a country and across the region. For instance, regional disparity on all fronts has been most blatant and conspicuous in Nepal. According to the *Human Development Report of Nepal 1998*, districts like Dang, Rolpa, Dhading, Baitadi, Dolpa and Jajarkot, considered to be the bastions of the Maoists, have human development index (HDI) values of less than 0.3 as against Kathmandu's 0.6. The gender-sensitive development index (GDI) further depresses the status of these districts. 'There is high level of disparity in human capabilities as well among the major caste and ethnic groups.'[13]

Similarly, though the number of industries has steadily risen in Nepal, the distribution pattern is remarkably skewed. Out of the total 1,679 operational manufacturing industries, over 70 per cent are located in the central development region, that too mostly in and around the Kathmandu Valley, 17 per cent in the eastern, 8 per cent in the western, and 3 and 2 per cent in the mid-western and far-western development regions respectively. Out of a total of 75 districts, 42 districts have some industries while the other 33 districts have none.[14] Again, the central development region (CDR), consisting of the capital city Kathmandu takes over 41 per cent of the total energy consumption as against 10 per cent of the far-western development region (FWDR).[15]

This is adequately reflected in the cottage and small-scale industries as well. For example, out of the 4,588 cottage and small-scale industries spread over different development regions which received loans from the commercial banks, almost 36 per cent were located in the central development region thereby constituting almost 47 per cent of the total loan disbursed (Rs. 498 million) in 1998–9. The eastern development region with 27 per cent of the industries and 24 per cent of the loan disbursed had the second highest concentration. The mid-western and far-western regions constituted hardly 10 per cent and 7 per cent of the industries and 7 per cent and 4 per cent respectively of the loans disbursed. These constant deprivations and discriminations have been starkly accompanied by the caste and ethnicity based usurption and monopolization of civil and political powers. This was recognized as late as 1990 in Nepal's constitution, which states that 'the State shall while maintaining the cultural divergence of the country, adopt a policy towards the strengthening of the national unity, promoting healthy and cordial social relations among the various religious groups, castes and class, community, linguistic groups of the society' [26 (2)].[16] These issues lie at the very heart of the ongoing violent Maoist movement.[17]

According to a study, the northern and eastern provinces of Sri

Lanka seemed to be the poorest in terms of per capita income in the year 2000.[18] The statistical data available with the Department of Census and Statistics (2003) indicated that in early 1980s, Sabragamuwa province was the poorest in terms of per capita income, followed by Uva province. However, in the 1990s these poor rankings went to the northern and eastern provinces. In 2000, the per capita income of the northern province was Rs. 37,206 as against the national average of Rs. 63,000.

Though the spread of net state domestic product (SDP) at current prices across various states in India may not be a good index of the inequality in the distribution of national income generation mainly on the grounds of sharp variations in the sizes, natural resource endowments and infrastructural facilities in these states, one can still refer to it for both the growth rates in the SDP and the geographical size-SDP performance in the total Indian context. However, regional imbalance has been a major cause of conflicts in India. This had in fact tended to increase gradually during the 1980s followed by a relatively steep increase in the early years of the reforms period and got consolidated in the rest of the 1990s. Table 12.1 shows the great variations in the projections of people below the poverty line in the states by the end of the Tenth Plan in 2006–7. It varies from 2 per cent in states like Gujarat, Haryana, Himachal Pradesh and Punjab to 41 per cent and 43 per cent respectively in Orissa and Bihar. There are studies that clearly show that inter-state inequality, as measured by the Gini-coefficient, has clearly increased.[19]

Pakistan has been in a vortex of a range of violence including that triggered by sectarian violence, jehads and also by Islamist Muttahida Majlis-e-Amal (MMA) and Al Qaida. The Baluch movement, the demand for Pakhtunistan, the demand for Sindh autonomy and the Muhajir movement have had their own course of violence, insurgency and terrorism. All these have strong elements of terrorism backed by competitive funding from both within and outside the country. The militants are armed to the teeth which is largely a fallout of the arms that had been supplied to the Mujahidins by the US to fight against the Soviet forces in 1980s. Many of the jehadi organizations which are now banned in both Pakistan and Afghanistan continue to receive copious Arab funds.

The constant conflict between the Baluch movement in

TABLE 12.1: INDIA: POVERTY PROJECTIONS FOR 2006–7

States	Rural % of Poor	Urban % of Poor	Combined % of Poor
Andhra Pradesh	4.58	18.99	8.49
Arunachal Pradesh	37.89	4.48	29.33
Assam	37.89	4.48	33.33
Bihar	44.81	32.69	43.18
Goa	N.A	N.A.	N.A.
Gujarat	2.00	2.00	2.00
Haryana	2.00	2.00	2.00
Himachal Pradesh	2.00	2.00	2.00
Jammu & Kashmir	N.A.	N.A.	N.A.
Karnataka	7.77	8.00	7.85
Kerala	1.63	9.34	3.61
Madhya Pradesh	28.73	31.77	29.52
Maharashtra	16.96	15.20	16.18
Manipur	37.89	4.48	30.52
Meghalaya	37.89	4.48	31.14
Mizoram	37.89	4.48	20.76
Nagaland	37.89	4.48	31.86
Orissa	41.72	37.46	41.04
Punjab	2.00	2.00	2.00
Rajasthan	11.09	15.42	12.11
Sikkim	37.89	4.48	33.78
Tamil Nadu	3.68	9.64	6.61
Tripura	37.89	4.48	31.88
Uttar Pradesh	24.25	26.17	24.67
West Bengal	21.98	8.98	18.30
All India	21.09	14.99	19.33

Source: Government of India, *Tenth Five Year Plan 2002-2007*, vol. 1, New Delhi: Planning Commission, 2002.

Baluchistan and the federal government of Pakistan has been primarily driven by both Baluchi sub-nationalism and the feeling that the development benefits have not been shared commensurately with the regions contribution. For instance, most of the major gas reserves including Sui, Pir, Koh and Marri are located in Baluchistan making it the largest supplier of gas in the country, yet it has the highest poverty ratio and lowest literacy rate among the provinces. The ongoing anti-terrorist military operation may only consolidate the flare-up between the Baluchistan Liberation Army (BLA) and the federal authorities. Gas pipelines in Sui have been under constant attack from the local tribes over the past years.[20]

In India, regional distribution of natural reserves is uneven (see Table 12.2). In fact, sharing of natural resources has been the most significant issue in many of the conflict situations. A number of states have demanded a share in the development resources commensurate with their contributions in terms of production, their natural resource exploitations, and overall contribution to the national income. The All Assam Students' Union and also the United Liberation Front of Assam (ULFA) have been highlighting the mismatch between Assam's rich resources, including huge reserves of minerals and oil, a large variety of forests, and the highly potential unharnessed economic sectors like water, and its character of a relatively backward state. The Assamese feel that the resources have been exploited without adequately sharing the benefits with the state. The two major resource-based industrial activities, viz., oil and plantation, have not really brought any substantive transformations in the state. The backward linkages of these industries are rather limited while their forward linkages are with industries located in the big metropolises elsewhere. The result has been the emergence of an enclave-type economy, i.e. a few modern industries in the midst of traditional industries with very little or no interaction between the two.[21]

TABLE 12.2: INDIA: REGIONAL DISTRIBUTION OF PRIMARY COMMERCIAL ENERGY RESOURCES

Region	Coal (mt)	Lignite (mt)	Crude Oil (mt)	Natural Gas (mcm)	Hydro power (TWH)
Northern	1.06	2.51	0.03	0	225.00
Western	56.90	1.87	519.47	516.42	31.40
Southern	15.46	30.38	45.84	80.94	61.80
Eastern	146.67	0	2.19	0.29	42.50
North-Eastern	0.89	0	166.17	152.00	239.30
Total	220.98	34.76	733.70	749.65	600.00

Source: *Tenth Five Year Plan*, New Delhi: Planning Commission, 2002.

The All Assam Students' Union unleashed a scathing attack on the union government for 'deliberately' keeping Assam deprived and not commensurately sharing the gains from the exploitation of its natural resources. Even as Assam lagged behind in industrialization and the number of unemployed grew, the head offices of all major public and private enterprises continued to be located outside Assam,[22] and forest resources plummeted from 39 per cent in 1951–2 to 31 per cent in 1993 of the total geographical area. A hard-hitting booklet *Eclipse in the East* appearing at the height of the agitation in early 1980s noted: 'Assam had been treated nothing better than a colony . . . the state has been fragmented beyond recognition. . . . The tea industry which produces 270 million kg of tea worth over Rs. 400 crore every year, is controlled from Calcutta and London.'

All these have very serious impacts on the economy of Assam. As the returns from private economic activities are not ploughed back, the generation of employment and income outside the government sector has been very dismal. The cream of development gets siphoned off to outside the state. This is how Assam has been steadily losing what Keynes calls the multiplier effect as expressed thus:

$$\Delta Y = \frac{1}{1-c}\Delta I_o$$

Where ΔY is change in income; c is marginal propensity to consume and ΔI_o is increase in investment, the value of multiplier (K) is:

$$\frac{1}{1-c}$$

According to this theory of income determination, income will increase by an amount which is K times the increase in investment. Since most of the returns on investment are not ploughed back, the multiplier will not be effective, and mainly because of the low income the marginal propensity to consume will be rather high.[23]

This outflow of multiplier has been witnessed historically in many countries including Bhutan and Nepal and in Indian states like Himachal Pradesh, Jammu & Kashmir, Uttaranchal, and the north-east region including the Darjeeling hills. A noted economist of the region wrote, 'the credit-deposit ratio being very low in the region, the banking sector transfers something like Rs. 5,000 crore from this region to other regions for investment. Because of prolonged insurgency in the region, despite abundance of natural resources (oil, gas, coal, granite, limestone, water and forest wealth) no outside investment has taken place. Indeed there was capital flight in the last eight years from the region'.[24]

It is difficult to monitor and quantify the resource transfer from Assam to other states mainly because of the nature of transfer, involvement of informal agencies, and the poor level of the economic activity-wise database and information. However, at the same time, it is observed that the regions afflicted by one or other forms of armed conflict do not show any particular correlations with the state and the extent of poverty prevailing in those regions. In other words, the popular belief that these conflicts could be associated with less poverty may not stand up to a full test. Some of the states where violence has been a strong feature, like Assam, Nagaland and Bihar, have the presence of a hefty percentage of people below the poverty line, whereas other conflict-ridden states (in varying degrees), like Andhra Pradesh, Jammu & Kashmir and Punjab, have comparatively a much lower percentage of people below the poverty line. This makes us broadly conclude that both situations, of high and low levels, of poverty, tend to generate conflicts and violence, although the combinations of other causal factors could be in sharp variance. In Punjab, it was the higher aspirations from its plateau-type of position that may have resulted in armed conflicts, whereas in states like Bihar, Assam and Nagaland, their inability to take off from the base itself could have triggered conflictual situations.[25]

The very distributive imbalances brought about by development intervention like the Green Revolution became a major source of conflict in India. In Punjab, the skewed distribution of the benefits of the Green Revolution became conspicuous, when just 20 per cent of rich Jat farmers grabbed more than 60 per cent of the total land. This skewed distribution had been acute in some other districts as well.[26] A study conducted to assess income distribution over six different categories of Punjabi farmers concluded that the level of mechanization largely paralleled the size of holdings. It showed that hiring out of assets, including equipment, draft animals and land, to the smaller farmers constituted almost 22 per cent of the non-farming income of Class 6. This only reflected the grossly unequal distribution of technological benefits.[27]

This uneven distribution of benefits was amply reflected in the caste structure also. The Jat capitalist farmers who are usually pitched against the Scheduled Castes (Mazhabis) have been the overwhelming beneficiaries. The Mazhabis along with other low-caste artisans like Lohar Sikhs (blacksmiths), carpenter Sikhs (Ramgarhias), Rai Sikhs, Labana Sikhs, Cheema Sikhs have developed their own 'culture of deprivation'. At the political level, their hostility against Akali capitalist farmers (and liking for the Congress (I) or communist parties) and their Nirankari background made them special targets of Sikh extremists, which forced them to fall into the Akali fold.[28]

The contents of the economic policy and programme in the Anandpur Sahib Resolution (ASR) made clear the basic reasons in this conflict. It demanded land ceiling at 30 standard acres instead of 17.50 acres, cheap inputs, abolition of excise duty on tractors, and remunerative agricultural prices. To have a wider appeal, it also talked about workers, middle-class employees, agricultural labour and educated unemployed. The resolution expressed very clearly the opposition of the capitalist farmers to traders and monopolists. It demanded the complete nationalization of trade in food grains and unrestricted movement of food grains in India.[29] The ASR also talked of fixing the price of agricultural produce and opposed the demarcation of food zones and the restrictions that go with it on the movement of food grains, and demanded that 'the whole country should be a single food zone'. It also demanded 'increased and cheaper power and irrigation facilities'.

SUSTENANCE OF TERRORISM

An interplay of a large number of endogenous and exogenous factors have sustained these terrorist activities. This section deals mostly with various 'economic' and 'commercial' bases, forms and channels that sustain terrorism in South Asia. Besides the massive funding by the diaspora communities and overt and covert assistance by the hostile neighbouring countries, the extent and implications of extortions and lootings have been enormous. These forcible tax raisings and extortions have taken place even in distant diaspora communities. In some cases the strategy has been to displace the population through violent actions so that in the short run they are able to mobilize resources for instant use, and acquired movable and immovable properties could be used for more violence in the long run. These have brought fortunes to the militants and even the local majority people. A typical case of this phenomenon is that of the Kashmiri Pandits in the Kashmir Valley of Jammu & Kashmir. Over 56,346 displaced Kashmiri migrant families have been living in camps in Jammu region, Delhi, and other states.[30] A range of similar emerging situations, particularly in the north-east region of India (Manipur, Nagaland, Meghalaya and Assam), can be cited. This 'cleansing' by the Bodos through plunder, arson, massacre, and persecution has forced a large number of the non-Bodos, particularly Adivasis (Santhals), Nepalese and Biharis in Kokrajhar district, to flee the area on a large scale.[31]

'Industry of terror' is what the victims call the entire complex matrix and intriguing modalities of abduction, extortion, and looting. This has been the backbone of insurgency in all the theatres of militancy in South Asia, and terrorists have used diverse instruments and modi operandi in the perpetrations of crimes. These techniques are sometimes highly complex and sophisticated and to a large extent institutionalized (see Table 12.3). They do it in the name of cleansing the system and to 'get rid of corruption' in the governments. Most of these incidents have taken place where there is marked decay in the political culture, steady erosion in the faith and confidence of the people in the systems of governance and when the emergence of the ultra-rich phenomenon among certain sections becomes very conspicuous.

The criticality of militants' operations in many parts is based on the tacit support, and complementary patronization of politicians and his sophisticated nexus between them and the militants. In many parts of north-east India, it is believed that no cabinet discussion and decision can be kept a secret. Most of the

TABLE 12.3: SOUTH ASIA: LOOTING, ABDUCTION AND EXTORTION—MODES AND TECHNIQUES

* Loot the banks and other public exchequers.
* Kidnap or abduct a person and ask for ransom.
* Serve notices to companies and agencies for contributions.
* Establish linkages with contractors or profiteering agencies for commissions on deals and projects mainly related to the government.
* Impose a tax on the movement of vehicles.
* Threaten households, politicians, and professionals with extermination and demand contributions from them.
* Raise contributions from particular localities, communities, and NGOs in the form of tolls, taxes, 'war taxes', 'protection money', 'patriotic tax', and even development security.
* Practise open extortion by forming a gang and going around the town from shop to shop.

decisions are known to the militant outfits much before their implementation.

Interestingly funding for some of the major terrorist attacks in other parts of the world has also been traced to the South Asian region. For instance, US investigators have reportedly 'traced the origin of the funding of 9/11 to financial accounts in Pakistan, where high-ranking and well-known Al Qaida operatives played a major role in moving the money forward, eventually into the hands of the hijackers located in the US'. The FBI estimated that the 9/11 attacks cost between $175,000 and $250,000, which paid for flight training, travel, and other expenses. This money reportedly flowed to the hijackers through associates in Germany and the United Arab Emirates.[32]

I. THE DIASPORA GROUPS[33]

One of the key elements that sustains terrorism in a particular situation has been the role of external support. This has been widely discussed. There are growing knowledge bases on this as the very nature of terrorism has grown into a massive conglomerate with an intrinsic international network. There are various ways that the phenomenon of external support to a terrorist movement or a group has been recorded. There are genuine difficulties in measuring the extent and impact of outside support because of both the nature and the mode of transactions. Terrorist groups in the region have sought varying forms of support from their diaspora ranging from safe-havens to weapons, and from political voice and diplomatic propaganda to resources and training and intelligence.

Diaspora groups—immigrant communities settled and established in other countries[34]—have played very active and effective roles in supporting at least some of the terrorist organizations and the causes propounded by them in South Asia. Examples abound, of such causes being facilitated by sophistication in communication technology, complexities in fund transfers, and the ability and commitment of the diasporas to support the cause in a consistent and prolonged manner. These terrorist groups have harnessed and fully exploited what Anderson calls 'long distance nationalism'.[35] The increasing influence of some of the diaspora groups on the policy makers of the countries where they are living is another crucial aspect. This is because these diaspora communities themselves are emerging as economic magnates with strong professional pools, and also the mere fact that they constitute significant vote banks. This type of influence on the host countries is in turn used to create leverages vis-à-vis the diasporas' countries of origins.

A recent study by the RAND Corporation noted that 'some of the most significant diasporas of today, like the Indians and Sri Lankan Tamils, have begun to exercise unprecedented clout in the affairs of their home countries, akin to the Jewish diaspora in the US' and that 'the more activist elements among these larger immigrant communities . . . have more rapid and visible means of calling attention to issues of interest in their home countries than ever before, thanks to the communication and information technology revolution.'[36]

The diasporas have injected a new set of trends in the entire context of support to insurgencies and conflictual dynamics in their homelands. These supports have been in terms of money, arms, propaganda and lobbying in international forums, and recruits back in their home countries. These supports have not only helped sustain the anti-state campaigns but also enhanced the insurgents' institutional and physical capabilities to thwart and withstand both counter-insurgency measures and other legislative actions. Punjab and Kashmir in India, the LTTE-led movement for an independent Elam in Sri Lanka, the Maoist movement in Nepal, all have received various and important forms of support from their respective migrant communities.

The role played by some sections of the Sikh diaspora in supporting the secessionist movement in Punjab during the 1980s is well recorded. A White Paper issued during the height of the violence in Punjab mentioned that:

> several secessionist Sikh organizations are operating abroad. The chief among them which have raised the slogan of Khalistan or a separate Sikh state are the National Council of Khalistan (NCK), Dal Khalsa, Babbar Khalsa and Akhand Kirtan Jatha. The NCK headed by Dr. Jagjit Singh Chauhan is active in the UK, West Germany, Canada and the USA. The Dal Khalsa activities are mainly in UK and West Germany, while the Babbar Khalsa is operating largely from Vancouver in Canada.[37]

In Pakistan, free education provided by madrasas or religious schools has attracted a large number of people. And at least some schools clearly inculcate extremism and violence in the younger minds as reflected in the orientation of formations like the Taliban. The ethnic group-based politico-terrorist formations like Muttahida Quomi Movement–Altaf Hussain (MQM-A) leading the Muhajir Quomi Movement, the sectarian formation based on Shia and Sunni sects like Tehrik-e-Jafria Pakistan and Sipah-e-Sahaba Pakistan (SSP), outfits primarily aimed at freeing Kashmir from India like the Lashkar-e-Toiba, and Osama bin Laden's Al Qaida network centred within Afghanistan have sustained because of the support base they have both within and outside the country. Besides the usual means of financing like narco-trafficking and front companies, they have widely exploited the instruments of globalization including communication through e-mail and websites and other satellite-based facilities.

Both 'nationality' (ethnicity) and 'religion' diasporas have actively supported terrorist elements in Pakistan. After the declaration by General Musharraf that 'Pakistan has a firm position of principle in the international battle against terrorism. We reject terrorism in all its forms and manifestations anywhere in the world'.[38] Pakistan made selective crackdowns on the financial assets of religious extremist organizations. As of

November 2001, Islamabad had frozen over $300,000 in terrorist-related assets in several banks.[39] Various newspapers indicated that the accounts worth Rs. 621.41 million of at least 15 groups and individuals including Osama bin Laden, Al-Rashid Trust (ART), Rabita Trust (RT), Harkat-ul-Mujahidin (HuM) and Jaish-e-Mohammad (JeM), had been frozen.[40]

The sustenance of the LTTE in Sri Lanka as one of the most sophisticated and deadliest insurgency groups in the world has a lot to do with the support of the Tamil diaspora. The LTTE commands massive support among the Tamil diaspora abroad. It has been a well-coordinated and sophisticated diasporic support conducted to a large extent by its International Secretariat headquartered in the UK. It is believed that as much as 90 to 95 per cent of the LTTE war budget comes from overseas.[41] The LTTE network, particularly at the international level, draws varieties of support and influence. The LTTE's publicity network and propaganda activities have covered almost 54 countries including the UK, France, Germany, Switzerland, Canada and Australia. Many sources of financial contributions are noticed: (a) direct contributions from migrant communities particularly from the UK, Canada, and Australia where there are large Tamil expatriate communities, and also Norway and Switzerland; (b) contributions given to NGOs, charities, and benevolent donor groups; (c) illegal trafficking of people mainly for jobs and settlement on a heavy commission basis; (d) investments made in legitimate, Tamil businesses; and (e) drug trafficking and arms smuggling, supplies and sales to other insurgent groups. There are estimates that all these provide at least $50 million a year.

These fund-raising campaigns themselves are conducted in an organized manner using complex instrumentalities. The LTTE is said to maintain a comprehensive database including head counts, educational qualifications, skills available, political affiliations, income levels, and employment patterns of the Tamil diaspora. For instance, for the Tamil migrants abroad a type of baseline 'tax' is imposed, as a minimum obligation of each family living in the respective host state. It is estimated that in Canada alone, the sum collected in 1999 ran to $240 a year per household (the equivalent of one Canadian dollar per day).[42] At home, a parallel 'war tax' is imposed on each household and other supporters. The LTTE's own overt structures like the 'Tamil Eelam Judiciary' and the 'Tamil Eelam Police' actually facilitate the fund-raising operations within the northern and eastern provinces of Sri Lanka.

It is also mentioned that the Tigers use both the 'voluntary method' and 'intimidation and coercion' to procure and extract funds both in LTTE-controlled areas in Sri Lanka and among the diaspora.[43] They forcibly tax both individuals and business in the name of Tamil Eelam and for keeping the families and properties of diasporas 'safe and secure' in their homeland. 'In Germany, ten LTTE members were caught extorting 50 Deutsche Marks per month from Tamil families. . . . They threatened to harm relatives who were still living in Sri Lanka if the money was not forthcoming. The ring grossed 200,000 DM per month.'[44] In another incident it was found that 'the new Toronto area levies would demand that Tamil business turn over 20 per cent of their profits. Lists of profitable businesses were drawn up . . .'.[45]

The euphoria and spontaneous support is noticed whenever there has been a major victory for the LTTE. For instance, after the Tigers' widely publicized capture of Elephant Pass in 2000, there were reports throughout Canada, Australia, and the UK of a major infusion of spontaneous donations. There are also instances of influential and rich individuals making contributions to the LTTE war chest.

There are several instances where the LTTE has siphoned off funds extended by the various donor agencies to the NGOs and other social organizations for development and other welfare activities. More seriously, there are substantive cases where the LTTE has raised money through organized human smuggling, mostly of refugees and aspiring migrants to developed countries. Sri Lankan newspapers as well as intelligence officials in Canada, Australia, and the UK have mentioned that the charges are in the range of $18,000 and $32,000 per transaction. Thailand has been an easy trafficking corridor used by the LTTE wherein the most sought after destination has been Canada because of its liberal immigration laws and the relatively easy integration of the large Tamil diaspora there.[46]

There are a number of reports that the LTTE raises money

through drug trafficking which is further facilitated by the clandestine arms-running through established corridors and efficient international networks that operate either directly through or very close to major drug producing and transit centres, including Myanmar, Thailand, Cambodia, southern China, Afghanistan, and Pakistan.[47]

Another major source of its funding has been the LTTE's investments in various gainful activities and involvement in trading and commercial ventures. The proxy ownership, *benami*, holdings and clandestine operations has been its *modus operandi* in ventures like 'gold and jewelry trade, wholesale commodity freight and distribution, and the provision of local Tamil computer, telephone, and bus services.' It is estimated that this fetched the LTTE almost $6.5 million for the period between October 1998 and October 1999.[48]

Hawala to avoid Foreign Exchange Regulation Act (FERA) is another channel for foreign funding. The JIC report also mentions the International Sikh Youth Federation (ISYF) which has been routinely sending money through *Hawala* channels to various Sikh fundamentalist groups in India.

II. SUPPORT FROM HOSTILE NEIGHBOURS

There are two very pertinent examples of support for terrorists from hostile neighbours. Firstly, as mentioned earlier, India's support to the Tamil militants in Sri Lanka is a widely known fact.[49] And the second example is that of Pakistan's involvement in abetting terrorism in Jammu & Kashmir in India. The economic costs for the involved countries in planning-instigating, financing, managing, maintaining and curbing have been enormous.

Though India maintains that its support was essentially guided by its changing threat perception and the security concerns emanating from Sri Lanka,[50] it did provide a major initial boost and substance to the Tamils' militant activities. A highly regarded Indian diplomat who was witness to the entire process later wrote: 'while Mrs. Gandhi's support for Sri Lankan Tamil aspirations was correct and justified, her policy of materially supporting Tamil militants separatists was wrong. India's interests and the Tamil cause which oriented her towards generating pressure on Jayawardene could have been pursued by political and diplomatic means instead of extending materials support to Tamil militants.'[51]

The foreign hand behind the entire Punjab cauldron has been a much debated issue. If the government and the media have pointedly proved the presence of foreign elements in Punjab, there have been an equal number of rebuttals from some sections of the Sikhs and the foreign countries that invariably figured in the Punjab agitation. The government apprehended that Pakistan was bent upon the dismemberment of India. In her long interview with the BBC immediately after Operation Blue Star in 1984, Indira Gandhi said, 'now one specific thing that came out in our press and which was told by some of [the] young men who were misguided enough to try and leave that they were excited to do this by what they saw on the Pakistan TV. . . . We are not saying it is a government plot. We are saying there are some external forces. I do not think anybody has used the word government . . . the CIA is active in a number of countries and there is no reason to think that it is not active here. But whether it is involved in this or not, I do not think, I have not been specifically asked nor have said anything about it.'[52]

The leftist leader M. Farooqi was more emphatic when he said, 'our party has been continuously exposing the designs of US imperialists and the Zia military regime to aid and abet the separatists (the Khalistanis in this case). All the more reason that a political solution should have been evolved in time to counter the conspiracies of the imperialists and their henchmen.'[53]

The capture of Chinese-made weapons was set up as incontrovertible proof of this assertion. Pakistan's political and military interests in Punjab were evident as many sophisticated weapons came through Pakistan meant for both the Sikh militants and also the smugglers and hired murderers generally used by politicians, dacoits and feudal forces.[54]

That arms and ammunitions continue to flow in even after Rs. 200 crore was invested on the first-ever border-fencing project is indicated by the recovery of 250 kg of RDX by the Punjab and

Haryana police in January 1996. The Babbar Khalsa alone, which claimed responsibility for assassinating Beant Singh, is estimated to have smuggled in over 150 kg of RDX. Police say that this is part of a consignment of nearly five quintals of RDX that was smuggled into Punjab during 1995 by the International Sikh Youth Federation, Babbar Khalsa, and the Khalistan Commando Force. This was an effort by the badly mauled terrorist outfits to regroup and launch a fresh round of militancy. The role of narcotics smugglers has also become more prominent in arms import.[55] An *India Today* report also made an interesting revelation that the 'interrogation of a Pakistani national, Sahib Mohi-ud-din, a smuggler turned gun-runner for the Punjab militants who was captured by the police revealed how during his seven gun-running trips to India in the past three years he had ferried consignments of narcotics and gold permitted by the ISI as a remuneration for smuggling weapons. According to him, the ISI is running a regular training centre for smugglers on how to negotiate obstacles during border crossing. For every gun-running trip, he was given Rs. 12,000 by the ISI handlers.'[56]

Pakistan's ISI involvement in the terrorism in Jammu & Kashmir and other parts, though consistently denied by the Pakistani government, remains well established and widely reported. The *Annual Report (2002-2003)* of the Union Home Ministry emphatically stated that approximately 60 to 70 per cent of the terrorists operating in J&K are from outside, and are 'under the direct control of Inter Services Intelligence (ISI), Pakistan's external intelligence agency', with local people 'playing the role of porters and guides'. The transfer of funds has been massive and mainly through *Hawala* transactions to avoid any detection.[57] 'Pakistan continues to fund terrorist organizations operating in J&K through various channels including the *Hawala* (non-banking route). Several cases have been detected and investigated in the last few months, which point to the involvement of Pakistan in funding the terrorist organizations.'[58]

Sometimes the transfers are reported to have been funnelled through Pakistani embassies and their officials both in India and abroad.[59] Many of these transfers are again reported to have been routed through charitable trusts and other welfare related institutions.[60] These transfers have been detected even after the 'strict vigil' by the security agencies both in India and abroad after the 9/11 terrorist attacks on the World Trade Centre in New York. Many militant group leaders face income-tax proceedings for having massive undisclosed income (see Table 12.4). They have accumulated wealth with which they fund foreign tours and maintain a large number of staff in their offices.[61]

The Joint Intelligence Committee (JIC) of India has provided ample evidence of the involvement of Pakistan's ISI. It mentioned that the ISI spent about Rs. 2.4 crore a month to sponsor its subversive activities in Jammu & Kashmir. The report, which for the first time identifies both sources and recipients of such funding, includes data supplied by the Intelligence Bureau (IB), the Research and Analysis Wing (RAW) and the Directorate of

TABLE 12.4: JAMMU & KASHMIR: PROCEEDINGS LAUNCHED UNDER INCOME TAX (IT) ACT AGAINST THE LEADERS OF MILITANT GROUPS

Name	Undisclosed Income (Rs.)	Recovery (Rs.)
Syed Ali Shah Gilani	31,719,070	19,031,442
Altaf Ahmed Shah, son-in-law of Gilani	5,794,700	3,476,820
Ghulam Mohammed Baba (political assistant of Gilani, a non-IT payee)	527,598	316,558
Baba Abdul Qayoom (brother of Ghulam Mohammed Baba, a non-IT payee)	1,940,736	1,164,441
Nazir Ahmed Baba (brother-in-law of Ghulam Mohammed Baba, a non-IT payee)	2,092,150	1,255,290
Abdul Karim Bhat (linked to Ayesha Andrabi of the Dukhtaraan-e-Millat)	4,230,000	2,538,000
Abdul Rashid Saraf (a conduit linked to Abdul Ghani Bhat, Hurriyat Chairman)	37,828,755	22,397,253

Source: Computed from official sources and reportage in the English Language Press of India by *South Asia Intelligence Review*, Institute for Conflict Management, vol. 1, no. 31, 17 February 2003, New Delhi.

Revenue Intelligence (DRI). The JIC has identified Pakistan, Syria, Iran and Libya as countries selectively supporting militancy for regional gains.[62] The presence of a large number of terrorist groups in Pakistan is revealed by the fact that accounts containing Rs. 621.41 million of 15 terrorist groups and individuals were frozen by its federal government. It also refused income tax exemptions to 10 non-governmental organizations (NGOs).[63]

Since over 60 per cent of the militants currently active in J&K are said to be of foreign origin, the funding source and pattern has also been mostly from outside. Besides the 'voluntary collections', over 90 per cent of the funding is from source in other countries including the ISI of Pakistan and Islamic organizations like the World Association of Muslim Youth, Rabit-e-Islami, World Kashmir Freedom Movement, Kashmir American Council, Kashmir Study Group and Friends of Kashmir, UK, etc.

The break-up of the sources of terrorist funding in Jammu & Kashmir has reportedly been mentioned as: direct from Pakistan—25 per cent, from narcotics—15 per cent, from illegal sale of arms—10 per cent, through counterfeit currency—10 per cent, through *zakat* (an Islamic tax) and donations—10 per cent, from international Islamic organizations and the Organization of Islamic Countries—20 per cent, and through extortions/bank robberies—10 per cent.

The extent of illegal arms recovery in Bangladesh in recent times is indicative of a new corridor and transit points of arms smuggling, an emerging centre of Islamist terrorist consolidation, and also the cross-border linkages of militants and terrorists. In June 2003, police seized 115 kg of 'high powered' explosives and 62,100 rounds of live bullets of Chinese rifles during separate raids in an unnamed village under Kahalu *upa-zila* (administrative unit) of the Bogra district.[64] Again, in April 2004, the Bangladesh police and coast guard seized a huge cache of arms in the area of the port city of Chittagong.[65] Such seizures were made in Dhaka too.[66] The Bangladesh Bank through a notification on 6 July 2004 has reportedly cautioned all banks and financial institutions against six accounts for their suspected links with the Al Qaida and Taliban and instructed them to freeze the account.[67] All of this is going to create a major conflict ground for the forces of globalization in India and the neighbouring countries.

III. EXTORTIONS AND LOOTINGS

The main sources of funding for the Maoists in Nepal have been bank robberies, voluntary donations, repatriation of funds collected from Nepalese working mostly in India but in other countries as well, extortions from rich businessmen, and tax collections in areas under Maoist control. For instance, a recent report mentioned that the 'Maoists have been collecting their "people's government tax" from tourists visiting Solukhumbu region more strictly. They are charging Rs. 1,000 from each tourist and more from American trekkers'.[68] The same report also makes it clear that the Maoists are collecting money from the NGOs also as the district Maoist chief mentioned that, 'money is being collected from the NGOs as they have very high overheads. . . . We have demanded a royalty of 15 per cent for every Rs. 100,000 and will spend the money on development activities for the villagers'. It is estimated that by 2001 the Maoists had 'looted Rs. 250 million from Banks and other "institutions" and if "donations" and "taxes" are added, its collection could be well over Rs. 5 billion'.[69] This is quite possible given the huge upkeep expenses required for its cadres. The strength of the Maoists as provided by the government in early 2003 is approximately 5,500 combatants, 8,000 militia, 4,500 cadres, 33,000 hard-core followers, and 200,000 sympathizers. The Maoist themselves maintain that they have the 'the formation of two divisions, seven brigades and 19 battalions', as well as 'around a hundred thousand strong people's militia as a recruiting base'.[70]

The amount of money looted in Jammu & Kashmir alone has been enormous (see Table 12.5). The mining industry has borne the brunt of extortions by the MCC in Jharkhand. The MCC has abducted a number of officials of the Hindustan Construction Company as the company failed to pay 'levy'. On 3 January 2004, the Ranchi district police arrested a conduit of the MCC collecting levies amounting to Rs. 800,000 each month from coal transporters on behalf of the MCC.[71]

For the Achik National Volunteer Council (ANVC) the brisk business done by Meghalaya in the export of coal, limestone and boulders (estimated to be Rs. 2 billion annually) with Bangladesh has been a very fertile revenue base. It raises annual taxes from

TABLE 12.5: JAMMU & KASHMIR: MONEY LOOTED BY TERRORISTS

Year	Amount Looted (Million Rs.)
1990	22.62
1991	6.23
1992	6.48
1993	8.35
1994	13.91
1995	15.00
1996	3.00
1997	1.47
1998	1.09
1999	2.40
2000	1.00
2001	4.38

Source: *SAIR*, New Delhi: Institute of Conflict Management, 13 January 2001.

the coal truckers in the east and west Garo Hills districts and takes hefty commissions from businessmen. The owner of a coalfield in Borsora complained that 'receiving demand notes, negotiating on the amount and the nature of payment has become a part of our business skill. When even the laborers working in the coal business are not spared, I can't think of defying the militants demand not only for the continuation of my business but also for my own safety'. It is also found that the militants no longer send their own men to collect the ransom. They engage college students, auto rickshaw drivers, common people and some of its overground members for this purpose. They even maintain bank accounts across the border.[72]

It is estimated that the PWG's rich coffers include a phenomenal 700 million rupees in extortions annually, mainly from the landowners, corrupt government employees, professionals, and businesses in their pockets of influence.[73]

The failure of the state to provide security has perforce brought bout peaceful coexistence between the militant outfits and ıe various business groups and companies. At times it is found that the payment of a 'maintenance grant' or 'security expenses' to the terrorist groups by the private companies has been well institutionalized. This was revealed when in 1997 the cultural secretary of ULFA, Pranati Deka, was arrested in Mumbai where she had been taken by Tata Tea Limited (TTL) for delivery of her baby in the local hospital. In September 2003, an extortion notice of Rs. 20 million was served on Hindustan Levers Limited's (HLL) Doomdooma division in Tinsukia district. In the previous rounds of such extortions a number of eminent tea planters had been abducted or killed.[74]

They call it legal collections. Otherwise how do they fight the army, maim and kill cadres of rival factions, send large delegations of 'NGOs' to Bangkok for negotiations? 'When a battalion of NGO representatives goes to Bangkok, it involves a huge expenditure. We have received complaints of such forcible collection of money at Dimapur. It is a terrible burden on the business community', the former Nagaland Chief Minister S.C. Jamir had stated in May 2002.[75]

IV. BUSINESS INTERESTS

Besides the known militants–politicians nexus, militancy, terrorism and insurgency have become a major rent-seeking activity. The involvement of these groups in investment and further accumulations of capital has been both unnoticed and massive. They have in a sense emerged as true multinational actors with investment and business interests spread over a large number of countries and sectors. This has been one of the key sustenance factors for many of these groups.

One of the much-talked about centres that breed militancy in Pakistan has been the 'madrasas', the seminaries traditionally and primarily meant to impart education and to supplement the governmental education system. Many madrasas inculcate extremism and a violent anti-Americanism in their students. 'In these schools, a rigid condemnation of Western culture, coupled with the local conditions of failing societies, produces young men inclined to support the same causes championed by Osama bin Laden and other terrorists.'[76] Some of them, including the Deobandi madrasas headquartered in Karachi, are doing roaring business and have now spread to the Barelvi and Shia seminaries too. This injection of huge money has weakened the hold of the Pakistani state over its own population.[77]

A home ministry report on the north-east militants in 2001 stated that, 'Muivah has bought 12,450 shares worth US $1,25,000 (equivalent to about Rs. 6 million) listed to an Irish multinational company, well known for the production of consumer goods'. The report also noted that the NSCN-IM had prepared a 'balance sheet' showing an expenditure of Rs. 200 million, but which actually amounted to US $500 million, as its chief had invested in real estate, shares, hotels, and the proprietorship of several companies.[78]

The involvement of the ULFA and NSCN cadres in drug and small-arms trafficking has been widely reported. Like the LTTE, the ULFA is also said to be running a number of business ventures including media consultancies, hotels, and garment factories both within India and in the neighbouring countries particularly Bangladesh. ULFA's budget for the year 2001 alone is estimated to be Rs. 31 crore.[79]

V. CONSTITUENCY OF INSTABILITY AND VIOLENCE

People, institutions, and agencies thrive in negative situations. This is why, over the years, one has found a very conspicuous pre-existence of vested constituencies that promote violence and instability. This is true in all the theatres of protracted militancy and insurgency in many parts of India.

In India–Pakistan relations, whatever stakeholdings they have, they are unfortunately all on the side of keeping the conflict alive; for example, the arms purchase lobby, smuggling syndicates, and the Dubai-based traders. In other words, the higher the possibility of conflict between India and Pakistan, the better and wider the opportunities and avenues for these, what we can call, 'negative stake holders', to maximize their gains. One can cite several examples to conclusively show that some of these agencies have been playing the Kashmir card only to perpetuate the narrow economic interests of these miniscule stakeholders.[80]

For instance, in the Kashmir Valley, three-way finances are poured in by the Indian government, cross-border donors, and foreign donors in the name of security, for instigating terrorism, and for people's welfare respectively. People who are directly benefited by the availability of these ample resources would naturally like the instability to continue if not deepen further. A *New York Times* report says that:

> Many of the activists have managed to exploit a bloated and unaccountable bureaucracy. Others are leaders of a separatist movement bankrolled by Pakistan and by Kashmiris abroad, or ex-militants who used the spoils of war to move from villages to big homes in Srinagar. Some profited from the largesse of intelligence agencies operating in the valley. Some Kashmiris made their money the old-fashioned way—through horticulture or handicrafts—while others took over the jobs or businesses that the valley's Pandits, or Hindus, driven out by Muslim militants left behind. . . . Srinagar and Jammu, the summer and winter capitals, are the only cities in the country where real estate prices have continuously risen in the last decade. . . . There are 21,000 cars in Srinagar alone—a fivefold increase from 1990. There were 560 private schools in the valley seven years ago; there are 1,360 now. . . . No one knows how much money for militants, carried in person or passed on through bank deposits, has come into the state. Some suspect that at least some of that money has been channeled through Jammu and Kashmir Bank, the most successful institution in the state and the most vivid emblem of Kashmir's boom. Since militancy began, its deposits have grown from $458 million to $2.29 billion.[81]

VI. TERRORISM: DISCERNING IMPACT

There is interesting theoretical literature which outlines the matrices of the economic impact of terrorism. One of the ways to more specifically express its impact on the international business environment is to put it in a framework of a series of concentric bands (circle) wherein the bands closest to the centre show primary impacts and the outermost band identifies a number of longer term issues. The bands in between indicate secondary impacts.[82] For instance, the response-generating impacts do represent the possible responses to the terrorist attacks as manifested in the stimulus of government spending, new controls on financial transactions, and migration, to induced changes in costs and individual behaviour (see Fig. 12.1).

Perhaps the easiest impacts to understand are the stimulatory effects of increased government expenditure. As this takes the

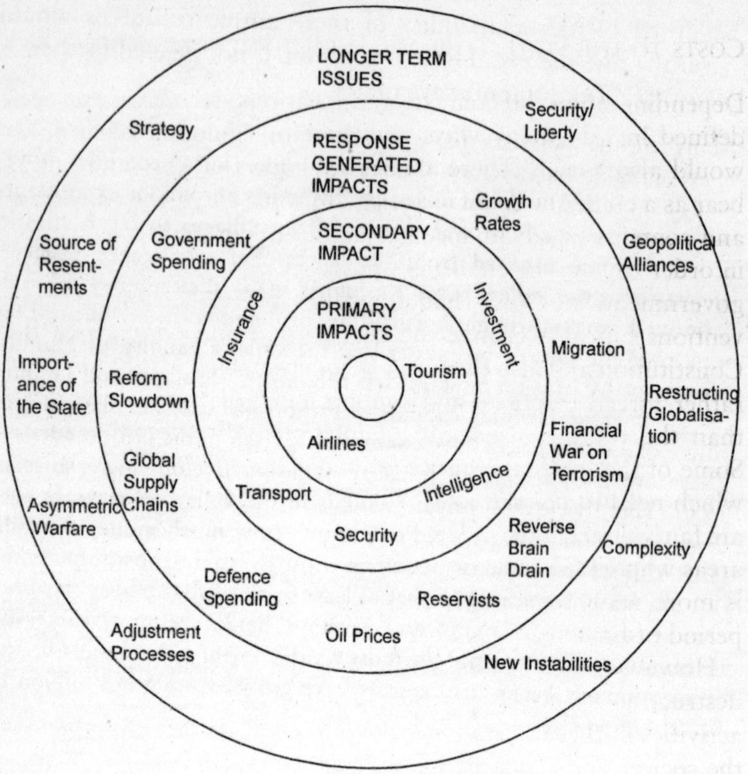

Source: Peter Enderwick, 'Terrorism and the International Business Environment', *AIB-Insights*, Special Issue, Academy of International Management, 2001.

FIG. 12.1: DISCERNING IMPACTS OF THE TERRORIST ATTACK ON THE INTERNATIONAL BUSINESS ENVIRONMENT

form of direct assistance to distressed industries such as airlines, underwriting of additional insurance and security costs, and increased military expenditure, these expenditures become both deflationary and unproductive. The resulting conflict may substantially increase internal displacement and lead to both forced and voluntary international migration.

COSTS TO THE STATE: DYNAMIC IMPACT PHENOMENON

Depending upon the contexts and locations, terrorism has been defined in very many ways and therefore its costs and impact would also vary.[83] There are several costs that the state has to bear as a consequence of terrorism. In some cases, the entire face and contents of governance has had to undergo transformation in order to face the challenges posed by terrorism. Some of the governments not only had to make special legislative interventions but also change the very format and contents of the Constitution and also the forms of governments. The States were rather forced to create and support a parallel apparatus other than the routine institution of internal and external security. Some of the internal security functions have certain dimensions which need to be addressed. Though the costs involved in these are fairly direct and to a large extent measurable, there are several areas where cost analysis becomes complex and enormous. This is more so when some of these costs are spread over a longer period of time.

However, these costs are beside the loss of human lives, destruction of public properties, and disruption of productive activities in the state and more importantly, the overall health of the society and economy in the long run. It has been the people who have had to suffer from both the state and the terrorists. People become a yam between two friction ridden rocks which only creates fire, terror and physical harm. It is extremely arduous and methodologically challenging to measure the real socio-economic, politico-strategic and environment-cultural impacts of terrorist violence and responses of the states both in terms of physical parameters and inter-generation adversities. Some of the dimensions of internal security functions are:

(i) intelligence gathering,
(ii) protection of political leaders,
(iii) guarding vital locations,
(iv) screening people at airports, and hardening target[84]
(v) frequent security checks and road blocks which create long delays and loss of productivity,
(vi) deployment of forces in the terrorist hit areas,

(vii) fighting a war against a terrorist group including buying arms, maintaining the forces and paying compensation packages to killed security personnel.

No literature is easily available on how much value, time, and effort have been lost in tackling the challenge of terrorism. More pertinently, in the face of massive onslaughts on the institutions of law and governance, most of the states ignore the fact that if the time devoted to tackling terrorism had been used instead to pursue development, there would have been much improvement in the socio-economic indicators and other development parameters. Similarly, if terrorism-led violence had not existed how much the society and economy would have progressed. More recently, India maintained that terrorism had been the 'key obstacle' in initiating and promoting a free trade regime in South Asia under the SAARC.[85] Given the socio-economic ramifications of free trade in the region, the opportunity costs in all these are estimated to be enormous.

In the wake of terrorism, depending on the size, resources, and capacity of the concerned states, the South Asian states have increasingly resorted to seeking both military and financial support from the regional and global-partner countries. This has definitely affected the economic independence of these countries. The erosion in national independence, intrusion into sovereignty and its long-term impact on diplomatic obligations, and political gratitude are serious and at times have pernicious fallouts. What has been more conspicuous is that these states are finding it increasingly difficult to match the changing tactics, transformed linkages, diverse strategies, and convoluted instruments that are found among the terrorist groups in the region.

There are several economic parameters on the basis of which we can assess the impact of violent conflicts and terrorism. These include destruction of infrastructure, increase in security-defence expenditure, destruction of factories and standing crops, stoppage of economic activities, and impact on tourism, production, export and import, growth in GNP, balance-of-payment position, and level of foreign exchange reserves and fiscal deficit. On the other hand, there are some factors that do indicate the indirect costs of such situations such as a general loss of confidence in the economy and the consequent inability to attract foreign investment, brain drain, displacement and migration, high transaction costs, and various kinds of economic distortions. Given these multidimensional facets of the destructive and dislocating impact, there are expectedly serious methodological difficulties in assessing and determining their exact cost. Experts have found it difficult to exactly and quantitatively isolate the terrorist factor in a chain of destructive actions.

A study revealed that livelihoods had been affected in a number of short- and long-term ways as a consequence of prolonged exposure to armed violence.[86] Some of the impacts noted across many case studies, included:

- fear, anxiety, suspicion, and insecurity
- forcible and voluntary displacement
- changes in occupation
- changes in expenditure patterns
- contribution to the polarization along ethnic and political lines
- impacts on the quality, delivery, and sustainability of developmental activities
- systematic erosion of the credibility of municipal and national governance

In the immediate aftermath of 9/11, some of the South Asian countries directly involved in the war on terrorism were affected both positively and negatively depending on their policies and strategic importance.[87] Some countries in the region had direct and immediate economic and financial benefits. For instance, the US wrote off $1 billion of Pakistan's foreign debt, as did the Paris Club creditors like Denmark and Commonwealth Development Corporation of UK, as a reward for Pakistan's 'support' in Afghanistan against the Taliban and Al Qaida. Further, despite a dismal economic performance and an alarming proportion of external debt, 'with the right nod from Washington', it also received substantive support from the IMF and other external inflows, concessional multilateral loans and grants. Most noteworthy was the rescheduling of its debt in the Paris Club which gave a rare 'stock' treatment to its debt usually extended only to 'Highly Indebted Poor Countries (HIPC)' in December 2001.[88] At one go this reduced the debt/service ratio of Pakistan from 21.3 per cent in 2000–1 to 13.1 per cent in 2001–2, and by mid

2004 Pakistan's foreign currency reserves had reached over $12 billion from a mere $3.3 billion in September 2001.[89]

Similarly, the peace initiative in Sri Lanka, which was partly triggered off by the 'war against terrorism', brought Sri Lanka a handsome aid package of US $3 billion pledged by various donors over a three-year period for rehabilitation, reconstruction, and growth generating reforms.[90]

Economic Costs: Some Instances

Though not many studies have been carried out in South Asia to assess and determine the costs of terrorism and related responses by the states, attempts are now being made to rigorously and empirically examine diverse macroeconomic impacts that are at least easily perceptible and largely measurable. At the same time, there are various other critical macro impacts which will unravel their real deleterious dimensions only over the next few years, that too if peace and normalcy are restored. At the present time, it is too early a proposition to assess the damages caused by this violent movement.

There are competitive or action-reaction based impacts also. Terrorism and counter-terrorism activities have led to costly competitive spending particularly in Pakistan and India, and, as Jagjit Singh says:

> This only proves that Indian counter-terrorism strategy of applying political-military pressure has significantly increased the costs to Pakistan of its mythical policy of 'low cost option' of pursuing terrorism under the nuclear umbrella . . . Islamabad has had to spend Rs. 2,000 crore extra during the last six months because of India's mobilisation and threat to exercise the option of using military force. This raised the Pakistan's military expenditure by 0.6 per cent of GDP in six months. In other words, Islamabad could have raised the allocations for health four times with this money.[91]

At the macro level, the first serious implication is usually further marginalization of certain regions and people that are extensively and intensively affected by the terrorism violence. The following subsections make an attempt to examine the macroeconomic impact of prolonged terrorist violence, the implications on defence and internal security budgets and also on a critical socio-economic activity like tourism.

I. MACRO SITUATIONS: THE IMPACT ASSESSMENT

While analysing the economic cost of war between the government, forces and the LTTE in Sri Lanka a study estimated the cost from 1983 to 1995 to be 131 per cent of 1995 GDP.[92] A more comprehensive study found the cost from 1983-1996 to be approximately 168 per cent of the 1996 GDP[93] (see Table 12.6). This is a huge sum for a developing economy with a per capita

TABLE 12.6: SRI LANKA: COMPOUND PRESENT VALUE (1996) OF ESTIMATED COST OF THE WAR 1984–96

(*Rs. million*)

Direct and Indirect Cost of War	Interest Rate (r = 0.05)	% of GDP: 1996[1]
Direct Cost		
Direct Government Military Expenditure	287,543	41.33
LTTE Military Expenditure	28,754	4.13
Govt. Expenditure on Relief Services[2]	20,742	2.98
Cost of Lost Infrastructure[2, 3]	93,584	13.45
Indirect Cost		
Lost Income due to Foregone Public Investment	59,884	8.61
Lost Income from Reduced Tourist Arrivals	118,365	17.01
Lost Earning due to Lost Foreign Investment	495,252	71.19
Lost Income due to Displacement (up to 1995)	38,229	5.49
Lost Income due to Lost Human Capital of Dead or injured Persons[4]	17,229	2.48
Output Foregone in the Northern Province in 1996[5]	9,031	1.30
Total	1,168,613	167.97

Notes: [1] Values as percentage of 1996 GDP are given in this column; [2] Due to lack of yearly data values given in the last two columns are not compounded; [3]This includes Rehabilitation and Reconstruction in the north and the east up to 1995 (85,034), Infrastructure in the Greater Colombo area up to 1996 (4,500), damages to houses in Jaffna in 1996 (4,050); [4]Income could also have been lost due to 'brain-drain'; however, because of data problem this cost is not included in the calculation; and [5]Cost of damage on top of damage to houses.

Source: N. Arunatilake, S. Jayasuriya and S. Kelegama, 'The Economic Cost of the War in Sri Lanka', *World Development*, vol. 29, no. 9, 2001.

income of less than US $1,000. In fact, per capita expenditure on defence in Sri Lanka is estimated to be the highest in South Asia.[94]

These studies have also highlighted how Sri Lanka consistently lost in terms of investment flows, tourist arrivals, slowing down of the reforms process and in becoming a regional hub. After the July 1983 communal violence in Colombo and the subsequent wars, many of the prospective investors including Motorola, Harris, Sony, Bank of Tokyo shied away from Sri Lanka. It was only in 1994 and 1999 that tourist arrival exceeded the 1982 figures—close to 410,000. Sri Lanka steadily eroded its chances of becoming a regional financial, shipping and aviation hub. The major economic activity of fishing suffered badly as two-thirds of the ocean fishing areas had restrictions on fishing.

In order to minimize the war risks, the Sri Lankan government had to provide extra market incentives to foreign investors sometimes at exorbitant cost to the state's exchequer. Investors demanded much a higher rate of return in any investment project to hedge their risks. On the other hand, foreign companies demanded excruciating entry facilitations. For instance, Caltex which took charge of Lanka Lubricants was given exclusive monopoly status in regard to the importation and distribution of lubricants till 2004. Similar arrangements had to be made with Shell in gas. These monopolistic situations naturally dislocated the market-oriented reforms, eroded the elements of competition, and closed the entry of others.

The economies of the war-torn eastern and the northern provinces have suffered the brunt of terrorism and violence. Since 1990 these provinces had been subject to severe economic embargoes on consumer, medicinal and intermediate goods particularly in the rebel-held areas. Certain goods were totally banned and some others had quantitative restrictions. In addition to this, lack of power supply from the national grid in the northern province severely affected all productive activities. Eventually the government lifted the economic embargo in January 2002. Kilinochchi, Mullaittivu, and areas in Mannar mainland are still not connected to the national grid.

In 1983, little more than 50,000 people were employed in the north and east in all types and sizes of industries, which was

8 per cent of the total employed in the industrial sector of the country. In terms of employment in the industrial sector, Jaffna employed 18,500, followed by Ampara 13,500, and Batticaloa 10,000. All these have literally vanished today.[95]

The following extract from the *Asia-Pacific Economic Update 2002* sums up how terrorism has affected the Sri Lankan economy in very recent years.[96]

> If it weren't for the crippling effects of the 18 year-old civil war, Sri Lanka would likely be one of Asia's top performers. But it's tough to run a successful economy when people are shooting at each other. For example in April and May of 2000, the Liberation Tigers of Tamil Eelam (LTTE) inflicted a series of defeats on the Sri Lankan armed forces. It sharply increased military spending. The military budget was lifted from Rs. 52 billion to a record Rs. 83 billion ($1 billion) for purchase of new warplanes, rocket launchers, and other hardware. Other government spending was cut and development projects put on hold. Unfortunately, spending cuts were not deep enough. So the government opted to borrow the money for the plus up in defense spending. Consequently, domestic government borrowing rose to 8.5 per cent of GDP in 2000 even though the target was 3 per cent. Repayments on state borrowings consume 32 per cent of government revenue. Total public debt rose to 97 per cent of GDP. Increased military spending, subsequent over-borrowing, and higher oil prices led to an exchange crisis in late 2000. The central bank faced an overvalued currency, capital flight, and low reserves. Foreign reserves ($950M) covered only six weeks of imports. Lacking any other solution, the government turned to the IMF. In return for a $253M IMF loan, Colombo had to implement market reforms—formerly delayed by popular opposition.

In Jammu & Kashmir, the extent of direct destruction, including of properties and social infrastructures, caused by militant activities has been enormous (see Table 12.7). This has also meant the killing of a large number of civilians, security forces personnel and terrorists. The physical and psychological costs of all these destructions and dislocations are beyond any quantitative measurement and analysis.

In Nepal, the nine-year-long conflict, besides causing the mindless killings and extensive displacement of people, has led to the gratuitous destruction of physical infrastructures including drinking water projects, buildings, communication installations,

TABLE 12.7: INDIA: DESTRUCTION OF PROPERTY BY MILITANTS IN JAMMU & KASHMIR

Year	Total Incident	Govt. Building	Education Buildings	Private House	Bridges	Shops	Hospital
1990	646	501	129	1,242	172	202	0
1991	391	45	24	819	24	83	0
1992	564	65	57	2,312	28	200	0
1993	662	98	46	1,110	34	400	0
1994	606	172	119	666	46	162	4
1995	688	127	133	1,814	16	402	2
1996	482	52	68	602	2	161	3
1997	259	13	11	437	5	67	1
1998	177	13	15	273	1	66	0
1999	136	7	9	284	2	6	0
2000	129	14	6	330	1	107	0
2001	274	30	16	419	2	77	1
2002	255	14	10	421	4	20	0
Total	5,269	1,151	643	10,729	337	1,953	11

Source: Ministry of Home Affairs, *Annual Report 2002-2003*, Government of India, New Delhi, 2003.

bridges, hydel projects and roads.[97] Violence has spread to all 75 districts in the country and the rural areas remain to a large extent delinked and paralysed. The World Bank mentions that the cost has been estimated at 8–10 per cent of GDP. More than one-third of Nepal's 3,900 village development committee (VDC) buildings have been destroyed, 19 districts (of a total of 75) are without telephone services, 250 post offices have been ruined and 6 airports have been closed. Nepal's National Planning Commission (NPC) estimates the direct damage to the impoverished economy at between US$ 300 million and 500 million. It puts the rehabilitation costs of damaged infrastructure alone at over USD 400 million. The costs of repeated economic blockades and frequent *bandhs* remain unestimated.

Many of the districts particularly in the western, mid-western and far-western regions, already had sharp and protracted disparity-led development stagnation. Though the economic growth rate has been more or less similar for last six to seven years, for the first time became negative in the second half of 2002 (see Table 12.8). This was the peak of the Maoists, attacks and confrontations with the state security forces.[98]

TABLE 12.8: NEPAL: GROSS DOMESTIC PRODUCT PERFORMANCE (% CHANGE OVER PREVIOUS YEAR)

Fiscal Years	Nominal GDP	Real GDP (1984–5 price)
1990–1	16.47	6.44
1991–2	24.81	4.62
1992–3	14.09	3.29
1993–4	15.87	7.90
1994–5	9.59	2.87
1995–6	14.01	5.70
1996–7	12.61	4.77
1997–8	7.48	3.37
1998–9	13.01	4.00
1999–2000	10.50	6.40
2000–1	7.30	4.90
2001–2	2.73	–0.46*
2002–3	5.88	2.28*

Note: * At 1994–5 prices.
Sources: Nepal Rashtra Bank, *Economic Report*, Kathmandu, various issues; Ministry of Finance, *Economic Survey*, Kathmandu, various issues and Central Bureau of Statistics, *Statistical Year Book of Nepal 2003*, Kathmandu.

The economic growth rate suffered very badly for the first time in 2001–2 as the agriculture sector grew by just 2.22 per cent, down from the previous year's 5.47 per cent. The non-agriculture sector recorded a negative growth rate of –2.09 per cent, a massive decline from the 4.28 per cent growth of the previous year. The Nepalese economy thus recorded a negative growth rate of –0.46 per cent in the fiscal year 2001–2.

Table 12.9 gives us a glance at the key economic indicators in the Nepalese economy. The rate of investment has shown a steady decline in the last six years. This is going to adversely affect economic activities in the country. Unless it is covered by both internal and external borrowing, slackness in the economic growth is inevitable. However, the loan repayment and interest component is already very high in the regular expenditure. Any pressure on the interest and loan components will drastically jack up the regular expenditure thereby severely distracting the economy from the development process.

TABLE 12.9: NEPAL: KEY ECONOMIC INDICATORS (AS PERCENTAGE OF GDP)

Heads	1995–6	1996–7	1997–8	1998–9	1999–2000	2000–1
Investment	27.32	25.34	24.84	20.48	23.38	23.01
Revenue	8.70	10.83	10.95	10.89	11.35	12.15
Regular Expenditure	8.66	8.62	9.03	9.08	9.13	10.65
Development Expenditure	10.03	9.46	9.62	8.34	8.40	9.74
Fiscal Deficit	5.55	5.12	5.91	5.26	4.67	5.86
Export (% change over previous year)	12.71	13.86	21.54	29.67	39.65	11.70
Import (% change over previous year)	16.92	25.65	–4.87	–1.66	24.00	6.60
GDP (Producers price in Rs. million)	248913	280513	300793	3042036	378033	408218

Sources: Nepal Rashtra Bank, *Economic Report*, Kathmandu, various issues, and Ministry of Finance, *Economic Survey*, Kathmandu, various issues.

Further, the external borrowing will have its own condition particularly when there is widespread apprehension about the ability of the Nepalese authorities to direct the resources to productive areas. This was true even during normal circumstances in the country. Although reconstruction and rebuilding funds may be extended by the donor agencies in the very near future, they would definitely come with harsh conditions attached particularly in the arena of governance and efficient utilization. At the Nepal Development Forum meeting, the donors raised the issues of growing corruption, inefficiency and lack of ownership in the development programmes in unambiguous and unequivocal terms. They all laid emphasis on a clean and effective administration.

Internal borrowing would also adversely affect the fiscal deficit which is already on the higher side. There could thus be a sharp rise in the level of unemployment. The inflationary tendency which could creep in the very near future may also affect poverty-alleviation related activities in the economy and could further undermine the already fragile competitive base of Nepalese products in the international market. The resultant devaluation of its currency vis-à-vis the hard currencies may be costly to the nation.

In the Indian state of Andhra Pradesh, the PWG's acts of violence and vandalism have hindered industrial growth and development in the state. 'The State is unable to achieve the expected development and growth due to their [the PWG's] anti-government stance.'[99] The implications of extortions have been many and varying. Firstly, it has shaken the business confidence of the people. Investment has gone down drastically and the private sector has literally withdrawn from the development process. Development efforts have become exclusive to the government. Further, businesses have either stayed away or moved to safer areas. For instance, in the PWG-infested areas of Karimnagar and Warangal districts in Andhra Pradesh, the *tendu* leaf (tobacco) contractors either did not bid for the annual contracts to collect the leaves or chose to do business in neighbouring Chattisgarh. This has undermined the very livelihood patterns of a large number of tribal farmers in forest areas, who collect the leaves on a seasonal basis and for whom this has been a major source of livelihood. Secondly, most of the government's contractors are also affected by the extortion of a substantial proportion of funds by the extremists. This has directly affected the quality of public works. A very critical dimension of the recurrence of terrorist violence is the de-concentration and diversion of the systems of governance from the core development dynamics. This contributes significantly to the persistence of the general level of backwardness in the region.

The terrorist attack on the Indian parliament on 13 December 2002 and the military mobilization that followed resulted in travel advisories being issued by western powers which further hurt investor sentiments. Tourism was badly affected. If Indian investors run for cover, which foreign investor will come? It injected a high degree of economic uncertainty.[100]

Interestingly, despite all the violence and instability, the Jammu & Kashmir region of India has one of the lowest poverty ratios in the county. The percentage of people living below the poverty line has been steadily coming down from, 40.83 per cent in 1973–4 to a low of 3.48 per cent in 1999–2000. This is also more or less, true of Punjab, another violence-torn state of India. Unlike Jammu & Kashmir, the other states affected by militancy and violence are in fact still reeling under deeper and extensive poverty (see Table 12.10).

TABLE 12.10: INDIA: PERCENTAGE OF POPULATION BELOW POVERTY LINE (ARRANGED IN DECREASING ORDER OF 1999–2000)

States	1973–4	1983	1993–4	1999–2000
Jammu & Kashmir	40.83	24.24	25.17	3.48
Punjab	28.15	16.18	11.77	6.16
Himachal Pradesh	26.39	16.40	28.44	7.63
Delhi	49.61	26.22	14.69	8.23
Haryana	35.36	21.37	25.05	8.74
Kerala	59.79	40.42	25.43	12.72
Gujarat	48.15	32.79	24.21	14.07
Rajasthan	46.14	34.46	27.41	15.28
Andhra Pradesh	48.86	28.91	22.19	15.77
Mizoram	50.32	36.00	25.66	19.47
Karnataka	54.47	38.24	33.16	20.04
Tamil Nadu	54.94	51.66	35.03	21.12
Maharashtra	53.24	43.44	36.86	25.02
West Bengal	63.43	54.85	35.66	27.02
Manipur	49.96	37.02	33.78	28.54
Uttar Pradesh	57.07	47.07	40.85	31.15
Nagaland	50.81	39.25	37.92	32.67
Arunachal Pradesh	51.93	40.88	39.35	33.47
Meghalaya	50.20	38.81	37.92	33.87
Tripura	51.00	40.03	39.01	34.44
Assam	51.21	40.47	40.86	36.09
Sikkim	50.86	39.71	41.43	36.55
Madhya Pradesh	61.78	49.78	42.52	37.43
Bihar	61.91	62.22	54.96	42.60
Orissa	66.18	65.29	48.56	47.15
All India	54.88	44.48	35.97	26.10

Note: The poverty line of Himachal Pradesh and expenditure distribution of Jammu & Kashmir are used to estimate poverty ratio of Jammu & Kashmir.

Source: Government of India, *Tenth Five Year Plan (2002–2007)*, New Delhi: Planning Commission.

TABLE 12.11: SOUTH ASIA: DEFENSE EXPENDITURE AND TRADE IN ARMS

ASIA	Military Expenditure				Armed Forces Personnel				Arms Trade			
	% of GNI		% of CGE		Total-Thousand		% of Lab F		Ex % of TX		Im % of TM	
	1992	1999	1992	1999	1992	1999	1992	1999	1992	1999	1992	1999
Bangla-desh	1.3	1.3	11.2	10.1	107	110	0.2	0.2	0.0	0.0	1.1	1.0
India	2.4	2.5	12.4	14.6	1270	1300	0.3	0.3	0.0	0.0	2.9	1.6
Nepal	1.0	0.8	6.0	5.7	35	35	0.4	0.3	0.0	0.0	0.0	0.0
Pakistan	7.0	5.9	27.9	27.9	580	590	1.4	1.2	0.4	0.1	6.6	9.7
Sri Lanka	3.7	4.7	13.2	18.4	110	110	1.5	1.3	0.0	0.0	0.3	0.7

Note: GNI: Gross National Income; CGE: Central Government Expenditure; Lab F: Labour Force; Ex: Exports, TX: Total Exports; TM: Total Imports.

Source: The World Bank, *World Development Indicators*, 2002.

As can be seen from Table 12.11, the military expenditure and number of armed forces is steadily increasing for the South Asian countries.

In the renewed violence in Karachi, trade and industry associations of the city, as indicated earlier, say they suffered a loss of more than 35 per cent in revenue generation in May 2004 alone. The chairman of the SITE Association of Industry, Mohammad Nisar Sheikhani, disclosed that a one-day strike causes a production loss of Rs. 100 to 120 million to industries. The government also suffers an estimated revenue loss of around Rs. 1.3 billion per day in Karachi alone. The livelihood of daily workers remains much affected.[101]

II. IMPACT ON DEFENCE EXPENDITURE

As the tactics and instruments of terrorism become more sophisticated and advanced the terrorist groups require heavy funding in order to acquire new techniques and technologies. Besides the standard terrorist tools like AK rifles and car bombs, the newer elements like jet aircrafts, weapons of mass destruction including chemical, biological and radiological materials, are increasingly used by them. Government forces and machineries have not only to match this but also pre-empt them. This has severe implications on the defense and internal security spending.

In Sri Lanka,[102] the steady escalations in the defence budget, mainly because of a number of military operations throughout the 1990s, also put tremendous pressure on the general public as the government introduced a national security levy of one per cent in 1992 for defence financing. In military strength, the number of army personnel increased from 30,000 in 1986 to 118,890 in 1996, navy from 3,960 to 11,831, air force from 3,700 to 12,292, and police from 21,000 to 80,000 during the same period.[103] The capture of the Elephant Pass by the LTTE in March/April 2000 and the subsequent fight by the Sri Lankan army further triggered a heavy dose of defence spending amounting to 6 per cent of GDP—the highest after 1983 (see Table 12.12). The government procured sophisticated defence equipment including multi-barrel rocket propel launchers.

An assessment of the impact on Pakistan's defence budget is complicated by the non-availability of a consistent and single data even from official sources. An analyst found that General Musharraf had given a figure of Rs. 151.6 billion for 2001–2 as against the figure of Rs. 149 billion given by the official *Economic Survey* of Pakistan, and a figure of Rs. 146 billion (2002–3) was given by the federal finance minister in his budget speech as against the Rs. 158 billion mentioned in the *Economic Survey* for the same period.[104]

Though the overall defence budget of India does indicate the general trend in the security situation as perceived by the national government, it does not give any clear-cut indications about the actual outlay and expenditure earmarked to deal with situations caused by terrorism, militancy, and insurgency. However, one could get much deeper insights from (i) the security budget of a particular terrorism-affected state government, (ii) the allocations made by the special commissions like the Finance Commission on maintaining law and order, and (iii) the grants extended by the union government to the affected states for relief and compensation and as special development packages.

In Jammu & Kashmir and the north-east region of India the huge cost involved in tackling militancy and terrorism has meant

TABLE 12.12: SRI LANKA: BUDGET DEFICITS AND EXPENDITURES ON DEFENCE

(*Rs. million*)

	1982	1983	1985	1990	1995	1998	1999	2000	2001
Government Expenditure	33,531	39,637	55,234	99,814	200,482	268,179	279,159	335,823	387,537
Budget Deficit as % of GDP	17.4	13.5	11.7	9.9	8.4	9.2	7.5	9.9	10.9
Defense – Recruitment	804	1,182	2,318	10,317	25,815	42,496	40,071	56,915	48,161
Defense – Capital	313	572	3,294	4,285	10,539	11,832	8,307	19,313	15,977
Defense – Total	1,117	1,754	5,612	14,602	36,354	54,328	4,878	76,228	64,138
GDP (Mkt. Price)	99,238	121,601	162,375	321,784	667,772	1,017,986	1,105,963	257,634	400,180
Def. Exp. as % of Govt Exp.	3.1	4.4	10.2	14.6	18.1	20.3	17.3	22.7	16.5
Def. Exp. as % of GDP	1.1	1.4	3.5	4.5	5.4	5.3	4.4	6.1	4.6

Source: Central Bank of Sri Lanka, *Annual Report*, various issues.

BOX 12.1: INDIA: SECURITY RELATED EXPENDITURE REIMBURSED BY THE UNION GOVERNMENT 1989–2002 IN JAMMU & KASHMIR

Assistance to Kashmiri migrants & related activities = Rs. 530.45 crore
Welfare activities = Rs. 362.79 crore
Security works & related activities = Rs. 233.23 crore
Election related additional security related expenditure = Rs. 192.00 crore
Additional expenditure on Police = Rs. 872.73 crore
Action Plan SRE = Rs. 166.65 crore
Total = Rs. 2357.85 crore

Source: Ministry of Home Affairs, *Annual Report 2002–2003*, New Delhi: Government of India, 2003.

the diversion of a significant portion of development budgets which could otherwise have been used for more productive activities. For instance, in Jammu & Kashmir, the reimbursement of security-related expenditure incurred by the state government since 1989 has cost the union government a whopping Rs. 2,357.85 crore during 1989–2002 (Box 12.1).

During the period 1997–8 to 2002–3 alone, the reimbursement of the security related-expenditure by the Union government in the north-eastern states amounted to over Rs. 760 crore[105] (see Table 12.13). On top of this, the modernization of their police forces with emphasis on supply of (i) arms and ammunition, (ii) vehicles, (iii) communication equipment, and (iv) other essential equipment has cost the union government over Rs. 284 crore during the same period (see Table 12.14).

Interestingly, as shown in Table 12.15, Nepal's defence and internal security expenditure as a percentage of regular expenditure has gone down by almost 10 percentage points, from 33 per cent in 1991–2 to 22 per cent in 2000–1. Though the high of 1990–1 could be attributed to the maintenance of the law and order situation in the country during and immediately after the restoration of multi-party democracy, the decline, particularly in the last six years, goes very contrary to general expectations.

However, the latest document does mention that the defence expenditure of Nepal to be 30 per cent of GDP in 2002–3.

TABLE 12.13: INDIA: REIMBURSEMENT OF SECURITY RELATED EXPENDITURE BY THE UNION GOVERNMENT IN THE NORTH EASTERN STATES

(*Rs. crore*)

State	Released in 1997–8	Released in 1998–9	Released in 1999–2000	Released in 2000–1	Released in 2001–2	Released in 2002–3*	Released Grand Total
Assam	131.91	78.86	52.17	63.97	92.86	68.01	487.78
Nagaland	0	35.61	17.88	7.50	12.71	16.92	90.62
Manipur	0	19.43	3.44	14.18	4.00	7.64	48.69
Tripura	0	28.55	17.53	15.00	27.70	29.85	118.63
Arunachal Pradesh	–	–	–	1.00	1.90	8.35	11.25
Meghalaya	–	–	–	3.21	00.60	0.95	4.76
Total	131.91	162.45	91.02	104.86	139.77	131.72	761.73

Note: *15 March 2003.

Source: Ministry of Home Affairs, *Annual Report 2002–2003*, New Delhi: Government of India, 2003.

TABLE 12.14: INDIA: CENTRAL ASSISTANCE FOR MODERNIZATION OF POLICE FORCES IN NORTH EASTERN STATES

(*Rs. crore*)

State	1997–8	1998–9	1999–2000	2000–1	2001–2	2002–3*	Total
Assan	17.10	6.64	22.72	22.45	18.21	15.61	102.73
Nagaland	6.16	1.08	4.52	6.51	5.93	15.88	40.08
Manipur	6.26	.98	5.54	6.51	3.62	11.49	34.40
Tripura	6.11	1.33	6.06	13.81	8.32	10.36	45.99
Meghalaya	–	1.22	4.74	6.35	3.25	4.88	20.44
Mizoram	–	.67	3.46	4.36	3.65	7.91	20.05
Arunachal	–	–	–	–	–	–	–
Pradesh	–	.56	3.86	5.38	.76	5.41	15.97
Sikkim	–	–	–	2.06	.89	1.74	4.69
Total	35.63	12.48	50.90	67.43	44.63	73.28	284.35

Note: * Upto 15 March 2003.

Source: Ministry of Home Affairs, *Annual Report 2002-2003*, New Delhi: Government of India, 2003.

TABLE 12.15: NEPAL: COMPONENTS OF REGULAR EXPENDITURE

(*Percentage*)

	1991–2	1994–5	1995–6	1996–7	1997–8	1998–9	1999–2000	2000–1
General Administration	14.44	9.6	8.9	9.65	8.76	8.65	8.55	8.04
Defence and Internal Security	33.04	21.58	21.65	21.71	21.83	22.32	23.05	22.35
Social Services	12.22	26.74	28.4	28.18	30.11	29.53	30.34	30.07
Economic services	6.71	8.18	9.29	9.01	8.77	8.79	8.20	6.90
Misc.	33.57	33.80	31.79	30.13	30.51	30.69	29.80	32.58
Total Regular Exp. (Rs. million)	8,172.6	16,606.7	18,714.2	20,969.0	23,218.3	26,389.9	29,271.4	37,772.3

Source: Nepal Rashtra Bank, *Economic Report*, Kathmandu, various issues.

Expectedly, the impact on development expenditure has been quite remarkable. There has been more or less an equal decline in the share of development expenditure as percentage of GDP in the last six years. Within the regular expenditure also economic services have recorded a declining trend. The then prime/finance minister, while presenting his budget for the year 2002–3, said that the government considered investment in security expenses as 'investment in peace.'[106] In fact, besides the social-services related expenditure, defence and internal security recorded the highest growth rate of over 22 per cent from 1994–5 to 2000–1. It recorded an almost 2.5-fold jump during the same period (see Table 12.16).

To combat Maoist violence and to 'streamline the security system', Nepal for the first time is literally resorting to 'militarization' of the country under the newly constituted 'unified command'. More sophisticated weapons have been inducted into the Royal Nepalese Army which has received huge military aid from the US, UK, and India. During 2002–3, $17 million had been committed by the US for defence equipment, while the UK and India provided 6.5 million pounds sterling and US $66 million respectively.[107] This is likely to drastically increase when the RNA expands and consolidates under the King dominated new political dispensation imposed in February 2005.

TABLE 12.16: NEPAL: TRENDS IN THE COMPONENTS OF REGULAR EXPENDITURE

(*Rs. million*)

	1994–5	2000–1	Increase in Value	Annual Growth Rate
General Administration	1,600	3,037.3	1.89 fold	14.97
Defense and Internal Security	3,585	8,444.9	2.35 fold	22.59
Social Services	4,441	11,360.0	2.5 fold	25.96
Economic Services	1,359	2,623	1.9 fold	15.50
Misc.	5,620	12,306	2.1 fold	19.82
Total Regular Expenditure (Rs. Million)	16,606.7	37,772.3	2.27 fold	21.24

Source: Nepal Rashtra Bank, *Economic Report*, Kathmandu, various issues.

III. IMPACT ON TOURISM

Terrorism and violence have always had a very substantive impact on tourism in South Asia. The revelation that the 9/11 terrorist strikes on the World Trade Centre in New York had its direct linkages with the Al Qaida and the Taliban in and around Afghanistan, and the subsequent actions against these forces in South Asia very adversely affected the movement of tourists to South Asia. This caused huge losses to the numerous businesses involved in tourism including hotels, restaurants, entertainment spots, travel agencies, and street vendors.

Sri Lanka has been the worst-hit country in terms of tourist arrivals mainly due to the deteriorated security situation. This has been triggered by separatist war in the north during 1983–2001, as well as the youth insurgency in the south during 1986–9. At present tourist receipts account for over US $250 million, which is 20 per cent of the country's service receipts and 3.4 per cent of current account receipts.[108] The sector also provides direct or indirect employment opportunities to 87,600 people, which is about 1.5 per cent of the total employment in the country.[109]

The boom that the tourism industry experienced after economic liberalization in 1977 came to an abrupt end in 1983. The number of tourist arrivals—400,000—in 2002, is as the same as it was 20 years ago.[110] It grew by 22 per cent per annum during 1976–82 but declined by 10 per cent per annum during 1983–9. During the past 20 years—1983–2002—the marginal growth of tourist arrivals in Sri Lanka (1.5 per cent per annum) remained far below world average as well as that of most of the countries in Asia.[111] However, the foreign exchange receipts from tourism have grown at 4.8 per cent per annum due to the increase in spending by an average tourist. Despite a few downturns in response to the decline in the industry resulting in a dramatic fall in the prices of tourism-related services, receipts per tourist have generally increased from US $360 in 1982 to US $645 in 2002 (see Fig. 12.2).

However, the signing of the Memorandum of Understanding (MoU) between the Sri Lankan government and the Tamil militants (LTTE) in February 2002 followed by a ceasefire, marked a revival of tourism as well. Tourist arrivals during the

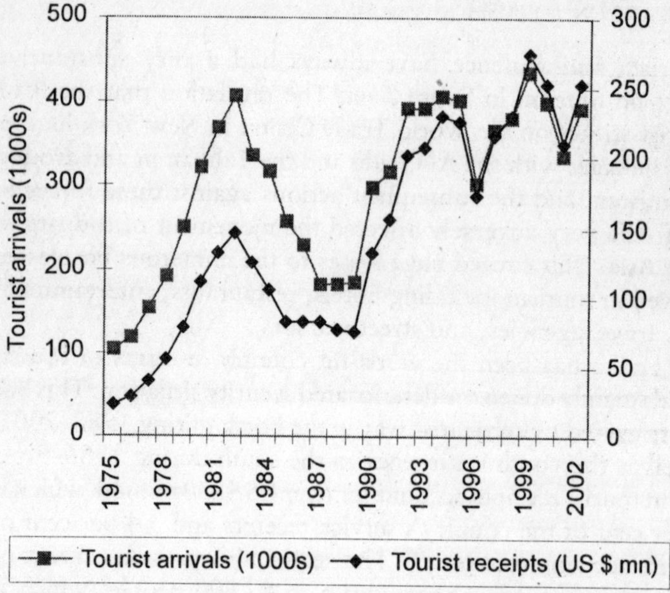

FIG. 12.2: SRI LANKA'S TOURIST ARRIVALS AND RECEIPTS 1975–2002

first half of 2003 increased by nearly 25 per cent as compared with tourist arrivals in the first half of the previous year.

At the micro level, the recent example of Karachi is interesting. The incidents of terrorism and unrest in the city have dearly cost its tourism industry. A newspaper report mentions that the 'leading hotels face a decline of 15–20 per cent in occupancy while smaller hotels register 50 per cent decline. . . . Manager Operations, Sarawan Hotel, Salim Shaikh said that room occupancy now ranges between 30–40 per cent as compared to 70–80 per cent earlier as people have stopped travelling to Karachi mainly from Lahore, Islamabad, Faisalabad, Gujranwala, Rawalpindi, Peshawar, etc.'.[112]

Tourism remains one of the worst-hit sectors in Jammu & Kashmir as well. Besides the decline in the arrival of tourists, a good extent of tourism-related infrastructure remains damaged and demolished. Even the number of domestic tourists to the Valley, which reached 490,215 in 1989, touched an all-time low of 322 in 1995. The number of foreign tourists went down from

TABLE 12.17: INDIA: TOURISTS ARRIVALS IN JAMMU & KASHMIR

Year	Kashmir Valley			Ladakh Region			Vaishno Devi	Amar-nathji
	Domestic	Foreign	Total	Domestic	Foreign	Total		
1997	7027	9111	16138	3991	12810	16801	4434233	79035
1998	99636	10247	109883	6792	15238	22030	4622097	149920
1999	200162	17130	217292	1905	9669	11574	4668340	114366
2000	104337	7575	111912	6217	11825	18042	5109575	173334
2001	66732	5859	72591	4260	15439	19699	5056919	119037
2002	17561	1698	19259	2376	4203	6579	2868946	110793

Source: Ministry of Home Affairs, *Annual Report 2002–2003*, New Delhi: Government of India, 2003.

67,762 in 1989 to 8,198 in 1995. The number of pilgrims visiting Amarnath had also shrunk considerably during the period 1990–7. However, the situation seems to have improved since the late 1990s (see Table 12.17).

The most noticeable and devastating impact of the Maoist movement in Nepal has been on the country's tourism industry. This impact has been doubly felt because of the significant level of dependence of the Nepalese economy on the tourism sector. Foreign exchange earned from tourism is as high as 15 per cent of Nepal's total foreign exchange earnings. The income from the tourism sector constitutes almost 5 per cent of the Nepalese GDP and 35–40 per cent of the total value of merchandise exports.[113]

Equally serious has been the gross underutilization of the tourism infrastructure in the country including travel agencies, hotels and restaurants, parks and recreational areas. The impact on the forward and backward linkage segments of the tourism industry including transport, communication, markets, and handicrafts has been widespread and very critical. A large section of the people attached to the tourism industry have remained out of jobs for the last few years. The social implications of this are well known.

Table 12.18 provides us with the tourist arrival figures from 1995–2000. The onset of multi-party democracy, liberalization of the Nepalese economy, and the vast improvement in the tourism-related infrastructure brought about a massive increase

TABLE 12.18: NEPAL: TOURIST ARRIVALS

Origin	1995	1996	1997	1998	1999	2000
Indian	117260	122512	133438	143229	140661	95915
Others	246135	271101	288419	320455	350843	367731
Total	363395	393613	421857	463684	491504	463646

Source: Nepal Rashtra Bank, *Economic Report*, Kathmandu, various issues; and Ministry of Finance, *Economic Survey*, Kathmandu, various issues.

in the number of tourists arriving in Nepal, from a mere 92,440 in 1975 to 2.92 lakhs in 1991, and then very sharply to almost 5 lakhs by 2000. However, the provisional estimates that are now available show that the number of tourist arrivals dropped below one lakh in 2002. This down trend had already started in 2000 and was strengthened by a number of factors including the Maoist violence, the anti-Indian incidents including the hijacking of Indian Airlines aircraft, arson resulting from the 'Hritik Roshan incident' and the royal massacre.

IV. WITHDRAWAL SYNDROME

One of the major fallouts of terrorist violence has been the withdrawal of development agencies, both national and international, from the affected areas. The development programmes have been disrupted and dislocated. In every developmental project or business transaction, the militants take the lion's share and what is left for development is so meager. A large number of development projects have been suspended or totally terminated halfway causing the state exchequer losses in the millions of rupees. After the NSCN-IM served an extortion note of Rs. 6 million on Oil India Limited (OIL), work at the Khumsai oil well in the Changlang district of Arunachal Pradesh was suspended, resulting in a loss of Rs. 200 to 300 million annually. The Border Road Task Force (BRTF) in Nagaland decided to indefinitely suspend work in the Wokha-Bokajan sector of the state following extortion and threats from 'armed miscreants'.

In Nepal, development activities in the Maoist-affected districts of Kailali, Jumla, Humla, Mugu, and Dolpa have been suspended by the donor agencies. The statement issued by the donor agencies mentioned that:

in response to increasing pressure on development programmes and workers, donor agencies issued their Basic Operating Guidelines in October 2003 setting out the principles for their engagement in Nepal. Development agencies have made it particularly clear that agencies neither register with nor contribute to Maoists organizations. Over the past few weeks, some Maoists in Nepalganj and Dhangadhi have made serious demands and threats against a number of development agencies, which are inconsistent with the Guidelines.

As a result of these actions, and our inability to ensure the safety of staff:

SNV, DFID and GTZ are forced to suspend all support to the Rural Community Infrastructure Worked programme in Humla, Mugu, Jumla and Dolpa with effect from 16 May. This will affect around 25000 people benefiting from the programme. Furthermore, SNV (the Netherlands Development Organisation) is forced to suspend all its activities in the Mid west.

Similarly, GTZ and DFID have no option but to suspend all support to Freed Kamaiya Food Security programmes activities in Kailali with effect from 16 May. This will affect 30,000 people benefiting from the programme.

WFP, in the absence of the required technical assistance normally provided by the above agencies, will also have to suspend its support to the Rural Community Infrastructure Works programme in the affected districts

Support to these programmes will restart when it is clear that staff can operate in a safe environment and according to the guidelines. We call upon the Maoists to uphold their stated commitment to respect the Geneva Conventions and not to carry out any physical action or exercise coercion against NGOs.[114]

Conclusion

In the South Asian context, most of the recorded violent movements have a strong economic content in terms of the triggering factors, instruments of sustenance, and immediate and long-term consequences. These economic matrices have local, national, cross border and international roots, linkages and ramifications.

These are manifested in a range of deprivation syndromes characterized by topographical variations, the imposition of ethno-religious superiority, practices like internal colonialism and the weak and limited reach of national governance. In many cases, the irrational and skewed sharing of natural resources and siphoning off of economic multiplier in contrasting economic geographies and the distributive imbalances of development gains have acted as a serious catalytic agent. Some of them are common yet the manifestations and directions are different and the degree of intensity largely varies. There are at the same time new trends of increasing international co-ordination for funding, arms supply and an effective demonstration of skills and prowess by the terrorist and other militant groups. These groups are doubly facilitated by their access to the most sophisticated means of communications and other frontier technologies.

An interplay of a large number of endogenous and exogenous factors have sustained these terrorist activities. In many cases retributions against the heavy clamp down by the state authorities have further fuelled their activities. Whereas the emergence of newer generation of fighters and the diasporic linkages including extensive commercial engagements of terrorist groups have sustained their programmes and actions. The diasporic communities have not only provided safe haven to fleeing voluntary and forced migrants and weapons but also space for diplomatic propaganda thereby consolidating the cause of 'long distance nationalism'. In many ways some of these militant groups could be called multinational actors particularly in terms of their investment and business interests spread over a large number of countries and sectors. All these together with the increasing ability of some of the diaspora groups to influence the policy makers of the countries where they are living have helped sustain the anti-state campaigns of the terrorist groups. This has enhanced their institutional and physical capabilities to thwart and withstand both counter-insurgency measures and other legislative actions.

The extortions and lootings have been the backbone of insurgency in all the theatres of militancy and terrorism in South Asia. The modi operandi of these criminal activities have been both covert and blatant. On the one hand, forcible tax raising is widely practiced, on the other hand the minority population is permanently displaced through violent actions to grab and acquire their movable and immovable properties. These have brought riches to the militants and even the local majority people. This is how the 'industry of terror', abduction, extortion and looting are institutionalized as a major rent seeking activity. This is heightened by a marked decay in the political culture, consolidation of militants–politician nexus and a steady erosion in the faith and confidence of the people in the systems of governance.

The support extended by hostile neighbours in both creating and sustaining terrorism is a well practiced phenomenon in this region. In all these the economic costs for planning-instigating, financing, managing, maintaining and curbing have been enormous for the involved countries.

What is most intriguing yet debilitating in this region which hosts the world's largest number of poverty-stricken and illiterate people is the conscious development and promotion of a strong constituency of instability and violence. Here people, institutions, and agencies thrive in negative situations like violence and instability. While the states actively participate in promoting such constituencies, the civil society only remains a relative spectator in the show of national power.

A quantitative analysis of economic costs of terrorism is a complex task. There are intricacies involved in the segmentation and analysis of economic costs in each violent and destructive event perpetrated by a terrorist attack. It is difficult to quantify or isolate the impact of such terrorist attacks particularly when complex socio-economic matrices and logistical intricacies are involved. However, the economic analysis if done in a more specific politico-social context, can actually help in understanding and making their policy applications more effective.

In the case of South Asia there have not been any serious and systematic attempts to study the economic impact of terrorism and insurgency despite the fact that this region has remained one of the most important theatres of terrorism, insurgency and other militant activities in the past. At the same time, there is some interesting theoretical literature that outline the matrices of the impact of terrorism. Perhaps the easiest impacts to understand and assess are the stimulatory effects of increased government expenditure. As this takes the form of direct assistance to distressed industries such as airlines, underwriting of additional insurance and security costs, and increased military expenditure, these expenditures become both deflationary and unproductive.

The South Asian countries have borne a range of costs as a consequence of terrorism and other militancy related violence. In some cases the entire system of governance has undergone transformation to combat terrorism and in others, special legislative interventions including the basic framework of the constitution and the very forms of governments have been undertaken. When the states have created a parallel apparatus other than the routine institution of internal and external security, the economic costs involved have been fairly direct and to a large extent measurable. At the same time, the enormous yet complex forward and backward costs that impinge upon the state and the society remain beyond any measurement. This is more so when these costs are spread over a longer period of time. Therefore, one finds it to be extremely arduous and methodologically challenging to measure the real socio-economic, politico-strategic and environment-cultural impacts of terrorist violence. There is serious dearth of literature that assess the value, time and effort that has been lost in tackling terrorism. We have not come across any instances in the region which could provide us an assessment of socio-economic gains that would have been triggered if time, monetary and other physical resources devoted to tackling of terrorism had been utilized in the development arena. In other words, how much did a violence ridden economy lose by way of withdrawals of projects and development participation by the national and international agencies?

In the wake of terrorism, depending upon the size, resources and capacity of the concerned States, the South Asian states have increasingly resorted to seeking both military and financial support from the regional and global partner countries. This has definitely impinged upon the economic independence of these affected countries. The erosion in national independence, intrusion into sovereignty and its long term impact on diplomatic obligations and political gratitude are serious and at times pernicious. Conspicuously these states are finding it increasingly difficult to match the changing tactics, transformed linkages, diverse strategies and convoluted instruments that are found among the terrorist groups in the region.

The very impact of terrorism and violent conflicts is both dynamic and varying. It is a phenomenon which acquires newer dimensions as the techniques and instruments of such terrorist violence undergo both structural and methodological transformations. Any serious assessment and evaluation of the impact of violent movement that is so widespread and scattered requires a systematic empirical enquiry. In many cases, there are serious time lags in the manifestations of the actual deleterious impact of such a violent situation. There are variables and parameters which would start expressing the magnitude of impact only in the long run when the pressures and pulls exert their full effect on them. Further, for the period in which the most concentrated violence took place the data and statistics from reliable sources including that from the government are yet to be published. There are instances where the States have played down the impact both by statistical manipulations and also by not releasing detailed information. Therefore, the assessment made in this paper are only very cursory and at times indicative rather than scientific and comprehensive. And the cost estimates are also very-tentative and could be far short of the real impact and burden. This definitely indicates the need to study the problematic in a much more comprehensive manner.

NOTES

1. Keki N. Daruwalla, 'Terrorism and National Security', in Satish Kumar (ed.), *India's National Security, Annual Review-2001*, New Delhi: Vikas, p. 328.
2. Robert G. Wirsing, 'South Asia: The Baluch Frontier Tribes of Pakistan', in Robert G. Wirsing (ed.), *Protection of Ethnic Minorities: Comparative Perspectives*, New York: Pergamon Press, 1981; Lawrence Ziring, 'Pakistan's Nationalities Dilemma: Domestic and International implications', in Lawrence Ziring (ed.), *The Subcontinent in World Politics: India, Its Neighbours and the Great Powers*, New York: Praeger, 1978.
3. Muchkund Dubey, 'Anatomy of terrorism in South Asia—I', *The Hindu*,

1 January 2003; Mahendra P. Lama, 'Separatism and Armed Conflicts in North-East India', in *Conflict and Violence in South Asia,* ed. K.M. de Silva, International Centre for Ethnic Studies, Sri Lanka: Kandy, 2000; B. Raman, 'Counter-Terrorism: The Indian Experience', Paper no. 649, 1 April 2003, South Asia Analysis Group, New Delhi, at the website http://www.saag.org/papers7/paper649.html

4. These included 8 civil servants and 36 business people, *Kuensel Online*, quoting Prime Minister Lyonpo Jigmi Thinley , 17 July 2004.
5. See William M. Landes, 'An Economic Study of US Aircraft Hijackings, 1961-76', *Journal of Law and Economics,* 21:1, 1978, pp. 1–31; Walter Enders, Todd Sandler and John Cauley, 'An Econometric Analysis of the Impact of Terrorism on Tourism' *KYKLOS,* 45:4, 1992, pp. 531–54; Nisha Arunatilake, Sisira Jayasuriya and Saman Kelegama, 'The Economic Cost of the War in Sri Lanka', *World Development,* 29:9 , September 2001, pp. 1483–1500; Muhammad Q. Islam and Wassim N. Shahin, 'Economic Methodology Applied to Political Hostage—Taking in Light of the Iran-Contra Affair', *Southern Economic Journal,* 1989, 55:4, pp. 1019–24; Walter Enders and Todd Sandler, 'Causality between Transnational Terrorism and Tourism: The Case of Spain', *Terrorism,* 14:1, pp. 49–58.
6. See William E. James, 'Indonesia's External Trade and Competitiveness: Assessing the Economic Costs of terrorism', paper presented at the USAID-CSIS Seminar on 'Economic Cost of Terrorism: Indonesia's responses', May 2002, Jakarta.
7. Bruce Hoffman, *Inside Terrorism*, New York: Columbia University Press, 1998; Paul Wilkinson and A.M. Stewart (eds.) , *Contemporary Research on Terrorism*, Aberdeen, UK: University of Aberdeen Press, 1987; Martha Crenshaw, 'Current Research on Terrorism: The Academic Perspective', *Studies in Conflict and Terrorism*, 15:1, 1992, pp. 1–11.
8. Todd Sandler and Walter Enders, 'An Economic Perspective of Transnational Terrorism', February 2002.
9. See, for instance, 'Terrorism and the International Business Environment', *Insights*—Special Electronic Issue ; http: // aib.msu.edu / publications / insights/insights_special.pdf
10. Report entitled 'The Economic Costs of Terrorism' prepared by the Joint Economic Committee led by Jim Saxton, United States Congress in May 2002, p. 1.
11. Gary Becker and Kevin Murphy, 'Prosperity will Rise out of the Ashes', *Wall Street Journal,* 29 October 2001, as quoted in 'The Economic Costs of Terrorism', p. 5.
12. For example, the Delhi-based Institute for Conflict Management has been able to disseminate a considerable amount of data and information on both the terrorist/insurgency violence and its large-scale national

and international ramifications. Similar efforts have been made by the South Asia Analysis Group in Madras, the Institute of Policy Studies in Colombo, and the University of Karachi.

13. *Nepal Human Development Report 1998*, Nepal South Asia Centre, Tripureshwar, Kathmandu, Nepal, 1998.
14. *Nepal and the World: A Statistical Profile*, Federation of Nepalese Chambers of Commerce and Industry, Kathmandu, 2003; Mahendra P. Lama, 'Indian Investment in Nepal in the Post Reforms Period', *The Indian Journal of Commerce*, New Delhi, April–June 1999.
15. For details see Mahendra P. Lama, Mohan Man Sainju and Q.K. Ahmad, 'Reforms and Power Sector in South Asia: Scope and Challenges for Cross Border Trade', in Mohsin Khan (ed.), *Economic Development in South Asia*, New Delhi: Tata McGraw Hill, 2005.
16. HMG, *The Constitution of Nepal*, Kathmandu.
17. See Harka Gurung, *Nepal: Social Demography and Expressions*, New Era, 1998.
18. T.M.Z.D. Wasantha Mutaliph and Anile D. Bandaranaike, 'A Provincial Estimation and Analysis of Regional Economic Activity in Sri Lanka 1996/2000', *Central Bank of Ceylon, Staff Studies*, vol. 31, no. 32, November 2002, Colombo.
19. M.S. Ahluwalia, 'Economic Performance of States in Post Reforms Period', *Economic and Political Weekly*, Mumbai, 6 May 2000.
20. In May 2004 alone, approximately 140 rockets were fired in Sui. On 3 May 2004, 3 Chinese engineers were killed and 11 persons, including 9 Chinese nationals, sustained injuries in a car-bomb attack. Kanchan Lakshman 'Balochistan: A Rising Insurgency', *SAIR*, vol. 3, no. 4, 9 August 2004.
21. Atul Sharma, 'Development Strategies in the North East in the context of Globalisation', unpublished seminar paper, 1995, p. 12; P.C. Barua (ed.) *Development Planning of North-East India*, Delhi: Mittal, 1990; P.D. Saikia and U. Phukan, *Rural Development in North-East India*, Delhi: B.R. Publishing, 1989.
22. Sanjib Baruah, *India Against Itself: Assam and Politics of Nationality*, New Delhi: Oxford University Press, 1999, pp. 150–1.
23. Mahendra P. Lama, 'Separatism and Armed Conflicts', in K.M. de Silva (ed.), *Conflict and Violence in South Asia*, Kandy: International Centre for Ethnic Studies, 2000.
24. Jayanta Madhab, 'North-East: Crisis of Identity, Security and Underdevelopment', *Economic and Political Weekly*, Mumbai, 6 February 1999.
25. Mahendra P. Lama, 'Stability and Instability in the Indian Economy—Challenges of Poverty', in D.D. Khanna (ed.), *Democracy, Diversity, Stability—50 Years of Indian Independence, Alleviation and Environmental Protection*, New Delhi: Macmillan, 1998; and see also

Mahendra P. Lama, 'Armed Conflicts by the Haves: A Case Study of Punjab', in Gerald Peris and S.W.R. de Samarasinghe (eds.), *History and Politics: Millennial Perspectives: Essays in Honour of Kingsley de Silva*, Colombo: Law and Society Trust, 1999.

26. Hamish Telford, 'The Political Economy of Punjab: Creating Space for Sikh Militancy', *Asian Survey*, University of California, Berkley, November 1992, pp. 976–7.
27. Size of operational holdings were defined as: class 1:1 to 2.49 acres; class 2:2.50 to 4.99 acres; class 3:5 to 7.49 acres; class 4:7.50 to 12.49 acres, class 5:12.50 to 24.99 acres; and class 6:25 or more acres. G.S. Bhalla and G.K. Chadha, 'Green Revolution and the Small Peasant: A Study of Income Distribution in Punjab Agriculture', *Economic and Political Weekly*, 15 May 1982, pp. 826–33.
28. Gopal Singh (ed.), *Punjab Today*, New Delhi: Intellectual Publishing House, 1987, p. 12.
29. Anandpur Sahib Resolution (ASR) adopted by the Akali Dal in October 1973. The Dal's open session at Ludhiana in October 1978 adopted twelve resolutions as its main demands. The major demands were greater autonomy, transfer of Chandigarh to Punjab, consideration of territorial disputes, proper distribution of Ravi–Beas waters and an All-India Gurudwara Act. Sucha Singh Gill and K.C. Singhal, 'Genesis of Punjab Problem', in Abida Samiuddin (ed.), *The Punjab Crisis: Challenge and Response*, New Delhi: Mittal Publication, 1985, pp. 46–7.
30. Ministry of Home Affairs, *Annual Report 2002-2003*, New Delhi, p. 27. As per the earlier estimate given by the Home Minister in Parliament, the number of registered Kashmiri migrants families was 29,074, Jammu region, and 19,338, Delhi. Home Minister L.K. Advani in the Lok Sabha on 22 December 1998, quoted by *Hindustan Times*, Delhi, 23 December 1998.
31. Mahendra P. Lama, 'Internal Displacement in India: Causes, Protection and Dilemmas', *Forced Migration Review*, no. 8, August 2000, Refugee Studies Centre, Oxford University.
32. John S. Pistole, Deputy Assistant Director of the Federal Bureau of Investigation's (FBI) counter-terrorism division, revealed this during his testimony to the Senate Governmental Affairs Committee in Washington on 31 July 2003. See *Hindustan Times*, 1 August 2003 and also *SAIR*, vol. 2, no. 3, 4 August 2003.
33. Daniel L. Byman, Peter Chalk, Bruce Hoffman, William Rosenan and David Brannan, *Trends in Outside Support for Insurgent Movement*, RAND's National Security Research Division, 2001.
34. For a review of diaspora politics, see Michael Shafer, *Deadly Paradigms: The Failure of U.S. Counterinsurgency Policy*, Princeton, N.J.: Princeton University Press, 1988, pp. 1–19; and Anthony D. Smith, 'Zionism and Diaspora Nationalism', *Israel Affairs*, vol. 2, no. 2, Winter 1995, pp. 321–46.

35. Benedict Anderson, *Long Distance Nationalism, World Capitalism and the Rise of Identity Politics*, Amsterdam: Centre for Asian Studies, 1992.
36. As quoted by Aziz Haniffa, '"Diasporas" growing clout over home countries', *Times of India*, 3 December 2001, which makes reference to this RAND Corporation study, 'Security Dynamics of Demographic Factors.'
37. 'White Paper on the Punjab Agitation', issued on 10 July 1984, in Virendra Grover (ed.), *The Story of Punjab: Yesterday and Today*, New Delhi: Deep and Deep, 1995, pp. 343–6.
38. Statement given by President Pervez Musharraf of Pakistan, following his meeting with President George Bush in Washington, 13 February 2002; ibid.
39. US Department of State, 'South Asia Overview', in *Patterns of Global Terrorism—2001*, released by the Office of the Coordinator for Counterterrorism, 21 May 2002.
40. *Jang*, 21 June 2003.
41. Daniel L. Byman et al., *Personal Correspondence with Sri Lankan Intelligence and Government officials*, Colombo, May 1999.
42. John Gunaratne, *A Decade of Confrontation: Sri Lanka and India in the 1980s*, Colombo: Stamford Lake, 2000, pp. 74–6. A figure of 300 UK pounds annually per family has also been quoted by Gunaratne for UK diaspora contributions.
43. http://www.satp.org/satporgtp/countries/shrilanka/terroristoutfits/LTTE.HTM
44. *Funding Terror: The Liberation Tigers of Tamil Eelam and their Criminal Activities in Canada and the Western World, Mackenzie Briefing Notes*, Toronto, 1995, p. 4, as quoted by Peter Kloos, 'A Secessionist Movement in an Age of Globalisation: The LTTE in Sri Lanka', seminar paper presented at the international seminar on Ethno-Sectarian Conflicts and Internal Dynamics of Regional Security in South Asia organized by Jawaharlal Nehru University, New Delhi, September 1996.
45. Ibid., p. 5.
46. For information in this paragraph, see Daniel L. Byman, Peter Chalk, Bruce Hoffman, Willian Rosenan, David Brannan, *Personal Correspondence and Interviews with UK, Canadian, Australian and Sri Lankan Intelligence and Diplomatic Officials*, London, Canberra, Ottawa and Bangkok, November–December 2000.
47. Kirthy Abeyesekera, *The Underworld of Sex, Crime and Drugs*, Colombo: Lakehouse, 1991.
48. John Gooneratne, *A Decade of Confrontation: Sri Lanka and India in the 1980s*, Pannipitiya, Sri Lanka: Stamford Lake, 2000.
49. Some of these were boldly and professionally reported by Shekhar Gupta in *India Today*, 31 March 1984, New Delhi, pp. 88–94, and Denzil Peiris in *South*, March 1985, pp. 13–15.

50. For elaborate descriptions and analyses of these issues see J.N. Dixit, *Assignment Colombo*, New Delhi: Konark, 1998, Chapter 5; S.D. Muni, *Pangs of Proximity: India and Sri Lanka's Ethnic Crisis*, New Delhi: Sage, 1993, pp. 165–83; and Gooneratne, *A Decade of Confrontation*, pp. 100–50.
51. J.N. Dixit, *Assignment Colombo*, New Delhi: Konark, 1998.
52. Samiuddin (ed.), *The Punjab Crisis: Challenge and Response*, New Delhi: Mittal Publication, 1985, pp. 302–3.
53. Ibid., p. 335.
54. T.G. Jacob, *Chaos in Nation Formation: Case of Punjab*, New Delhi: Odyssey Press, 1990, p. 11.
55. Ramesh Vinayak, 'Punjab: Uphill Task', *India Today*, New Delhi, 15 February 1996, p. 145.
56. Ibid., pp. 145–47.
57. *Hawala* financial system which originated in the early medieval commerce in the Near and Middle East primarily to coordinate economic interactions among various groups developed against the backdrop of a lack of formal regulatory systems. The Koran's ban on charging interest—the *riba*—is said to have further boosted this system as an alternative to the market-oriented economic structures. *Hawala* can be found as a legal concept as early as 1,327. *Hawala* in its original form served as a simple delegation payment or transfer of a claim. This was to minimize the transaction costs as much as possible. Debt between two parties could be transferred to a third party through mutual consent even when the parties were in different locations. The money is transferred through a code and *Hawala* intermediary and within a very short period of time. There are usually no bookkeeping notes and the financial intermediary does not depend on a complicated infrastructure. This can operate well behind the façade of legal businesses. The *Hawala* financial institutions of today are, however, dramatically different from the traditional ones. Matthias Schramm and Markus Taube, 'The Institutional Foundations of Al Qaida's Global Financing System'.
58. Government of India, Ministry of Home Affairs, *Annual Report 2002–2003*, pp. 15-16.
59. The expulsion of Pakistan's Charge d'Affaires Jalil Abbas Jilani in February 2003 by the Government of India after the Delhi Police formally filed documents charging him with passing on Rs. 370,000 to Anjum Zamruda Habib, a key member of the far-right women's organization, the Khawateen Markaz, was widely reported. The money, police investigators say, was to be passed on to Abdul Gani Bhat, the head of the principal anti-India political coalition in Kashmir, the All-Parties Hurriyat Conference (APHC). The APHC's representative in New Delhi, Sabir Ahmad Dar, was also arrested along with Habib.
60. In 1998, Jammu & Kashmir Police discovered that the Pakistan embassy

in Saudi Arabia had been passing money to the Hizb-ul-Mujahidin through Jamaat-e-Islami affiliated charities like the Kashmir Medicare Trust and the Muslim Welfare Society. Mohammad Nazir, an ethnic Kashmiri employed in the Pakistan embassy in Jeddah, moved the funds through a Dubai-based businessman of Kashmiri origin, Mohammad Shafi Mir. The Hizb also regularly received funds gathered in the United States and United Kingdom by activists like Ayub Thakur and Ghulam Nabi Fai. See Praveen Swami, 'APHC: The Nexus with Terror', *South Asia Intelligence Review*, Institute for Conflict Management, vol. 1, no. 31, 17 February 2003, New Delhi. It is stated that over 90 per cent of the funding is from other countries and Islamic organizations like the World Association of Muslim Youth, Rabit-e-Islami, World Kashmir Freedom Movement, Kashmir American Council, Kashmir Study Group and Friends of Kashmir, and ISI in Nepal. Bhabani Dikshit, 'Free flow of funds sustains terrorism', *The Daily Excelsior*, 17 April 2002, http: // www.hvk.org /articles /0402 /133.html, URL: http:// www.dailyexcelsior.com / 02apr17 /edit.htm#3.

61. The APHC itself files no tax returns. It runs offices in New Delhi and Srinagar, funds the domestic and international travel of its leaders, and pays salaries to some 40 employees—a not inconsiderable expense. Organizations like the Jamaat-e-Islami, the Lashkar-e-Toiba (LeT) and Jaish-e-Mohammad (JeM) raise substantial public funds in Pakistan. See Swami, 'APHC: The Nexus with Terror'; see also *Frontline*, Madras, 1997.
62. http://www.satp.org.
63. Official documents made available to parliament revealed that the bank accounts of many individuals and organizations stand frozen, including that of Osama bin Laden, Al-Rashid Trust (ART), Rabita Trust (RT), Harkat-ul-Mujahidin (HuM) and Jaish-e-Mohammed (JeM). *Jang*, Islamabad, 21 June 2003.
64. *www.dailystarnews.com*, Dhaka, 29 June 2003. This is a new route different from the traditional Cambodia-Thailand-Andaman Sea-Cox's Bazaar circuit that has long been in operation. The pressure to move away from the traditional routes has been increasing and the new river route through the Jamuna to the Brahamputra is used by ULFA and ATTF and also the vulnerable 22-km land stretch of the Siliguri corridor in north Bengal.
65. *The Hindu*, New Delhi, 26 April 2004. Previously, in January 2004, Bangladesh Rifles (BDR) seized 32 anti-tank mines, 6 rocket-launchers, 10 rocket-launcher cell chargers and equipment for 14 rocket-launcher cells, after an encounter with some terrorists (with suspected links to the Arakanese rebels in Myanmar) at Lemuchhari in the Bandarban district of Chittagong Hill Tracts (CHT), on 1 January 2004. *The Daily Star*, 2 January 2004.

66. Four AK-47 assault rifles, 2 revolvers, 20 hand grenades, 4 time bombs, a large number of AK-47 bullets and explosives were seized after an encounter with a criminal gang at Kuril Badda on 30 November 2003, *Daily Star*, 1 December 2003.
67. The suspected accounts are of Mohammad bin Mohammad Abdelhedi, Kamal Darraji, Mohammad El Mahfoudi, Imed bin Bechir Jamali, Habib bin Ahmad Louviri and Chabanne bin Mohamed Trabelsi. Of them, Mahfoudi is Moroccan while the others are reportedly Tunisian, *New Age Bangladesh*, Dhaka, 9 July 2004.
68. 'Trekker Tax', *Kantipur*, 16 May 2004, reproduced in *Nepali Times,* Kathmandu, 21–7 May 2004.
69. Deepak Thapa, 'Day of the Maoist', *Himal South Asia*, Kathmandu, vol. 14, no. 5, May 2001.
70. Press release given by chairman of the Communist Party of Nepal (Maoist) and leader of the insurgency, Pushpa Kamal Dahal aka Prachanda, 5 October 2003.
71. In December 2003, the MCC demanded Rs. 70 million from the management of the Steel Authority of India Ltd. (SAIL)-owned Meghahatuburu mine in Jharkhand's West Singhbhum district. They also stormed the Indian Aluminium Company facilities at Bagdu in Lohardaga district destroyed property and took away Rs. 104,000 in cash. Nihar Nayak, 'Left Wing Extremism: Synchronized Onslaught', *South Asia Intelligence Review*, vol. 2, no. 28, 26 January 2004.
72. Ibid.
73. P.V. Ramana, 'Andhra Pradesh: A Blow to the Bastion, but Naxalites Still a Force', *South Asia Intelligence Review*, Institute for Conflict Management, vol. 1, no. 37, 31 March 2003, New Delhi.
74. Tata Tea is one the biggest stakeholders in Assam's tea industry. Earlier, in 1990, HLL had to close down its operations in the state as it did not succumb to pressures. It also publicly decried such demands of terrorist groups and indicted the state and the Union Government for their inaction. Bibhu Prasad Routray, 'Assam: Resisting Extortion—HLL Leads the Way', *SAIR*, vol. 2, no. 13, 13 October 2003.
75. Ibid.
76. Testimony on Counterterrorism and South Asia by Ambassador Michael A. Sheehan, Coordinator for Counterterrorism U.S. Department of State, before the House International Relations Committee on 12 July 2000.
77. *Daily Times*, Karachi, 19 February 2003, http://www.alternatives.ca/article393.html
78. Quoted by Sashinungla, 'Nagaland: The Dynamics of Extortion', *South Asia Intelligence Review*, vol. 2, no. 22, New Delhi, 15 December 2003.
79. Estimation by Jaideep Saikia as quoted by Bobby Sarangthem, *United Liberation Front of Assam (ULFA)*, University of Pune, 2003.

80. Mahendra P. Lama, 'Designing Economic Confidence Building Measures: Roie of India in South Asia', in *India's Pivotal Role in South Asia,* New Delhi: CASAC, September 2000. For example, how some of the best known multinationals located in Pakistan with stakes in the Kenyan tea industry have consistently used the Kashmir card to block tea import from India is conclusively discussed in the author's monograph on *Regional Economic Cooperation in South Asia: A Commodity Approach,* Society for Peace, Security and Development Studies, Department of Defence and Strategic Studies, University of Allahabad, 1997. See also article on 'Integrating the Tea Sector in South Asia: New Opportunities in the Global Market', *South Asian Survey,* Delhi, January–June 2001.
81. Amy Waldman, 'Border Tension a Growth Industry for Kashmir', *New York Times*, 18 October 2002, http: // www. arches.uga.edu /~sga/ readings / kashmir_ growth_ industry.htm
82. Peter Enderwick, 'Terrorism and the International Business Environment', Academy of International Management, *AIB-Insights,* Special Issue, 2001.
83. The European Union provisionally agreed in December 2001 that 'terrorist offences' constitute those 'intentional' acts that may 'seriously damage a country or an international organisation' when committed with the aim of 'seriously intimidating a population . . . unduly compelling a government or an international organization to perform or abstain from performing any act, or seriously destabilizing or destroying the fundamental, political, constitutional, economic or social structures of a country or an international organisation.'

    On the other hand, under the Indian Prevention of Terrorism Act (POTA), a terrorist act is defined as an act committed by a person or persons with the intention of threatening the unity, integrity, security or sovereignty of India or striking terror that results in death or injuries (or likelihood thereof), destruction or damage to property, disruption of essential supplies or services, damage or destruction of equipment to be used for the defence of India or for other purposes of government, or detention of any person with the intention of compelling the Government of India to abstain from or do any act. A terrorist act also includes the raising of funds intended for the purpose of terrorism. Key-Note Address by K.C. Pant, Deputy Chairman, Planning Commission on 'Combating Terrorism' at the International Plenary Conference to mark the Golden Jubilee of the Parliament of India on 22 January 2003 at Central Hall, Parliament House, New Delhi, as available on the website: http://planningcommission.nic.in/aboutus/speech/dch218.pdf.

    There are attempts to put the terrorism debate in what is called new issues impacting security and expressed in the term 'Grey Area

Phenomena' (GAP), that covers a broad spectrum of activities including terrorism, intra-state conflict, drug trafficking, money laundering, religious extremism, environmental degradation, ethnic 'cleansing', and transnational crime. For detailed discussions of the GAP see Max G. Manwaring, *Grey Area Phenomena: Confronting the New World Disorder*, Boulder, Colo: Westview Press, 1993. See also J.F. Holden-Rhodes and Peter Luphsa, 'Horseman of the Apocalypse: Grey Area Phenomena and the New World Order', in *Global Dimensions of High Intensity Crime and Low Intensity Conflict*, ed. Graham H. Turbiville, University of Illinois at Chicago and Office of International Criminal Justice, 1995; and Peter Chalk, 'Grey-Area Phenomena in Southeast Asia: Piracy, Drug Trafficking and Political Terrorism', *Canberra Papers on Strategy and Defense*, no. 123, Canberra: Australian National University Strategic and Defense Studies Centre, 1997.

84. Besides the physical inconvenience and loss of time, the cost of such screenings has been enormous. A study estimated the costs of mandatory screening in the US at $194.2 million for the period 1973–6, W.M. Landes, 'An Economic Study of US Aircraft Hijacking, 1961-1971', *Journal of Law and Economics*, 1978, no. 21, pp. 1–31; Another study estimated the cost of $ 3.24 million to $ 9.25 million to deter a single hijacking, Grant Wardlaw, *Political Terrorism: Theory, Tactics, and Counter-Measures*, New York: Cambridge University Press, 1989.
85. India's External Affairs Minister Natwar Singh stated this after the 25th Council of Ministers Meeting of the South Asian Association for Regional Cooperation (SAARC) in Islamabad on Tuesday, 20 July 2004, as reported by AFP.
86. Dipankar Banerjee and Robert Muggah, *Small Arms and Human Insecurity*, Colombo: Regional Centre for Strategic Studies, 2002.
87. Farzana Nosab, 'Global Economic Implications of 9/11 Attacks', *Strategic Studies,* vol. 22, no. 3, Autumn 2002, Islamabad, Institute of Strategic Studies: p. 207.
88. Besides Egypt, Poland and Yugoslavia, Pakistan was the fourth non-HIPC country to receive this treatment which takes into account the entire outstanding stock (principal and accumulated arrears) and re-profiles it to over an extended period of time. Government of Pakistan, *Economic Survey 2002–2003*, Ministry of Finance, Islamabad, p. 152.
89. Ibid., p.147.
90. Central Bank of Sri Lanka, *Annual Report 2003*, Colombo, see also Jehan Perera, 'Peace Process: A Little Arm-twisting', *SAIR,* vol. 1, no. 41, 28 April 2004. In total package worked out by the donors at the Tokyo Conference in June 2003 was to the tune of $4.5 billion. One-third of this amount was meant for rehabilitation and re-construction in the Tamil areas of north and east provided the peace process could be advanced within the framework laid down by the donors.–Editor).

91. Jasjit Singh, 'High price of "low cost" terror', http: // meaindia. nic.in /opinion / 2002 / 06 / 17o03.htm
92. Saman Kelegama, 'Economic Cost of Conflict in Sri Lanka', in R. Robert (ed.), *Creating Peace in Sri Lanka: Civil War and Reconciliation*, Washington DC: Brookings Institution Press, 1999.
93. N. Arunatilake, S. Jayasuriya, and S. Kelegama, 'The Economic Cost of the War in Sri Lanka', *World Development*, vol. 29, no. 9, 2001.
94. World Bank, *Sri Lanka-Recapturing Missed Opportunities*, Washington DC: SASPR, 2000.
95. These issues have been discussed in greater detail in a report entitled 'India-Sri Lanka Land Bridge Project: Assessment of Economic and Social Impact', prepared by a India–Sri Lanka Joint Research Team led by Mahendra P. Lama in 2003.
96. *Asia-Pacific Economic Update 2002*, vol. 1, United States Pacific Command, http://www.pacom.mil/publications.
97. World Bank, *Nepal Country Assistance Strategy, 2004-2007*, Washington, 2003. Also see, Yubaraj Ghimire, 'Uncertain Truce', *SAIR*, vol. 1, no. 29, 3 February 2003; Ajai Sahni, 'Nepal: How not to Fight an Insurgency', *SAIR*, vol. 2, no. 21, 8 December 2003; Lok Raj Baral, 'Insurgency, Development and Destruction', *SAIR*, vol. 2, no. 28, 26 January 2004, and Keshab Poudel, 'Maoists Overrun the Hinterland', *SAIR*, vol. 2, no. 47, 7 June 2004.
98. Nepal Rashtra Bank, *Economic Report*, Kathmandu, various issues; Ministry of Finance, *Economic Survey*, Kathmandu, various issues.
99. This was stated by state Chief Minister Chandrababu Naidu while speaking in Warangal district on 19 November 2002. The PWG, with a significant presence in many of the 23 districts of Andhra Pradesh, is supposed to have set up 'special guerrilla zones' in north Telengana, south Telengana, Nallama and the north coastal regions. Sanjay K. Jha, 'The Maoist Maze', and 'The Compact Revolutionary Zone', *South Asia Intelligence Review*, Institute for Conflict Management, vol. 1, nos. 1 and 34, 10 March 2003.
100. Sanjay Baru, 'War, Terrorism and Economic Uncertainty', *Financial Express*, 14 February 2003.
101. Kanchan Lakshman, 'Pakistan: Terror and the Economy', *SAIR*, vol. 2, no. 48, 14 June 2004.
102. Saman Kelegama, 'Sri Lankan Economy of War and Peace', *Economic and Political Weekly*, 23–9 November, vol. 37, 2002, pp. 4678–85; D. Dunham, and S. Kelegama, 'Does Leadership Matter in the Economic Reform Process? Liberalisation and Governance in Sri Lanka, 1989–93', *World Development*, vol. 25, no. 2, 1997.
103. K.M. de Silva, *Sri Lanka Country Paper*, International Conference on Conflict & Conflict resolution in South Asia, International Centre for Ethnic Studies, Kandy, July 1997.

104. Ayesha Siddiqa, 'There can be no accountability without transparency', *The Friday Times*, September 2003.
105. These include expenditure incurred by the state governments on transportation, new vehicles/bullet-proofing of new/existing vehicles, purchase of automatic/semi-automatic weapons along with ammunition, bullet-proof jackets and other protective gear, and procurement of the latest communication equipment both mobile and static, bomb detectors, explosive detectors, computers, etc. It also includes expenditure on capital works, on jails and detention centres attached to police stations, special training provided to state police and prison administration personnel for counter-insurgency purposes, raising India Reserve Battalions, provisions for CPMFs/army deployment, ex-gratia grant and gratuitous relief to the victims of extremist violence, and transporting arrested militants to jails outside the state or those arrested from outside the state to the state by special flights, etc.
106. Prime Minister Sher Bahadur Deuba presented this budget in 2002 a few months before his government was dismissed by the King for the first time in October 2002.
107. Lok Raj Baral, 'Insurgency, Development and Destruction', *SAIR*, vol. 2, no. 28, 26 January 2004.
108. Central Bank of Sri Lanka, *Annual Reports*, various issues, Colombo.
109. Ibid.
110. The tourism figures in Sri Lanka reported in this study, unless otherwise stated, are from the Sri Lanka Tourist Board (2002), *Annual Statistical Report of Sri Lanka Tourism 2002*, Colombo.
111. D.A.C. Silva, 'Sustainable Tourism Development in Sri Lanka', thesis, Vrije University, Amsterdam, 2002, p. 75.
112. More than 61 people were killed in May 2004 alone in Karachi, *Dawn*, Islamabad, 9 June 2004.
113. Mahendra P. Lama, 'The Maoist Movement in Nepal: The Economic Implications', in Sridhar Khatri and Gert W. Kueck (eds.), *Terrorism in South Asia: Impact on Development and Democratic Process*, New Delhi: Shipra, 2003.
114. This press statement was signed by the heads of GTZ, SDC, CIDA, DFID, SNV, JICA, and Ambassadors of the European Union, Norway, Denmark and Finland. *The Himalayan Times*, Katmandu, 10 May 2004.

13. Responding to Terrorism: An Overview

S.D. Muni

In the case studies and comparative perspectives in this volume, various aspects of strategies pursued in South Asia in responding to and coping with terrorism have been discussed. We should attempt to see the broader picture that emerges from this discussion. There have been sharp differences among South Asian countries about understanding terrorism as also in dealing with it. And yet there is a considerably larger common ground in the strategies followed by the South Asian countries in responding to their individual as well as collective challenges of terrorism. Let us identify and evaluate some of these common features.

TERRORISM

Whichever way one looks at it, terrorism is the philosophy and thought behind the use of terror as an instrument, a means in the pursuance of political goals generally expressed through conflicts and violence. Not all violence may be treated as terror, but any violence or even fear inflicted on unarmed, innocent people, is terrorism. Elimination of terrorism, therefore, is essentially the elimination of violence and conflicts, and this cannot be done without addressing the causes, roots, and sources from where such conflicts originate and arise. Almost all the contributors in this study agree that these conflicts are rooted in political marginalization, socio-economic deprivation and discrimination, caste, religion, regional and cultural suppression, neglect, and so on. The key to understanding these conflicts is the transition from such neglect, deprivation, and discrimination to the precipitation of violent conflicts. Such transition is neither unilinear nor uniform in different situations. In fact every conflict has its own specificities and unique characteristics.

These specificities and characteristics are reflected in organization of the insurgencies, leadership, support bases, sources of arms, funding, ideological inspiration, political and diplomatic endorsement, social and political context in which the conflict emerges and evolves, the nature of regimes that confront the insurgencies, and so on. In terms of substantive issues that arise from the patterns of deprivation and discrimination which constitute the root causes of conflicts, two categories stand out distinctly. One encompasses conflicts that are systemic, aiming at the transformation of the socio-political order. They range from the Maoists insurgency in Nepal to the Naxalites in India and also the JVP revolt in Sri Lanka. The last one also had a strong ethnic orientation. The other category may broadly be described as that of ethnic and religious origins where a common thread may be the separatist character of the revolt. The demand of a separate state is voiced in many of these conflicts.

The characteristics of conflicts in South Asia and elsewhere have been immensely influenced, even shaped, by the spread of globalization. This influence of globalization has been both positive and negative. Negatively, the improved systems of information and communication, easy access to arms and training resources, institutionalized overt as well as covert means of financial transactions, and globally spread diaspora have greatly helped in the intensification and persistence of conflicts. On the positive side, the states confronting terrorism have also been facilitated by globalization in harnessing international support. The international community has become increasingly willing and capable of intervening in conflicts, fighting terrorism, and resolving conflicts. Not many conflicts have been resolved or terrorism rooted out through the intervention of the international community, but the growing significance of this development must be taken note of. In particular, after the 9/11 developments, even international organizations, including the UN, have come forward to strengthen collective efforts for fighting terrorism. It may not be out of place here to underline that South Asia experiences both 'global terrorism' as well as regional and local terrorism. The scene of global terrorism is evident along the

Pakistan–Afghanistan border. Pakistan's role first in becoming a hub of 'global terrorism' and now in countering this terrorism is being increasingly acknowledged. From India's perspective, terrorism in Kashmir is clearly and closely linked to the forces of 'global terrorism', though in Pakistan and some of the western and other countries, there may be a tendency to view the Kashmir situation as a result of the bilateral dispute between India and Pakistan, with historical roots in the partition and the manner of transfer of power to India and Pakistan from the British colonial empire.

A notable common thread in South Asian terrorism that emerges out of the case studies in this volume, is the nexus of politics and terrorism. In all the cases studied, politicians in India, Pakistan, Nepal, Sri Lanka, and Bangladesh are shown to have links with terrorists. These links are established, played upon, and exploited in the course of the struggle for power by the politicians. The use of terrorism in the local political power struggles range from mobilization of electoral support to physical elimination of opponents. The nexus of politics and crime in South Asia also feeds into the rise and persistence of terrorism. Three stark examples of the politics-terrorism nexus are; (i) royal patronage of the Maoists in Nepal during the first five years of the insurgency, i.e. during 1996–2001, to discredit political parties and democratic governance; (ii) President Premadasa's collaboration with the LTTE during 1989–90 in Sri Lanka to drive the Indian Peace Keeping Force out; and (iii) the Pakistani state's (especially its Inter Services Intelligence–the ISI) full patronage and protection to jehadi forces operating in Afghanistan until 11 September 2001, and Jammu & Kashmir till date. This nexus, however, is more insidious and widespread in South Asia, leaving no country unaffected and is clearly discernible at all levels of political operations.

There are analysts and policy makers in South Asia who do not give much weight to the 'root-causes' aspect when it comes to dealing with terrorism. They emphasize more on the visible and operational aspects of terrorism and argue that if the structure, leadership, resources, and capabilities of the terrorist groups are destroyed by the use of force, terrorism will be crippled down, even if the root causes of deprivation and discrimination are not addressed. They also argue that addressing the root causes is a long-term and often uncertain remedy. If terror is not confronted forcefully and urgently, it will spread, get entrenched and become powerful. Getting to 'root-causes' amounts to not countering and combating terrorism. There may be a point in these arguments, and if one looks at the resolution of the Punjab insurgency in India, it appears persuasive. But then, if force is the real answer to terrorism and conflicts, why has it not succeeded elsewhere in so many other cases? We will come to this issue again later. It is however conceded even by the opponents of the 'root-causes' approach that use of force alone in combating terrorism will not serve the purpose. That political processes must be initiated and pursued simultaneously with the use of force. For instance, in the case of Punjab in India, the holding of elections played a critical role in coping with the insurgency. The conclusion of other political deals like the Rajiv–Longowal Agreement also created helpful conditions. Destroying the structure of terrorism—its capabilities, leadership, organization, credibility, etc.—may give respite from violence and restore peace and order for a while, but for any enduring resolution of terrorism-generating conflicts, the root causes have to be addressed, grievances and alienation have to be mainstreamed and redressed.

Responses: Use of Force

In responding to the challenge of terrorism, the South Asian states have shown a strong inclination towards the use of force; though this use of force is generally mingled with the feeble use of other strategies as political and constitutional accommodation and the developmental approach. Dependence on the use of force comes to states naturally and out of urgency because the rise of terrorism loudly announces the precipitation of a security crisis. The first and immediate response when such a crisis has been perceived, has to be the use of force because all other responses need patience, planning, and a longer gestation time. Terrorism challenges the credibility and legitimacy of the state and as such it cannot be seen to be slow in its response. The use of force is also a reflex action of what the state knows best and finds convenient to resort to. In all the terrorism-generating conflicts in South Asia, use of force has been, continues to be, and perhaps will remain a dominant form of response. But this has not yielded the desired results except in very very few cases, Punjab in India, for instance. In a way, the success story of combating terrorism in Punjab is not entirely due to the use of force, though it is generally projected as such. Even in the case of Punjab, political action, particularly holding elections and an agreement between the central government and the local Punjabi leadership, also played a very important role in ending the insurgency.

What the Punjab case, however, brings out clearly is that use of force starts becoming effective only when it is employed as a well-planned and carefully calibrated strategy. This became possible in the Punjab only after 1987; until then the use of force was more in the nature of a 'crude over-reaction' (e.g. Operation Blue Star). Ruthless and unplanned use of force may in fact strengthen terrorist forces, reinforce insurgencies, and erode the credibility of the state. Of this there are several examples, i.e. in Jammu & Kashmir, India's north-east, Maoist spread in Nepal after the Romeo (1995) and Kilo Sierra (1998) operations, and Sri Lanka after the pogrom of July 1983 and 'Operation Liberation' (April–May 1987) against the Tamils.

In the nature of the use of force, the instruments are also of critical significance. When the state starts the use of force as a conscious strategy, the police often become the first casualty, which is unfortunate because the police are the best source of local intelligence. Army and paramilitary forces are mostly unaware of local conditions. Following the induction of paramilitary and armed forces, the South Asian states have often felt the need to create integrated commands for operational efficiency. Their induction also escalates the levels of violence and drives the terrorist forces to seek better weapons and uglier means of violence. There are examples of the use of air and sea power in South Asia in combating terrorism. In Sri Lanka, the induction of air power by the IPKF in Jaffna University under 'Operation Pawan' during October–November 1987 proved disastrous for the IPKF due to poor intelligence. Prior and subsequent to this, the use of air power in Sri Lanka by the Sri Lankan forces as well as the IPKF inflicted heavy casualties even on innocent people. Similarly, the induction of helicopter gunships in Nepal in fighting the Maoists has also inflicted heavy casualties on innocent people. In Pakistan, the coordinated operations of the US and Pakistani forces along the Pakistan–Afghanistan frontier areas after 9/11 have witnessed the use of most sophisticated and heavy weaponry in anti-terrorist operations at the cost of civilian casualties. The problem of the induction of air power and heavy weaponry is that, being fired from a distance, it cannot distinguish between a terrorist and an innocent person.

The important factor that is often missed is the adequacy and appropriateness of the force structure to be used in countering terrorism. The nature of the insurgency, the terrain, motivation, clearly defined objectives and targets, need for coordination, etc., are the critical inputs that should be carefully assessed in planning the use of force. But such efforts are made rarely if at all. In the absence of such efforts, use of force has either become counter-productive or it has failed to deliver the desired results, as is evident in most of the cases. The ultimate goal of the use of force cannot be the elimination of terrorism, but of crippling the capabilities of the terrorists so as to force them to come to the negotiating table. This makes it necessary that the use of force be carefully calibrated with the overall political objective of bringing the terrorists and insurgents into the mainstream of political and social life.

The use of force also needs politico-legal provisions in the form of special acts and powers for the armed forces to be put in place. In all the South Asian countries such special provisions have been enacted (see Data Paper by P.V. Ramana). Some of these provisions have raised strong protests because they have been abused, like the Armed Forces Special Powers Act in India's north-east (Manipur agitation during 2004). The legislative provisions for combating terrorism curb the freedoms of ordinary citizens and make the armed forces less accountable. The Royal Nepal Army has often insisted on the imposition of emergency before launching its anti-Maoists operations. The RNA spokesman Brig. Gen. Deepak Gurung, appreciating King Gyanendra's action of taking over power on 1 February 2005 and the imposition of emergency said:

Now we can solely go after the Maoists in a single minded manner without having to worry what's going to happen on the streets, peoples' agitation. We can solely direct our resources and energy towards them. Definitely, we can deal with the Maoists in a decisive manner. Our main aim will be to force them to come to talks.

The consequences of unplanned or improperly planned use of force have been many and diverse in South Asia. The worst of these has been the huge backlash of innocent deaths and human rights violations, for which the states are answerable, though there may be no accountability for the terrorists. However, since the terrorists are also seeking international recognition and support, they are also brought under scrutiny and are held accountable by international and national human rights organizations and movements. Innocent people are killed, women raped, and children orphaned by the indiscriminate use of force. A whole set of implications for the gender in particular and society in general are created. The international community, both of state and non-state actors, comes into play and pressures are generated on the states. Most of the South Asian states have set up national human rights commissions, generally under international pressure. Nepal has also been forced, in April 2005, to allow monitoring by the UN Human Rights Commission of its social situation. These violations have brutalized societies, created trauma and psycho-sociological distortions, and pushed social harmony backwards by years and decades.

The use of force as a terrorism-combating strategy has also had serious economic effects. The defence burden of countries facing the menace of terrorism has grown, and this has disturbed the smaller countries more than the bigger ones like India. In Nepal and Sri Lanka, the increased defence burden has been at the cost of the economic and social sectors, as resources had to be diverted. Assistance comes to meet the demands of these sectors but seldom is such assistance adequate. Pakistan presents us with a unique experience in this respect because fighting terrorism in collaboration with the US has helped it to secure economic support, manage its debt burden, raise resources for selected social development activities like education and health, and even attract investments. In Nepal and Sri Lanka, the intensification of their respective conflicts has hampered economic activities like trade and commerce, and production and agriculture. It has also adversely affected tourist inflows which are so critical for economic activity. Internal war zones have also been affected adversely, in the flow of food and agriculture products from production centres to the markets. The long-term costs are often not calculated properly, because such costs also include destruction of economic infrastructures like roads, power projects, schools, administrative buildings, etc., by the terrorists. The costs of rehabilitation and reconstruction are also staggering in the areas where damage to the economic infrastructure and human settlements has been extensive.

In the area of political systems, the military approach has also tended to strengthen and legitimize autocratic systems and authoritarian power structures. In Sri Lanka, during the early 1980s, the Tamil insurgency facilitated constitutional changes which concentrated power in the hands of the president. For the past ten years it has been realized that the presidential system with an all-powerful president has been helpful neither in finding a solution to the Tamil problem nor in the restoration of stability and order in Sri Lanka. In the case of Pakistan and Nepal, it is obvious that undemocratic military rule and autocratic monarchy respectively, have succeeded in consolidating their hold on their respective societies. The king of Nepal even dared to concentrate more powers in his hands in the name of combating Maoist terrorism. In Pakistan, General Musharraf's role in combating the Taliban and Al Qaida has helped him in diffusing the pressure for a fully democratic and civilian role in the immediate context. The king of Nepal may be deriving his due lessons from Pakistan's experience.

POLITICAL AND CONSTITUTIONAL ACCOMMODATION

It was mentioned earlier that, together with the 'use of force', the South Asian states have also responded to terrorism-generating conflicts through offers of political and constitutional accommodation, but the latter strategy has not been dominant as a whole at the regional level. The two South Asian countries which have taken recourse to political and constitutional accommodation towards the insurgencies and terrorism are India and Sri Lanka. An obvious reason behind this could be that both have always been democratic countries and therefore more susceptible to popular accountability. There is also a stronger tradition to follow the political and constitutional road in conflict resolution in these countries since their respective freedom struggles. There is comparatively greater sensitivity to the rule of law, at least in public perception, in these countries than in their South Asian neighbours.

India's strategy of political and constitutional accommodation facilitated conflict resolution in at least three insurgency situations. One was the Tamil identity crisis during the early 1960s which was diffused by evolving the three-language formula, and the other two were the Punjab and Mizo insurgencies where the offer of power-sharing at the provincial level and the use of constitutional resilience played a positive role in resolving the conflicts. In the Punjab, the Akali Dal came to power and in Mizoram, the erstwhile rebel leader Laldenga formed the government. In both cases the Congress party, which was ruling at the centre, had to quit power at the provincial levels. The political approach was also evident in Jammu & Kashmir when, in the September 2002 elections, the defeat of the central government's ally, the National Conference was accepted as a positive development towards turning the corner in the terrorism-affected state. The constitutional question of autonomy is still very critical in Kashmir and some real accommodation will have to be made of the Kashmiri aspirations in this regard if the situation there has to be stabilized. Constitutional and political issues, including those of extended territorial boundaries for Nagaland, are also on the table in the central government's negotiations with the Naga group, led by Issac Muivah.

Unlike India, in Sri Lanka an additional factor behind a sustained political approach has been the Sri Lankan state's incapacity to take the LTTE on militarily. The LTTE, at least after 1987, seems to have been able to create a myth of its military invincibility. Before 1987, India had made it very clear that it would not allow a military solution to the Tamil problem. Recall the intervention in May 1987 with MIG fighter planes and loaves of bread (bread bombs). Therefore, there were compulsions rather than voluntary choice in Sri Lanka's case to seek a political and constitutional way out of the Tamil insurgency. Due to these compulsions, the Sri Lankan government has lacked sincerity in engaging itself seriously on political and constitutional issues. This was evident in the lack of proper implementation of the District Development Council (DDC) idea during 1983–4; and the 19th Amendment after 1987. The Indo-Sri Lanka Agreement of July 1987 also has a detailed provision for political and constitutional accommodation of the Tamils' genuine demands, which remains unimplemented till date. The Sri Lankan government's lack of sincerity in accommodating the Tamil aspirations is a consequence of internal politics both within the Sinhala mainstream political parties and in the Tamil groups. Sinhala competitive politics has not allowed the ruling party, particularly the SLFP, to show accommodation towards the Tamils. Earlier, the UNP had blocked President Kumaratunga's efforts in this direction; now even an ally of the SLFP, the JVP is doing so to reflect its ethnic prejudices. The LTTE has also been equally guilty in not letting the political and constitutional process advance by refusing to get engaged in such a process. The LTTE wants to keep its option of a separate state and sole representation of the Tamil community intact, and for this reason it is not enthusiastic about any final political and constitutional settlement within the framework of a United Sri Lanka. It is even refusing to start serious negotiations on political and constitutional issues.

A preference for political and constitutional accommodation in resolving the terrorism-generating conflicts is also voiced by other countries. In Bangladesh, a political way out was found for the Chakma insurgency in the Chittagong Hill Tracts (CHT) area. This was underpinned by arrangements to assure the protection of the cultural identity to the Chakmas. In Pakistan, the political approach is not compatible with the framework of the 'global war on terrorism', pursued in collaboration with the US. No serious initiative has been taken to approach the conflicts with Muhajirs, the sectarian strife between the Shias and Sunnis, or even in Baluchistan. In view of the state's alliance with the religious extremists and terrorists, the only political approach on the part of the state could be to distance itself from them, rather than accommodate them. Pakistan has distanced itself from the Taliban and Al Qaida, the 'global terrorists', but it is finding it hard to do the same with its own local, home-grown terrorists. In Nepal, the demand for a new constitution to be framed by an elected constituent assembly is central to the resolution of the Maoist insurgency. But the king cannot accept it because any new constitution would erode the status of the monarchy in Nepal. The Maoists' insurgency is linked to the demand for the restructuring of the Nepali state, making its present incumbents averse to permitting any drastic alteration of the existing power balance among the communities and social groups. The king may be open to some amendments in the prevailing constitution but not more than that.

The External Dimension

There is an unavoidable external dimension to the challenge of terrorism in South Asia, primarily due to the integrated nature of the region—unnatural borders, socio-economic contiguities and the cultural identities across these borders—and also because of globalization which has played a significant role in the spread of terrorism. No internal conflict is truly internal. There is now an international resolve to fight the forces of terrorism, particularly after 9/11, as reflected in a number of UN Resolutions like 1373 of September 2001, and 1430, 1438, 1440 and 1450 of October–December 2002.

In meeting the challenge of terrorism in South Asia, the external dimension impinges at three levels: bilateral, regional and international. The importance of bilateral cooperation in responding to terrorism is highlighted by the cross-border nature of terrorism and its spillover, dictated by the geo-strategic structure of the region and the conscious strategic use of conflicts and insurgencies in one country by a neighbouring country. Almost all the South Asian countries have been victims as well as culprits of cross-border terrorism in relation to their neighbours at one stage or another. However, there is no parallel to the consistency and dedication with which Pakistan has identified itself with insurgency and terrorism against India in Jammu & Kashmir primarily, but also in the north-east and the Punjab.

The most striking example of bilateral cooperation in combating terrorism has been presented by Bhutan which carried out military operations against Indian insurgent groups' with sanctuaries in Bhutan. These operations took place in December 2003. There have been other examples in this category of bilateral cooperation, like Myanmar's 'Golden Bird' operations in 1995 which were coordinated with India to flush out Naga insurgents who were operating along the Indo–Myanmar borders. India also extended this cooperation to Sri Lanka when it sent the IPKF to fight the LTTE and helped the Sri Lankan government in the implementating the 1987 Agreement on the resolution of the Tamil issue. There are people in India who think aloud that such cooperation should be extended to Nepal to deal with the Maoist insurgency. India had extended all possible help to Nepal in the early 1950s to contain the internal rebellion led by K.I. Singh. There are no prospects of bilateral cooperation between India and Bangladesh to contain the activities of insurgents from India's north-east (Bodos, ULFA, and the Kamatapur Liberation Organization) who are using Bangladesh's territory for sanctuary and support. The case of Bangladesh is something like that of Pakistan in supporting Indian insurgents and terrorists.

These contrasting cases underline the fact that for close bilateral cooperation in dealing with terrorism militarily, one of two preconditions is essential: the level of political and strategic understanding between the cooperating countries should be of a very high order; and or, the neighbouring country cooperating with the terrorism-afflicted country should see such cooperation as in its own interest. Let us illustrate this point with the examples of Bhutan–India and India–Sri Lanka cooperation in combating terrorism. A close treaty-bound political and strategic understanding has existed between India and Bhutan for a long time. However, Bhutan had its own constraints of sovereignty and force capability which prevented it from undertaking terrorism–combating operations for nearly six to seven years. It came forward to extend the required cooperation only when it realized that the Indian insurgents were not going to be persuaded by anything less than the use of force to vacate Bhutan. And further, the continuation of such sanctuaries in Bhutanese territory was becoming a serious threat to Bhutan's own security interests. Similarly, in Sri Lanka's case, India committed itself to the July 1987 Agreement, including sending the IPKF to disarm the LTTE to ensure that there was no separate Tamil state in Sri Lanka and that the Sri Lankan government did not invite the strategic presence of extra-regional powers in the Island. In the absence of these preconditions, it may be unrealistic to expect that any meaningful bilateral cooperation to combat terrorism could have been ensured.

Since close political and strategic understanding does not exist amongst all the South Asian countries, it may be unrealistic to expect any meaningful cooperation at the regional level in combating terrorism. The SAARC Convention on Suppression of Terrorism was first concluded in 1987. But the lack of political will among the member countries did not allow this convention even to be ratified by all the members. The convention was taken up for reinforcement at the Kathmandu SAARC Summit in 2002. However, as long as a lack of political will persists and as long as member countries continue to use terrorism and internal conflicts in neighbouring countries to further their own security and strategic interests, it may not be possible to have even a normal level of regional cooperation. The South Asian regional geo-strategic structure is such that the basic thrust of cooperation in the field of combating terrorism, including sharing of intelligence and curbing of illegal financial and arms transactions amongst the regional terrorist groups, has to be implemented bilaterally. At the regional level, a general commitment can be made and a framework of cooperation can be evolved. Developmental co-operation within the regional framework, which may strengthen the socio-economic capabilities of the SAARC members in responding to terrorism also cannot be pursued smoothly and expeditiously in the absence of bilateral political and strategic understanding. There have been very significant developments in India–Pakistan relations as a result of General Musharraf's visit to India in April 2004. The two traditionally adversarial neighbours have committed to ensuring that terrorism will not be allowed to disrupt their nascent peace process. If such understanding gathers strength and momentum, the prospects of a regional approach in responding to terrorism will improve considerably.

At the extra-regional level, the role of the international community in conflict-resolution and dealing with terrorism has been significantly enhanced over the past decade. In particular, the spread of globalization, the emergence of the unipolar world order, and the cascading impact of 9/11 events have combined to make 'suppression of terrorism' a priority global security agenda. At the international and regional organizations, mechanisms are evolved and enforced to curb terrorism-promoting activities both by the defiant state and by the interested non-state actors. Several UN resolutions and regional commitments may be recalled in this respect, including those related to financial flows, arms supplies and drug trafficking involving terrorist organizations and insurgencies. These efforts are providing a multilateral framework for responding to terrorism, which is strengthening and supplementing the responses at local and regional levels. South Asian countries have benefited considerably from these international efforts.

An important multilateral initiative that is gathering momentum is the emergence of developmental assistance donors as peacemakers. In a given terrorism-generating conflict prone country, the donors are coordinating their efforts, through the offer of financial initiatives, diplomatic engagement, and political persuasion to bring the parties to such conflicts to the negotiating table for resolution of the issues involved. The offer and denial of assistance, both financial and military, is being used to nudge the parties to the conflict towards a peace process, and the parameters of such a peace process are also being defined by the donors. The leadership and guidance in these efforts is generally provided by the US, with active support from Japan and the European Union. In South Asia, Sri Lanka and Nepal have become direct targets of the donors' peacemaking initiatives.

This initiative in the case of Sri Lanka started with the Oslo Declaration issued on 25 November 2002, after a conference of several government representatives from 'the Asia-Pacific region, North America and Europe'. The representatives of both the Sri Lanka government and the LTTE were present at this conference. The Oslo Declaration identified the basic requirements of a 'lasting peace' in Sri Lanka and proposed a donors conference to focus on 'longer-term financial assistance and . . . efforts at donor co-ordination'.[1] This was followed by two conferences each in Washington in April and in Tokyo in June 2003. The

Tokyo Declaration promised, over a period of four years, from 2003–6, 'a cumulative estimated amount in excess of US $4.5 bn'. This assistance was 'closely linked to substantial and parallel progress in the peace process towards the fulfillment of the objectives agreed upon by the parties in Oslo'. The international community took upon itself to 'monitor and review' the progress in the peace process.[2] However, this assistance has not yet started flowing. The LTTE refused to participate in the Tokyo Conference and seems to be stuck on its priority for interim authority in the north and east regions of the Island. It is also not forthcoming on the political aspects of conflict-resolution unless the authority for the north and east is bestowed on it. Political priorities are naturally a conditioning concern for the rehabilitation and reconstruction of the conflict-prone areas. The economic incentives have not been able to make a dent in the political positions, and in the meanwhile, terrorist violence persists in Sri Lanka.

In the case of Nepal, at the initiative of the US and the UK, the donors met at a conference in London in December 2002, to offer multilateral support for the resolution of the Maoist insurgency. Multilateral committees of the donors were set up to raise funds and monitor three areas: (i) defence and security, (ii) the political issues involved, and (iii) developmental requirements in the Maoists' dominated areas. Unlike Sri Lankan case, the Nepalese government and the Maoists did not participate in this conference, though the government of Nepal has welcomed this initiative as it is aimed primarily at strengthening the state's capabilities to meet the Maoists' challenge. Here again the initiative has not succeeded much, though assistance to Nepal has been flowing from multilateral and diverse sources. The problem is that much of the conflict zone in rural areas is dominated by the Maoists and it is becoming increasingly difficult for international agencies to carry on with the developmental work without the approval of the insurgents.

Related to the international efforts in strengthening the states' responses to terrorism in South Asia is the role of third parties in conflict-resolution, through direct mediation or indirect facilitation in the peace process. Offers of a third party's role in the conflict-resolution have been numerous, ranging from non-state actors and states to international organizations, particularly the UN. Conflicts in Kashmir, Nepal, and Sri Lanka have been targeted for this. However, there is only one active third-party role in terrorism-generating South Asian conflicts; the one in Sri Lanka. Norway has been playing the role of facilitator since 2000, beginning a peace process between the LTTE and the Sri Lankan government. Its most spectacular achievement so far has been the ceasefire since February 2002, which is holding despite its fragility and frequent breaches. The Tsunami disaster which struck Sri Lanka in December 2004 has brought the promise of economic assistance for rehabilitation and reconstruction worth US $2 billion. The management of the flow of this assistance has further strengthened Norway's facilitation efforts to bring the two warring sides to work together for the larger good of the Sri Lankan people.

The involvement of the international community in general and the role of third parties in particular in conflict-resolution in South Asia raises many questions, the most important of which are related to the stakes and interests, as also to the objectivity and neutrality of the 'third party' in resolving a given conflict. These stakes and interests are often defined in terms of the universal values of peace, stability, and development which are suspect in the eyes of one or the other party involved in the conflict. India has been generally averse to the involvement of 'third parties' in any conflict involving itself. It also has strong reservations when prospects of such involvement arise in its sensitive neighbourhood, though we may hasten to add that Norway's facilitation role started after India's approval, and India continues to support this role within the framework that it should not exceed 'facilitation'. India is also not inclined to favour any third-party role in Nepal including by the UN. Since the US is seen to be actively interested in most of these 'third party' initiatives, its interests are linked to the overall strategy of waging 'war on global terrorism'. It is important to recall here that India, through diplomatic persuasion and engagement, tried to mobilize US pressures on Pakistan to ensure that Pakistan's support for cross-border terrorism in Jammu & Kashmir is drastically reduced.

The third-party role is vulnerable to the charges of intervention and partiality at any stage when one finds this role to be not in one's narrowly defined self-interests. If a great power is involved as a 'third party', or is backing a third party, the questions of sovereignty and 'favouritism' are raised. Norway has come under such attack in Sri Lanka from diverse quarters, including President Kumaratunga as well as the ruling coalition partner, the JVP. The US and General Musharraf have come under heavy criticism in Pakistan for their anti-terror coalition against the Taliban and Al Qaida. The 'third party' involvement when not based on a broader political consensus tends to divide political opinions. This weakens the state's political will to fight terrorism. As a consequence, it also helps the terrorist organizations gain legitimacy and mobilize internal and countervailing international support in the name of preserving 'genuine' national interests. However, in the situation of stalemated conflicts, the prospects of the third-party role making a constructive contribution are promising provided such a role is defined and pursued after careful planning and with the support of a broader consensus among the parties involved in the conflict.

Prospects

South Asia's dominant strategy to respond to terrorism will continue to be based on the use of force. This cannot succeed in producing the desired result unless pursued simultaneously with political and constitutional accommodation as well as economic and developmental efforts. In pursuing these latter strategies, the states need to work on a sustained basis to address the root causes of terrorism. Governance has to be improved and consensual politics has to be pursued. This is easier said than done.

The coming years will also see increasing engagement of the international community in responding to the challenge of terrorism. South Asian countries will have to learn to live with this aspect, a product of growing globalization and an assertive unipolar world order. The South Asian states will have to evolve strategies that can engage the international community at both multilateral and individual state levels in a constructive manner in conflict resolution endeavours without distorting their own priorities.

Notes

1. Text of Oslo Declaration, made available by the Sri Lankan High Commission in India.
2. Text of the Tokyo Declaration, 10 June 2003.

14. Data Paper on Terrorism in South Asia

P.V. Ramana

SOUTH ASIAN TERRORIST GROUPS: EXTRA-REGIONAL PROSCRIPTION

Designated Foreign Terrorist Organisations, USA

Al Qaida
Lashkar-e-Taiba (LT)
Lashkar-i-Jhangvi (LJ)
Liberation Tigers of Tamil Eelam (LTTE)
Harakat-ul-Mujahidin (HUM)
Jaish-e-Mohammed (JEM)

Other Terrorist Organisations, USA

Al-Badr Mujahidin
Communist Party of Nepal (Maoist)/United People's Front
Hizb-i-Islami Gulbuddin
Hizb-ul-Mujahidin
Jamiat-ul-Mujahidin
Harakat-ul-Jihad-i-Islami (HUJI)
Harakat-ul-Jihad-i-Islami/Bangladesh (HUJI-B)
Sipah-i-Sahaba
People's War Group
Maoist Communist Centre

Source: Patterns of Global Terrorism 2002 Executive Summary, United States Department of State, April 2003, pp. 33-4.

AID Agencies Designated as Terrorist Support Organizations

Al Akhtar Trust

Al-Rashid Trust
Ummah Tameer-e-Nau

Source: US Department of State
http://usinfo.state.gov/is/Archive/2004/Apr/02-337975.html

UNITED KINGDOM

Al Qaida
Babbar Khalsa (BK)
Harakat Mujahidin (HM)
International Sikh Youth Federation (ISYF)
Lashkar-e-Taiba (LT)
Jaish-e-Mohammed (JEM)
Liberation Tigers of Tamil Eelam (LTTE)

Source: Home Office of the Government of United Kingdom
http://www.homeoffice.gov.uk/terrorism/threat/groups/index.html

CANADA

Babbar Khalsa
Babbar Khalsa International
International Sikh Youth Federation
Lashkar-e-Taiba
Lashkar-e-Jhangvi
Jaish-e-Mohammed
Al Qaida
Harkat-ul-Mujahidin

Source: Public Safety and Emergency Preparedness, Canada
www.psepc-sppcc.gc.ca/national_security/counter-terrorism/Entities_e.asp

AUSTRALIA

Al Qaida
Harakat-ul-Mujahidin
Jaish-i-Mohammed
Lashkar-e-Taiba

Lashkar-i-Jhangvi
Liberation Tigers of Tamil Eelam

Source: Listing of Terrorist Organisations, Australian National Security; Attorney-General's Department
http://www.nationalsecurity.gov.au/www/agdHome.NSF

EUROPEAN UNION

Babbar Khalsa
International Sikh Youth Federation (ISYF)
Lashkar-e-Taiba (LET)/Pashan-e-Ahle Hadis

Source: Official Journal of the European Union
http://www.statewatch.org/news/2003/sep/terrlistexEUSept03.pdf

NATIONAL LEGISLATION

Name of Act	Year of Enactment	Current Status	Remarks
India			
Terrorist and Disruptive Activities (Prevention) Act	1985	Defunct	Last amended in 1993; Allowed to lapse in 1995
Terrorist Affected Areas (Special Courts) Amendment Act	1985		Originally enacted in 1984
Prevention of Terrorism Act	2002	In operation	Applicable in the States that wish to implement the law. Significantly, the Jammu & Kashmir government announced that it would not implement the law in the State
Maharashtra Control of Organised Crime Act	1999	In operation	
Andhra Pradesh Control of Organized Crime Act	2001	In operation	

Arunachal Pradesh Control of Organized Crime Act	2002	Defunct	The Act was repealed after the Gegong Apang-led Government took office in August 2003
Disturbed Areas (Special Courts) Act	1976	In operation	It extends to the whole of India except the state of Jammu and Kashmir
Armed Forces (Assam and Manipur) Special Powers Act	1958	In operation	Originally enacted in 1958. In operation as amended in 1972. Enables certain special powers to be conferred upon members of the armed forces in disturbed areas in the states of Assam and Manipur
Armed Forces (Punjab and Chandigarh) Special Powers Act	1983		
Chandigarh Disturbed Areas (Amendment) Act	1989		Originally enacted in 1983 as Chandigarh Disturbed Areas Act
Punjab Disturbed Areas Act	1983		
Armed Forces (Jammu and Kashmir) Special Powers Act	1990	In operation	
Assam Maintenance of Public Order Act	1953		
Assam Preventive Detention Act	1980		
Nagaland Security Regulation	1962	In operation	
Unlawful Activities (Prevention Amendment) Act	1969	In operation	Originally enacted in 1967
Anti-Hijacking (Amendment) Act	1994	In operation	Originally enacted in 1982
Extradition (Amendment) Act	1993	In operation	Originally enacted in 1962

National Security (Amendment) Act	1988	In operation	Originally enacted in 1980
Prevention of Money Laundering Act	2002	In operation	The Act seeks to track the flow of funds to India to finance terrorism and narcotics through illegal money transfer channels including *Hawala*
Preventive Detention (Continuance) Act	1957	In operation	Originally enacted in 1950
Public Interest Disclosure (Protection of Informers) Act	2002	In operation	
SAARC Convention (Suppression of Terrorism) Act	1993	In operation	
Suppression of Unlawful Acts Against Safety of Civil Aviation (Amendment) Act	1994	In operation	Originally enacted in 1982
Bangladesh			
Telecommunications Act	2001		Amendment sought to Section 30 to enable interception e-mail
Public Safety (Special Provisions) Act	2000	Repealed by the Khaleda Zia-led coalition regime on 2 April 2002.	Provides for trials by special tribunal for offences like toll extraction, kidnapping, ransom, and damaging vehicles
Special Powers Act	1974	In operation	Provides special measures for prevention of certain prejudicial activities and for conducting more speedy trial and effective punishment for certain grave offences

Suppression of Terrorism Act	1992	Enacted for limited period	
Section 54 CrPC	1898	In operation	Allows for arrest without warrant and preventive detention
Offences Disrupting Law and Order (Summary Trial) Act or Speedy Trial Act	2002	In operation	
Joint Drive Indemnity Act	2003	Enacted for specific objectives	
Money Laundering Prevention Act	2002	In operation	
Second Amendment Act	1973		Article 33 of the Constitution amended to provide for enacting preventive detention laws
Section 124 A, Bangladesh Penal Code Sedition Act	1860	In operation	
The Special Security Force Ordinance	1986		Established a security force which is to be under the direct command of the president and controlled and administered by a director who may be invested with the powers of the chief of army staff in respect of operations of the force
Section 99A of the Code of Criminal Procedure	1898		If the administration considers any publication to be prejudicial to the security of the State, it may take action under Section 99A of the Code of Criminal Procedure to ban and seize all copies of that publication

Law and Order Disruption Crimes (Speedy Trial) Act	2002	Operational status uncertain	(i) Speedy or summary trial of those involved in causing hindrance to normal movements of air, road, rail or water transport; mugging; illegal toll collection; vandalism; and so forth; (ii) Improvement in law and order situation in short time
Nepal			
Terrorist and Destructive Activities (Control and Punishment) Ordinance 2060	Introduced in year 2002	Renewed in April 2004 for another six months in the absence of the House of Representatives	Under this Act, security forces can detain anyone suspected of being a 'terrorist' or having any links with 'terrorists' for a maximum of 90 days without an arrest warrant
Terrorist and Disruptive Activities (Control and Punishment) Act	2002	In operation	
Public Safety Act	1990	In operation	As amended in 1991. Allows for people to be held in preventive detention for a period up to 90 days 'to prevent them from taking any action which could have an adverse effect, among others, on the security or order and tranquility of the country'. The Home Ministry can extend this period for another 90 days and a further extension up to 12 months from the original date of issue can be obtained,

			subject to the approval of an advisory board established under the Act
Public Safety Regulations	Issued immediately after the June 2001 regicide	In operation	These regulations empower the chief district officers or officials on their behalf to order an individual or a group under solitary confinement or limit their movement to certain areas if officials are 'convinced' that the suspects are about to harm the country's sovereignty, integrity or infringe law and order
Anti-State Crimes and Penalties Act	1989	In operation	
Local Administration Act 2028	1990	Amended in year 2002	Grants special powers to security forces. The Act has the potential to lead to arbitrary arrest and detention
Article 115 Clause 1 of the Constitution of the Kingdom of Nepal 1990	1991	Currently in operation	'If a grave emergency arises in regard to the sovereignty or integrity of the Kingdom of Nepal or the security of any part thereof, whether by war, external aggression, armed rebellion or extreme economic disarray, His Majesty may by proclamation, declare or order a state of emergency in respect of the whole of the Kingdom of Nepal or of any specified part thereof'

Pakistan			
Terrorist Affected Areas (Special Courts) Act	1991		Extended the authority of Speedy Trial Courts and gave police more powers to use weapons
Anti Terrorism Act	1997	Amended in January 2004 in the light of UNSC Resolutions on raising minimum and maximum punishment for offences relating to the financing of terror and making it a non-bailable offence	'Provide for the prevention of terrorism, sectarian violence and for speedy trial of heinous offences and for matters connected therewith and incidental thereto'
Anti-Terrorism Ordinance (Amendment) Ordinance	1999		Amended the Anti-Terrorism Act 1997
Pakistan Armed Forces (Acting in Aid of the Civil Power) Ordinance	1998		Originally promulgated to establish military courts in Sindh to try MQM activists. Amended in January 1999 to extend the establishment of military courts throughout the country. In February 1999, the Supreme Court ruled that the military courts were illegal, and transferred the cases to Anti-Terrorism Courts

Prevention of Anti-National Activities, Act	1947		
West Pakistan Maintenance of Public Order Act	1960		
Sri Lanka			
Public Security Ordinance	1947	In operation	
Prevention of Terrorism Act	1979	In operation	
Emergency Regulations	1996	In operation	Section 5 of the PSO empowers the President to make Emergency Regulations 'as they appear to be necessary or expedient'

Source: Online, especially English language media reports from the respective countries, and offline library resources.

GROUPS PROSCRIBED UNDER TERRORISM LAWS IN SOUTH ASIAN COUNTRIES

India

1. Babbar Khalsa International
2. Khalistan Commando Force
3. Khalistan Zindabad Force
4. International Sikh Youth Federation
5. Lashkar-e-Taiba/Pasban-e-Ahle Hadis
6. Jaish-e-Mohammed/Tahrik-e-Furqan
7. Harkat-ul-Mujahidin/Harkat-ul-Ansar/Harkat-ul-Jehad-e-Islami
8. Hizb-ul-Mujahidin/Hizb-ul-Mujahidin Pir Panjal Regiment
9. Al-Umar-Mujahidin
10. Jammu and Kashmir Islamic Front

11. United Liberation Front of Assam (ULFA)
12. National Democratic Front of Bodoland (NDFB)
13. People's Liberation Army (PLA)
14. United National Liberation Front (UNLF)
15. People's Revolutionary Party of Kangleipak (PREPAK)
16. Kangleipak Communist Party (KCP)
17. Kanglei Yaol Kanba Lup (KYKL)
18. Manipur People's Liberation Front (MPLF)
19. All Tripura Tiger Force
20. National Liberation Front of Tripura
21. Liberation Tigers of Tamil Eelam (LTTE)
22. Students Islamic Movement of India
23. Deendar Anjuman
24. Communist Party of India (Marxist-Leninist)–People's War, all its formations and front organizations
25. Maoist Communist Centre (MCC), all its formations and front organisations
26. Al Badr
27. Jamiat-ul-Mujahidin
28. Al Qaida
29. Dukhtaran-e-Millat (DEM)
30. Tamil Nadu Liberation Army (TNLA)
31. Tamil National Retrieval Troops (TNRT)
32. Akhil Bharat Nepali Ekta Samaj (ABNES)

Source: Text of Prevention of Terrorism Act, 2002.

NEPAL

Communist Party of Nepal (Maoist) (CPN-M)

PAKISTAN

1. Sipah-e-Sahaba Pakistan (SSP)
2. Tehrik-e-Jafria Pakistan (TJP)
3. Jaish-e-Mohammed (JeM)
4. Lashkar-e-Taiba (LeT)
5. Tanzim Nifaz-e-Shariat-e-Mohammadi (TNSM)
6. Millat-e-Islami Pakistan (formerly SSP)
7. Khuddam-i-Islam (formerly JeM)

8. Islami Tehrik-e-Pakistan (formerly TJP)
9. Jamiat-ul-Ansar (formerly Harkat-ul-Mujahidin)
10. Hizbul Tehrir (Part of Khilafat Movement)
11. Jamaat-ul-Furqan (sister organization of JeM)

Source: Text of President Pervez Musharraf's address to the nation, 12 January 2002; *Dawn*, Karachi, 16 November 2003 and 21 November 2003.

Sri Lanka

Liberation Tigers of Tamil Eelam (LTTE)
(currently a de-proscribed group)

Bangladesh

Purba Banglar Communist Party (Janajuddha group)
Biplobi Communist Party
Sarbahara Party (Mrinal group)
Sarbahara Party (Jabbar faction)
Bangladesher Communist Party (Hoque)
Bangladesher Sarbahara Party (Kamrul)
Bangladesher Sarbahara Party (Zia)
JSD Gano Bahini (greater Jessore area)
Srama Jibi Mukti Andolon (greater Kustia area)

Source: English language media reports from Bangladesh various issues and online resources relating to Bangladesh.

RESOLUTIONS OF THE UNITED NATIONS SECURITY COUNCIL RECOMMENDING MEASURES AGAINST TERRORISM

Resolution No.	Date	Indicative content	Recommended action
S/RES/1535(2004)	26 March 2004	Threats to international peace and security caused by terrorist acts	Revitalises Counter-Terrorism Committee and recommends creation of the office of Counter Terrorism Executive Directorate to enhance the ability of the Committee in implementing Resolution No. 1373
S/RES/1526(2004)	30 January 2004	Threats to international peace and security caused by terrorist acts	Improve implementation of measures imposed by paragraph 4 (b) of resolution 1267 (1999), paragraph 8 (c) of resolution 1333 (2000), and paragraphs 1 and 2 of resolution 1390 (2002) against Osama bin Laden, members of Al Qaida and Taliban and other individuals, groups, undertakings and entities associated with them
S/RES/1456(2003)	20 January 2003	High-level meeting of the Security Council: combating terrorism	All States must take urgent action to prevent and suppress all active and passive support to terrorism, and in particular comply fully with all relevant resolutions of the Security Council, in particular resolutions 1373, 1390 and 1455
S/RES/1455(2003)	17 January 2003	On improving implementation of measures imposed by paragraph 4 (b) of Resolution 1267 (1999), paragraph 8 (c)	Improve implementation of measures imposed by paragraph 4 (b) of resolution 1267 (1999), paragraph 8 (c) of resolution 1333 (2000) and paragraphs 1 and 2 of resolution 1390 (2002)

(contd.)

Resolution No.	Date	Indicative content	Recommended action
		of Resolution 1333 (2000) and paragraphs 1 and 2 of Resolution 1390 (2002) on measures against the Taliban and Al Qaida	
S/RES 1452(2002)	20 December 2002	On implementation of measures imposed by paragraph 4 (b) of Resolution 1267 (1999) and paragraph 1 and 2 (a) of Resolution 1390 (2002)	Decides that the provisions of paragraph 4 (b) of resolution 1267 (1999), and paragraphs 1 and 2 (a) of resolution 1390 (2002), do not apply to funds and other financial assets or economic resources that have been determined by the relevant State(s) to meet specific expenses and, therefore, consider and approve requests for extraordinary expenses
S/RES/1450(2002)	13 December 2002	On the obligations of state parties to the International Convention for the Suppression of Terrorist Bombings and the Convention for the Suppression of Unlawful Acts against the Safety of Civil Aviation	Condemns in the strongest terms the terrorist bomb attack at the Paradise Hotel in Kikambal, Kenya, and the attempted missile attack on Arkia Israeli Airlines flight 582 departing Mombasa, Kenya, on 28 November 2002 as well as other recent terrorist acts in various countries. . . . Urges all States, in accordance with their obligations under resolution 1373 (2001), to cooperate in efforts to find and bring to justice the perpetrators, organizers and sponsors of these terrorist attacks
S/RES/1438(2002)	14 October 2002	Condemning the bomb attacks in Bali, Indonesia, on 12 October 2002.	Urges all States, in accordance with their obligations under resolution 1373 (2001), to cooperate in efforts to find and bring to justice the

			perpetrators, organizers and sponsors of these terrorist attacks
S/RES/1377(2001)	12 November 2001	Recalls its resolutions 1269 (1999), 1368 (2001) and 1373 (2001)	Calls on all States to take urgent steps to implement fully resolution 1373 (2001), and to assist each other in doing so, and underlines the obligations on States to deny financial and all other forms of support and safe haven to terrorists and those supporting terrorism
S/RES/1373(2001)	28 September 2001	On international cooperation to combat threats to international peace and security caused by terrorist acts	Measures for suppressing the financing of terrorism. Recommends the establishment of the Counter-Terrorism Committee (CTC), comprising 15 members, to monitor the implementation of resolution 1373 by and all states and attempts to enhance their capability to combat terrorism
S/RES/1363(2001)	30 July 2001	On the establishment of a mechanism to monitor the implementation of measures imposed by resolutions 1267 (1999) and 1333 (2000)	Establish a mechanism to monitor implementation of measures imposed by resolutions 1267 (1999) and 1333 (2000); assist States bordering Afghanistan under Taliban control and other States to enhance their capacity to implement measures imposed by resolutions 1267 (1999) and 1333 (2000)
S/RES/1333(2000)	19 December 2000	On Measures against the Taliban	Demands the Taliban to comply with resolution 1267 (1999), shut down all terrorist training camps, and asks member states to implement specific measures against the Taliban
S/RES/1267(1999)	19 October 1999	On international cooperation in the fight against terrorism	Asks all member to fully implement all anti-terrorism conventions they are parties to, adhere to at the earliest to which they are yet not parties, (contd.)

Resolution No.	Date	Indicative content	Recommended action
			and implement, cooperate in suppressing terrorism, as well as take measures to prevent as well as suppress the financing of terrorism
S/RES/1267(1999)	15 October 1999	On Measures against the Taliban	Asks the Taliban to turn in Osama bin Laden, stop providing sanctuary to international terrorists and member states to implement measures that would help in implementing the directives to the Taliban
S/RES/1054(1996)	26 April 1996	Sanctions against Sudan	Imposes sanctions against Sudan for failing to extradite to Ethiopia the three terrorists who made a failed assassination attempt on Egyptian President Hosni Mubarak on 26 June 1995. Asks all member states and other states to reduce diplomatic presence in Sudan and deny entry to Sudanese officials
S/RES/1044(1996)	31 January 1996	Extradition of terrorists for attempting to assassinate the Egyptian President	Asks Sudan to extradite the terrorists who made an attempt to assassinate Egyptian President Mubarak
S/RES/748(1992)	31 March 1992	Sanctions against Libya	Asks Libya to turn in the terrorists who had blown up a Pan Am aircraft, and asks all Member states and other states to deny entry to Libyan officials into their territory, and imposes air restrictions and arms embargo on Libya

Source: http://www.un.org/terrorism sc.htm

SPECIAL FORCES IN SOUTH ASIAN COUNTRIES

BANGLADESH

Rapid Action Battalion (RAB)

RAB was formed as an elite special force to curb terrorism and to deal with the deteriorating law and order situation in the country. Members of the force would be recruited from among the serving members of all the 'disciplined forces of Bangladesh'—including the armed forces, police, Bangladesh Rifles and Ansars, the last two being paramilitary forces.[1] The strength of the force has been reported to be 500.[2] Media reports of July 2003 said, besides, that 23 Rapid Action Teams were already in operation in the country, and each team consisted of 12 members. The number of teams could be expanded as when the need was felt. It would function under the framework of rules made in the context of the Armed Police Battalion Act 2003. It can be deployed across the country and would function under the supervision of the Inspector General of Police. The RAB will have the same powers and functions as police officers enjoy under the Criminal Procedure Code, including investigation.[3]

The RAB Bill received the President's assent on 12 July 2003.

On that day, the President assented to the act Armed Police Battalions (Amendment Act 2003), which was earlier, passed by parliament. It proposed for establishment of RAB, replacing the Armed Police Battalions Ordinance 1979. Seven battalions of RAB with the headquarters comprise 5,521 personnel. The seven battalions will include four battalions deployed in Dhaka Division, one battalion each will be deployed in Chittagong, Khulna and Rajshahi divisions. An Additional Deputy Inspector General or equivalent will act as the Commanding Officer of a Battalion and a Major or equivalent as Company Commander.

Sources: *Daily Star*, Dhaka, 10 July 2003 and 13 July 2003, http://www.bangla.net/newage/1006031/front.html and M. Jahangir Alam, 'Row over ranks affects RAB', *The New Nation*, 13 April 2004.

INDIA

National Security Guards (NSG)

The NSG is a special force and its members are also known as the Black Cats, following the black uniform they wear. Its members are drawn from the three services of the Indian Armed Forces, as well as from paramilitary forces such as the Border Security Force. Units of the NSG are trained to foil terrorist attacks and hijacking. It was formed in 1984. The NSG has two complementary elements, viz., Special Action Group comprising Army personnel and Special Rangers Group comprising personnel drawn from the Central Para Military Forces and State Police Forces.

The NSG is tasked with handling counter-terrorism, anti-kidnapping, anti-sabotage, anti-hijacking, hostage rescue and VIP security. The NSG is also used extensively in the anti-terrorist role vis-à-vis: Neutralization of specific terrorist threats in vital installations or any given area; Engaging and neutralizing terrorists in specific situations; handling hijack situations involving piracy in the air and on the land; and rescue of hostages in kidnap/abduction situations.

Rashtriya Rifles (RR)

The RR was formed in 1990. Its units come under four Counter-Insurgency Force Headquarters. Victor Force looks after Anantnag and Pulwama districts in the south Kashmir Valley, Kilo Force looks after Kupwara and Baramulla districts in the north Kashmir Valley. Both these are under the operational control of the 15 Corps. The Delta Force looks after Doda district and the Romeo Force Poonch and Rajouri districts. These two forces come under the operational control of the 16 Corps. Each force is headed by a GOC-in-C with the rank of major general.

Grey Hounds (GH)

Raised in 1989, the GH is an elite force in the southern Indian state of Andhra Pradesh (AP), created especially to tackle the left-wing extremist insurgency in that state. It has scored numerous significant successes against the Naxalites and has become a role model for police in many Indian states. Though there were proposals to form such units in other states on the lines of the GH, such proposals have not fructified till date.

Its main objective is to deal effectively with the left-wing extremist violence on the law and order front and other situations arising out of unforeseen situations. The GH is maintained as a youthful force by drawing personnel from various departments of AP police for a fixed tenure. The Unit is headed by an Inspector General of Police and all other officers and men are drawn on deputation from various organisations of the AP Police. They are imparted specialised training in field craft and weapons' handling and emphasis is given to developing high standard of physical fitness and mental alertness. This unit offers its services to other states apart from AP. They started commando training since June 2000 to Police Personnel from other states of Maharashtra, Madhya Pradesh, Bihar, Chhattisgarh, Jharkhand, Orissa, and West Bengal.

Source: Official Website of the Andhra Pradesh Police; www.apstatepolice.org.

Andhra Pradesh Special Police (APSP)

APSP battalions are deployed to provide protection to police stations in Andhra Pradesh from attacks by the left-wing extremists.

Special Security Branch (SSB)

The SSB, presently known as the *Shasastra Seema Bal*, which is approximately 35,000-strong, is an elite semi-intelligence corps that carries out border patrols on the Nepal and Chinese borders along with India's Intelligence Bureau.

SSB was set up in early 1963 in the wake of the Indo–China conflict of 1962 for promoting national integration and security consciousness among the people of border areas in NEFA, North Assam, North Bengal, Hills of Uttar Pradesh (now Uttranchal), Himachal Pradesh, Jammu and Ladakh to strengthen defence preparedness. The sphere of activities of the organization was subsequently extended to Manipur, Tripura and Jammu (1965), Meghalaya (1975), Sikkim (1976), Rajasthan and Gujarat (1985), Rajasthan and Gujarat, Manipur and Mizoram (1988), South Bengal, Nagaland (1989), Nubra Valley, Rajouri and Poonch district of Jammu & Kashmir (1990–1). SSB has since January, 2001 been entrusted with the task of a border guarding force on the entire 1,751 km stretch of Indo–Nepal border in the states of Uttranchal, Uttar Pradesh, Bihar, West Bengal and Sikkim. The uniformed personnel are deployed along [the] Indo–Nepal Border for Border Management and the civilian component in the hinterland for collection of information having a bearing on India's security concerns and also for undertaking civic action and perception management activities.

Source: Official Website of the SSB at http://www.ssb.nic.in/history.html.

NEPAL

Armed Police Force (APF)

The APF was formed in the year 2001 by enacting the Armed Police Force Act, 2001. The King of Nepal, Gyanendra, on 18 December 2003, inaugurated the headquarters of the Armed Police Force at Halchowk, Kathmandu Valley, which was built at a cost of NR.96m. The strength of the APF in 2003 November was estimated to be at 16,000.[4] It is envisaged that the force would eventually have a strength of 20,000.

The Armed Police Force has been leading the battle against the Maoist insurgents. This force has a variety of modern American and British equipment. Its chief was assassinated in January 2003.

SRI LANKA

Special Task Force (STF)

Set up in 1983, the STF is the para-military arm of the Sri Lanka Police, deployed essentially for Counter Terrorist and Counter Insurgency operations within the country. They are also deployed in the close protection Units providing security for VVIP's and at key installations. The nucleus of the STF was formed after drawing on Policemen already in service and having them trained by the Army in the handling of Infantry weapons and given basic training in 'jungle operations'. The first few Platoons formed were deployed mainly to provide support for Police Station[s] in the north of Sri Lanka. As the STF grew in numbers, they took on the added responsibilities of providing protection to Key Installations in the Colombo District and providing personnel for the protection of the President, Prime Minister and several Ministers of the Cabinet.

Source: http://www.police.lk/divisions/stf.html.

PAKISTAN

Special Services Group (SSG)

Formed in 1966, it consists of three battalions and one independent company. The headquarters for the SSG was established at Cherat. Each battalion consists of 700 men and is led by a Lieutenant Colonel. The SSG is capable of carrying out the following missions: counter-terrorism, unconventional warfare, counter-insurgency, security for very important people and places, reconnaissance, raids, and riverine operations.

NOTES

1. http://www.hrw.org/press/2003/06/bangla060403.htm
2. http://www.assam.org article.php?sid=258&PHPSESSID=97a765052fee8485cb45f7745d8a2a93
3. http://www.bangla.net/newage/100603/front.html
4. Chitra Tiwari, 'Violence soars after Nepal peace talks fail in Nepal', ailhttp://www.washingtontimes.com/world/20031031-094214-1174r.htm

MULTILATERAL AND REGIONAL CONVENTIONS ON TERRORISM

Convention	Place, Date and Year	Countries signed
UN Conventions deposited with the Secretary General of the United Nations		
Convention on the Prevention and Punishment of Crimes against Internationally Protected Persons, including Diplomatic Agents	New York, Adopted by the General Assembly on 14 December 1973	Bhutan, India, Maldives, Nepal, Pakistan, Sri Lanka
International Convention against the Taking of Hostages	New York, Adopted by the General Assembly 17 December 1979	Bhutan, India, Nepal, Pakistan, Sri Lanka
International Convention for the Suppression of Terrorist Bombings	New York, Adopted by the General Assembly on 15 December 1997	India, Nepal, Maldives, Pakistan, Sri Lanka
International Convention for the Suppression of the Financing of Terrorism	New York, Adopted by the General Assembly on 9 December 1999	Bhutan, India, Sri Lanka
UN Conventions deposited with other depositories	Date and Year, Depository	
Convention on Offences and Certain Other Acts Committed on Board Aircraft	Signed at Tokyo on 14 September 1963 Deposited with the Secretary-General of the International Civil Aviation Organization (ICAO)	Bhutan, India, Maldives, Nepal, Pakistan, Sri Lanka
Convention for the Suppression of Unlawful Seizure of Aircraft	Signed at The Hague on 16 December 1970. Deposited with the Governments of the Russian Federa-	

	tion, the United Kingdom and the United States of America	
Convention for the Suppression of Unlawful Acts against the Safety of Civil Aviation	Signed at Montreal on 23 September 1971. Deposited with the Governments of the Russian Federation, the United Kingdom and the United States of America	Bangladesh, Bhutan, India, Maldives, Nepal, Pakistan, Sri Lanka
Protocol on the Suppression of Unlawful Acts of Violence at Airports Serving International Civil Aviation, supplementary to the Convention for the Suppression of Unlawful Acts against the Safety of Civil Aviation	Signed at Montreal on 24 February 1988. Deposited with the Governments of the Russian Federation, the United Kingdom and the United States of America and with the Secretary-General of ICAO	India, Maldives, Pakistan, Sri Lanka
Convention for the Suppression of Unlawful Acts against the Safety of Maritime Navigation	Done at Rome on 10 March 1988. Deposited with the Secretary-General of the International Maritime Organization (IMO)	
Protocol for the Suppression of Unlawful Acts against the Safety of Fixed Platforms Located on the Continental Shelf	Done at Rome on 10 March 1988. Deposited with the Secretary-General of IMO	
Convention on the Marking of Plastic Explosives for the Purpose of Detection	Signed at Montreal on 1 March 1991. Deposited with the Secretary-General of ICAO	India, Maldives, Pakistan, Sri Lanka
Regional Convention		
SAARC Regional Convention on Suppression of Terrorism	Signed at Kathmandu on 4 November 1987. Deposited with the Secretary-General	Bangladesh, Bhutan, India, Maldives, Nepal, Pakistan, Sri Lanka

of the South Asian Association for Regional Cooperation (SAARC)

Source: United Nations Treaty Collection, accessible from the Disarmament and Terrorism page at the website of the UN, www.un.org.

SUMMARY OF CONVENTIONS

CONVENTION ON THE PREVENTION AND PUNISHMENT OF CRIMES AGAINST INTERNATIONALLY PROTECTED PERSONS, INCLUDING DIPLOMATIC AGENTS, NEW YORK, 14 DECEMBER 1973

The Convention applies to the crimes of direct involvement or complicity in the murder, kidnapping, or attack, whether actual, attempted or threatened, on the person, official premises, private accommodation or means of transport of diplomatic agents and other 'internationally protected persons'. Internationally protected persons are defined as Heads of State or Government, Ministers for Foreign Affairs, State officials and representatives of international organizations entitled to special protection in a foreign State, and their families.

States Parties have obligations to establish their jurisdiction over the offences described, make the offences punishable by appropriate penalties, take alleged offenders into custody, prosecute or extradite alleged offenders, cooperate in preventive measures, and exchange information and evidence needed in related criminal proceedings. The offences referred to in the Convention are deemed to be extraditable offences between States Parties under existing extradition treaties, and under the Convention itself.

INTERNATIONAL CONVENTION AGAINST THE TAKING OF HOSTAGES, NEW YORK, 17 DECEMBER 1979

The Convention applies to the offence of direct involvement or complicity in the seizure or detention of, and threat to kill, injure or continue to detain a hostage, whether actual or attempted, in order to compel a State, an international intergovernmental organization, a person or a group of persons, to do or abstain from doing any act as an explicit or implicit condition for the release of the hostage.

Each State Party is required to make this offence punishable by appropriate penalties. Where hostages are held in the territory of a State Party, the State Party is obligated to take all measures it considers appropriate to ease the situation of the hostages and secure their release. After the release of the hostages, States Parties are obligated to facilitate the departure of the hostages. Each State Party is obligated to take such actions as may be necessary to establish jurisdiction over the offence of taking of hostages.

States Parties have obligations to establish their jurisdiction over the offences described, make the offences punishable by appropriate penalties, take alleged offenders into custody, prosecute or extradite alleged offenders, cooperate in preventive measures, and exchange information and evidence needed in related criminal proceedings. The offences referred to in the Convention are deemed to be extraditable offences between States Parties under existing extradition treaties, and under the Convention itself.

INTERNATIONAL CONVENTION FOR THE SUPPRESSION OF TERRORIST BOMBINGS, NEW YORK, 15 DECEMBER 1997

The Convention applies to the offence of the intentional and unlawful delivery, placement, discharge or detonation of an explosive or other lethal device, whether attempted or actual, in, into or against a place of public use, a State or Government facility, a public transportation system or an infrastructure facility, with the intent to cause death or serious bodily injury, or extensive destruction likely to or actually resulting in major economic loss. Any person also commits an offence if that person participates as an accomplice in any of these acts, organizes others to commit them or in any other way contributes to their commission. The Convention does not apply where an act of this nature does not involve any international elements as defined by the Convention.

States Parties are required to establish jurisdiction over and make punishable, under their domestic laws, the offences described, to extradite or submit for prosecution persons accused of committing or aiding in the commission of the offences, and to assist each other in connection with criminal proceedings under the Convention. The offences referred to in the Convention are deemed to be extraditable offences between States Parties under existing extradition treaties, and under the Convention itself.

INTERNATIONAL CONVENTION FOR THE SUPPRESSION OF THE FINANCING OF TERRORISM, NEW YORK, 9 DECEMBER 1999

The Convention applies to the offence of direct involvement or complicity in the intentional and unlawful provision or collection of funds, whether attempted or actual, with the intention or knowledge that any part of the funds may be used to carry out any of the offences described in the Conventions listed in the Annex, or an act intended to cause death or serious bodily injury to any person not actively involved in armed conflict in order to intimidate a population, or to compel a government or an international organization to do or abstain from doing any act. The provision or collection of funds in this manner is an offence whether or not the funds are actually used to carry out the proscribed acts. The Convention does not apply where an act of this nature does not involve any international elements as defined by the Convention.

The Convention requires each State Party to take appropriate measures, in accordance with its domestic legal principles, for the detection and freezing, seizure or forfeiture of any funds used or allocated for the purposes of committing the offences described. The offences referred to in the Convention are deemed to be extraditable offences and States Parties have obligations to establish their jurisdiction over the offences described, make the offences punishable by appropriate penalties, take alleged offenders into custody, prosecute or extradite alleged offenders, cooperate in preventive measures and counter-measures, and exchange information and evidence needed in related criminal proceedings. The offences referred to in the Convention are deemed to be extraditable offences between States Parties under existing extradition treaties, and under the Convention itself.

CONVENTION ON OFFENCES AND CERTAIN OTHER ACTS COMMITTED ON BOARD AIRCRAFT, TOKYO, 14 SEPTEMBER 1963

The Convention applies to offences and other acts prejudicial to good order and discipline on board an aircraft, committed while the aircraft is in flight or on the surface of the high seas or of any other area outside the territory of any State. It does not apply to State aircraft, for example, aircraft used in military, customs and police services.

The purpose of the Tokyo Convention is to protect the safety of the aircraft and of the persons or property thereon and to maintain good order and discipline on board. The aircraft commander, members of the crew and, in specific circumstances, even passengers on board, are empowered to prevent the commission of such acts and to disembark the person concerned. The aircraft commander may also disembark the offender or, if the offence is serious, deliver him to the competent authorities of a Contracting State when the aircraft lands. The Convention protects the aircraft commander and any crew member or passenger assisting him in imposing the measures he finds necessary from any proceedings in respect of actions taken by them.

The State of registration of the aircraft is competent to exercise jurisdiction over offences and acts committed on board. Each Contracting State is obliged to take the necessary measures to establish its jurisdiction as the State of registration. The Convention does not eliminate existing or future jurisdiction in States other than the State of registration. A Contracting State which is not the State of registration may not interfere with an aircraft in flight in order to exercise its criminal jurisdiction over an offence committed on board except in certain cases, for instance, the offence has been effected in the territory of the State overflown, the offence has been committed by or against a national or permanent resident of that State, and the offence is against the security of that State.

CONVENTION FOR THE SUPPRESSION OF UNLAWFUL SEIZURE OF AIRCRAFT, THE HAGUE, 16 DECEMBER 1970

The Convention defines the act of unlawful seizure of aircraft, and the Contracting States have undertaken to make such an offence punishable by severe penalties. Under the provisions of The Hague Convention a State is obliged, whether or not it is the State of registration, to take such measures as may be necessary to establish its jurisdiction over the offence in the case where the alleged offender is present in its territory and it does not extradite him. If there is no extradition treaty between the States concerned and the offender is in the territory of a Contracting State and that State refuses to extradite the offender, then it must submit the case to its competent authorities for the purpose of prosecution under its criminal law.

The Convention requires any Contracting State in which the aircraft or its passengers or crew are present to facilitate the continuation of the journey of the passengers and crew as soon as possible and to return the aircraft and its cargo to the persons lawfully entitled to possession without delay.

CONVENTION FOR THE SUPPRESSION OF UNLAWFUL ACTS AGAINST THE SAFETY OF CIVIL AVIATION, MONTREAL, 23 SEPTEMBER 1971

The Convention deals with acts other than those covered by the Tokyo and The Hague Conventions. The Montreal Convention defines a wide spectrum of unlawful acts against the safety of civil aviation and the Contracting States have undertaken to make these offences punishable by severe penalties. The Convention contains detailed provisions on jurisdiction, custody, prosecution and extradition of the alleged offender similar to those of The Hague Convention. Like the Tokyo and The Hague Conventions, the Montreal Convention does not apply to aircraft used in military, customs or police services. This Convention attempts to establish a form of universal jurisdiction over the offender, as provided in Article 5(1) of the Convention. The scope of the Convention is primarily determined in terms of the 'international element' provided in Article 1, sub-paragraphs 1(a), (b), (c), (d) and (e). The Convention applies, irrespective of whether the aircraft is engaged in international or domestic flight, only as provided in Article 4(2) of the Convention, namely, if:

(a) the place of take-off or landing, actual or intended, of the aircraft is situated outside the territory of the State of registration of the aircraft; or

(b) the offence is committed in the territory of a State other than the State of registration of the aircraft.

In the case of air navigation facilities mentioned in Article 1, sub-paragraph 1(d), the Convention applies only if the facilities destroyed, damaged, or interfered with are used in international air navigation.

CONVENTION ON THE PHYSICAL PROTECTION OF NUCLEAR MATERIAL, VIENNA, 3 MARCH 1980

The Physical Protection Convention has a twofold objective: it establishes levels of physical protection required to be applied to nuclear material used for peaceful purposes while in international nuclear transport and it also provides for measures against unlawful acts with respect to such material while in international nuclear transport as well as in domestic use, storage and transport.

Although the levels of physical protection prescribed in the Convention are required to be applied only to nuclear material used for peaceful purposes while international nuclear transport, other provisions of the Convention (e.g. the requirements that relate to making specified acts punishable offences under national law, to establishing jurisdiction over those offences and to prosecuting or extraditing alleged offenders) apply also to nuclear material used for peaceful purposes while in domestic use, storage and transport. Accordingly, States Parties to the Convention are obliged to make punishable under their national law the intentional commission of offences with respect to nuclear material as listed in its Article 7, in particular, intentional commission of: acts without lawful authority dealing with nuclear material causing or likely to cause death or serious injury or damage to any person or property; theft or robbery of nuclear material; embezzlement or fraudulent obtaining of nuclear material; demands for nuclear material by any form of intimidation; threats to use nuclear material to cause death or serious injury or damage to any person or property; or threats to steal nuclear material to compel a person, international organization or State to do or refrain from doing any act. The Convention also contains specific rules on jurisdiction and extradition.

PROTOCOL ON THE SUPPRESSION OF UNLAWFUL ACTS OF VIOLENCE AT AIRPORTS SERVING INTERNATIONAL CIVIL AVIATION, SUPPLEMENTARY TO THE CONVENTION FOR THE SUPPRESSION OF UNLAWFUL ACTS AGAINST THE SAFETY OF CIVIL AVIATION, MONTREAL, 24 FEBRUARY 1988

The Protocol adds to the definition of 'offence' given in the Montreal Convention of 1971 unlawful and intentional acts of violence against persons at an airport serving international civil aviation which cause or are likely to cause serious injury or death and such acts which destroy or seriously damage the facilities of such an airport or aircraft not in service located thereon or disrupt the services of the airport; the qualifying element of these offences is the fact that such an act endangers or is likely to endanger safety at that airport. These offences are punishable by severe penalties, and Contracting States are obliged to establish jurisdiction over the offences not only in the case where the offence was committed in their territory but also in the case where the alleged offender is present in their territory and they do not extradite him to the State where the offence took place.

CONVENTION FOR THE SUPPRESSION OF UNLAWFUL ACTS AGAINST THE SAFETY OF MARITIME NAVIGATION, ROME, 10 MARCH 1988

The Convention applies to the offences of direct involvement or complicity in the intentional and unlawful threatened, attempted or actual endangerment of the safe navigation of a ship by the commission of any of the following acts: seizure of or exercise of control over a ship by any form of intimidation; violence against a person on board a ship; destruction of a ship or the causing of damage to a ship or to its cargo; placement on a ship of a device or substance which is likely to destroy or cause damage to that ship or its cargo; destruction of, serious damaging of, or interference with maritime navigational facilities; knowing communication of false information; injury to or murder of any person in connection with any of the preceding acts. The Convention applies to ships navigating or scheduled to navigate into, through or from waters beyond the outer limit of the territorial sea of a single State, or the lateral limits of its territorial sea with adjacent States, or when the alleged offender is found in the territory of a State Party.

The Convention does not apply to warships, ships owned or operated by a State when being used as a naval auxiliary or for customs or police purposes or ships that have been withdrawn from navigation or laid up.

The offences referred to in the Convention are deemed to be extraditable offences and States-parties have obligations to establish their jurisdiction over the offences described, make the offences punishable by appropriate penalties, take alleged offenders into custody, prosecute or extradite alleged offenders, cooperate in preventative measures, and exchange information and evidence needed in related criminal proceedings.

PROTOCOL FOR THE SUPPRESSION OF UNLAWFUL ACTS AGAINST THE SAFETY OF FIXED PLATFORMS LOCATED ON THE CONTINENTAL SHELF, ROME, 10 MARCH 1988

The Protocol applies to the offences described in the Convention for the Suppression of Unlawful Acts against the Safety of Maritime Navigation when committed in relation to a 'fixed platform', defined as an artificial island, installation or structure permanently attached to the sea-bed for the purpose of exploration or exploitation of resources or for other economic purposes.

States-parties have obligations in relation to establishing their jurisdiction over the offences described, making the offences punishable by appropriate penalties, taking alleged offenders into custody and prosecuting or extraditing them.

CONVENTION ON THE MARKING OF PLASTIC EXPLOSIVES FOR THE PURPOSE OF DETECTION, MONTREAL, 1 MARCH 1991

The Convention requires each State Party to prohibit and prevent the manufacture in its territory of unmarked plastic explosives.

Plastic explosives will be marked by introducing during the manufacturing process any one of the detection agents defined in the Technical Annex to the Convention. The Convention also requires each State Party to prohibit and prevent the movement into or out of its territory of unmarked explosives and to exercise strict and effective control over the possession of any existing stocks of unmarked explosives. Stocks of plastic explosives not held by authorities performing military and police functions are to be destroyed or consumed for purposes not inconsistent with the objectives of the Convention, marked or rendered permanently ineffective, within a period of three years from the entry into force of the Convention in respect of the State concerned.

The Convention also establishes an International Explosives Technical Commission, experts in the field of manufacture or detection of, or research in, explosives. The Commission will evaluate technical developments relating to the manufacture, marking and detection of explosives, report its findings, through the Council of ICAO, to all States Parties and international organizations concerned, and propose amendments to the Technical Annex to the Convention, as required.

United Nations Conventions Deposited with the Secretary-General of the United Nations

Convention on the Prevention and Punishment of Crimes against Internationally Protected Persons, including Diplomatic Agents.

International Convention against the Taking of Hostages, adopted by the General Assembly of the United Nations on 17 December 1979.

International Convention for the Suppression of Terrorist Bombings, adopted by the General Assembly of the United Nations on 15 December 1997.

Arabic Chinese English French Russian Spanish Status Summary. International Convention for the Suppression of the Financing of Terrorism, adopted by the General Assembly of the United Nations on 9 December 1999.

UNITED NATIONS CONVENTIONS DEPOSITED WITH OTHER DEPOSITARIES

(Please note that the status of each convention is made available by the relevant depositary.)

Convention on Offences and Certain Other Acts Committed on Board Aircraft, signed at Tokyo on 14 September 1963. (Deposited with the Secretary-General of the International Civil Aviation Organization.)

Convention for the Suppression of Unlawful Seizure of Aircraft, signed at The Hague on 16 December 1970. (Deposited with the Governments of the Russian Federation, the United Kingdom and the United States of America.)

Convention for the Suppression of Unlawful Acts against the Safety of Civil Aviation, signed at Montreal on 23 September 1971. (Deposited with the Governments of the Russian Federation, the United Kingdom and the United States of America.)

Convention on the Physical Protection of Nuclear Material, signed at Vienna on 3 March 1980. (Deposited with the Director-General of the International Atomic Energy Agency.)

Arabic Chinese English French Russian Spanish Status Summary.

Protocol on the Suppression of Unlawful Acts of Violence at Airports Serving International Civil Aviation, supplementary to the Convention for the Suppression of Unlawful Acts against the Safety of Civil Aviation, signed at Montreal on 24 February 1988. (Deposited with the Governments of the Russian Federation, the United Kingdom and the United States of America and with the Secretary-General of the International Civil Aviation Organization.)

Convention for the Suppression of Unlawful Acts against the Safety of Maritime Navigation, done at Rome on 10 March 1988. (Deposited with the Secretary-General of the International Maritime Organization.)

Protocol for the Suppression of Unlawful Acts against the Safety of Fixed Platforms Located on the Continental Shelf, done at Rome on 10 March 1988. (Deposited with the Secretary-General of the International Maritime Organization.)

Convention on the Marking of Plastic Explosives for the Purpose of Detection, signed at Montreal on 1 March 1991. (Deposited with the Secretary-General of the International Civil Aviation Organization.)

Regional Conventions on Terrorism

SAARC Regional Convention on Suppression of Terrorism, signed at Kathmandu on 4 November 1987. (Deposited with the Secretary-General of the South Asian Association for Regional Cooperation.)

Source: http://untreaty.un.org/English/Terrorism.asp.

PROFILES OF TERRORIST GROUPS

Official name	Other names	Country (area of activities)	Year founded	Leader
(1)	(2)	(3)	(4)	(5)
Al Badr	Al Badr Mujahidin	J&K, India; Azad Kashmir; Pakistan, Afghanistan	1998	Lukmaan (founder), presently led by Bakht Zameen
Jamiat-ul-Mujahidin (Break away faction of Hizb-ul-Mujahidin)	Break away faction of Hizb-ul-Mujahidin	J&K, India; Afghanistan	1990	Hilal Ahmed Mir (founder), presently led by Engineer Mohammad Salah (chief commander)
Al Qaida	Dukhtaran-e-Kashmir	J&K, India	1987	Ayesha Andrabi alias Kulsun alias Didi alias Raji is the Presiden; Nahida Nasreen is Gen. Secretary
Dukhtaran-e-Millat (DeM)				
Lashkar-e-Taiba/Pasban-e-Ahle Hadis	Jamaat-ud-Dawaa	J&K, India; Azad Kashmir; Pakistan, Afghanistan, Iraq, Chechnya, USA, Britain, Bosnia	1990	Hafiz Mohammad Sayeed
Jaish-e-Mohammed/ Tahrik-e-Furqan	Khaddamul Islam	J&K, India; Azad Kashmir; Pakistan, Afghanistan	2000	Maulana Masood Azhar
Harkat-ul-Mujahidin/ Harkat-ul-Ansar/Harkat-ul-Jehad-e-Islami		J&K, India; Parts of all provinces in Pakistan, especially in Punjab and North-West Frontier province	1993	

(contd.)

(1)	(2)	(3)	(4)	(5)
Hizb-ul-Mujahidin/Hizb-ul-Mujahidin Pir Panjal Regiment		J&K, India; Afghanistan; Azad Kashmir; Pakistan	1989	Mohammad Yusuf Shah alias Syed Salahuddin, chief, Gazi Nasiruddin, chief commander (operations), Kashmir Valley (killed on 16 January 2004)
Jammu and Kashmir Islamic Front		J&K, Delhi, Gujarat, and some other isolated pockets of India; Kathmandu in Nepal; and Dhaka in Bangladesh	1995	Bilal Ahmed Beg, chairman
United Liberation Front of Assam (ULFA)		Primarily in Asam, India; Bhutan	1979	Bhimakanta Buragohain, founder; Arbind Rajkhowa, chairman, Paresh Baruah, 'commander-in-chief'
National Democratic Front of Bodoland (NDFB)	Originally founded as Bodo Security Force	Primarily in Asam, India	1988	Ranjan Daimary, founder and president
People's Liberation Army (PLA), constitutent of Manipur People's Liberation Front (MPLF)		Primarily in Manipur, India	1978	Irengbam Chaoren
United National Liberation Front (UNLF), constitutent of Manipur People's Liberation Front (MPLF)		Primarily in Manipur, India	1964	Rajkumar Meghen, chairman

People's Revolutionary Party of Kangleipak (PREPAK), constitutent of Manipur People's Liberation Front (MPLF)		Primarily in Manipur, India	1977	R.K. Tulachandra, founder; Achamba, chairman, Tajila, commander-in-chief
Kangleipak Communist Party (KCP)		Manipur, India	1980	Ibohanbi, founder
Kanglei Yaol Kanba Lup (KYKL)	Founded through the merger of merger of United National Liberation Front (UNLF) Oken faction, People's Revolutionary Party of Kangleipak (PREPAK) Meiraba faction, and Kangleipak Communist Party (KCP) Pishak faction	Manipur, India	1994	Achou Toijamba, chairman; Tojamba and Oken, joint chiefs of the military commission
Manipur People's Liberation Front (MPLF)	The MPLF is a 'common platform' under which UNLF, PLA and PREPAK operate			
All Tripura Tiger Force	Former cadres of the Tripura National Volunteers regrouped to constitute the ATTF	Tripura, India; Bangladesh	1990	Ranjit Debbarma

(contd.)

(1)	(2)	(3)	(4)	(5)
National Liberation Front of Tripura	Split leading to formation of TRA in 1993, split in 2000 leading to formation of BNCT, vertical split in 2001 leading to formation of Debbarma and Jamatiya factions	Tripura, India; Bangladesh	1989	Nayanbasi Jamatiya and Biswamohan Debbarma are heading two NLFT factions
Liberation Tigers of Tamil Eelam (LTTE)		Sri Lanka	1976	Velupillai Prabhakaran
Students Islamic Movement of India		Bases and supporters in several pockets of Assam, West Bengal, Bihar, Uttar Pradesh, Gujarat, Maharashtra, Madhya Pradesh, Tamil Nadu, Andhra Pradesh, Karnataka; University campuses and affilitaes; sympathisers among the expatriate population in the Gulf	1977	Mohammad Ahmadullah Siddiqi, founder; Shahid Badar Falah, chairman till arrested in 2001; presently headed by General Secretary Safdar Nagori
Deendar Anjuman	Sect founded in Karnataka, India	Parts of Karnataka, Andhra Pradesh and Maharashtra	1924	Hazrat Moulana Deendar Channabasaveshwara Siddiqui, founder; Sayyid

				Imam, chief; Syed Zia-u Hassan, spiritual leader Sundaram, founders; Maran chief
Communist Party of India (Marxist-Leninist)—People's War	People's War Group (PWG)	Several pockets of Andhra Pradesh, a few pockets in Karnataka, large tracts of Chhattisgarh, pockets of Maharashtra and Madhya Pradesh, southern Orissa, northern West Bengal, parts of Jharkhand and Chhattisgarh, pockets of influence and or presence in Uttar Pradesh, Uttaranchal, Delhi, Punjab, Haryana and Rajasthan, India	1980	Kondapalli Seetharamaiah (founder). Muppala Lakshmana Rao, General Secretary, Nambala Kesava Rao, Chief of the People's Guerrilla Army
Maoist Communist Centre of India (MCCI)	Originally founded ad Dakshin Desh in 1969, renamed MCC in 1975. Renamed MCCI in 2001	Parts of Bihar and Jharkhand, a few pockets in West Bengal and Orissa and minimal presence in Uttar Pradesh	1975	Amulya Sen and Kanhai Chaterjee, founding leaders; pramod Mishra, Sanjay Dusadh, current leaders
Tamil National Retrieval Troops (TNRT)	Operating under the name Tamizhar Vidhuthalai Iyakkam after proscription	Parts of Tamil Nadu, inclduing in Chennai, India	1984-85	Pulavar Kaliyaperumal, Thamizharasan and Anbazhagan alias

(contd.)

(1)	(2)	(3)	(4)	(5)
Tamil Nadu Liberation Army (TNLA)	Naxalite leders of CPI-ML Tamil Nadu State unit split and founded Tamil Nadu Communist Party-Marxist-Leninist (TNCP-ML), whose armed wing is the TNLA	Isloated pockets in Tamil Nadu, some Tamil speaking areas of Karnataka, India	1980s	Ravi alias P. Ravichandran, founder, an accused in the killings of PERLF leader Padmanabha and assassination of Rajiv Gandhi
Babbar Khalsa International (BKI)	Split in 1992 with the formation of the Parmar faction	USA, Canada, UK, Germany, France, Belgium, Norway, Switzerland and Pakistan	1980	Sukhdev Singh Babbar and Talwinder Singh Parmar, founders; Wadhwa Singh, chief
Khalistan Commando Force		Punjab, India		
Khalistan Zindabad Force		Punjab, India		
International Sikh Youth Federation	Split into several factions	Among supporters in UK, North America, Canada and other Western European countries; in Punjab in the past, office in Pakistan	1984	Amrik Singh, Jasbir Singh Rode (nephew of Bhindranwale), Lakhbir Singh Rode, chief
Akhil Bharatiya Nepali Ekta Samaj		Northern Bengal and is active in north-east India, Uttar Pradesh and Bihar,	1979	Ram Prasad Sharma, President; Raju Nepali, Gen. Secretary; Amrit

		in areas inhabited by ethnic Nepalese, and in stretches bordering Nepal.		Thapa, Vice-President
Sipah-e-Sahaba Pakistan (SSP)	Earlier termed Anjuman Sipah-e-Sahaba; now known as Millat-i-Islamia	Several parts of all four provinces in Pakistan; Sargodha, Bahawalpur, Jhang, Multan and Muzaffargarh towns are strongholds	1985	Maulana Haq Nawaz Jhangvi, Maulana Zia-ur-Rehman Farooqi, Maulana Eesar-ul-Haq Qasmi and Maulana Azam Tariq established the SSP, founders; Allama Ali Sher Ghazni, Patron-in-Chief, Maulana Zia-ul-Qasmi chairman of the Supreme Council
Tehreek-e-Jaferia Pakistan (TJP)	Originally termed Tehreek Nifaz Fiqah-e-Jafria; Now known as Tehrik-e Islami		1992	Allama Syed Sajid Ali Naqvi, chief
Tehreek-e-Nafaz-e-Shariat-e-Mohammadi (TNSM)	Split from SSP	Tribal areas of North-West Frontier Province, especially in Swat and and adjoining districts of NWFP	1992	Maulana Sufi Mohammad, chief
Lashkar-e-Jangvi (LeJ)		Across Pakistan	1996	Muhammad Ajmal alias Akram Lohri, commander-in-chief (Saalar-i-Ala)

(contd.)

PROFILES OF TERRORIST GROUPS (contd.)

Official name (1)	Cadre (6)	Ideology strength (7)	Objective(s) (8)	Financing (9)	Weapons holding (10)	Activities (11)
Al Badr	200	Islamist	Merge J&K with Pakistan	ISI, voluntary donations in Pakistan and PoK.		Attacks on Indian security forces, known to have deployed suicide squads
Jamiat-ul-Mujahidin (Break away faction of Hizb-ul-Mujahidin)	Few hundreds	Islamist	Favour acceession of J&K to Pakistan	ISI		Attacks on Indian security forces, known to have deployed suicide squads
Al Qaida						
Dukhtaran-e-Millat (DeM)	350	Islamist	Favours accession of J&K with Pakistan	Known to have received money through *Hawala* (illegal money transfer from a London-based person,		Protests and demonstrations to observe Islmiac way of life by women, against extra-judicial killings by security forces and against objection-able literature Hawala transactions

				Ayub Thakur; part of the money is believed to have been given by the ISI.		
Lashkar-e-Taiba/ Pasban-e-Ahle Hadis	500-1000	Islamist	Merge J&K with Pakistan	Saudi Arabia, Kuwait, Pakistan-based Ahle Hadis sect industrialists, ISI, Al Qaeda	AK series; RPG; Mortars;	Attacking Indian security forces, vital installations and symbols of Government, massacre of Hindus, suicide attacks
Jaish-e-Mohammed/ Tahrik-e-Furqan	500-1000	Islamist of the Deobandi school	Merge J&K with Pakistan	Pakistan, Azad Kashmir Government, ISI, Al Qaida	RPGs, Assault Rifles and Mortars	Attacks on Indian Secirity Forces and vital installations, symbols of Government, Killing civilians, suicide attacks
Harkat-ul-Mujahidin/Harkat-ul-Ansar/Harkat-ul-Jehad-e-Islami	800 cadres and 10,000 sympathisers	Islamist		Sympathisers in Saudi Arabia, other Gulf and Islamic states, Pakistan, J&K		

(1)	(6)	(7)	(8)	(9)	(10)	(11)
Hizb-ul-Mujahidin/Pir Panjal Regiment	1500	Islamist	Merge J&K with Pakistan	ISI, voluntary donations in Pakistan , J&K and Azad Kashmir, *Hawala*.	AK series; RPG; Mortars	Attacks on Indain security forces, civilians and vital installations
Jammu and Kashmir Islamic Front	50	Islamist	Libaeration of Kashmir through Armed struggle, right to self-determination	ISI, Khalistan Zindabad Force	AK series; RPG; Mortars; Explosive Devices	Perpetrated bomb blasts in Delhi and at least one in Rajasthan
United Liberation Front of Assam (ULFA)	500-700		Establish an independent, socialist state of Assam	Extortion, ISI, Donations	AK series, Explosive Devices	Attacks on security forces, bomb blasts at vital istallations, muder and abductions for ransom, extortion
National Democratic Front of Bodoland (NDFB)	3,500		Establish sovereign Bodoland, discontinue the use of Devanagari	Extortion		Attacks on security forces, abductions for ransom, murder

			script and implement roman script		
People's Liberation Army (PLA), constitutent of Manipur People's Liberation Front (MPLF)	Four Divisions		Liberate Manipur, form a revolutionary front stretching across the whole of India's north-east and unify all ethnic groups	Extortion	Attacks on security forces, extortion
United National Liberation Front (UNLF), constitutent of Manipur People's Liberation Front (MPLF)		Socialist	Establish independent, socialist Manipur	Extortion	Attacks on civilians and troops
People's Revolutionary Party of Kangleipak (PREPAK), constitutent of Manipur People's Liberation Front (MPLF)	200		Expulsion of non-natives from Manipur and function as the most genuine revolutionary organisation	Extortion	Attacks on civilians and troops; Imposing a moral code

(contd.)

(1)	(6)	(7)	(8)	(9)	(10)	(11)
Kangleipak Communist Party (KCP)	40	Communist	Expulsion of non-natives from Manipur	Extortion		Attacks on civilians, troops and imposing a moral code
Kanglei Yaol Kanba Lup (KYKL)		North East nantionalism, described by the group as one-for-all, all-for-one	'rebuild' the Manipuri society by clearing it of all vices like immoral activities, drug trade and corruption.	Extortion		Attacks on civilians and state installations
Manipur People's Liberation Front (MPLF)						
All Tripura Tiger Force	600		Expel Bengali-speaking immigrants who entered Tripura after 1956, Restore land to tribals, delete names of those who entered Tripura after 1956 from electoral rolls	Extortion		

National Liberation Front of Tripura	Biswamohan-550; Nayanbasi-250		Liberating Triputa from Indian neo-colonilism, forging distinct and independent Tripuri identity	Extortion		Attacks on civilians and state installations;
LTTE	about 7,000		Sovereign Tamil state	Tamil Diaspora; 'Taxation' in north and east		Attacks on civilians and state installations; non-LTTE tamils
Students Islamic Movement of India	400 full-time cadres, 20,000 supporters	Extremist, militant Islam	Proselytise, wage jehad for the cause of Islam; establish Dar-ul-Islam (land of Islam) by either forcefully converting everyone to Islam or by violence.	Internal fund raising, donations from Assembly of Muslim Youth (WAMY), Riyadh and International Islamic Federation of Students' Organizations (IIFSO), Kuwait; ISI		Propagating Islamic values and way of life among children and youth, training programmes, and propaganda

(contd.)

(1)	(6)	(7)	(8)	(9)	(10)	(11)
Deendar Anjuman	100 missionaries and 15,000 followers	Sufi	Proselytise, convert India into Islamic state			Annual inter-religious dialogue, propagation, bomb blasts, spread religious hatred and create communal tensions
Communist Party of India (Marxist-Leninist)—People's War	3,500 armed, underground cadres	Marxist, Leninist, Maoist	Herald New Democratic Revolution through protracted people's war, on the lines of the Chinese Revolution	Extortion, abductions for ransom, sympathisers, looting banks, real estate business		Attacking security forces through guerrilla tactics, murders, abductions, burglaries, destrution of private and public property and forced occupation of land
Maoist Communist Centre (MCC)	1,000 armed cadres and several thousand over-ground supporters and aympathisers	Maoist ideology	Form people's government through armed struggle following the dictums of Mao	Extortion, internal fund raising		Attacking security forces through guerrilla tactics, murders, abductions, destrution of private and public property and forced occupation of land

Tamil National Retrieval Troops (TNRT)	Secessionist	Form independent Tamil Nadu through armed struggle			
Tamil Nadu Liberation Army (TNLA)	Secessionist	Independent Tamil Nadu to later encompass area in Sri Lanka that consitute the LTTE's notion of Tamil Eelam			Minor explosions, looting banks, attacking and looting police stations for weapons
Babbar Khalsa International (BKI)	Secessionist	Independent Sikh state of Khalistan	Robberies; Sikh Diaspora		Responsible for the explosion of Air India flight Kanishka off the Lockerbie coast, assassination of Punjab Chief Minister Beant Singh, explosions and killings, fund raising and propaganda

(contd.)

(1)	(6)	(7)	(8)	(9)	(10)	(11)
Khalistan Commando Force						
Khalistan Zindabad Force						
International Sikh Youth Federation		Secessionist	Independent Sikh homeland of Khalistan	und raising among diaspora		Fund raising among diaspora
Akhil Bharatiya Nepali Ekta Samaj	Unspecifed		proliferation of greater Nepal idea	Nepalese Diaspora		A front for the Maoist insurgents of Nepal
Sipah-e-Sahaba Pakistan (SSP)	1,00,000 registered activists	Sunni, sectarian	Declare Pakistan a Sunni state, oppose Shia domination		Sophisticated arms	Targeted killings and massacre of worshippers at mosques, attacks on security force personnel
Tehreek-e-Jaferia Pakistan (TJP)		Shia, sectarian	Create society based on 'pure Islam', protect social, political and religious rights of Shiites, propaganda of Shiite ideas, coordination of all Pakistani Shiite organisa-	Shiite community in Pakistan, Iran as well as certain commercial groups.	Sophisticated arms	Targeted killings, attacks on Sunnis

			tions and fight imperialism, establish Islamic egalitarianism and social justice.			
Tehreek-e-Nafaz-e-Shariat-e-Mohammadi (TNSM)		Wahabi; rejects democracy as being un-Islamic	Militant enforcement of Islamic law; imposition of shariat in Pakistan	Internal fund raising	Kalashnikovs, grenades, rocket launchers, missiles, swords	Clashes with security forces, fought alongside the Taliban against US-led coalition forces, lay seige to government offices, running three FM stations, parallel courts
Lashkar-e-Jangvi (LeJ)	300	Deoband, Sunni sectarian	Aims to transform Pakistan into a Sunni state, primarily through violent means.	Internal fund raising, support from Deobandi groups and sources in Saudi Arabia.	Ak series rifles; Grenades; High-intensity explosives	Sectarian killings of Shias, fought against the Soviets in Afghanistan, made an attempt on the life of the them Premier, Nawaz Sharief, assisted the Al Qaida in exploding car bombs; Suicide bombings

Note: The PWG and MCCI have merged on 21 September 2004 to found the Communist Party of India (Maoist) (CPI-Maoist). Muppalla Lakshmana Rao alias Ganapathy is the General Secretary of the Central Committee (provisional) of the new outfit. —Author.

Contributors

SAMINA AHMED is senior researcher at International Crisis Group (ICG).

LOK RAJ BARAL is Executive Chairman of Nepal Centre for Contemporary Studies, Kathmandu, Nepal. He is a former Professor of Political Science at Tribhuvan University, Kathmandu and also former Ambassador of Nepal to India.

WASBIR HUSSAIN is Consulting Editor of *The Sentinel*, Guwahati, Assam, and Associate Fellow, Institute for Conflict Management, New Delhi.

VIJENDRA SINGH JAFA is a retired Indian Administrative Service officer. He had served for many years in the Indian north-eastern states of Assam, Meghalaya and Mizoram.

ABUL KALAM is professor of International Relations at Dhaka University, Dhaka, Bangladesh.

MAHENDRA P. LAMA is Professor of South Asian Studies at the School of International Studies, Jawaharalal Nehru University, New Delhi.

KETHESHWARAN (KETHESH) LOGANATHAN is with Centre for Policy Alternatives, Colombo, Sri Lanka.

S.D. MUNI is Professor of South Asian Studies at School of International Studies, Jawaharlal Nehru University, New Delhi. He also served as India's Ambassador to Laos (1997–99).

V.R. RAGHAVAN is a retired Lieutenant General and was the

Indian Army's Director General of Military Operations. He is currently, President, Centre for Security Analysis, Chennai and Director of Delhi Policy Group.

P.V. RAMANA is Research Fellow at Observer Research Foundation, New Delhi.

AJAI SAHNI is Executive Director, Institute for Conflict Management & South Asia Terrorism Portal; Editor, *South Asia Intelligence Review*; Executive Editor, *Faultlines: Writings on Conflict & Resolution*.

AYESHA SIDDIQA is a senior freelance journalist in Pakistan. She has also been contributing to the *Jane Defence Weekly*.

DEEPAK THAPA is a senior journalist in Nepal.

Index